Compiled by Günter Beer

THE PEPIN PRESS / AGILE RABBIT EDITIONS

AMSTERDAM AND SINGAPORE

Tarifa-Infos
Anreise
tarifa.ch

Wohnen **Standort**

With special thanks to Magda Garcia Masana
from LocTeam S.L., Barcelona

Compiled and edited by Günter Beer
(www.webdesignindex.org)

Cover, CD label and book design by Pepin van Roojen
Layout by Kathi Günter and Sarah David-Spickermann
CD master by Günter Beer and Sarah David-Spickermann

Introduction by Pepin van Roojen
Translations by LocTeam, Barcelona (German, Spanish, French, Italian and Portuguese), and The Big Word, Leeds (Japanese, Chinese and Korean).

ISBN 90 5768 063 7
The Pepin Press – Agile Rabbit Editions

The Pepin Press BV
P.O. Box 10349
1001 EH Amsterdam
The Netherlands

Tel +31 20 4202021
Fax +31 20 4201152
mail@pepinpress.com
www.pepinpress.com

10 9 8 7 6 5 4 3 2
2008 07 06 05 04

Manufactured in Singapore

Contents

Free CD-Rom in the inside back cover

On peut s'asseoir..

KIXA
"SOMETIMES I THINK ABOUT SOMETHINGS...
SOMETIMES THEY CAN TO BE COME TRUE"
WORKS 00 01 02 03 04 05 06

Thank you for buying this fourth edition of our annual *Web Design Index*. Since its inception in the year 2000, this series has developed into one of the most important publications in its field. Year after year it provides an accurate overview of the state of the art in web design.

As in the previous volumes, this book presents a selection of 1002 outstanding web pages. With each page, the URL is indicated. The names of those involved in the design and programming of the sites are stated as follows:

D design
C coding
P production
A agency
M designer's e-mail address

In the inside back cover, you will find a CD-ROM containing all the pages, arranged according to their location in this book. You can view them on your monitor with a minimum of loading time, and access the Internet to explore the selected site in full.

Web design can range from single-page sites with simple layouts, to sophisticated structures featuring the latest capabilities. Selection for the *Web Design Index* is based on design quality, innovation, and effectiveness – regardless of complexity. So, in this book, you will find examples of all conceivable forms and styles.

Submissions

The *Web Design Index* is published annually. Should you wish to submit or recommend a design for consideration for the next edition, please access the submission form at www.webdesignindex.org.

The Pepin Press/Agile Rabbit Editions

The Pepin Press/Agile Rabbit Editions publishes a wide range of books and CD-ROMs with visual reference material and ready-to-use images for designers, for Internet applications as well as high-resolution printed media. For more information, please visit www.pepinpress.com.

Herzlichen Dank für den Kauf dieser vierten Ausgabe unsers jährlichen *Web Design Index*. Seit Beginn dieser Serie im Jahr 2000 hat sich diese zu einer der wichtigsten Veröffentlichungen in diesem Bereich entwickelt. Jahr für Jahr bietet dieses Werk einen genauen Überblick über die neuesten Entwicklungen im Webdesign.

Wie auch in den vorangegangenen Bänden enthält auch das vorliegende Buch eine Auswahl von 1002 erstklassigen Webseiten. Für jede Webseite ist auch die entsprechende URL angegeben. Die Namen der für Design und Programmierung der Sites verantwortlichen Personen sind mit folgenden Codes verzeichnet:

D Design
C Code
P Produktion
A Agentur
M E-Mail-Adresse des Designers

In der hinteren Umschlagseite finden Sie eine CD-ROM mit allen Seiten, geordnet nach deren Platzierung im vorliegenden Buch. Sie können diese mit äußerst kurzen Ladezeiten auf dem Bildschirm anzeigen oder diese im Internet aufrufen, um die gesamte Site zu erkunden.

Webdesign reicht von Sites mit nur einer Seite und sehr einfachem Layout bis hin zu komplexen Strukturen mit den neuesten Funktionen. Die Auswahl für den *Web Design Index* basiert auf der Qualität des Designs, dem Innovationsgrad und der Wirkung und ist von der Komplexität unabhängig. Daher enthält das vorliegende Buch Beispiele aller nur erdenklichen Arten und Stile von Webdesigns.

Einreichungen

Der *Web Design Index* ist eine jährliche Publikation. Wenn Sie ein Design für die nächste Ausgabe einreichen oder empfehlen möchten, verwenden Sie bitte das Teilnahmeformular auf www.webdesignindex.org.

The Pepin Press/Agile Rabbit Editions

The Pepin Press/Agile Rabbit Editions veröffentlicht eine breite Palette an Büchern und CD-ROMs mit visuellem Referenzmaterial und sofort verwendbaren Bildern für Designer, Internet-Applikationen sowie hoch auflösende Print-Medien. Weitere Informationen entnehmen Sie bitte der Website www.pepinpress.com.

Nous vous remercions d'avoir fait l'acquisistion de cette quatrième édition annuelle de l'*Index de modèles de sites Web*. Depuis ses débuts en 2000, cette collection est devenue l'une des publications les plus importantes de son secteur et propose chaque année un aperçu exhaustif des toutes dernières tendances dans la conception de sites Web.

Comme dans les volumes précédents, cet ouvrage présente une sélection de 1002 sites Web exceptionnels. L'URL de ces sites est à chaque fois mentionnée. Les noms des responsables du design et de la programmation des sites sont mentionnés selon le code suivant :

D design
C codage
P production
A agence
M adresse e-mail du designer

Un CD-ROM inclus à l'intérieur de la quatrième de couverture contient toutes les pages Web dans l'ordre de leur apparition dans le livre. Il vous permettra de les visualiser sur votre ordinateur avec un temps de chargement minimum et d'accéder à Internet pour explorer en détail le site choisi.

Le design Web reprend des ouvrages très divers, des sites à page unique à la mise en page simple aux systèmes plus sophistiqués exploitant les toutes dernières fonctionnalités. La sélection des sites pour l'*Index de modèles de sites Web* se base sur la qualité de leur design, leur caractère novateur et leur efficacité – quelle que soit leur complexité. Vous trouverez donc dans cet ouvrage des exemples de tous les styles et formes imaginables de sites Web.

Candidatures

l'*Index de modèles de sites Web* paraît chaque année. Si vous souhaitez soumettre ou recommander un site Web pour notre prochaine édition, vous pouvez remplir le formulaire de candidature que vous trouverez à l'adresse www.webdesignindex.org.

The Pepin Press/Agile Rabbit Editions

Les éditions Pepin Press/Agile Rabbit publient un vaste choix de livres et de CD-ROM reprenant des documents visuels de référence et des images prêtes à l'emploi pour l'usage des designers, pour les applications destinées à l'Internet ainsi que tout support imprimé haute définition. Pour en savoir plus, consultez la page www.pepinpress.com.

Vi ringraziamo per aver acquistato la quarta edizione del *Indice del Disegno Web*, la pubblicazione annuale che a partire dal 2000, anno della sua prima uscita, è diventata un punto di riferimento nel settore, offrendo ogni anno una rassegna accurata sullo stato dell'arte del web design.

Come nei precedenti volumi, il libro presenta una selezione di 1002 pagine web straordinarie. Per ogni pagina web viene indicata la direzione URL. I nomi delle persone che hanno partecipato alla concezione e alla programmazione dei siti sono preceduti dalle seguenti abbreviazioni:

D design
C codifica
P produzione
A agenzia
M indirizzo e-mail dei disegnatori

All'interno della copertina posteriore troverete un CD-ROM che contiene tutte le pagine web sistemate secondo l'ordine di apparizione nel libro. Appaiono sul monitor in pochissimo tempo e permettono di accedere alla pagina selezionata per navigare nel sito desiderato.

Il web design può variare da semplici siti con una sola pagina a strutture sofisticate elaborate secondo le ultime tecniche. Il criterio di selezione utilizzato per il *Indice del Disegno Web* si basa sulla qualità del design, sull'innovazione e sull'efficacia, indipendentemente dalla complessità. Così, in questo libro, troverete degli esempi di ogni forma e stile possibile.

Candidature

Indice del Disegno Web è una pubblicazione annuale. Se volete presentare o raccomandare una creazione perché venga inclusa nella prossima edizione, potete accedere al modulo di candidatura nel sito www.webdesignindex.org.

The Pepin Press/Agile Rabbit Editions

The Pepin Press/Agile Rabbit Editions pubblica una vasta gamma di libri e CD-ROM con materiale informativo ed immagini per designer, per applicazioni Internet, e anche per mezzi stampa ad alta risoluzione. Per ulteriori informazioni potete visitare il sito www.pepinpress.com.

Gracias por adquirir esta cuarta edición del *Índice de diseño de páginas web*. Desde su aparición en el año 2000, esta serie se ha convertido en una de las publicaciones más importantes de su sector. Año tras año muestra una visión detallada del estado del diseño de páginas web.

Como en los volúmenes anteriores, esta edición presenta una selección de 1.002 magníficas páginas web (junto a cada una de ellas se indica la dirección URL correspondiente). Los nombres de quienes han participado en el diseño y la programación de cada sitio se citan de la siguiente manera:

D diseño
C codificación
P producción
A agencia
M correo electrónico del diseñador

En el interior de la contracubierta encontrará un CD-ROM que contiene todas las páginas web, ordenadas según aparecen en este libro. Si lo desea, puede verlas en su monitor (el tiempo de descarga es mínimo) y acceder a Internet para explorar en su totalidad el sitio web seleccionado.

El diseño de páginas web abarca desde sitios formados por una sola página de composición sencilla hasta complicadas estructuras con las más novedosas técnicas. Los criterios de selección de este índice se basan en la calidad, la innovación y la eficacia del diseño, sin tener en cuenta su complejidad; por lo tanto, en este libro encontrará ejemplos de todas las formas y estilos que pueda imaginar.

Sugerencias

El *Índice de diseño de páginas web* se publica de forma anual. Si desea sugerir o recomendar un diseño para que se tenga en cuenta para la próxima edición, rellene el formulario de sugerencias que aparece en la dirección www.webdesignindex.org.

The Pepin Press/Agile Rabbit Editions

La editorial The Pepin Press/Agile Rabbit Editions publica una gran variedad de libros y CD-ROM con material de referencia visual e imágenes destinados a diseñadores, aplicaciones de Internet y medios impresos de alta resolución. Si desea obtener más información visite www.pepinpress.com.

Obrigado pela compra da quarta edição do nosso *Catálogo de Web Design* anual. Desde o seu início em 2000, esta série evoluiu para uma das publicações mais importantes da sua área. Ano a ano, proporciona com exactidão uma descrição geral do estado da arte em web design.

Tal como nos volumes anteriores, este livro apresenta uma selecção de 1002 páginas web notáveis. Cada página inclui a indicação do URL. Os nomes das pessoas envolvidas no design e na programação dos sites encontram-se indicados do seguinte modo:

D design
C codificação
P produção
A agência
M endereço de e-mail do designer

No interior da contracapa, encontrará um CD-ROM com todas as páginas, organizadas de acordo com a sua localização neste livro. Poderá visualizá-las no seu monitor com um tempo de carregamento mínimo e aceder à Internet para explorar na totalidade o site seleccionado.

O *Catálogo de Web Design* pode variar de sites de uma página com formatos simples para estruturas sofisticadas que apresentam as capacidades mais avançadas. A selecção para o *Catálogo de Web Design* é feita com base na qualidade de design, inovação e eficácia, independentemente da complexidade. Por isso, poderá encontrar neste livro exemplos de todas as formas e estilos concebíveis.

Envios
O *Catálogo de Web Design* é publicado anualmente. Caso pretenda submeter um design a consideração para a próxima edição ou fazer uma recomendação, aceda ao respectivo formulário em www.webdesignindex.org.

The Pepin Press/Agile Rabbit Editions
A Pepin Press/Agile Rabbit Editions publica um vasto leque de livros e CD-ROMs com material de consulta visual e imagens prontas-a-utilizar para designers, aplicações de Internet, e suporte impresso de alta resolução. Para obter informações adicionais, visite o endereço www.pepinpress.com.

본 연도별 웹 디자인 인덱스의 제 4 판을 구매해 주셔서 감사합니다. 2000년에 발간이 시작된 이후, 이 시리즈는 이 분야에서 가장 중요한 출판물 중의 1개로 발전했으며 해마다 웹에서 웹 디자인에서 정확한 최신의 개관을 제공해주고 있습니다.

이전의 판에서와 같이, 이 책은 선별된 1002개의 현저한 웹 페이지를 보여줍니다. 각 페이지와 더불어, URL은 표시됩니다. 사이트의 디자인과 프로그래밍에 관련되는 것들의 이름은 다음과 같이 정해집니다:

D 디자인
C 코딩
P 생산
A 에이전시
M 디자이너의 이메일 주소

뒷 표지 내부 쪽에서, 여러분은 이 책 내에서의 그들의 위치에 따라 배열된 모든 페이지를 포함하는 CD-ROM을 발견할 것입니다. 여러분은 최소의 로딩 시간을 가진 모니터상에서 그것들을 볼 수 있으며, 선별된 사이트를 완전하게 검색하기 위해서 인터넷에 접근할 수 있습니다.

웹 디자인은 단순한 레이아웃을 가진 한 페이지짜리 사이트에서부터 최신 능력을 특징으로 하는 세련된 구조까지의 범위가 있습니다. 웹 디자인 인덱스를 위한 선별조건은 복잡성과 관계없이 디자인 품질, 혁신 및 효과성을 기초로 합니다. 그러므로 이 책에서, 여러분은 모든 생각할 수 있는 형태와 양식의 예를 발견할 것입니다.

제출
웹 디자인 인덱스는 매년 출판됩니다. 어러분이 다음 판에 대한 고려로서 디자인을 제출하거나 추천하기를 원하신다면, www.webdesignindex.org에서 제출 형태에 접근해 주시기 바랍니다.

페핀출판사 / 기민한 토끼그림 판
페핀출판사 / 기민한 토끼그림 판은 고해상도 인쇄매체뿐 아니라 디자이너 및 인터넷 응용을 위한 시각적인 참고 자료와 바로 사용이 가능한 이미지를 가진 다양한 범위의 서적과 CD-ROM을 출판합니다. 상세한 정보를 구하려면 www.pepinpress.com을 방문하시기 바랍니다.

感謝你購買這本《網頁設計索引》年刊第四版。從2000年它誕生起，本系列已發展成為同行業最重要的出版物之一，每年都會對網頁設計的最新趨勢進行準確概述。

同前面幾卷一樣，本書展示了1002張精彩的網頁。對每張網頁都提供有URL。網站設計和程式設計中所用的名稱約定如下：

D 設計
C 編碼
P 作品
A 代理商
M 設計者的電郵地址

在本書的封底內頁，你會發現一張CD-ROM，它包含了全書內容，其編排順序與本書一致。你可以最短的時間裝在電腦上，然後在顯示螢幕上進行瀏覽，也可以連線網際網路，以全螢幕方式瀏覽所選網站。

網頁設計從單層的單頁網站到具有最新性能的複雜結構的網站。《網頁設計索引》的篩選標準是根據設計品質、創意及效率 – 而不管複雜程度如何。因此在本書中，你可以找到所有可能的樣式和風格的實例。

提 交
《網頁設計索引》每年出版一次。如果你希望在下一輯中提交或推薦網頁設計，請訪問 www.webdesignindex.org 獲得提交表格。

The Pepin Press/Agile Rabbit Editions 出版社
The Pepin Press/Agile Rabbit Editions 出版了大量的書籍和 CD-ROM，為設計師、網路應用以及高清晰度的印刷性媒體提供直觀的參考材料和圖片素材。

欲獲得更多資訊請訪問 www.pepinpress.com.。

ウェブデザイン年鑑の第4版をお求め頂き誠にありがとうございます。2000年に企画開始となったこのシリーズも、今ではこの分野の最も重要なレビュー誌となり、ウェブデザインの現状の正確な概覧として好評を頂いております。

前年度に引き続き、今回も1002の優れたウェブサイトを選んでおとどけします。各サイトのURLも併せて掲載いたしました。サイトのデザイン及びプログラミングに関わった人名は、以下の記号で示しています：

D デザイン
C コード化
P 制作
A 代理店
M デザイナーのE-メール

裏表紙の内側にはCD-ROMが入っており、この本での収録順に従って全掲載ウェブサイトに関する情報が含まれています。短い時間でロードした後は、ご自身のPCモニターで掲載のウェブサイト全てにインターネットによるアクセスができます。

ここに含まれるウェブサイトのデザインは、レイアウトの単純な1ページのサイトから、最新技術を駆使し洗練された構造を持つサイトまで、実に様々です。ウェブデザイン年鑑では、そのサイトがどのくらい複雑かではなく、デザインの質、画期性、効果に注目して掲載サイトを選んでいます。従ってこの年鑑では、あらゆる形態やスタイルのサイトをご覧になることでしょう。

応募について
ウェブデザイン年鑑は年次刊行されています。次回の年鑑にご自身のウェブデザインを応募なさりたい方、ウェブデザインの推薦をなさりたい方は、www.webdesignindex.org.からダウンロードできる応募用紙でお申し込み下さい。

ペピン・プレス/アジール・ラビット・エディションについて
ペピン・プレス/アジール・ラビット・エディションは、インターネットのアプリケーションや高解像度印刷媒体で使用できる、デザイナー向けのビジュアル資料やレディーメード素材付きの書籍及びCD-ROMを幅広く手がけています。
詳細についてはwww.pepinpress.comでご覧下さい。

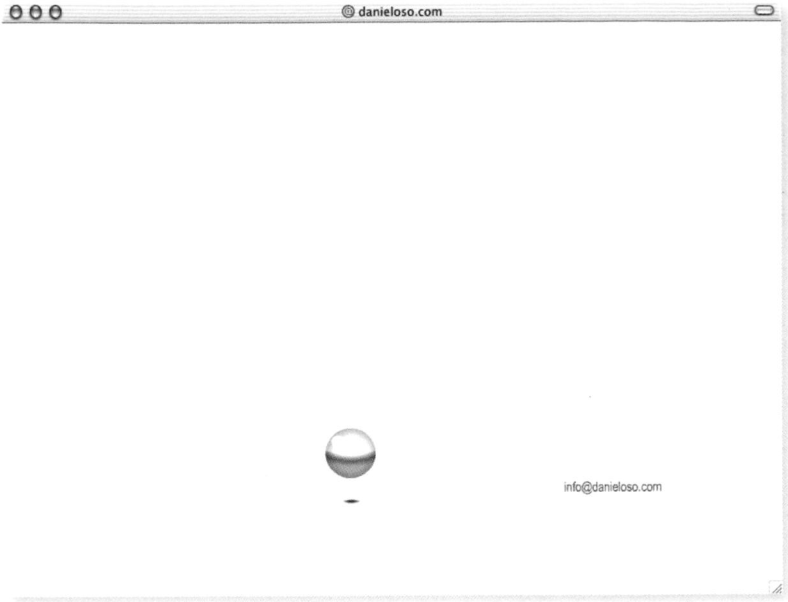

WWW.DANIELOSO.COM
D: DANIEL BERNARDO
A: DIAGRAMA, **M:** 123@DANIELOSO.COM

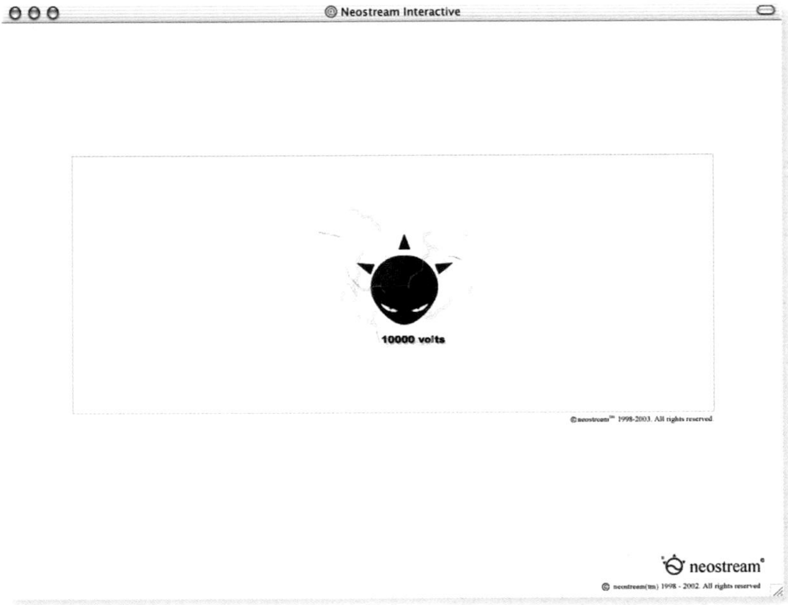

WWW.NEOSTREAM.COM

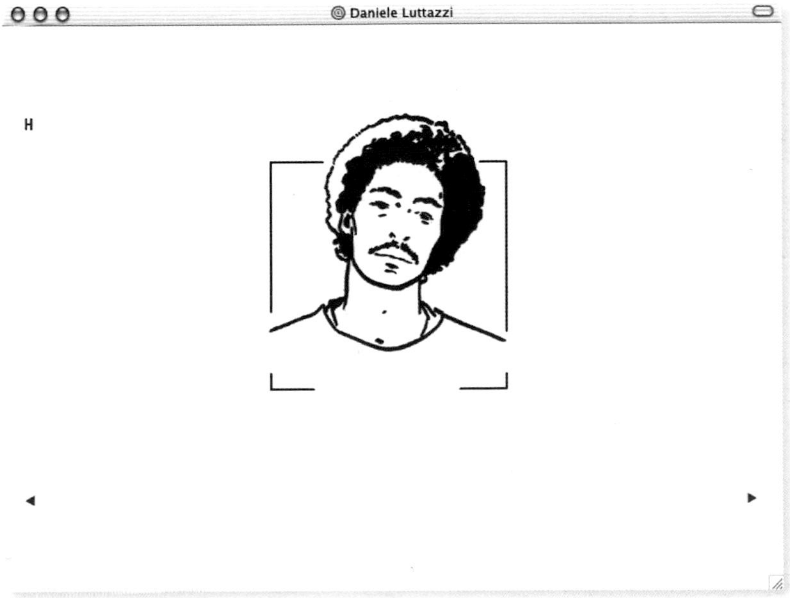

WWW.DANIELELUTTAZZI.IT
D: DANIELE LUTTAZZI, **C:** FILIPPO IMBRIGHI, **P:** KRASSNER ENTERTAINMENT
A: KRASSNER ENTERTAINMENT, **M:** SHELDRAKE@LIBERO.IT

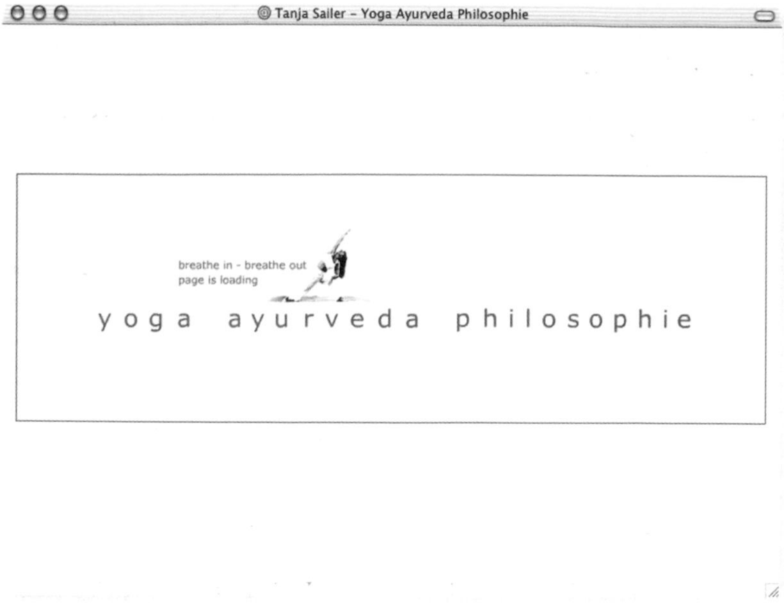

WWW.TANJA-SAILER.DE
D: MARIO STÖCKINGER
M: FLOYD@MAYASIGN.DE

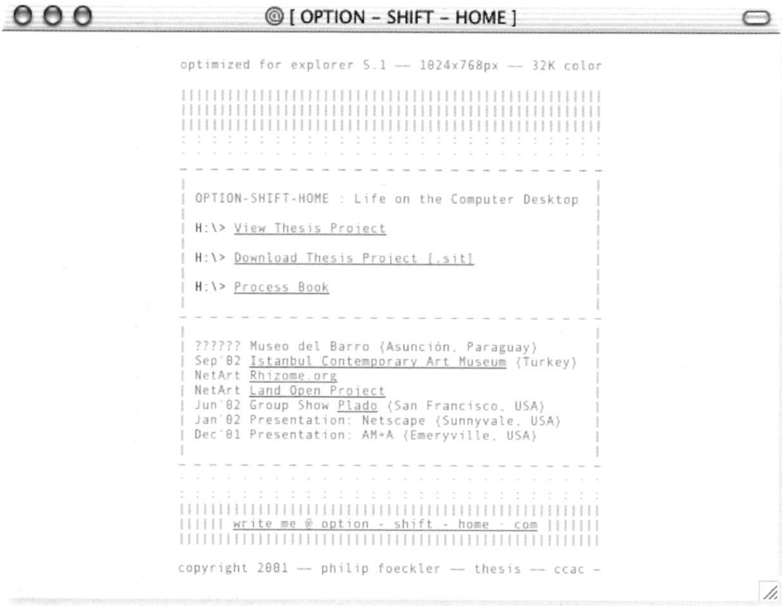

WWW.OPTION-SHIFT-HOME.COM
D: PHILIP FOECKLER
M: PHILIP@POCKETART.COM

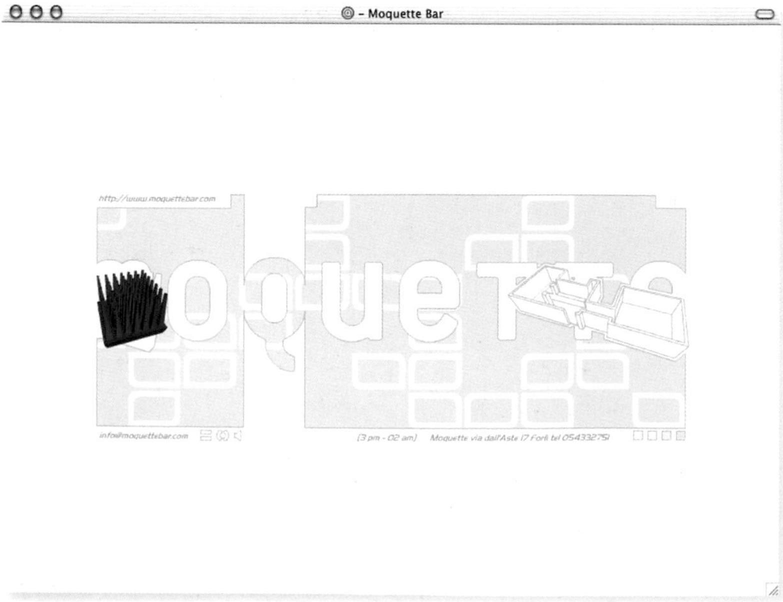

WWW.MOQUETTEBAR.COM
D: LUCA SANTOLAMAZZA
A: LSDESIGN, **M:** ELLESSE_D@LIBERO.IT

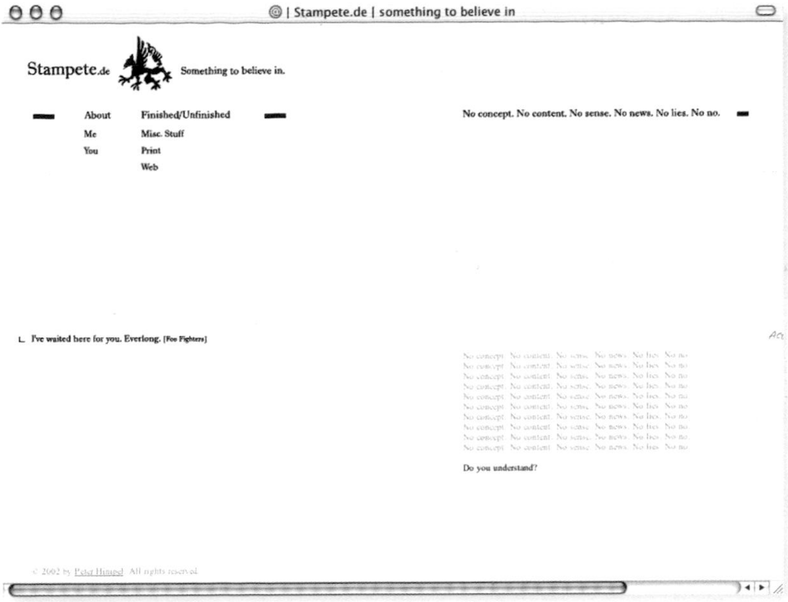

WWW.STAMPETE.DE
D: PETER HIMPEL

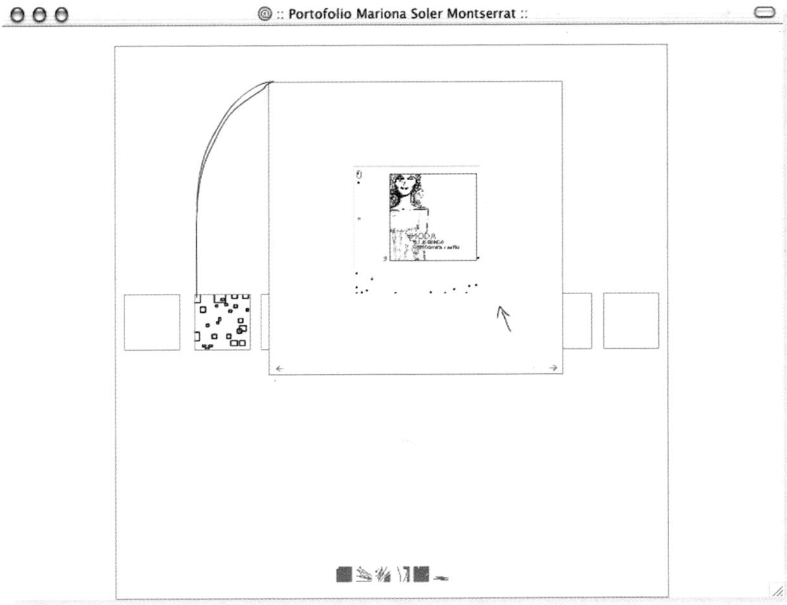

WWW.ES.GEOCITIES.COM/BOOK_MARIONA
D: MARIONA, **C:** XAVI
M: MARIONA_SOLER@HOTMAIL.COM

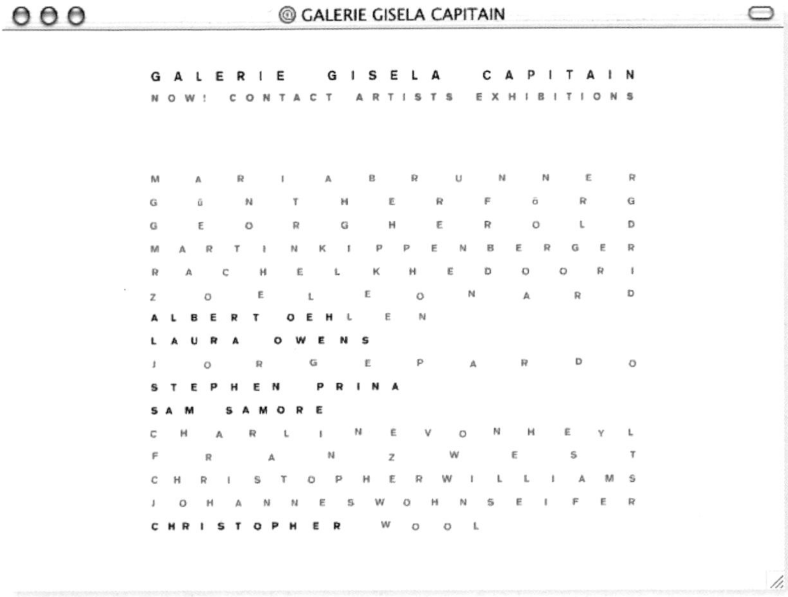

WWW.GALERIE-CAPITAIN.DE
D: STUDIO ORANGE
A: STUDIO ORANGE, **M:** DIRK@STUDIOORANGE.DE

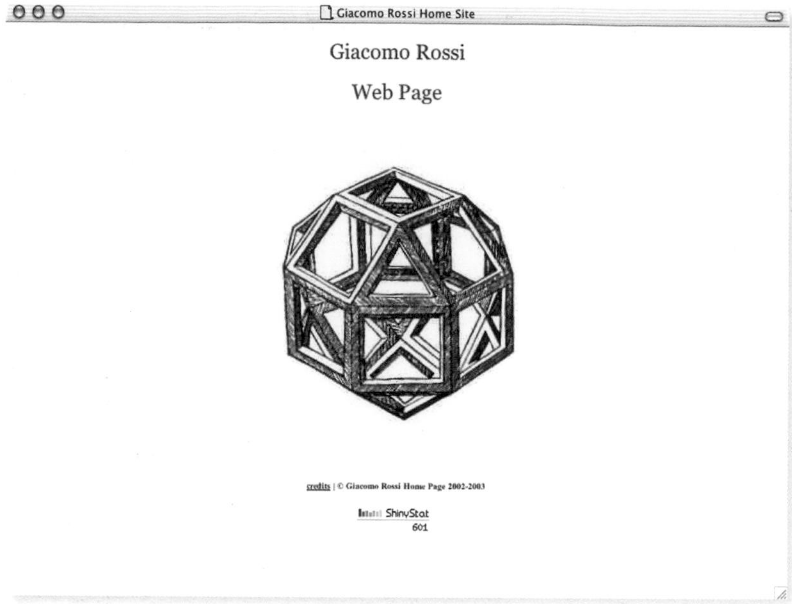
Giacomo Rossi Home Site
Giacomo Rossi
Web Page
ShinyStat
601

WWW.GIACOMO.ALTERVISTA.ORG
D: GIACOMO ROSSI
A: GIACOMO ROSSI, **M:** GIACOMO.ROSSI@LIBERO.IT

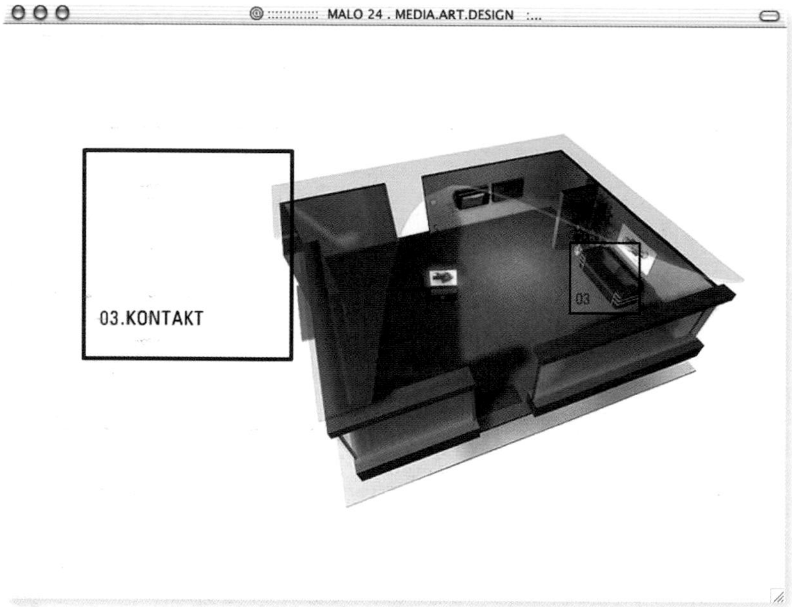
MALO 24 . MEDIA.ART.DESIGN
03.KONTAKT
03

WWW.MALO24.DE
D: MICHAEL LOEW, SASCHA MAERZ, **C:** MICHAEL LOEW SASCHA MAERZ, **P:** MALO24
A: MALO24, **M:** INFO@MALO24.DE

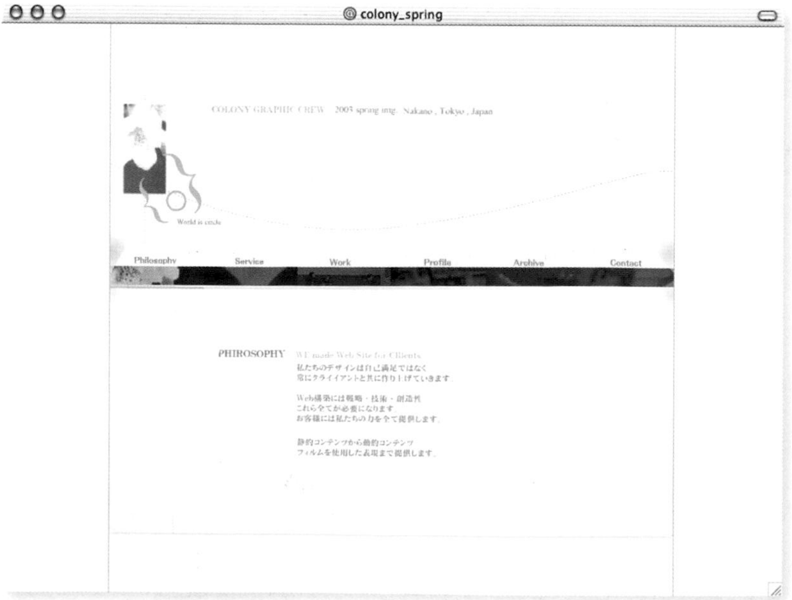
colony_spring
Philosophy
Service
Work
Profile
Archive
Contact
PHIROSOPHY

WWW.ARTISANSTREAM.COM/0301DHW/ONOE/
D: HIRONORI ONOE
A: COLONY GRAPHIC, **M:** HIRO212@MSN.COM

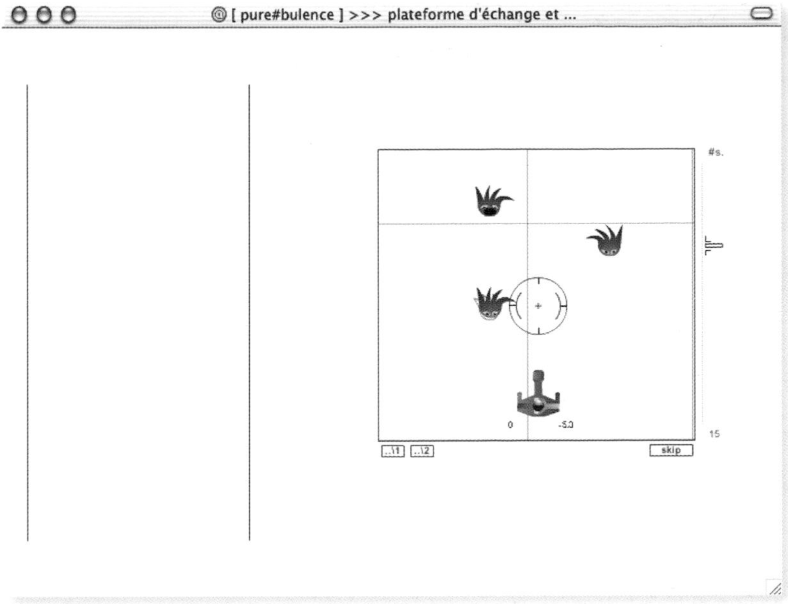

PERSO.WANADOO.FR/STEPHAN.VIENNET/PUREBULENCE
D: STEPHAN VIENNET
M: STEPHAN.VIENNET@WANADOO.FR

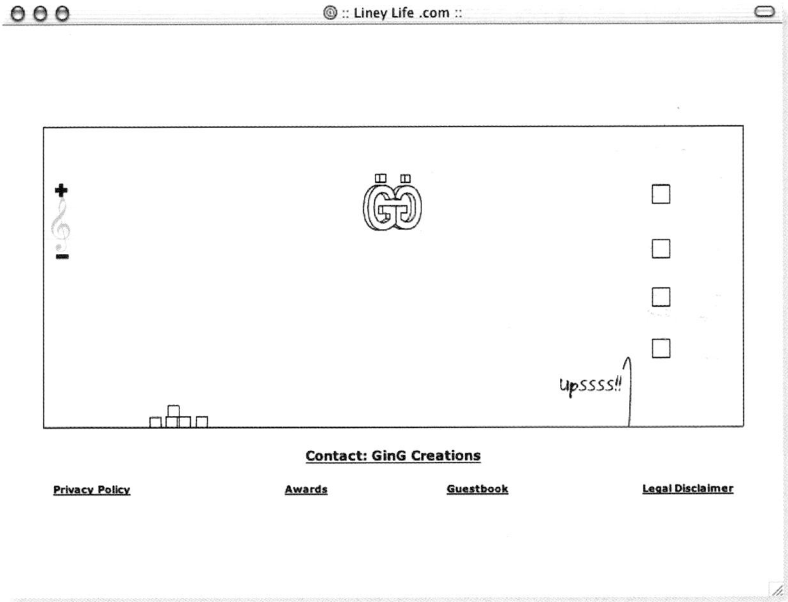

WWW.LINEYLIFE.COM
D: FRANCO VELLA
A: GING CREATIONS, **M:** FRANCO@GINGCREATIONS.COM

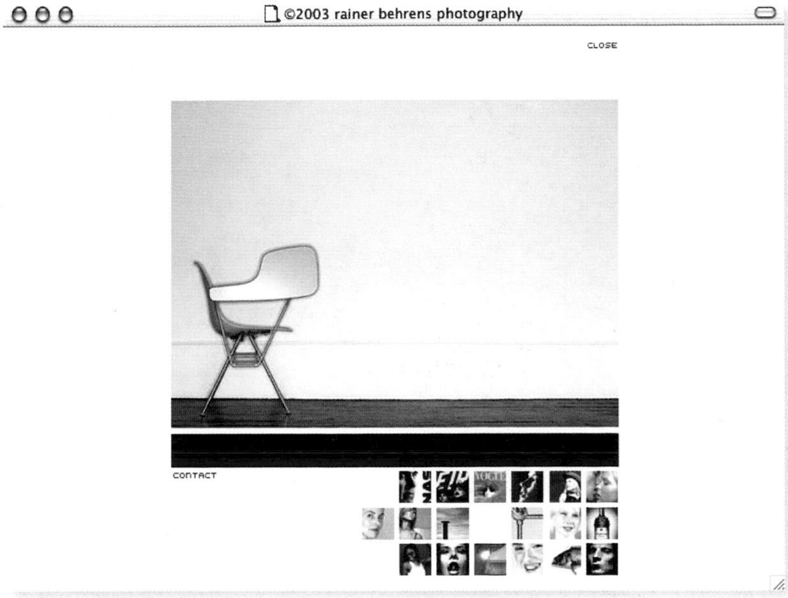

WWW.RAINERBEHRENS.COM
D: RAINER BEHRENS
A: RAINER BEHRENS PHOTOGRAPHY, **M:** WEBDESIGN@RAINERBEHRENS.COM

WWW.PONTANO.IT
D: MIA PONTANO
M: INFO@PONTANO.IT

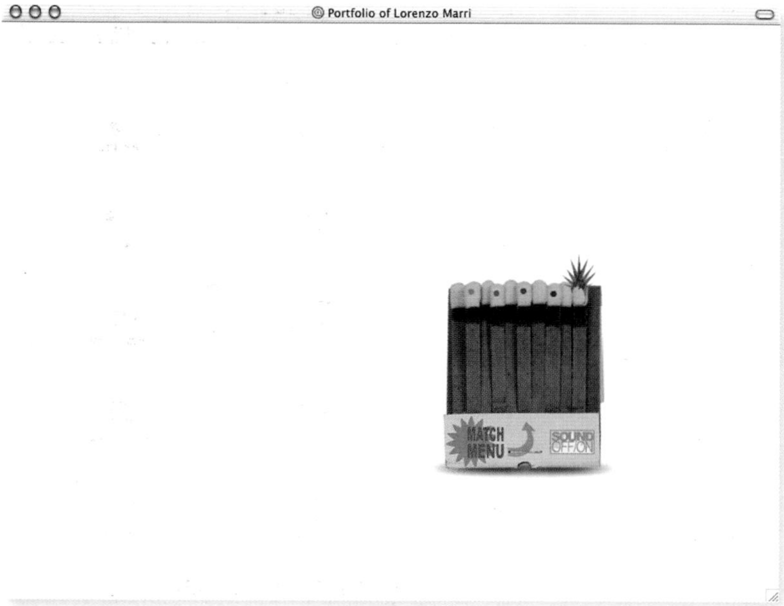

WWW.TRINITYNETWORLD.ORG/LORENZO/
D: LORENZO MARRI
M: LORENZOMARRI@HOTMAIL.COM

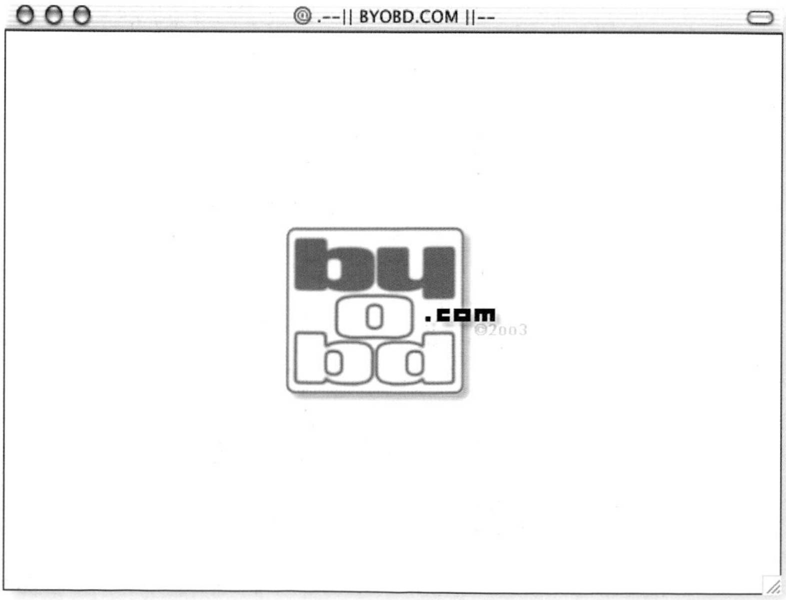

WWW.BYOBD.COM
D: OLIVER BISKO
A: BYOBD, **M:** OB@BYOBD.COM

Dänecke - Labels and More | Flexodruck | Stri...
Wer macht aus der Wurst die echte Herta?

WWW.DAENECKE.COM
D: THOMAS RICKER, **C:** JÜRGEN EBBING
A: PROSALES GMBH, **M:** J.EBBING@MEDIAHAUS.DE

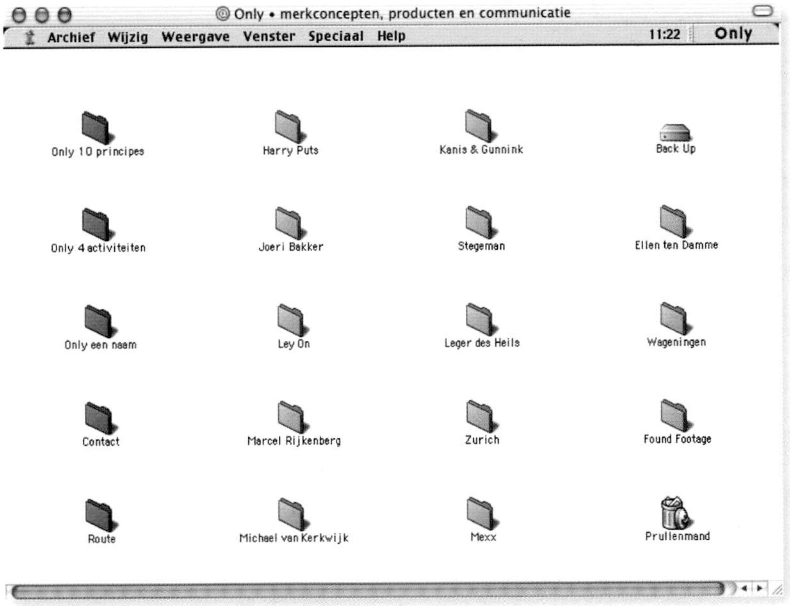
Only • merkconcepten, producten en communicatie
Archief Wijzig Weergave Venster Speciaal Help
11:22
Only
Only 10 principes
Harry Puts
Kanis & Gunnink
Back Up
Only 4 activiteiten
Joeri Bakker
Stegeman
Ellen ten Damme
Only een naam
Ley On
Leger des Heils
Wageningen
Contact
Marcel Rijkenberg
Zurich
Found Footage
Route
Michael van Kerkwijk
Mexx
Prullenmand

WWW.ONLY.NL
D: DENNIS VAN DEN BRINK
A: ONLY, **M:** DENNIS@ONLY.NL

OUT! Web 4 You

WWW.WEB4U.OUTWEB.NL
D: P.J.H.M. HENDRIKX
A: WEBPUNT.NL, **M:** P.HENDRIKX@WEBPUNT.NL

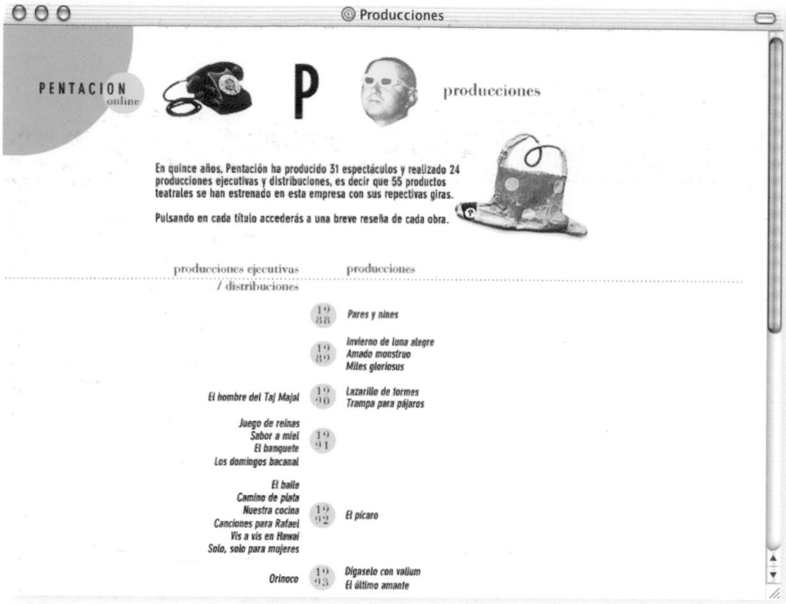

WWW.PENTACION.COM
D: DAVID SUEIRO
A: DSDG, **M:** DAVID@SUEIRO.COM

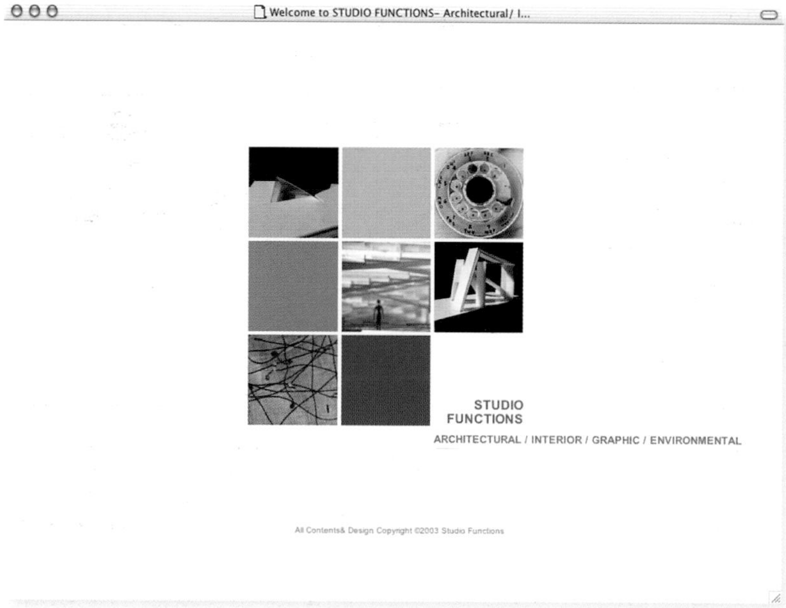

STUDIOFUNCTIONS.COM
D: BENJAMIN PAGE , **P:** PETER M. WENZEL
A: STUDIO FUNCTIONS, **M:** BPAGE@STUDIOFUNCTIONS.COM

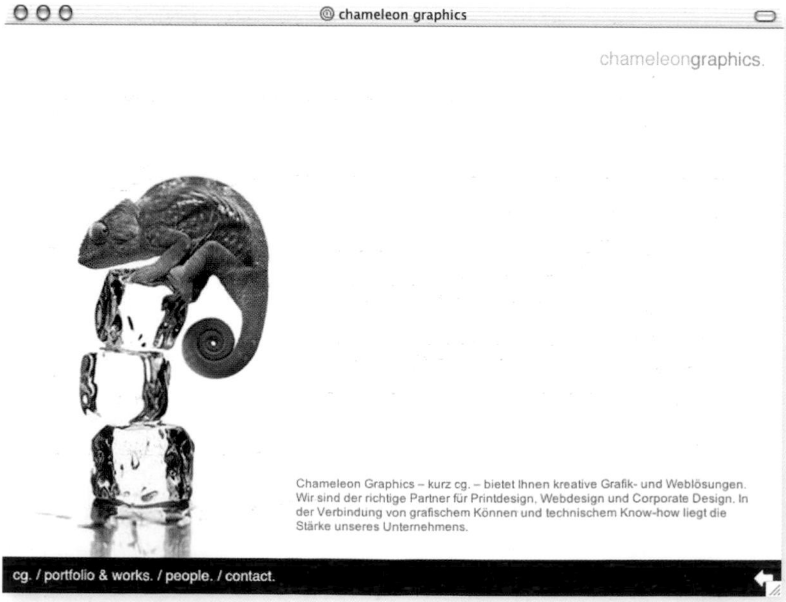

chameleon graphics
chameleongraphics.
Chameleon Graphics – kurz cg. – bietet Ihnen kreative Grafik- und Weblösungen. Wir sind der richtige Partner für Printdesign, Webdesign und Corporate Design. In der Verbindung von grafischem Können und technischem Know-how liegt die Stärke unseres Unternehmens.
cg. / portfolio & works. / people. / contact.

WWW.CHAMELEONGRAPHICS.CH
D: MICHEL SEELIGER
A: CHAMELEON GRAPHICS GMBH, **M:** INFO@CHAMELEONGRAPHICS.CH

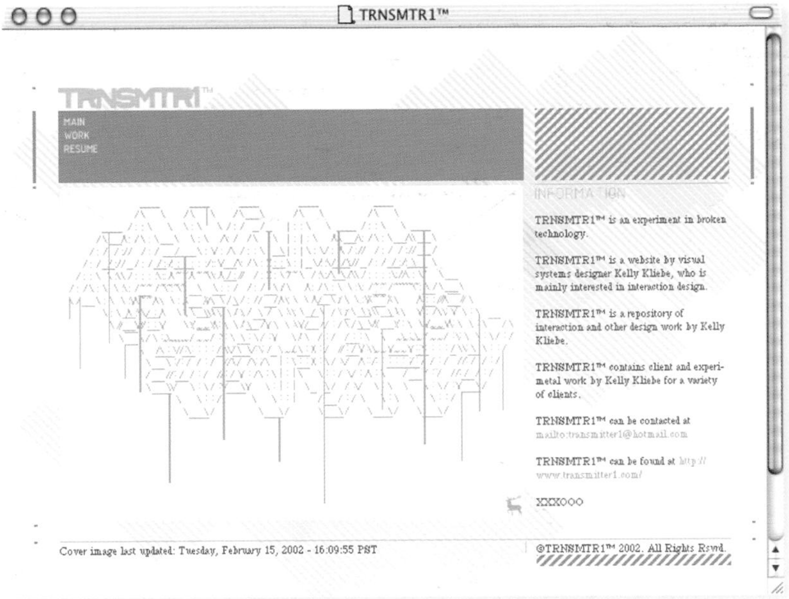

WWW.TRANSMITTER1.COM
D: KELLY KLIEBE
A: TRNSMTR1, **M:** TRANSMITTER1@HOTMAIL.COM

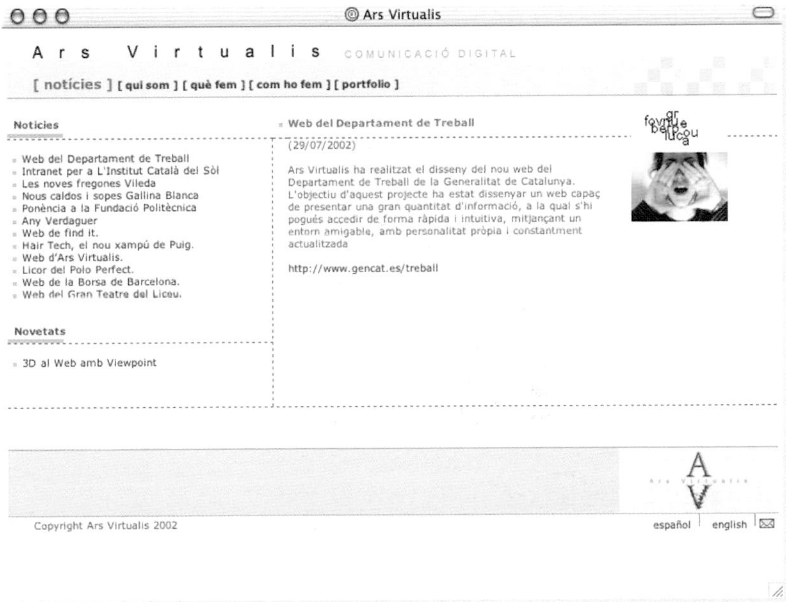

WWW.ARSVIRTUALIS.COM
A: ARS VIRTUALIS, **M:** ARSVIRT@ARSVIRTUALIS.COM

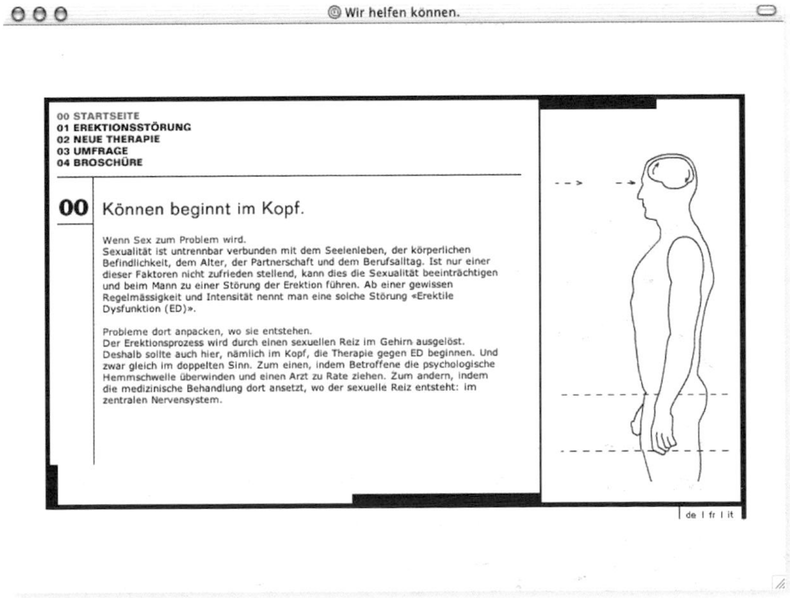

WWW.WIR-HELFEN-KOENNEN.CH/
D: OLIVER FENNEL, **C:** MARC RINDERKNECHT
A: JUNG VON MATT/LIMMAT AG, **M:** MARC.RINDERKNECHT@JVM.CH

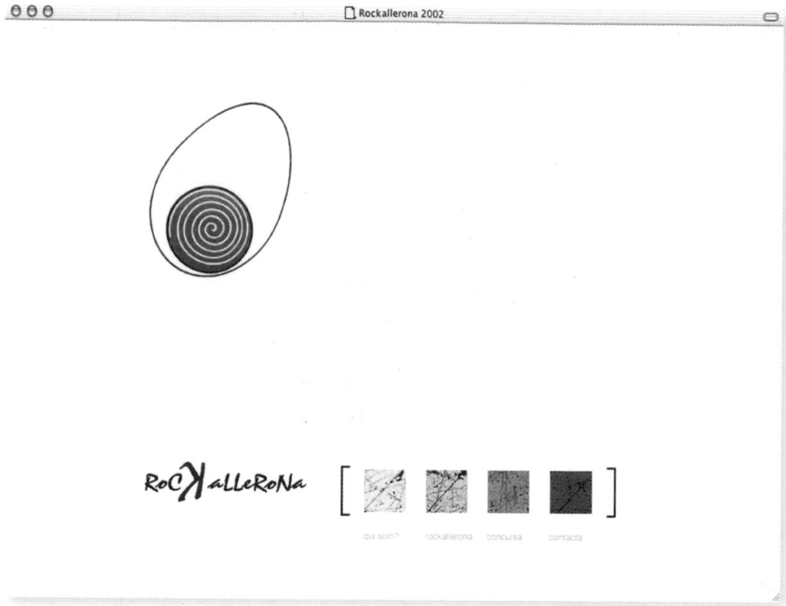
Rockallerona 2002
RoCKalleRoNa

WWW.ROCKALLERONA.COM
D: LLUÍS BERTRANS BUFÍ
M: LLUIS@ROCKALLERONA.COM

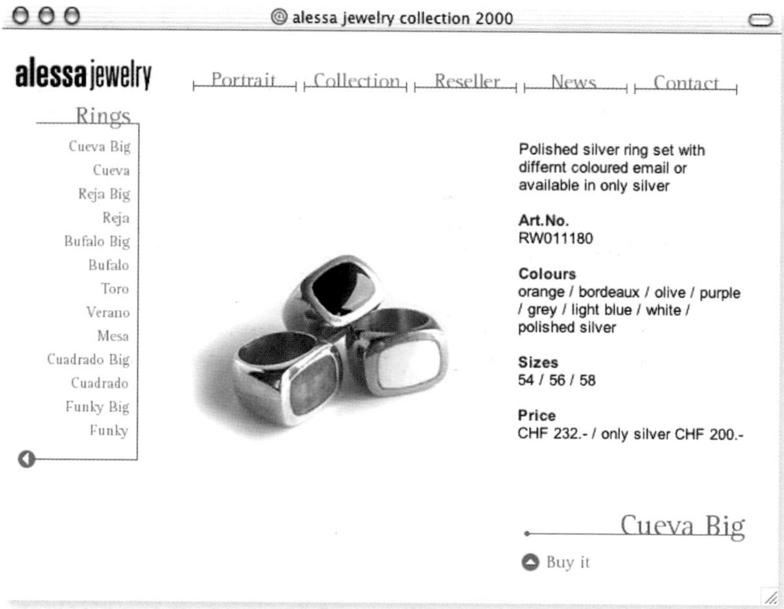
alessa jewelry collection 2000
alessajewelry
Portrait
Collection
Reseller
News
Contact
Rings
Cueva Big
Cueva
Reja Big
Reja
Bufalo Big
Bufalo
Toro
Verano
Mesa
Cuadrado Big
Cuadrado
Funky Big
Funky
Polished silver ring set with differnt coloured email or available in only silver
Art.No.
RW011180
Colours
orange / bordeaux / olive / purple / grey / light blue / white / polished silver
Sizes
54 / 56 / 58
Price
CHF 232.- / only silver CHF 200.-
Cueva Big
Buy it

WWW.ALESSAJEWELRY.COM
D: DOMINIC TIMMIS, **C:** PETER ULRICH, **P:** PETER ULRICH
A: NEXUS - CREATIVE COMPANY, **M:** INFO@NCC.CH

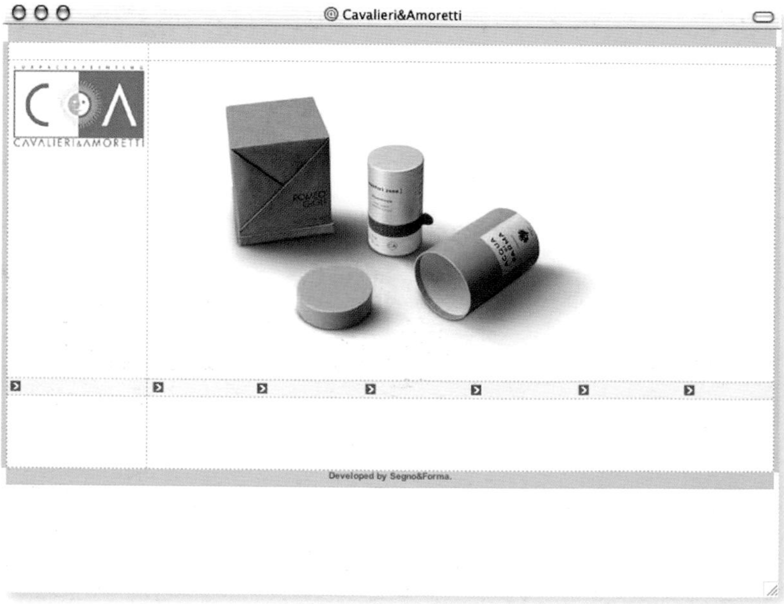
Cavalieri&Amoretti
CAVALIERI&AMORETTI
Developed by Segno&Forma.

WWW.CAVALIERIEAMORETTI.COM
D: DANIELE LODI RIZZINI, **C:** DANIELE GIUSTI, **P:** DANIELE LODI RIZZINI
A: SEGNO&FORMA, **M:** DANIELE@SEGNOEFORMA.IT

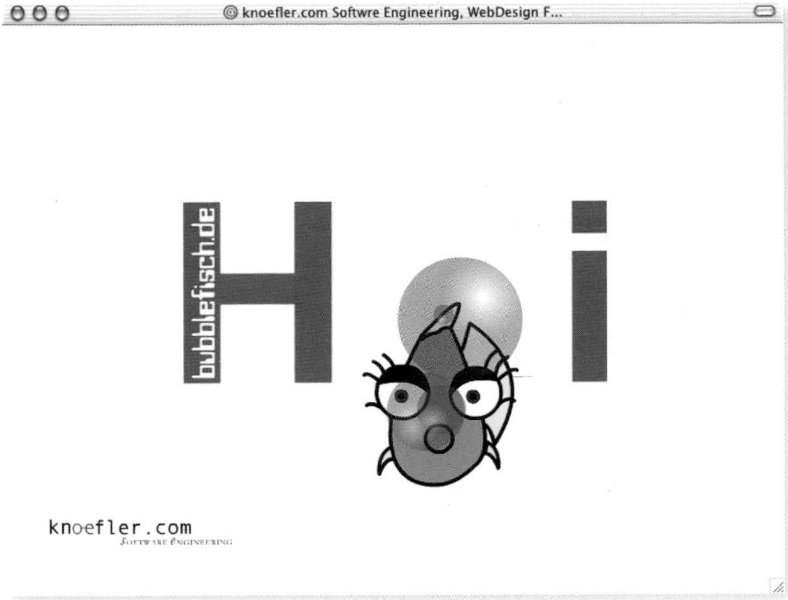

WWW.BUBBLEFISCH.DE
D: SÖNKE KNÖFLER
A: KNOEFLER.COM, **M:** SKNOEFLER@KNOEFLER.COM

WWW.MY-FAVORITE-THINGS.WEBMEN.DE/BLACK_DESIRE/ALL_BLACK_DESIRE.HTML
D: MICHAEL RIPP
A: POOL-WEBDESIGN, **M:** INFO@POOL-WEBDESIGN.DE

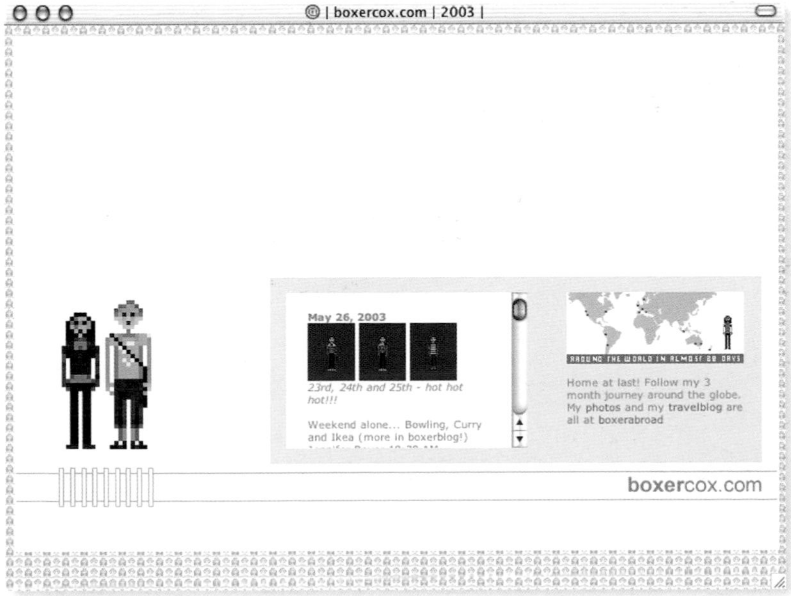

WWW.BOXERCOX.COM
D: JEN BOXER
A: BOXERCOX, **M:** JEN@BOXERCOX.COM

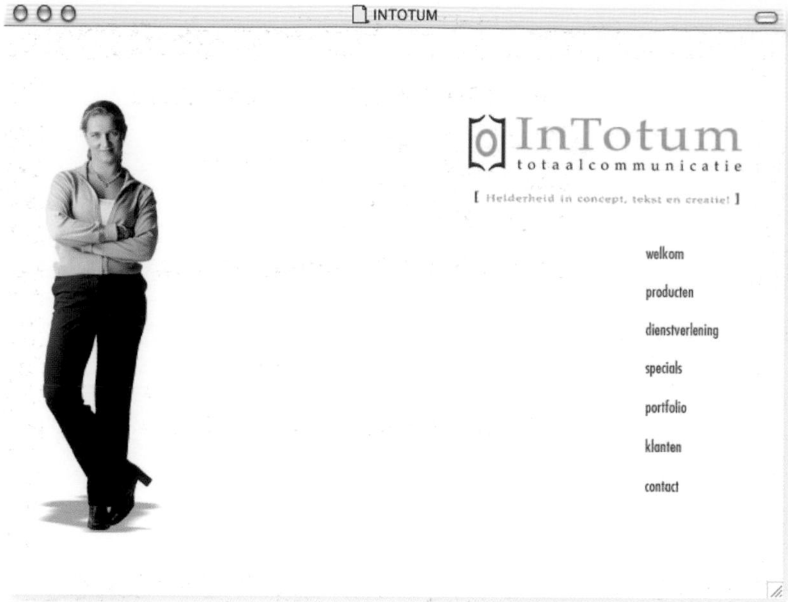

WWW.INTOTUM.NL
D: LEO HAMERS
A: YAIKZ!, **M:** INFO@YAIKZ.NL

WWW.CAPELLADESDISSENY.COM
D: FRANCESC CAPELLADES PUIG, **C:** JORDI GRANDIA CEBOLLERO
A: CAPELLADES DISSENY, **M:** FRANK@CAPELLADESDISSENY.COM

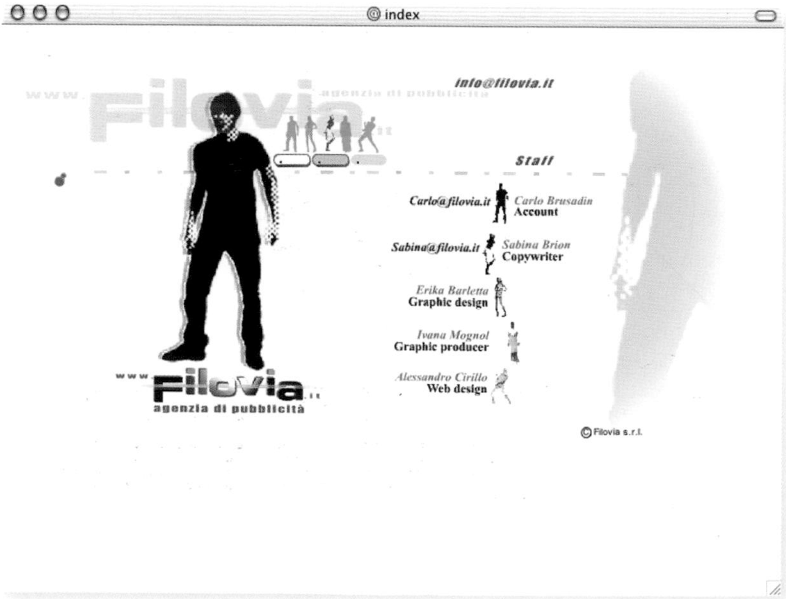

WWW.FILOVIA.IT
D: ALESSANDRO CIRILLO
A: AGENZIA PUBBL. FILOVIAS.R.L., **M:** ALESFLY@TISCALINET.IT

WWW.SERENAMOTTARELLA.COM
D: SERENA MOTTARELLA
M: INFO@SERENAMOTTARELLA.COM

WWW.IMAGOS.ORG
D: MODE MARTÍNEZ
A: NEOMODE, **M:** SABINOMODE@HOTMAI.COM

WWW.ABARGON.COM
D: THE WHOLE ABARTEAM
A: ABARGON, **M:** JCARIAS@ABRGON.COM

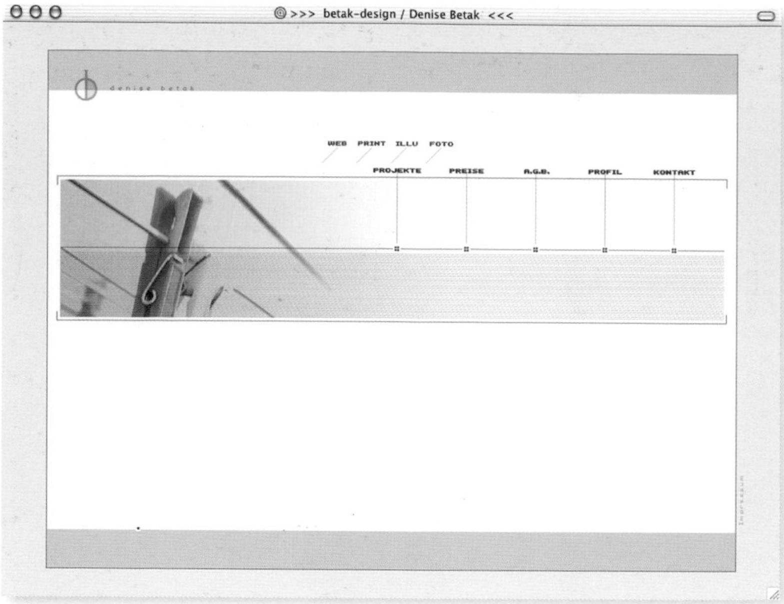

WWW.BETAK-DESIGN.DE
D: DENISE BETAK
A: DENISE BETAK DESIGN, **M:** GIANLUCA.DONADONI@ESIRION.DE

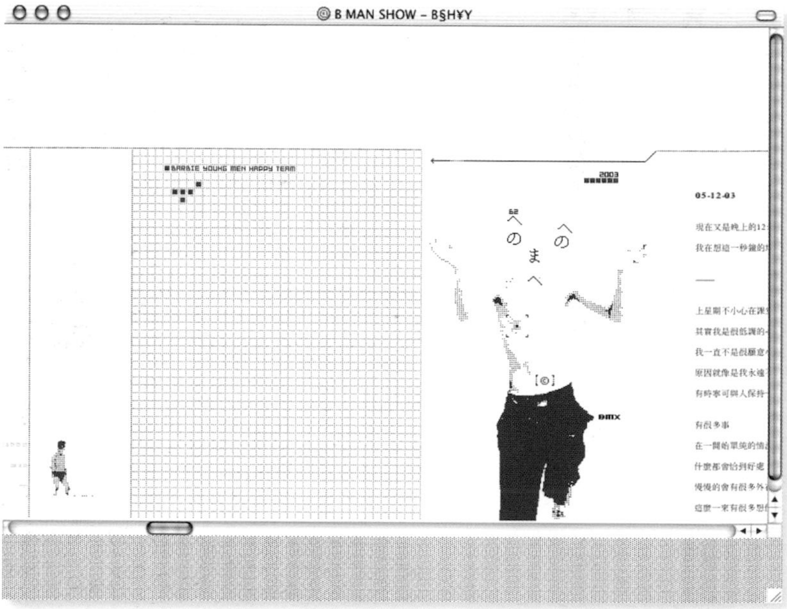

WWW.62BINGO.IDV.ST
D: BINGO
M: BINGO.721@YAHOO.COM.TW

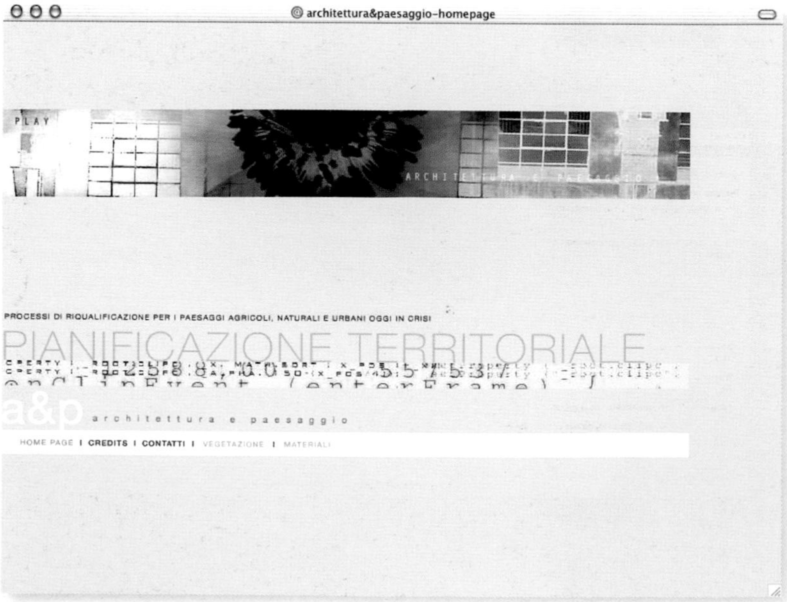

WWW.ARCHITETTURAEPAESAGGIO.IT
D: GRAZIANO DE ROSSI
M: GDEROSSI@ALMA.IT

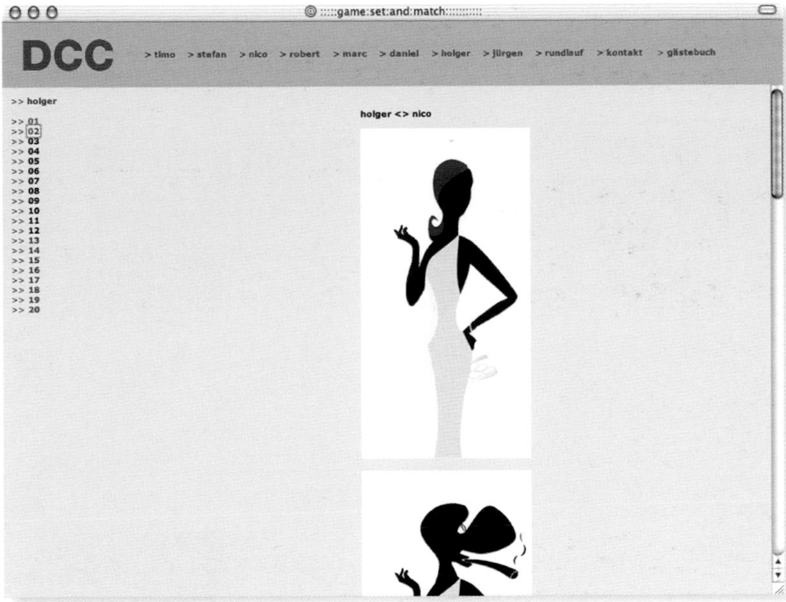

WWW.DIGITALCENTERCOURT.COM
D: NICO HENSEL, **C:** NICO HENSEL, **P:** TIMO BRAUCHLE
A: ACROFUZZ.DE I LICHTPUNKT.BIZ, **M:** NH@LICHTPUNKT.BIZ

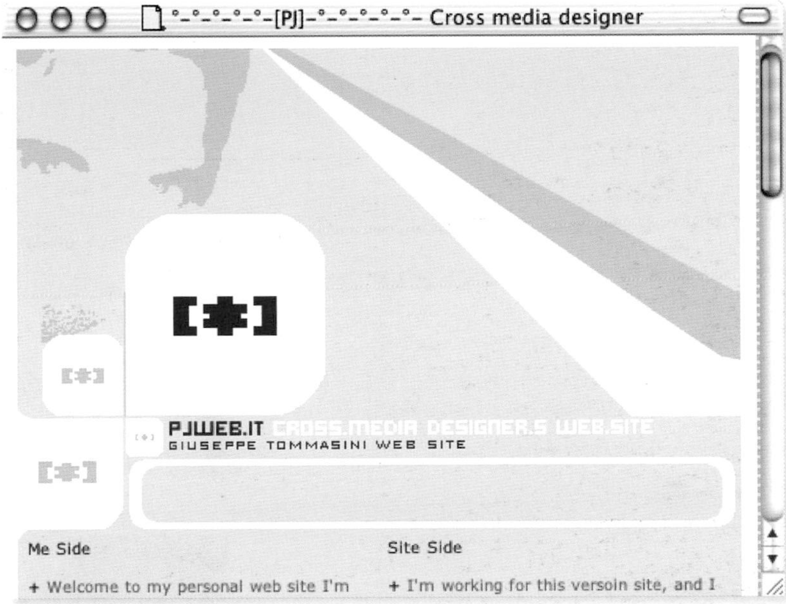

WWW.PJWEB.IT
D: TOMMASINI GIUSEPPE
M: WEBMASTER@PJWEB.IT

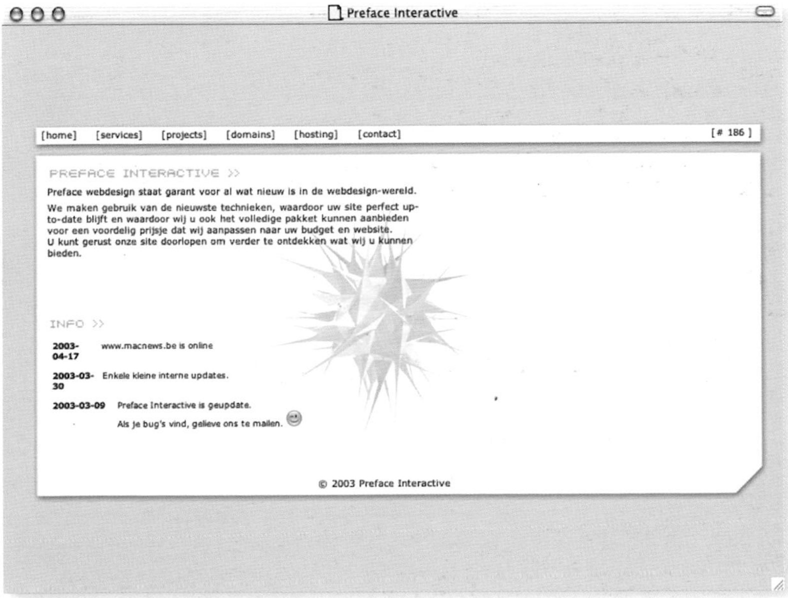

WWW.PREFACE.BE
D: SAM VAN MALLEGHEM, **C:** DRIEK DESMET
M: DRIEK@PREFACE.BE

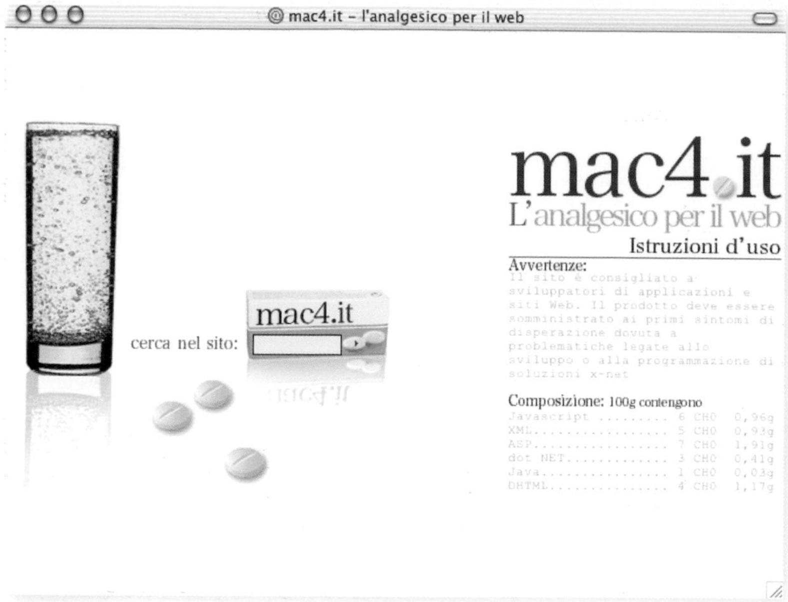

WWW.MAC4.IT
D: ALESSANDRO DI LELIO, **C:** MATTEO CASATI, **P:** MATTEO CASATI
M: M.CASATI@MAC4.IT

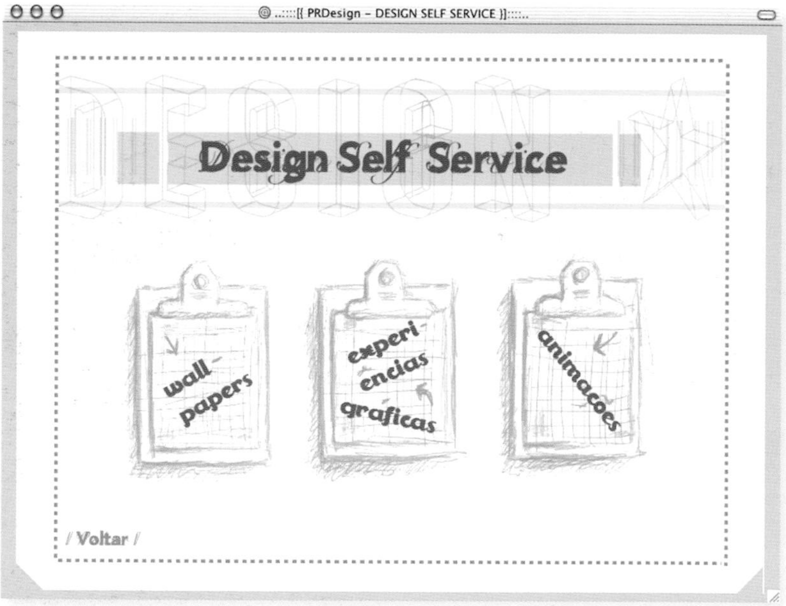

WWW.PRDESIGN.COM.SAPO.PT
D: PEDRO RODRIGUES
A: PRDESIGN

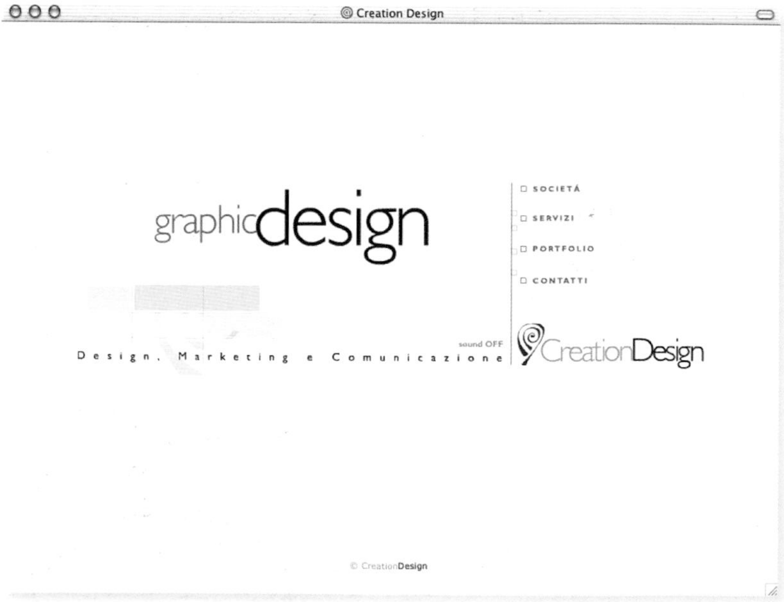

WWW.CREATIONDESIGN.IT
D: GIORGIO FACOETTI
A: CREATION DESIGN, **M:** G.FACOETTI@CREATIONDESIGN.IT

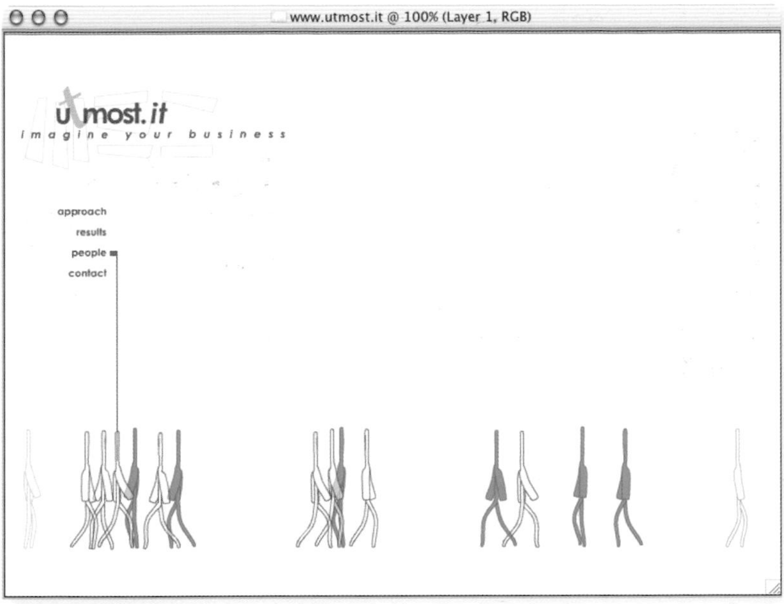

WWW.UTMOST.IT
D: TOMAS MEGHI
M: INFO@UTMOST.IT

WWW.VIVELANOURRITURE.BE
D: LEEN DE SMEDT
A: BALLY-HOO, **M:** INFO@BALLY-HOO.BE

WWW.FERMINPEREZ.COM
D: FERMÍN PÉREZ PRADOS
M: FERMIN@FERMINPEREZ.COM

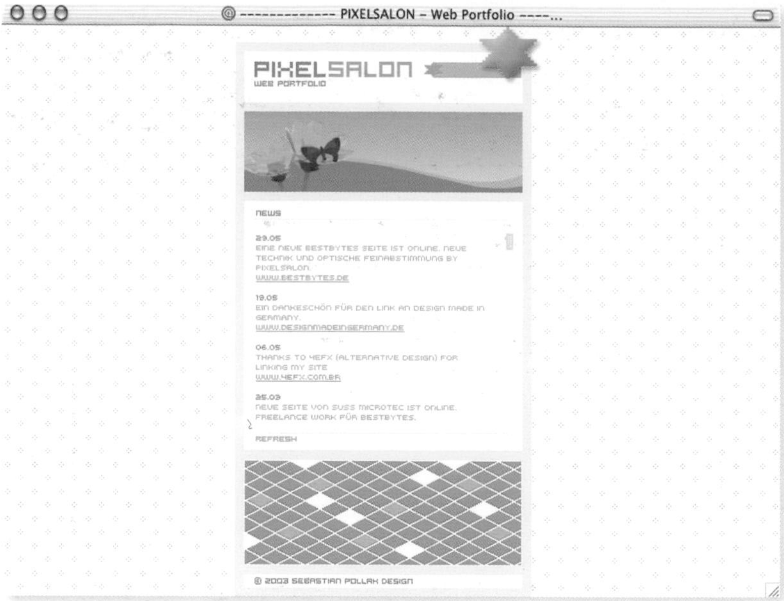

PIXELSALON - Web Portfolio
PIXELSALON
WEB PORTFOLIO
NEWS
29.05
EINE NEUE BESTBYTES SEITE IST ONLINE. NEUE TECHNIK UND OPTISCHE FEINABSTIMMUNG BY PIXELSALON.
WWW.BESTBYTES.DE
19.05
EIN DANKESCHÖN FÜR DEN LINK AN DESIGN MADE IN GERMANY.
WWW.DESIGNMADEINGERMANY.DE
06.05
THANKS TO 4EFX (ALTERNATIVE DESIGN) FOR LINKING MY SITE
WWW.4EFX.COM.BR
25.03
NEUE SEITE VON SUSS MICROTEC IST ONLINE. FREELANCE WORK FÜR BESTBYTES.
REFRESH
© 2003 SEBASTIAN POLLAK DESIGN

WWW.PIXELSALON.DE
D: SEBASTIAN POLLAK
M: SEBASTIAN@PIXELSALON.DE

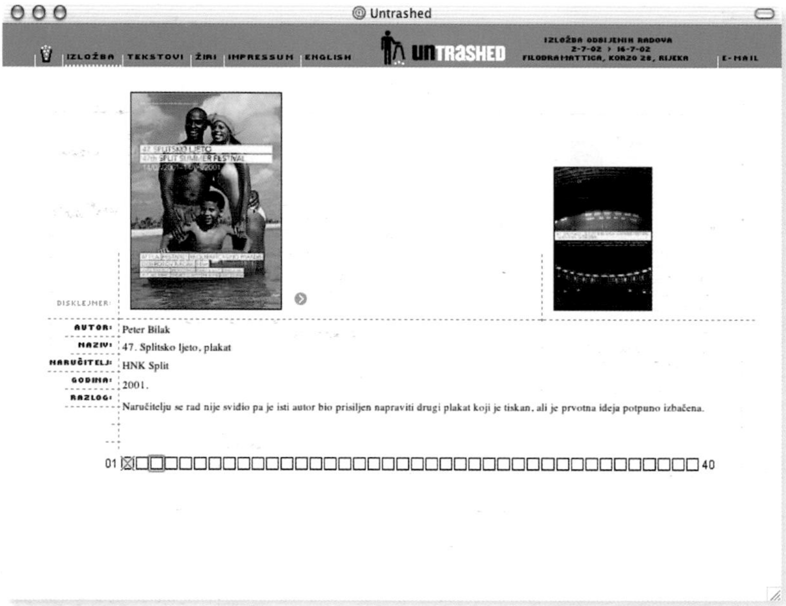

Untrashed
IZLOŽBA
TEKSTOVI
ŽIRI
IMPRESSUM
ENGLISH
UNTRASHED
IZLOŽBA ODBIJENIH RADOVA
2-7-02 > 16-7-02
FILODRAMMATTICA, KORZO 28, RIJEKA
E-MAIL
DISKLEJMER:
AUTOR: Peter Bilak
NAZIV: 47. Splitsko ljeto, plakat
NARUČITELJ: HNK Split
GODINA: 2001.
RAZLOG: Naručitelju se rad nije svidio pa je isti autor bio prisiljen napraviti drugi plakat koji je tiskan, ali je prvotna ideja potpuno izbačena.
01
40

WWW.UNTRASHED.COM
D: IGOR SKUNCA, **C:** PETRA ZLOVIC
A: INVENT - MULTIMEDIA STUDIO, **M:** IGOR@INVENT.HR

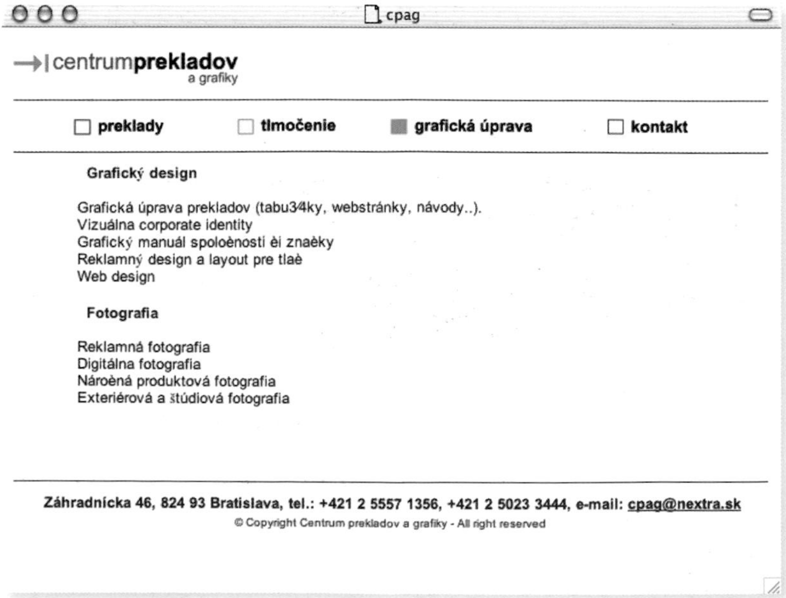

cpag
centrumprekladov
a grafiky
preklady
tlmočenie
grafická úprava
kontakt
Grafický design
Grafická úprava prekladov (tabu34ky, webstránky, návody..).
Vizuálna corporate identity
Grafický manuál spoloènosti èi znaèky
Reklamný design a layout pre tlaè
Web design
Fotografia
Reklamná fotografia
Digitálna fotografia
Nároèná produktová fotografia
Exteriérová a štúdiová fotografia
Záhradnícka 46, 824 93 Bratislava, tel.: +421 2 5557 1356, +421 2 5023 3444, e-mail: cpag@nextra.sk
© Copyright Centrum prekladov a grafiky - All right reserved

WWW.HOME.NEXTRA.SK/CPAG
D: JAN ONDREJKA
M: ONDREJKA@AFAD.SK

WWW.PROCTA.DE
D: MARCO GATZSCH
A: PROCTA INTERNET SOLUTIONS, **M:** MARCO.GATZSCH@PROCTA.DE

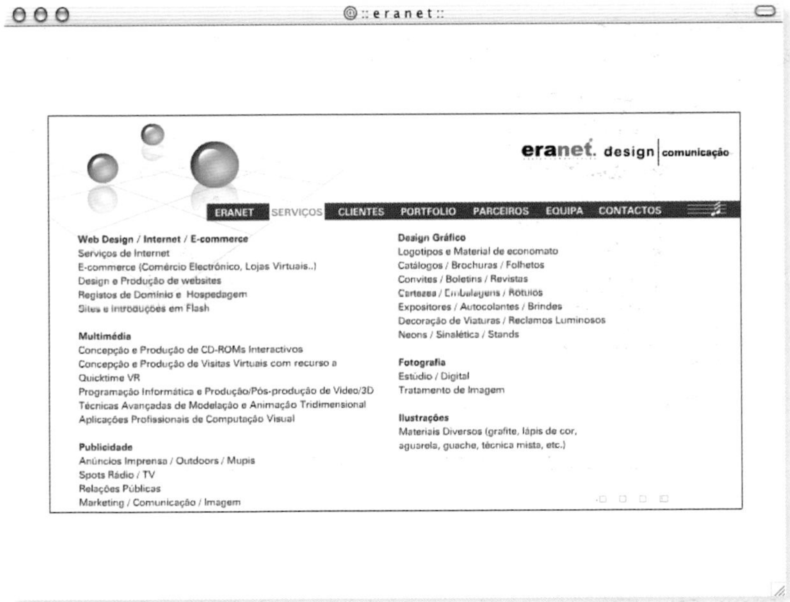

WWW.ERANET.PT
D: ISABEL CUNHA, **P:** ERANET
A: ERANET, **M:** ISABEL.CUNHA@ERANET.PT

WWW.LEONARDOGRECO.IT
D: LUCA BIANCONI, **C:** LUCA BIANCONI
A: MODULAB, **M:** MODULAB@LIBERO.IT

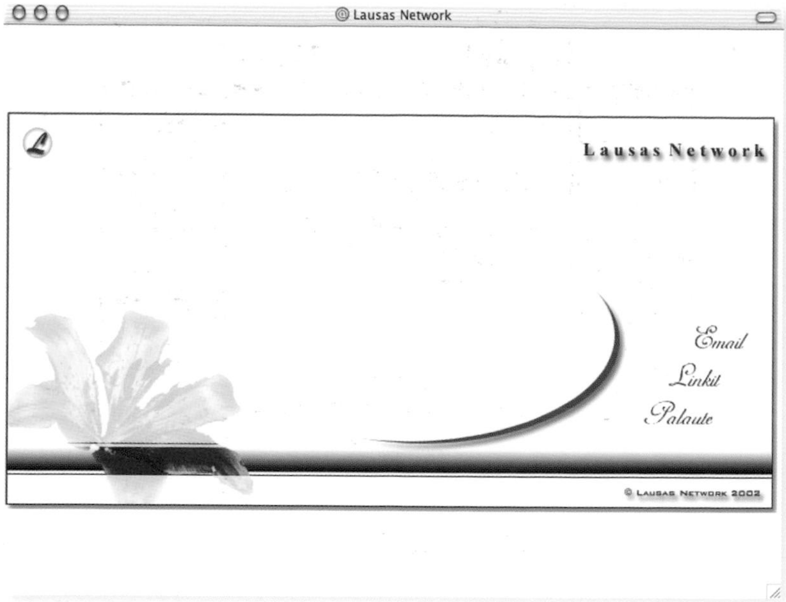

Lausas Network
Lausas Network
Email
Linkit
Palaute
© Lausas Network 2002

WWW.LAUSAS.NET/
D: VICTOR LAUSAS
A: LAUSAS NETWORK, **M:** VICTOR@LAUSAS.NET

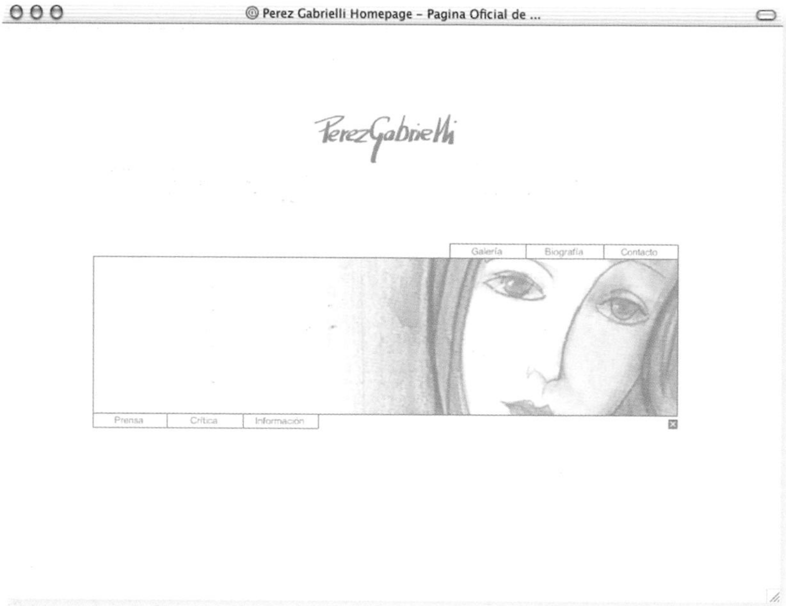

Perez Gabrielli Homepage - Pagina Oficial de ...
PerezGabrielli
Galeria
Biografia
Contacto
Prensa
Critica
Informacion

WWW.PEREZGABRIELLI.COM
D: RICARDO CABALLERO
A: PEREZ GABRIELLI, **M:** AGENT@PEREZGABRIELLI.COM

MAGELLAN Netzwerke GmbH - Die Netzwerk Spezia...
MAGELLAN
Netzwerke GmbH
Bitte wählen Sie aus:
LAN/WAN Systemlösungen
Security
Sprach-/Datenintegration
Netzwerk Management & Analyse
Consulting
Training
Das Unternehmen
Die MAGELLAN Netzwerke GmbH hat sich auf Netzwerktechnologie und Datenkommunikation spezialisiert.
Als herstellerunabhängiges Systemhaus bieten wir an unseren Standorten Köln, Essen, Hamburg und München unseren Kunden individuelle Lösungen.
Weitere Informationen...

WWW.MAGELLAN-NET.DE
D: DIRK BEHLAU
A: PIXELEYE INTERACTIVE, **M:** DIRK@PIXELEYE.DE

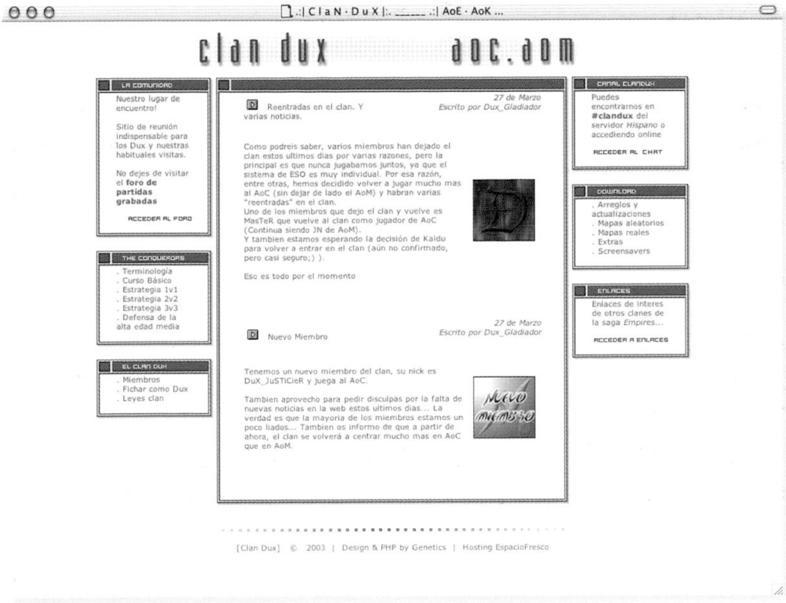

WWW.CLANDUX.COM
D: HUMBERT TORROELLA NAVARRO
A: ESPACIO FRESCO, **M:** GENETICS@CLANDUX.COM

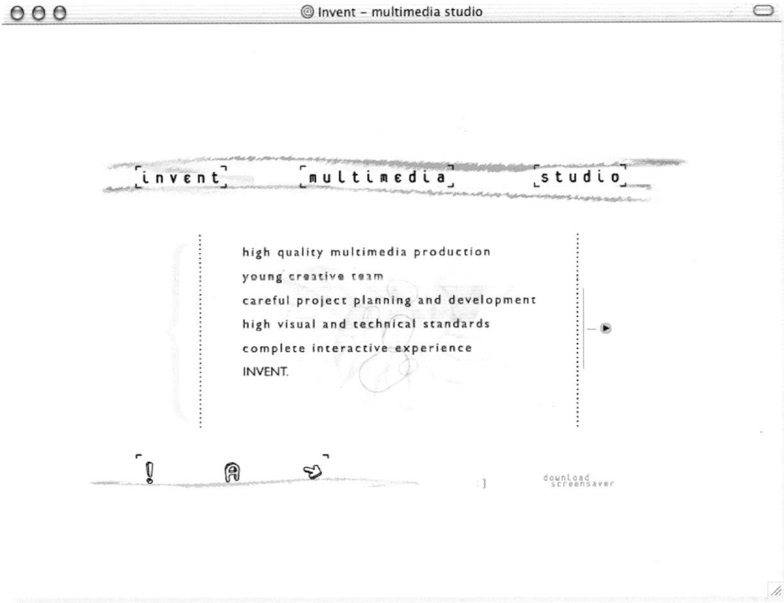

WWW.INVENT.HR
D: IGOR SKUNCA, **C:** PETRA ZLOVIC
A: INVENT - MULTIMEDIA STUDIO, **M:** IGOR@INVENT.HR

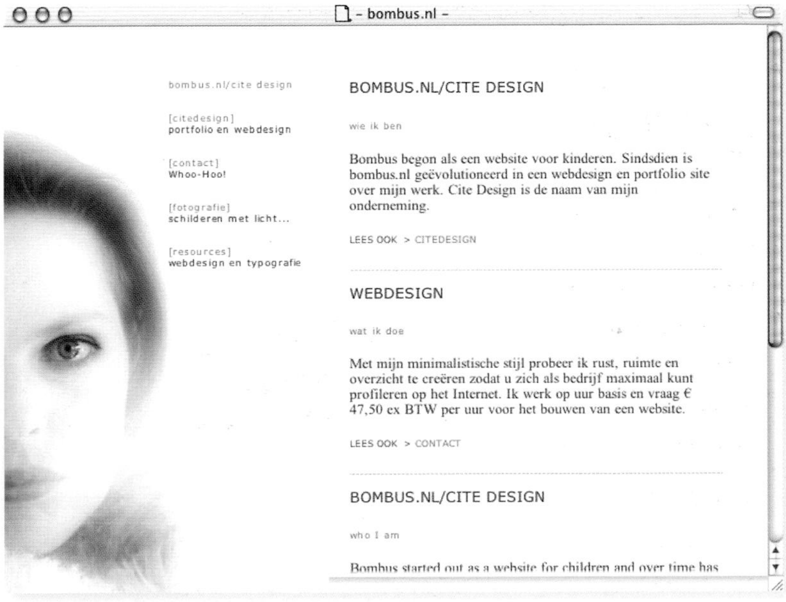

WWW.BOMBUS.NL
D: DANIËLLE MOLENAAR
A: BOMBUS, **M:** BOMBUS@BOMBUS.NL

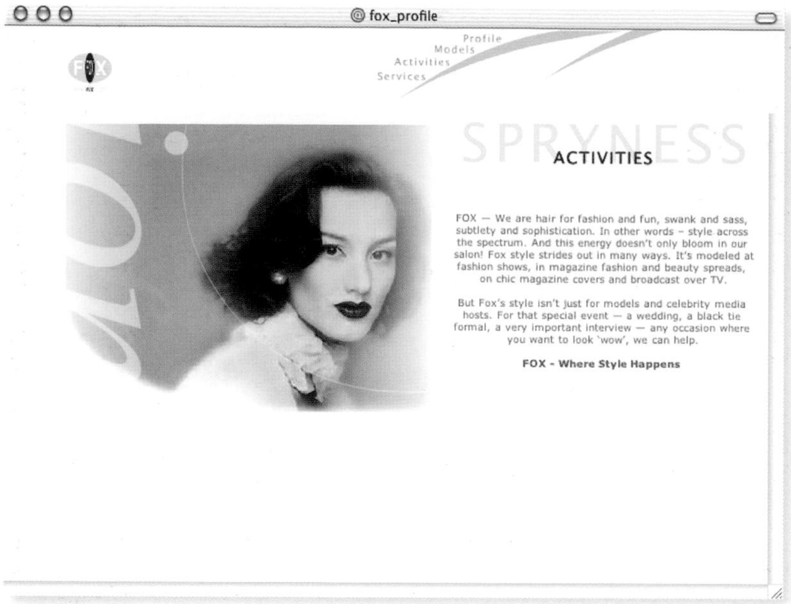

fox_profile
Profile
Models
Activities
Services
SPRYNESS
ACTIVITIES
FOX — We are hair for fashion and fun, swank and sass, subtlety and sophistication. In other words – style across the spectrum. And this energy doesn't only bloom in our salon! Fox style strides out in many ways. It's modeled at fashion shows, in magazine fashion and beauty spreads, on chic magazine covers and broadcast over TV.
But Fox's style isn't just for models and celebrity media hosts. For that special event — a wedding, a black tie formal, a very important interview — any occasion where you want to look 'wow', we can help.
FOX - Where Style Happens

WWW.FOXHAIR.COM
D: DEXTER TEOH
M: TEOHCSD@SPH.COM.SG

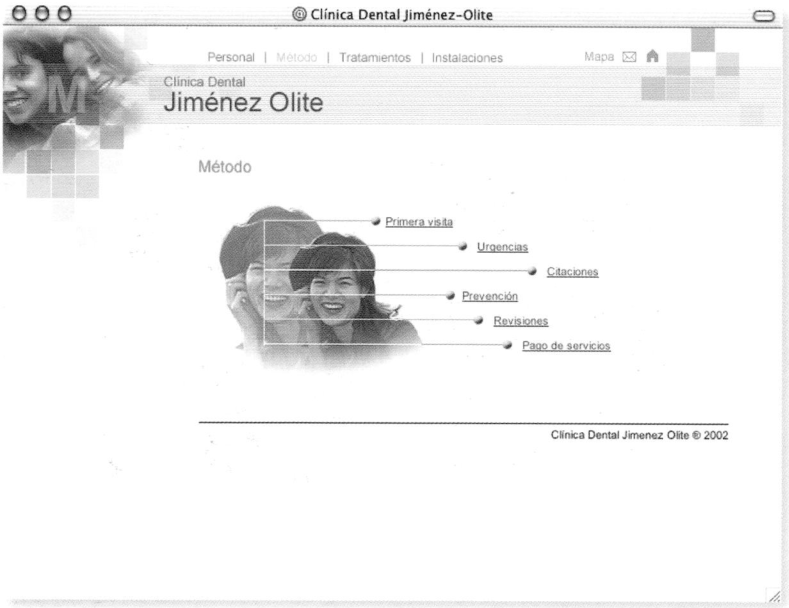

WWW.JIMENEZ-OLITE.COM
D: SANTI SALLÉS
A: TUNDRABCN, **M:** INFO@TUNDRABCN.COM

WWW.STYLEHOTELS.NET
D: SANTI SALLÉS
A: TUNDRABCN, **M:** INFO@TUNDRABCN.COM

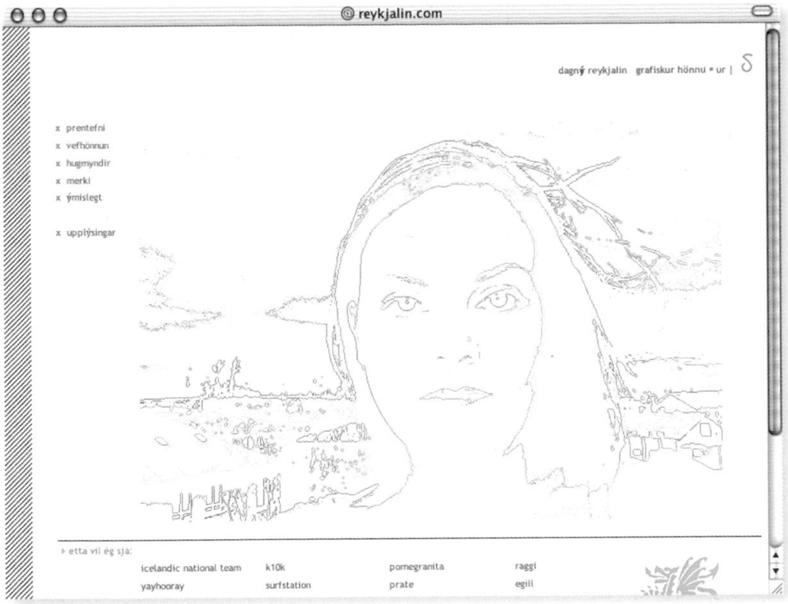

WWW.REYKJALIN.COM
D: DAGNY REYKJALIN
M: DAGNY@REYKJALIN.COM

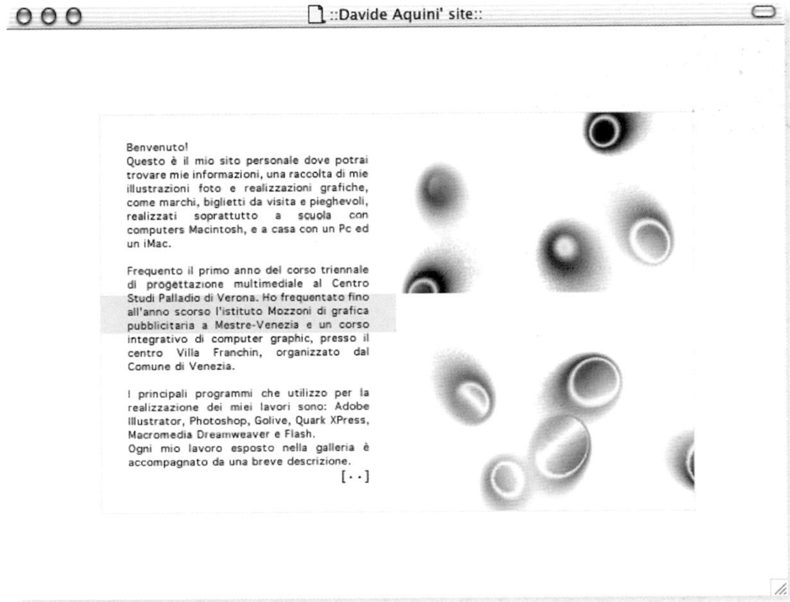

WWW.WHYNET.INFO/DAVIDE
D: DAVIDE G. AQUINI
M: DAVIDE@WHYNET.INFO

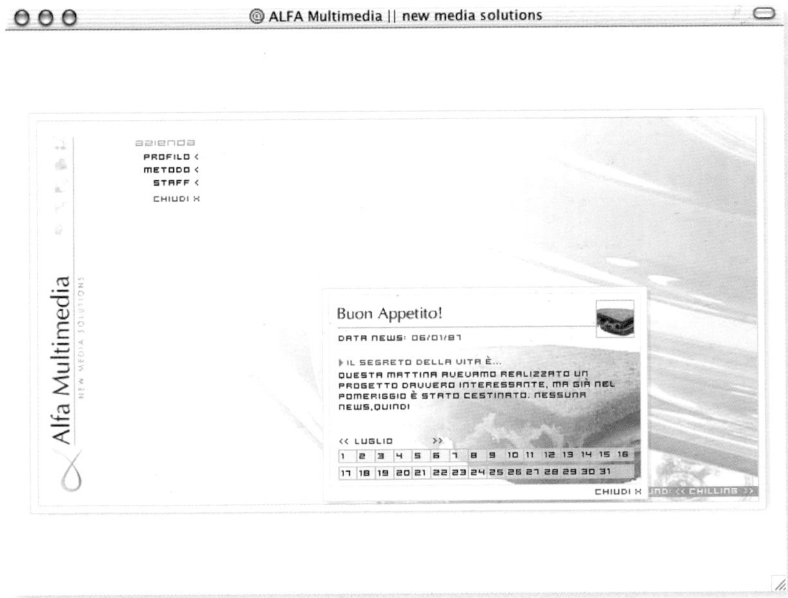

WWW.ALFAMULTIMEDIA.IT
D: GABRIELE DI LORENZO
A: ALFA MULTIMEDIA, **M:** WEBMASTER@ALFAMULTIMEDIA.IT

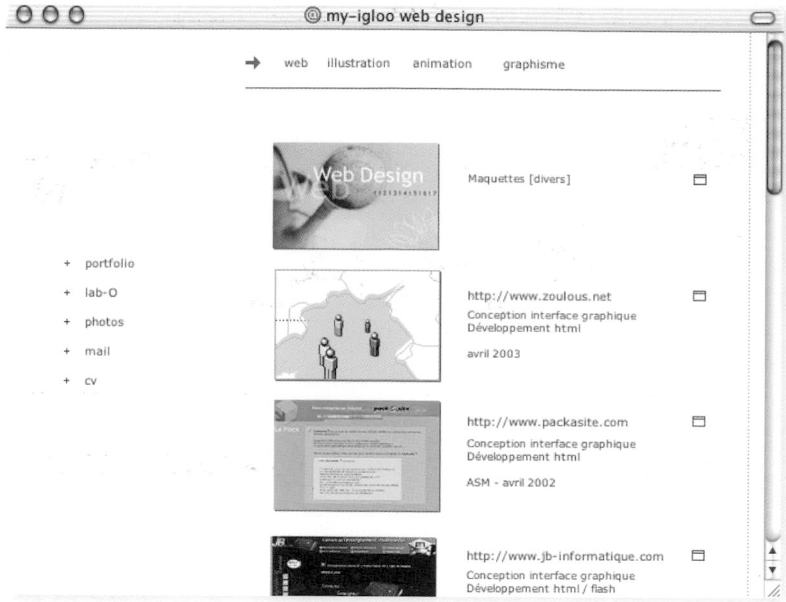

WWW.MY-IGLOO.COM
D: VALERIE LEBLANC
M: VAL@MY-IGLOO.COM

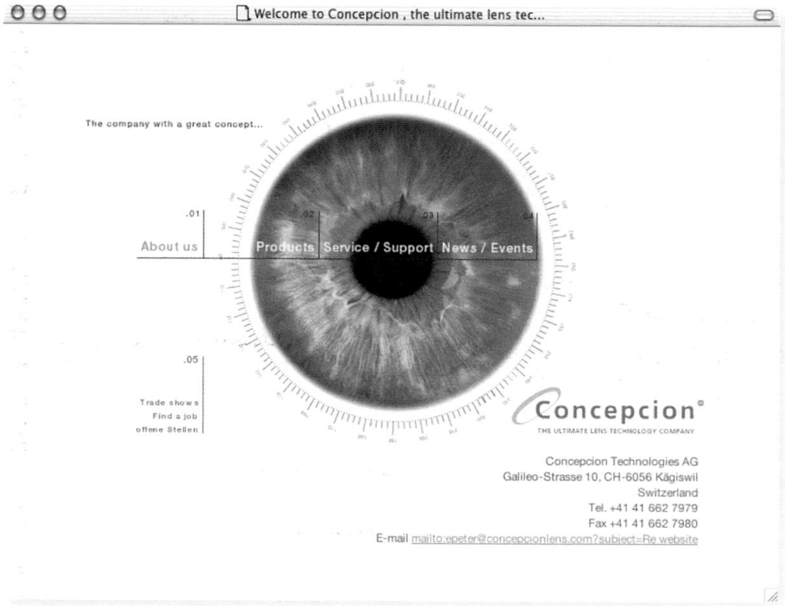

WWW.CONCEPCIONLENS.COM
D: DOMINIC TIMMIS, **C:** DOMINIC TIMMIS, **P:** PETER ULRICH
A: NEXUS - CREATIVE COMPANY, **M:** INFO@NCC.CH

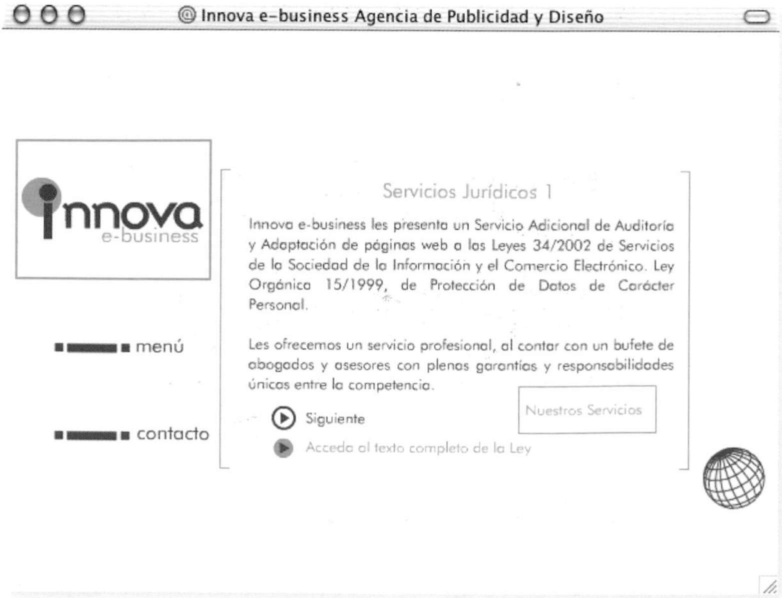

WWW.IEBS.ES
D: DAVID TOLEDO
A: NNOVA E-BUSINESS, **M:** DAVIDTOLEDO@IEBS.ES

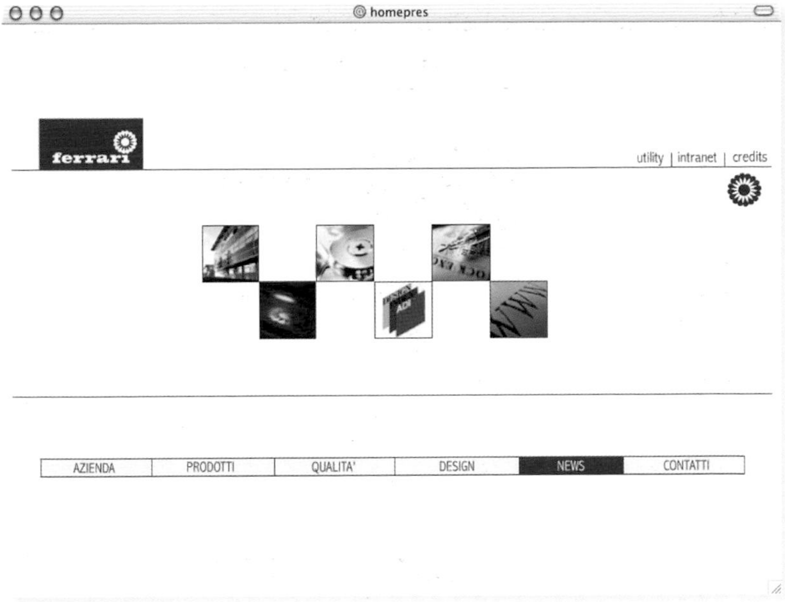

WWW.FERRARISPA.IT
D: BOROZAN VANJA, **C:** AMBROSINI MASSIMILIANO, **P:** MATERICA
A: MATERICA, **M:** AINAV@VIRGILIO.IT

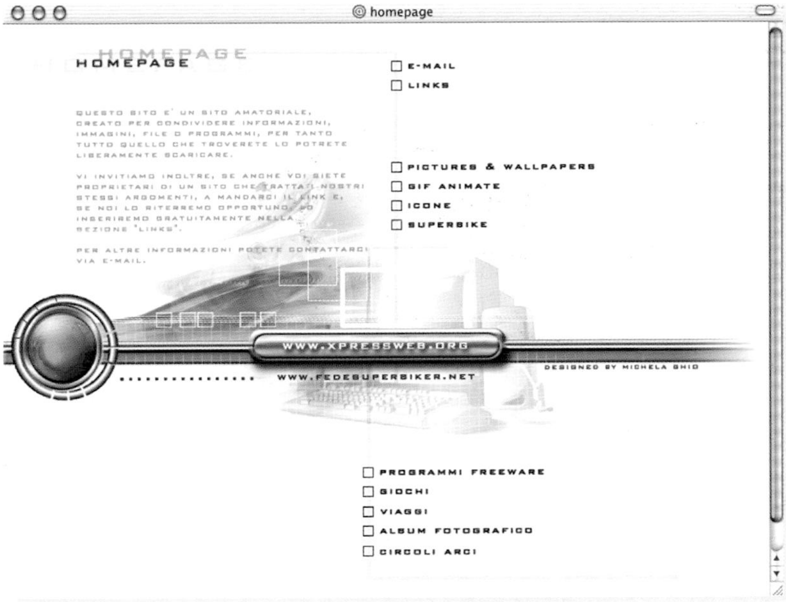

WWW.XPRESSWEB.ORG
D: MICHELA GHIO
M: POSTMASTER@XPRESSWEB.ORG

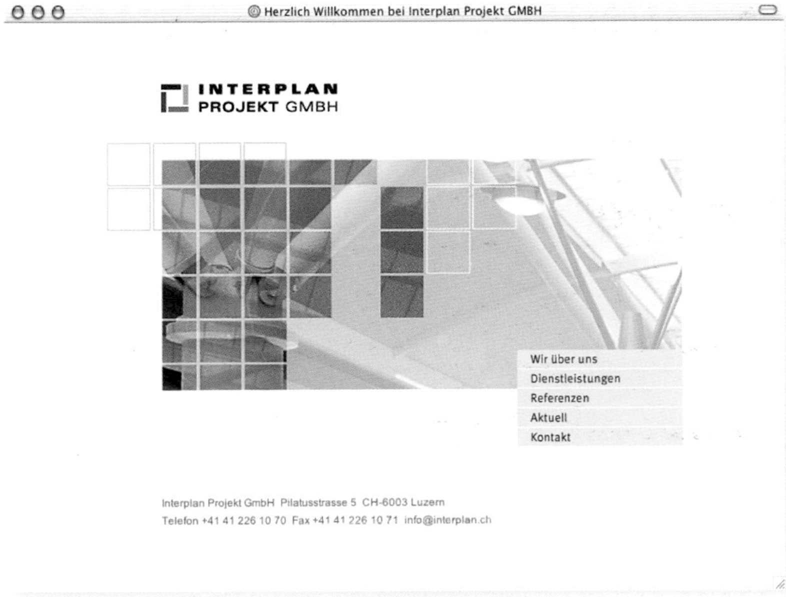

WWW.INTERPLAN.CH
D: CORNEL BETSCHART, **C:** CORNEL BETSCHART, **P:** PETER ULRICH
A: NEXUS - CREATIVE COMPANY, **M:** INFO@NCC.CH

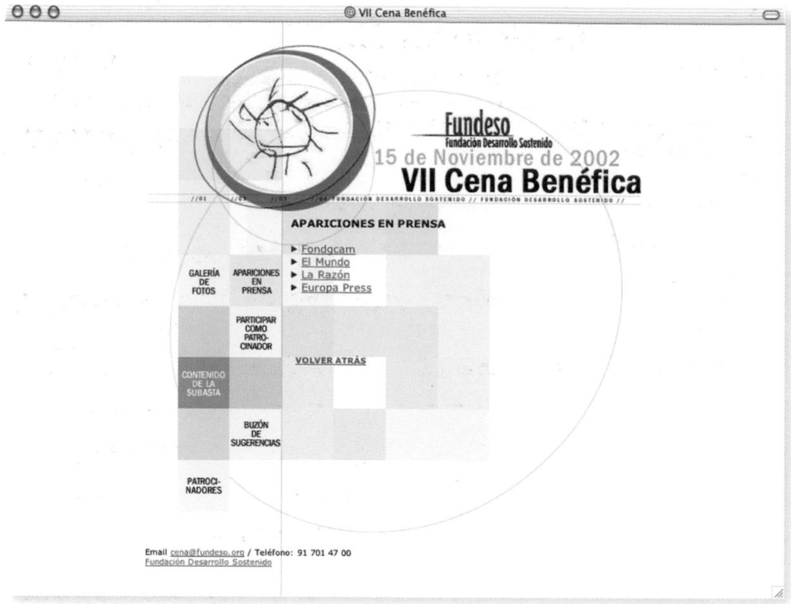

WWW.FUNDESO.ORG/CGI-BIN/CENA/MEDIA.PL?PRO=INDEX
D: DAVID NAVARRO GOMEZ
A: ENK3 COMUNICACION, **M:** NAVARRO@ENK3.COM

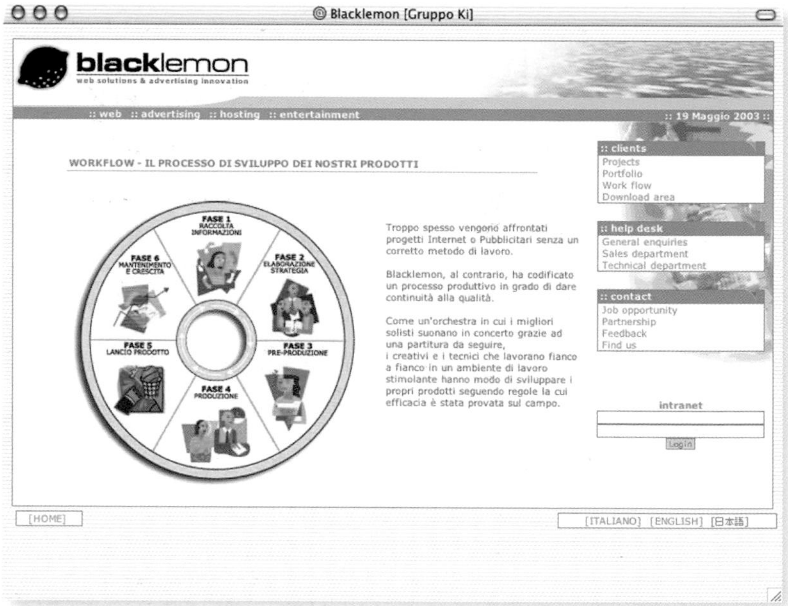

WWW.BLACKLEMON.COM
D: NICOLA BELLOTTI
A: BLACKLEMON, **M:** INFO@BLACKLEMON.COM

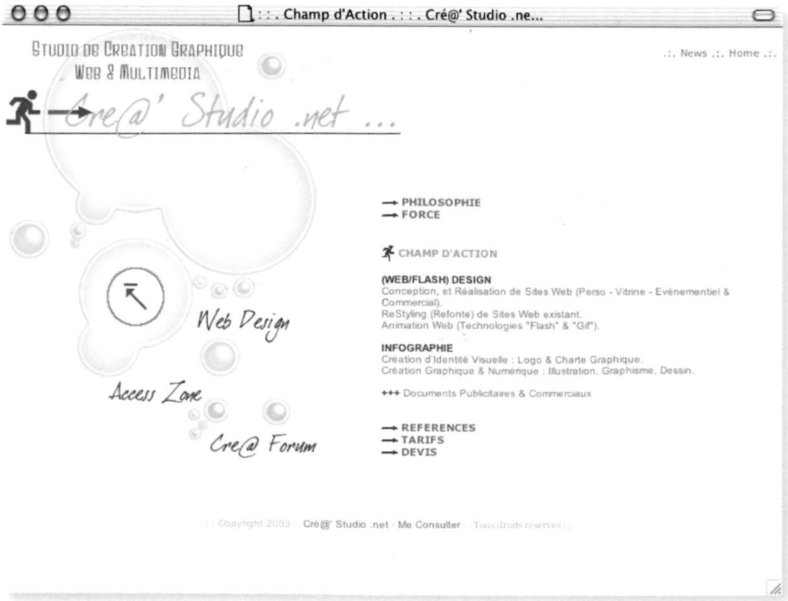

WWW.CREASTUDIO.NET
D: LAURENT SÉVERINE
M: NELLSSS@CREASTUDIO.NET)

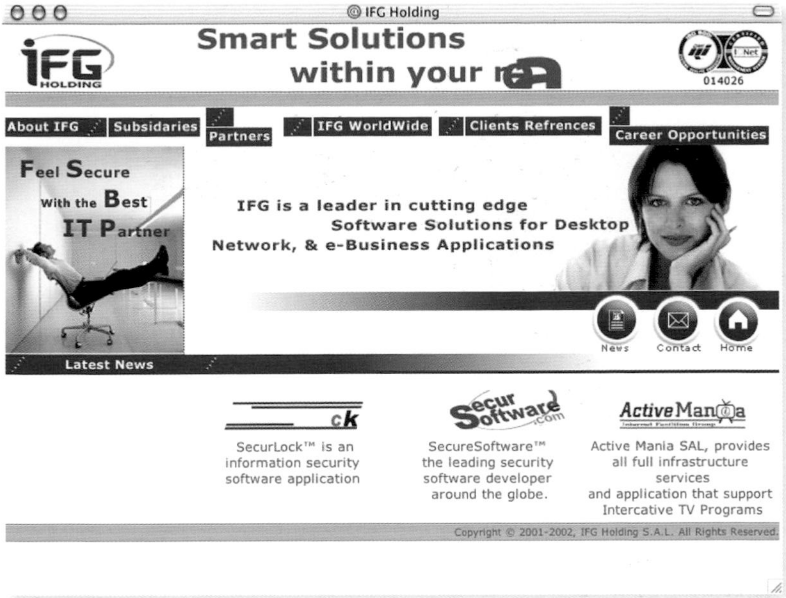

WWW.IFGHOLDING.COM
D: KHALIL EL HAJJAR, **C:** KHALIL EL HAJJAR, **P:** IFG WEB DEPARTMENT
M: KHALIL.HAJJAR@IFSAL.COM

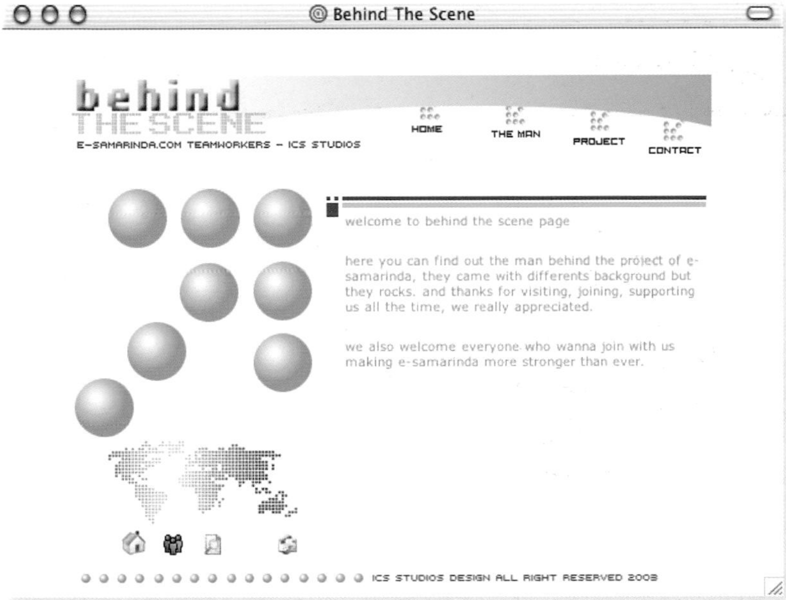

WWW.ICS.E-SAMARINDA.COM
D: CIPZ
A: ICS STUDIOS, **M:** CIPZ@MSN.COM

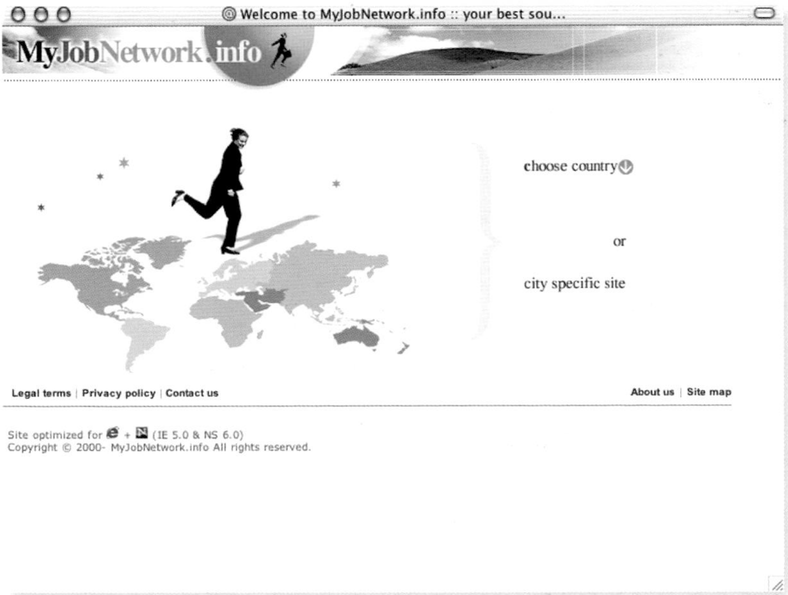

WWW.E-MYCAREER.COM
D: CATALIN ILINCA, **C:** HKMSOFT CORPORATION, **P:** HKMSOFT CORPORATION
A: MEDIA9, **M:** OFFICE@MEDIA9.RO

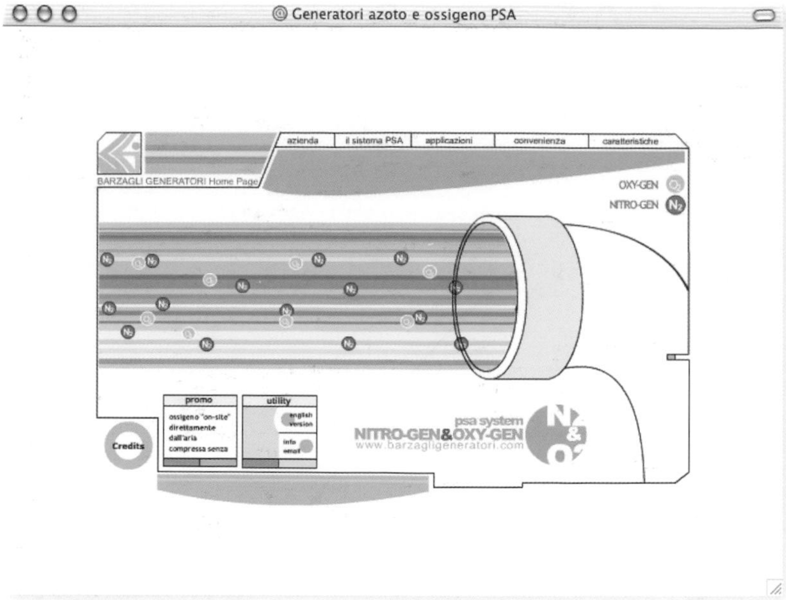

WWW.BARZAGLIGENERATORI.COM
D: MICHELE CATANI
M: MICHECAT@LIBERO.IT

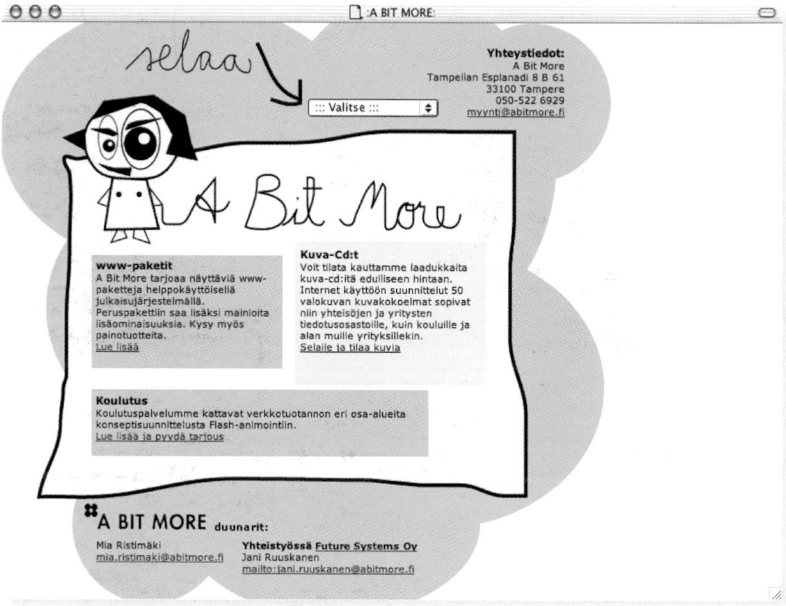

WWW.ABITMORE.FI
D: MIA RISTIMÄKI
A: A BIT MORE, **M:** MIA@ABITMORE.FI

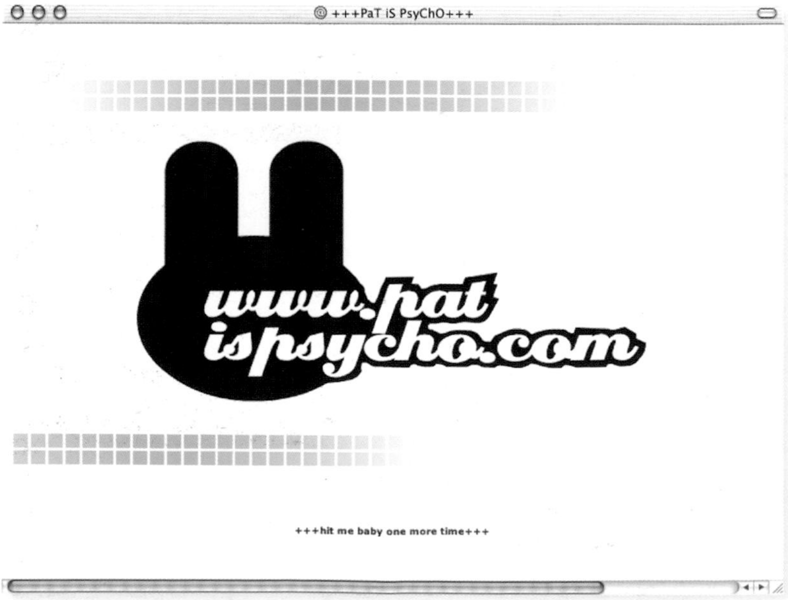

WWW.GEO.YA.COM/PATISPSYCHO
D: PATRICIA COLAO
M: ZEDZIBBON@HOTMAIL.COM

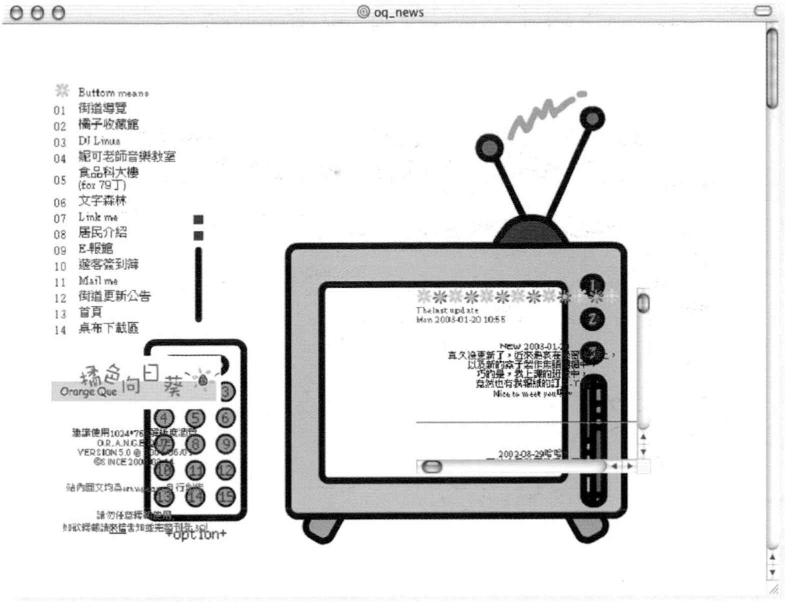

WWW.QUE.IDV.TW
D: QUE
A: PINMO VISUAL STUDIO, **M:** QUEORANGE@HOTMAIL.COM

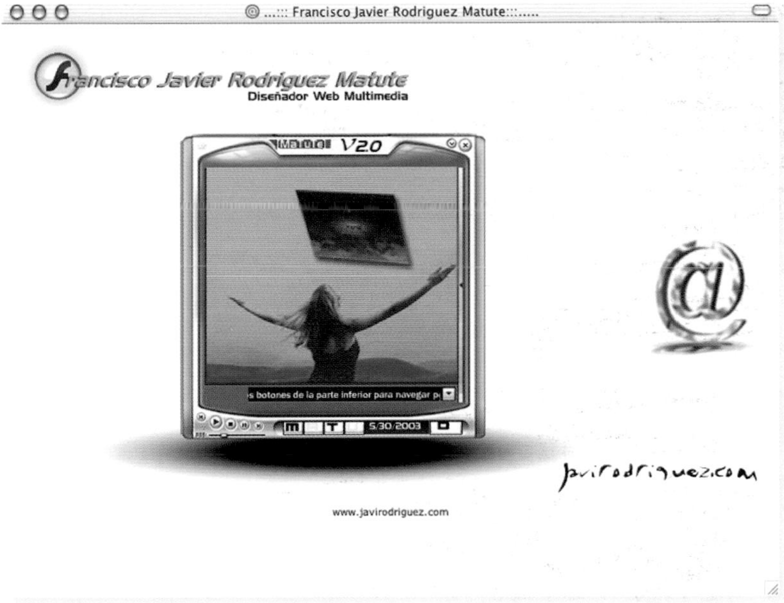

WWW.JAVIRODRIGUEZ.COM
D: FCO JAVIER
M: MATUTE@SUPERCABLE.ES

WWW.MONOGRAFICO.NET
D: DRAKE, **C:** DRAKE, **P:** LUAN MARK
A: ILOGIK INDUSTRIES, **M:** RAUL@ILOGIKINDUSTRIES.COM

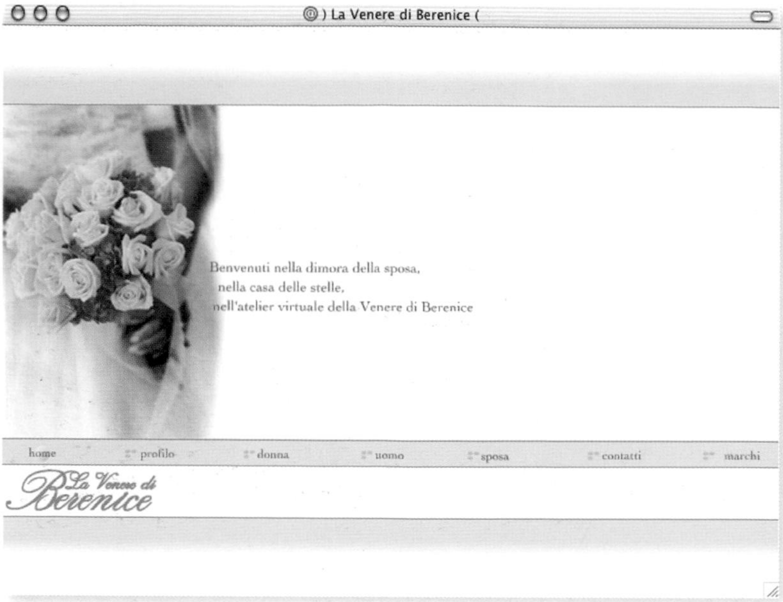

WWW.LAVENEREDIBERENICE.COM
D: MARCO TRAMONTANO, **C:** MARCO TRAMONTANO, **P:** TURNE
A: MARCOTRAMONTANO.COM, **M:** CONTATTI@MARCOTRAMONTANO.COM

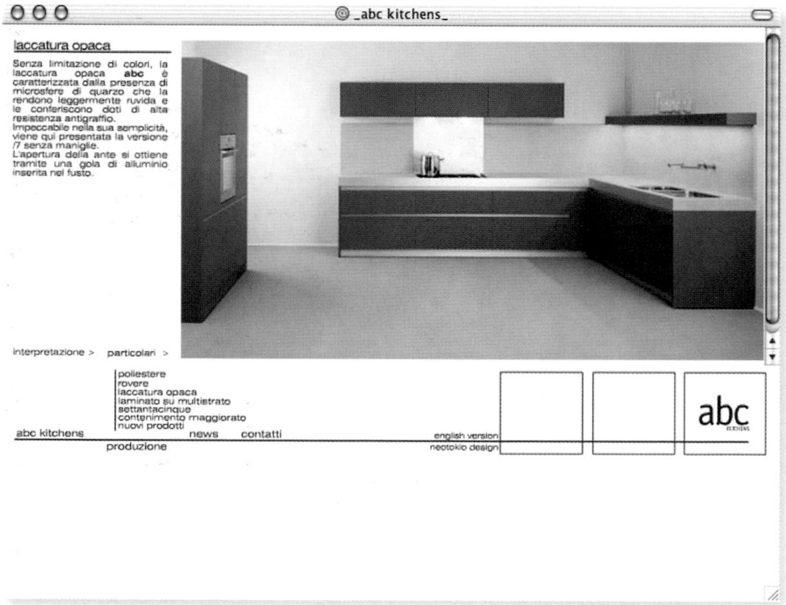

WWW.ABCCUCINE.IT
D: ROSARIO VALENTE
A: NEOTOKIO DESIGN, **M:** INFO@NEOTOKIODESIGN.COM

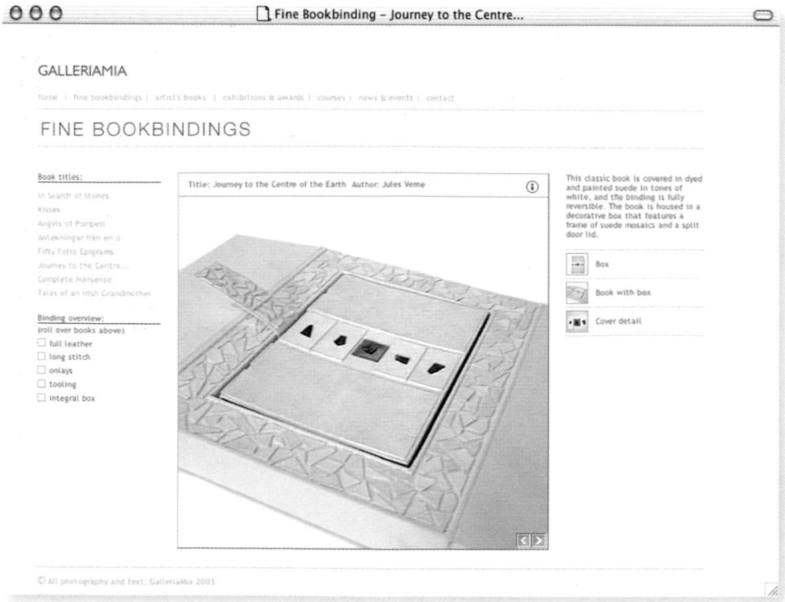

WWW.GALLERIAMIA.NET
D: NICK JONES, **C:** NICK JONES, **P:** MIA LEIJONSTEDT
M: INFO@NICKJONES.COM

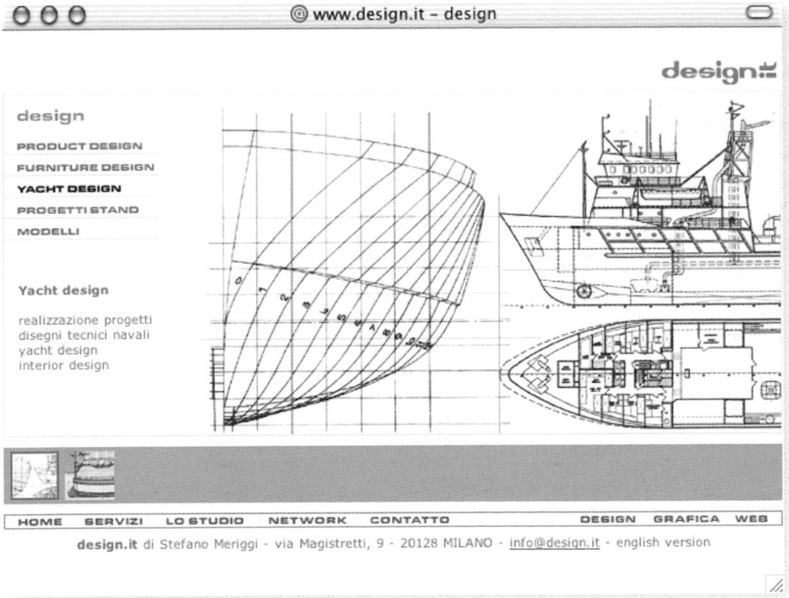

WWW.DESIGN.IT
D: STEFANO MERIGGI
A: DESIGN.IT, **M:** INFO@DESIGN.IT

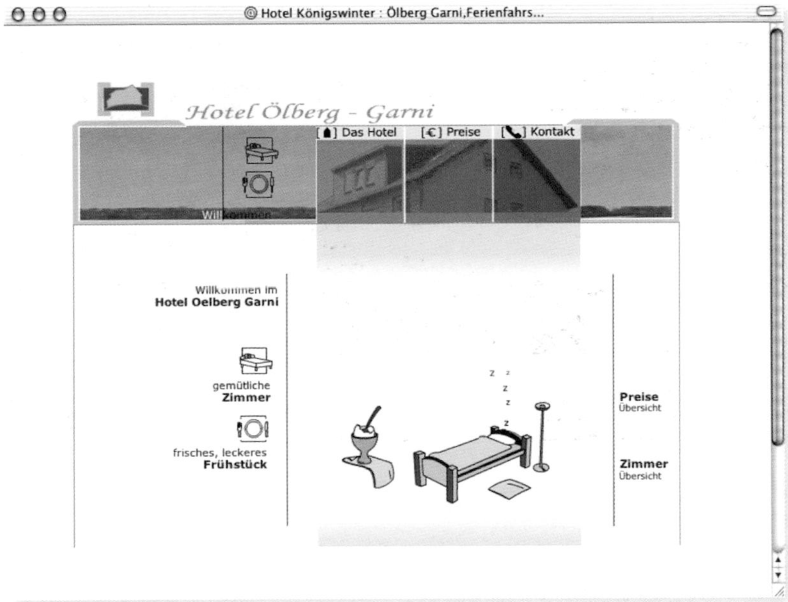

WWW.HOTEL-OELBERG.DE
D: ANDREAS V. OETTINGEN
A: UVIP.MEDIA INTERNET CONSULTING, **M:** AVOETTINGEN@UVIP-MEDIA.DE

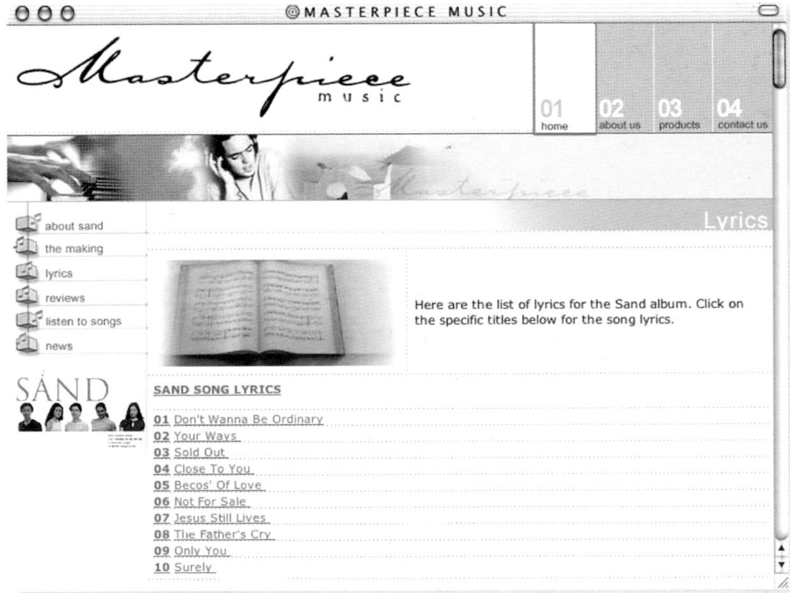

WWW.MASTERPIECEMUSIC.COM.MY
D: JASMINE HOR MYN-LI, **C:** ESOLVED.COM, **P:** ESOLVED.COM
A: ESOLVED.COM, **M:** JASZY76@YAHOO.COM

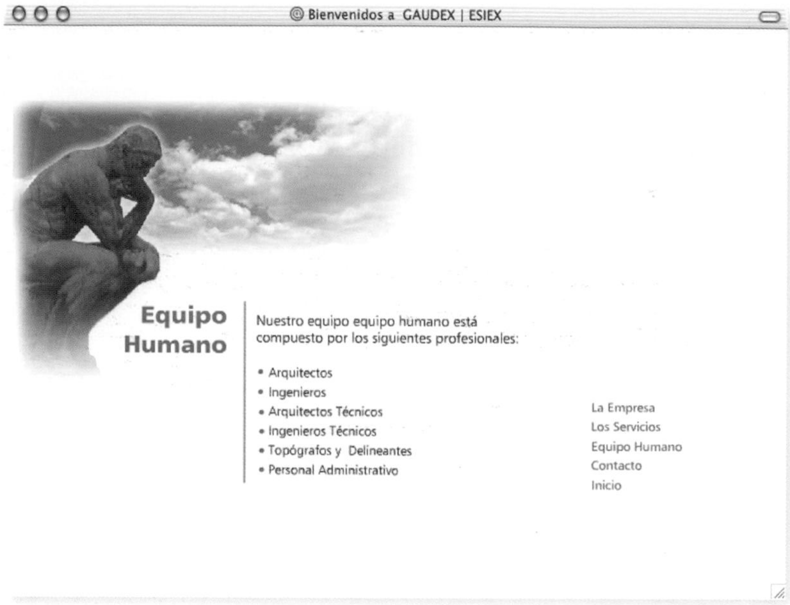

WWW.GAUDEX.COM
D: ALONSO RAMÓN & RAFAEL CASTAÑO
A: RAMÓN & CASTAÑO | ESTUDIO DE DISEÑO, **M:** INFO@GAUDEX.COM

WWW.CAMMAERT.COM/GRAPHIC_ALGAS.HTML
D: JUAN CARLOS CAMMAERT
M: JC@CAMMAERT.COM

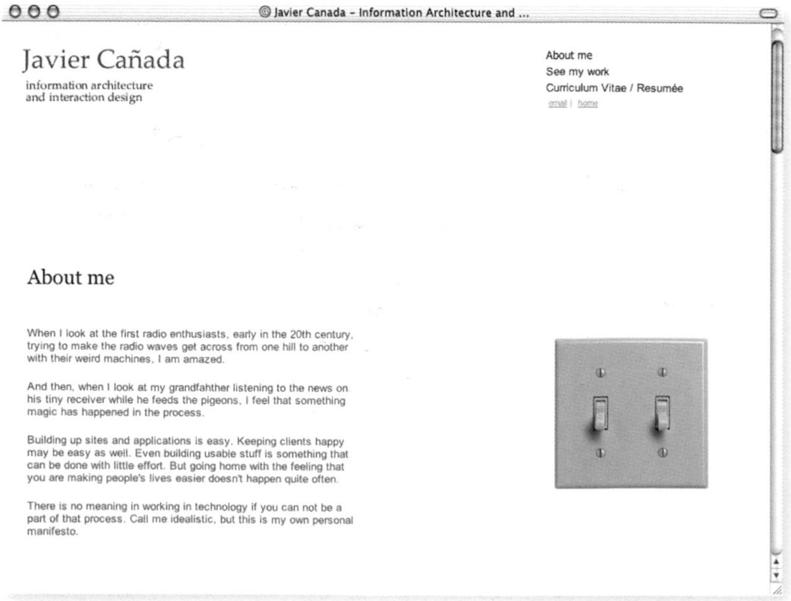

Javier Canada - Information Architecture and ...
Javier Cañada
information architecture and interaction design
About me
See my work
Curriculum Vitae / Resumée
About me
When I look at the first radio enthusiasts, early in the 20th century, trying to make the radio waves get across from one hill to another with their weird machines, I am amazed.
And then, when I look at my grandfahther listening to the news on his tiny receiver while he feeds the pigeons, I feel that something magic has happened in the process.
Building up sites and applications is easy. Keeping clients happy may be easy as well. Even building usable stuff is something that can be done with little effort. But going home with the feeling that you are making people's lives easier doesn't happen quite often.
There is no meaning in working in technology if you can not be a part of that process. Call me idealistic, but this is my own personal manifesto.

WWW.TERREMOTO.NET/JAVIER
D: JAVIER CAÑADA
M: JAVIER@TERREMOTO.NET

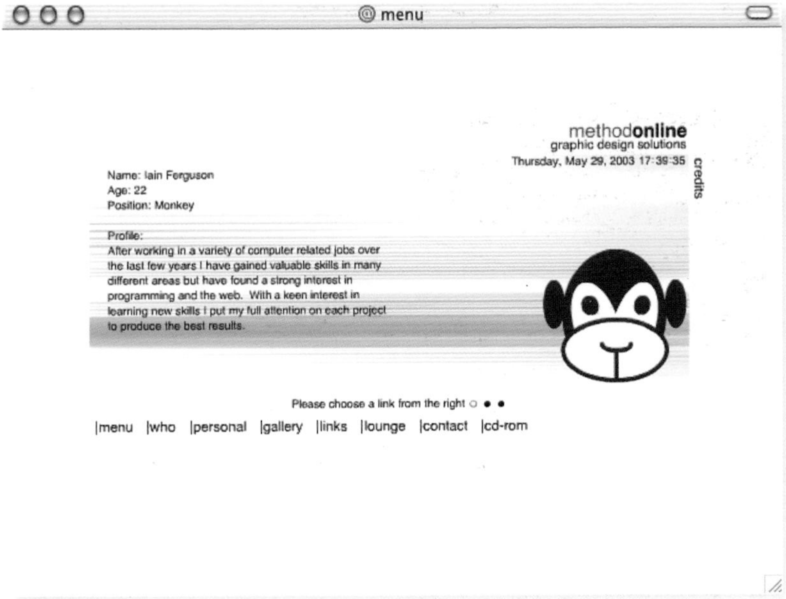
@ menu
methodonline
graphic design solutions
Thursday, May 29, 2003 17:39:35
credits
Name: Iain Ferguson
Age: 22
Position: Monkey
Profile:
After working in a variety of computer related jobs over the last few years I have gained valuable skills in many different areas but have found a strong interest in programming and the web. With a keen interest in learning new skills I put my full attention on each project to produce the best results.
Please choose a link from the right
|menu |who |personal |gallery |links |lounge |contact |cd-rom

WWW.METHOD.ORG.UK
D: JAMES ROBERTS
A: METHOD, **M:** JAMES@METHOD.ORG.UK

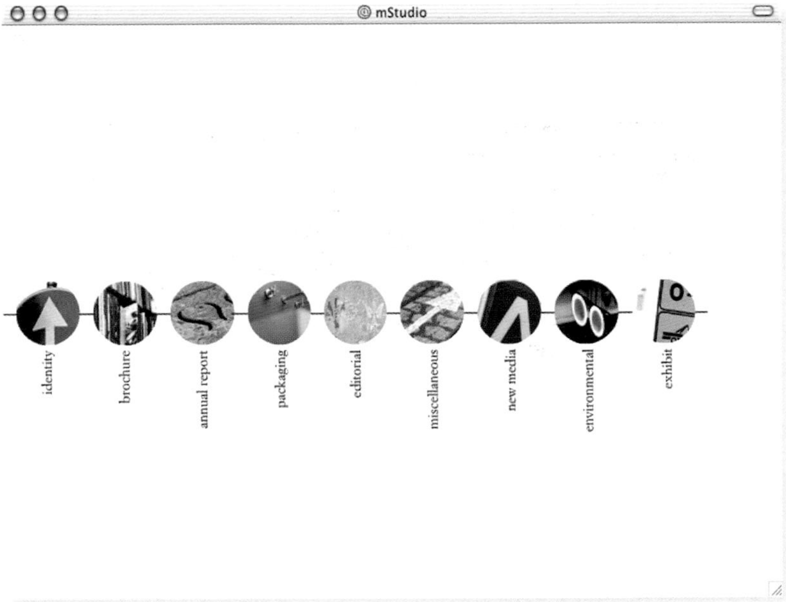
@ mStudio
identity
brochure
annual report
packaging
editorial
miscellaneous
new media
environmental
exhibit

WWW.MSTUDIOMILANO.IT
D: MARCO MIRABELLA
A: MSTUDIO SRL, **M:** MSTUDIO@MSTUDIOMILANO.IT

@ ++++++MECHAvision++++++
/GRAPHIC DESIGN :::::::::: 1 :: 2 :: 3 :: 4 :: 5 :: 6 :: 7 /PHOTOGRAPHY :::::::::: 1 :: 2 :: 3 :: 4 :: 5 :: /ILLUSTRATIONS :::::::::: 1 :: 2 :: 3 :: 4 :: 5 ::
/WEBSITES :::::::::: 1 :: 2 :: 3 :: 4 :: 5 :: /ANIMATIONS FLASH ::::::::::1 :: 2 :: 3 :: 4 :: 5 :: /CONTACT
Welcome to MECHAvision.com
Bienvenue sur MECHAvision.com
MECHAVISION.COM
mechavision All contents copyright (c)

WWW.MECHAVISION.COM
D: JEAN-JACQUES FREDERIC
M: FREDJJ@WANADOO.FR

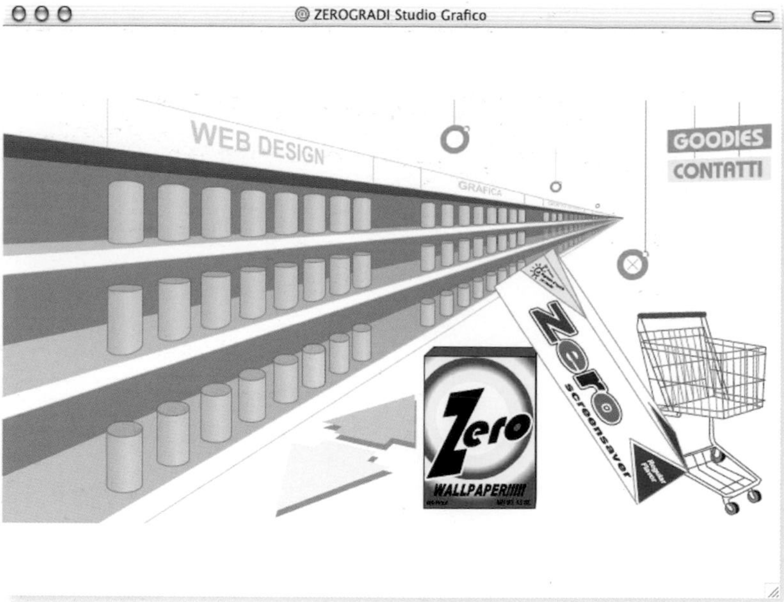

WWW.ZEROGRADI.IT
D: ZEROGRADI
A: ZEROGRADI, **M:** INFO@ZEROGRADI.IT

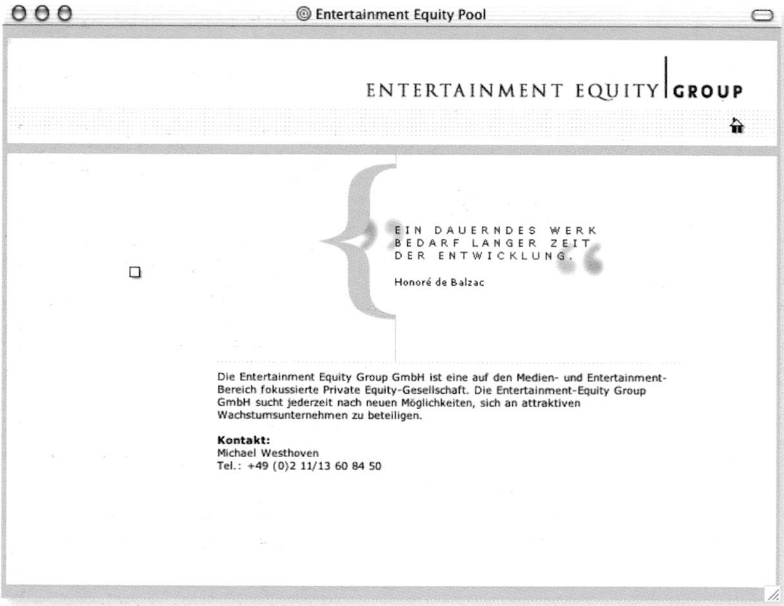

WWW.ENTERTAINMENT-EQUITY.COM
D: ULRIKE BUNK, **P:** ELECTRIC UMBRELLA
A: SENN.SANDER WERBEAGENTUR, **M:** BUNK@SENNSANDER.DE

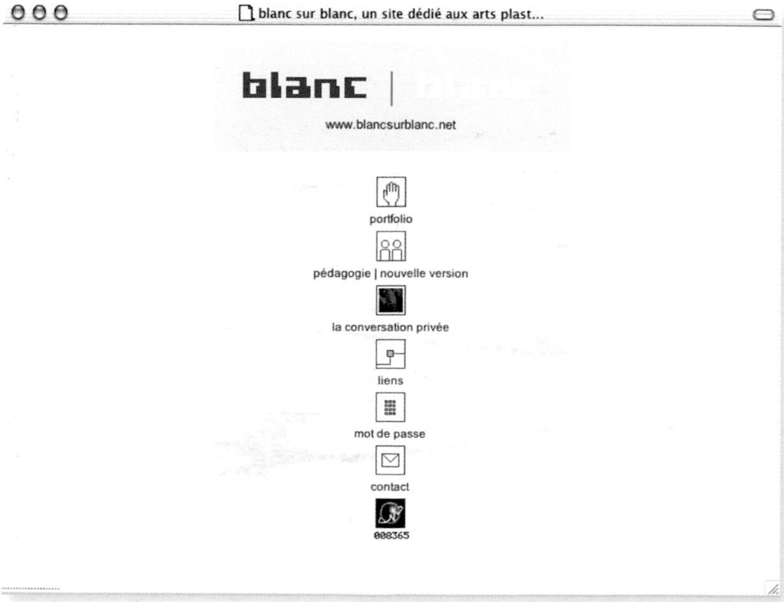

WWW.BLANCSURBLANC.NET
D: GAILLE MANU
M: EGAILLE@EXCITE.COM

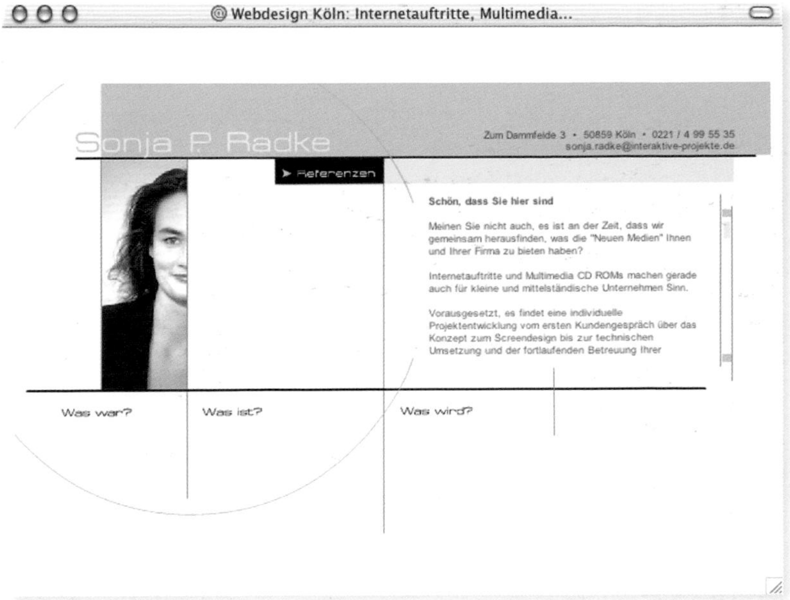

WWW.NEWMEDIASTYLE.DE
D: SONJA RADKE, **C:** OLIVER MANZ, **P:** SONJA RADKE
A: SONJA RADKE - INTERAKTIVE PROJEKTE, **M:** SONJA.RADKE@NEWMEDIASTYLE.DE

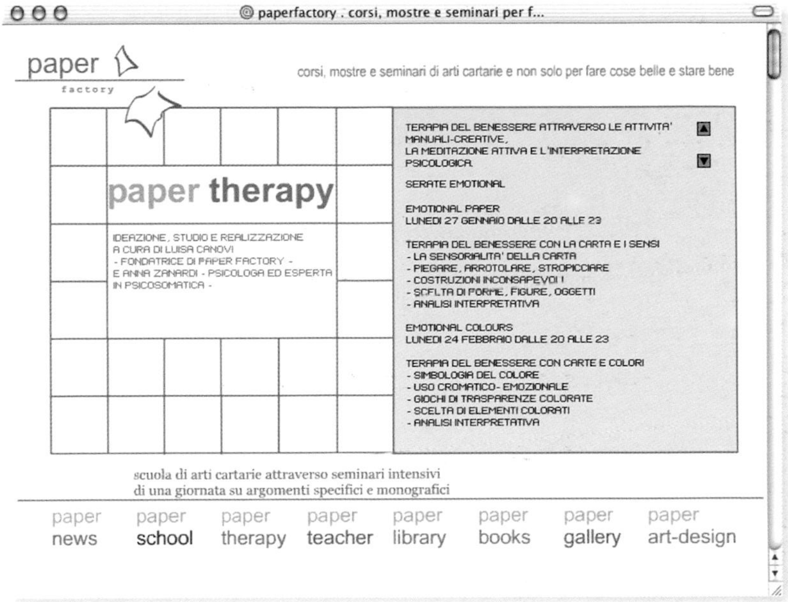

WWW.PAPERFACTORY.IT
D: ELENA CASARTELLI
M: LENSKY@LIBERO.IT

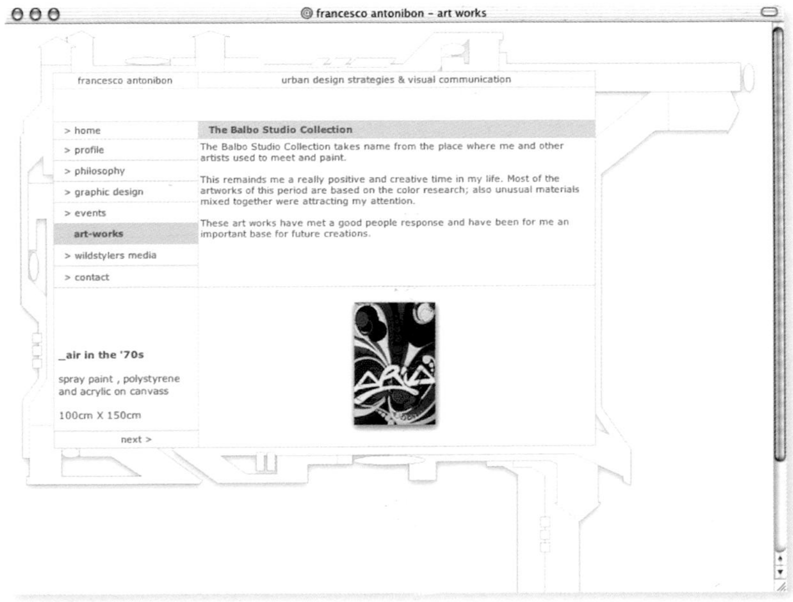

WWW.ANTONIBON.INFO/ANTONIBON_HOME_ITA.HTML
D: FRANCESCO ANTONIBON
M: FRANCESCO@ANTONIBON.INFO

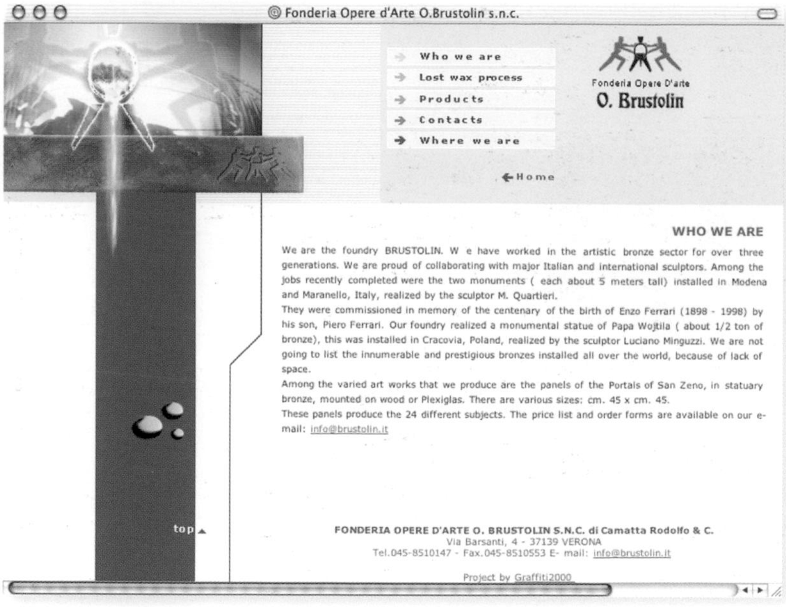

WWW.BRUSTOLIN.IT
D: LUCA CATTOI
A: LINEA WEB GRAFFITI 2000 S.P.A., **M:** CATTOI@GRAFFITI2000.COM

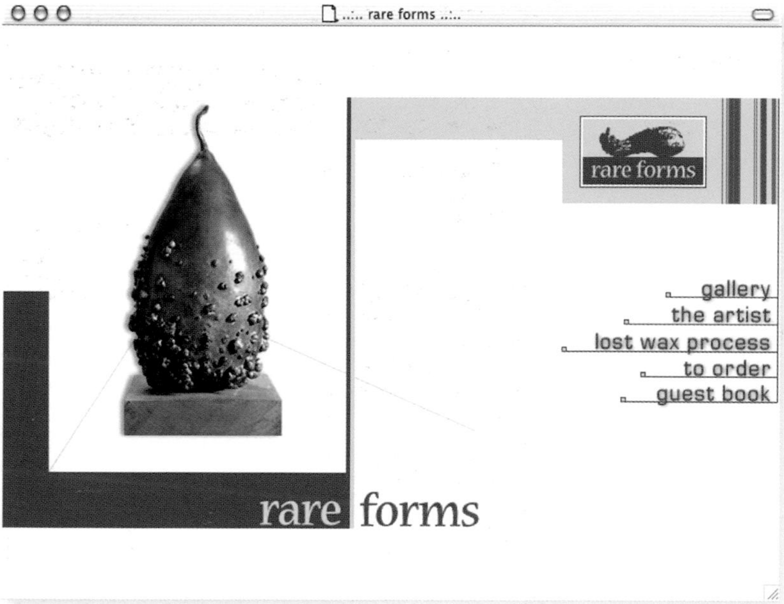

WWW.RAREFORMS.COM
D: NIKOLAI ZAUBER
A: NIKOLAI.NL, **M:** NZAUBER@HOTMAIL.COM

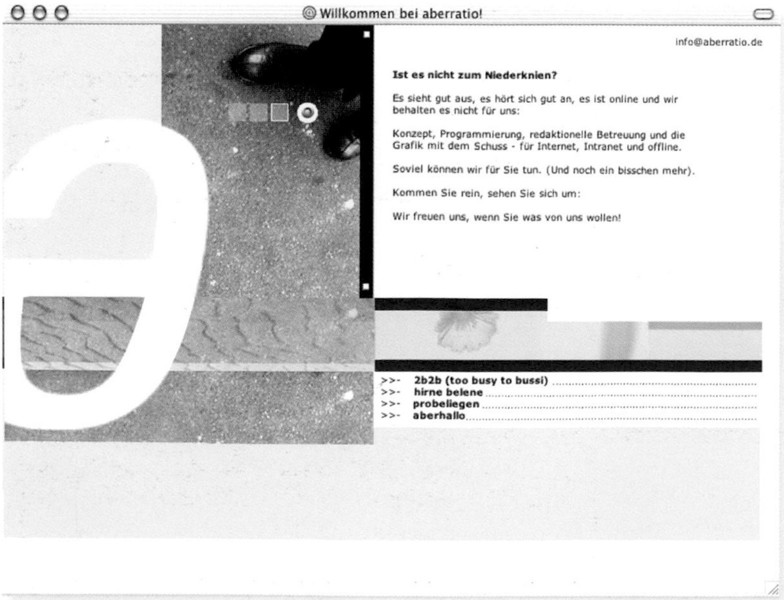

WWW.ABERRATIO.DE
D: GOLDGEIST HAMBURG
A: GOLDGEIST HAMBURG, **M:** WWW.GOLDGEIST.COM

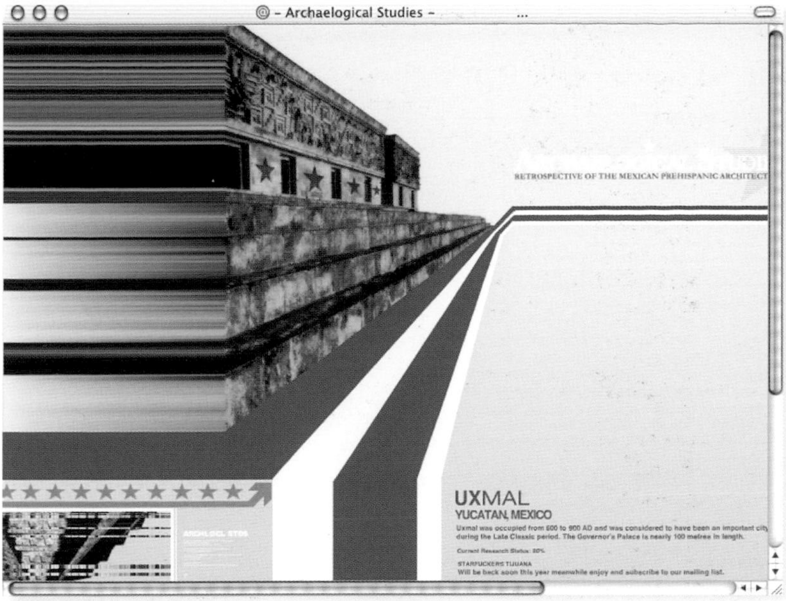

WWW.STARFUCKERS.ORG
D: DANIEL MENESES
M: DANIEL@STARFUCKERS.ORG

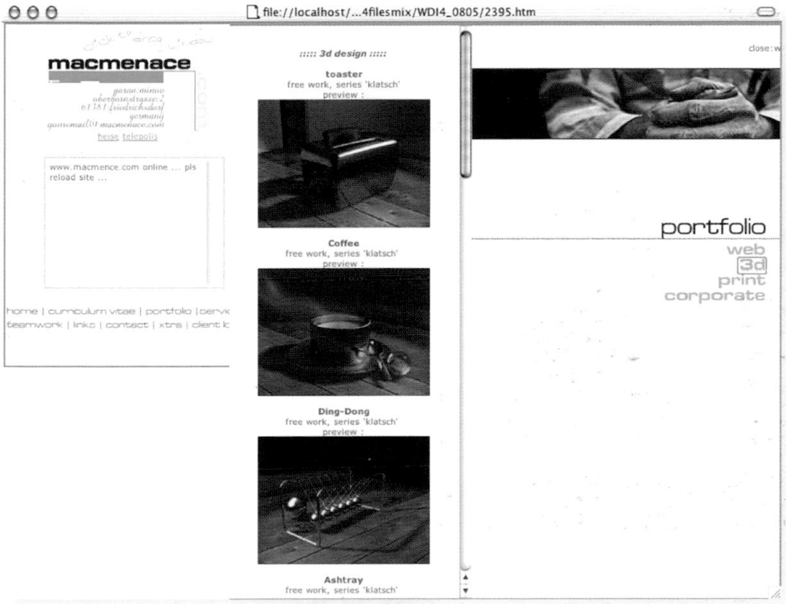

WWW.MACMENACE.COM
D: GORAN MINOV
A: MACMENACE.COM, **M:** YOUREMAIL@MACMENACE.COM

WWW.3IES.IT
D: ANDR3A
A: 3IES, **M:** TRE_IES@YAHOO.IT

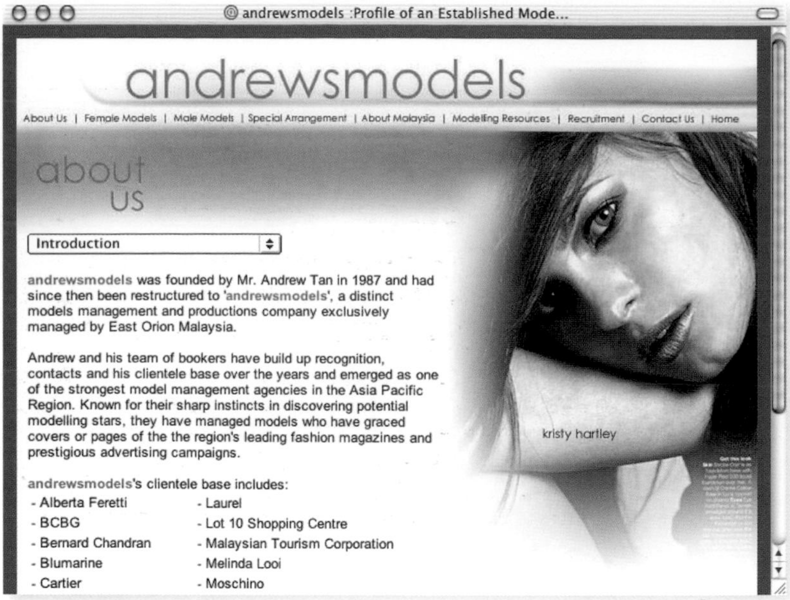

WWW.ANDREWSMODELS.COM
D: EUGENE FOO
A: MIRNET, **M:** JINYEN@MIRNET.COM.MY

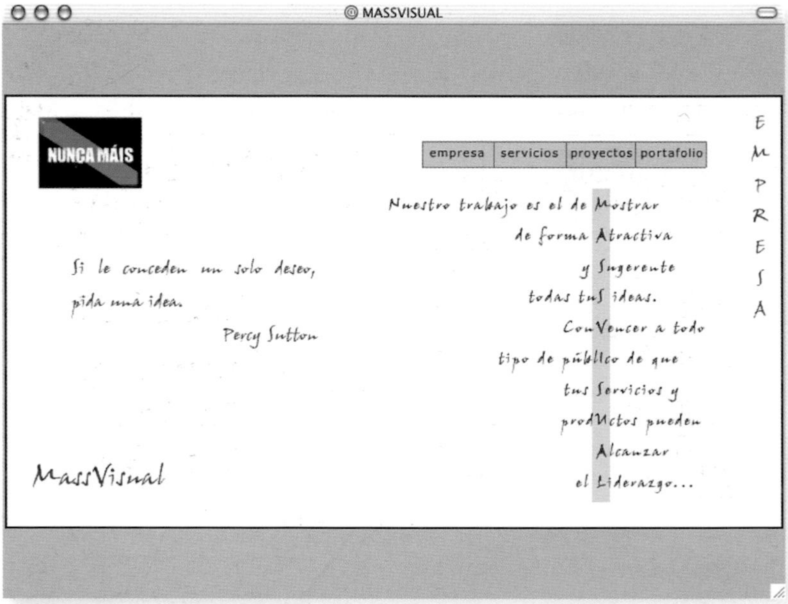

WWW.MASSVISUAL.COM
D: ISAAC GONZÁLEZ, **C:** JUAN F. VIDAL, **P:** ISAAC GONZÁLEZ
A: MASSVISUAL, **M:** GERENTE@MASSVISUAL.COM

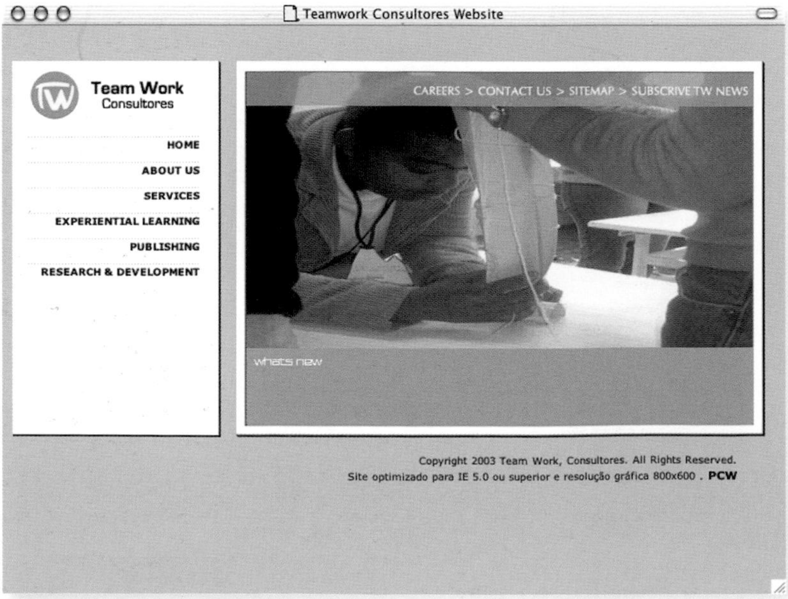

WWW.TEAMWORK.PT
D: ANA GRANJA
A: PCW, **M:** PAULA.GRANJA@LABOLIMS.COM

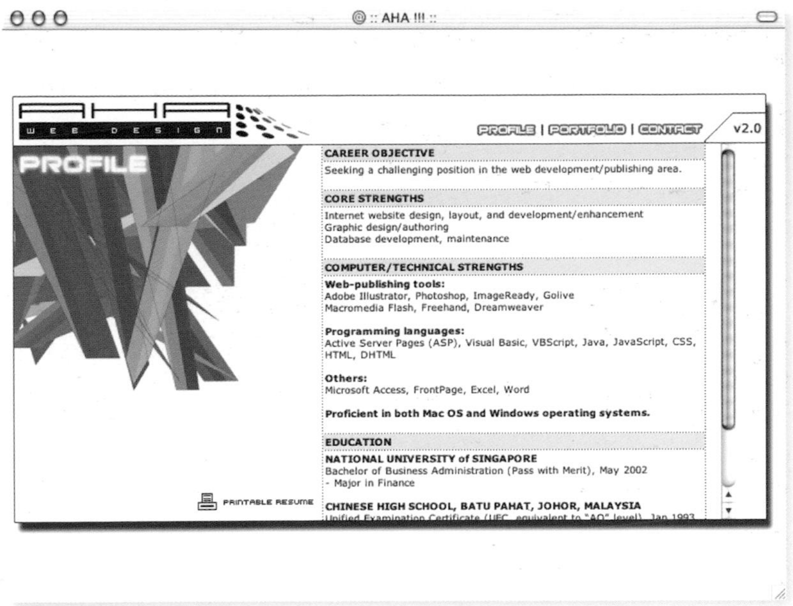

WWW.HOMEPAGE.MAC.COM/KWHOO
D: KOK WEI HOO
A: AHA WEB DESIGN, **M:** KWHOO@MAC.COM

WWW.TOMASBELLO.COM
D: DIOGO MELO, **C:** GUSTAVO MELO, **P:** DOISMAISDOIS.COM
A: DOISMAISDOIS.COM, **M:** INFO@DOISMAISDOIS.COM

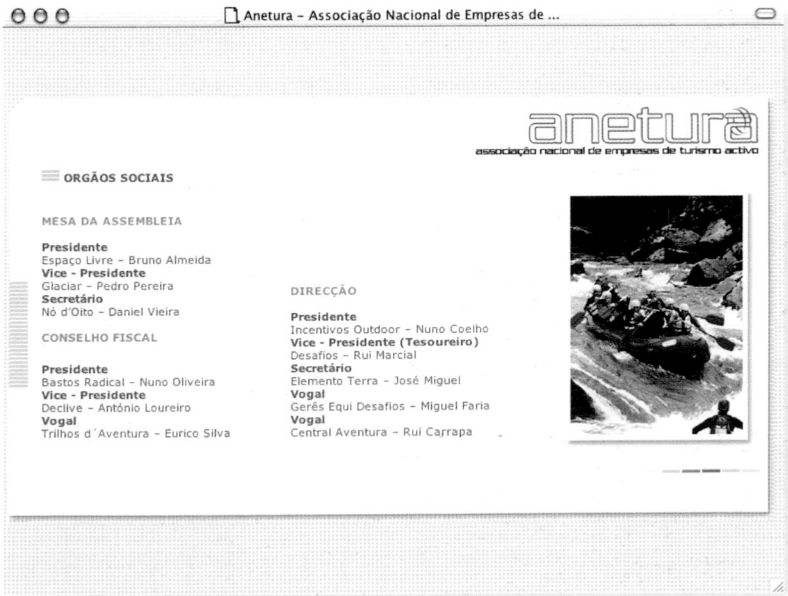

WWW.ANETURA.COM
D: ANA GRANJA
A: PCW, **M:** PAULA.GRANJA@LABOLIMS.COM

SENSOCOMUM.com, web services & consulting, ld...
SENSOCOMUM.com
BEM-VINDO SERVIÇOS CASE-STUDIES CARREIRAS CONTACTOS ENGLISH
O QUE É A SENSOCOMUM.com?
É uma oportunidade de o deixar explorar-nos - sim, a nós - as pessoas que todo o dia e toda a noite se sentam em frente a ligações de alta velocidade, construindo, programando, redesenhando, atribuindo permissões a ficheiros, todas as tarefas técnicas associadas à construção de sites, à sua manutenção, dedicadas a fazê-los crescer, a par de trabalhos mais conceptuais como marketing e posicionamento de mercado.
O QUE FAZEMOS?
Web Design/Construção/Integração
Pegue num site, elimine a retórica, e tudo o que pode ver são exactamente as coisas que podemos facilmente fazer para si - sistemas de publicação open-source, comunidades que correm de servidores Linux em qualquer ambiente de alojamento. Podemos especificá-lo, construí-lo, mantê-lo ou construir qualquer coisa completamente diferente que faça exactamente o que pretende. Fazemos igualmente upgrade de redes, construímos aplicações online e administração de bases de dados. Todo o trabalho feito de modo rápido e eficiente a custo fixo ou numa base horária, com tabelas flexíveis.
Marketing/Relações Públicas/Identidade Corporativa
Nunca gastamos um cêntimo em publicidade ou relações públicas com este site, mas contudo, chegou até nós. Como é que fizemos isto? Bem, é segredo. Mas se nos contactar, explicamos-lhe tudo. (dica: não tem nada a ver com o gasto de milhões de euros em branding e campanhas de marketing, mas tudo a ver com aproveitar as capacidades de raiz da Internet. Sim, é verdade: guerrilha marketing.)
SENSOCOMUM.com, Lda.
Rua Brito Capelo, 97-2º G/H
4450-072 Matosinhos
Portugal
Telf/Fax: +351 22 938 83 50
E-mail: info@sensocomum.com
WHO ARE WE?
We are a coalition of consultants, designers, industrial designers, programmers, journalists and marketeers with experience in dealing with complex problems and deploying optimum solutions.
If you need help and think you can use what we do, please contact us.

WWW.SENSOCOMUM.COM
D: FILIPE MIGUEL TAVARES
A: SENSOCOMUM.COM, **M:** FMT@FMTAVARES.NET

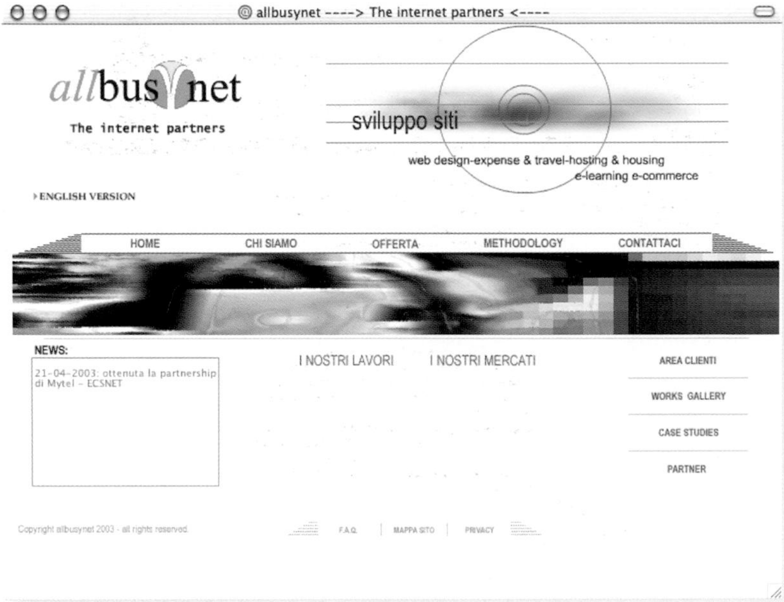

WWW.ALLBUSYNET.COM
D: FRANCESCO SERRAPEDE, **C:** FRANCESCO SERRAPEDE, **P:** ALLBUSYNET
M: SERRAPEDE@TISCALI.IT

SECNET: Kompetenzen
SECNET
Home I Kompetenzen I Typo3 I Kontakt
IT Casting
Wir pflegen ein leistungsfähiges Netzwerk von Web-Spezialisten für alle Arten von Anforderungen. Wir finden für Sie den geeigneten Partner im entsprechenden Themensegment.
Kommunikation
Wir sprechen die Sprache, der Nerd's*, Marketingexperten und CEO's. Mit dieser Fähigkeit können wir den kommunikativen Anforderungen und Änderungen im Projektverlauf stehts für alle Beteiligten verständlich machen und auf einen gemeinsamen Nenner bringen.
Strategieplanung
Was sind die Bedürfnisse von Morgen? Welche Entwicklungen können an Ihren Bedürfnissen vorbeigehen? Welchen Aufwand und welches technologische "Gehabe" können Sie sich ersparen?
Secnet bietet kompetente Beratung für KMU, Grosskonzerne und Einzelpersonen an.

WWW.SECNET.CH
D: RENE FRITZ, **P:** LEANDER SEYFFER
A: COLORCUBE, **M:** SEYFFER@SECNET.CH

WWW.DEUTSCHES-FILMMUSEUM.DE
D: HELLER, **C:** HELLER, **P:** DEUTSCHES FILMMUSEUM
M: SYSADMIN@DEUTSCHES-FILMMUSEUM.DE

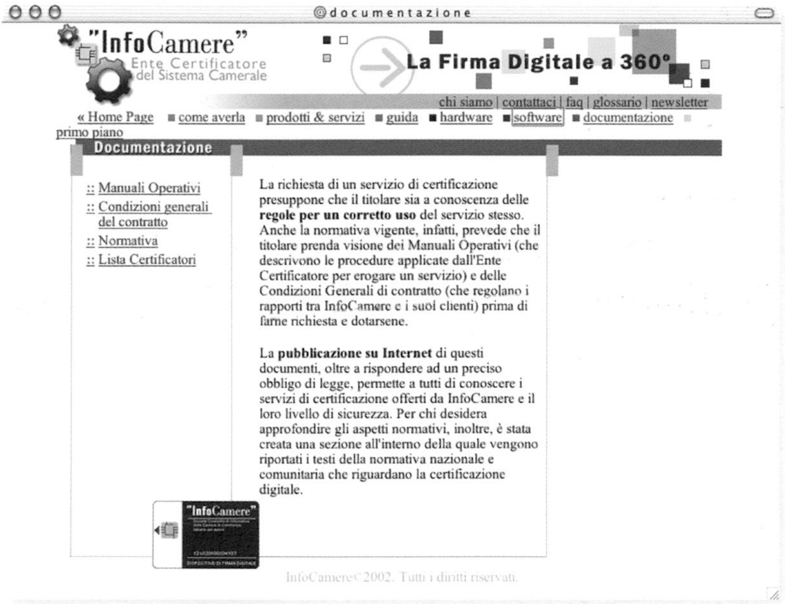

WWW.CARD.INFOCAMERE.IT
D: MARCO SEBASTIANI, **C:** MARCO SEBASTIANI, **P:** INFOCAMERE
A: INFOCAMERE, **M:** MARCO.SEBSTIANI@INFOCAMERE.IT

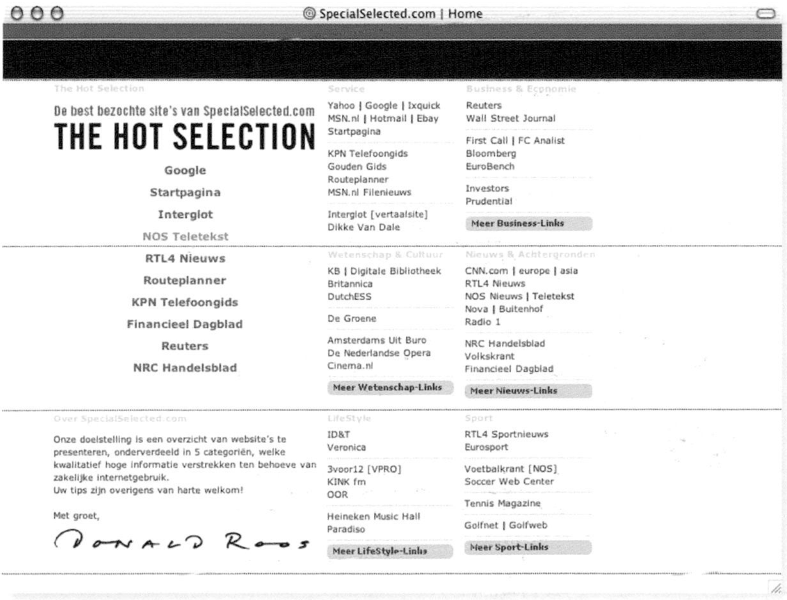

WWW.SPECIALSELECTED.COM
D: DONALD ROOS
A: OTHERWAYS, **M:** DONALD.ROOS@OTHERWAYS.NL

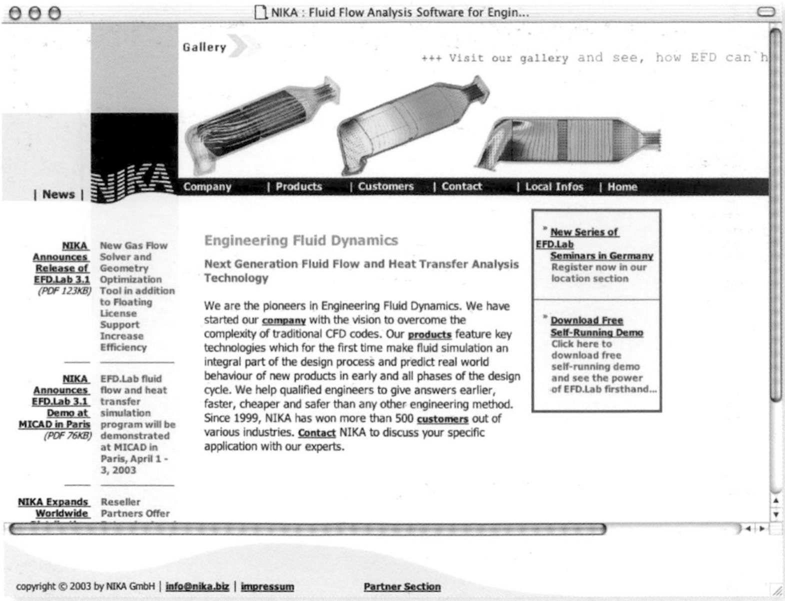

WWW.NIKA.BIZ
D: STEFAN FELDHINKEL
A: NIKA GMBH, **M:** SFELDHINKEL@NIKA.BIZ

WWW.EUROKARTENSYSTEME.DE
D: RICHARD PAUKERT, **C:** ULLRICH DOTTERWEICH
A: ZENTROPY PARTNERS GMBH, **M:** RPAUKERT@ZENTROPYPARTNERS.DE

WWW.PULSESOLUTIONS.COM
D: SANDEEP RATHOD, MANDAR PATIL, **C:** JIGAR MEHTA, **P:** MANOJ MANGHANI
A: PULSESOLUTIONS, **M:** SANDEEPRATHOD@HOTMAIL.COM

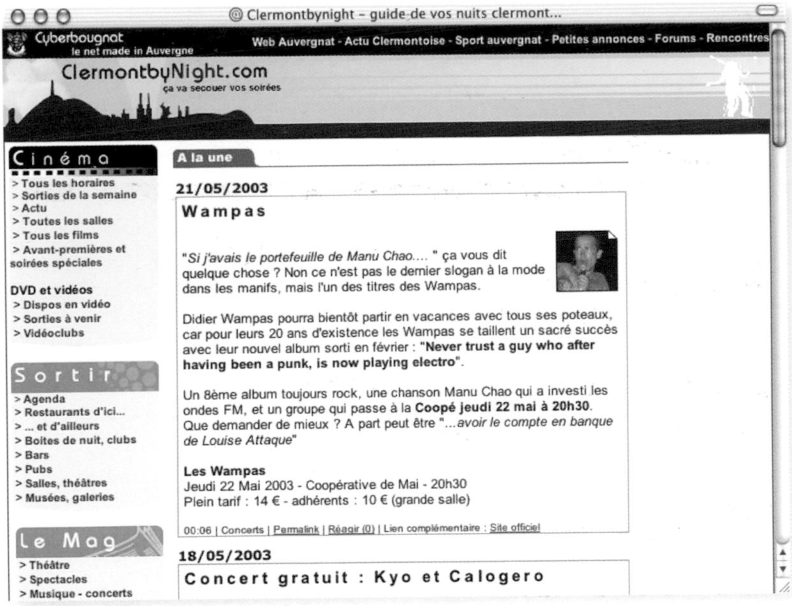

WWW.CLERMONTBYNIGHT.COM
D: BERTRAND SOULIER
M: BERTRAND@CYBERBOUGNAT.NET

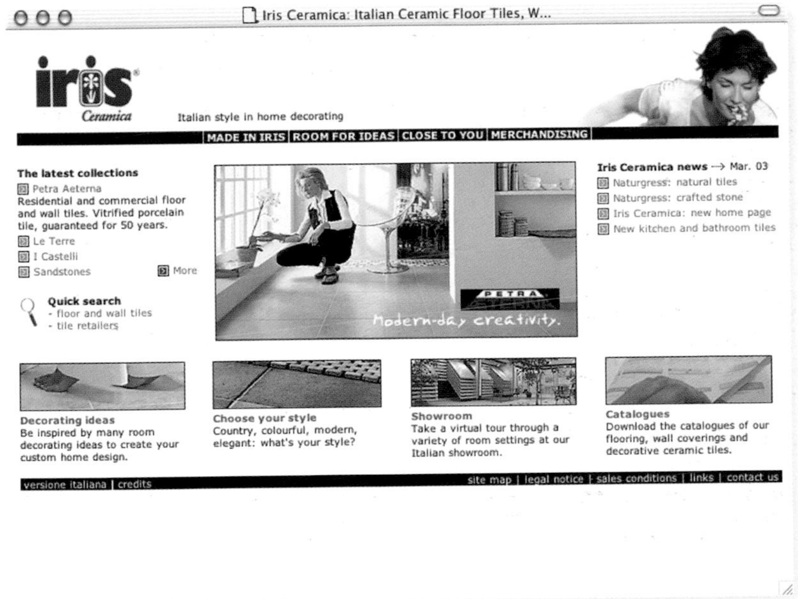

WWW.IRISCERAMICA.COM
D: ALBERTO MONTEVERDI, **C:** MASSIMILIANO CARULLI, **P:** GIOVANNA CARDELLA
M: ALBERTO@MONSWERK.COM

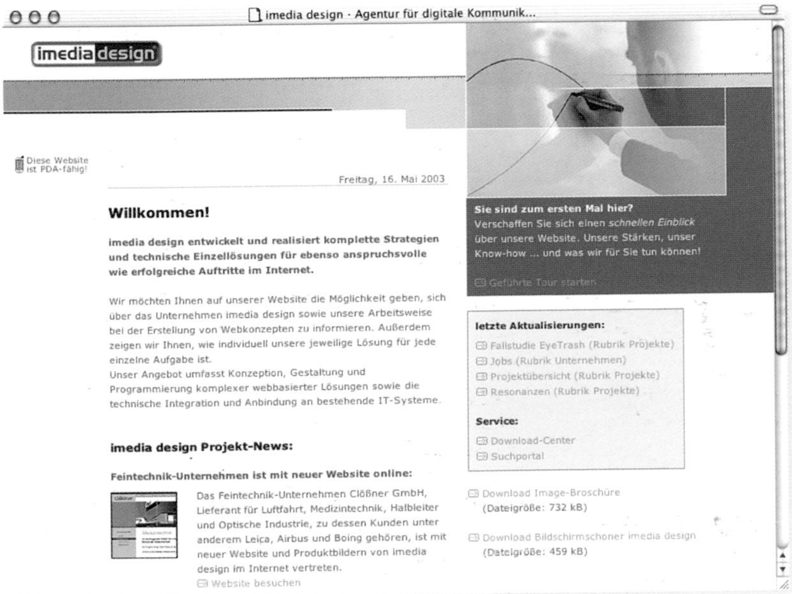

WWW.IMEDIA-DESIGN.DE
D: MICHAEL RINN
A: IMEDIA DESIGN, **M:** INFO@IMEDIA-DESIGN.DE

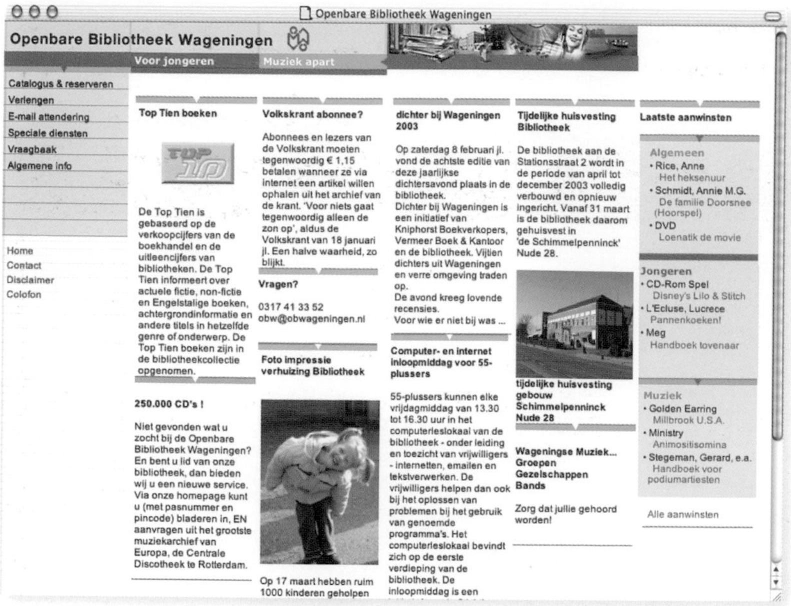

WWW.OBWAGENINGEN.NL
D: BOR BORREN, **C:** BOR BORREN/CONTRAST, **P:** WOLF KNAB WESITE ARCHITECTUUR
A: BORREN COMMUNICATIE & DESIGN, **M:** BOR@BORREN.NL

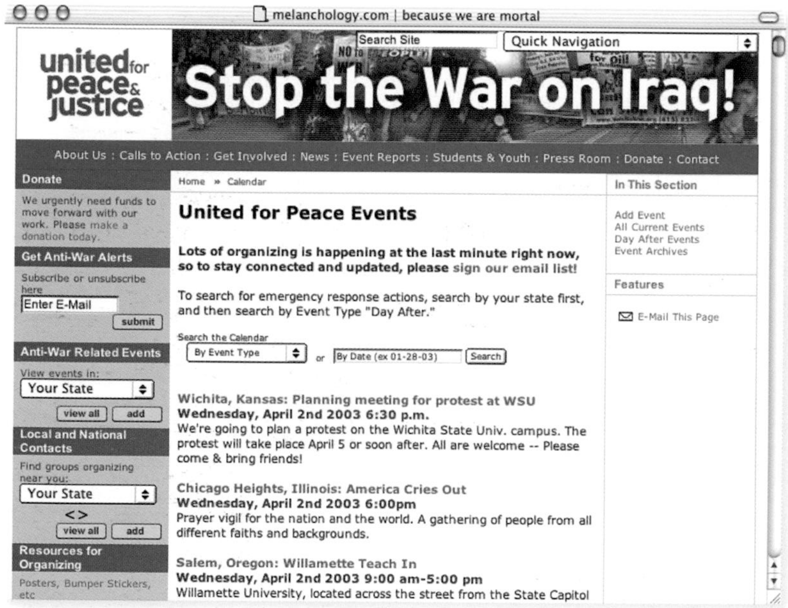

WWW.MELANCHOLOGY.COM
D: CHRISTOPHER NILSSON
A: MELANCHOLOGY, **M:** CREEP@MELANCHOLOGY.COM

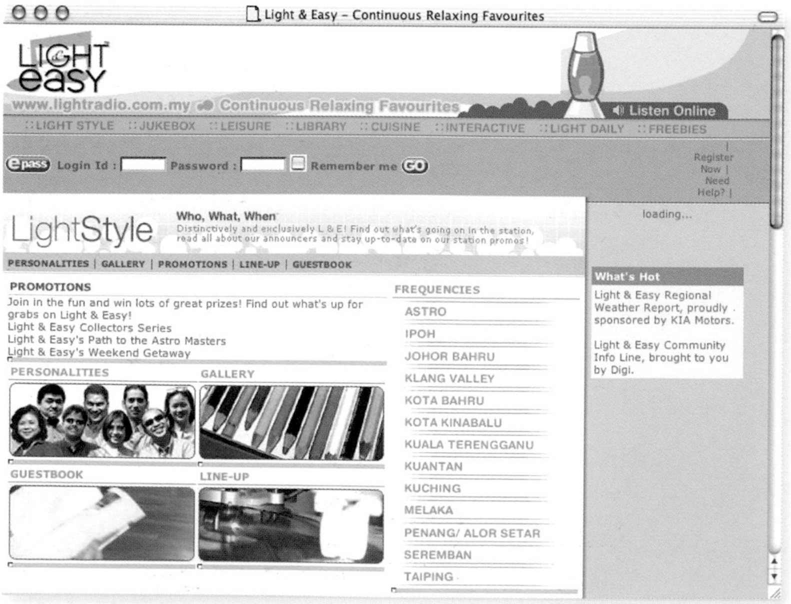

WWW.LIGHTRADIO.COM.MY
D: KAKIT TAN, **C:** NICOLE KONG SUI YEE, **P:** HAZLAN HUSSEIN
A: AMP SDN BHD, **M:** KAH-KIT_TAN@ASTRO.COM.MY

WWW.PRIMAVERASOFT.PT
D: PEDRO MATOS, **C:** PRIMAVERA SOFTWARE
A: PALETA DE IDEIAS, **M:** PEDRO.MATOS@PALETADEIDEIAS.PT

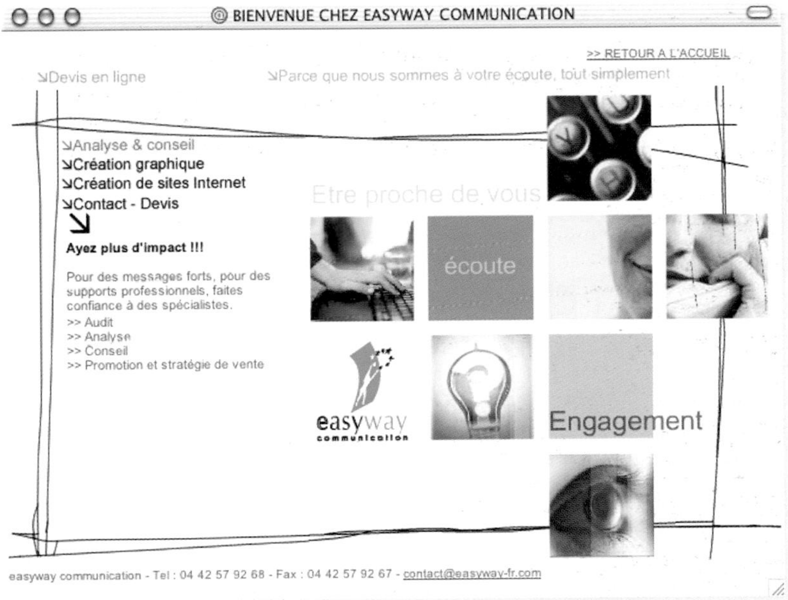

WWW.EASYWAY-FR.COM
D: VALERIE IBANEZ
A: EASYWAY COMMUNICATION, **M:** VALERIE.IBANEZ@WANADOO.FR

WWW.LINDKVIST.COM
D: ANDREAS LINDKVIST
A: LINDKVIST.COM, **M:** ANDREAS@LINDKVIST.COM

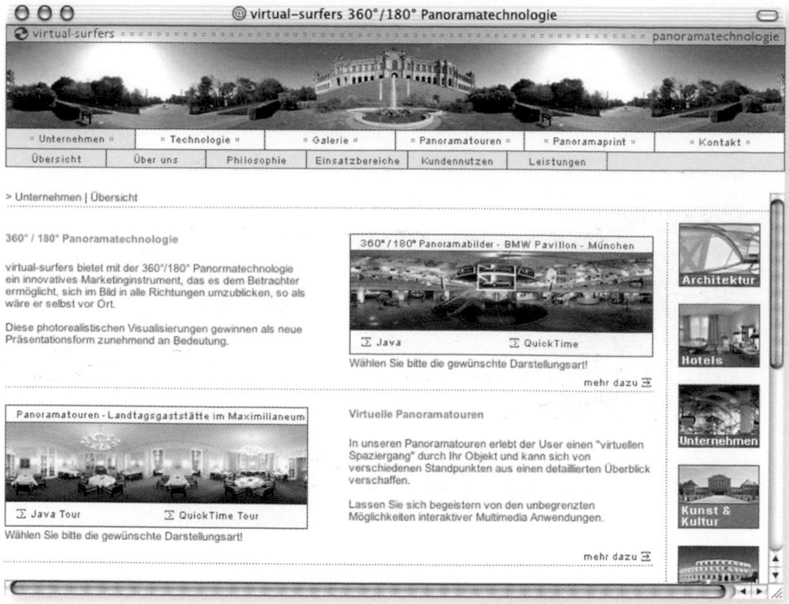

WWW.VIRTUAL-SURFERS.COM
D: CHRISTINA ROTTNER, **C:** STEPHAN VON BRESSENSDORF, **P:** S. V. BRESSENSDORF
A: VIRTUAL-SURFERS GMBH ::PANORAMATECHNOLOGIE ::, **M:** INFO@VIRTUAL-SURFERS.COM

WWW.ESPACIOFRESCO.COM
D: HUMBERT TORROELLA NAVARRO
A: ESPACIO FRESCO, **M:** DESIGN@ESPACIOFRESCO.COM

WWW.REDSPARK.NL
D: BURNEY VAN LEENEN
A: RED SPARK, **M:** BURNEY@REDSPARK.NL

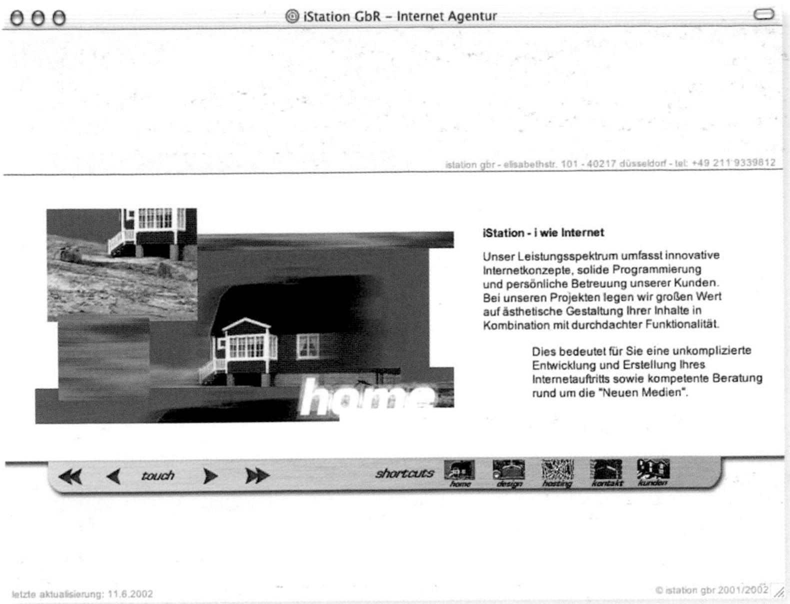

iStation GbR - Internet Agentur
istation gbr - elisabethstr. 101 - 40217 düsseldorf - tel: +49 211 9339812
iStation - i wie Internet
Unser Leistungsspektrum umfasst innovative Internetkonzepte, solide Programmierung und persönliche Betreuung unserer Kunden. Bei unseren Projekten legen wir großen Wert auf ästhetische Gestaltung Ihrer Inhalte in Kombination mit durchdachter Funktionalität.
Dies bedeutet für Sie eine unkomplizierte Entwicklung und Erstellung Ihres Internetauftritts sowie kompetente Beratung rund um die "Neuen Medien".
home
touch
shortcuts
home
design
hosting
kontakt
kunden
letzte aktualisierung: 11.6.2002
© istation gbr 2001/2002

WWW.ISTATION.DE
D: RENÉ FREI, **C:** PETER BRENNER
A: ISTATION GBR, **M:** R.FREI@ISTATION.DE

WWW.GRAPHIXEL.COM
D: BULENT INCE, **M:** WWW.GRAPHIXEL.COM

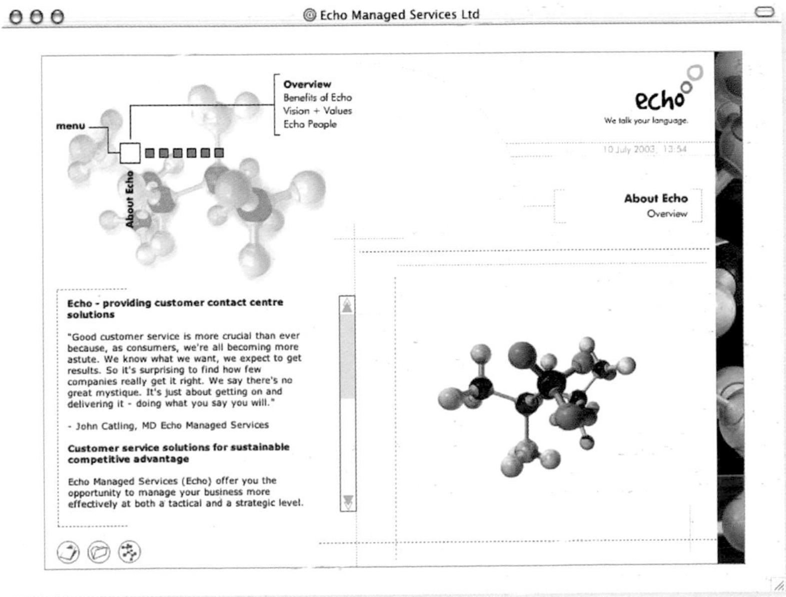

WWW.ECHO-MS.COM/MAIN.ASP
D: GERALD GLOVER, **C:** TOM ELGAR
A: TWOBELOWZERO, **M:** GEZ@TWOBELOWZERO.NET

Skipintro
SKIPINTRO
u zoekt ..?
Skipintro is een bureau op het kruispunt van reclame en internet. Ons werk behelst voornamelijk webvertising en websites in alle soorten en maten, maar we maken ook graag uitstapjes in andere media. Wij werken rechtstreeks voor opdrachtgevers, maar ook voor reclamebureaus. Wij geloven niet in onzin, wel in goede ideeën en in stevig doorwerken.
RIJKSMUSEUM CAMPAGNE
FROM OUR MAN ON THE SPOT
DIRK JENSMA
LAATSTE NIEUWS
EERDERE INTRO'S

WWW.SKIPINTRO.NL
D: YACCO VIJN
A: SKIPINTRO, **M:** INFO@SKIPINTRO.NL

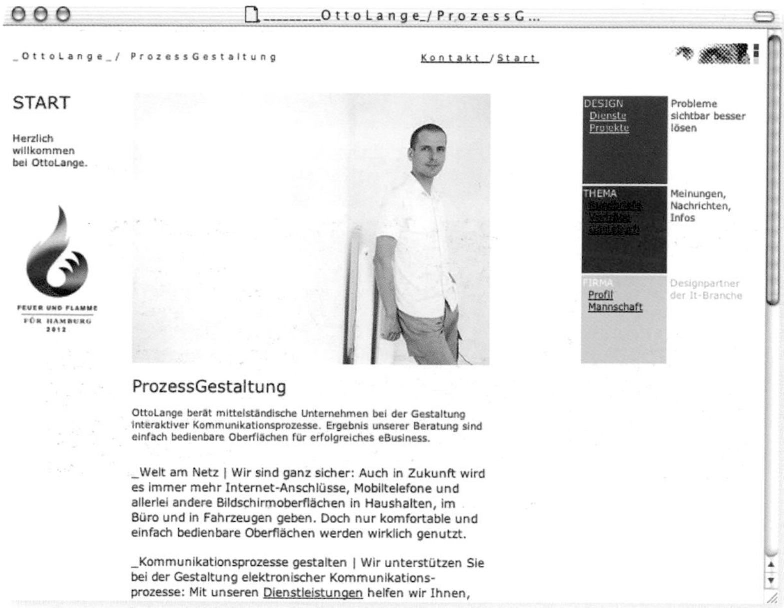

OttoLange/ProzessG...
OttoLange/ ProzessGestaltung
Kontakt /Start

Herzlich willkommen bei OttoLange.
FEUER UND FLAMME FÜR HAMBURG 2012

Meinungen, Nachrichten, Infos

Mannschaft

OttoLange berät mittelständische Unternehmen bei der Gestaltung interaktiver Kommunikationsprozesse. Ergebnis unserer Beratung sind einfach bedienbare Oberflächen für erfolgreiches eBusiness.
_Welt am Netz | Wir sind ganz sicher: Auch in Zukunft wird es immer mehr Internet-Anschlüsse, Mobiltelefone und allerlei andere Bildschirmoberflächen in Haushalten, im Büro und in Fahrzeugen geben. Doch nur komfortable und einfach bedienbare Oberflächen werden wirklich genutzt.
_Kommunikationsprozesse gestalten | Wir unterstützen Sie bei der Gestaltung elektronischer Kommunikations-prozesse: Mit unseren Dienstleistungen helfen wir Ihnen,

WWW.OTTOLANGE.DE
D: JENS LANGE / STEFANIE PINGEL
A: OTTO LANGE, **M:** STEFANIE_PINGEL@HAMBURG.DE

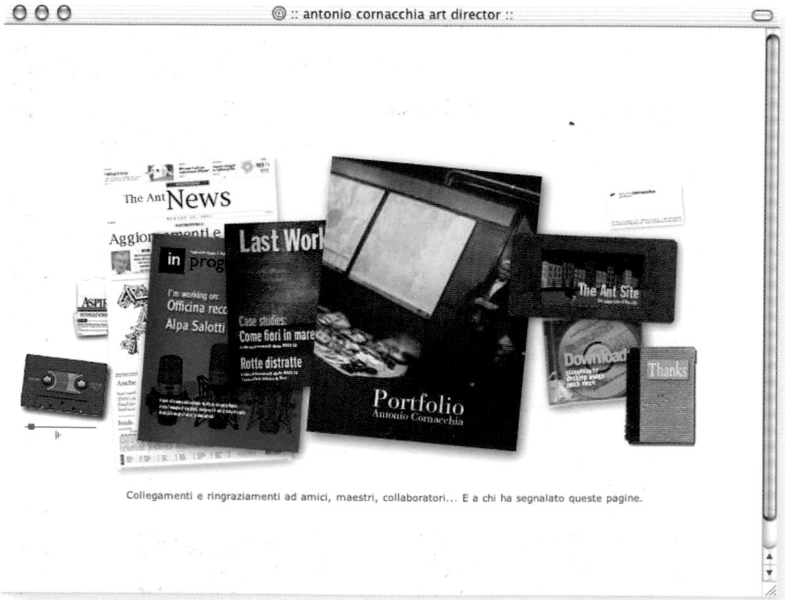

Collegamenti e ringraziamenti ad amici, maestri, collaboratori... E a chi ha segnalato queste pagine.

WWW.ANTONIOCORNACCHIA.COM
D: ANTONIO CORNACCHIA
M: ANTONIO@ANTONIOCORNACCHIA.COM

WWW.LEFTLOFT.COM
D: LEFTLOFT
A: LEFTLOFT, **M:** INFO@LEFTLOFT.COM

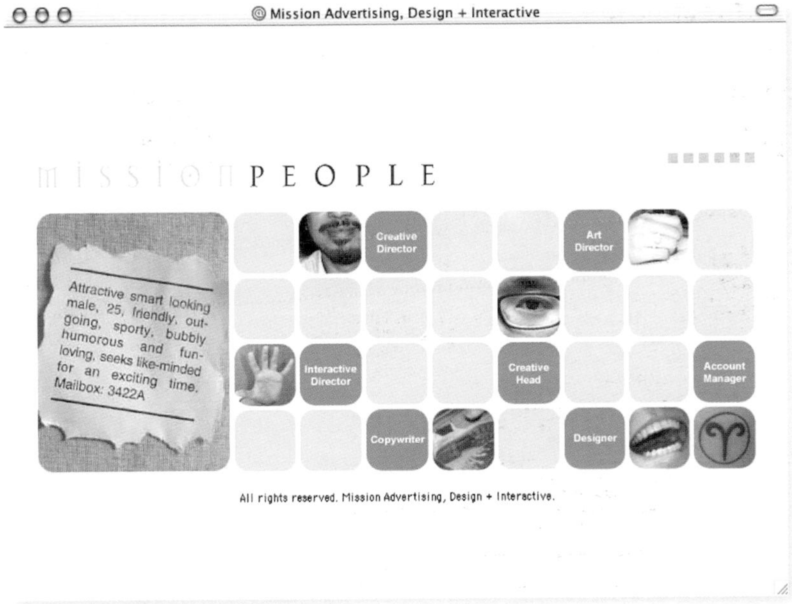

WWW.MISSION.COM.SG
D: ALLISON, **C:** ERNEST, P: KHOR
A: MISSION INTERACTIVE, **M:** ERNEST@MISSION.COM.SG

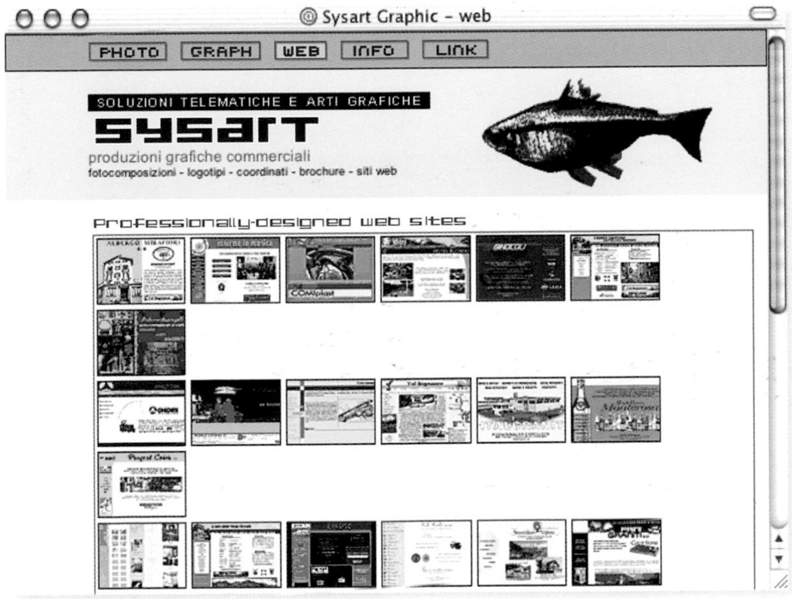

WWW.SYSART.IT
D: RICCARDO FAGGIANA
M: INFO@PARSITE.COM

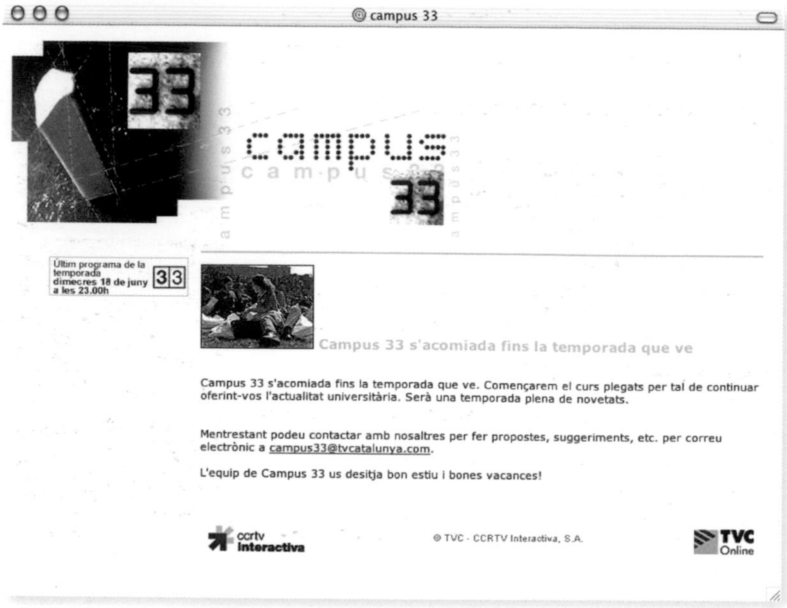
campus 33
campus
c a m p u s 3 3
Últim programa de la temporada dimecres 18 de juny a les 23.00h
Campus 33 s'acomiada fins la temporada que ve
Campus 33 s'acomiada fins la temporada que ve. Començarem el curs plegats per tal de continuar oferint-vos l'actualitat universitària. Serà una temporada plena de novetats.
Mentrestant podeu contactar amb nosaltres per fer propostes, suggeriments, etc. per correu electrònic a campus33@tvcatalunya.com.
L'equip de Campus 33 us desitja bon estiu i bones vacances!
ccrtv interactiva
© TVC - CCRTV Interactiva, S.A.
TVC Online

WWW.TVCATALUNYA.COM/CAMPUS33
D: MICK WALSH
A: WALSH PRODUCTIONS INC. , **M:** INFO@WPINYC.COM

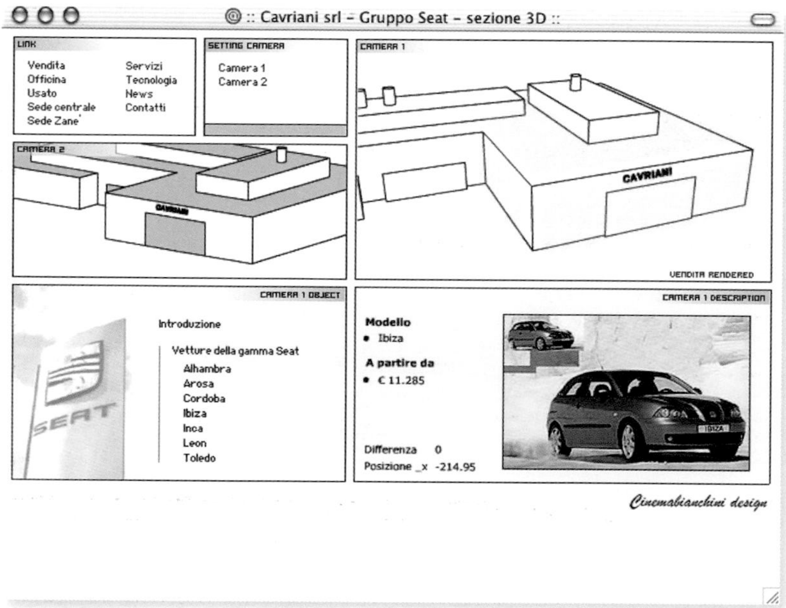
:: Cavriani srl - Gruppo Seat - sezione 3D ::
LINK
Vendita
Officina
Usato
Sede centrale
Sede Zane
Servizi
Tecnologia
News
Contatti
SETTING CAMERA
Camera 1
Camera 2
CAMERA 1
CAMERA 2
CAVRIANI
VENDITA RENDERED
CAMERA 1 OBJECT
Introduzione
Vetture della gamma Seat
Alhambra
Arosa
Cordoba
Ibiza
Inca
Leon
Toledo
CAMERA 1 DESCRIPTION
Modello
Ibiza
A partire da
€ 11.285
Differenza 0
Posizione _x -214.95
Cinemabianchini design

WWW.CAVRIANI.IT
D: DEL BEN NICOLA
A: CINEMABIANCHINI - DESIGN AGENCY, **M:** INFO@CINEMABIANCHINI.IT

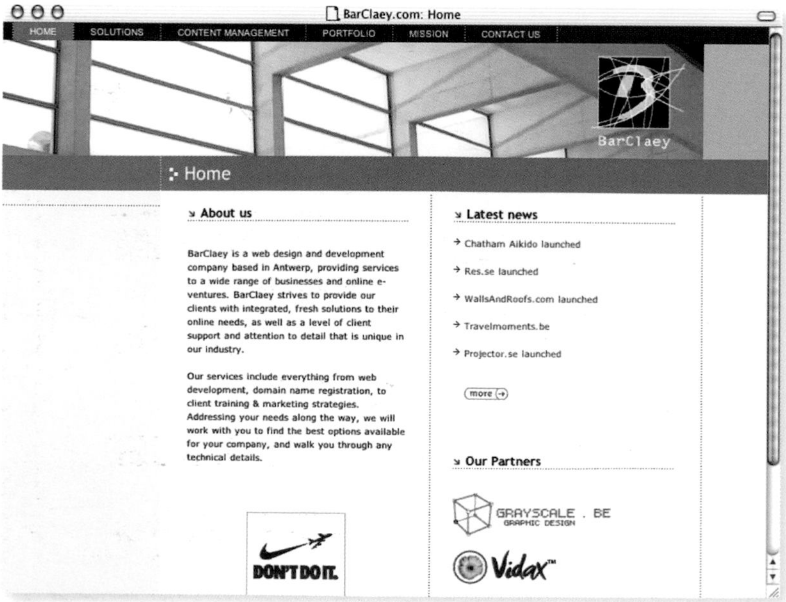
BarClaey.com: Home
HOME
SOLUTIONS
CONTENT MANAGEMENT
PORTFOLIO
MISSION
CONTACT US
BarClaey
Home
About us
BarClaey is a web design and development company based in Antwerp, providing services to a wide range of businesses and online e-ventures. BarClaey strives to provide our clients with integrated, fresh solutions to their online needs, as well as a level of client support and attention to detail that is unique in our industry.
Our services include everything from web development, domain name registration, to client training & marketing strategies. Addressing your needs along the way, we will work with you to find the best options available for your company, and walk you through any technical details.
Latest news
Chatham Aikido launched
Res.se launched
WallsAndRoofs.com launched
Travelmoments.be
Projector.se launched
more
Our Partners
GRAYSCALE . BE
GRAPHIC DESIGN
Vidax
DON'T DO IT.

WWW.BARCLAEY.COM
D: BARCLAEYS
A: BARCLAEY.COM, **M:** INFO@BARCLAEY.COM

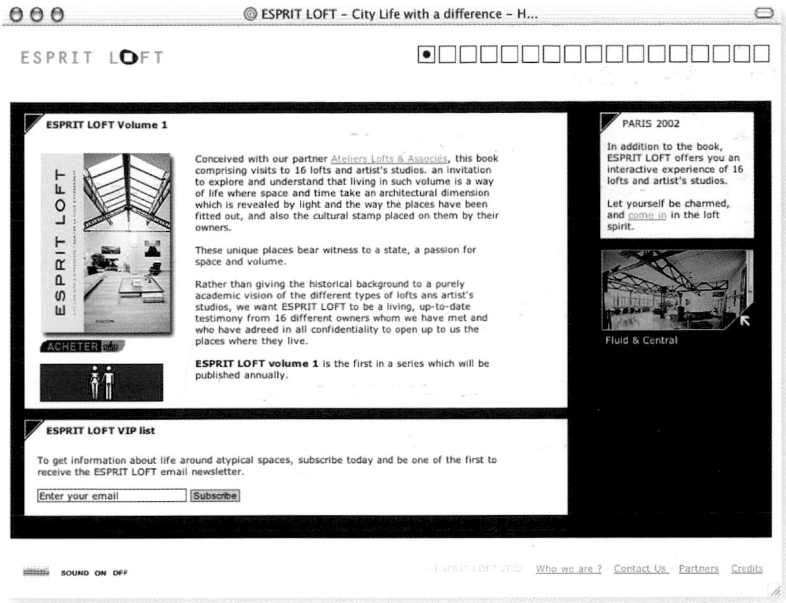

ESPRIT LOFT - City Life with a difference - H...
ESPRIT LOFT
ESPRIT LOFT Volume 1
Conceived with our partner Ateliers Lofts & Associés, this book comprising visits to 16 lofts and artist's studios, an invitation to explore and understand that living in such volume is a way of life where space and time take an architectural dimension which is revealed by light and the way the places have been fitted out, and also the cultural stamp placed on them by their owners.
These unique places bear witness to a state, a passion for space and volume.
Rather than giving the historical background to a purely academic vision of the different types of lofts ans artist's studios, we want ESPRIT LOFT to be a living, up-to-date testimony from 16 different owners whom we have met and who have adreed in all confidentiality to open up to us the places where they live.
ESPRIT LOFT volume 1 is the first in a series which will be published annually.
ACHETER
PARIS 2002
In addition to the book, ESPRIT LOFT offers you an interactive experience of 16 lofts and artist's studios.
Let yourself be charmed, and come in in the loft spirit.
Fluid & Central
ESPRIT LOFT VIP list
To get information about life around atypical spaces, subscribe today and be one of the first to receive the ESPRIT LOFT email newsletter.
Enter your email
Subscribe
SOUND ON OFF
Who we are ? Contact Us Partners Credits

WWW.ESPRIT-LOFT.COM
D: JÉRÔME DE VRIES
A: ESPRIT LOFT, **M:** CONTACT@ESPRIT-LOFT.COM

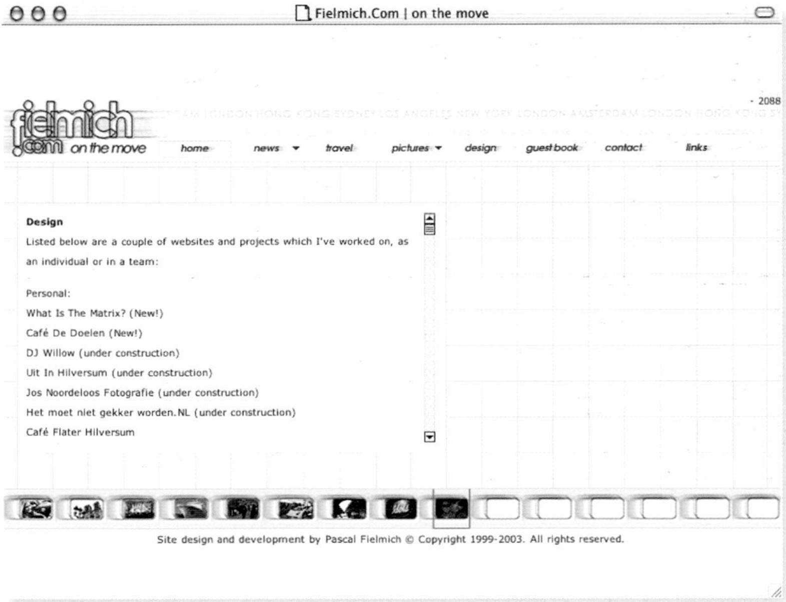

WWW.FIELMICH.COM
D: PASCAL FIELMICH
M: PASCAL@FIELMICH.COM

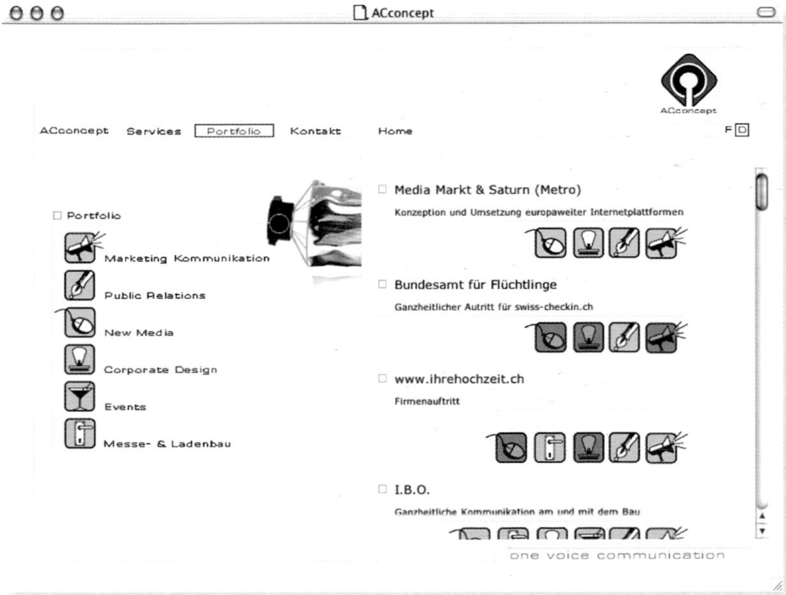

WWW.ACCONCEPT.CH
D: PATRICK SASSINE
A: ACCONCEPT, **M:** P.SASSINE@ACCONCEPT.CH

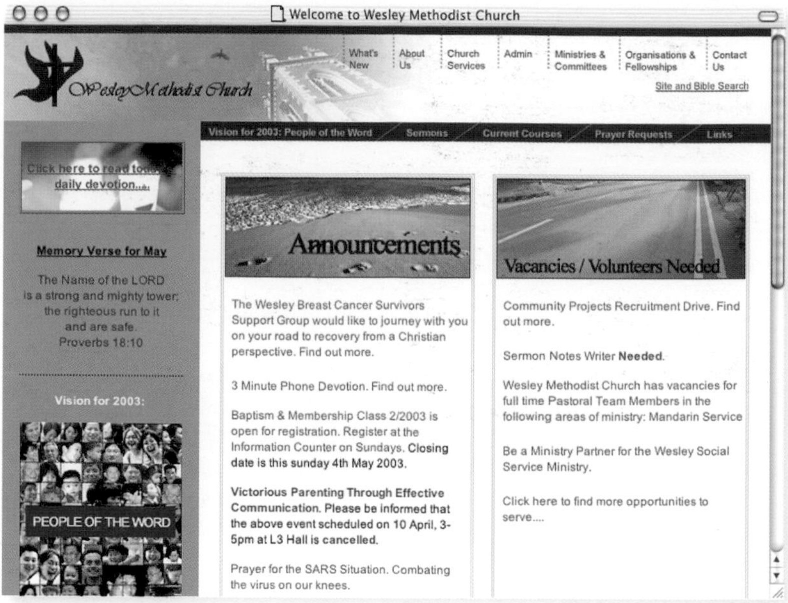

WWW.WESLEYMC.ORG
D: ADELE CHAN, **C:** CHRIS TAN
A: ASHER AND HOUSE, **M:** ADELE@ASHERANDHOUSE.COM

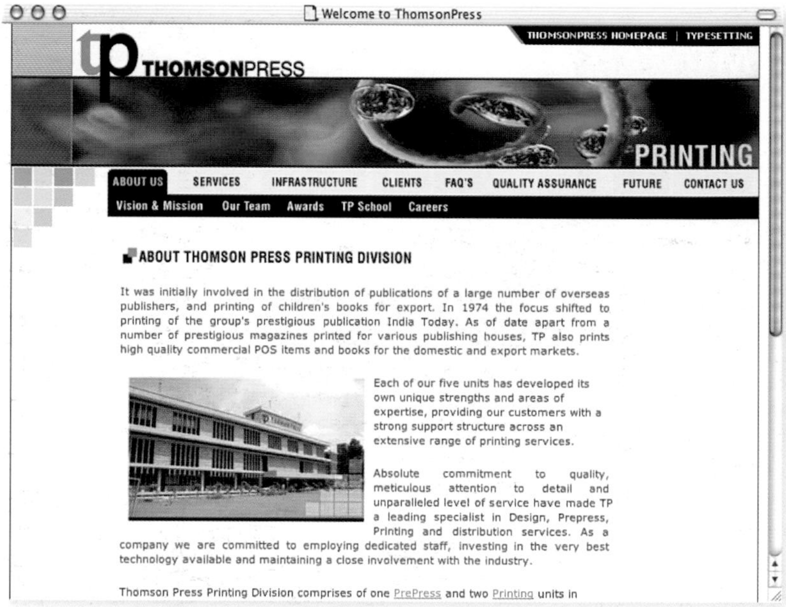

WWW.THOMSONPRESS.COM
D: SANJEEV SHARMA, **C:** ASHISH LAHORI, **P:** KALLI PURI
A: ITGO, **M:** SANJEEV.SHARMA@NAUKRI.COM

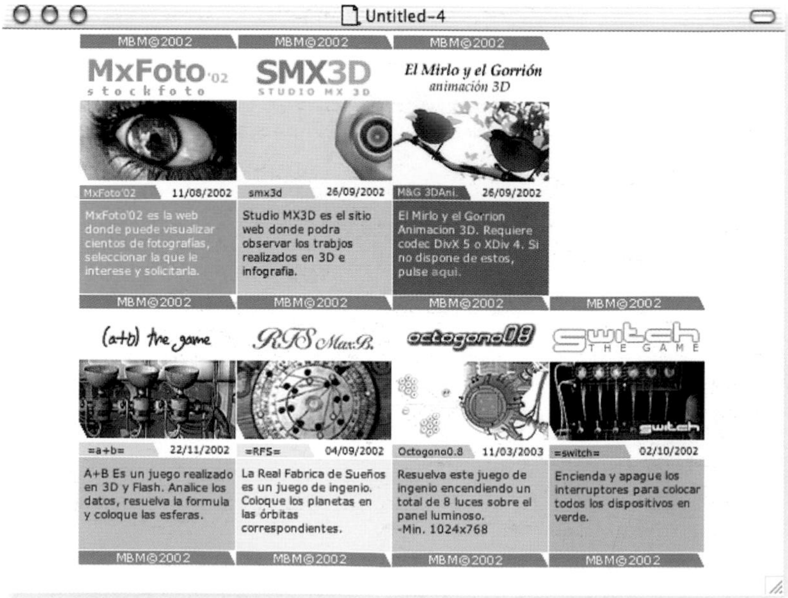

WWW.MAXBRIENZA.COM
D: MAX BRIENZA
A: SMX, **M:** WEBMASTER@MAXBRIENZA.COM

WWW.FORDRACING.PT
D: JOAO FERNANDES, **C:** JOAO FERNANDES, **P:** RUTE FRANÇA
A: VIEW., **M:** JOAO.FERNANDES@VIEW.PT

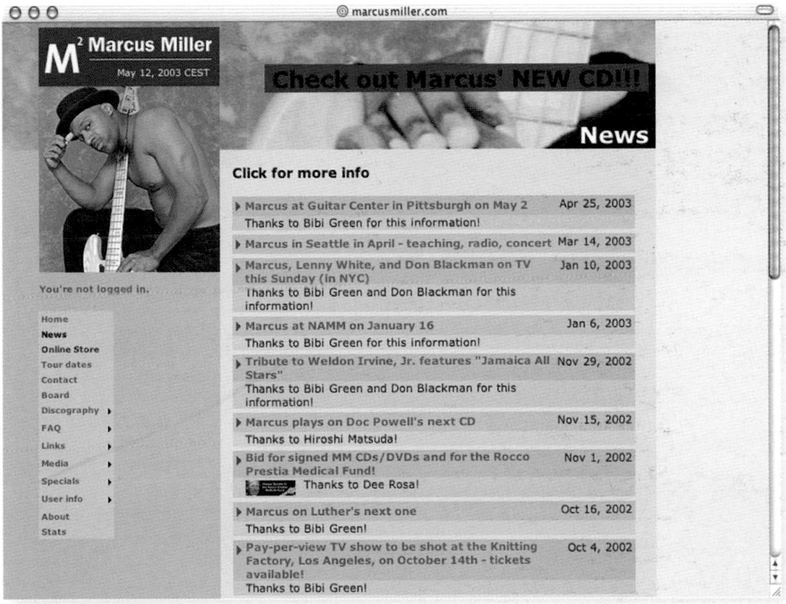

WWW.MARCUSMILLER.COM
D: MANFRED SPILLER, **P:** NORMAL NULL
A: NORMAL NULL, **M:** NULL@NORMAL-NULL.DE

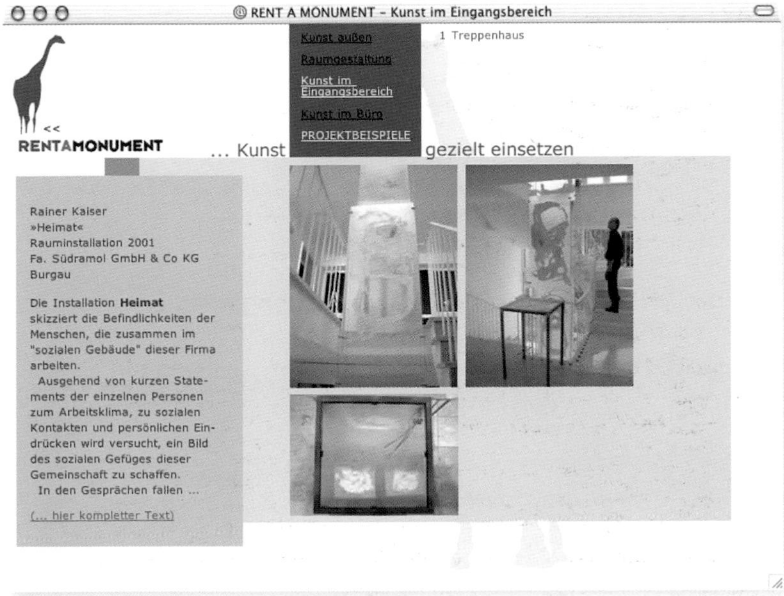

WWW.RENT-A-MONUMENT.DE
D: PIT KINZER
M: KUNSTPROJEKTE@PITKINZER.DE

WWW.DELOS.FANTASCIENZA.COM
D: SILVIO SOSIO
A: SOLID, **M:** SILVIO@SOSIO.IT

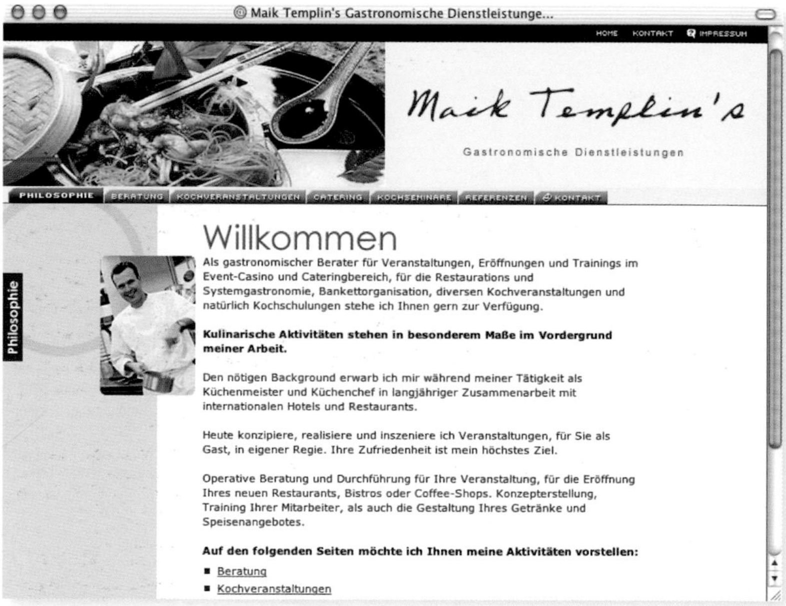

MAIK-TEMPLIN.DE
D: DINO PANNOZZO

WWW.STRATEGICEDGE.CO.UK
D: MIGUEL ALVAREZ / MICHAEL JENNINGS, **P:** MIGUEL ALVAREZ
A: RUBBER BAND GRAPHIC DESIGN, **M:** MIGUELAAV@YAHOO.CO.UK

WWW.MEXDESIGN.COM
D: LUIXN, **C:** ANA ISABEL PEREZ CORNEJO, **P:** ANA ISABEL PEREZ CORNEJO
A: MEXDESIGN.COM, **M:** WEBMASTER@MEXDESIGN.COM

WWW.DESIGNADDICT.COM
D: NICOLAS GLINOER
A: WALKING MEN, **M:** N@WALKINGMEN.COM

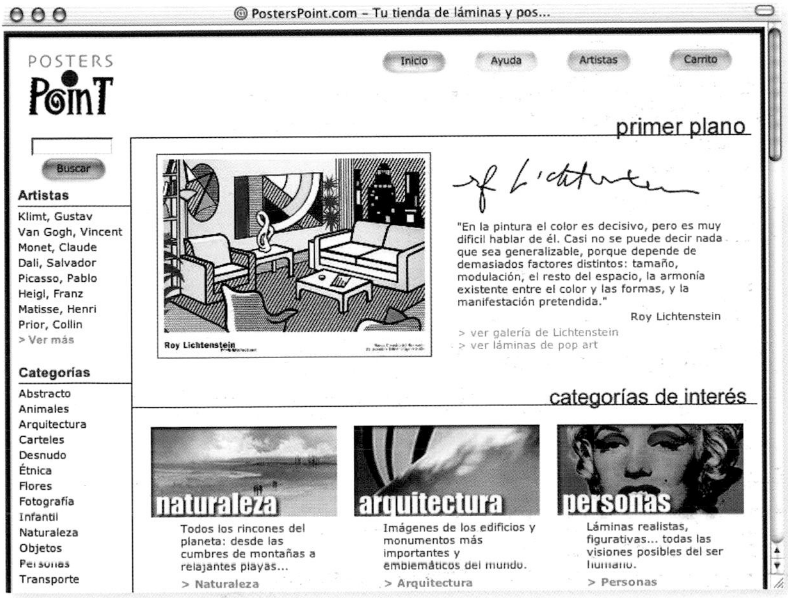

WWW.POSTERSPOINT.COM
D: CARLOS ZARAGOZA KOBLISCHEK
A: PLENUMWEB, **M:** INFO@PLENUMWEB.COM

WWW.NUOVEMODELLE.COM
D: DR. NICOLA BELLOTTI, **C:** DR. GHITA PASQUALI, **P:** DR. NICOLA BELLOTTI
A: BLACKLEMON, **M:** NUOVEMODELLE@BLACKLEMON.COM

WWW.LASTER.IT
D: LUCA DI FIORE
M: DIFIOREL@TISCALI.IT

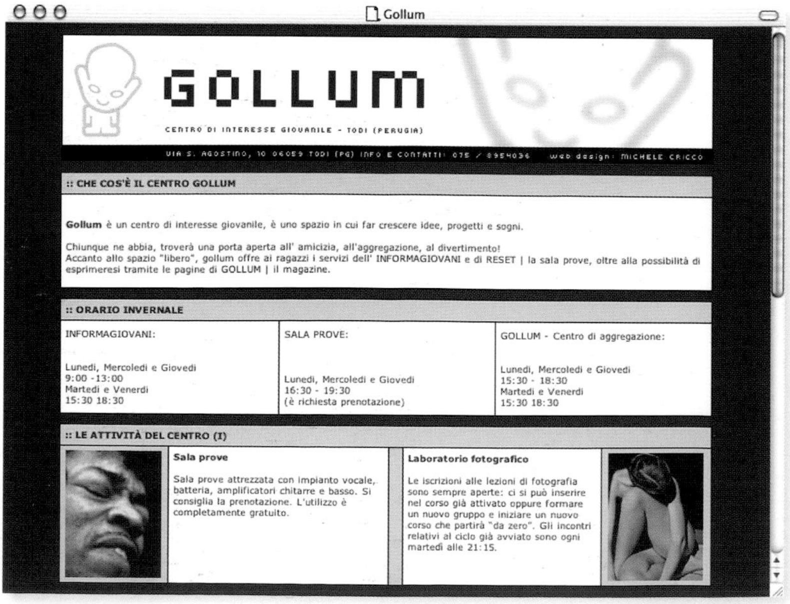

WWW.GOLLUMTODI.CJB.NET
D: MICHELE CRICCO
M: MIKIJESTER@YAHOO.COM

WWW.CHILEARTE.CL
D: FELIPE MOLINA
A: CHILEARTE.CL, **M:** FORTACHITO@HOTMAIL.COM

WWW.FILATELI.COM.BR
D: SILVIO TELES
A: ENOVA, **M:** WEBMASTER@FILATELI.COM.BR

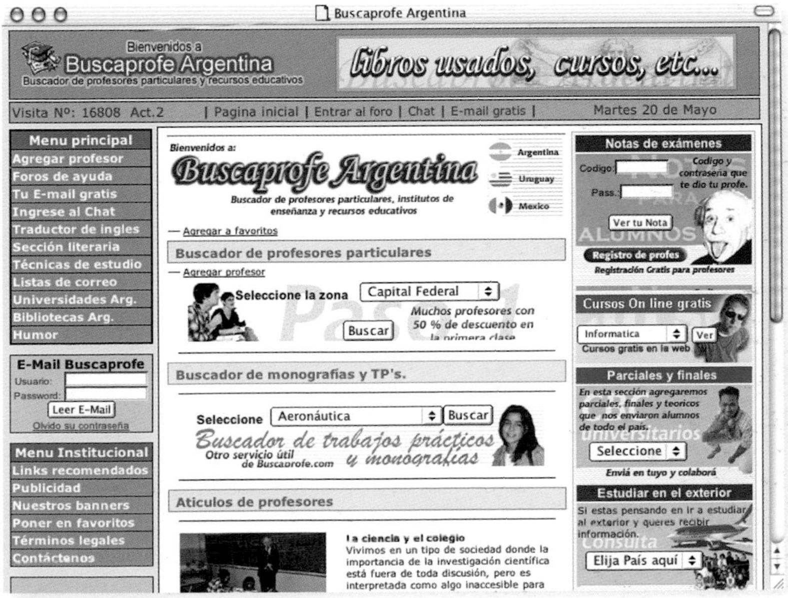

WWW.BUSCAPROFE.COM.AR
D: MAURO GENE
M: MAUROG@MATBA.COM.AR

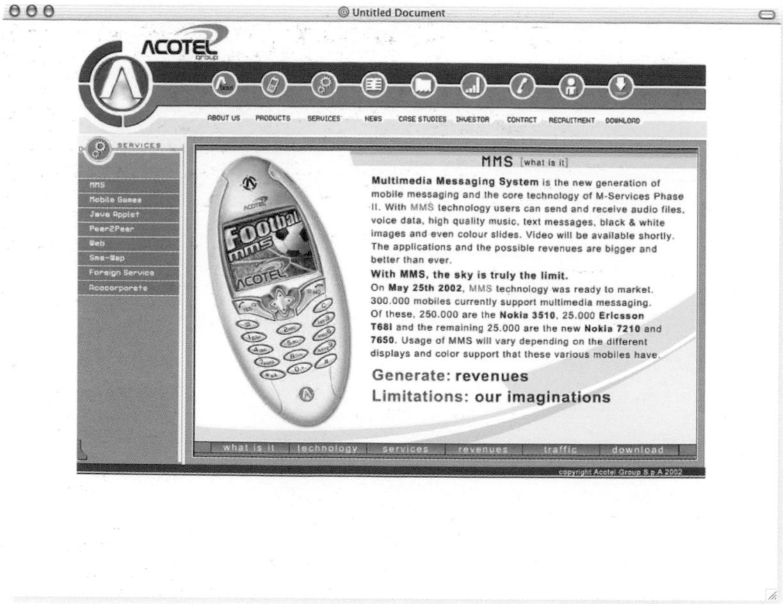

WWW.ACOTEL.COM
D: MAURIZIO DI GIOVANPAOLO, **C:** RICCARDO RIDENTI, **P:** ACOTEL GROUP
A: ACOTEL GROUP, **M:** DAVIDE.CARNEVALE@ACOTEL.COM

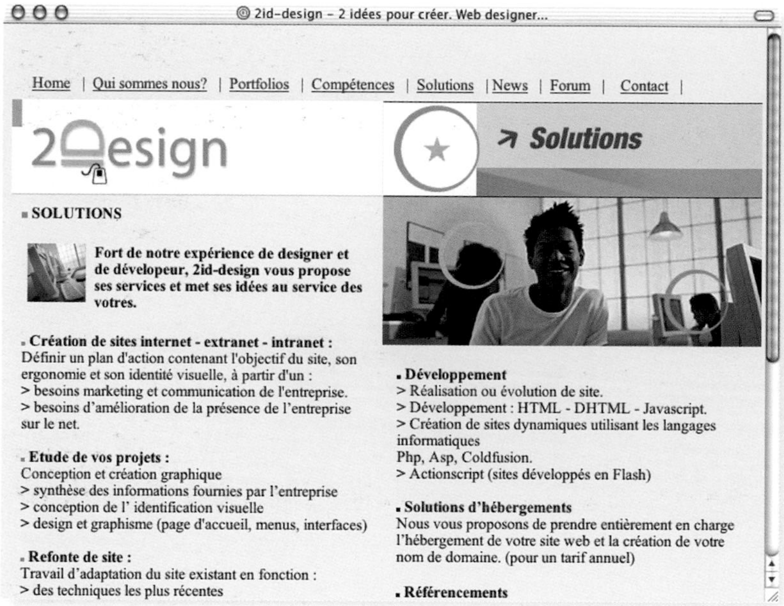

WWW.2ID-DESIGN.COM
D: NICOLAS STEPHANE
A: 2ID-DESIGN, **M:** DESIGNER@2ID-DESIGN.COM

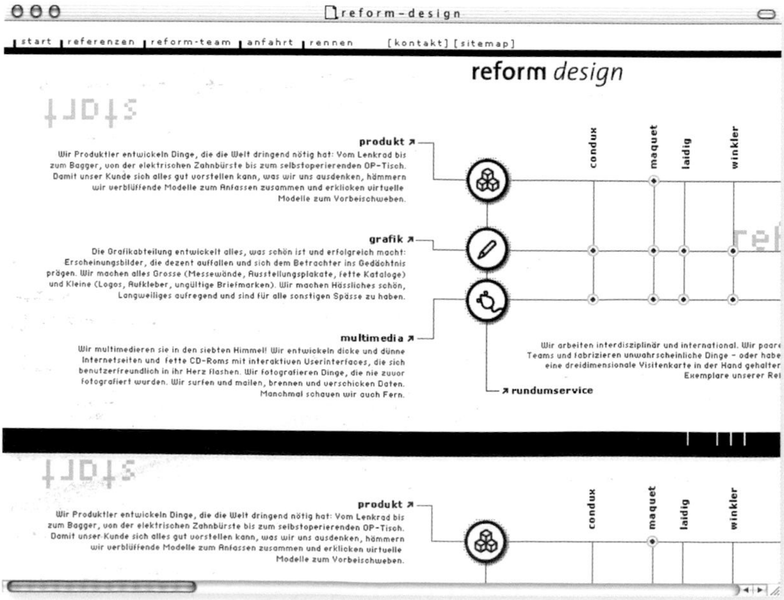

WWW.REFORM-DESIGN.DE
D: REFORM DESIGN
A: REFORM DESIGN, **M:** ANDREAS.KULL@REFORM-DESIGN.DE

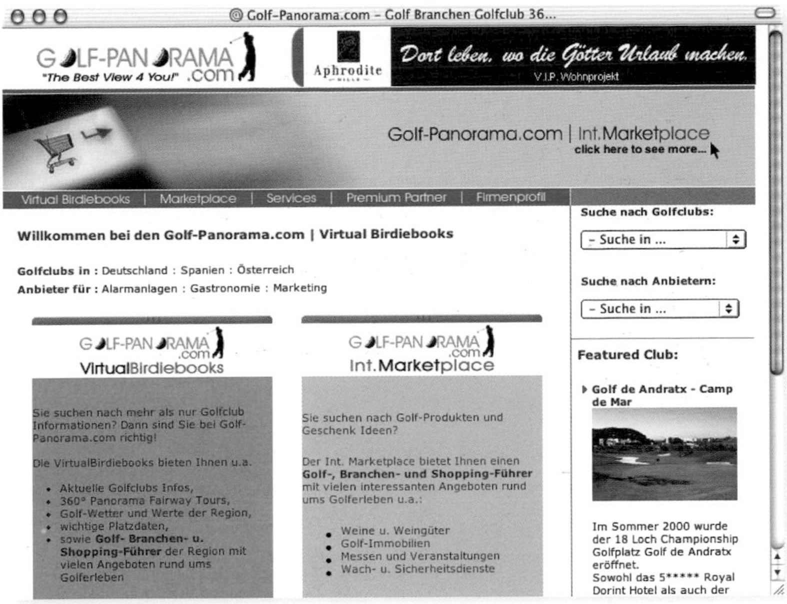

WWW.GOLF-PANORAMA.COM
D: ANDREAS POELL, **C:** KEITH ROWELL, **P:** ANDREAS POELL / IMS GMBH
A: APOELL.COM, **M:** HOME@APOELL.COM

WWW.ATECON.COM
D: BORJA BELLOD
A: IMAGEN CONSULTING, **M:** INFO@NETIMAGEN.COM

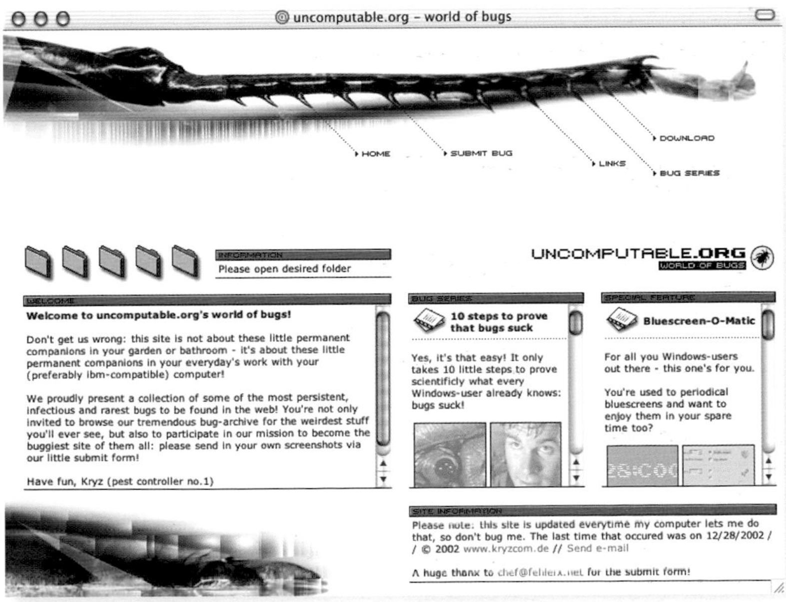

WWW.UNCOMPUTABLE.ORG
D: CHRISTOPH RENNE
A: KRYZCOM INC., **M:** CHEF@KRYZCOM.DE

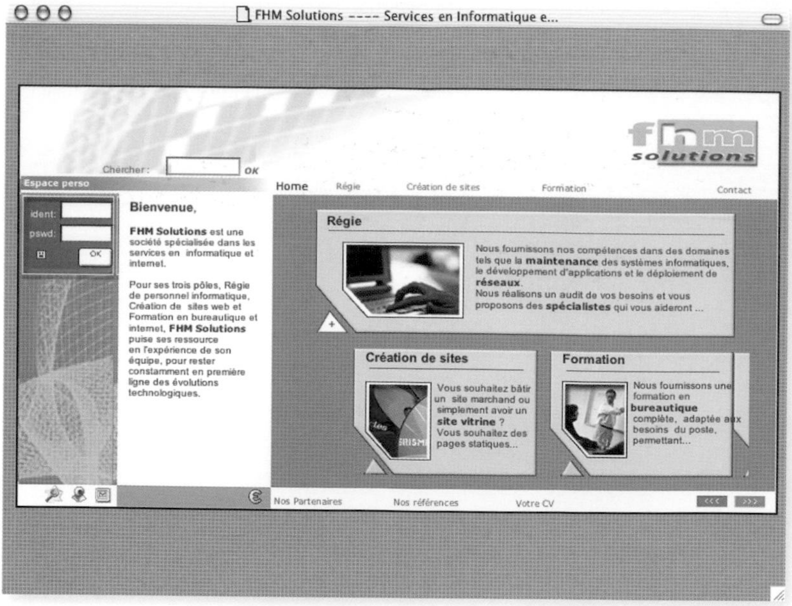

WWW.FHMSOLUTIONS.COM
D: FRANCIS GILLAIN
A: FHMSOLUTIONS, **M:** FGILLAIN@FHMSOLUTIONS.COM

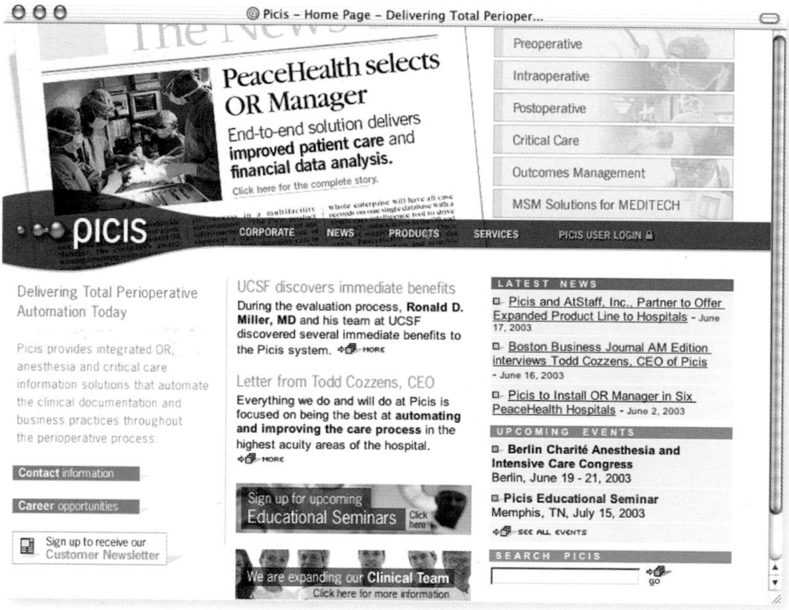

WWW.PICIS.COM
D: JUAN CARLOS CAMMAERT
M: JC@CAMMAERT.COM

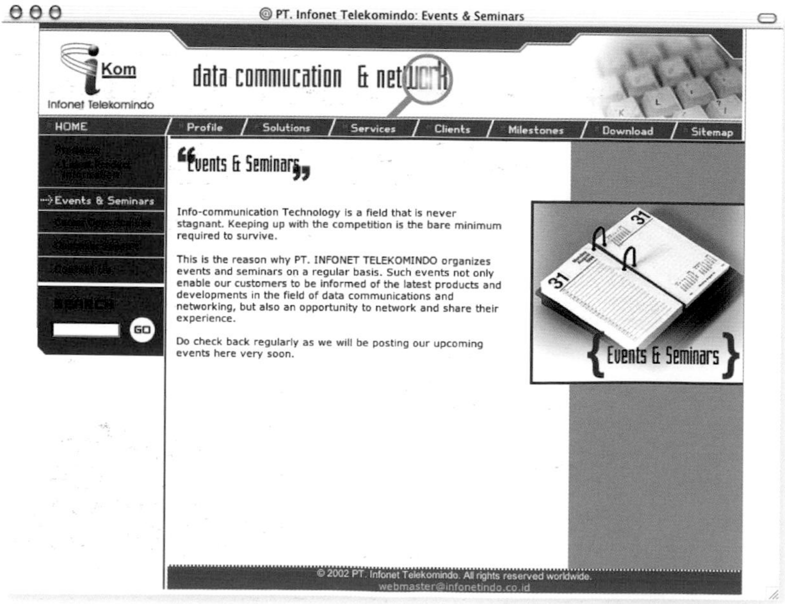

WWW.INFONET-TELEKOMINDO.COM
D: ROSALINE DJAYASUKMANA
A: DE-CAFE WEB & GRAPHIC DESIGN, **M:** DESIGN@DE-CAFE.COM

WWW.C3.HU
D: GEZA NYIRY
M: MAIL@NYK.HU

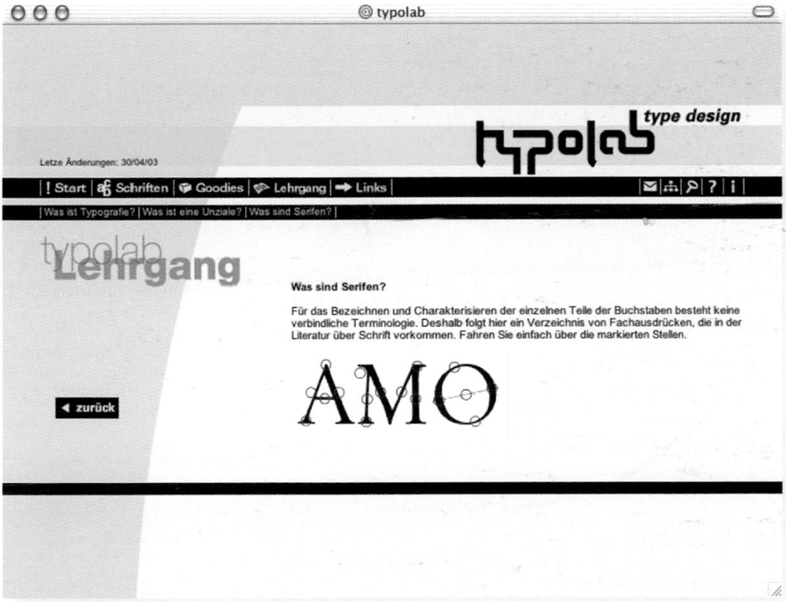

WWW.TYPOLAB.CH
D: HANSPETER PFISTER
M: HP.PFISTER@GMX.NET

WWW.ITOMI.IT
D: ANTONIO MORO
M: ANTONIO@ITOMI.IT

WWW.ARTUROELENA.COM
D: ANA BELÉN ALVAREZ, **C:** ENRIQUE VALENTÍN
A: GRAPHA, **M:** INFO@GRAPHA.NET

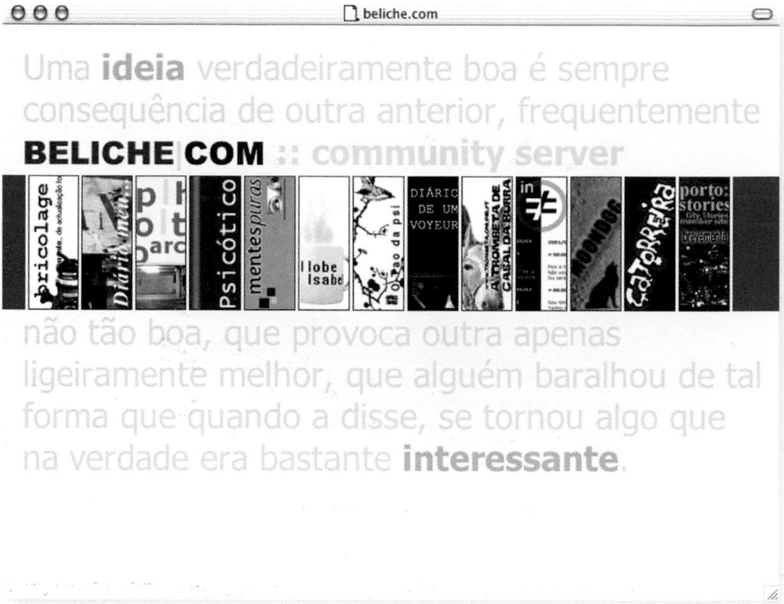

beliche.com
Uma ideia verdadeiramente boa é sempre consequência de outra anterior, frequentemente
BELICHE COM :: community server
não tão boa, que provoca outra apenas ligeiramente melhor, que alguém baralhou de tal forma que quando a disse, se tornou algo que na verdade era bastante interessante.

WWW.BELICHE.COM
D: FILIPE MIGUEL TAVARES
A: FMTAVARES.NET, **M:** FMT@FMTAVARES.NET

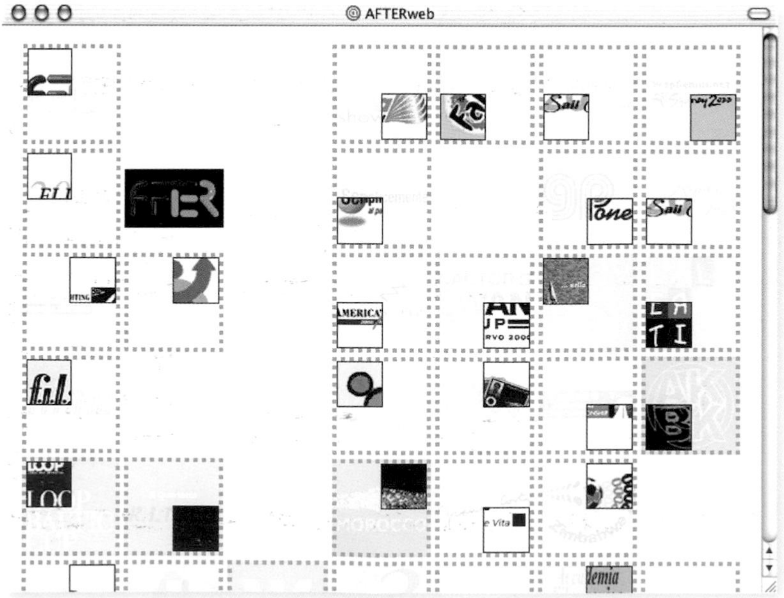

WWW.AFTERWEB.COM
D: SIMONA DI SILVIO, **C:** AFTER S.R.L., **P:** ANDREA FILACCHIONI
A: AFTER S.R.L., **M:** ANDREA.FILACCHIONI@AFTER.IT

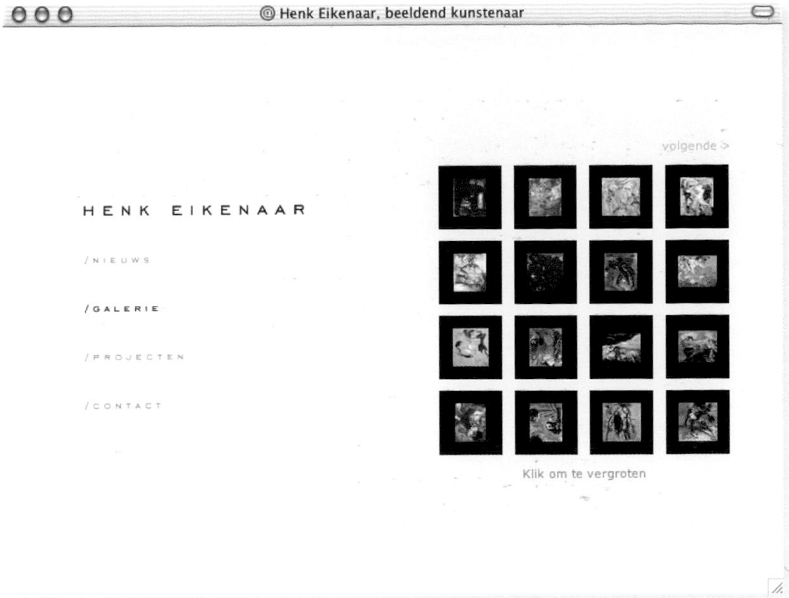

WWW.HENKEIKENAAR.NL
D: SJOERD EIKENAAR, **C:** JOOST GIELEN
M: JOOST@FRESHHEADS.COM

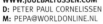

WWW.JUULBALTUSSEN.COM
D: PETER PAUL CORNELISSEN
M: PEPA@WORLDONLINE.NL

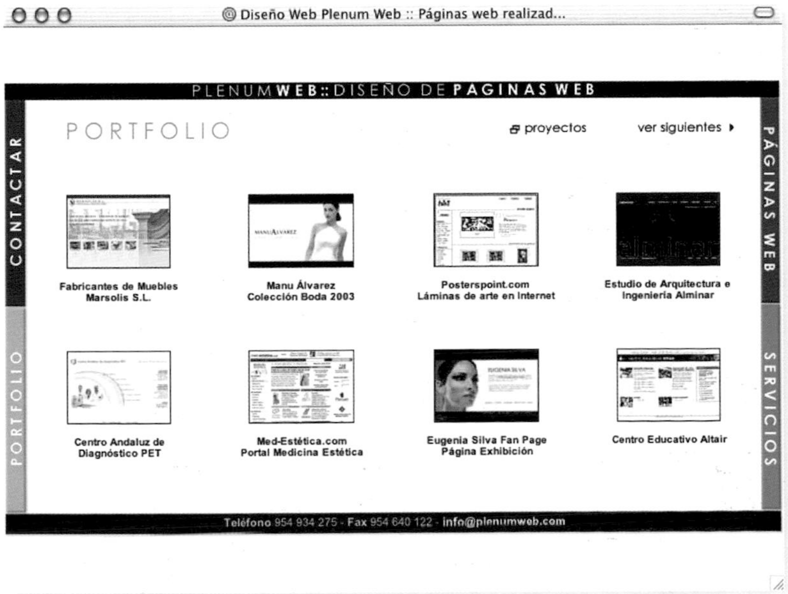

WWW.PLENUMWEB.COM
D: CARLOS ZARAGOZA KOBLISCHEK
M: CARLOSZK@PLENUMWEB.COM

LiberArte: Comunidad virtual para la promoció...
liber-arte.com
{ Quiénes somos } { Cómo navegar } { Normas } { Respuestas } { Registro } { Contactar }
Últimos eventos.
1/2 día en la escena.
Plaza de San Francisco.
Desde el día: 7/05/03
Hasta el día: 7/05/03
Acción decorados sorprende con una performance dedicada al teatro. Para realizar una obra de teatro hacen falta muchas personas y mucho trabajo, más del que se ve en la representación. Esta performance intenta hacer hincapié en todo lo que rodea a la obra. Se pretende reflejar con esta acción que hay que aunar muchos criterios, muchas ilusiones, muchos sueños para desempeñar una obra de teatro, incluso el público, pues si no hay nadie al otro lado del escenario la representación pierde su sentido más intrínseco que es el ofrecer un espectáculo. En este punto se cerraría el círculo de la acción donde, escultores, actores, música y transeúntes participan de la acción en sí, cada uno representando su papel, aportando su grano de arena en la realización de uno de los entretenimientos más antiguos en un marco que también tiene sus siglos de historia. Ofrecerá espectáculos escultóricos, teatrales, de música e imagen e integrará a los transeúntes en las actividades.
Buscar
<< ::: >>
Artistas
Pintura
Escultura
Fotografía
Cine
Teatro
Música
Literatura
Artesanía
NetArt
Gráfica
Suscríbete
Tu nombre
Tu email
Enviar
Exposiciones
Actual
Permanente
Servicios
Agenda
Charlas

WWW.LIBER-ARTE.COM
D: JESÚS FEÁS MUÑOZ
A: PÍXIMA INTERNET, **M:** JFEAS@PIXIMA.NET

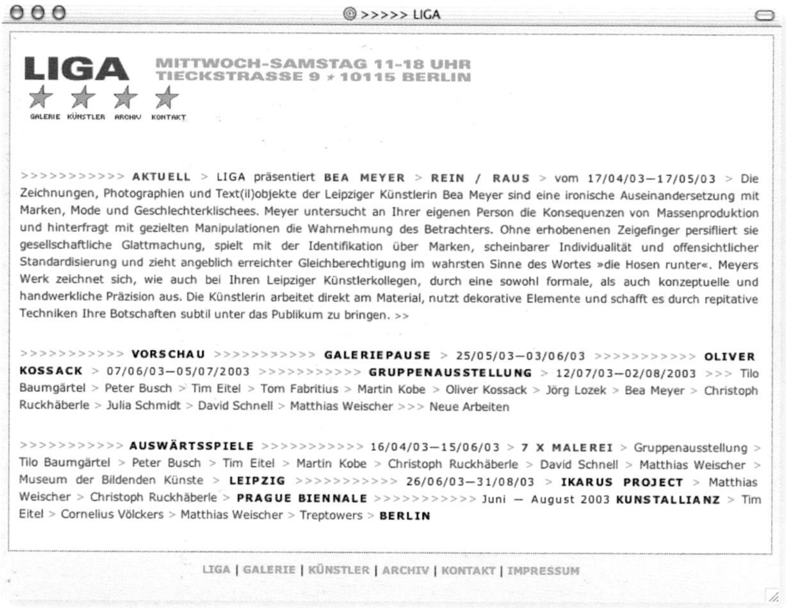
>>>>> LIGA
LIGA
MITTWOCH-SAMSTAG 11-18 UHR
TIECKSTRASSE 9 * 10115 BERLIN
GALERIE KÜNSTLER ARCHIV KONTAKT
>>>>>>>>>>> AKTUELL > LIGA präsentiert BEA MEYER > REIN / RAUS > vom 17/04/03–17/05/03 > Die Zeichnungen, Photographien und Text(il)objekte der Leipziger Künstlerin Bea Meyer sind eine ironische Auseinandersetzung mit Marken, Mode und Geschlechterklischees. Meyer untersucht an Ihrer eigenen Person die Konsequenzen von Massenproduktion und hinterfragt mit gezielten Manipulationen die Wahrnehmung des Betrachters. Ohne erhobenenen Zeigefinger persifliert sie gesellschaftliche Glattmachung, spielt mit der Identifikation über Marken, scheinbarer Individualität und offensichtlicher Standardisierung und zieht angeblich erreichter Gleichberechtigung im wahrsten Sinne des Wortes »die Hosen runter«. Meyers Werk zeichnet sich, wie auch bei Ihren Leipziger Künstlerkollegen, durch eine sowohl formale, als auch konzeptuelle und handwerkliche Präzision aus. Die Künstlerin arbeitet direkt am Material, nutzt dekorative Elemente und schafft es durch repitative Techniken Ihre Botschaften subtil unter das Publikum zu bringen. >>
>>>>>>>>>>> VORSCHAU >>>>>>>>>>> GALERIEPAUSE > 25/05/03–03/06/03 >>>>>>>>>>> OLIVER KOSSACK > 07/06/03–05/07/2003 >>>>>>>>>>> GRUPPENAUSSTELLUNG > 12/07/03–02/08/2003 >>> Tilo Baumgärtel > Peter Busch > Tim Eitel > Tom Fabritius > Martin Kobe > Oliver Kossack > Jörg Lozek > Bea Meyer > Christoph Ruckhäberle > Julia Schmidt > David Schnell > Matthias Weischer >>> Neue Arbeiten
>>>>>>>>>>> AUSWÄRTSSPIELE >>>>>>>>>>> 16/04/03–15/06/03 > 7 X MALEREI > Gruppenausstellung > Tilo Baumgärtel > Peter Busch > Tim Eitel > Martin Kobe > Christoph Ruckhäberle > David Schnell > Matthias Weischer > Museum der Bildenden Künste > LEIPZIG >>>>>>>>>>> 26/06/03–31/08/03 > IKARUS PROJECT > Matthias Weischer > Christoph Ruckhäberle > PRAGUE BIENNALE >>>>>>>>>>> Juni – August 2003 KUNSTALLIANZ > Tim Eitel > Cornelius Völckers > Matthias Weischer > Treptowers > BERLIN
LIGA | GALERIE | KÜNSTLER | ARCHIV | KONTAKT | IMPRESSUM

WWW.LIGA-GALERIE.DE
D: ANNA-LENA VON HELLDORF, SIMONE WASSERMANN, MARIO RÖHRLE, **C:** MARIO RÖHRLE
M: MITARBEITER@EMERCO.DE

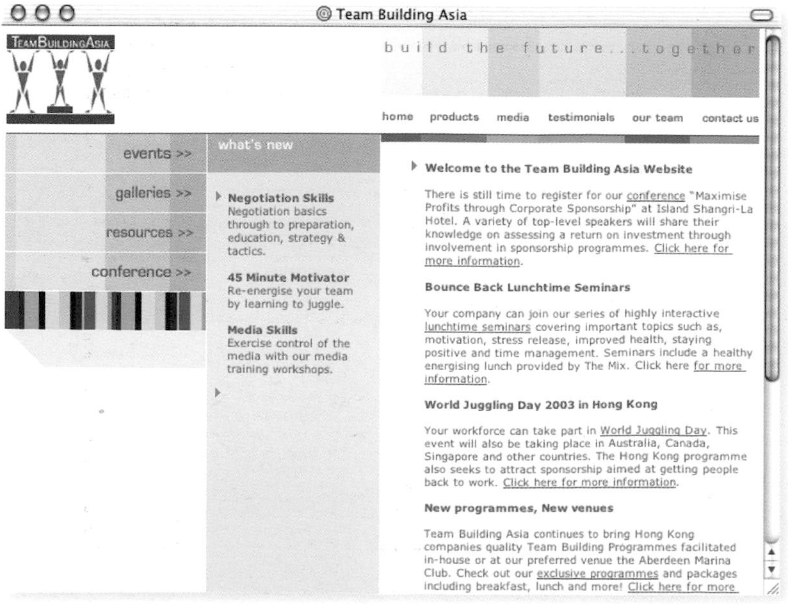
Team Building Asia
TEAMBUILDINGASIA
build the future...together
home products media testimonials our team contact us
events >>
galleries >>
resources >>
conference >>
what's new
Negotiation Skills
Negotiation basics through to preparation, education, strategy & tactics.
45 Minute Motivator
Re-energise your team by learning to juggle.
Media Skills
Exercise control of the media with our media training workshops.
Welcome to the Team Building Asia Website
There is still time to register for our conference "Maximise Profits through Corporate Sponsorship" at Island Shangri-La Hotel. A variety of top-level speakers will share their knowledge on assessing a return on investment through involvement in sponsorship programmes. Click here for more information.
Bounce Back Lunchtime Seminars
Your company can join our series of highly interactive lunchtime seminars covering important topics such as, motivation, stress release, improved health, staying positive and time management. Seminars include a healthy energising lunch provided by The Mix. Click here for more information.
World Juggling Day 2003 in Hong Kong
Your workforce can take part in World Juggling Day. This event will also be taking place in Australia, Canada, Singapore and other countries. The Hong Kong programme also seeks to attract sponsorship aimed at getting people back to work. Click here for more information.
New programmes, New venues
Team Building Asia continues to bring Hong Kong companies quality Team Building Programmes facilitated in-house or at our preferred venue the Aberdeen Marina Club. Check out our exclusive programmes and packages including breakfast, lunch and more! Click here for more

WWW.TEAMBUILDINGASIA.COM
D: MARC SCOTT, **C:** MARC SCOTT, **P:** TEAM BUILDING ASIA
A: MUSE INTERNATIONAL, **M:** RICHARD@MUSE-INTERNATIONAL.COM

Quo Hotels
QUO PUERTADELSOL
Get comfortable, you will feel fine.
Placed in the historical, cultural and commercial centre of Madrid, an emblematic building from the beginning of the XXth century with unique views to the city, that's where is located Quo Puerta del Sol Hotel. Totally restored, designed and equipped to offer you a perfect stay: high technology, design furniture, vanguard atmosphere, welcome amenities... and a professional and efficient customer service.
ROOMS | SERVICES | LOCATION | TRANSPORTS | e-mail

WWW.HOTELESQUO.COM
D: DAVID SUEIRO
A: DSDG, **M:** DAVID@SUEIRO.COM

design & lifestyle magazin

Quickinfo:
Sceyelines (sprich: Skylines) ist das neue Design & Life-style Magazin von Dirk Behlau (mit Unterstützung von Jens Franke).

Interviews:
Francois Chalet, Furi Furi, Buro Destruct, Die Gestalten Verlag, Galileo Design, DIK,

WWW.SCEYELINES.DE
D: DIRK BEHLAU, **C:** DIRK BEHLAU / JENS FRANKE
A: PIXELEYE INTERACTIVE, **M:** DIRK@DIRKBEHLAU.DE

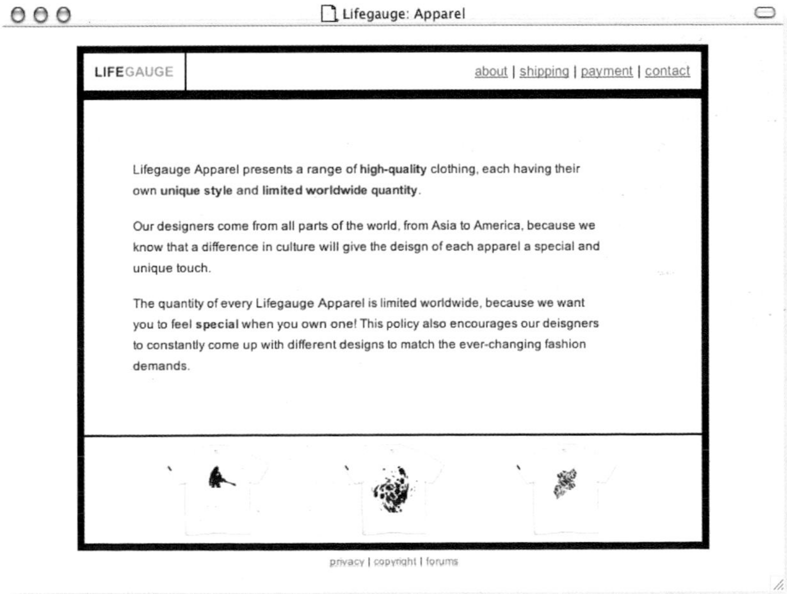

Lifegauge: Apparel
LIFEGAUGE
about | shipping | payment | contact
Lifegauge Apparel presents a range of high-quality clothing, each having their own unique style and limited worldwide quantity.
Our designers come from all parts of the world, from Asia to America, because we know that a difference in culture will give the deisgn of each apparel a special and unique touch.
The quantity of every Lifegauge Apparel is limited worldwide, because we want you to feel special when you own one! This policy also encourages our deisgners to constantly come up with different designs to match the ever-changing fashion demands.
privacy | copyright | forums

WWW.LIFEGAUGE.COM
D: FELIX SIM
M: FELIX@LIFEGAUGE.COM

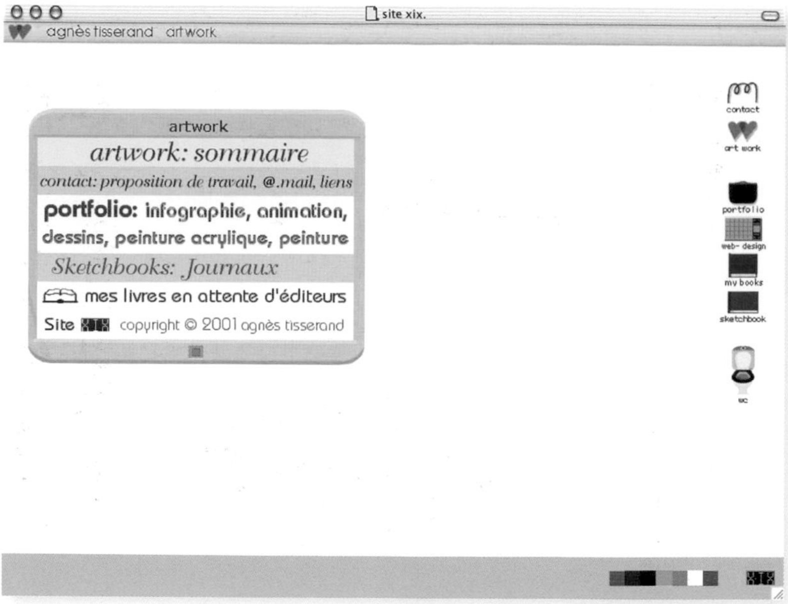

PERSO.CLUB-INTERNET.FR/XIX
D: AGNES TISSERAND
A: XIX, **M:** XIX@CLUB-INTERNET.FR

WWW.PRIMERAPERSONA.COM/LETRASPEQUENAS
D: ANNA MARIA LOPEZ LOPEZ
A: ANNA-OM-LINE - FASHIONMAS DESIGN SERVICES, **M:** ANNA@FASHIONMAS.COM

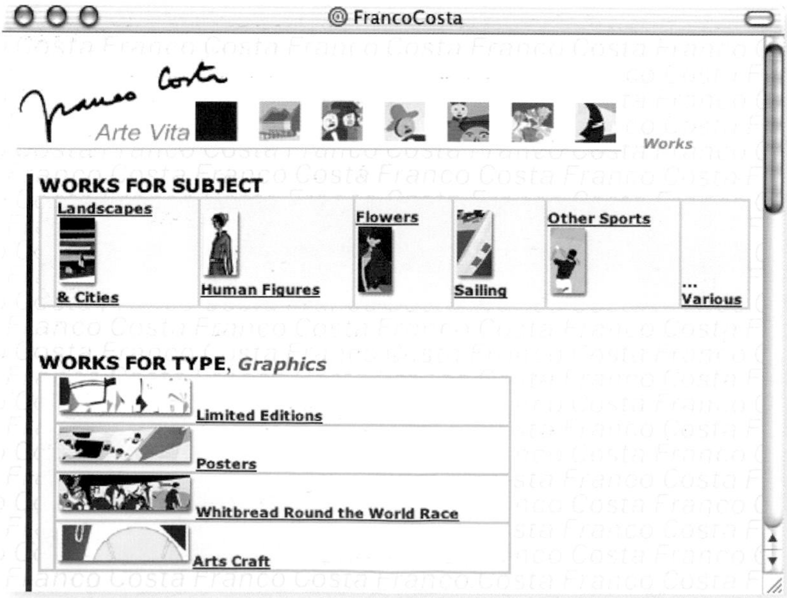

WWW.FRANCOCOSTA.IT
D: SIMONA DI SILVIO, **C:** AFTER S.R.L., **P:** ANDREA FILACCHIONI
A: AFTER S.R.L., **M:** ANDREA.FILACCHIONI@AFTER.IT

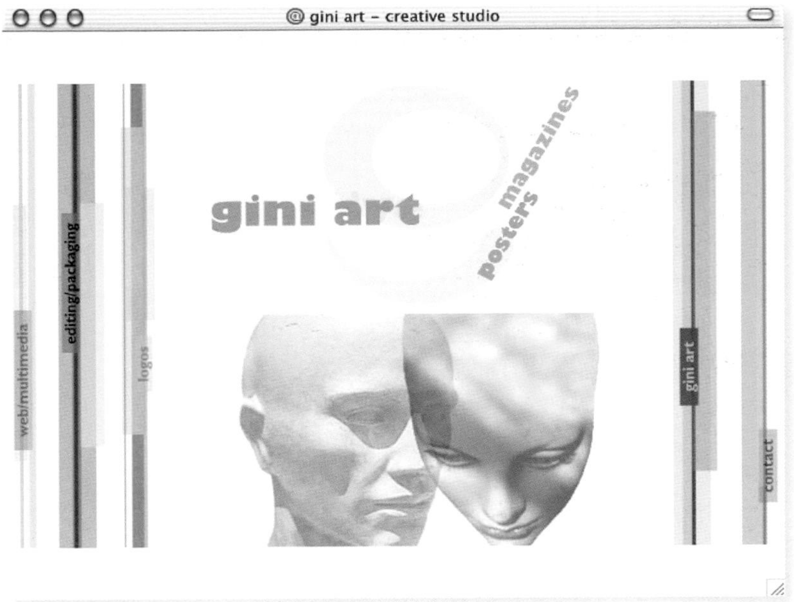

WWW.GINI-ART.NET
D: GIOVANNI CARA
M: GIO@GINI-ART.NET

WWW.ELEVA-COMUNICACION.COM
D: DAVID VÁSQUEZ MARTHAN
A: ELEVA COMUNICACIÓN, **M:** INFO@ELEVA-COMUNICACION.COM

WWW.REFRESH.PT/DEFAULTFULL.HTM
D: HELDER VASCONCELOS, **C:** RICARDO MACHADO, **P:** SERGIO TAVARES
A: GO WEB, LDA, **M:** INFO@GOWEB.PT

Parrot Interactive Graphic design, Multimedia...
PARROT
ADVERTISING, COMMUNICATIONS AND INTERACTIVE MEDIA
Shortcuts
Graphic design
• corporate
• logotype
• printing
Interactive media
• cd-rom/dvd
• sound/vision
• presenting
Website design
• webdesign
• html-edit
• the clients
Information
• overall info
• references
• parrot chat
• contact us
Welcome at Parrot Interactive media
Welcome! You have reached the renewed Parrot Interactive web pages. Please take your time to explore this pages! New in lay-out design and functionality. Via this presentation Parrot Interactive would like to present you an overview of the various disciplines wich are available for your company.
Why Parrot Interactive as a partner
Every company, yours also is unique and therefore deserves a special approach. Parrot Interactive is here to assist you in any way we can, making the best possible product. Your request will be dealt with thoughtfully and quickly, whether it's about creating a logo or a corporate identity. Satisfaction guaranteed!
Your targets are our targets
To give you a complete overview, we decided to break our disciplines into three separate pieces as shown by the buttons on the left-hand side. We invite you to take a tour and discover a few examples of our recent work.
Samples of recent work
Parrot Downloads → Ultimate SlotZone
Download our new casinogame Ultimate SlotZone 10.10
Play up to 4 different slotmachines and wander yourself in a real casino
Compatible with Windows 98, 2000, XP and Mac OS 9 up to MacOS X
Copyright © 2003 Parrot Interactive media, Inc. All rights reserved.

WWW.PARROT.NL
C: GER VERSTEEG
A: PARROT INTERACTIVE MEDIAÔ, **M:** TALKTO@PARROT.NL

Hana Zelenková - kandidát ÈSSD do Senátu
▸ úvodní stránka ▸ fotogalerie ▸ životopis ▾ akce ▸ program ▸ zeptejte se mne ▸ média
Rehabilitovat Senát v oèích veøejnosti dá mnoho práce
"Øada lidí tvrdí, že Senát není potøebná instituce. Samozøejmì, každý má nárok na vlastní názor. Faktem však je, že pokud zde byl zaveden systém dvoukomorového parlamentu, a ten byl ustaven demokratickým způsobem, odhlasovali jej ti, kdo dostali ve volbách platný mandát od volièù, je tøeba tento stav respektovat. Faktem pak také je, že právì systém dvoukomorového parlamentu není žádnou neovìøenou novinkou èi experimentem, vždy? se staèí podívat napøíklad na Velkou Británii. Také tam fungují dvì komory a nikdo si nemyslí, že by jedna z nich byla ménì významná.
Mohla bych zde hovoøit o Senátu jako o pojistce, opit mohu uvést øadu pøípadù, kdy tak skuteènì
PaedDr. Hana Zelenková
kandidátka ČSSD do Senátu
webmaster PRONETmedia

WWW.HANAZELENKOVA.CZ
D: KUBICEK MICHAL
A: PRONETMEDIA, **M:** CEO@PRONETMEDIA.CZ

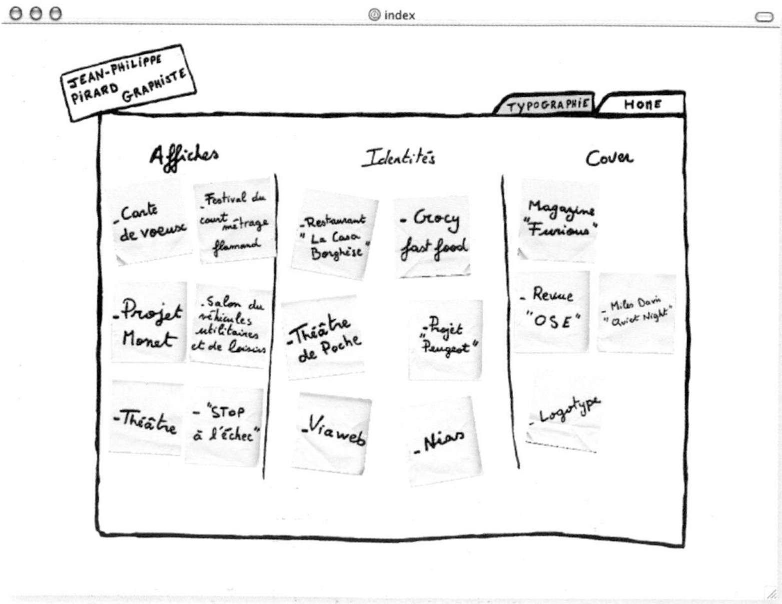
index
JEAN-PHILIPPE PIRARD GRAPHISTE
TYPOGRAPHIE
HOME
Affiches
Identités
Cover

WWW.PEPPERMINT.CC
D: JEAN-PHILIPPE PIRARD
A: PEPPERMINT, **M:** NATHALIE.VONAU@PEPPERMINT.CC

WWW.VERSO-LAUSANNE.CH
D: FRED HATT
A: TANGRAM, **M:** INFO@TANGRAM-DESIGN.CH

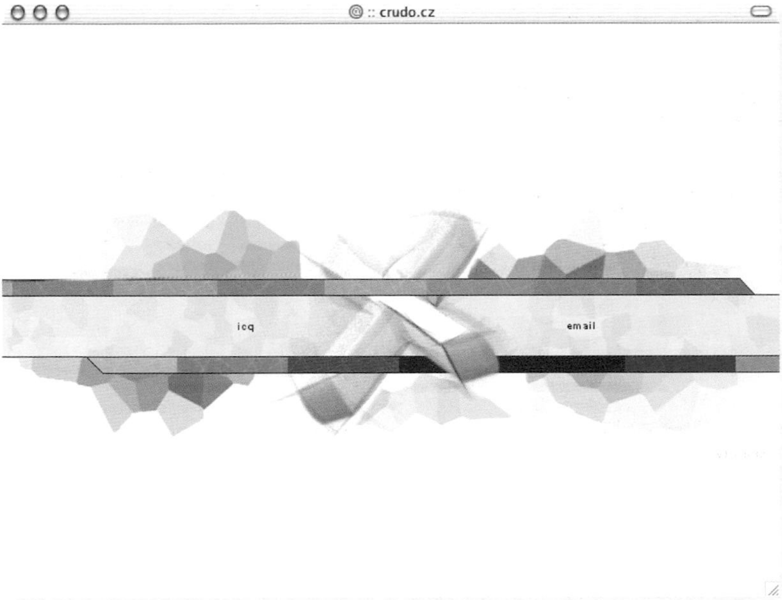

CRUDO.CZ
D: CRUDO
A: CRUDO, **M:** CRUDO@CRUDO.CZ

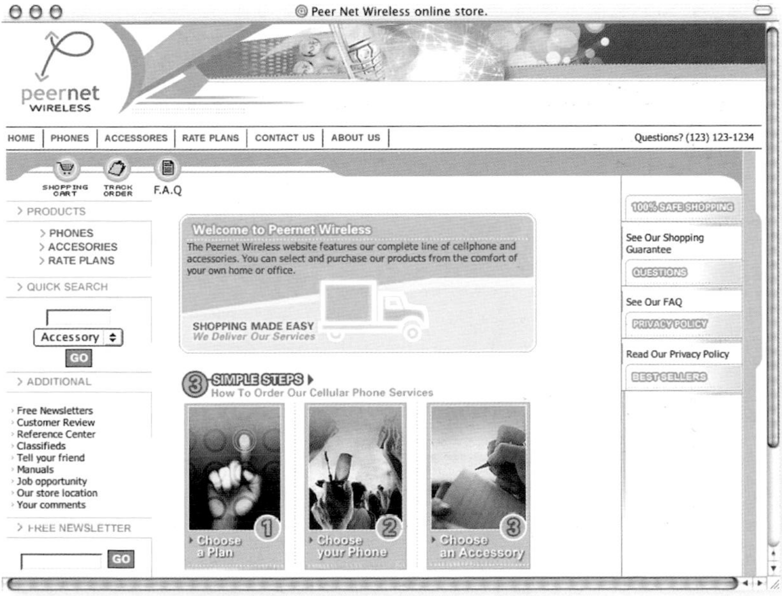

WWW.PEERNETWIRELESS.COM
D: JASMINE HOR MYN-LI, **C:** ESOLVED.COM, **P:** ESOLVED.COM
A: ESOLVED.COM, **M:** JASZY76@YAHOO.COM

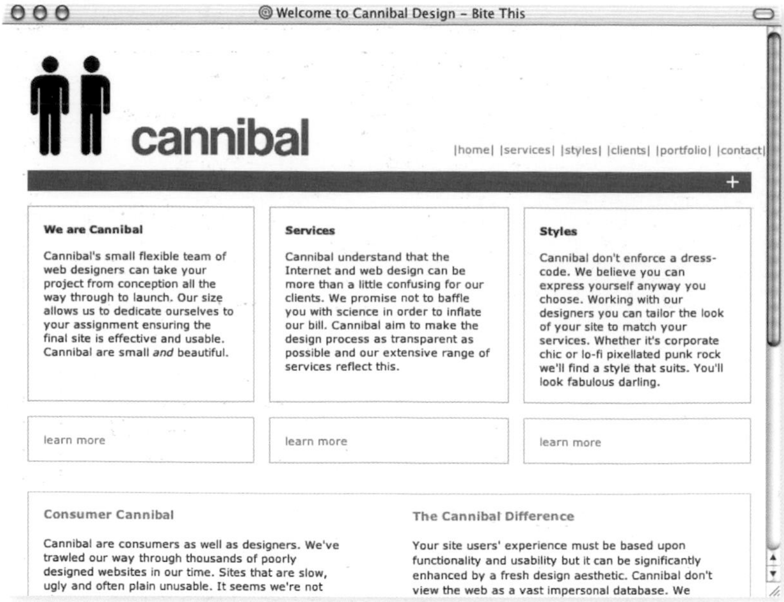
Welcome to Cannibal Design - Bite This
cannibal
|home| |services| |styles| |clients| |portfolio| |contact|
We are Cannibal
Cannibal's small flexible team of web designers can take your project from conception all the way through to launch. Our size allows us to dedicate ourselves to your assignment ensuring the final site is effective and usable. Cannibal are small and beautiful.
Services
Cannibal understand that the Internet and web design can be more than a little confusing for our clients. We promise not to baffle you with science in order to inflate our bill. Cannibal aim to make the design process as transparent as possible and our extensive range of services reflect this.
Styles
Cannibal don't enforce a dress-code. We believe you can express yourself anyway you choose. Working with our designers you can tailor the look of your site to match your services. Whether it's corporate chic or lo-fi pixellated punk rock we'll find a style that suits. You'll look fabulous darling.
learn more
learn more
learn more
Consumer Cannibal
Cannibal are consumers as well as designers. We've trawled our way through thousands of poorly designed websites in our time. Sites that are slow, ugly and often plain unusable. It seems we're not
The Cannibal Difference
Your site users' experience must be based upon functionality and usability but it can be significantly enhanced by a fresh design aesthetic. Cannibal don't view the web as a vast impersonal database. We

WWW.CANNIBALDESIGN.CO.UK
D: STEVEN KEY, RICHARD HALL
A: CANNIBAL , **M:** RICHCANNIBAL@HOTMAIL.COM

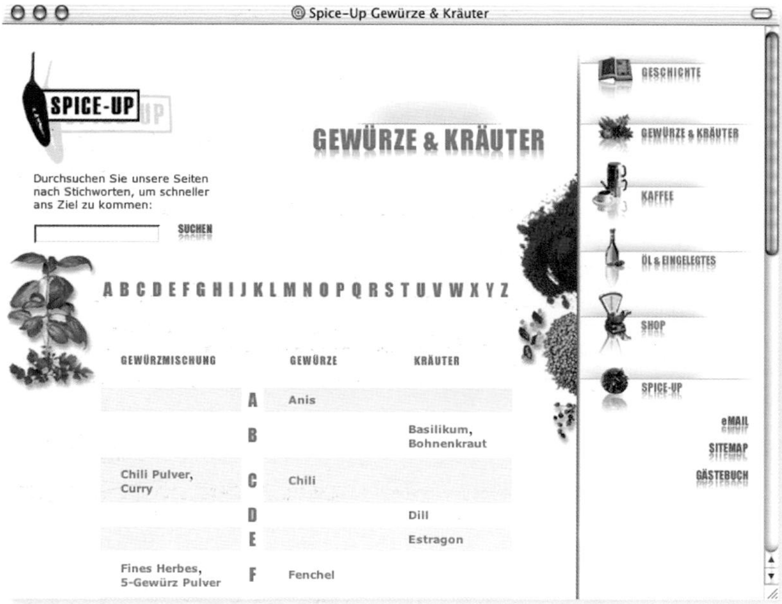
Spice-Up Gewürze & Kräuter
SPICE-UP
GEWÜRZE & KRÄUTER
Durchsuchen Sie unsere Seiten nach Stichworten, um schneller ans Ziel zu kommen:
SUCHEN
A B C D E F G H I J K L M N O P Q R S T U V W X Y Z
GEWÜRZMISCHUNG
GEWÜRZE
KRÄUTER
A Anis
B Basilikum, Bohnenkraut
Chili Pulver, Curry C Chili
D Dill
E Estragon
Fines Herbes, 5-Gewürz Pulver F Fenchel
GESCHICHTE
GEWÜRZE & KRÄUTER
KAFFEE
ÖL & EINGELEGTES
SHOP
SPICE-UP
eMAIL
SITEMAP
GÄSTEBUCH

WWW.SPICE-UP.DE
D: JESSIKA BÄTZ, **C:** JESSIKA BÄTZ, **P:** WEB-ACTS
A: WEB-ACTS, **M:** INFO@WEB-ACTS.DE

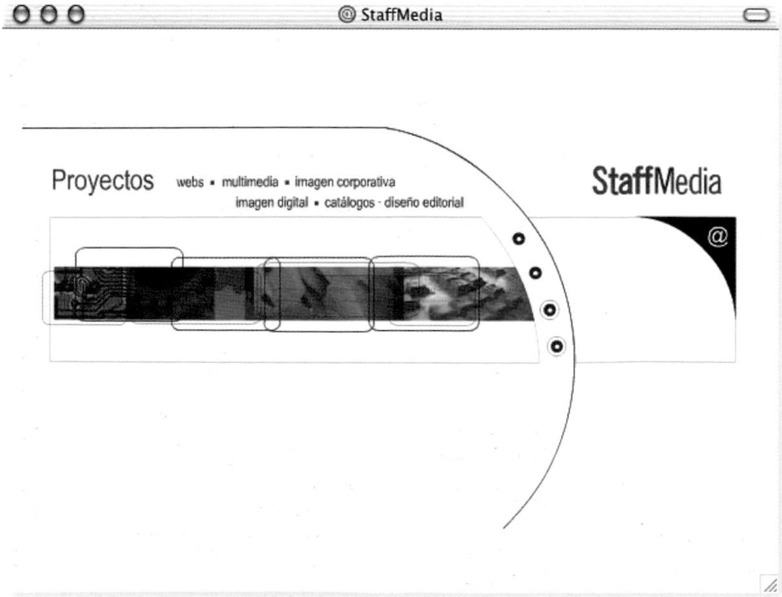
StaffMedia
Proyectos
webs • multimedia • imagen corporativa
imagen digital • catálogos · diseño editorial
StaffMedia
@

WWW.STAFFMEDIA.COM
D: JOSEP AÑOLS / EVA OROZCO, **C:** OSCAR BORDES, **P:** RAQUEL DE LA ENCARNACIÓN
A: STAFFMEDIA, **M:** STAFF@STAFFMEDIA.COM

WWW.URBANSCRIBE.CJB.NET
D: LUKE WILKINS
A: URBAN SCRIBE MULTIMEDIA, **M:** WILKINS@URBANSCRIBE.CJB.NET

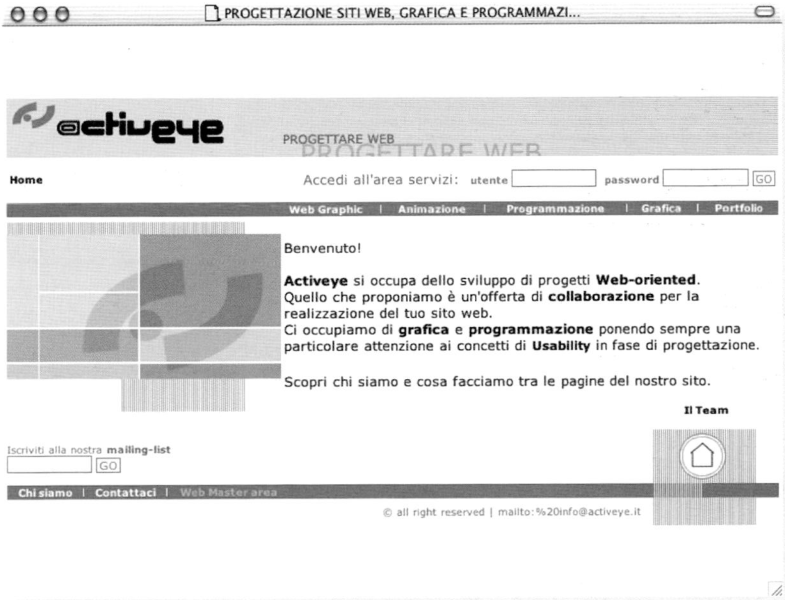

WWW.ACTIVEYE.IT
D: LUCA MASTRANGELO, **C:** GIACOMO LOTTA, **P:** ACTIVEYE
A: ACTIVEYE, **M:** INFO@ACTIVEYE.IT

WWW.GESTAZION.COM
D: RAMIRO SUEIRO

WWW.NICINGRAM.COM/FOLIO/URBAN_TEXTURES/URBAN_TEXTURES.HTM
D: JEN BOXER
A: NICINGRAM.COM, **M:** JEN@BOXERCOX.COM

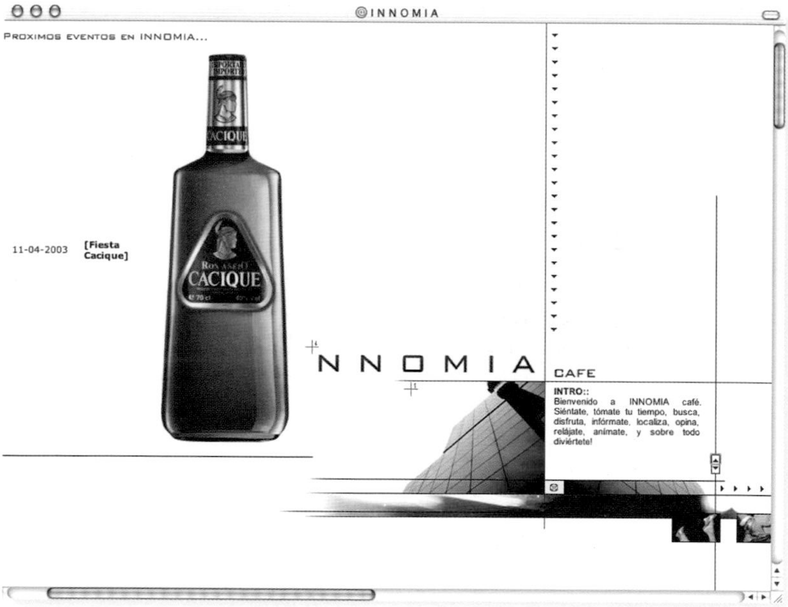

WWW.INNOMIA.COM
D: CARLOS ALBERTO RODRÍGUEZ LAGO, **C:** CARLOS ALBERTO RODRÍGUEZ LAGO
A: SHYLEX TELECOMUNICACIONES, **M:** EIKO@SHYLEX.COM

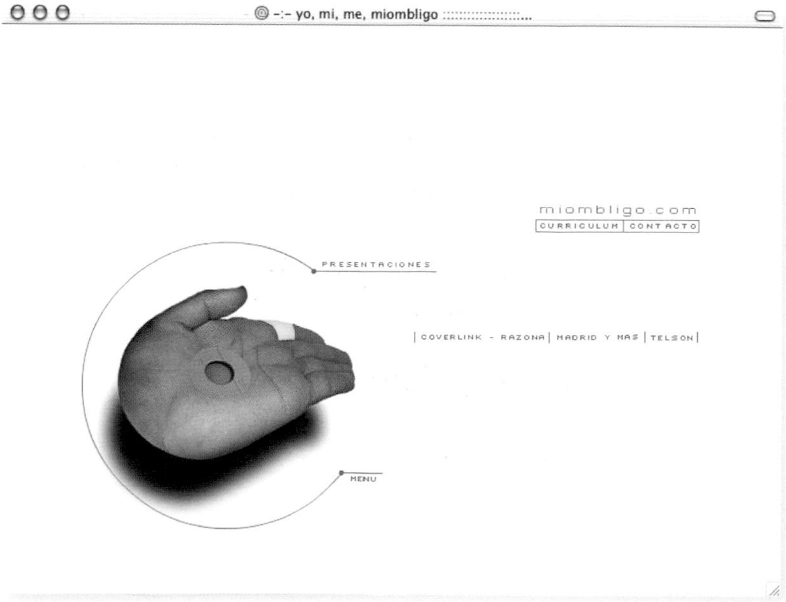

WWW.MIOMBLIGO.COM
D: SANTIAGO NÚÑEZ
A: MIOMBLIGO.COM, **M:** INFO@MIOMBLIGO.COM

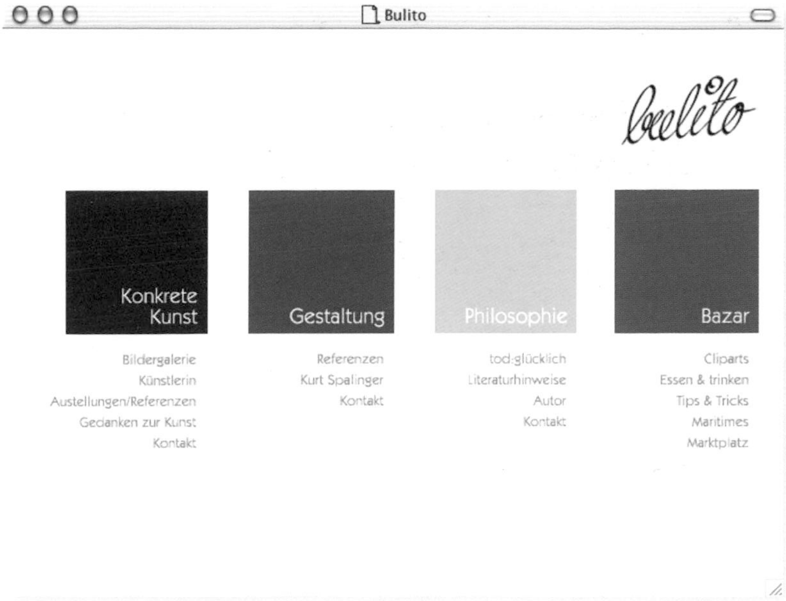
Bulito
Konkrete Kunst
Gestaltung
Philosophie
Bazar
Bildergalerie
Künstlerin
Austellungen/Referenzen
Gedanken zur Kunst
Kontakt
Referenzen
Kurt Spalinger
Kontakt
tod:glücklich
Literaturhinweise
Autor
Kontakt
Cliparts
Essen & trinken
Tips & Tricks
Maritimes
Marktplatz

WWW.BULITO.CH
D: KURT SPALINGER, **C:** ANDREAS JOHANNSEN, **P:** SYNKRON A/S
A: BULITO DESIGN, **M:** BULITO@BULITO.CH

Daniel Kästel - Steuerberatung - Auswahlseite
DANIEL KÄSTEL
Steuerberater & Dipl. Betriebswirt
Büro
Beratung
Kontakt
Impressum

WWW.KAESTEL.DE
D: BEN BUSCHFELD
A: BUSCHFELD.COM - GRAPHIC AND INTERFACE DESIGN, **M:** MAIL@BUSCHFELD.COM

Bitesite
bite
FOOD
DRINKS
WEB
MARKT 34/36 - 5211 JX 'S-HERTOGENBOSCH
T. 073 6840400 - BITESITE@PLEIN79.NL

WWW.BITESITE.NL
D: LEO HAMERS
A: YAIKZ!, **M:** INFO@YAIKZ.NL

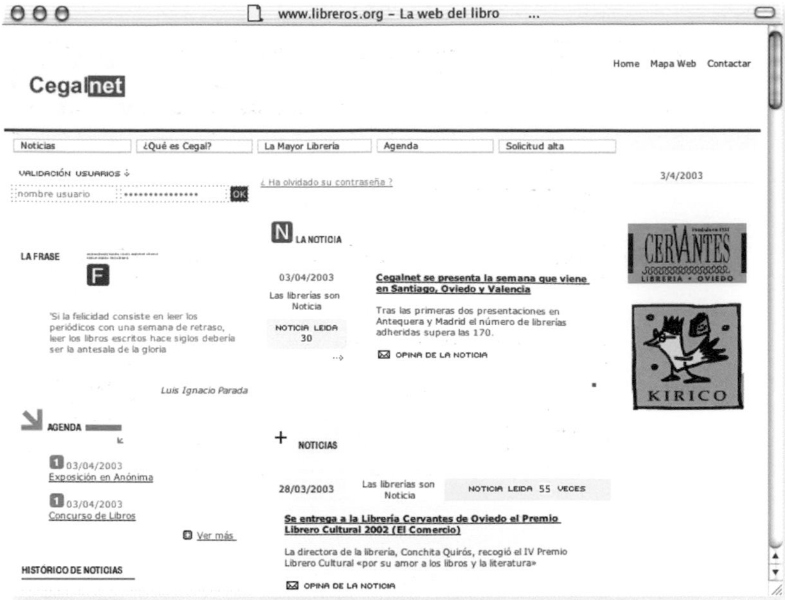

WWW.LIBREROS.ORG
D: ANTONIO BALLESTEROS QUEREJETA, **C:** LAURA BENITO, EVA DEL RIO, **P:** CEGAL
A: NHT-NORWICK, **M:** ABALLESTEROS@NHT-NORWICK.NET

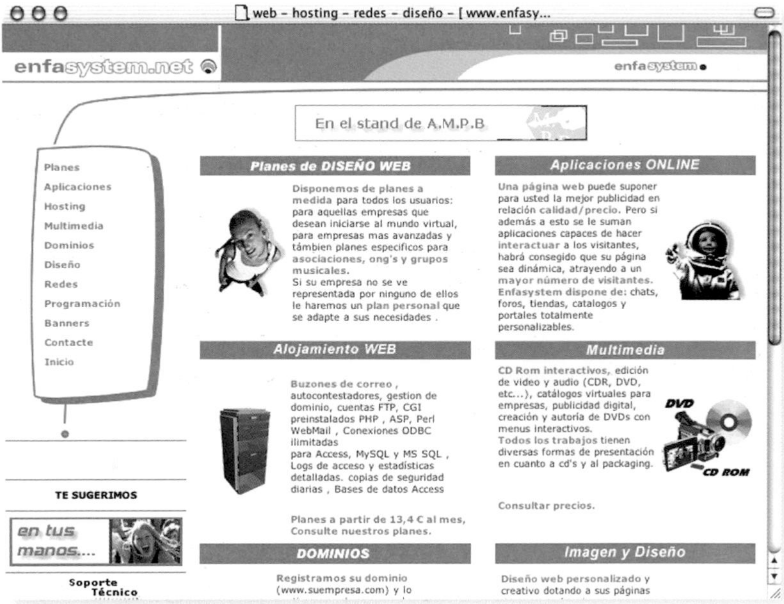

WWW.ENFASYSTEM.NET
D: JUANMA GIMEMEZ, **P:** JUANCARLOS CORDERO
A: ENFASYS-DESIGN, **M:** JUANMA@ENFASYSTEM.NET

WWW.VENTANANORTE.COM
D: JOSÉ MANUEL CARRERO ALEA
A: ZASME, **M:** CONTACTO@VENTANANORTE.COM

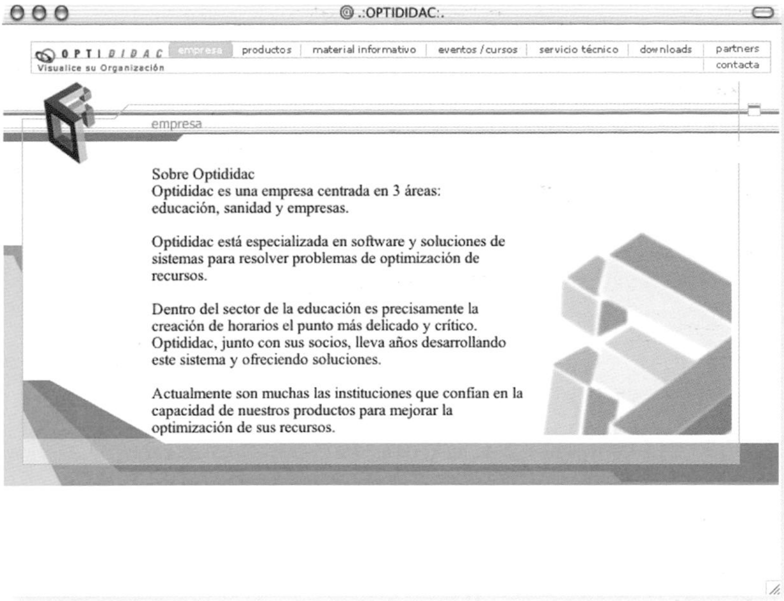

WWW.OPTIDIDAC.COM
D: ANA BELEN ALVAREZ TROITIÑO, **C:** ENRIQUE VALENTIN
A: GRAPHA, **M:** CRISTOBAL@GRAPHA.NET

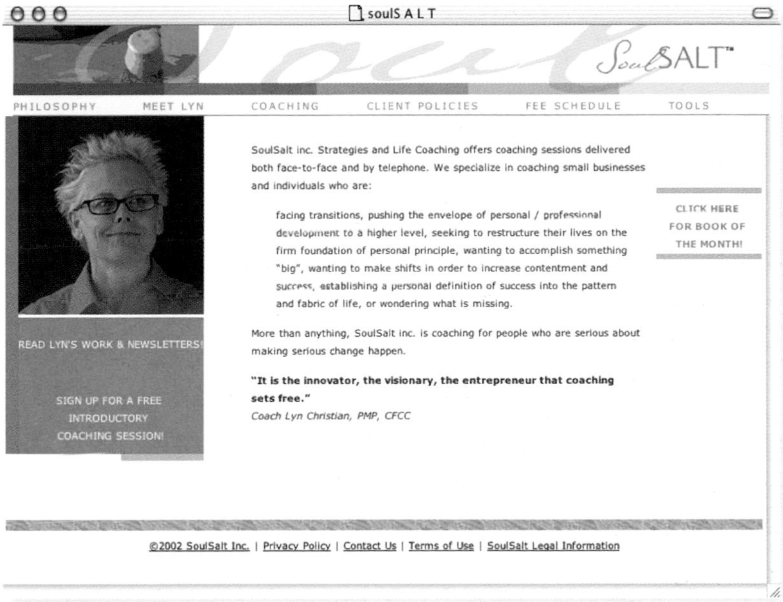

WWW.SOULSALT.COM
D: BRANT SKOUSEN
M: BSKOUSEN@FCPC.COM

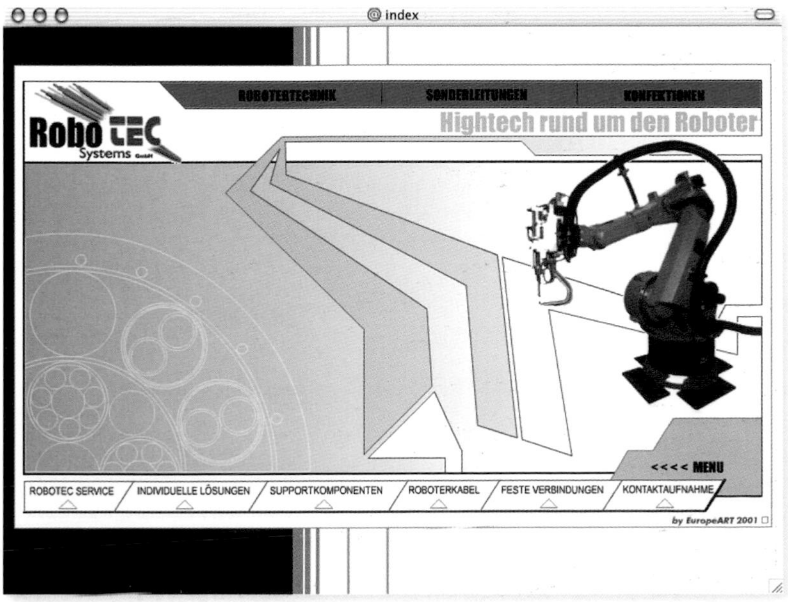

WWW.ROBOTEC-SYSTEMS.DE
D: JOSE BAÑEZ SORIA
A: EUROPEART WEB SERVICES S.L., **M:** JOSE@EUROPEART.COM

WWW.REVERSODASBERNARDAS.COM
D: WASHINGMACHINE
A: WASHINGMACHINE, **M:** WASHINGMACHINE@IP.PT

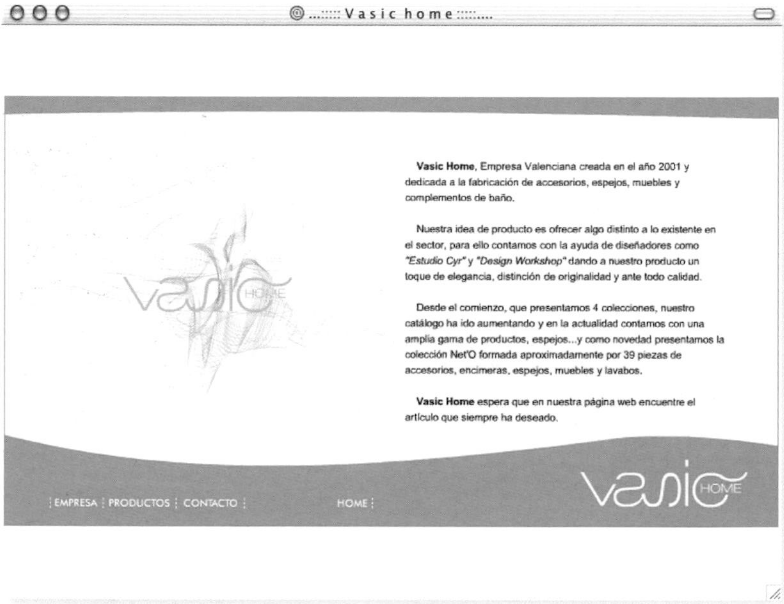

WWW.VASIC-HOME.COM
D: ALEX AYGÜES/PEDRO NAVARRO, **C:** PEDRO NAVARRO, **P:** VASIC HOMEACCESORIOS BAÑO
A: ÄMULTIMEDIA, **M:** MULTIMEDIA@ADISSENY.COM

WWW.CONSULTANCY.CH
D: MARC SCHMITT, **C:** MARC SCHMITT UND ROMAN ROCHEL, **P:** ROCHEL&SCHMITT GBR
A: ROCHEL&SCHMITT GBR, **M:** SCHMITT@CONSULTANCY.CH

WWW.ALUMINIUM.CZ
D: TOMAS BROUSIL, **C:** RADEK ZIGLER, **P:** ALUMINIUM
A: ALUMINIUM, **M:** RADEK.ZIGLER@ALUMINIUM.CZ

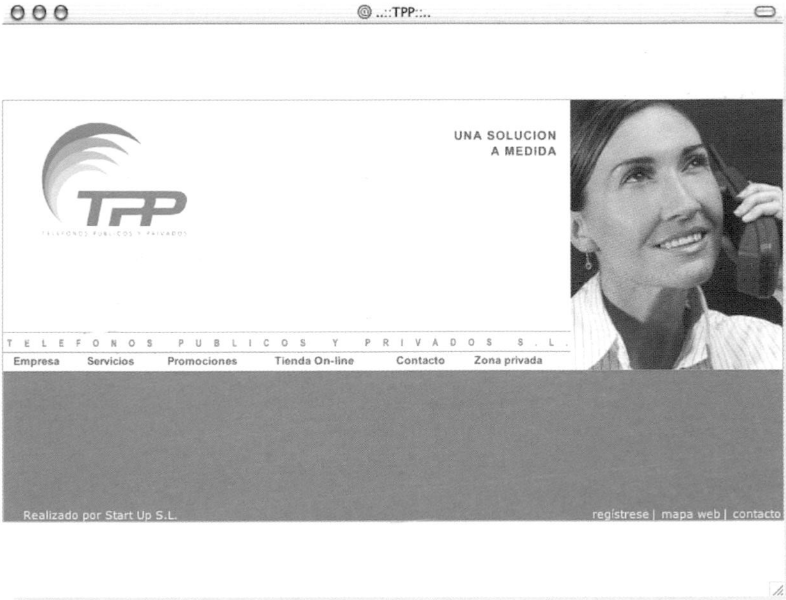

WWW.GRUPOTPP.COM
D: BERNARDO BARAGAÑO MOSLARES
A: START UP S.L., **M:** FONDAQUE@YAHOO.ES

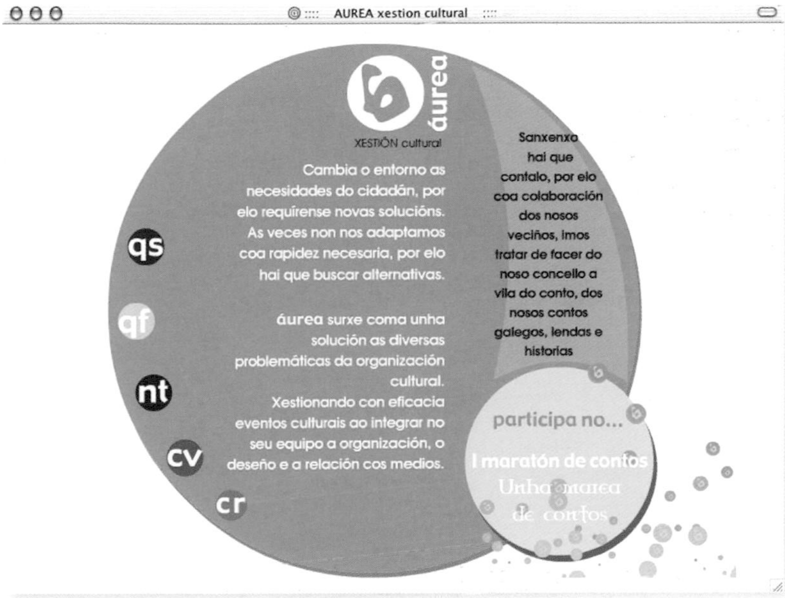

WWW.AUREACULTURA.COM
D: MAR SANDE
A: AUREA, **M:** WEBMASTER@AUREACULTURA.COM

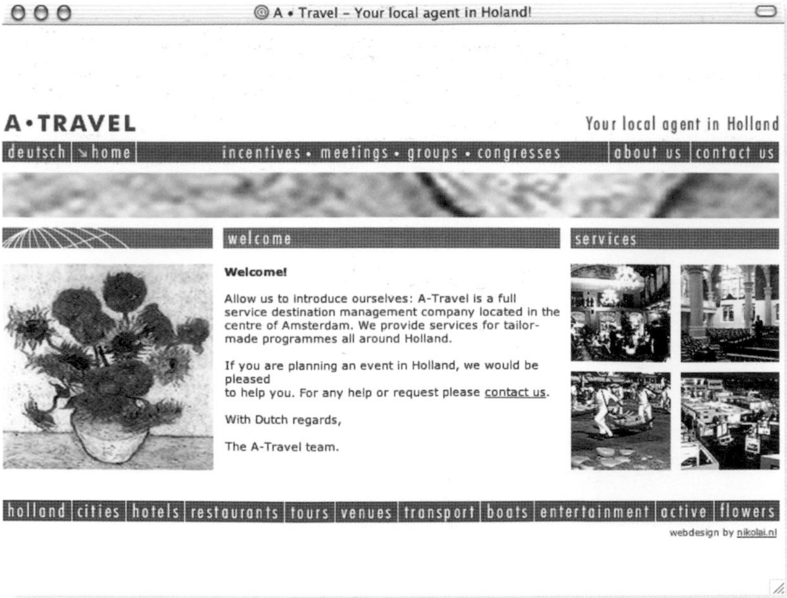
@ A • Travel – Your local agent in Holand!
A•TRAVEL
Your local agent in Holland
deutsch | home | incentives • meetings • groups • congresses | about us | contact us
welcome
services
Welcome!
Allow us to introduce ourselves: A-Travel is a full service destination management company located in the centre of Amsterdam. We provide services for tailor-made programmes all around Holland.
If you are planning an event in Holland, we would be pleased
to help you. For any help or request please contact us.
With Dutch regards,
The A-Travel team.
holland | cities | hotels | restaurants | tours | venues | transport | boats | entertainment | active | flowers
webdesign by nikolai.nl

WWW.A-TRAVEL.NL
D: NIKOLAI ZAUBER
A: NIKOLAI.NL, **M:** INFO@NIKOLAI.NL

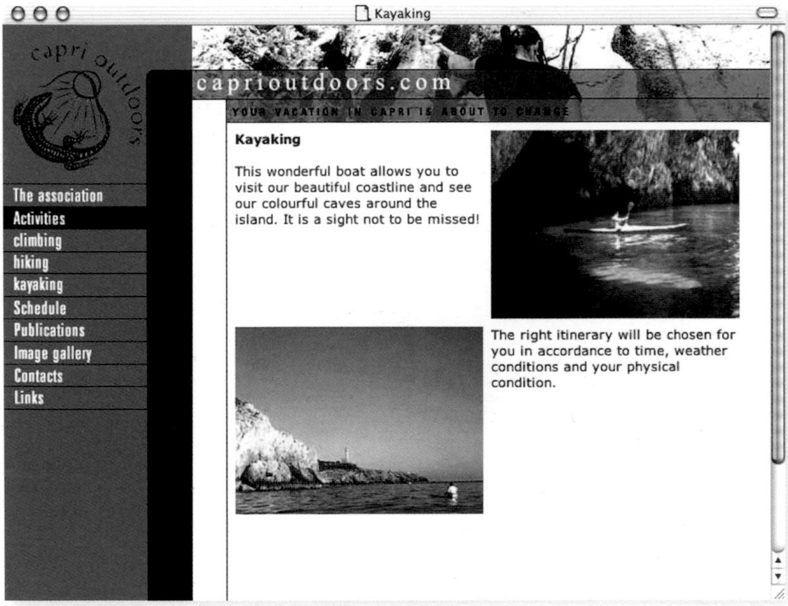
Kayaking
capri outdoors
caprioutdoors.com
YOUR VACATION IN CAPRI IS ABOUT TO CHANGE
The association
Activities
climbing
hiking
kayaking
Schedule
Publications
Image gallery
Contacts
Links
Kayaking
This wonderful boat allows you to visit our beautiful coastline and see our colourful caves around the island. It is a sight not to be missed!
The right itinerary will be chosen for you in accordance to time, weather conditions and your physical condition.

WWW.CAPRIOUTDOORS.COM
D: MARINA CAPOBIANCO
M: MARINA.CAPOBIANCO@LIBERO.IT

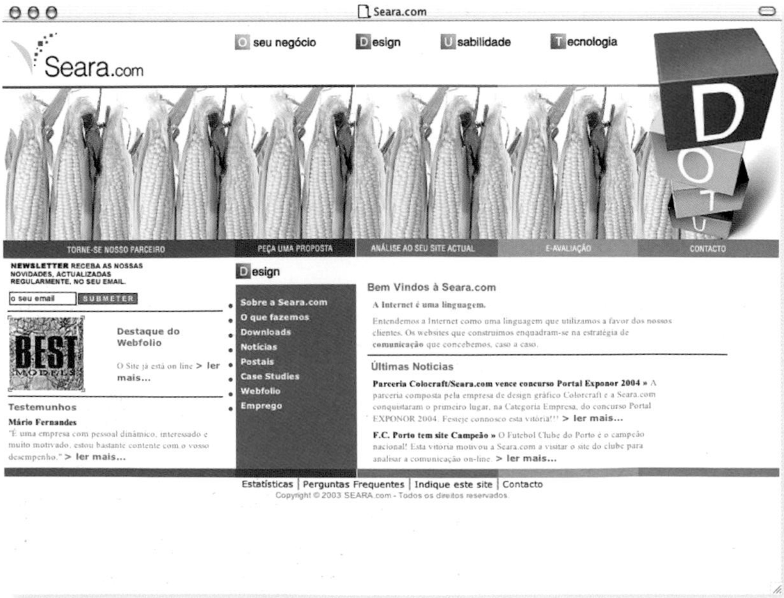
Seara.com
Seara.com
O seu negócio
Design
Usabilidade
Tecnologia
TORNE-SE NOSSO PARCEIRO
PEÇA UMA PROPOSTA
ANÁLISE AO SEU SITE ACTUAL
E-AVALIAÇÃO
CONTACTO
NEWSLETTER RECEBA AS NOSSAS NOVIDADES, ACTUALIZADAS REGULARMENTE, NO SEU EMAIL.
SUBMETER
Destaque do Webfolio
Testemunhos
Mário Fernandes
Design
Sobre a Seara.com
O que fazemos
Downloads
Notícias
Postais
Case Studies
Webfolio
Emprego
Bem Vindos à Seara.com
Últimas Notícias
Estatísticas | Perguntas Frequentes | Indique este site | Contacto

WWW.SEARA.COM
D: SEARA.COM
A: SEARA.COM, **M:** PAULACRUZ@SEARA.COM

WWW.WOLTERSMANN.DE
D: CHRISTIAN BRINDÖPKE
A: 5050 FIFTYFIFTY FILM + NEUE MEDIEN, **M:** CHRISTIAN@5050MEDIA.DE

WWW.DIGILANDER.IOL.IT/ZAPATELLI
D: ROBERTO SARTINI
M: RO.SA@LIBERO.IT

WWW.INKLUDE.COM
D: INKLUDE TEAM
A: INKLUDE , **M:** INFO@INKLUDE.COM

WWW.KEIDESIGN.NET
D: ANDREA ALIBARDI
M: ANDREA@KEIDESIGN.NET

WWW.ROYALIND.COM
D: AMARIN VEJCHAROEN, **C:** INETASIA TEAM, **P:** RIC SHREVES
A: INETASIA, **M:** RSHREVES@INETASIA.COM

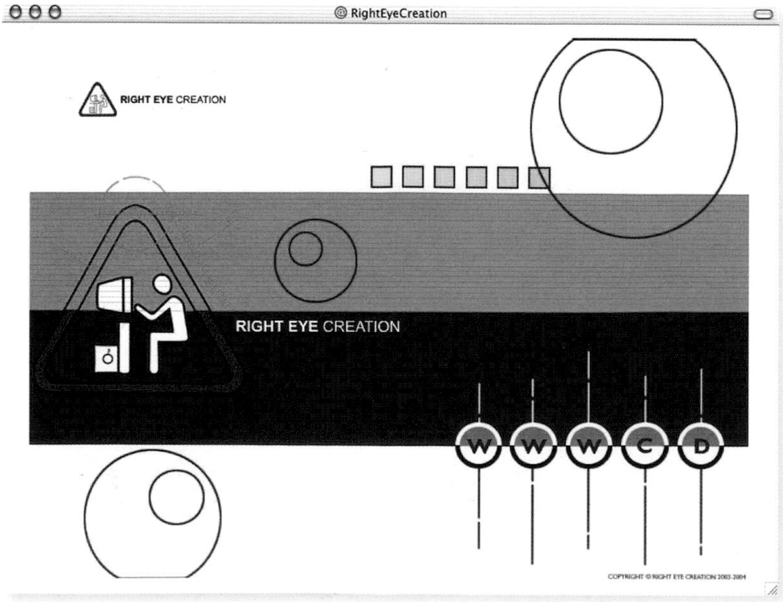

WWW.RIGHTEYECREATION.COM
D: ALISTAIR JAMESON, **C:** ALISTAIR JAMESON, **P:** ALISTAIR JAMESON, JONATHAN JAMESON
A: RIGHT EYE CREATION, **M:** WEB@RIGHTEYECREATION.COM

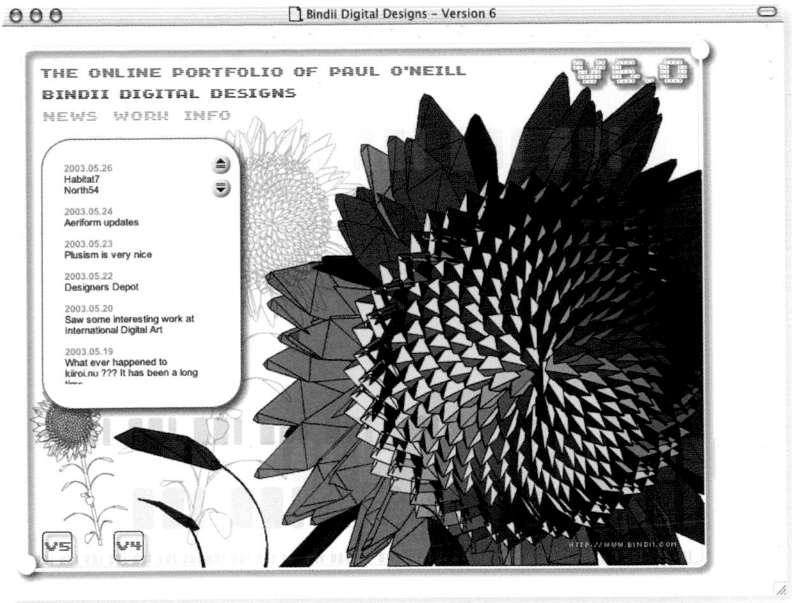

WWW.BINDII.COM
D: PAUL O'NEILL
M: DESIGN@BINDII.COM

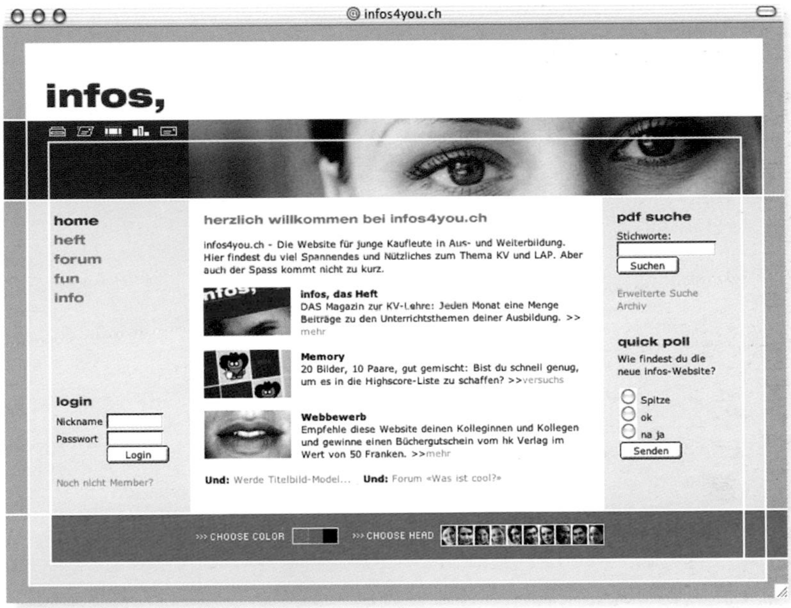

WWW.INFOS4YOU.CH
D: CHRISTOPH LOHRI
A: MAXOMEDIA, **M:** CHRISTOPH.LOHRI@HKVERLAG.CH

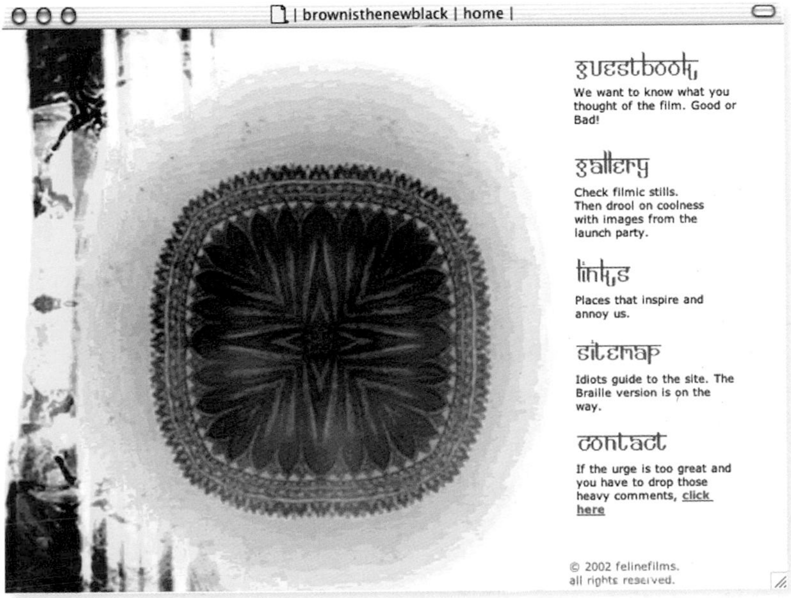

WWW.BROWNISTHENEWBLACK.COM/INDEX2.HTML
D: JEN BOXER
A: NICINGRAM.COM, **M:** JEN@BOXERCOX.COM

WWW.ANDREISPOSE.IT
D: STEFANO LUCHERINI, **C:** MATTEO GRAMIGNI, **P:** DESIGN BLU
A: ZONA ZERO, **M:** INFO@ZONAZERO.IT

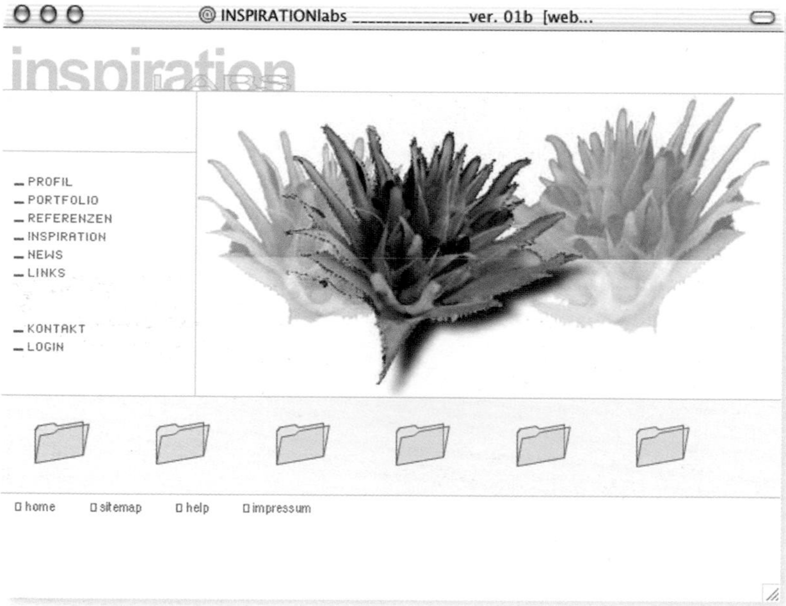

WWW.INSPIRATIONLABS.DE
D: ALEXANDER KNAPSTEIN
A: INSPIRATIONLABS, **M:** A.KNAPSTEIN@INSPIRATIONLABS.DE

WWW.IMAGESTORIES.COM
D: AL DRANGAJOV
A: FOURTHCOLOR.COM, **M:** FB@IMAGESTORIES.COM

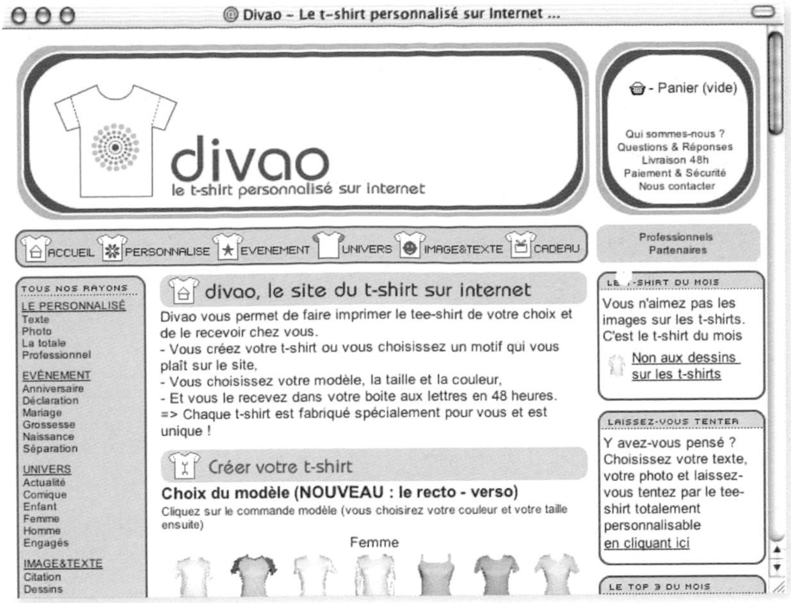

WWW.DIVAO.COM
D: MYRIAM LEYMARIE
M: CONTACT@MGRAFIK.COM

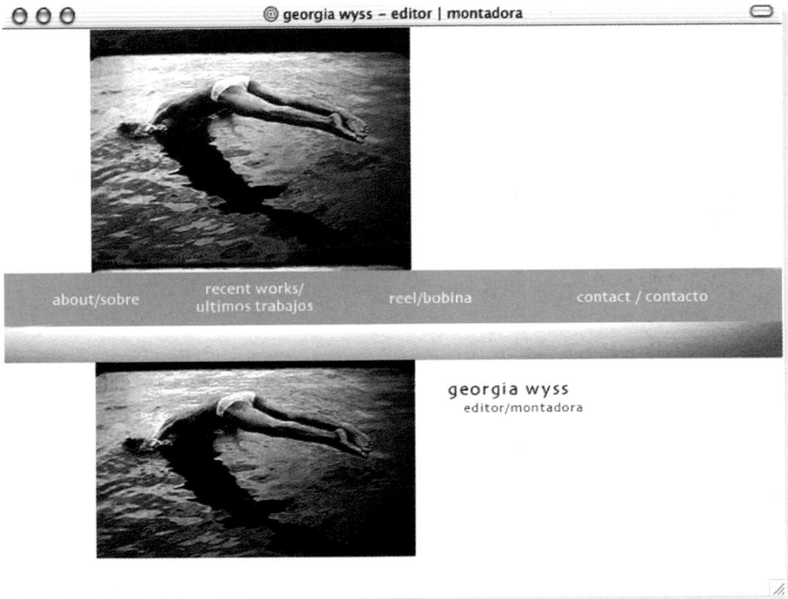

WWW.WPINYC.COM/GEORGIA/HOME.HTML
D: MICK WALSH
A: WALSH PRODUCTIONS, INC., **M:** INFO@WPINYC.COM

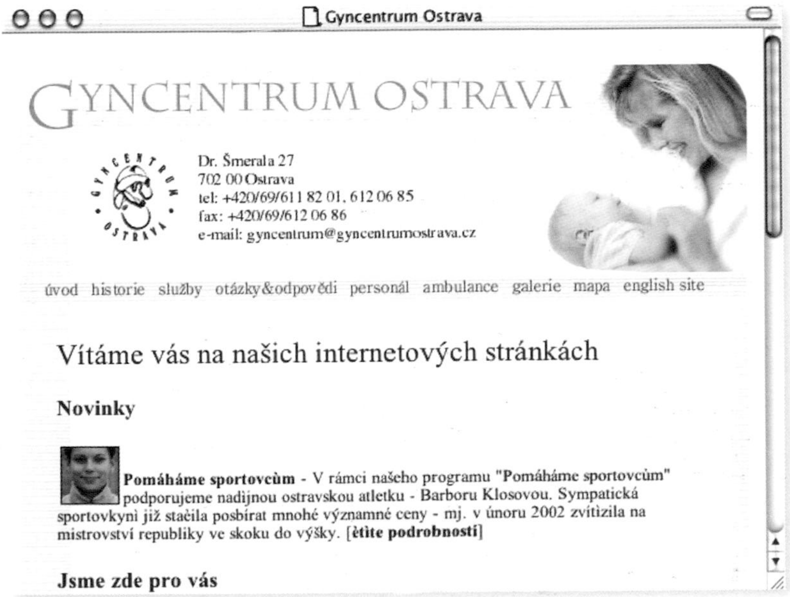

WWW.GYNCENTRUMOSTRAVA.CZ
D: MICHAL, **C:** KUBICEK
A: PRONETMEDIA, **M:** CEO@PRONETMEDIA.CZ

WWW.BENZIN.NET
D: THOMAS BRUGGISSER / MICHEL FRIES, **C:** SCHMID ROGER,
A: GRAFIKTRAKTOR.CH, **M:** MAILS@ROGER-SCHMID.CH

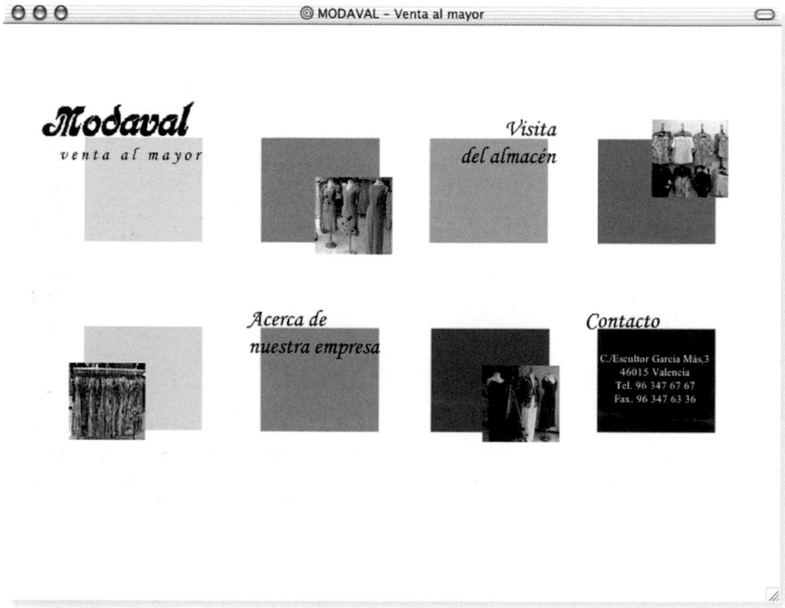

WWW.MODAVAL.COM
D: MÉRIAM ESPUNA
A: EUROPA 3, **M:** MERIAMEG2000@YAHOO.FR

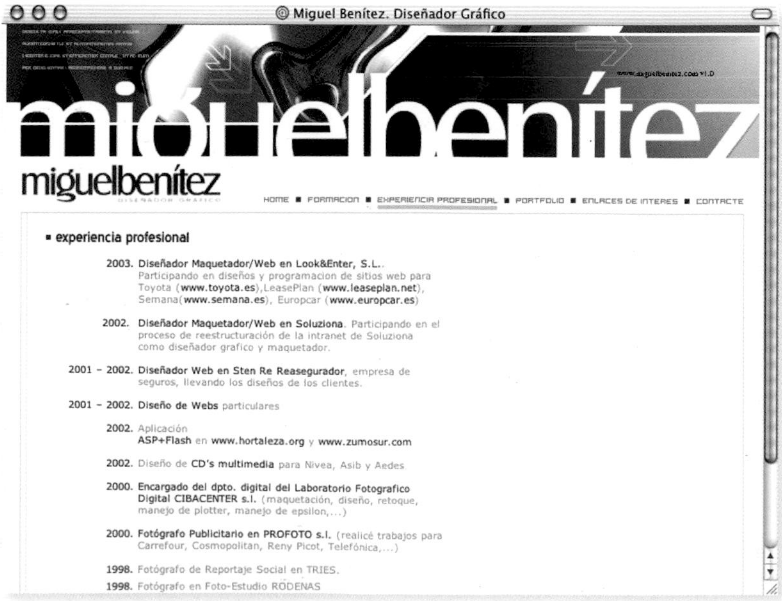

WWW.MIGUELBENITEZ.COM
D: MIGUEL ANGEL BENÍTEZ
M: INFO@MIGUELBENITEZ.COM

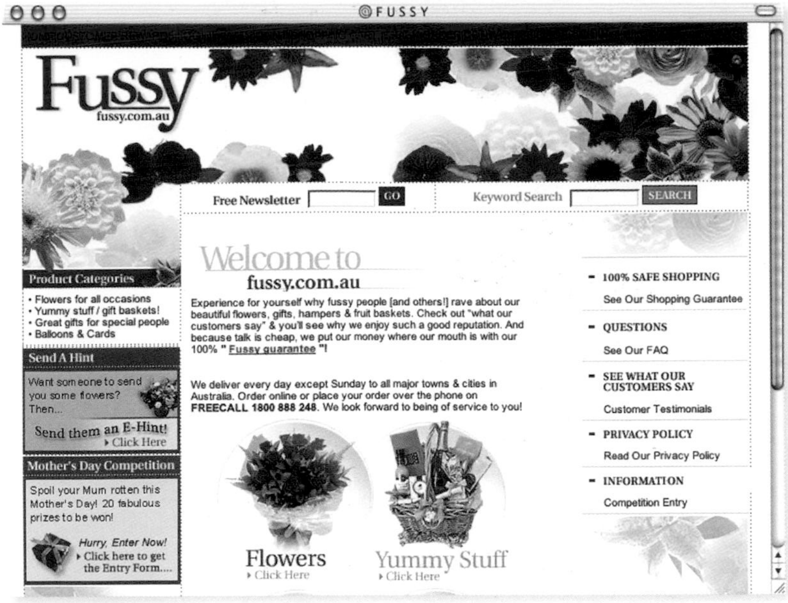

WWW.FUSSY.COM.AU
D: JASMINE HOR MYN-LI, **C:** ESOLVED.COM, **P:** ESOLVED.COM
A: ESOLVED.COM, **M:** JASZY76@YAHOO.COM

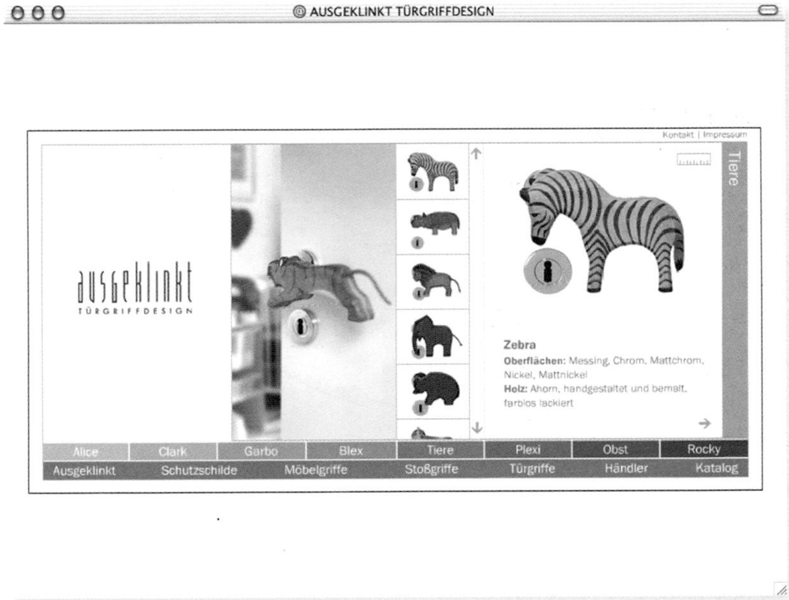

WWW.AUSGEKLINKT.DE
D: HAJO WEINSCHENK, KAI WEISSER, **C:** KAI WEISSER
A: FILEWERK/ ICONS OF, **M:** JUTTA.MEINECKE@FILEWERK.DE

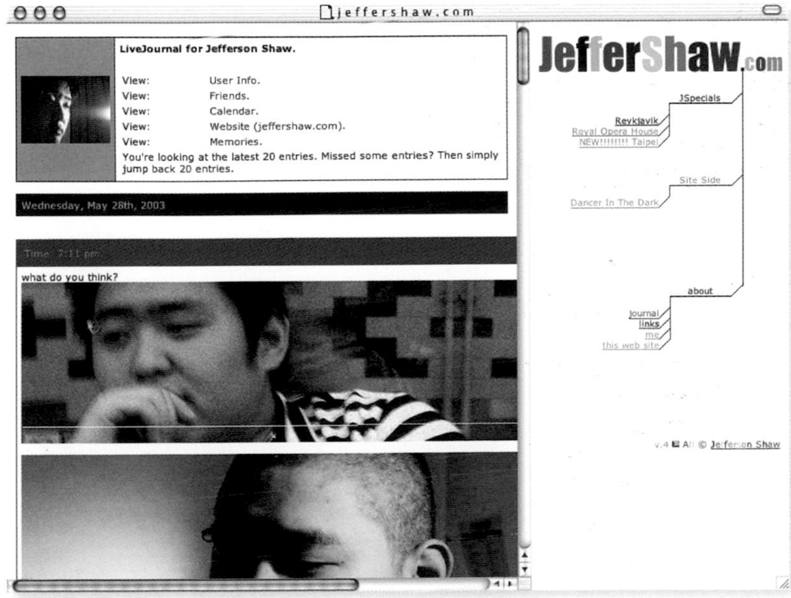

WWW.JEFFERSHAW.COM
D: JEFFERSON SHAW
M: JEFFERSHAW@HOTMAIL.COM

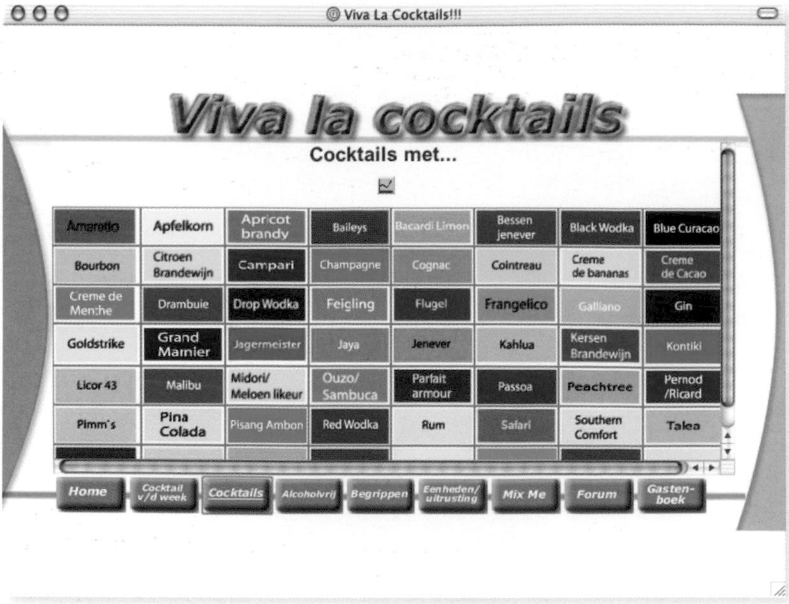

WWW.VIVALACOCKTAILS.NL
D: HILVERDA
M: INFO@VIVALACOCKTAILS.NL

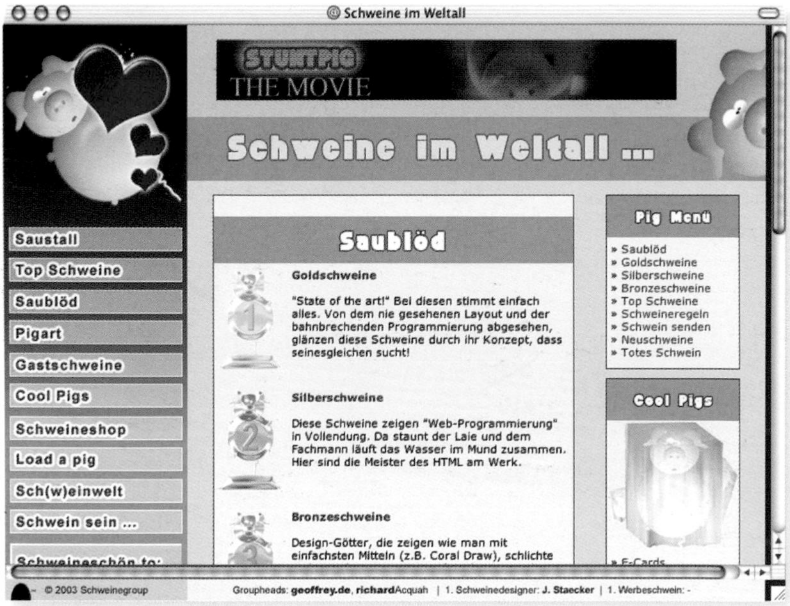

WWW.SCHWEINEIMWELTALL.DE
D: RICHARD ACQUAH , **C:** RONALD HAHN, **P:** JAN STAECKER, MARTIN RÖVEKAMP
M: ACQUAH@WEB.DE

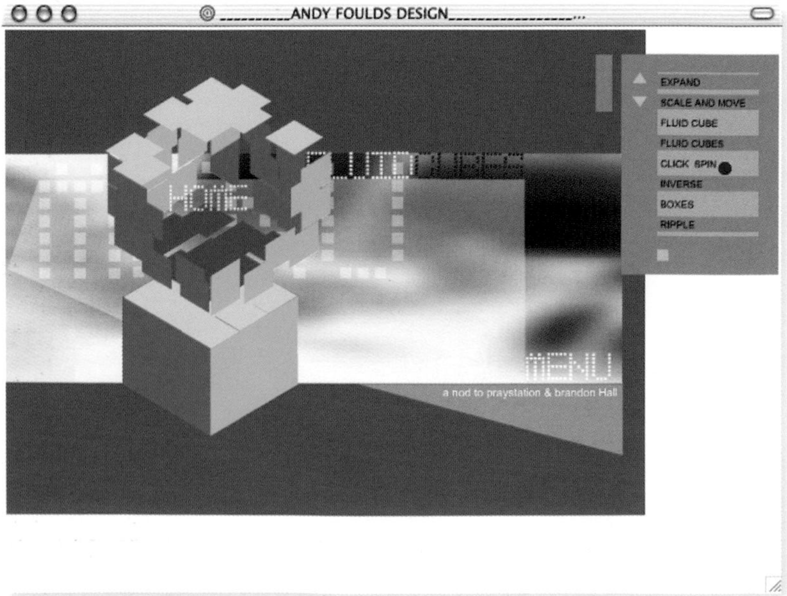

WWW.ANDYFOULDS.CO.UK
D: ANDY FOULDS
M: ANDY@ANDYFOULDS.CO.UK

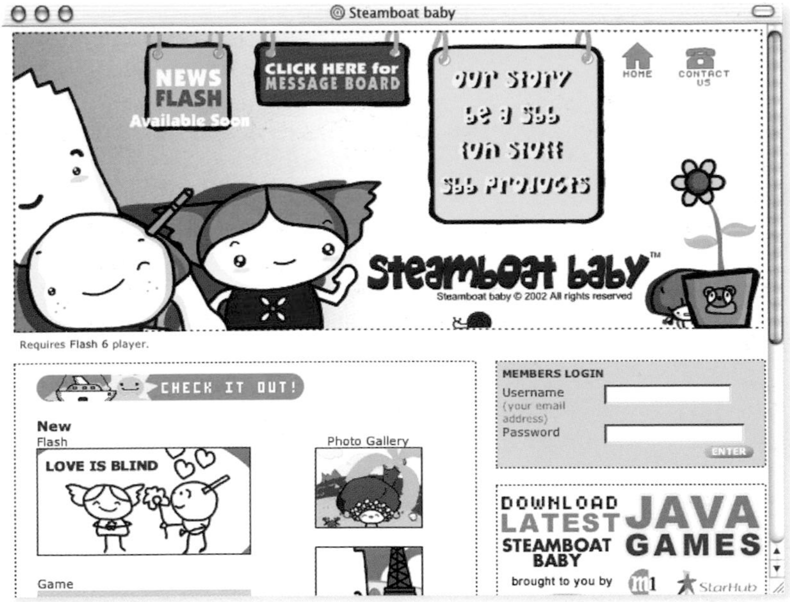

WWW.STEAMBOATBABY.COM
D: JOHN FOO, **C:** ACTIVATE STUDIO TEAM, **P:** JOHN FOO
A: ACTIVATE INTERACTIVE PTE LTD, **M:** GEORGINA@ACTIVATE.COM.SG

WWW.JK.CO.NZ
D: IAN BRAYSHAW, **C:** MATT CLARKSON
A: INSPIRED WEB SOLUTIONS, **M:** IAN@IWS.CO.NZ

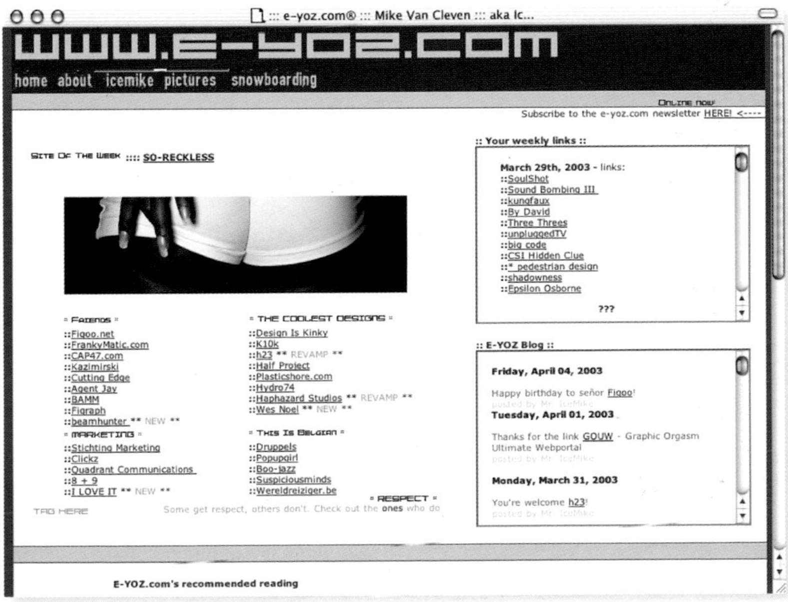

WWW.E-YOZ.COM
D: MIKE VAN CLEVEN
M: MIKE@E-YOZ.COM

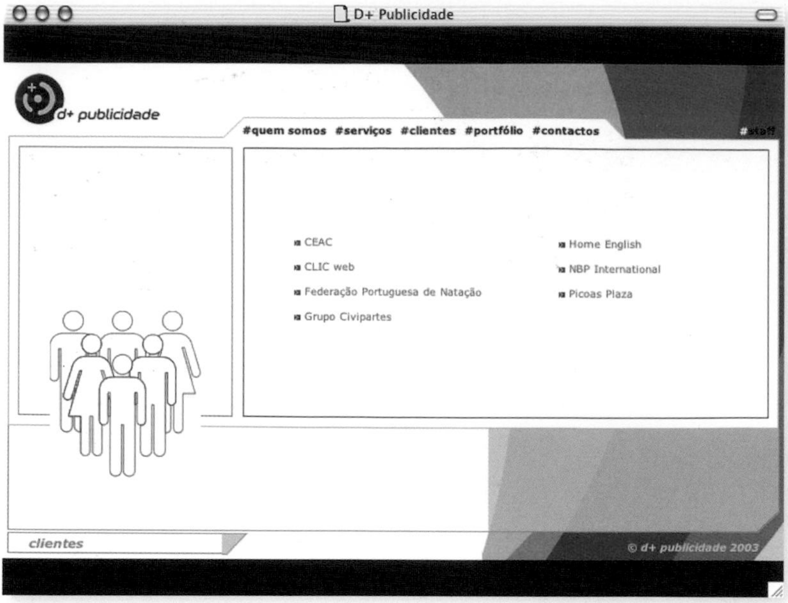

WWW.DMAISPUBLICIDADE.PT
D: MARCELO VIEIRA
A: D+ PUBLICIDADE, **M:** DMAIS@DMAISPUBLICIDADE.PT

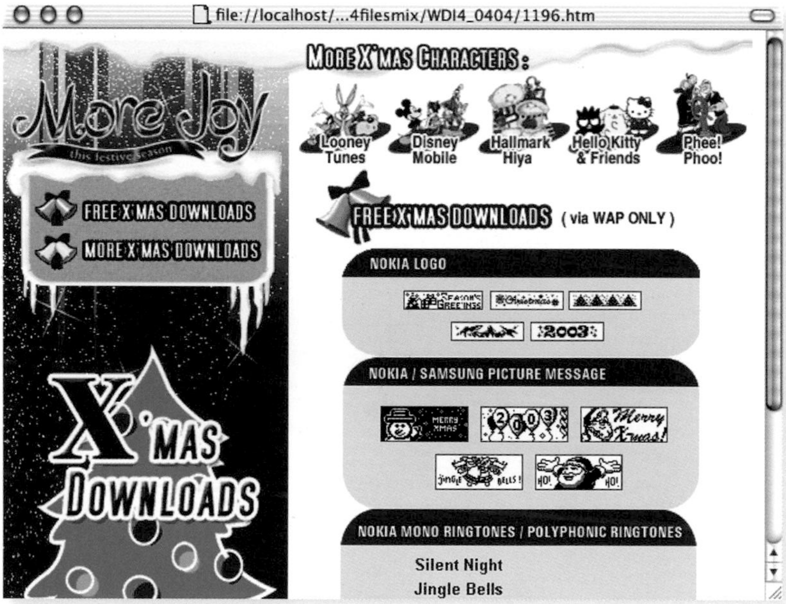

WWW.HOME.SINGTEL.COM/DOWNLOADS/XMAS/INDEX.HTML
D: IVAN MP TAN, SARAH HO, **C:** LYNDONN OH, **P:** PAUL KAN
A: AC'LAIM, **M:** IVAN@ACLAIM.COM.SG

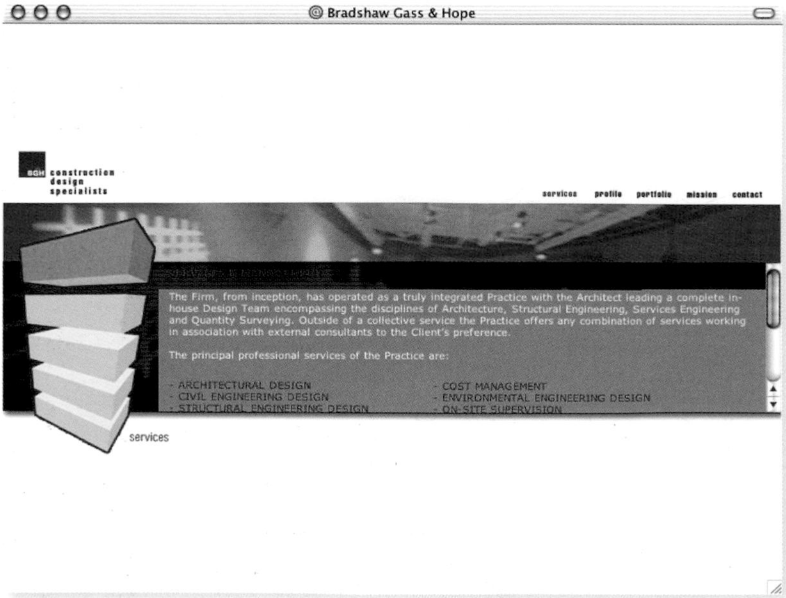

WWW.BGHBOLTON.CO.UK
D: JOHN SCHOFIELD, **C:** PHILIP JEFFS
A: THE TICKLE GROUP, **M:** JOHN@TICKLE.CO.UK

Prime Yachts
PRIME YACHTS
why prime yachts
introduction
why prime yachts
who
charter
brokerage
management & refit
contact
Prime Yachts was established to fulfill several yachtsmen's needs and dreams. Our inside knowledge of the challenges each yachtsmen faces helped us identify solutions to tackle these in the utmost efficient manner.
We listen to our clients concerns and as professional advisors our objective is to satisfy them with both excellent service and individual solutions tailored to their particular needs.
These days selling, buying or chartering a yacht is highly competitive. Prime Yachts has established reputable relationships in the yacht world to supply its clients with a full range of opportunities and exposure. Our success lies on adequate innovative strategies. Our aim is to make your dreams really come true!
www.primeyachts.com

WWW.PRIMEYACHTS.COM
D: DIOGO MELO, **C:** DIOGO MELO, **P:** DOISMAISDOIS.COM
A: DOISMAISDOIS.COM, **M:** RCAMARINHA@TVTEL.PT

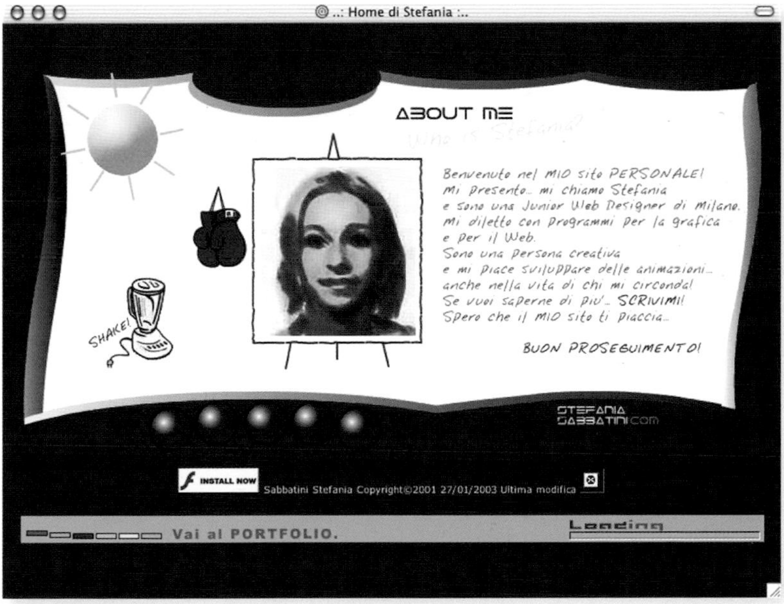
..: Home di Stefania :..
ABOUT ME
Benvenuto nel MIO sito PERSONALE!
mi presento... mi chiamo Stefania
e sono una Junior Web Designer di Milano.
mi diletto con programmi per la grafica
e per il Web.
Sono una persona creativa
e mi piace sviluppare delle animazioni...
anche nella vita di chi mi circonda!
Se vuoi saperne di più... SCRIVIMI!
Spero che il MIO sito ti piaccia...
BUON PROSEGUIMENTO!
SHAKE!
STEFANIA SABBATINI.COM
INSTALL NOW
Sabbatini Stefania Copyright©2001 27/01/2003 Ultima modifica
Vai al PORTFOLIO.
Loading

WWW.STEFANIASABBATINI.COM
D: STEFANIA SABBATINI
M: STE@STEFANIASABBATINI.COM

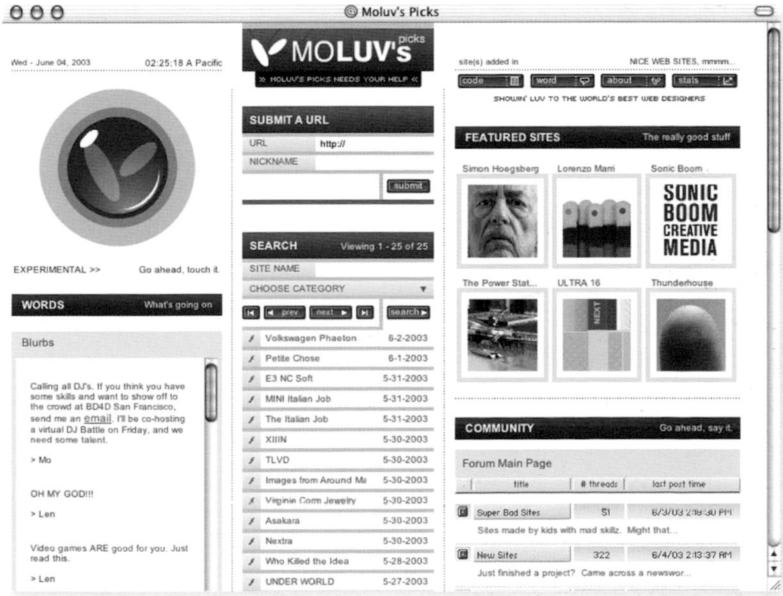
Moluv's Picks
MOLUV's picks
SUBMIT A URL
URL http://
NICKNAME
submit
SEARCH Viewing 1 - 25 of 25
SITE NAME
CHOOSE CATEGORY
FEATURED SITES The really good stuff
Simon Hoegsberg
Lorenzo Mari
Sonic Boom
SONIC BOOM CREATIVE MEDIA
The Power Stat...
ULTRA 16
Thunderhouse
EXPERIMENTAL >> Go ahead, touch it.
WORDS What's going on
Blurbs
COMMUNITY Go ahead, say it.
Forum Main Page
Volkswagen Phaeton 6-2-2003
Petite Chose 6-1-2003
E3 NC Soft 5-31-2003
MINI Italian Job 5-31-2003
The Italian Job 5-31-2003
XIIIN 5-30-2003
TLVD 5-30-2003
Virginie Corm Jewelry 5-30-2003
Asakara 5-30-2003
Nextra 5-30-2003
Who Killed the Idea 5-28-2003
UNDER WORLD 5-27-2003

WWW.MOLUV.COM
D: MAURICE WRIGHT
A: MOLUV, **M:** MAURICE@MOLUV.COM

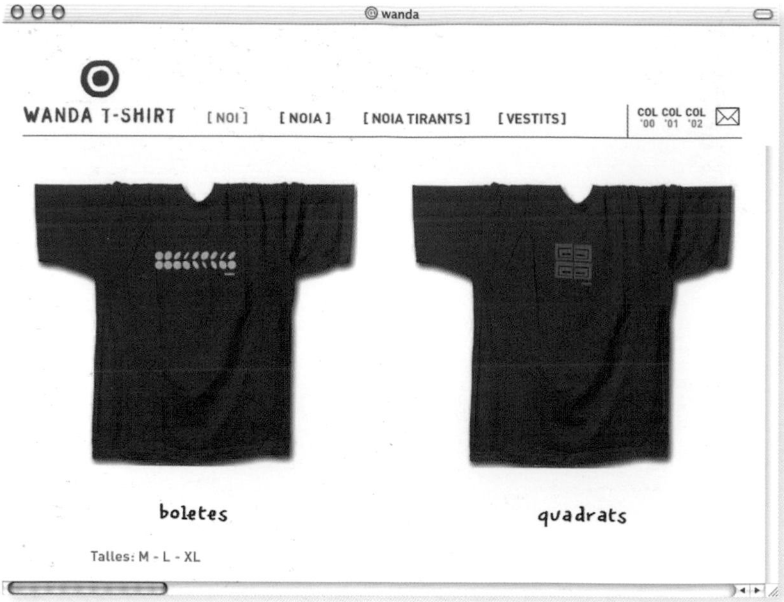

WWW.WANDAT-SHIRT.COM/
D: NATHALIE GARCIA
M: NATHALIE@ZINK.ES

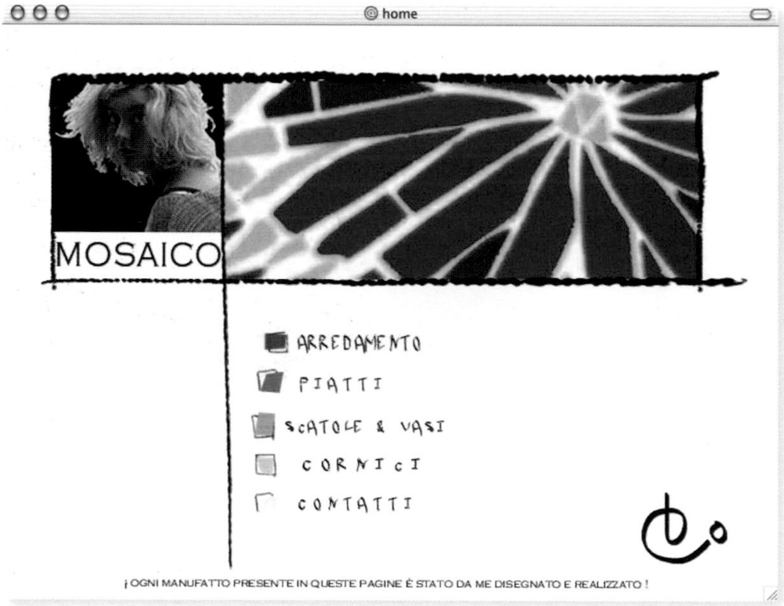

WWW.ELIL.IT
D: GABRIELE CAVAZZANO
M: GCVZ@YAHOO.IT

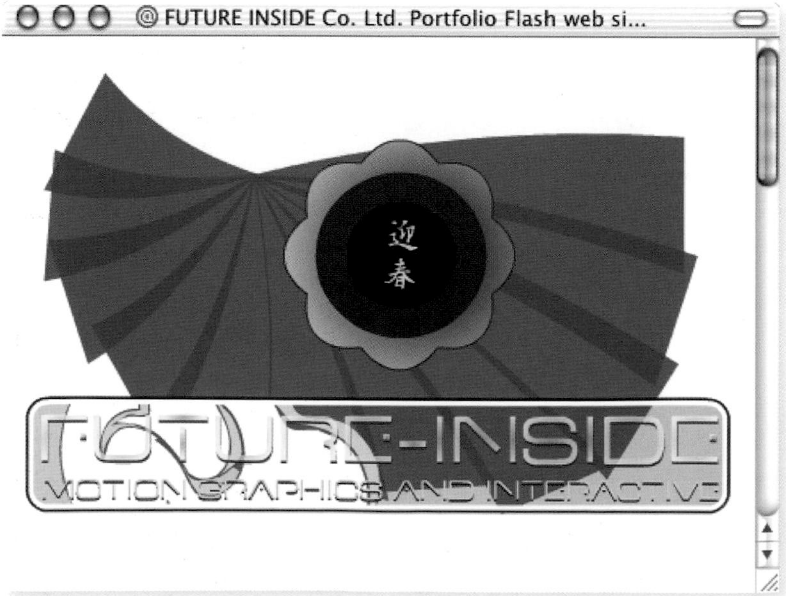

WWW.FUTURE-INSIDE.COM
D: GIORGIO REY
A: FUTURE INSIDE CO. LTD, **M:** GREY@FUTURE-INSIDE.COM

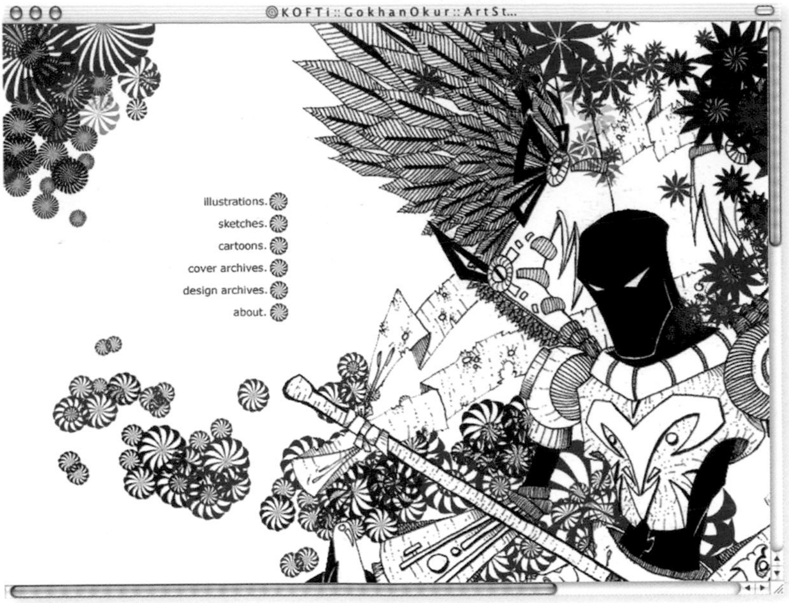

WWW.KOFTI.COM
D: GOKHAN OKUR
M: OKURGOKHAN@HOTMAIL.COM

WWW.SIOW.COM.TW/MICK
D: MICK HUANG
M: MICK0802@MS54.HINET.NET

WWW.BALBURDIA.COM
D: ADRIANO ESTEVES, **C:** ALEXANDRE R. GOMES
A: MUSICDROPS.COM, **M:** ADRIANO@MUSICDROPS.COM

WWW.NUNOMARTINS.COM
D: NUNO MARTINS
M: NUNO@NUNOMARTINS.COM

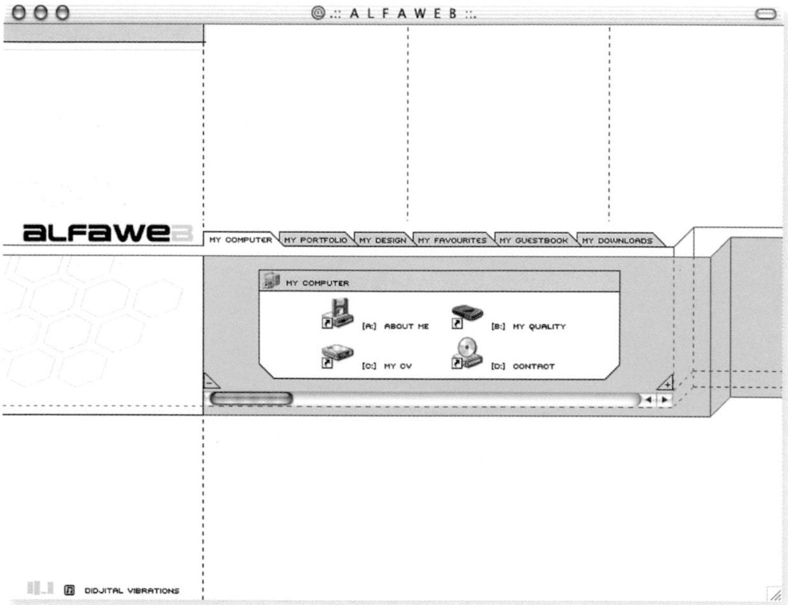

WWW.ALFAWEB.AT
D: ALEXANDER FALSCHLEHNER
A: ALFAWEB.AT, **M:** WEBMASTER@ALFAWEB.AT

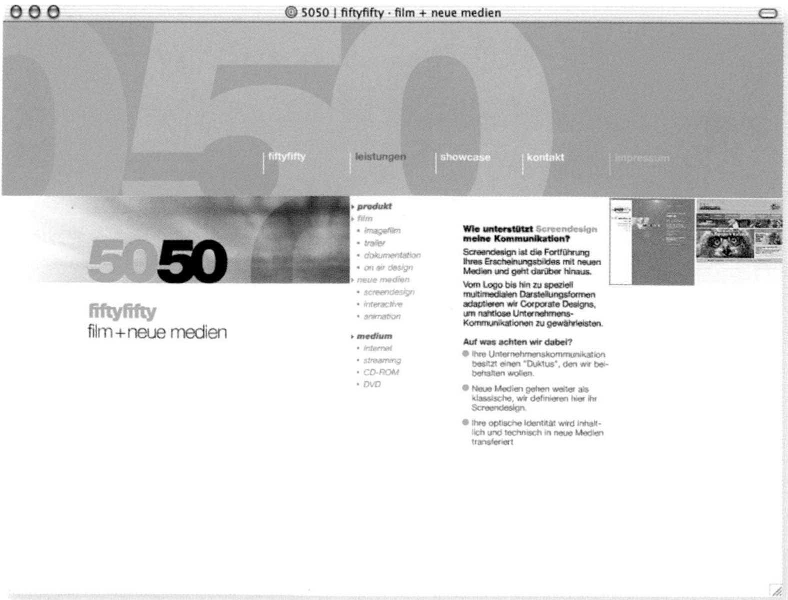

WWW.5050MEDIA.DE
D: CHRISTIAN BRINDÖPKE
A: 5050 FIFTYFIFTY FILM + NEUE MEDIEN, **M:** CHRISTIAN@5050MEDIA.DE

WWW.DWYER.DE
D: CARL J. DWYER
M: CONTACT@DWYER.DE

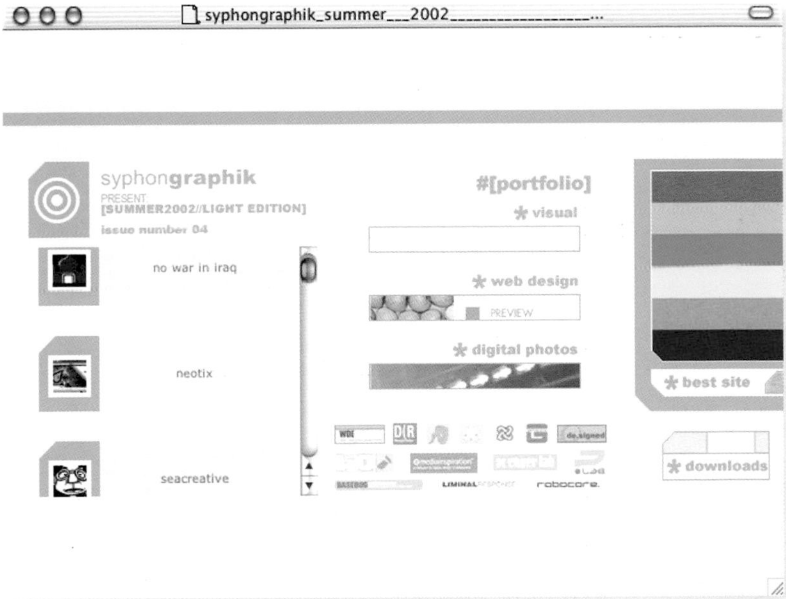

WWW.SYPHONGRAPHIK.IT
D: GLORIA CHIAVISTELLI
M: GLORIA@SYPHONGRAPHIK.IT

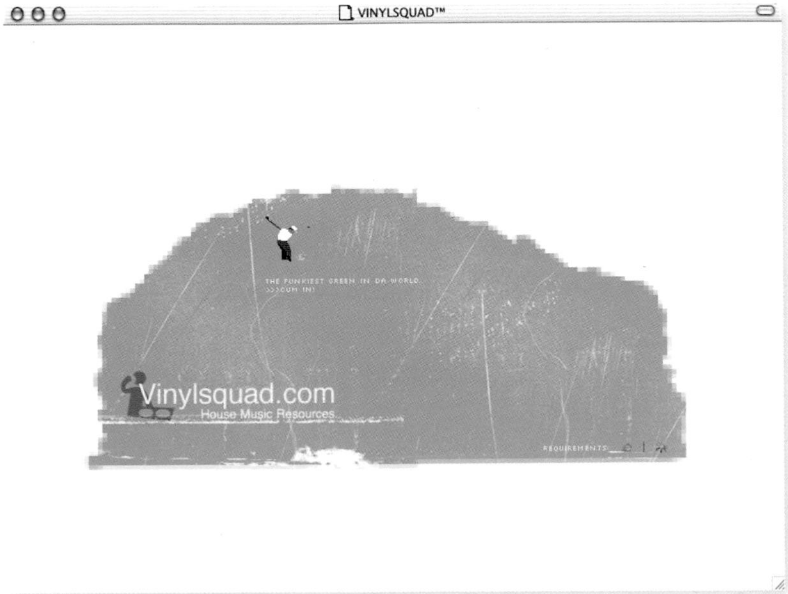

WWW.VINYLSQUAD.COM
D: OLIVER CLOPPENBURG, **C:** HANNES HOESS, SASCHA SPONHOLZ
A: DESTROY CPU, **M:** OLIVER@DESTROYCPU.COM

WWW.THEVISIONIS.IT
D: EMANUELA ROGU
M: EM@THEVISIONIS.IT

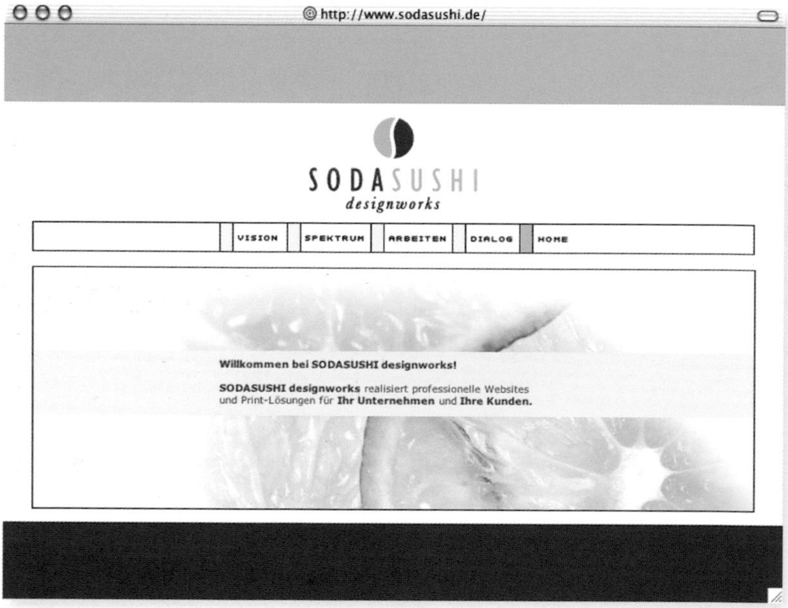

WWW.SODASUSHI.DE
D: STEFAN KRUSCHE
A: SODASUSHI DESIGNWORKS, **M:** KRUSCHE@SODASUSHI.DE

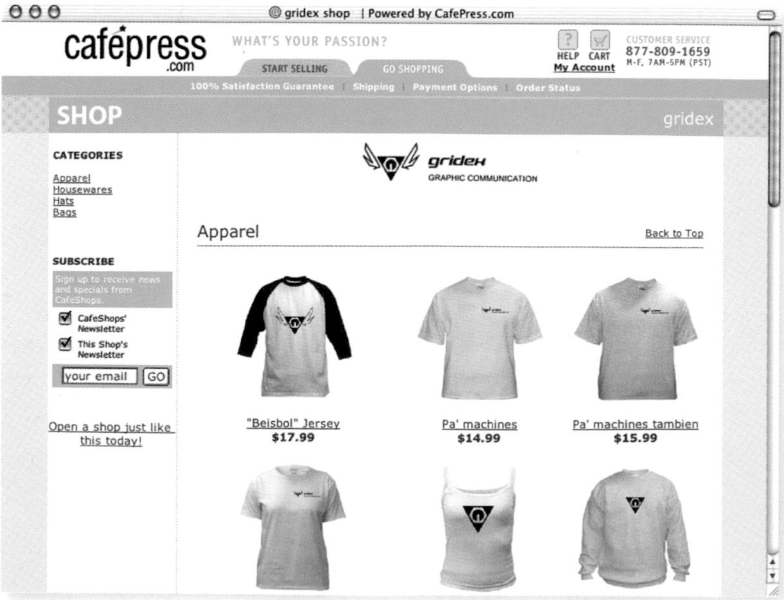

WWW.GRIDEX.COM
D: ABRAHAM GONZALEZ
M: ARRAKIS@MATHMOS.COM.MX

Tutors Exchange - www.tx.com.sg
24hrs Hotline
7000 862 9380
(Standard Local Toll, No Extra Charges)
Tutors Exchange
http://www.tx.com.sg
Welcome to Tutors Exchange!
If you're looking for a tutor to coach you to academic excellence, this is the place to be. Tutors Exchange has a vast network of qualified tutors to suit every student's needs.
Call us today at our Hotline: 7000 862 9380 for a discussion on your tutoring needs or Get A Tutor here.
Get A Tutor
About Us | How We Work | Get A Tutor | Be A Tutor
中文版
Home | About Us | How We Work | Get A Tutor | Be A Tutor | Contact Us
24hrs Hotline: 7000 862 9380 (Standard Local Toll, No Extra Charges)

WWW.SIMPLYTHEBEST.COM.SG
D: YU HSIANG WONG
A: EPISODE 12 PTE LTD, **M:** YUHSIANG@EPISODE12.COM

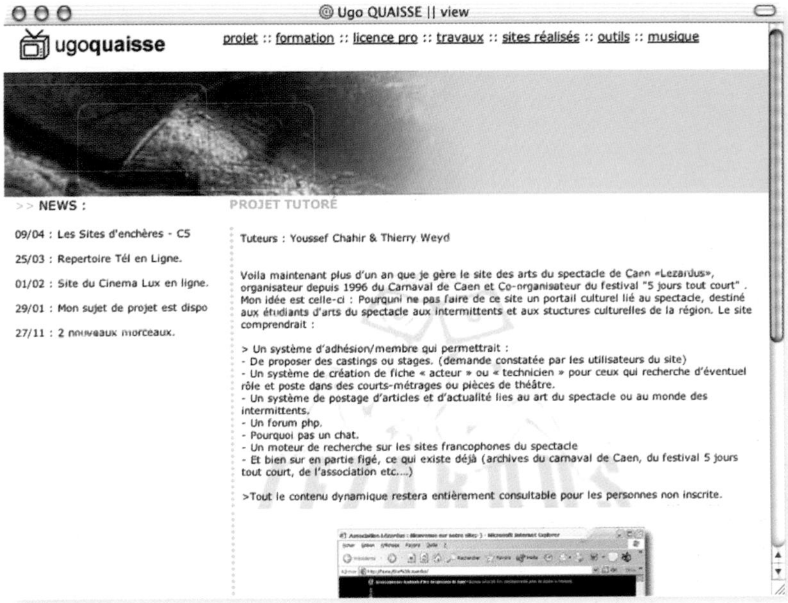
Ugo QUAISSE || view
ugoquaisse
projet :: formation :: licence pro :: travaux :: sites réalisés :: outils :: musique
>> NEWS :
09/04 : Les Sites d'enchères - C5
25/03 : Repertoire Tél en Ligne.
01/02 : Site du Cinema Lux en ligne.
29/01 : Mon sujet de projet est dispo
27/11 : 2 nouveaux morceaux.
PROJET TUTORÉ
Tuteurs : Youssef Chahir & Thierry Weyd
Voila maintenant plus d'un an que je gère le site des arts du spectacle de Caen «Lezardus», organisateur depuis 1996 du Carnaval de Caen et Co-organisateur du festival "5 jours tout court" . Mon idée est celle-ci : Pourquoi ne pas faire de ce site un portail culturel lié au spectacle, destiné aux étudiants d'arts du spectacle aux intermittents et aux stuctures culturelles de la région. Le site comprendrait :
> Un système d'adhésion/membre qui permettrait :
- De proposer des castings ou stages. (demande constatée par les utilisateurs du site)
- Un système de création de fiche « acteur » ou « technicien » pour ceux qui recherche d'éventuel rôle et poste dans des courts-métrages ou pièces de théâtre.
- Un système de postage d'articles et d'actualité lies au art du spectacle ou au monde des intermittents.
- Un forum php.
- Pourquoi pas un chat.
- Un moteur de recherche sur les sites francophones du spectacle
- Et bien sur en partie figé, ce qui existe déjà (archives du carnaval de Caen, du festival 5 jours tout court, de l'association etc....)
>Tout le contenu dynamique restera entièrement consultable pour les personnes non inscrite.

WWW.USERS.INFO.UNICAEN.FR/~UQUAISSE
D: UGO QUAISSE
A: HI!-POPULATION, **M:** UGO.QUAISSE@LAPOSTE.NET

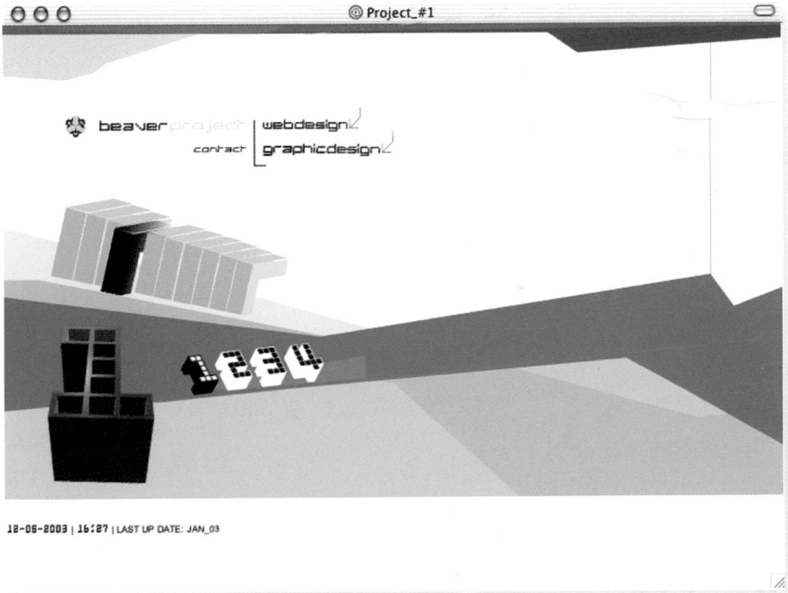
Project_#1
beaver project
webdesign
contact
graphicdesign
1234
12-06-2003 | 16:27 | LAST UP DATE: JAN_03

WWW.BEAVERPROJECT.COM
D: PEDRO SILVA
A: BEAVER PROJECT, **M:** PEDROSILVA@BEAVERPROJECT.COM

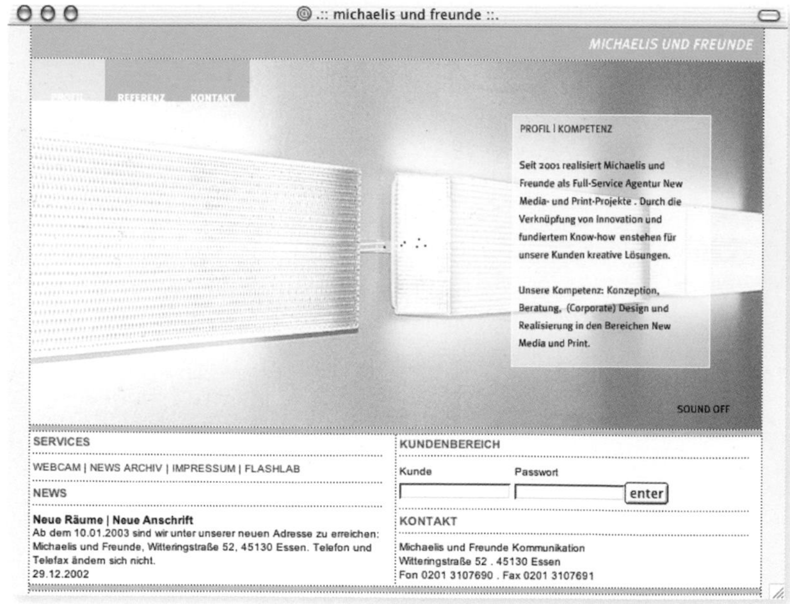

WWW.MICHAELIS-FREUNDE.DE
D: ANDRE MICHAELIS
A: MICHAELIS UND FREUNDE, **M:** KONTAKT@MICHAELIS-FREUNDE.DE

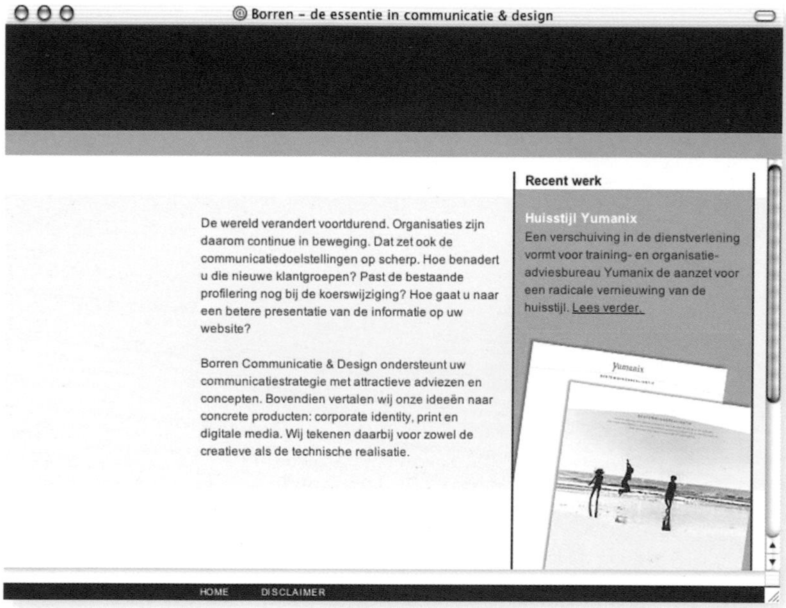

WWW.BORREN.NL
D: BOR BORREN, **C:** BOR BORREN, **P:** BOR BORREN/ANNEMIJN ZUMBRINK
A: BORREN COMMUNICATIE & DESIGN, **M:** BOR@BORREN.NL

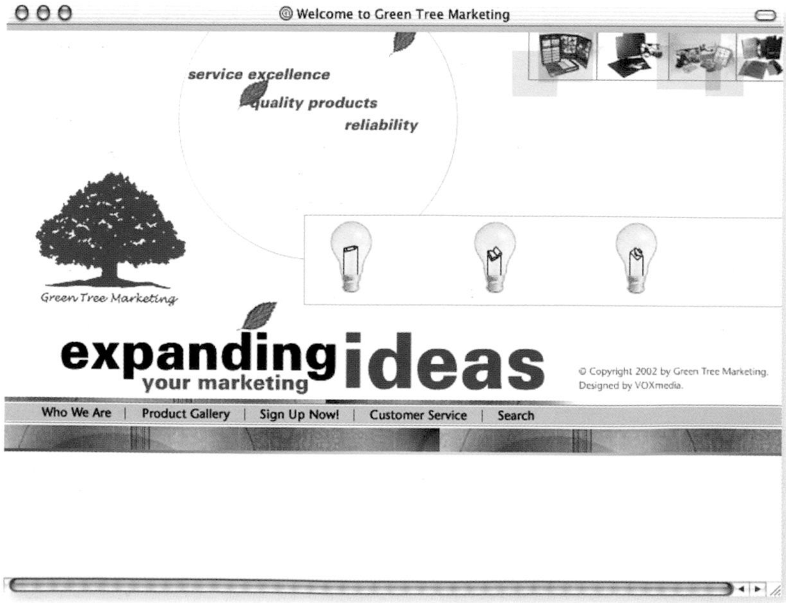

WWW.GREENTREE.COM.SG
D: KALINDA LOW, **C:** RAGHU
A: VOXMEDIA PTE LTD, **M:** JOE@VOXMEDIA.COM.SG

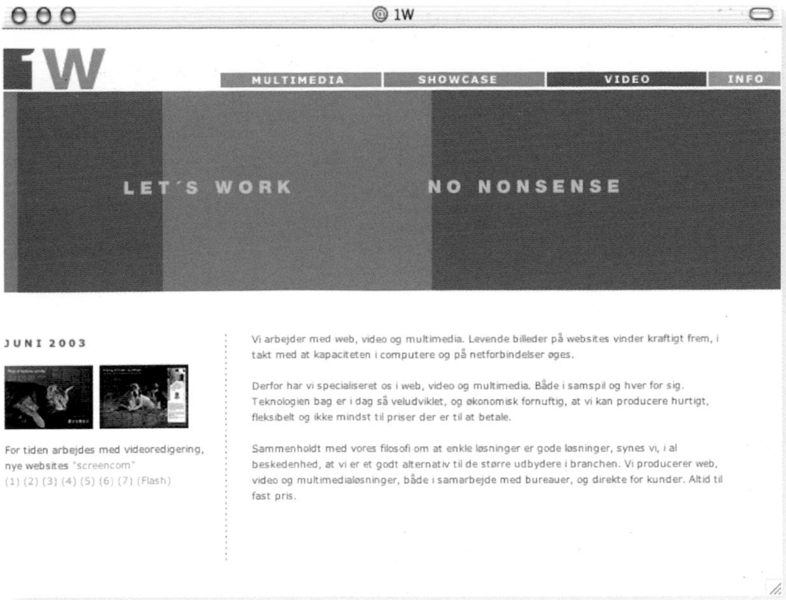
@ 1W
1W
MULTIMEDIA
SHOWCASE
VIDEO
INFO
LET´S WORK
NO NONSENSE
JUNI 2003
For tiden arbejdes med videoredigering, nye websites "screencom"
(1) (2) (3) (4) (5) (6) (7) (Flash)
Vi arbejder med web, video og multimedia. Levende billeder på websites vinder kraftigt frem, i takt med at kapaciteten i computere og på netforbindelser øges.
Derfor har vi specialiseret os i web, video og multimedia. Både i samspil og hver for sig. Teknologien bag er i dag så veludviklet, og økonomisk fornuftig, at vi kan producere hurtigt, fleksibelt og ikke mindst til priser der er til at betale.
Sammenholdt med vores filosofi om at enkle løsninger er gode løsninger, synes vi, i al beskedenhed, at vi er et godt alternativ til de større udbydere i branchen. Vi producerer web, video og multimedialøsninger, både i samarbejde med bureauer, og direkte for kunder. Altid til fast pris.

WWW.1W.DK
D: HENRIK LANDMARK, **P:** HENRIK LANDMARK
A: WWW.1W.DK

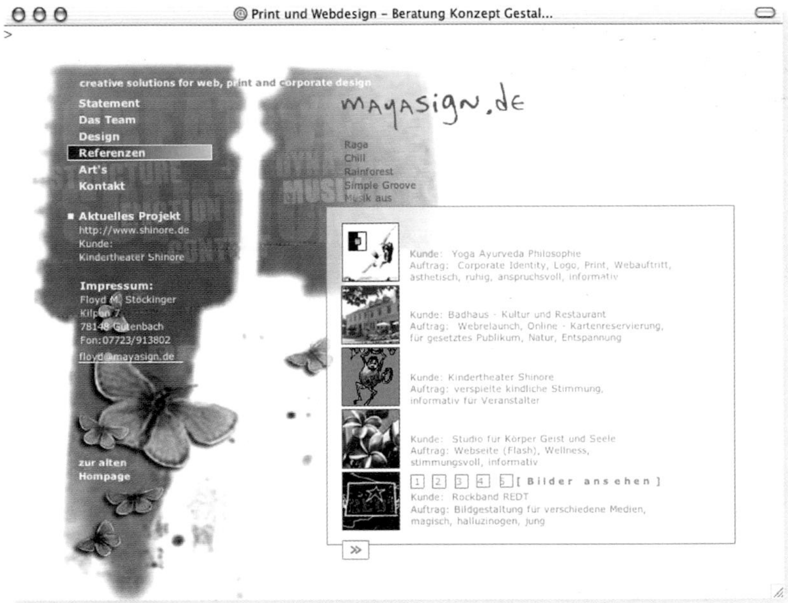

WWW.MAYASIGN.DE
D: MARIO STÖCKINGER
M: FLOYD@MAYASIGN.DE

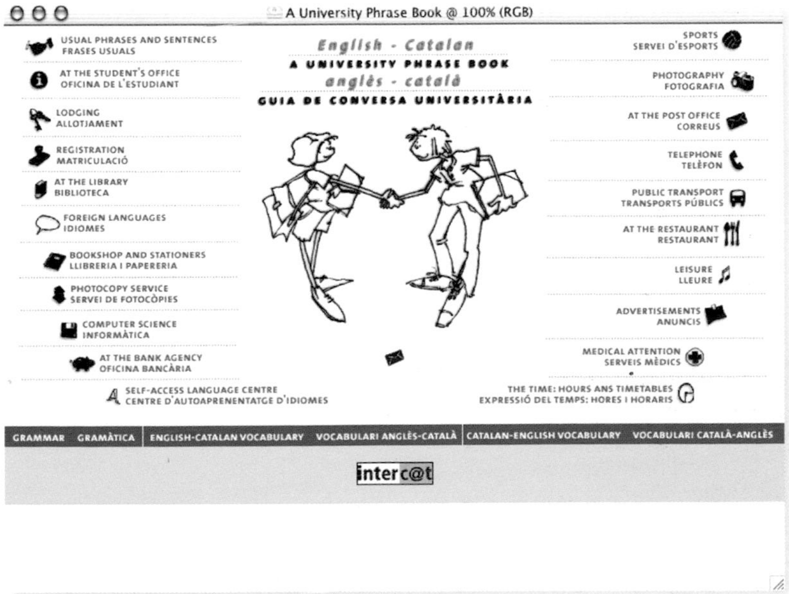

WWW.INTERCAT.GENCAT.ES
D: DIDIER GORON, **C:** NATHALIE GARCIA, **P:** ENRIC BAJUELO
A: ZINK COMUNICACIO, **M:** DIDIER.GORON@ZINK.ES

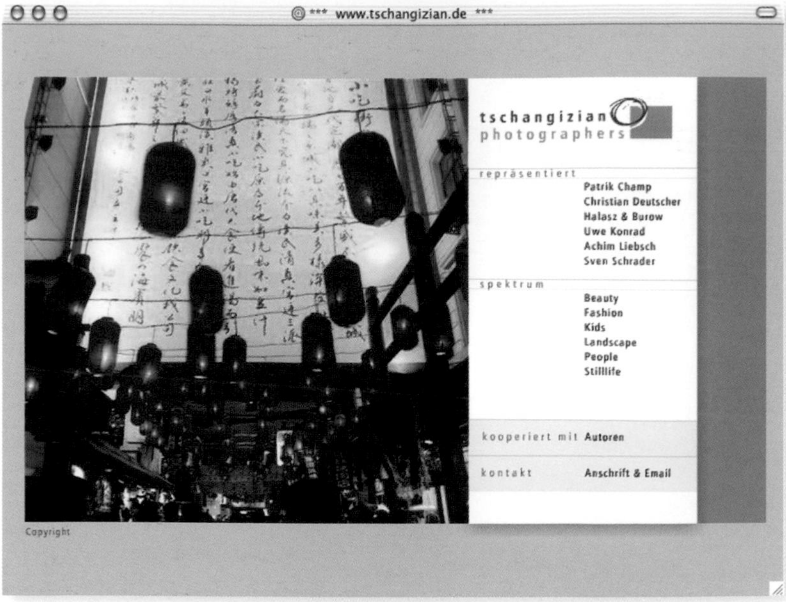

WWW.TSCHANGIZIAN.DE
D: LXFX
A: LXFX, **M:** ALEX@LXFX.DE

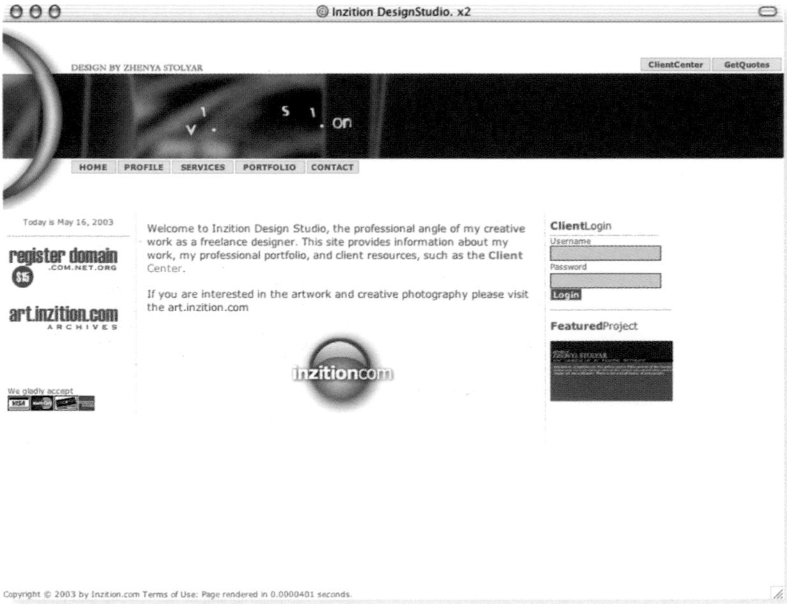

WWW.INZITION.COM
D: GENE STOLYAR
A: INZITION, **M:** INZITION@INZITION.COM

WWW.IN-BLEU.COM
D: IMELDA GUNAWAN
A: BLE:U, **M:** BLEU@IN-BLEU.COM

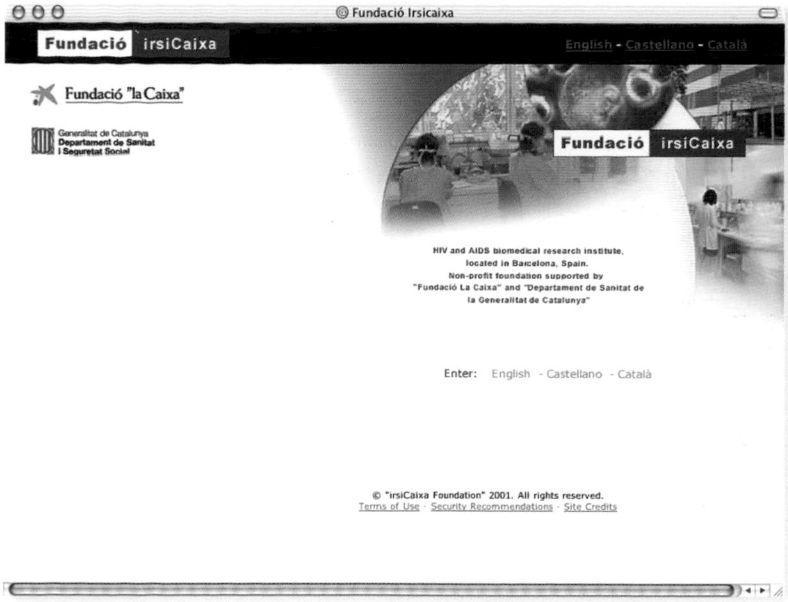

WWW.IRSICAIXA.ORG
D: MICK WALSH
A: WALSH PRODUCTIONS, INC., **M:** INFO@WPINYC.COM

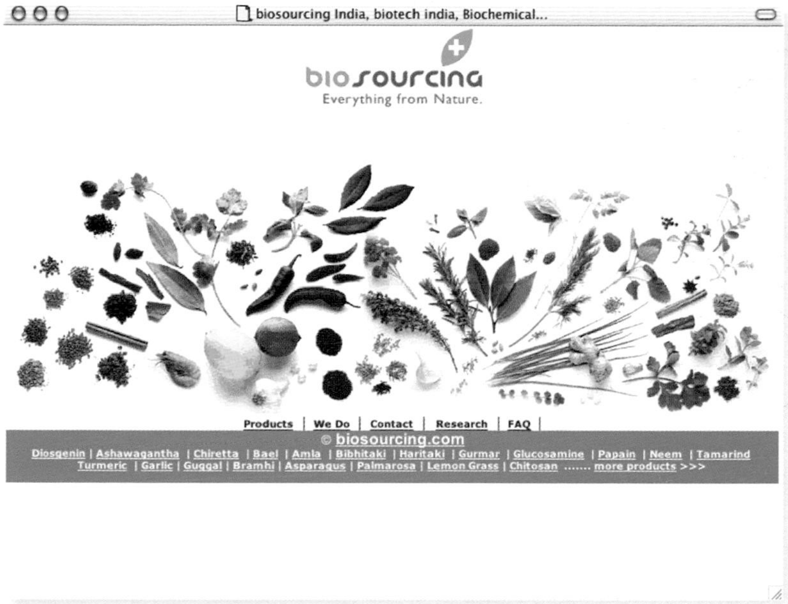

WWW.BIOSOURCING.COM
D: FIROZ, **C:** SIDHARTH, **P:** SIDHARTH
A: FIROZART, **M:** SIDHARTH@BIOSOURCING.COM

WWW.LAURAGUTIERREZ.NET
D: LAURA GUTIÉRREZ GARCÍA
M: INFO@LAURAGUTIERREZ.NET

WWW.FESTIVALDIROMA.ORG/EFA
D: FABIO LATTANZI ANTINORI, **C:** GIANLUCA DEL GOBBO, **P:** KITONB EXTREME THEATRE
A: FLYER, **M:** FABIO@TOXICDESIGNSTUDIO.COM

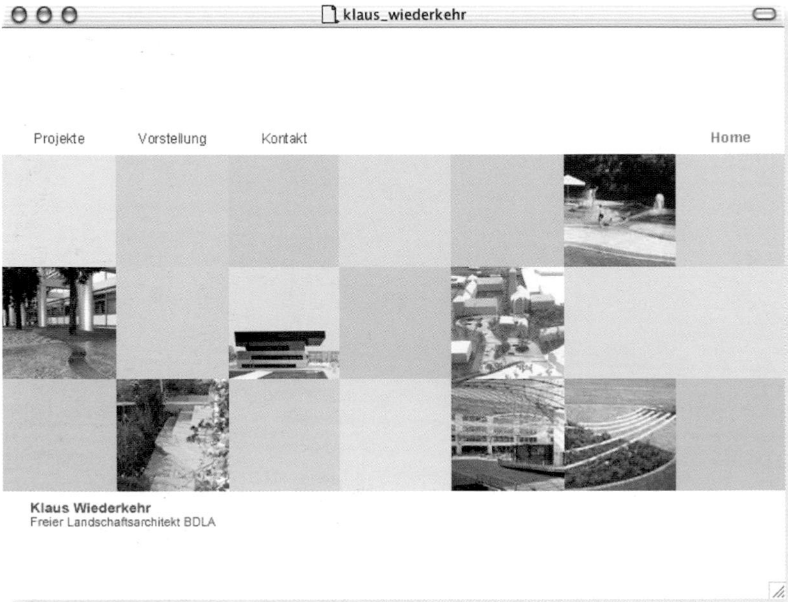

WWW.WIEDERKEHR.BIZ
D: MARKUS WEISMANN, MATTI WIRTH
A: MM, **M:** MATTIWIRTH@WEB.DE

WWW.TWIRL.IT
D: ROBERTA CASALIGGI, **C:** GIULIO PONS
A: TWIRL, **M:** INFO@TWIRL.IT

WWW.TUERCA.CL
D: ALEJANDRO RADEMACHER
A: ARBOL DE COLOR, **M:** XFIGUEROA@ARBOLCOLOR.CL

WWW.NETGAMECAIXANOVA.COM
D: IVAN RUBIO PARDO, **C:** JUAN ANTONIO ESPINA, **P:** MASIMPACTO.COM
A: LAB713

WWW.IMBASA.COM
D: EMMA REIXACH COLL
A: ESPA DPT. IMAGEN Y COMUNICACIÓN, **M:** EREIXoo@ESPA.COM

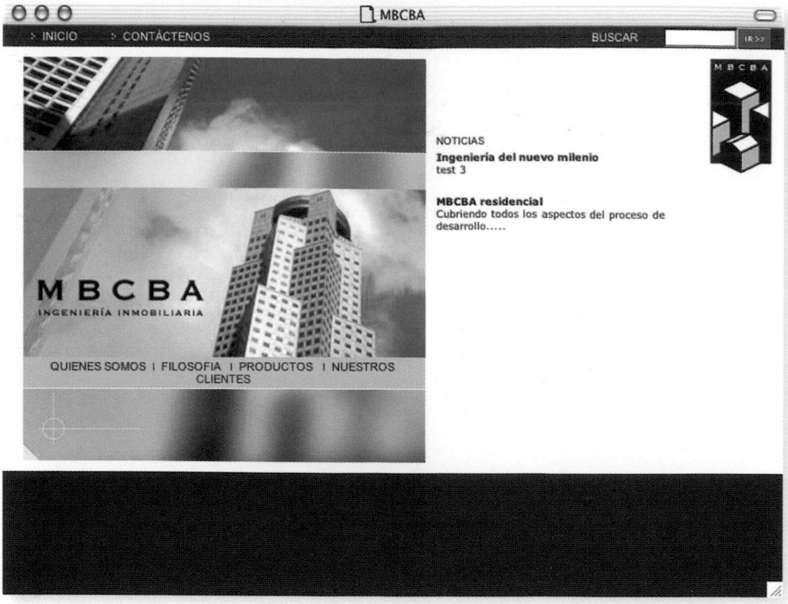

WWW.MBCBA.COM
D: ABARTEAM, **C:** RICARDO PACHECO
A: WAREBOX, **M:** LREYES@WAREBOX.COM

WWW.ANALITICAVETERINARIA.COM
D: MIGUEL ZORRAQUINO, **C:** ALFREDO ÁLVAREZ, **P:** ANALÍTICA VETERINARIA
A: ZORRAQUINO DESIGN STUDIO, **M:** DESIGN@ZORRAQUINO.COM

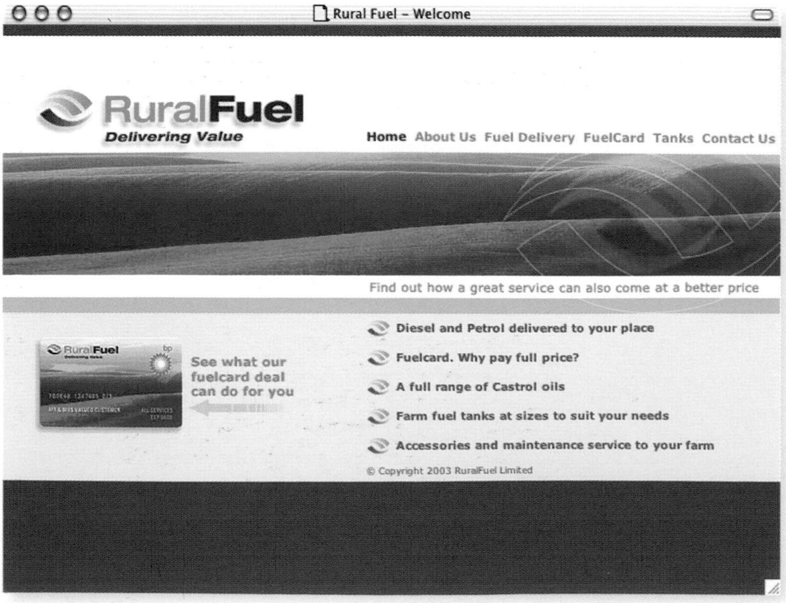

WWW.RURALFUEL.CO.NZ
D: IAN BRAYSHAW
A: INSPIRED WEB SOLUTIONS, **M:** IAN@IWS.CO.NZ

WWW.DECORNATURA.COM
D: EMILIO GARCIA VAZ
A: EDISSENY.COM*, **M:** INFO@EDISSENY.COM

WWW.ASCO.DE
D: ADY PRATIOTO, **C:** ADY PRATIOTO, **P:** ASCO GMBH
A: ASCO GMBH, **M:** A.PRATIOTO@ASCO.DE

WWW.PRINCE091280.COM
D: MARK WONG
A: HKSAR, **M:** MW091280@SINAMAN.COM

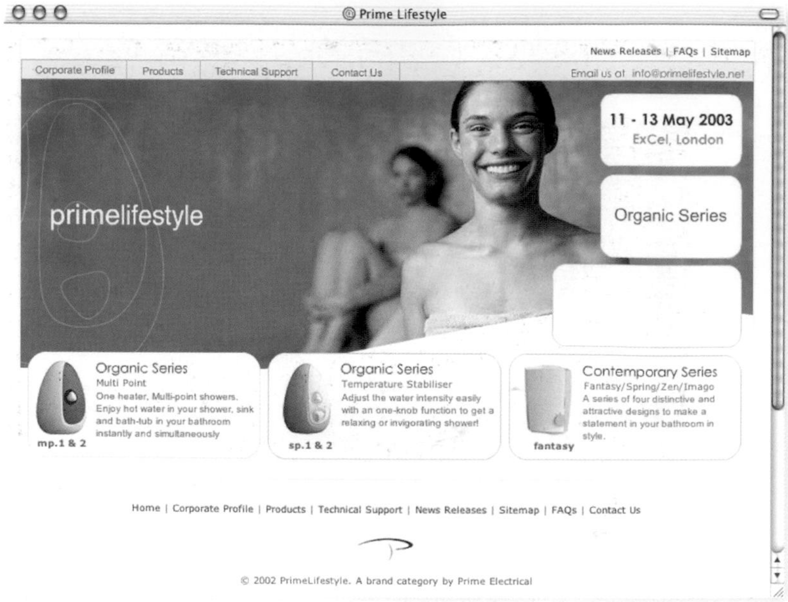

WWW.PRIMELIFESTYLE.NET
D: KEN CHAN, **C:** RAYMOND LIAN, **P:** ALDRICH KOH
A: MEEK, **M:** SKIN@PACIFIC.NET.SG

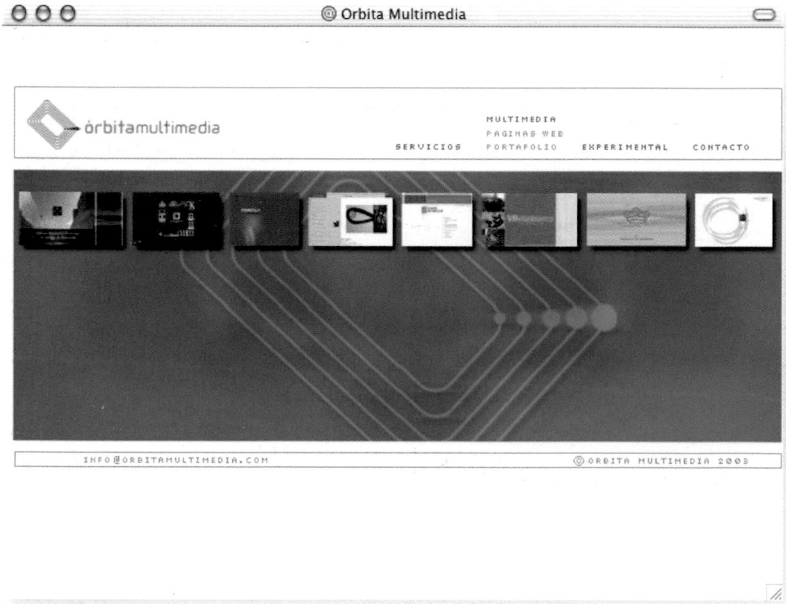

WWW.ORBITAMULTIMEDIA.COM
D: AMAIA TORRE TACCOLA
A: ORBITA MULTIMEDIA, **M:** INFO@ORBITAMULTIMEDIA.COM

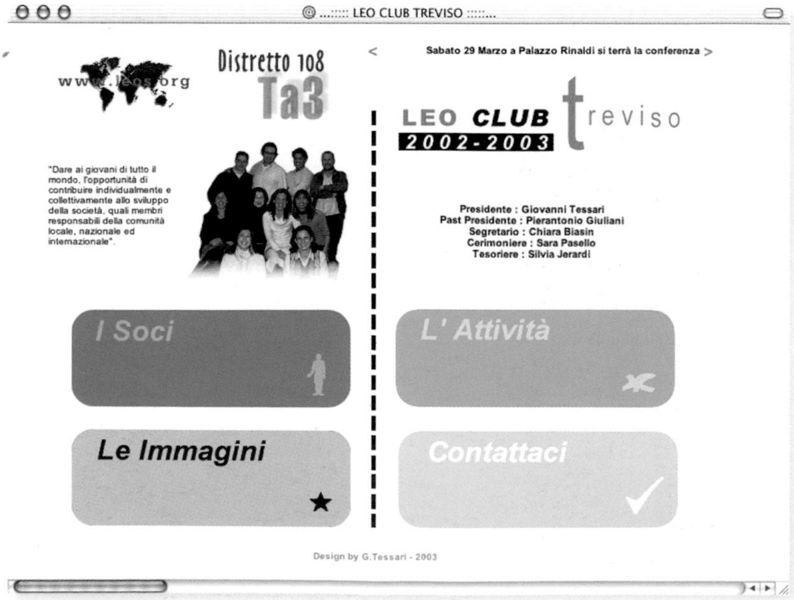

WWW.LEOTREVISO.IT
D: GIOVANNI TESSARI
M: GTEX2@LIBERO.IT

WWW.JPKAY.COM
D: JOHN PETER KAYTROSH
A: JP KAYTROSH CO., **M:** JPKAYTROSH@HOTMAIL.COM

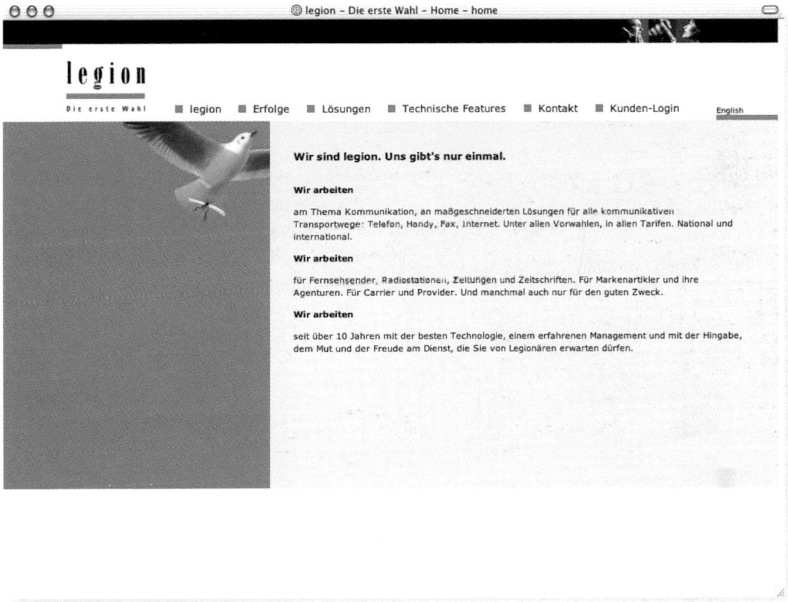

WWW.LEGION.DE
D: JOCHEN GUMPERT, **C:** UWE BOKELBRINK, **P:** ABERRATIO GMBH
A: ABERRATIO GMBH, **M:** JOCHEN@ABERRATIO.DE

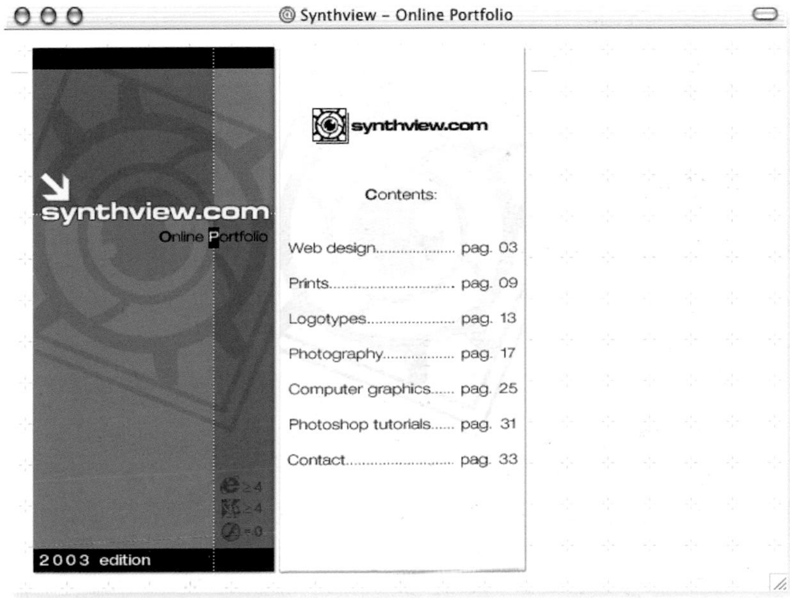

WWW.SYNTHVIEW.COM
D: JAN TONELLATO
A: SYNTHVIEW, **M:** INFO@SYNTHVIEW.COM

WWW.VEFUR.IS
D: OSKARSDOTTIR THRUDUR, **C:** VEFUR SOFTWARE SOULUTIONS LTD. ICELAND
M: VEFUR@VEFUR.IS

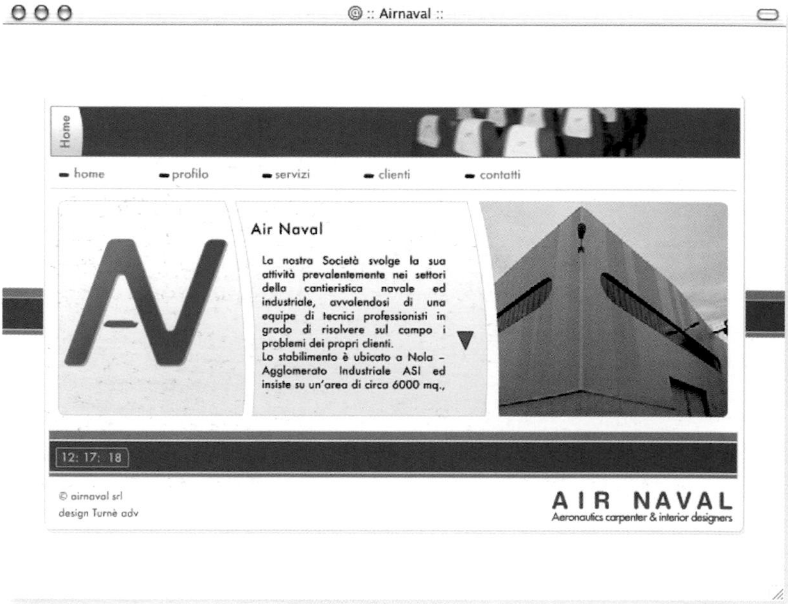

WWW.AIRNAVAL.IT
D: MARCO TRAMONTANO, **C:** MARCO TRAMONTANO, **P:** TURNE
A: MARCOTRAMONTANO.COM, **M:** CONTATTI@MARCOTRAMONTANO.COM

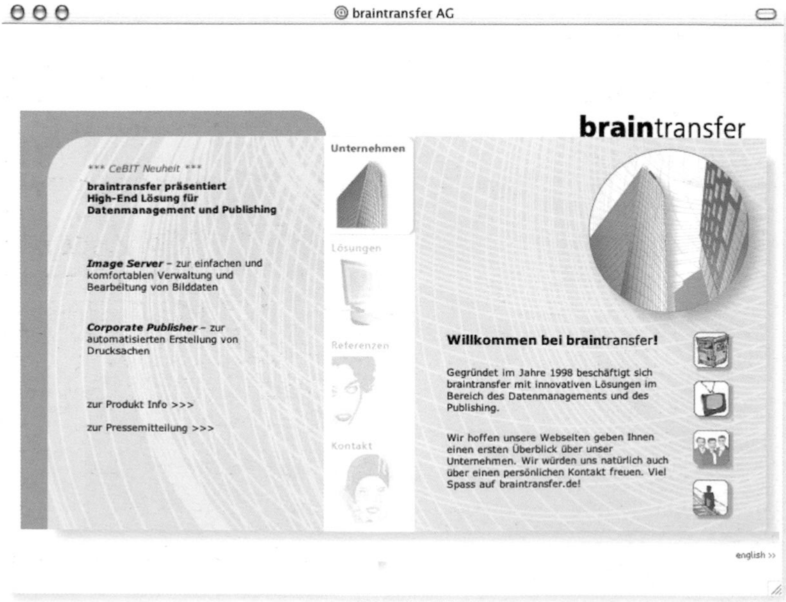

WWW.BRAINTRANSFER.DE
D: BURAK YILDIRIM, **C:** OLAF KREITZ, **P:** OLAF KREITZ
A: BRAINTRANSFER AG, **M:** BURAK.YILDIRIM@BRAINTRANSFER.DE

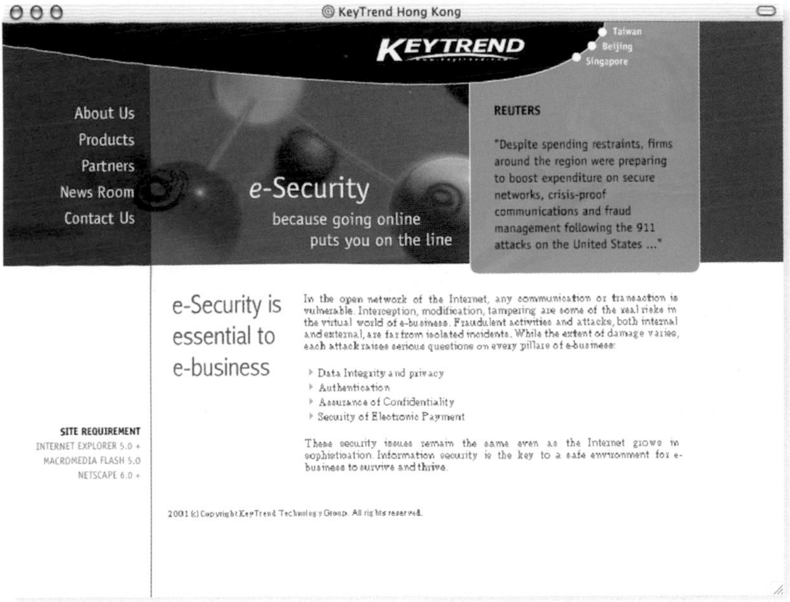

WWW.KEYTREND.COM.HK
D: GABRIEL TAN
A: KEYTREND (HK) TECHNOLOGY, **M:** GABRIEL@DAILOW.COM

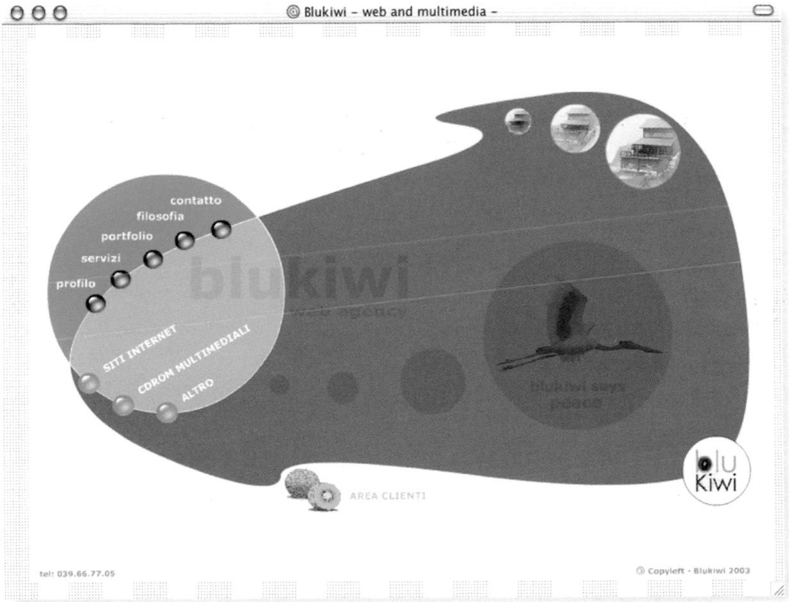

WWW.BLUKIWI.IT
D: ALESSANDRO MAURI, **C:** DIEGO PASQUADIBISCEGLIA, **P:** ALEXANDER TER KUILE
A: BLUKIWI, **M:** INFO@BLUKIWI.IT

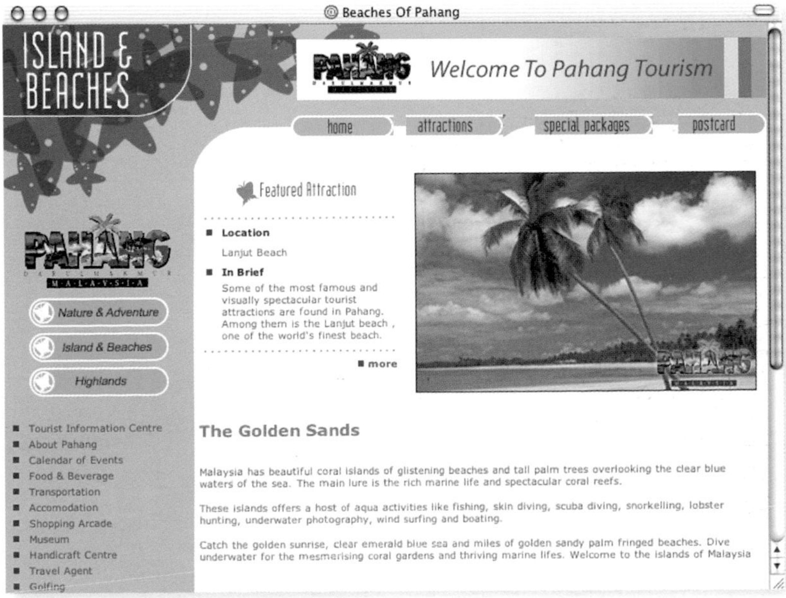

WWW.PAHANGTOURISM.COM
D: ISMAIL ISZARIZAL, **C:** SHAHARANI@JUNAIDY BIN MANSUR
A: EHSAN EBIZ SDN. BHD., **M:** ISZARIZAL@EHSAN-E.BIZ

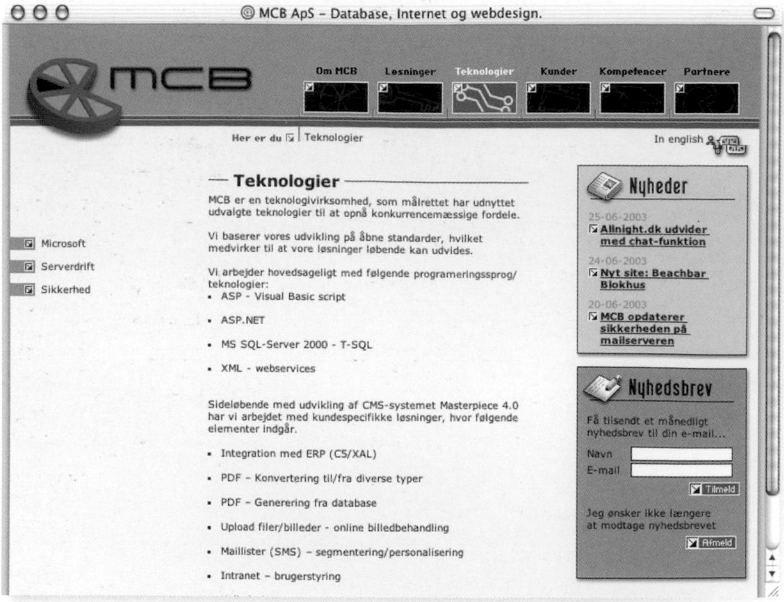

WWW.MCB.DK
D: ANNE BANK LINDBERG, **C:** JANUS KLOK LAURITSEN, **P:** THOMAS KRAGELUND
A: MCB, **M:** ANNE@MCB.DK

WWW.DESIGN.GANJINEH.COM
D: SCHAHRYAR FEKRI
A: GANJINEH DESIGN, **M:** SFEKRI@GANJINEH.COM

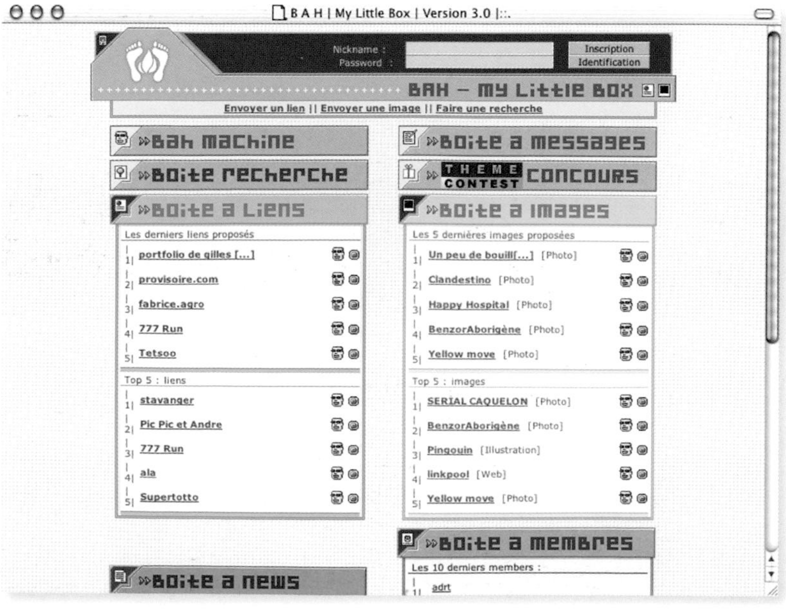

WWW.BAH.BE
D: MATHIEU BAZELAIRE
M: MATHIEU.BAZELAIRE@BAH.BE

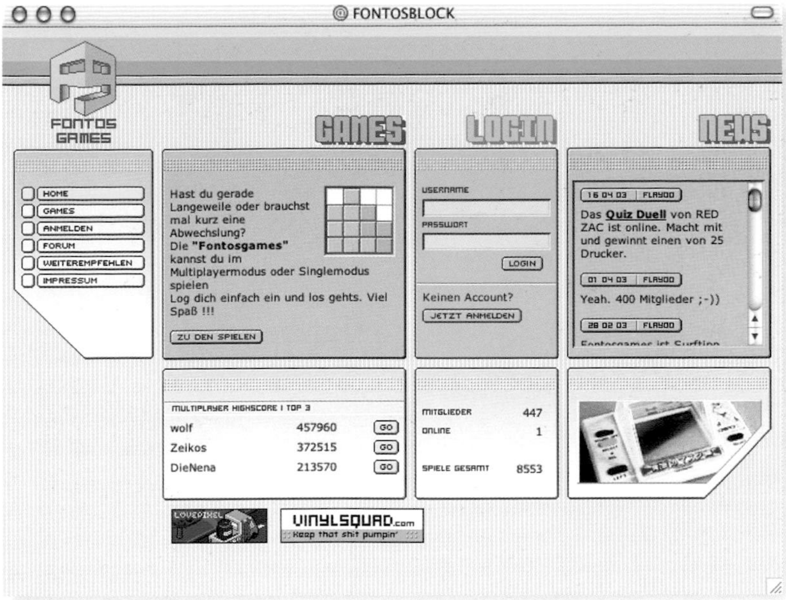

WWW.FONTOSBLOCK.DE
D: HANNES HÖß, ALI RASTAGAR, **C:** HANNES HÖß
A: IDEA GROUP HAMBURG, **M:** FLAYOO@HH01.COM

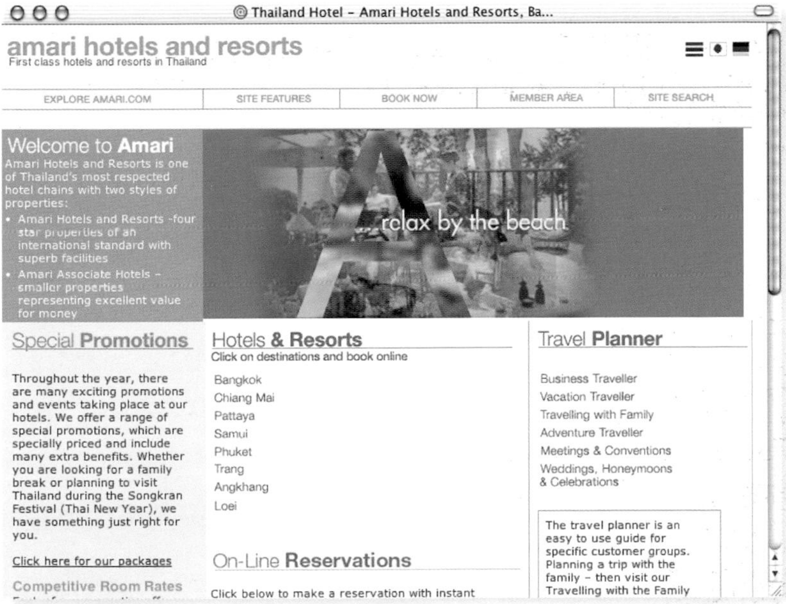

WWW.AMARI.COM
D: AMARIN VEJCHAROEN, **C:** INETASIA TEAM, **P:** RIC SHREVES
A: INETASIA, **M:** RSHREVES@INETASIA.COM

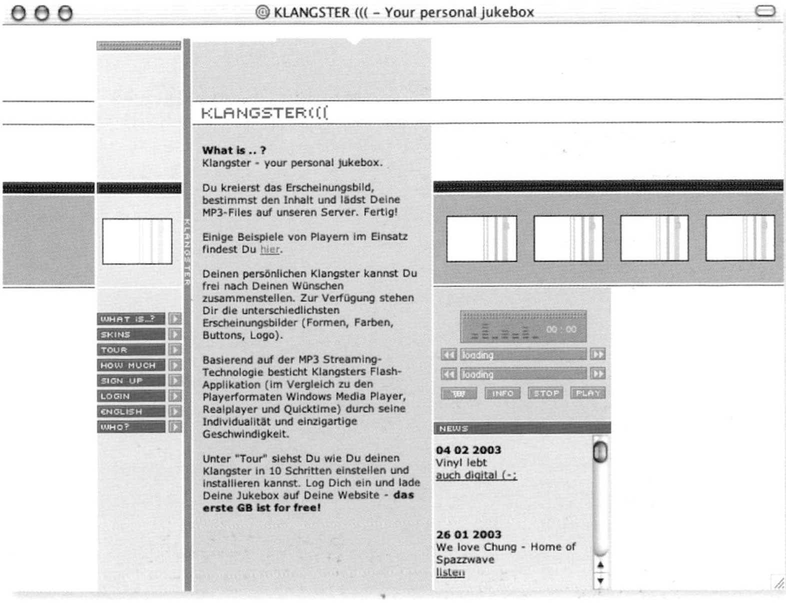

WWW.KLANGSTER.DE
D: HANNES HOESS
A: SUPERREAL DIGITAL MEDIA GMBH, **M:** HANNES@SUPERREAL.DE

WWW.ANNA-OM-LINE.COM
D: ANNA MARIA LOPEZ LOPEZ
A: FASHIONMAS DESIGN SERVICES, **M:** ANNA@FASHIONMAS.COM

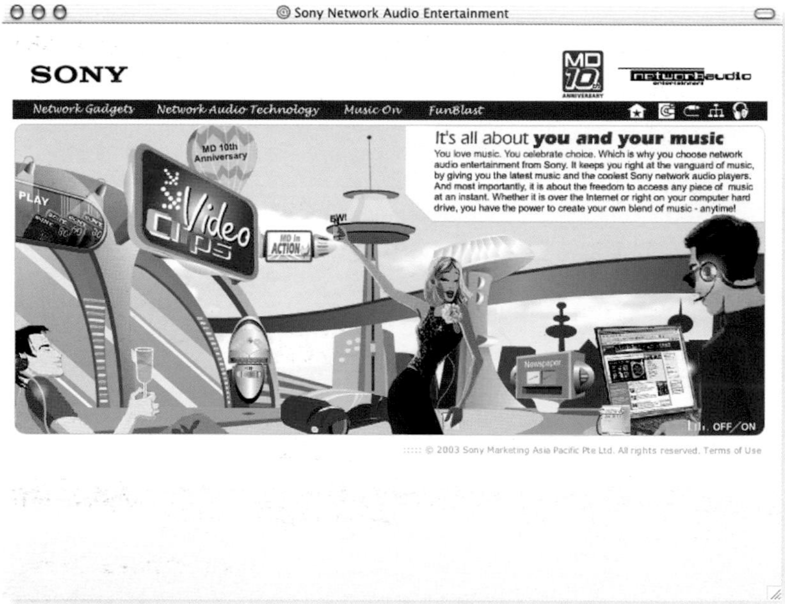

WWW.SONY-ASIA.COM/NETWORKAUDIO
D: STEPHANIE NG, DAVID TEO, TEE, **C:** DAVID TEO, TEE, AGNES, **P:** NG, STEPHANIE
A: ACTIVATE INTERACTIVE PTE LTD, **M:** STEPHANIE@ACTIVATE.COM.SG

WWW.ACTIVEPERKS.COM
D: JOHN FOO, **C:** ACTIVATE STUDIO TEAM, **P:** JOHN FOO
A: ACTIVATE INTERACTIVE PTE LTD, **M:** GEORGINA@ACTIVATE.COM.SG

WWW.GRUPSAGESSA.COM
D: JOSEP GARCIA CABALLÉ, **C:** JOSEP GARCIA CABALLÉ, **P:** GRUP SAGESSA
A: GRUP SAGESSA, **M:** PGARCIA@GRUPSAGESSA.COM

WWW.SCP-MUSIC.COM
D: MARIO DONADONI, **C:** MASSIMILIANO LO PORCHIO, **P:** STEFANO CASTAGNA
A: NITENS, **M:** INFO@NITENS.COM

WWW.BUNAC.ORG
D: JOHN LOYDALL
A: DEVELOP DESIGN, **M:** JOHN@DEVELOPDESIGN.CO.UK

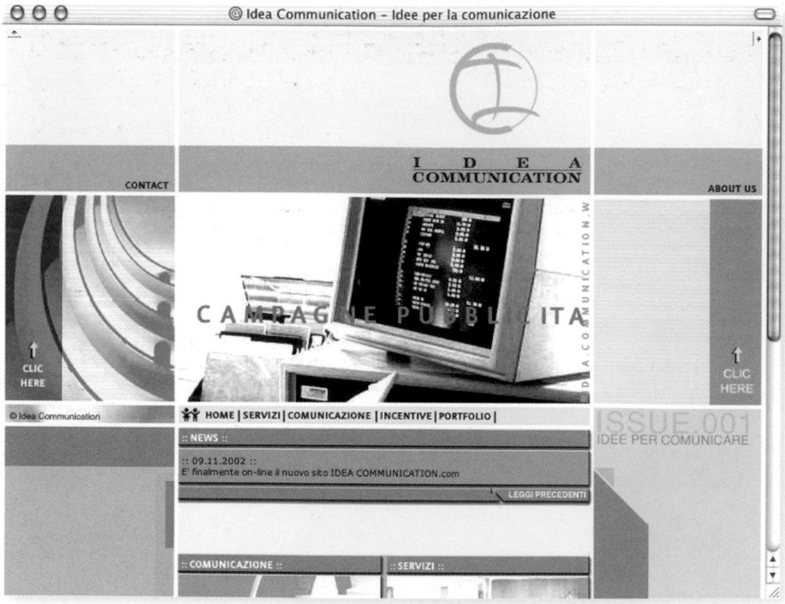

WWW.IDEACOMMUNICATION.COM
D: ALESSANDRO CAPPELLETTI
A: ALESSANDRO CAPPELLETTI, **M:** CAPPELLETTI@INFINITO.IT

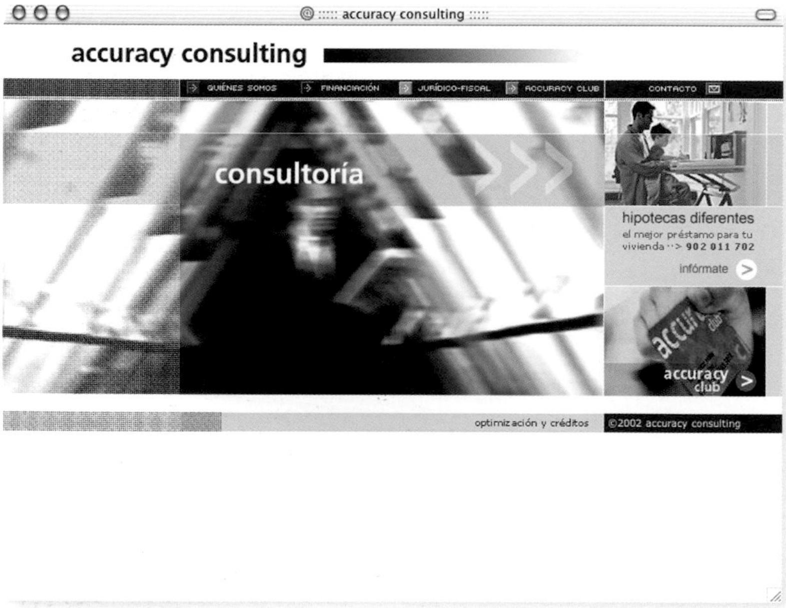

WWW.ACCURACYCONSULTING.COM
D: PATRICIA FUENTES
A: BLUE PLANET, **M:** INFO@BLPLANET.COM

WWW.OXBOWEB.COM
D: JULIEN DUCAMP, **C:** ORCHID NETWORK
M:GDEVOLDER@OXBOW.FR

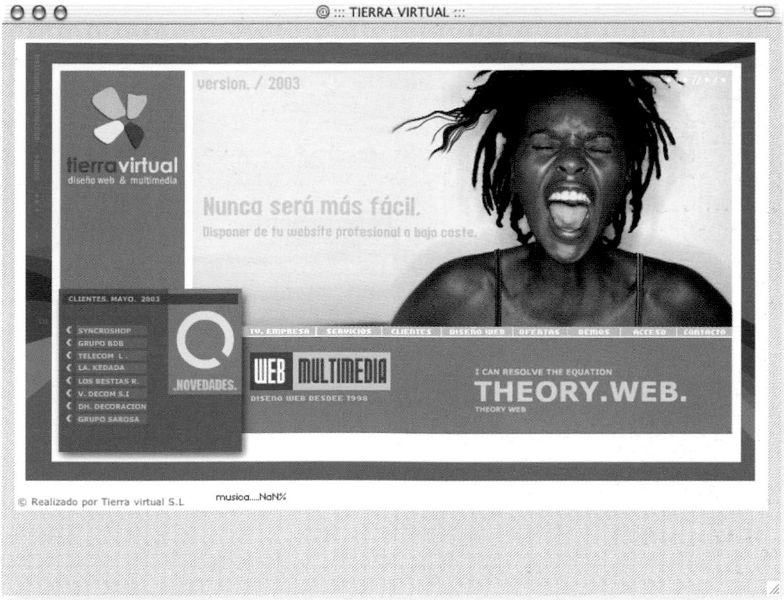

WWW.TIERRAVIRTUAL.NET
D: JESSICA TRAVIESO SUAREZ, **C:** JESSICA TRAVIESO SUAREZ, **P:** OSCAR PEREZ PINAZO
A: TIERRA VIRTUAL S.L, **M:** INFO@TIERRAVIRTUAL.NET

WWW.D-NOISE.NET
D: KIKE R. RIVERA
A: D-NOISE, **M:** CONTACTO@D-NOISE.NET

WWW.SHAMROCK.ORG
A: WALSH PRODUCTIONS, INC.
M: INFO@WPINYC.COM

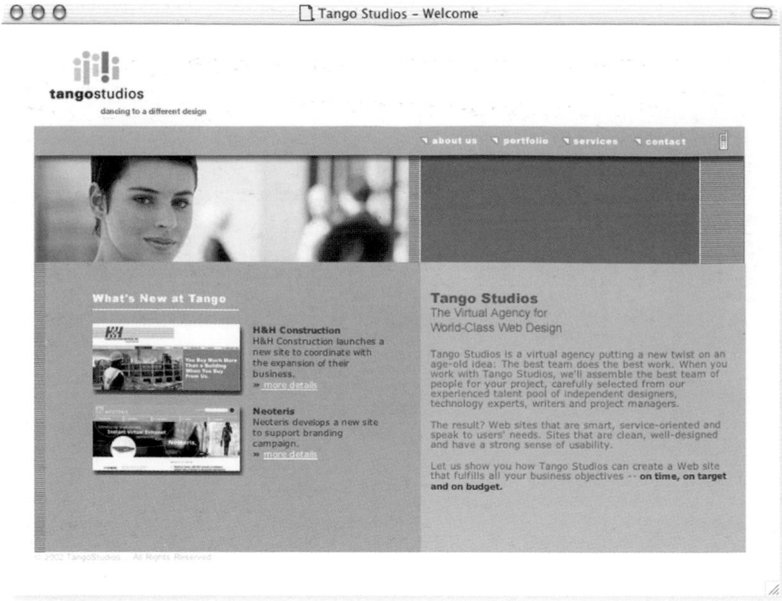

WWW.TANGOSTUDIOS.COM
D: DAN WARFIELD
A: TANGO STUDIOS, **M:** WARFIELD@TANGOSTUDIOS.COM

WWW.RACCOON.ES
D: MIGUEL ANGEL BENÍTEZ, **C:** MIGUEL ANGEL BENÍTEZ, **P:** PABLO NAVARRO RUBIO
M: INFO@MIGUELBENITEZ.COM

WWW.TELECOM-LEVANTE.COM
D: JESSICA TRAVIESO SUAREZ
A: TIERRA VIRTUAL S.L, **M:** INFO@TIERRAVIRTUAL.NET

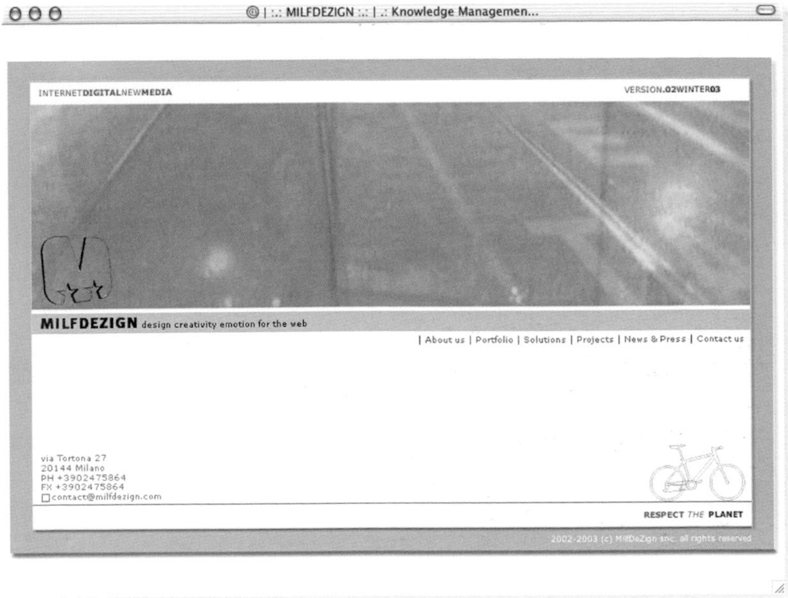

WWW.MILFDEZIGN.COM
D: LORENZO PREVIATI , MANUELA ZAVATTARO, **C:** GIANMARIA DALBONI, **P:** MILFDEZIGN
A: MILFDEZIGN, **M:** L8@MILFD3SIGN.COM

WWW.ARMANISOFT.CH
D: ARMIN MÜLLER, **C:** ARMIN MÜLLER
A: INGENIEURBÜRO ARMIN MÜLLER, **M:** AM@ARMANISOFT.CH

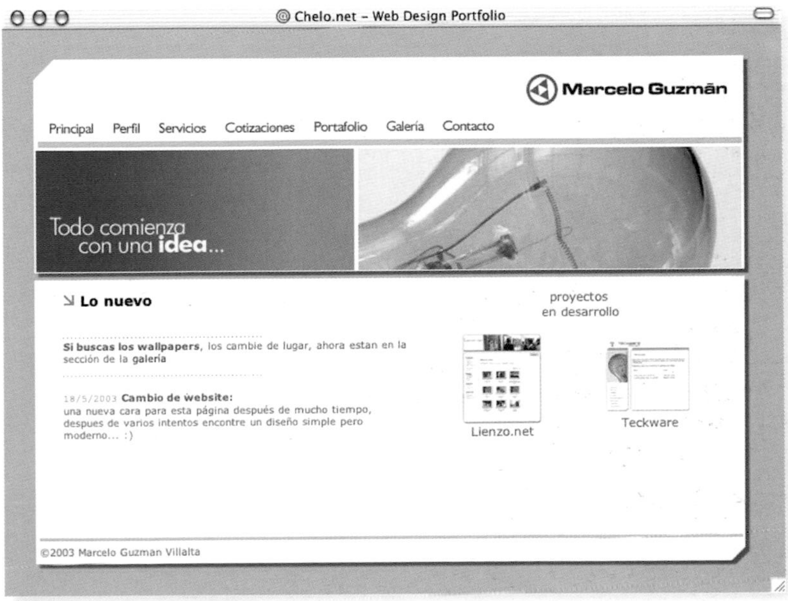

WWW.ARCEL.PT
D: FLÁVIO GOMES
A: ORBITALWEB, **M:** FLAVIO@ORBITALWEB.PT

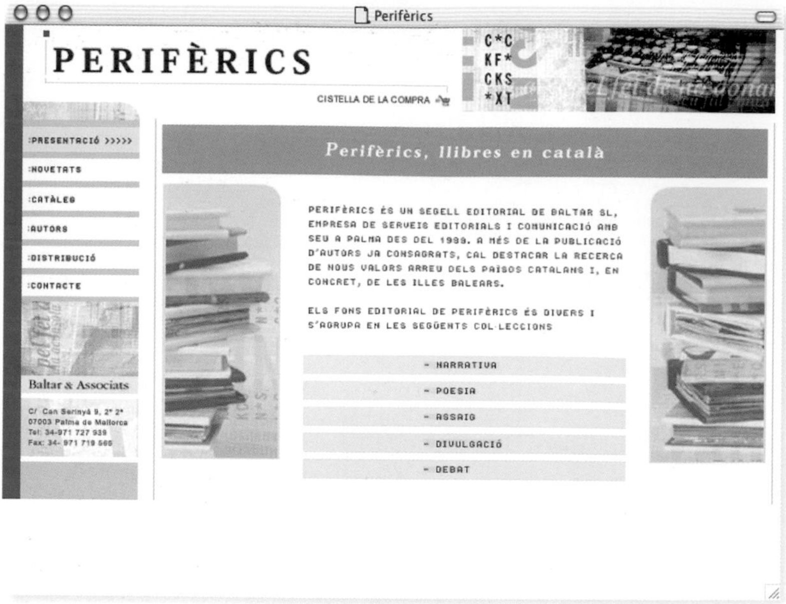

WWW.PERIFERICS.COM
D: WEBFACTORY INTERNET SL
A: WEBFACTORY INTERNET SL, **M:** WF@WEB-FACTORY.COM

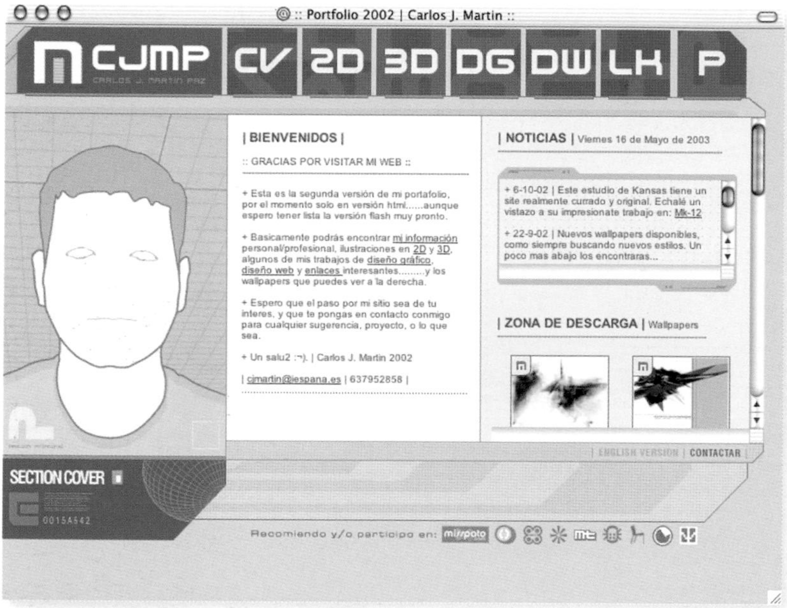

WWW.IESPANA.ES/CJMARTIN
D: VER ARRIBA, **C:** VER ARRIBA
M: CJMARTIN@IESPANA.ES

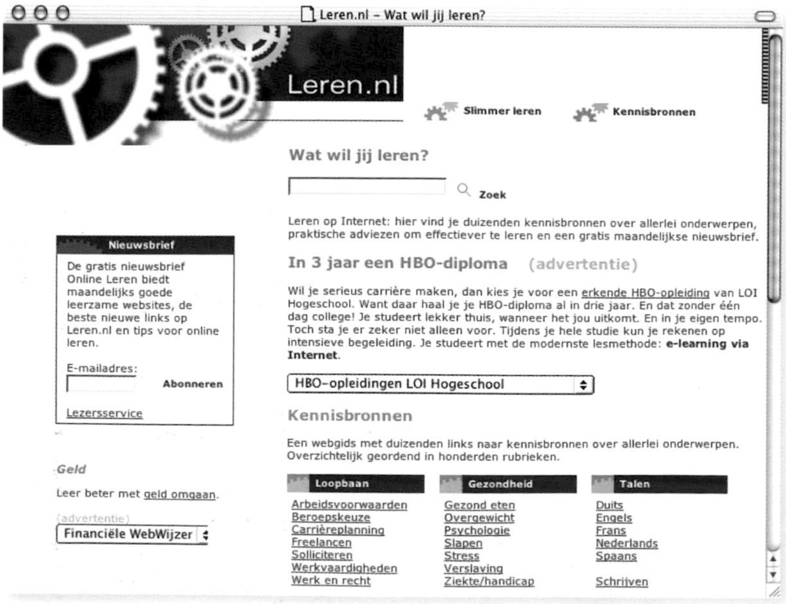

WWW.LEREN.NL
D: D. VAN DONGEN, **C:** D. VAN DONGEN & R. PIJLMAN
A: CONK, **M:** WEBMASTER@CONK.NL

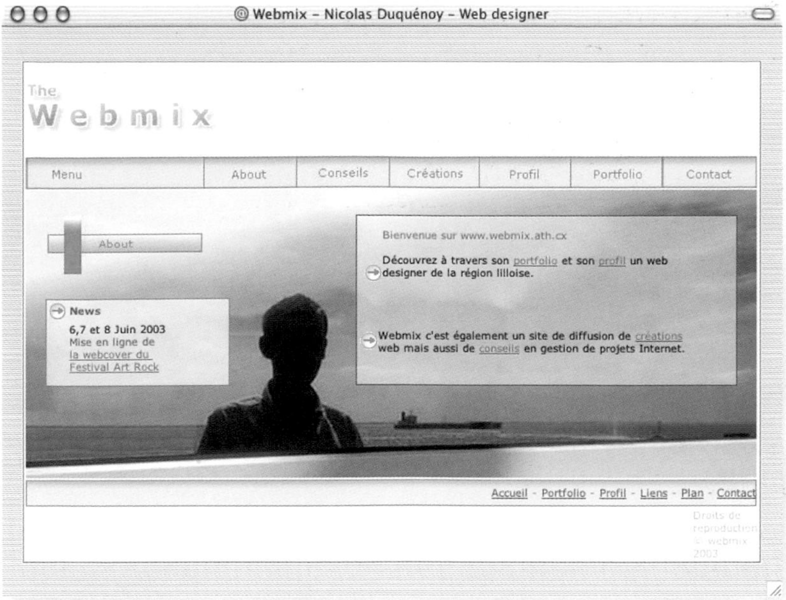

WWW.WEBMIX.ATH.CX
D: NICOLAS DUQUENOY
M: N.DUQUENOY@FREE.FR

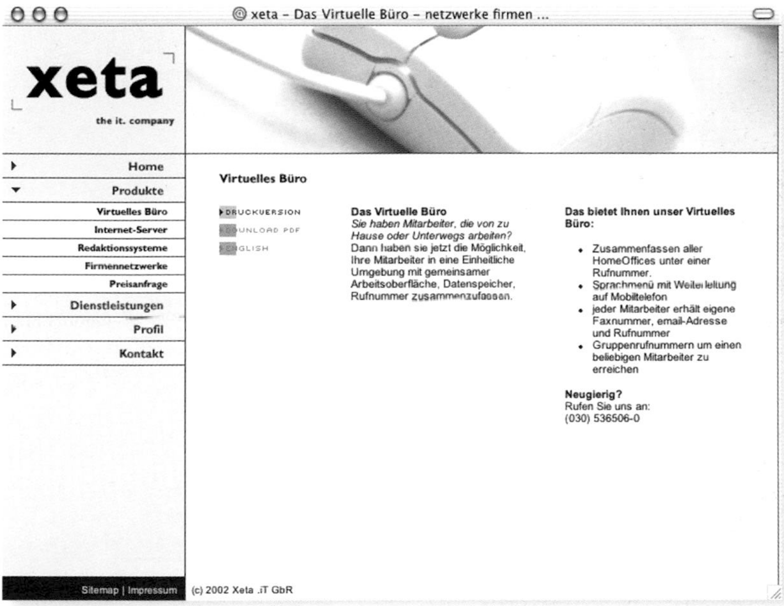

WWW.XETA.IT
D: PHILIP HOHN, **C:** PHILIP HOHN, NIKOLAI CIESLAK, **P:** PHILIP HOHN
A: XETA - THE .IT COMPANY, **M:** HOHN@XETA.IT

WWW.DECIMO.PT
D: NUNO CABRAL, **C:** JORGE BESSA
A: DECIMO, **M:** PEDROTOMAS@CCO.PT

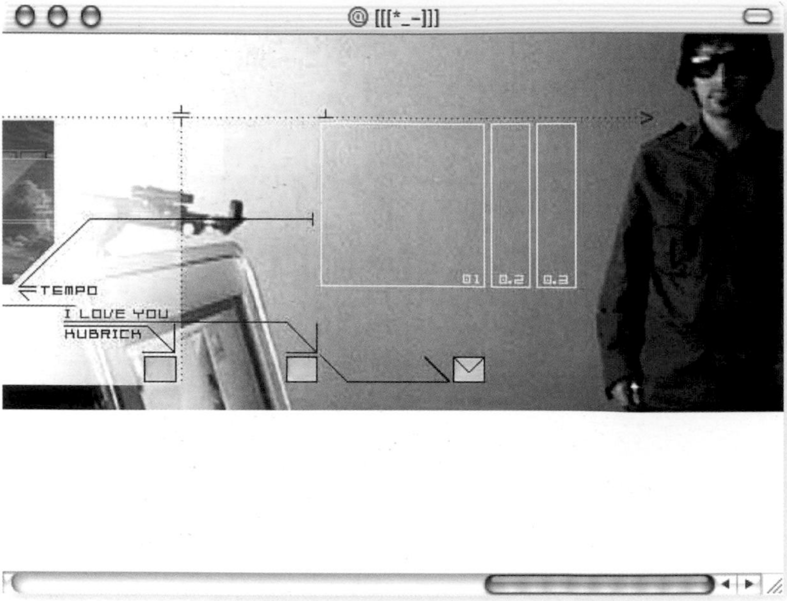

WWW.ANATOMICO.CL
D: LUIS BARRERA
A: ANATOMICO, **M:** ANATOMICO@ANATOMICO.CL

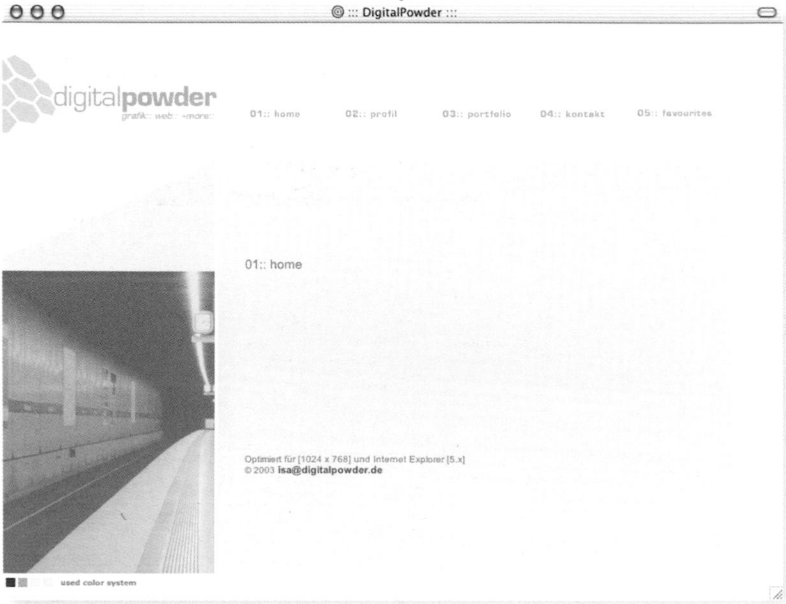

WWW.DIGITALPOWDER.DE
D: ISABEL WEIHERMANN
M: ISA@DIGITALPOWDER.DE

WWW.HABITATHOTELES.COM
A: ARS VIRTUALIS
M: ARSVIRT@ARSVIRTUALIS.COM

WWW.KYNETOS.COM
D: GIACOMO GIANCARLO
A: KYNETOS, **M:** PRESS@KYNETOS.COM

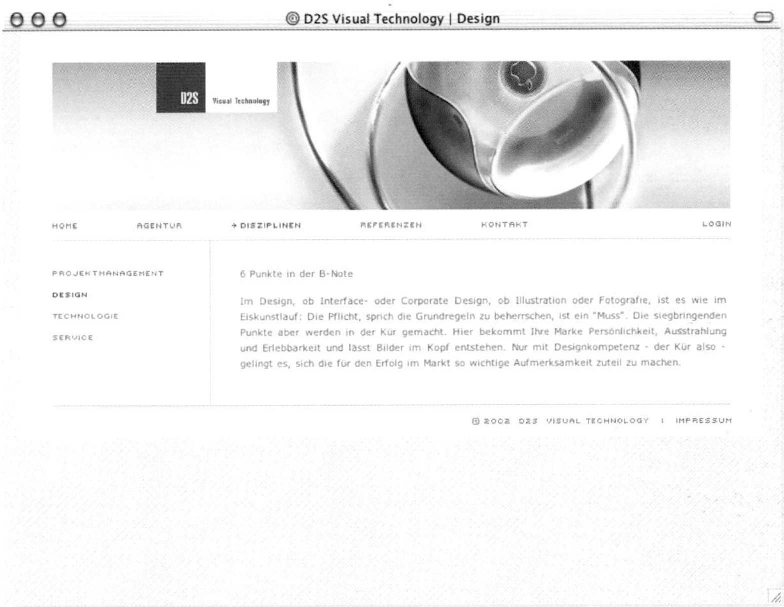

WWW.D2S.DE
D: ALFRED SCHNEIDER, **C:** ANDREW SCHMIDT, **P:** D2S VISUAL TECHNOLOGY
A: D2S VISUAL TECHNOLOGY, **M:** DESIGN@D2S.DE

WWW.2SDESIGN.WEB.PT
D: NUNO SOARES, **C:** NUNO SOARES, CRISTINA CORREIA
A: 2SDESIGN, **M:** SOARES29@IOL.PT

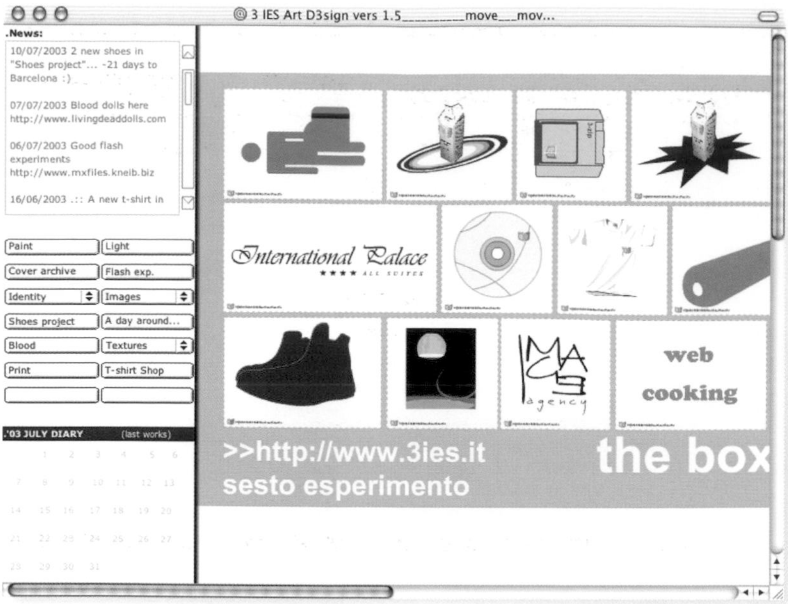

WWW.3IES.IT
D: ANDREA CUCCHI
M: TRE_IES@YAHOO.IT

WWW.MOVIFLEX.COM
D: ALBERTO GOMBAU, **C:** GUILLERMO GOMBAU
A: PROYECTO GRÁFICO, **M:** INFO@PROYECTOG.COM

WWW.FUTURA-AER.COM
D: ANTONIO FERNANDEZ-COCA
A: FERNANDEZCOCA.COM, **M:** ANTONIO@FERNANDEZCOCA.COM

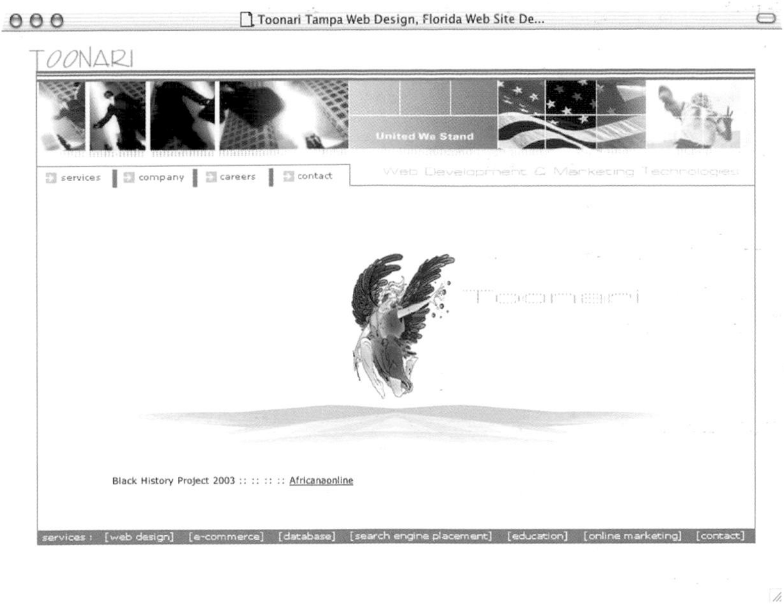

WWW.TOONARI.COM
D: SHEROL NORTHOVER, **C:** KARHRMAN ZIEGENBEIN, **P:** PAULINE NORTHOVER
A: TOONARI CORP, **M:** INFO@TOONARI.US

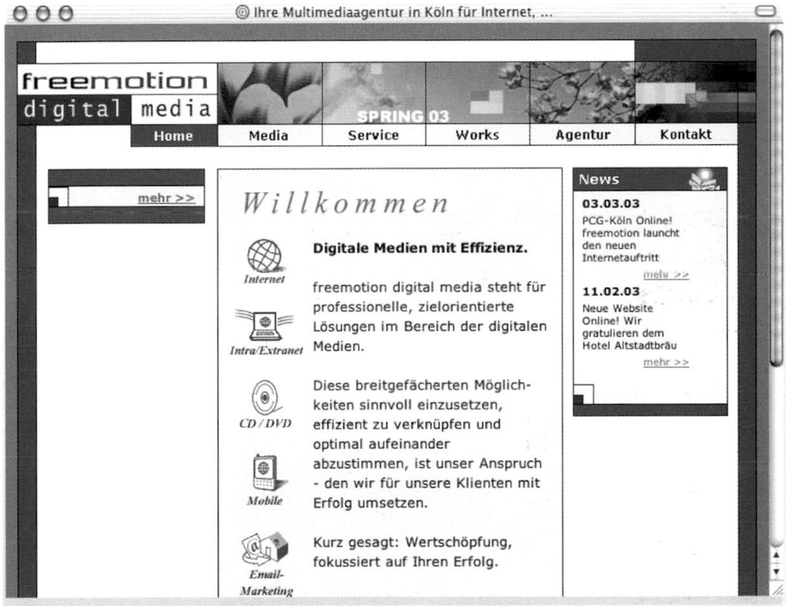

WWW.FREEMOTION.DE
D: DANIEL SCHÄFER, **C:** C.KRÖGER
A: FREEMOTION DIGITAL MEDIA, **M:** SCHAEFER@FREEMOTION.DE

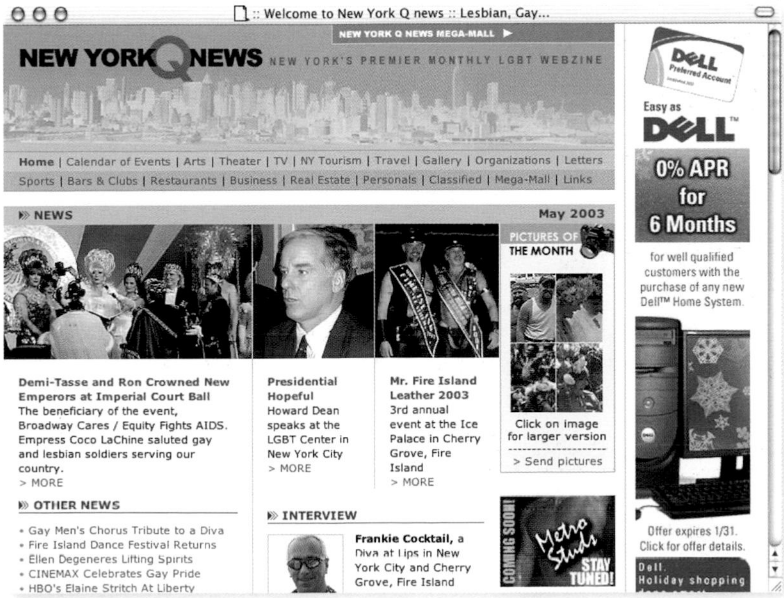

WWW.NEWYORKQNEWS.COM
D: MARCO HERRERA, **C:** CJ MINGOLELLI
A: CIRCA5859, **M:** MARCO@CIRCA5859.COM

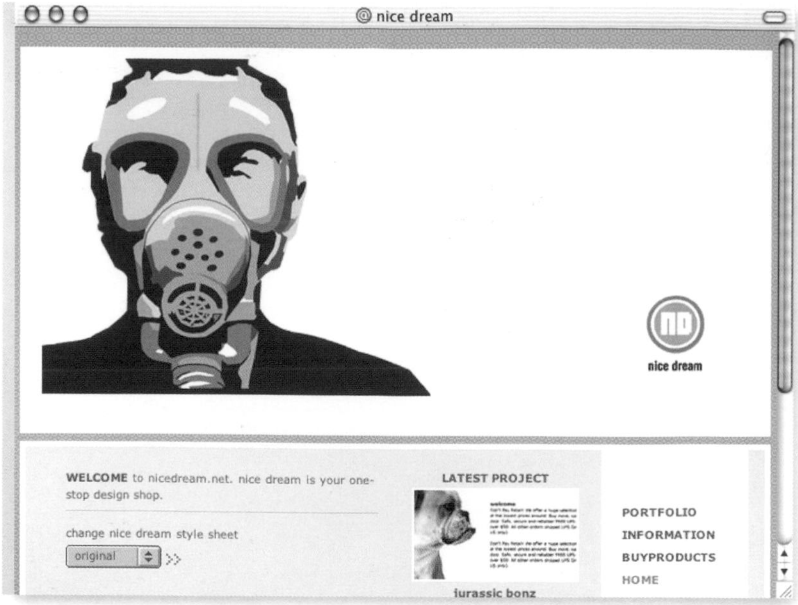

WWW.NICEDREAM.NET
A: NICE DREAM,
M: INFO@NICEDREAM.NET

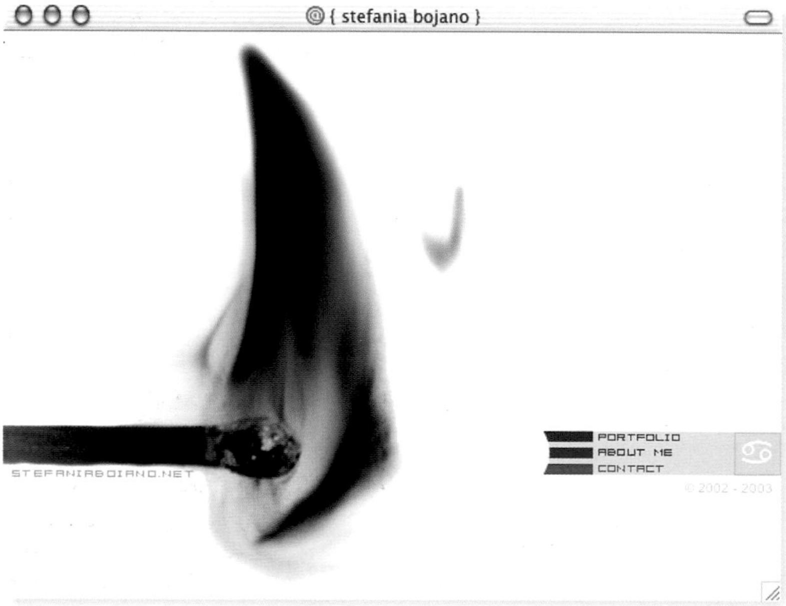

WWW.STEFANIABOJANO.NET
D: STEFANIA BOJANO
M: STEF@STEFANIABOJANO.NET

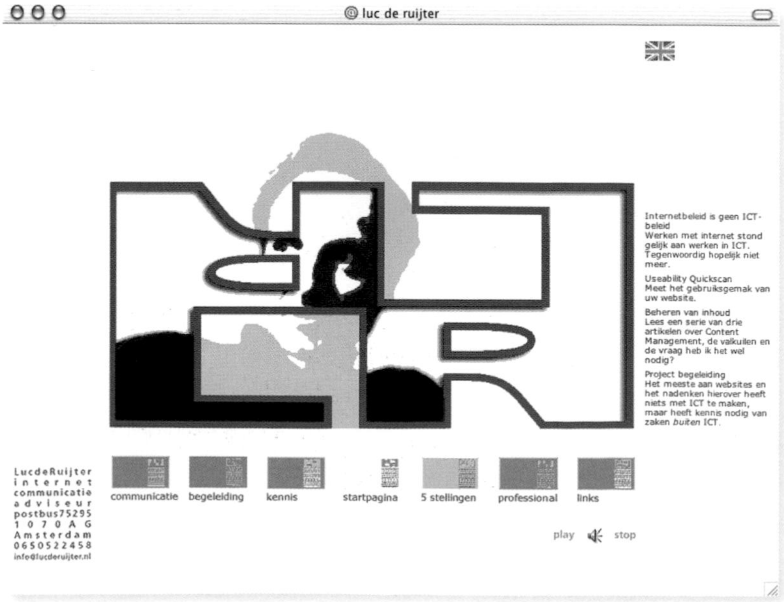

WWW.LUCDERUIJTER.NL
D: LUC DE RUIJTER
A: LUC DE RUIJTER AIC, **M:** INFO@LUCDERUIJTER.NL

WWW.PETERLINIDESIGN.IT
D: MATTEO PETERLINI DESIGN
A: MATTEO PETERLINI DESIGN, **M:** MATTEO@PETERLINIDESIGN.IT

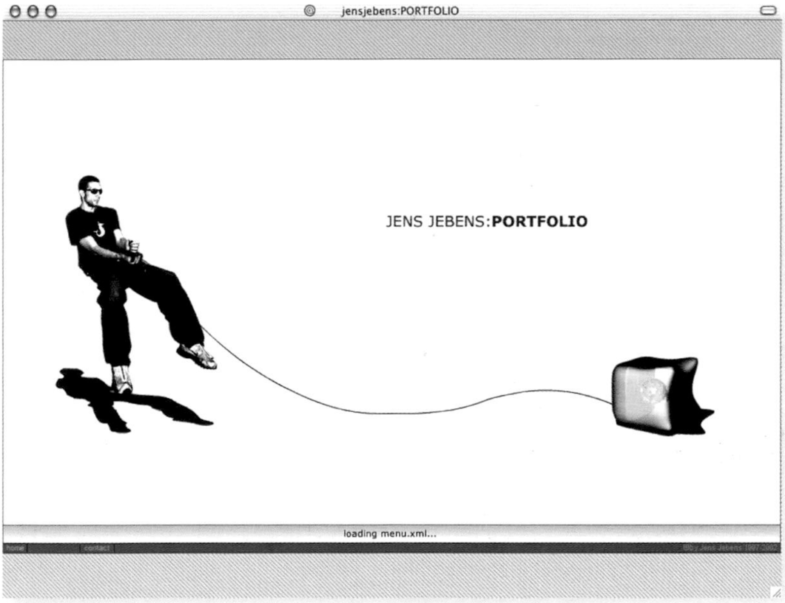

WWW.JJ80.COM
D: JENS JEBENS
A: JJ80, **M:** JJ80@JJ80.COM

WWW.CHANDENG.NET
D: DAO NGAM
M: CHAND@CHANDENG.NET

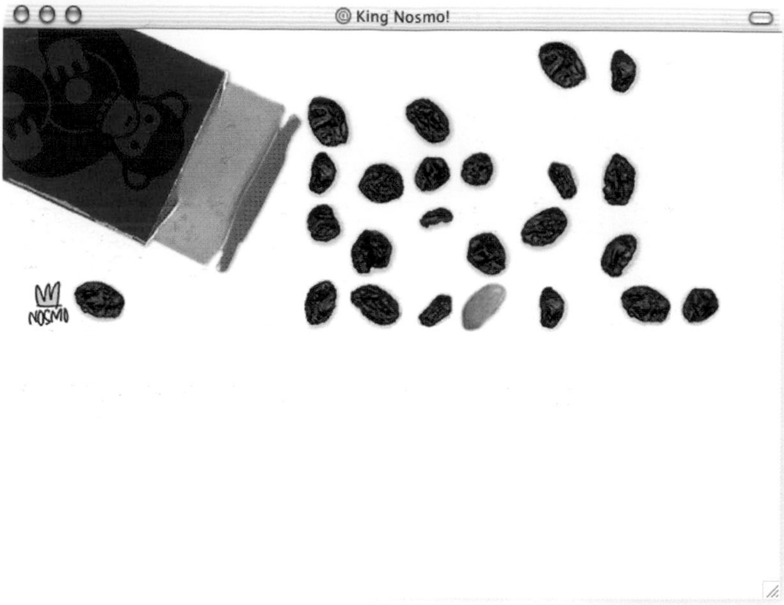

WWW.KINGNOSMO.COM
D: TOMAS DE RITA, KASPER STROMMAN
M: TOMAS@KINGNOSMO.COM

WWW.TAMTAMODE.COM/PRES.HTML
D: BASILE ANDREA, **C:** GIANFRANCO LOSANNO, **P:** TAMTAMODE
A: BASILE ADVERTISING, **M:** CONTACT@ANDREABASILE.IT

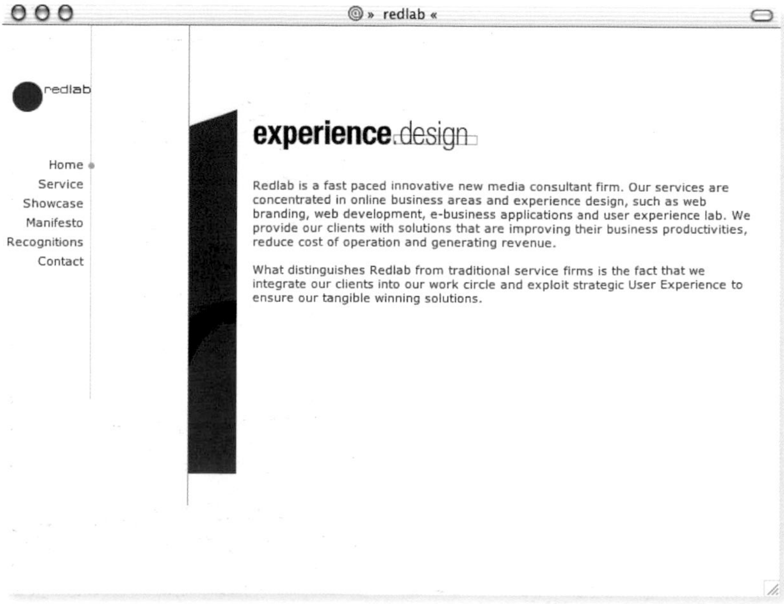

WWW.REDLAB.BIZ
D: AMORNTHEP CHIMPLEENAPANONT, **P:** SUVITA CHARANWONG
A: REDLAB CO., LTD., **M:** INFO@REDLAB.BIZ

WWW.DUNASTUDIO.COM
D: LUCA BARTOLINI
M: LUKLAB@ARUBA.IT

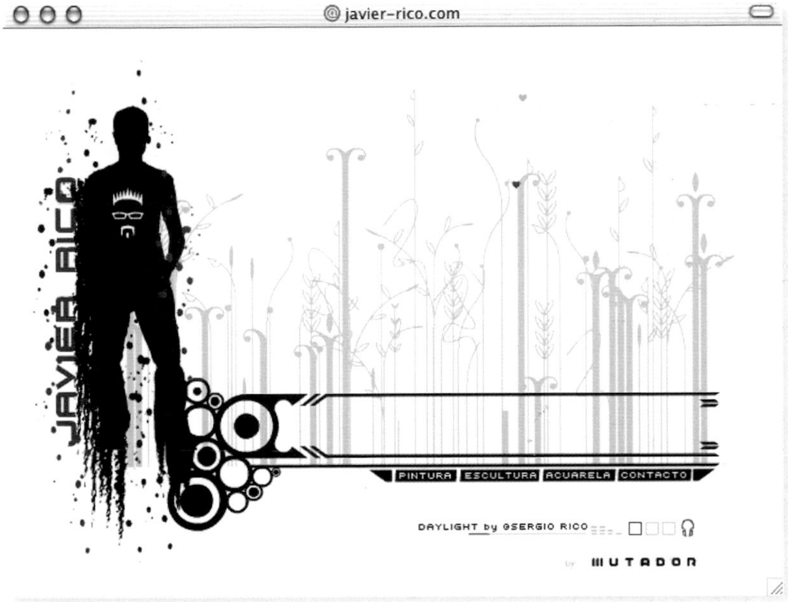

WWW.MUTADOR.COM/JAVIER_RICO
D: JAVIER RICO ASCARIZ, **C:** JAVIER RICO ASCARIZ, **P:** MUTADOR
A: MUTADOR, **M:** INFO@MUTADOR.COM

WWW.SORTED.RU
D: JASON MOORE
A: PIXELPLAYMEDIA, **M:** JASON@PIXELPLAYMEDIA.COM

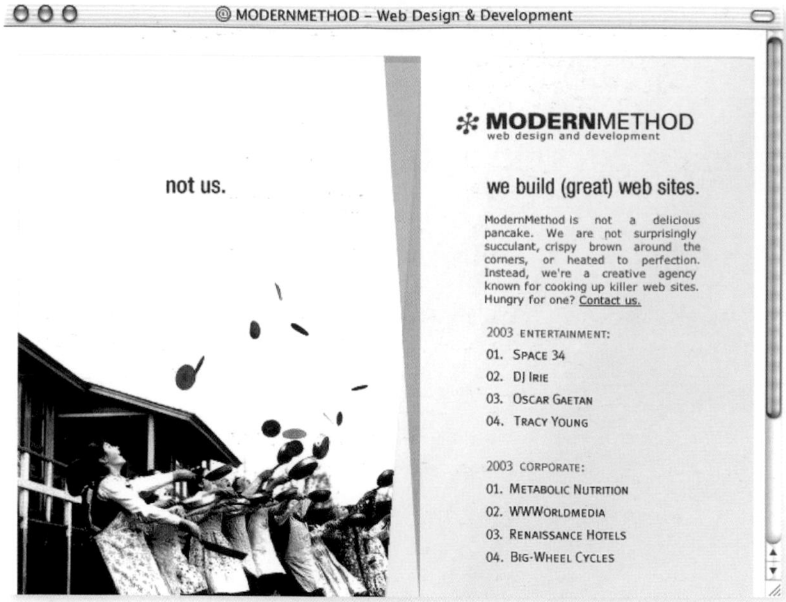

WWW.SORTED.RU
D: JASON MOORE
A: PIXELPLAYMEDIA, **M:** JASON@PIXELPLAYMEDIA.COM

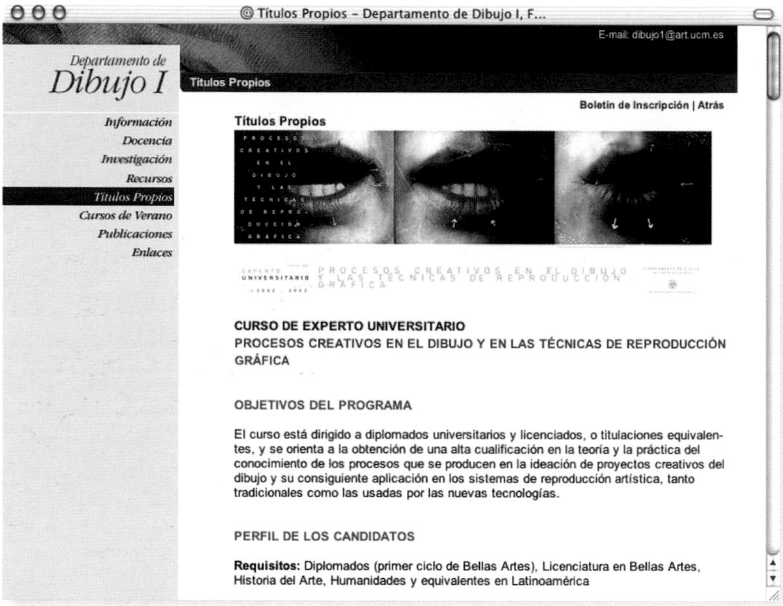

WWW.UCM.ES/INFO/DIBUJO1
D: RAÚL GÓMEZ VALVERDE
A: GOMEZVALVERDE.COM, **M:** RAUL@GOMEZVALVERDE.COM

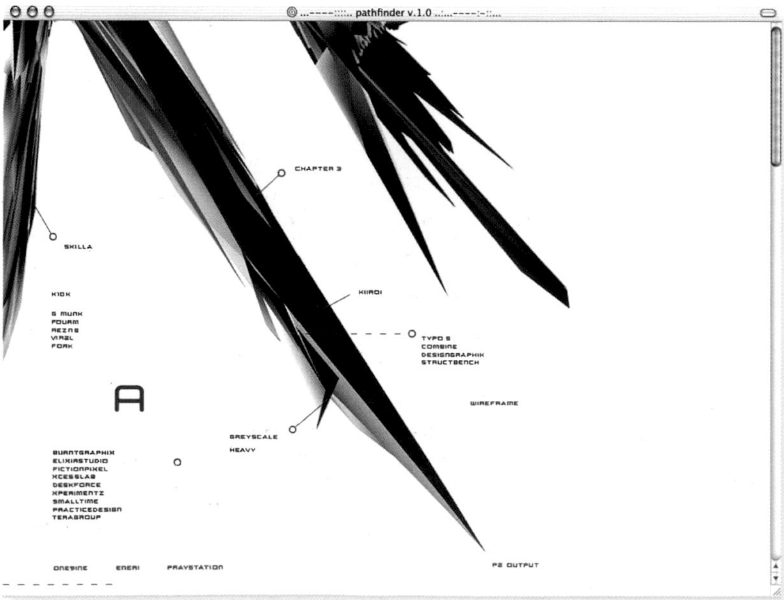

WWW.PATHFINDER.LI
D: MATTHIAS GILLE
M: MATTHIAS@XTENSIVE.DE

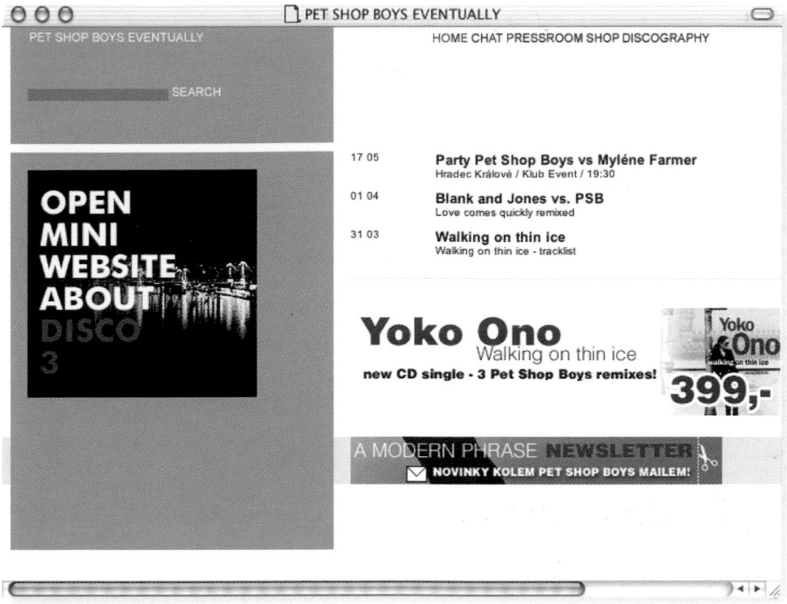

WWW.PETSHOPBOYS.CZ
D: RADEK VASICEK
M: RADEKV@YAHOO.COM

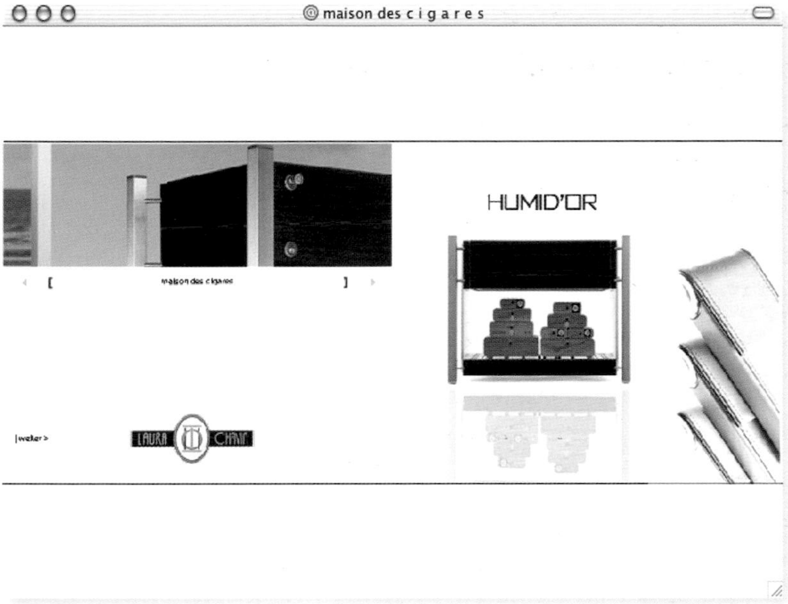

WWW.MAISON-DES-CIGARES.COM
D: HERWART KONNERTH
A: ITV2, M: MAIL@ITV2.DE

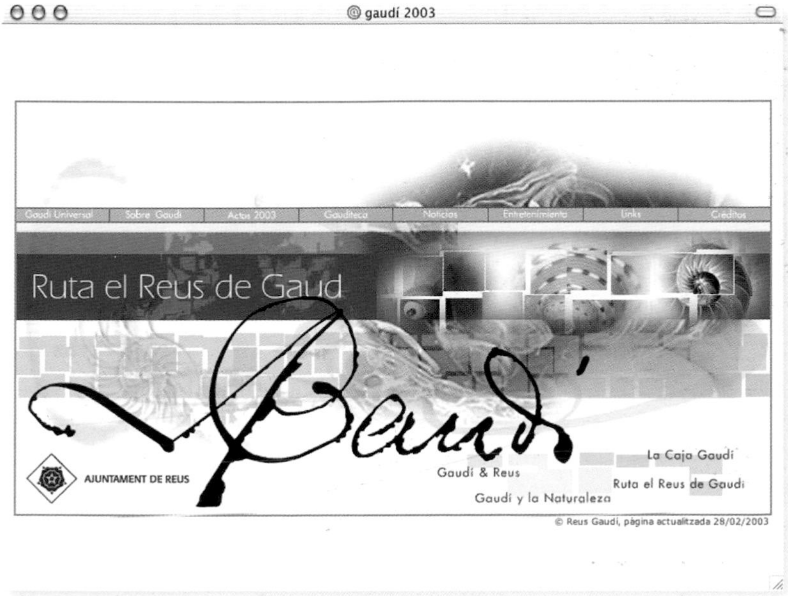

WWW.REUSGAUDI2002.ORG
D: ASIER LOPEZ CABAÑAS
A: PRAGMA AGÈNCIA DE PUBLICITAT.GENERAL, **M:** PRAGMA@PRAGMAPUBLICITAT.COM

WWW.KIRIO.IT
D: PIETRO LENA, **C:** MILO MANEO
A: KIRIO S.R.L., **M:** MILO.MANEO@KIRIO.IT

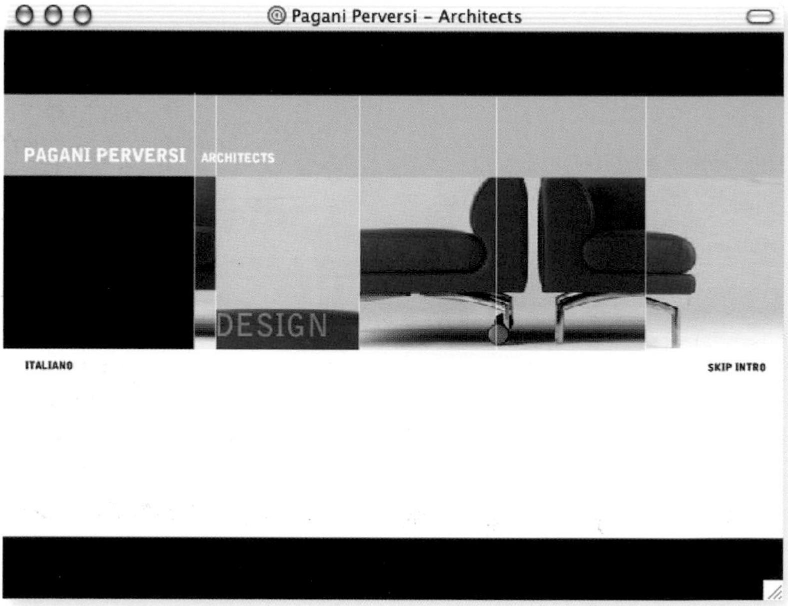

WWW.PAGANIPERVERSI.COM/HOME.HTML
D: MONICA FACCIO, **C:** DIREWEB, **P:** PAGANI E PERVERSI ARCHITETTI ASSOCIATI
A: DESIGNWORK, **M:** MONICA@DESIGNWORK.IT

WWW.RVMPOST.COM
D: TJERJA GEERTS
A: ESENCIA IDENTITY DESIGN, **M:** TG@ESENCIADESIGN.COM

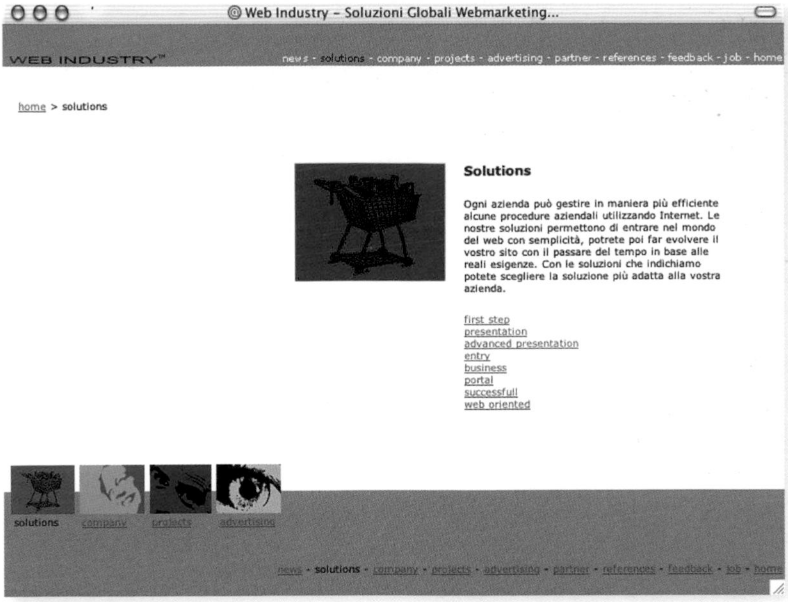

WWW.WEBINDUSTRY.IT
D: ALESSANDRO RUBINI, **C:** NICOLA CRAPIS, **P:** WEB INDUSTRY
A: WEB INDUSTRY SRL, **M:** ALESSANDRO@WEBINDUSTRY.IT

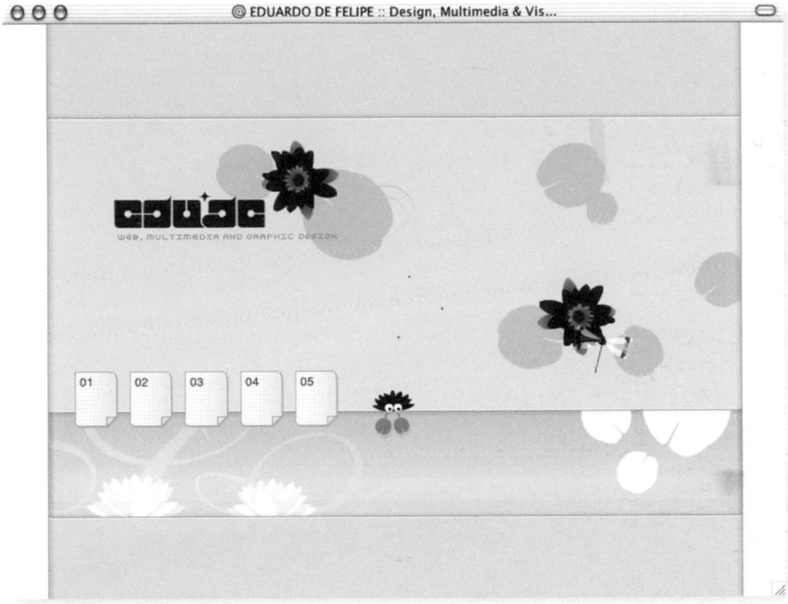

WWW.ELELEC.COM
D: EDUARDO DE FELIPE, **C:** LUIS MARTÍNEZ
A: ELEC, **M:** EDUARDO@ELELEC.COM

WWW.ORISBORSE.IT/INDEX3.HTML
D: ALFREDO ESPOSITO, **C:** MARCO POLLICE, **P:** CIRO VECCHIARINI
A: KOINE ARTE & COMUNICAZIONE, **M:** EXXPO@LIBERO.IT

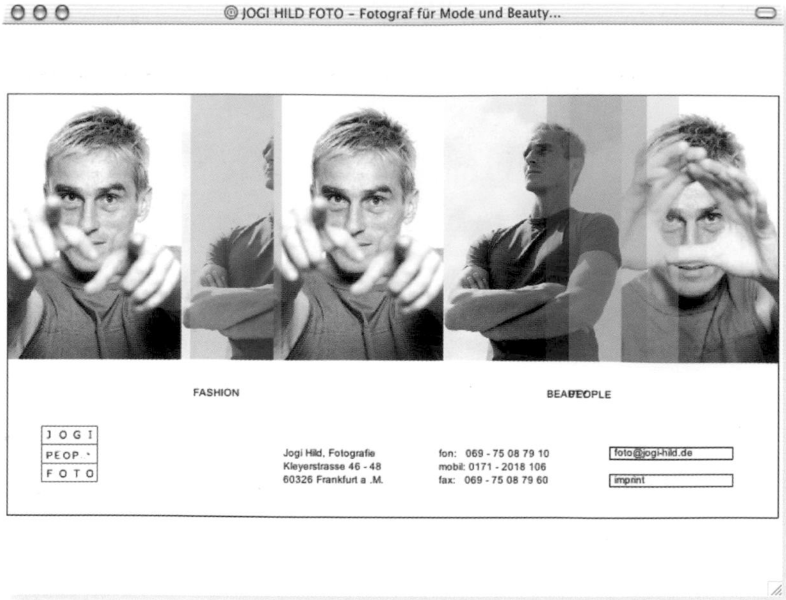

WWW.JOGI-HILD.DE
D: GABI UND CARL MÜLLER, **C:** SÖNKE KNÖFLER, **P:** SÖNKE KNÖFLER
A: MODERNE REKLAME, **M:** SKNOEFLER@KNOEFLER.COM

WWW.GABLUE.COM.MY
D: HENRY YAP
M: YEVAJO@HOTMAIL.COM

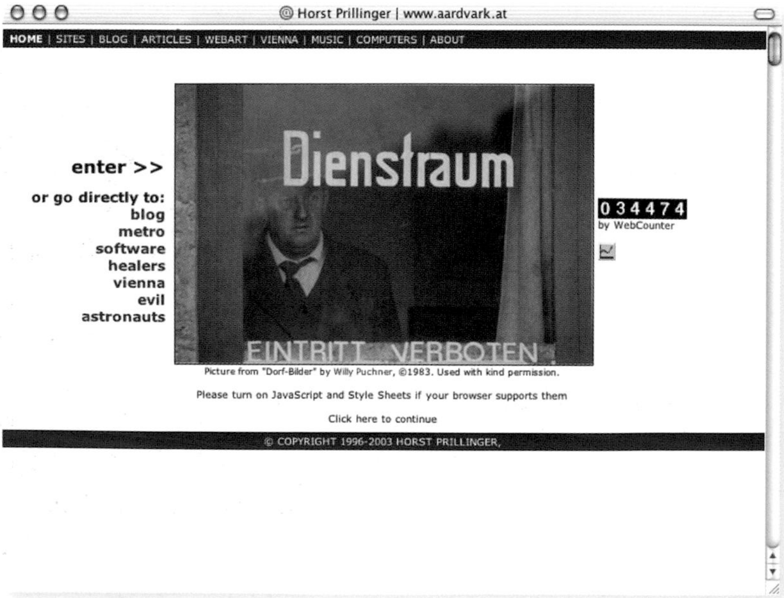

WWW.AARDVARK.AT
D: HORST PRILLINGER
M: HORSTP@MAC.COM

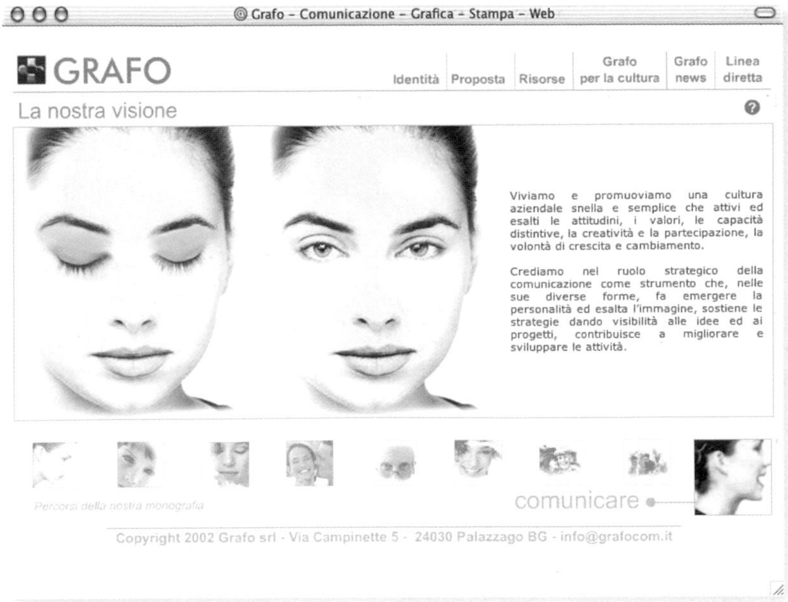

WWW.GRAFOCOM.IT
D: MASSIMILIANO ROSSI
A: GRAFO, **M:** WEB@GRAFOCOM.IT

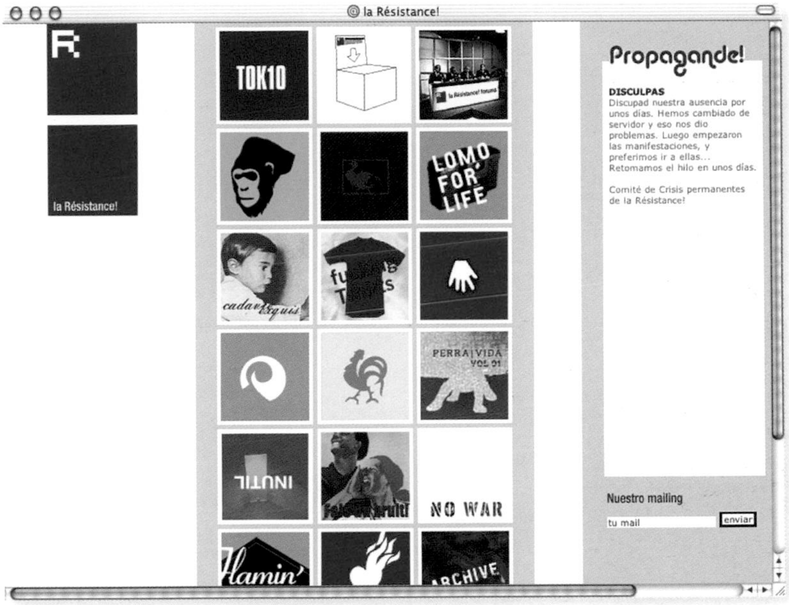

WWW.RESISTANTS.ORG
D: OTTODIETRICH, **C:** PIERRE PARTOUZE, **P:** PIERRE PARTOUZE
A: OTTODIETRICH, **M:** OTTODIETRICH@RESISTANTS.ORG

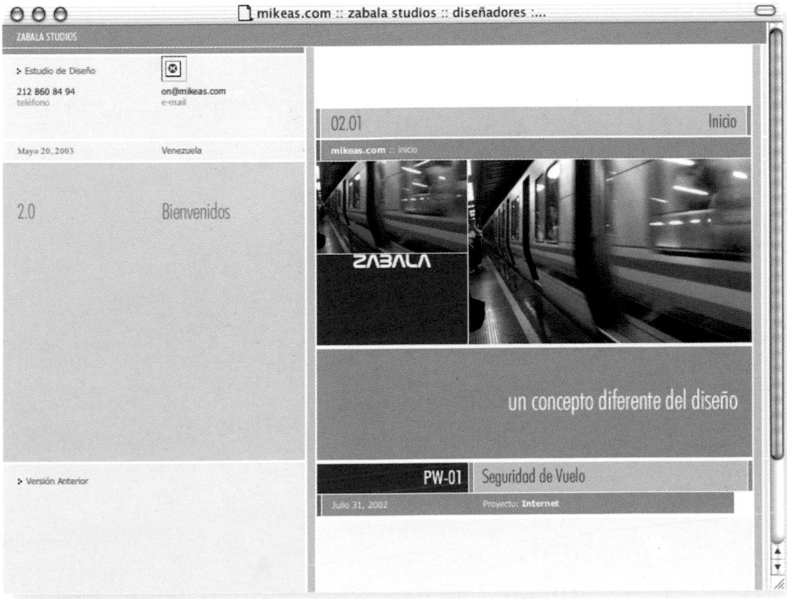

WWW.ZABALASTUDIOS.COM
D: MIGUEL ANGEL ZABALA
M: INFO@ZABALASTUDIOS.COM

WWW.PLAYING-ARTS.DE
D: HARRY HAUBER, HEINZ GRASMUECK, **C:** HAUBER, GRASMUECK, **P:** CHRISTOPH RIEMER
A: DTVR, **M:** HAUBER@DTVR.DE

WWW.TYPOGESTALTER.CH
D: URS BUESSER
A: T TYPOGRAFISCHE GESTALTUNG, **M:** TYPO@TYPOGESTALTER.CH

WWW.MAIALANDIA.COM
D: ANA GRANJA
A: PCW, **M:** PAULA.GRANJA@LABOLIMS.COM

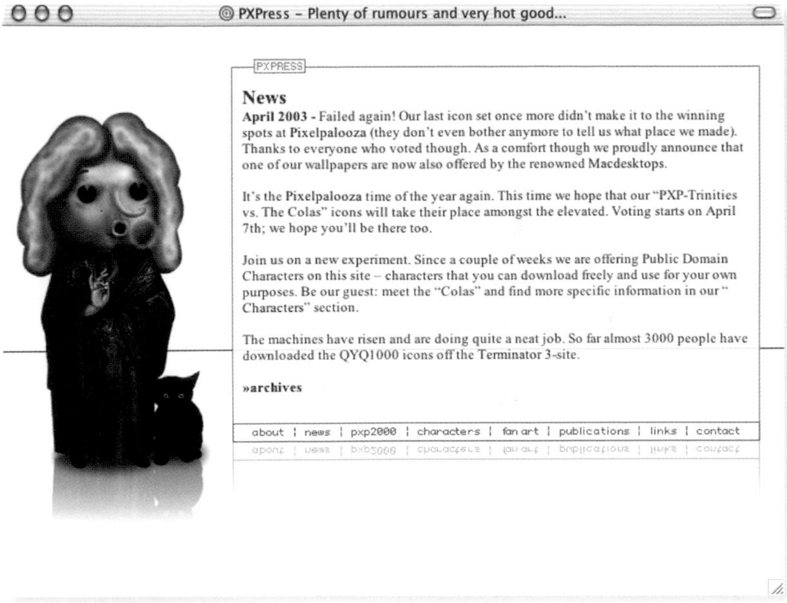

@ PXPress - Plenty of rumours and very hot good...
PXPRESS
News
April 2003 - Failed again! Our last icon set once more didn't make it to the winning spots at Pixelpalooza (they don't even bother anymore to tell us what place we made). Thanks to everyone who voted though. As a comfort though we proudly announce that one of our wallpapers are now also offered by the renowned Macdesktops.
It's the Pixelpalooza time of the year again. This time we hope that our "PXP-Trinities vs. The Colas" icons will take their place amongst the elevated. Voting starts on April 7th; we hope you'll be there too.
Join us on a new experiment. Since a couple of weeks we are offering Public Domain Characters on this site – characters that you can download freely and use for your own purposes. Be our guest: meet the "Colas" and find more specific information in our " Characters" section.
The machines have risen and are doing quite a neat job. So far almost 3000 people have downloaded the QYQ1000 icons off the Terminator 3-site.
»archives
about | news | pxp2000 | characters | fan art | publications | links | contact

WWW.PXPRESS.COM
D: HEIKO KIENDL-MÜLLER
A: PXPRESS, **M:** HM@PXPRESS.COM

WWW.KMSTUDIO.IT
D: FEDERICO MANCINI, **C:** ALESSANDRO BALASCO, **P:** FRANCESCO KURHAJEC
A: KMSTUDIO, **M:** FEDERICO@KMSTUDIO.IT

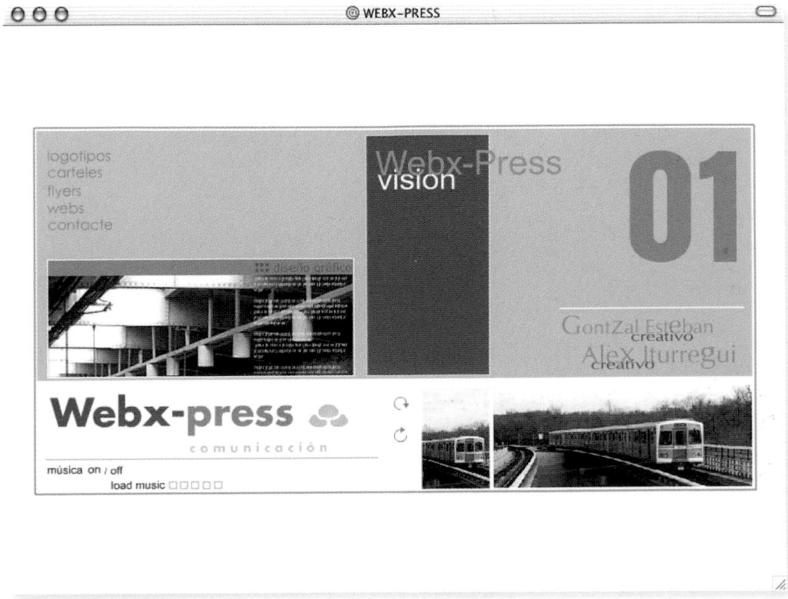

WWW.WEBX-PRESS.NET
D: GONZALO ESTEBAN
A: WEBX-PRESS, **M:** WEBX-PRESS@WANADOO.ES

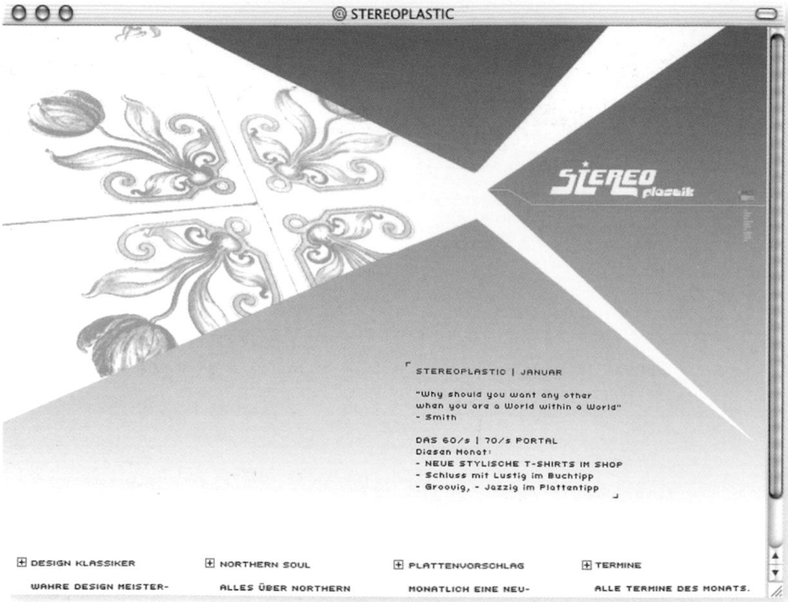

WWW.STEREOPLASTIC.COM
D: OTTO MIKE JOHN
A: MOD73 | URBAN INFLUENCED MEDIA ||, **M:** MOTTO@MOD73.COM

WWW.SINAPSISPROJECTS.COM
D: RAFAEL LEÓN DEL RÍO & PATRICIA FUENTES JAVATO, **C:** RAFAEL LEÓN DEL RÍO
A: SINAPSIS PROJECTS, **M:** RAFAEL@SINAPSISPROJECTS.COM

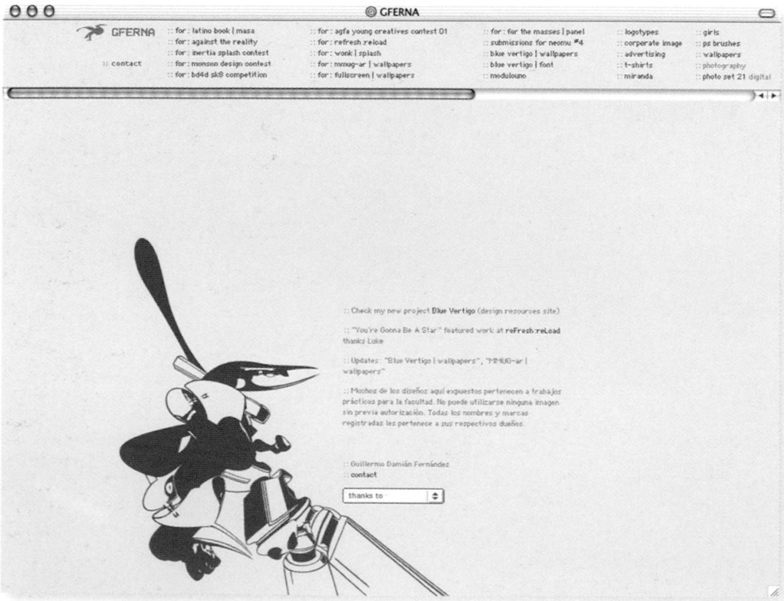

WWW.GFERNA.COM.AR
D: GUILLERMO DAMIÁN FERNÁNDEZ
A: GFERNA, **M:** GFERNA91@CIUDAD.COM.AR

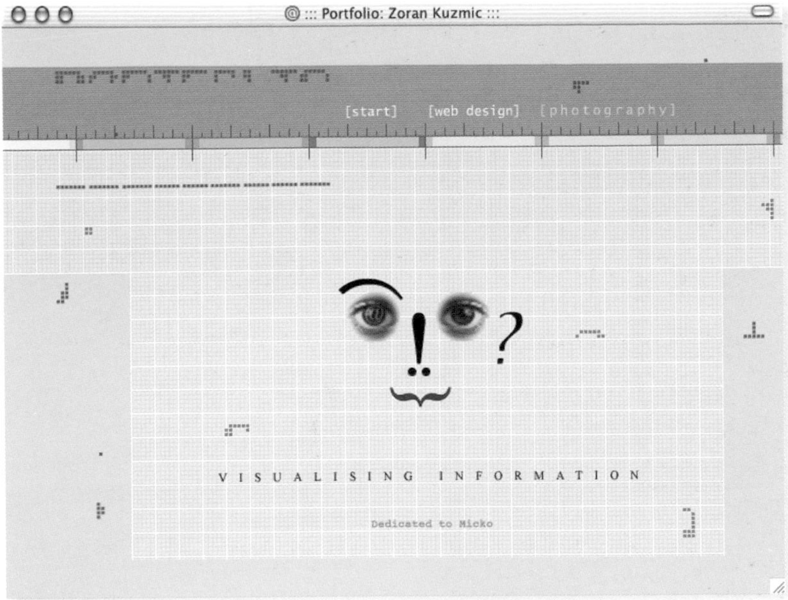

WWW.ZORANPLANET.COM
D: ZORAN KUZMIC
M: ZORAN_K@HOTMAIL.COM

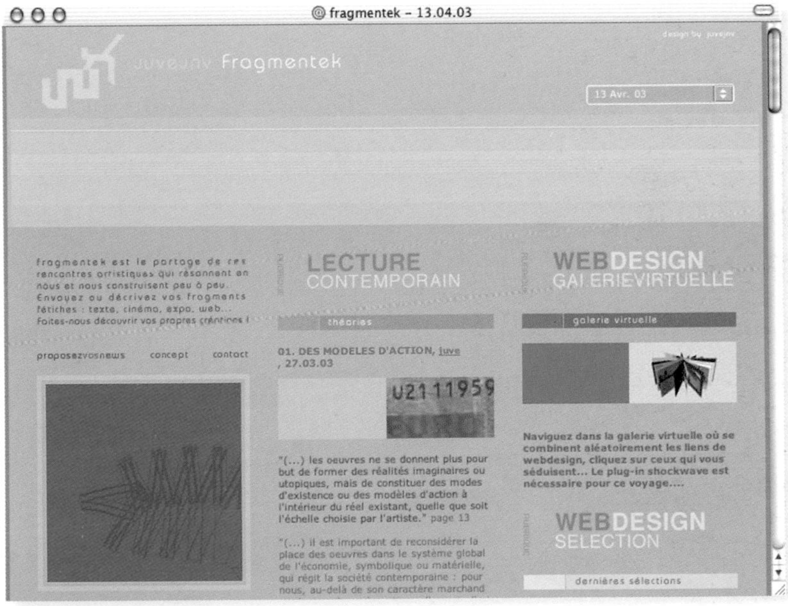

WWW.FRAGMENTEK.NET
D: JULIETTE NICOLAS-VULLIERME , **C:** LEMONDE BENOIT ET ACHARD LAURENT
M: JUVEJNV@FREE.FR

WWW.CRON-TSP.COM
D: ALVARO CALDERA VALENCIA, **C:** JORDI NIETO , **P:** ALVARO CALDERA VALENCIA
M: ACALDERA@CRON.CL

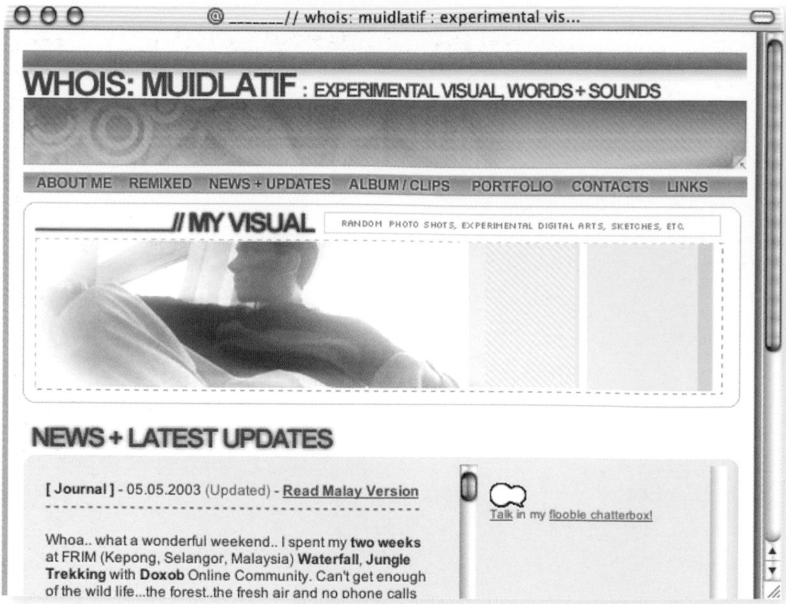

WWW.MUIDLATIF.COM
D: MUID LATIF
M: MUID@LYCOS.COM

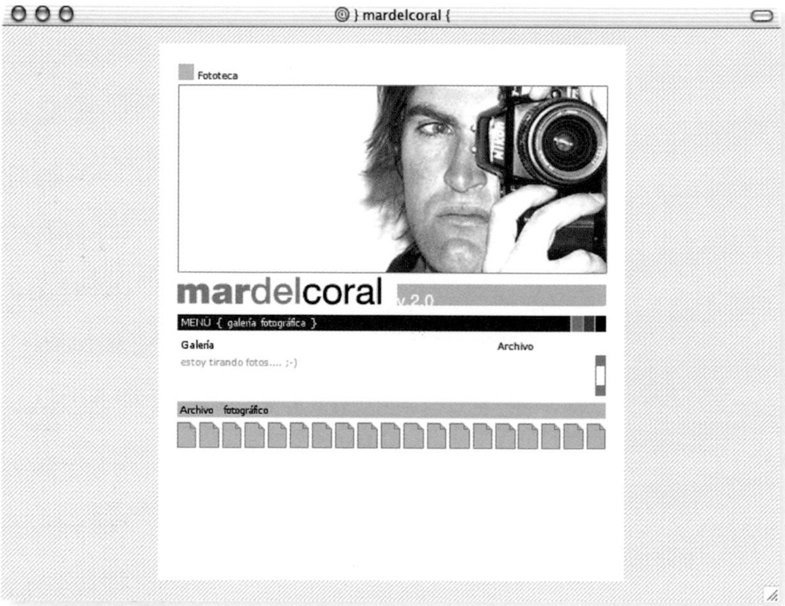

WWW.MARDELCORAL.COM
D: DANI MARTÍ PERNIN
M: DANI@MARDELCORAL.COM

WWW.SILBERMILCH.COM
D: ALEXANDER BRAUN
A: SILBERMILCH*, **M:** SILBER@SILBERMILCH.COM

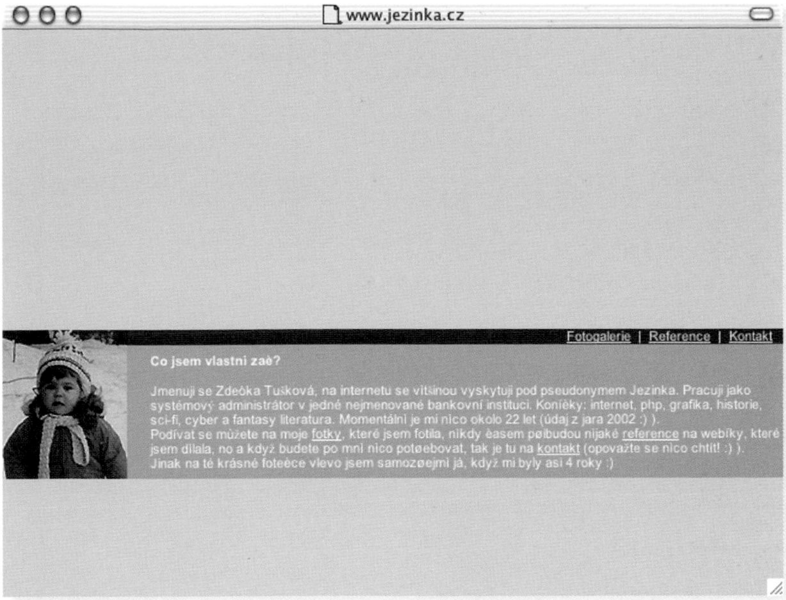

WWW.JEZINKA.CZ
D: JEZINKA
M: JEZINKA@JEZINKA.CZ

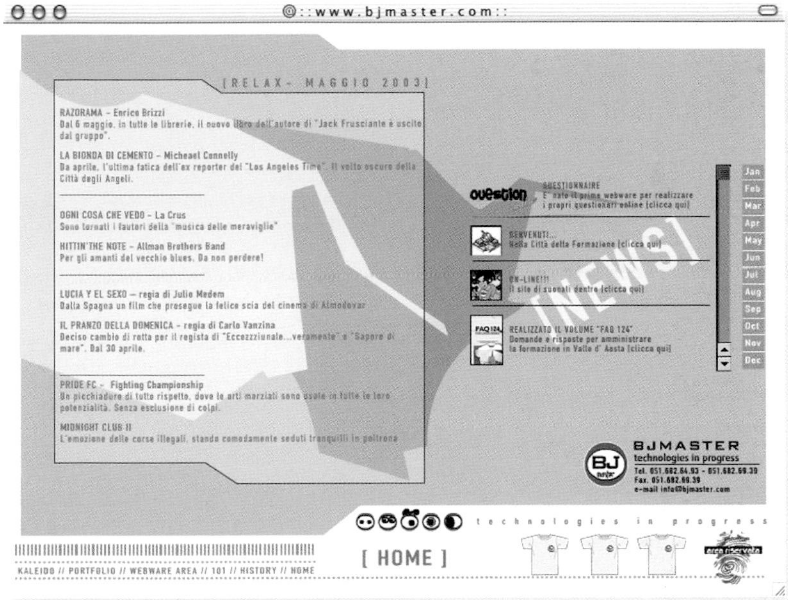

WWW.BJMASTER.COM
D: SARA GOVONI, **C:** GABRIELE BONGIOVANNI, **P:** GIUSEPPE OTTANI
A: BJMASTER, **M:** SARA@BJMASTER.COM

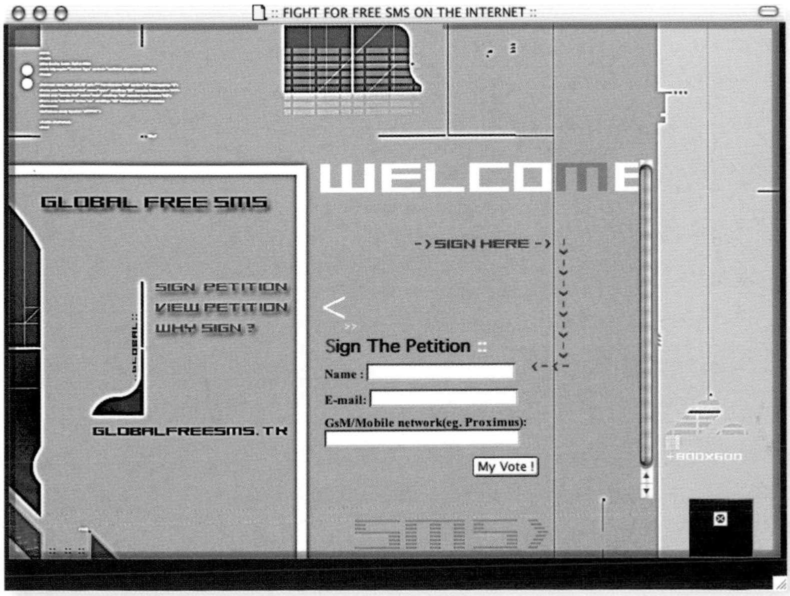

WWW.GLOBALFREESMS.TK
D: TIM VERHEES
M: JUNKCHASER@HOTMAIL.COM

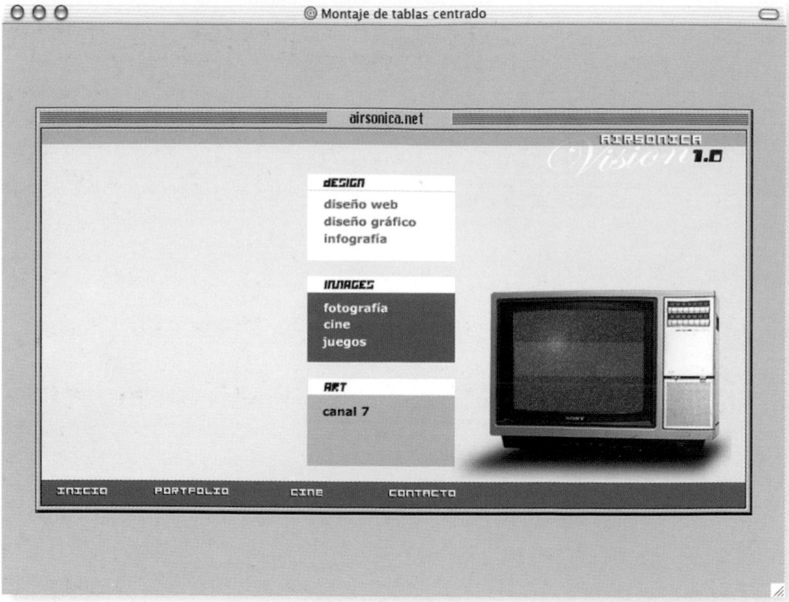

WWW.AIRSONICA.NET
D: JUAN ALONSO LOPEZ INIESTA
A: AIRSONICA.NET, **M:** ARTE@AIRSONICA.NET

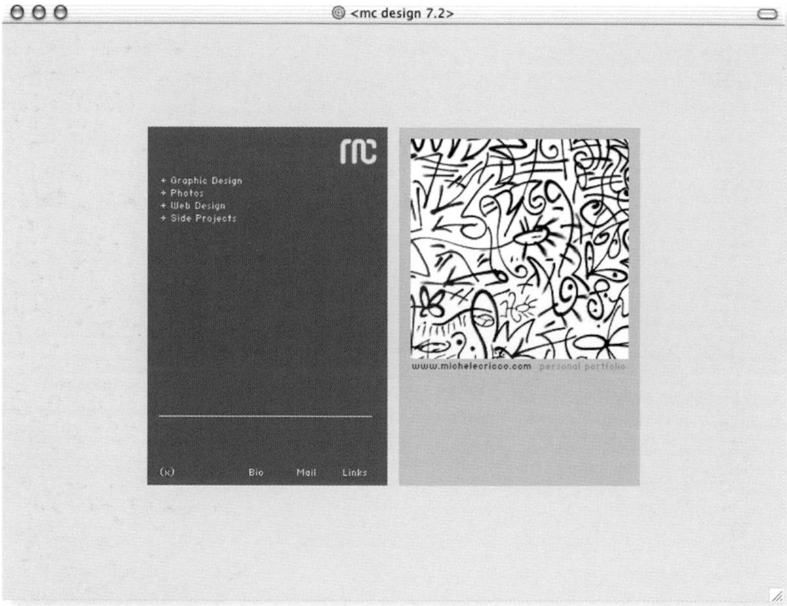

WWW.MICHELECRICCO.COM
D: MICHELE CRICCO
M: MIKIJESTER@YAHOO.COM

WWW.STUDIOMODACAPELLI.IT
D: ALESSANDRO RUBINI
A: WEB INDUSTRY SRL, **M:** ALESSANDRO@WEBINDUSTRY.IT

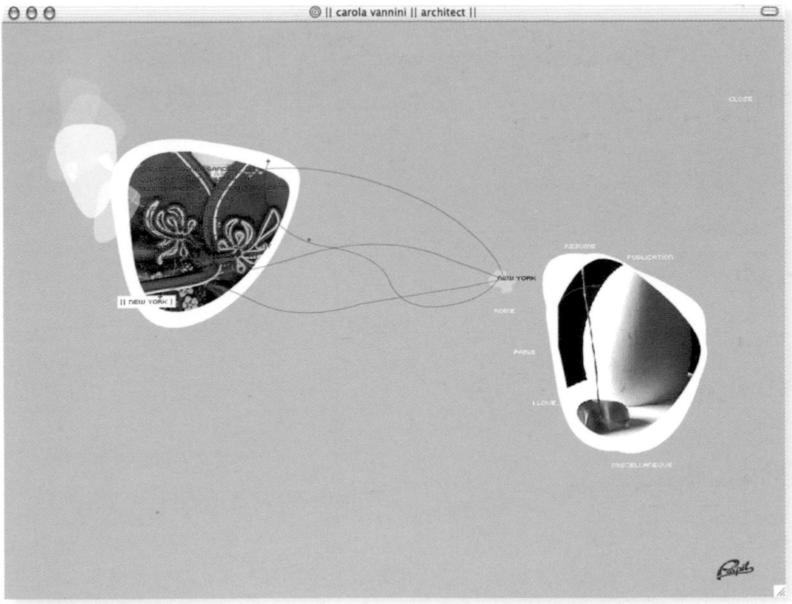

WWW.CAROLAVANNINI.COM
D: STEFANO PEDRETTI
A: PULPIT, **M:** PEDRO@PULPIT.IT

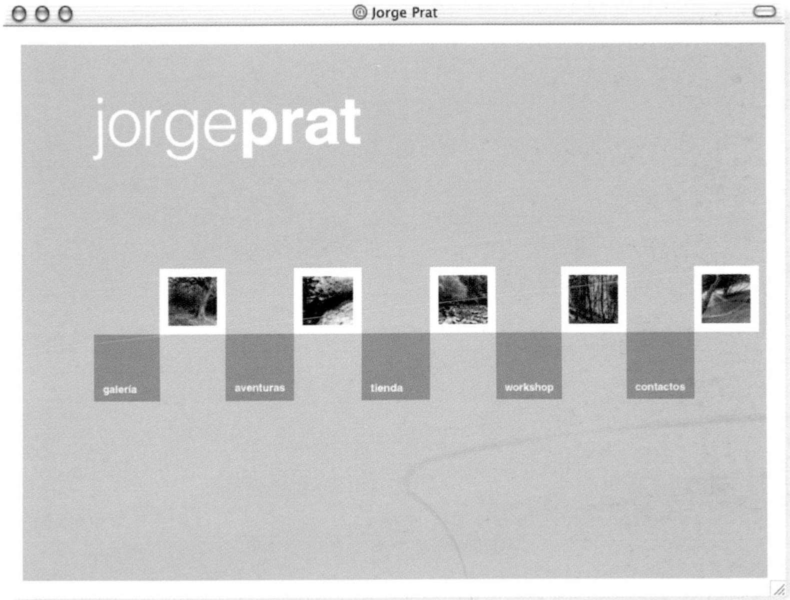

WWW.JORGEPRAT.CL
D: OVO LTDA.
A: OVO LTDA., **M:** OVO@OVO.CL

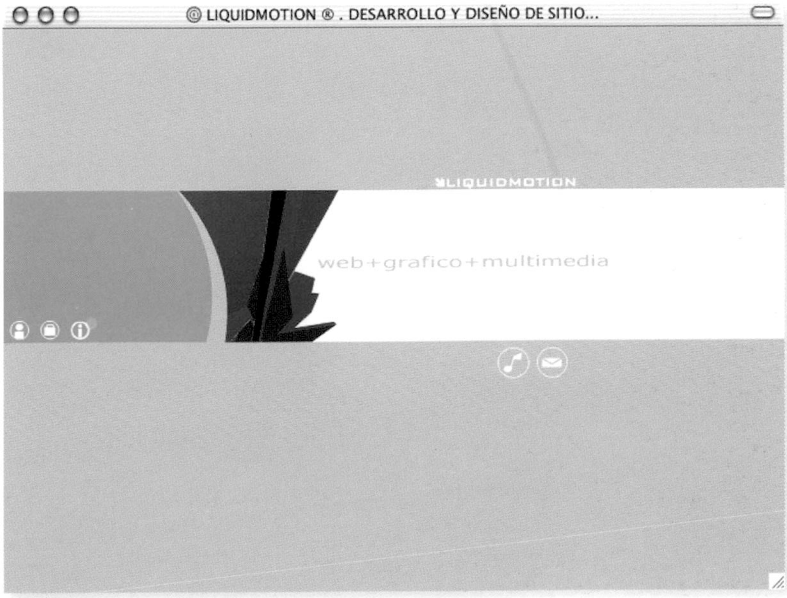

WWW.LMOTION.COM
D: LUIS ZUNO
A: LIQUIDMOTION, **M:** LUIS.ZUNO@LMOTION.COM.MX

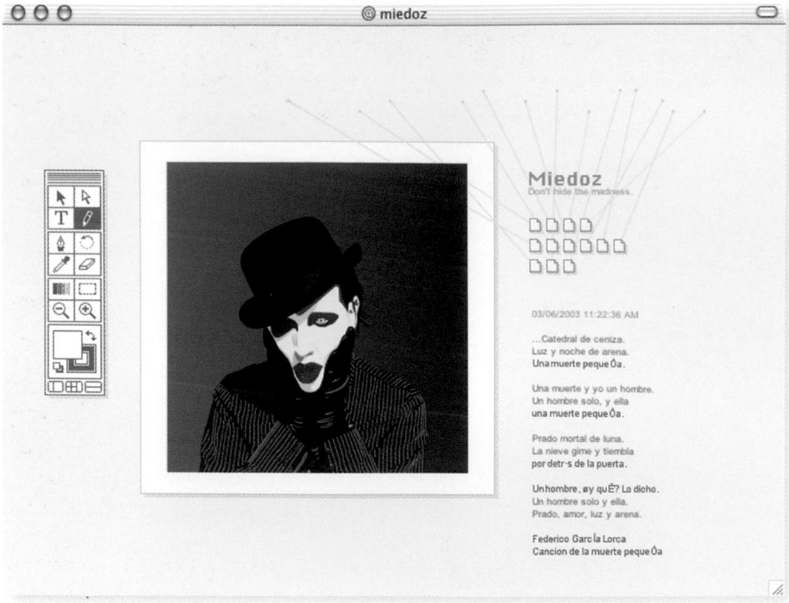

WWW.MIEDOZ.COM
D: MIEDOZ
M: INFO@MIEDOZ.COM

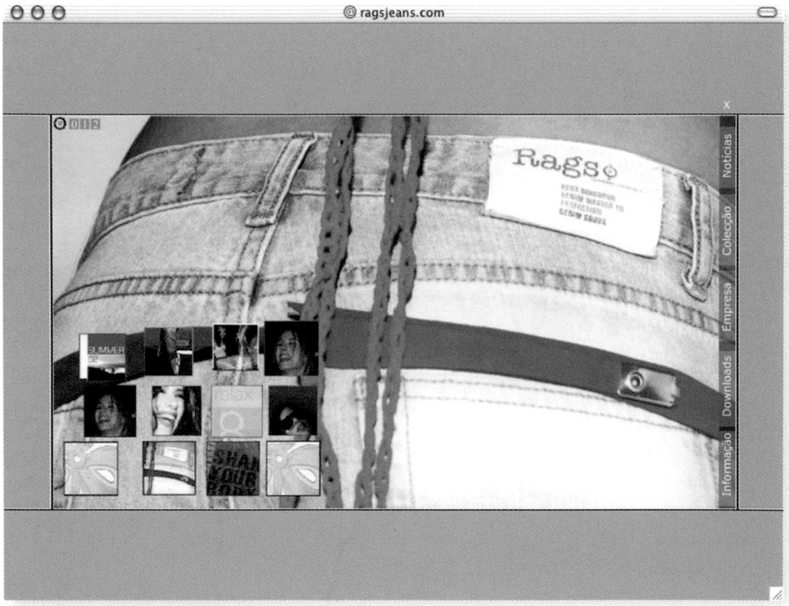

WWW.RAGSJEANS.COM
D: MIGUEL VAZ
A: PAGONGSKI.COM, **M:** ME@PAGONGSKI.COM

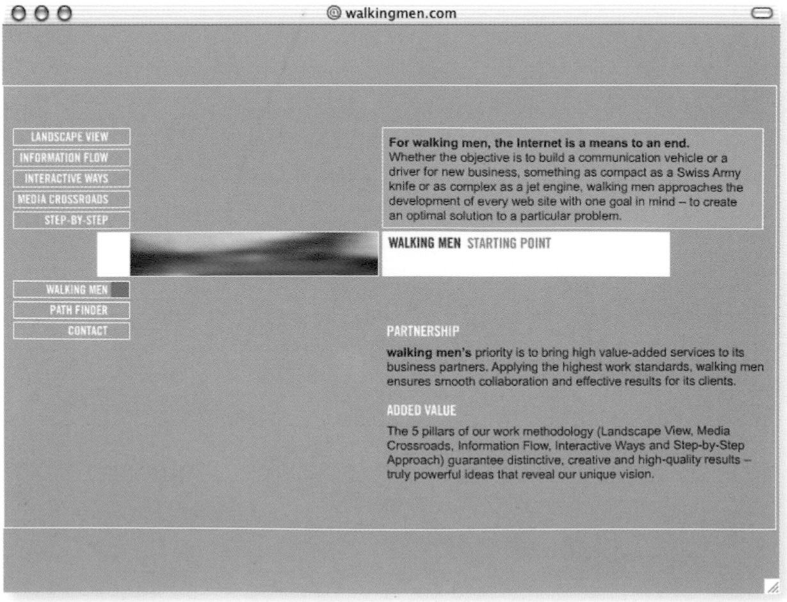

WWW.WALKINGMEN.COM
D: NICOLAS GLINOER
A: WALKING MEN, **M:** N@WALKINGMEN.COM

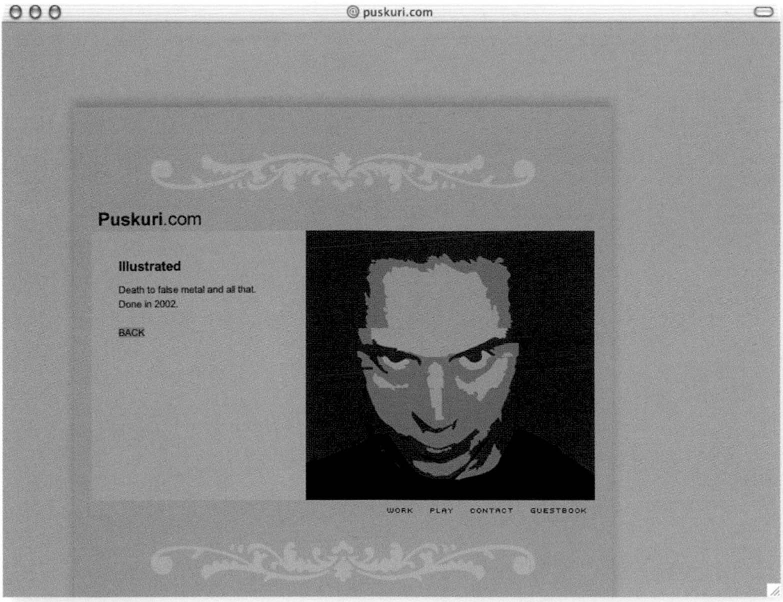

WWW.PUSKURI.COM
D: NIKO KAURANEN
M: NIKO@PUSKURI.COM

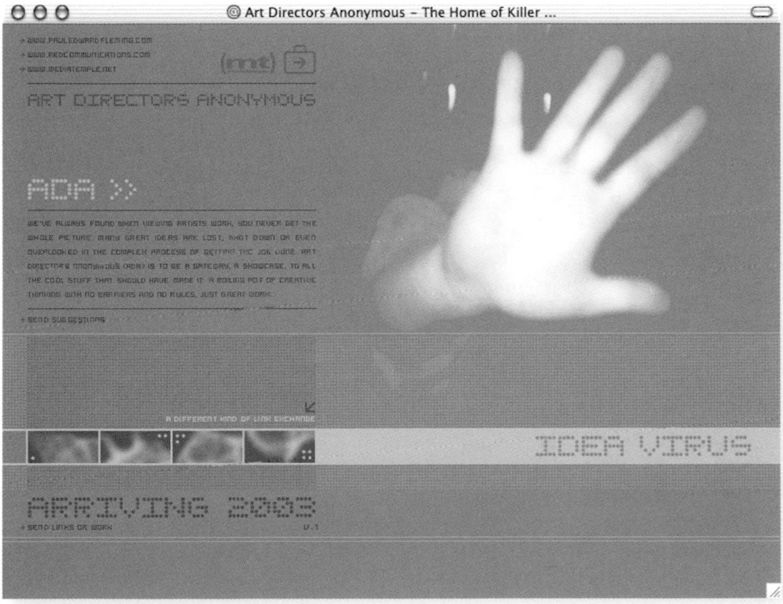

WWW.ARTDIRECTORSANONYMOUS.COM
D: ART DIRECTORS ANONYMOUS, **C:** PAUL FLEMING, **P:** PAUL FLEMING
A: RED COMMUNICATIONS, **M:** PAUL@REDCOMMUNICATIONS.COM

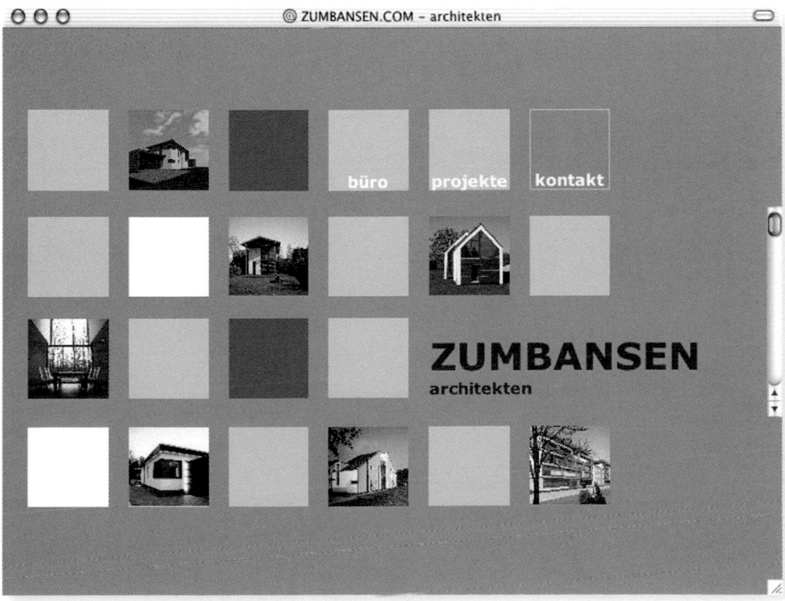

WWW.ZUMBANSEN.COM
D: HANNO DENKER, **C:** MARK LEEWE, **P:** WERK01
A: WERK01.DE, **M:** HANNO@WERK01.DE

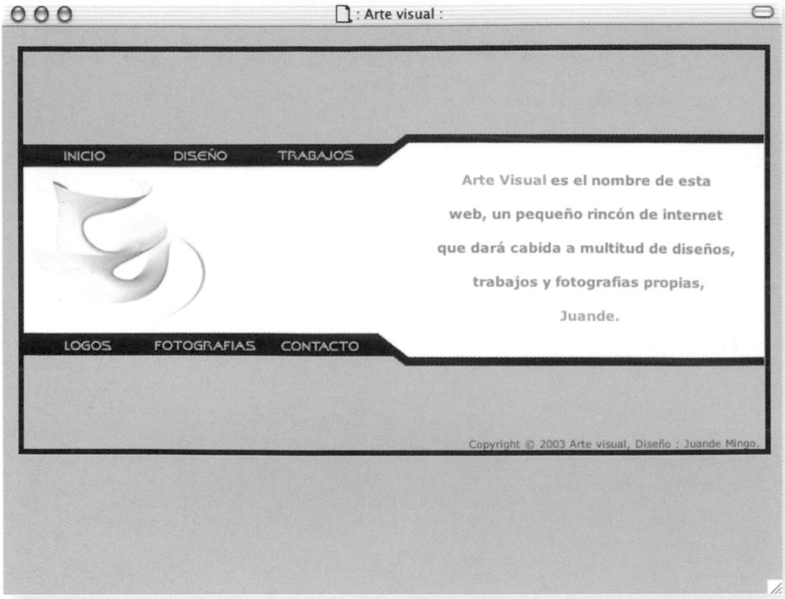

WWW.ARTEVISUAL.TK
D: JUANDE MINGO GONZALEZ
A: ARTE VISUAL, **M:** JUANDE1980@YAHOO.ES

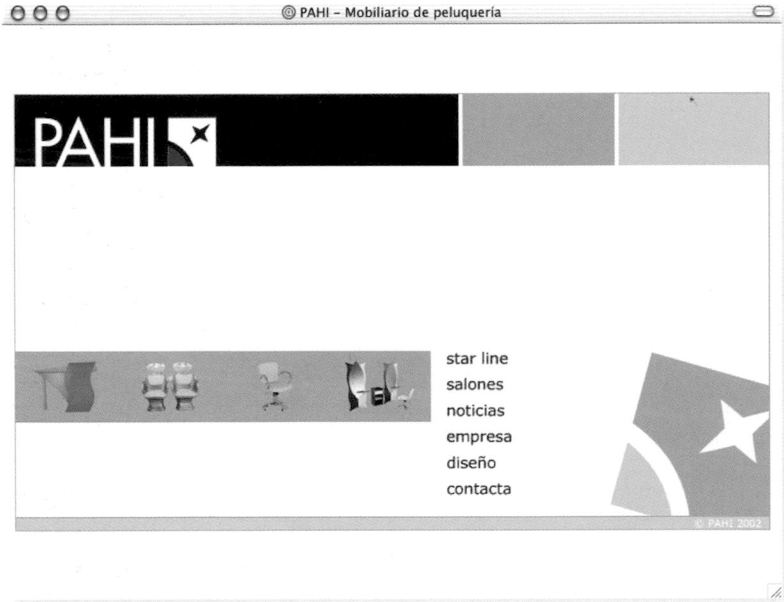

WWW.PAHI.COM
D: PAU MORENO MARTÍN
M: PAU@PATATABRAVA.COM

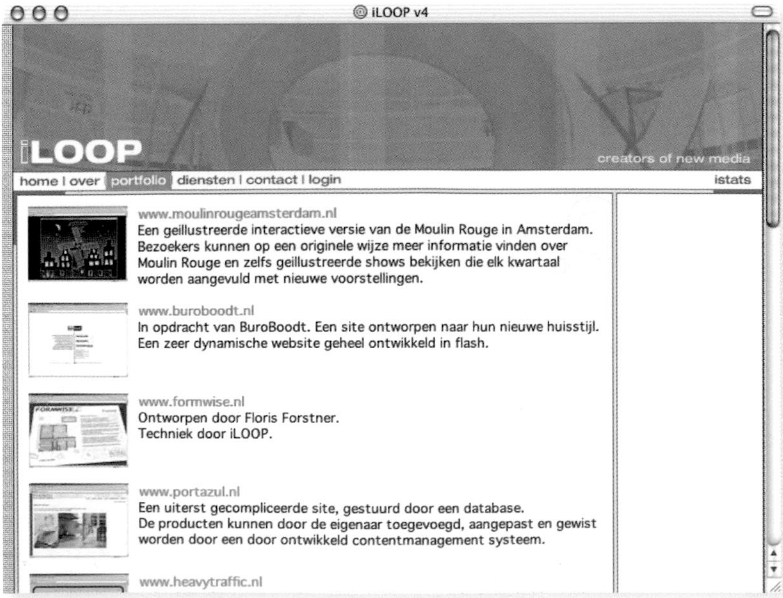

WWW.ILOOP.NL
D: DRIES DUIVES, **C:** NIELS BURGHARD, **P:** ILOOP
A: ILOOP, **M:** INFO@ILOOP.NL

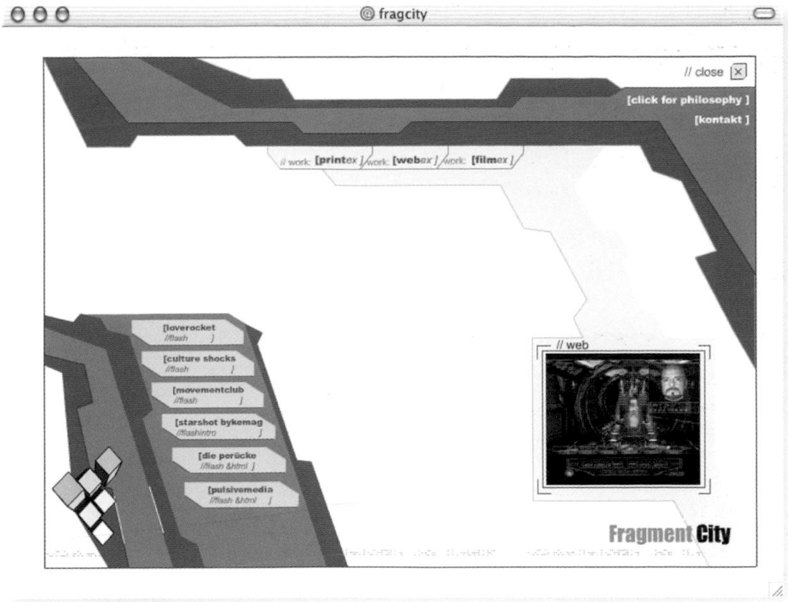

WWW.FRAGMENTCITY.DE
D: MARC FEHSE, **C:** FRAG-CITY-WORKERS, **P:** MARC FEHSE
A: DAS FRAGMENT, **M:** RAFFA_DE@YAHOO.DE

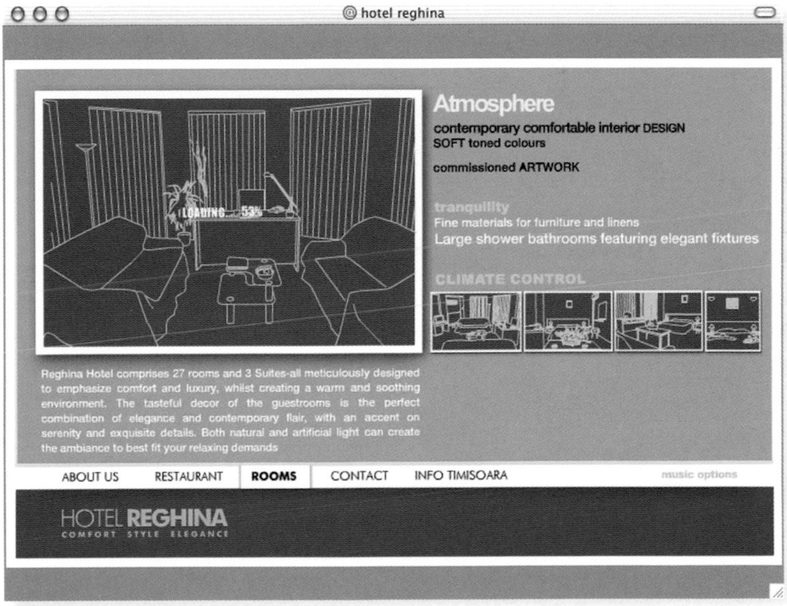

WWW.HOTEL-REGHINA.RO
D: VLAD ARDELEANU, **C:** VLAD ARDELEANU, **P:** OVIDIU HRIN
A: SYNOPSYS MEDIA, **M:** TUTSILVIA@XNET.RO

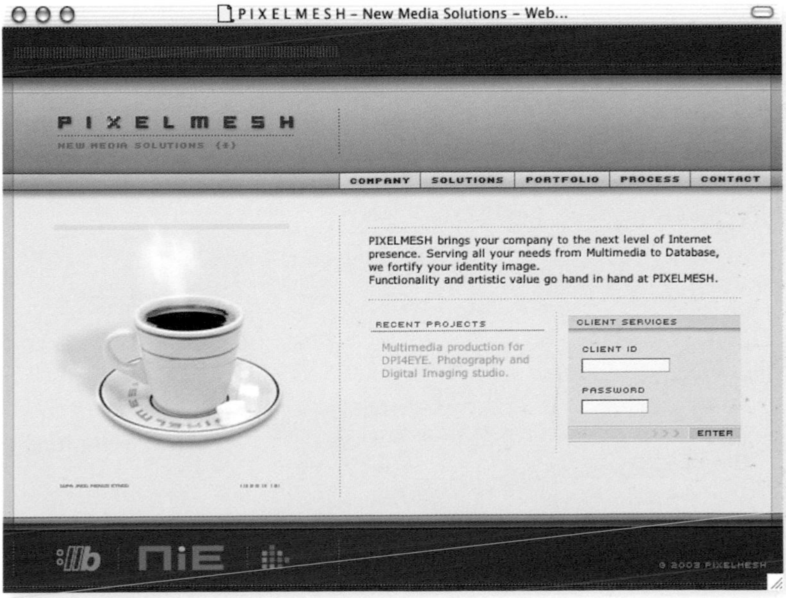

WWW.PIXELMESH.COM
D: JAREK STARENDA, **C:** RALPH BIELOBRADEK, **P:** JAREK STARENDA
A: PIXELMESH, **M:** JSTAR@PIXELMESH.COM

WWW.PEOPLEATTHEPEAK.COM
D: SAMANTHA CHONG, **C:** ALEX CHONG, **P:** JASON LOW
A: SCH'ANG DESIGN, **M:** JASON@SCHANG.COM

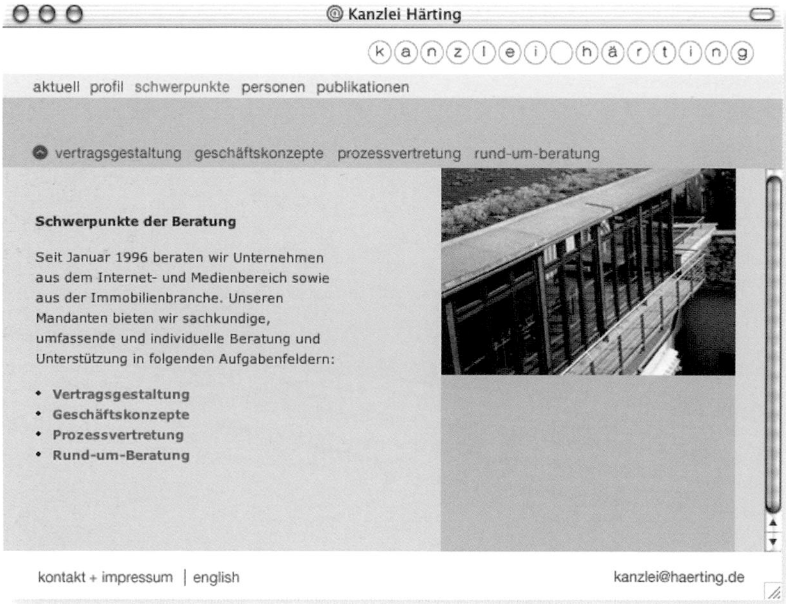

WWW.HAERTING.DE
D: BEN BUSCHFELD
A: BUSCHFELD.COM - GRAPHIC AND INTERFACE DESIGN, **M:** MAIL@BUSCHFELD.COM

WWW.PITKINZER.DE
D: PIT KINZER
M: KUNSTPROJEKTE@PITKINZER.DE

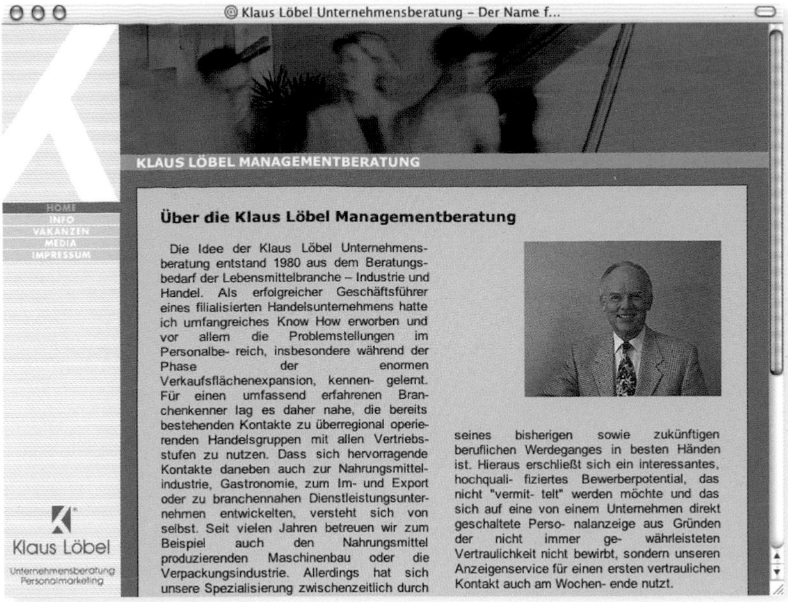

WWW.LOEBEL.DE
D: ANDREAS SPERWIEN
A: SPERWIEN DESIGN, **M:** INFO@HHCONCEPT.DE

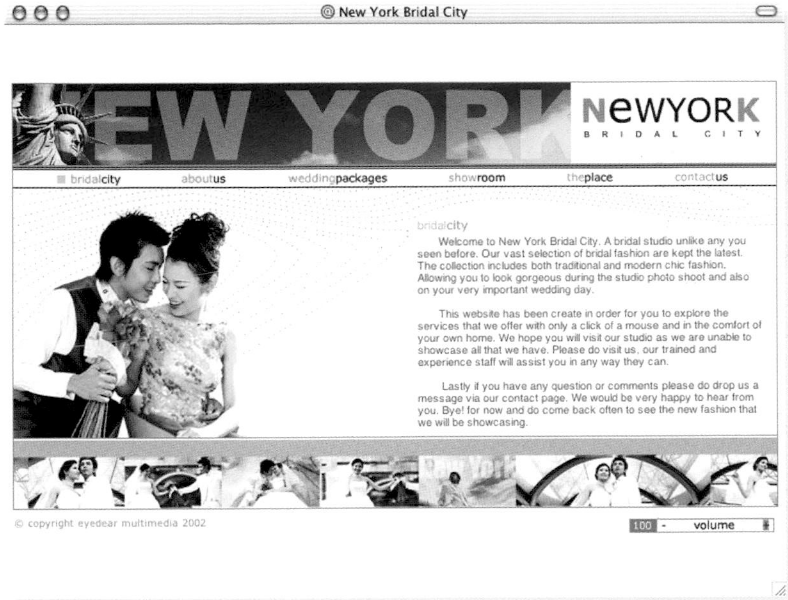

NEWYORKBRIDALCITY.COM
D: MOONLY KOAY
A: EYEDEAR, **M:** KGALAXIA@HOTMAIL

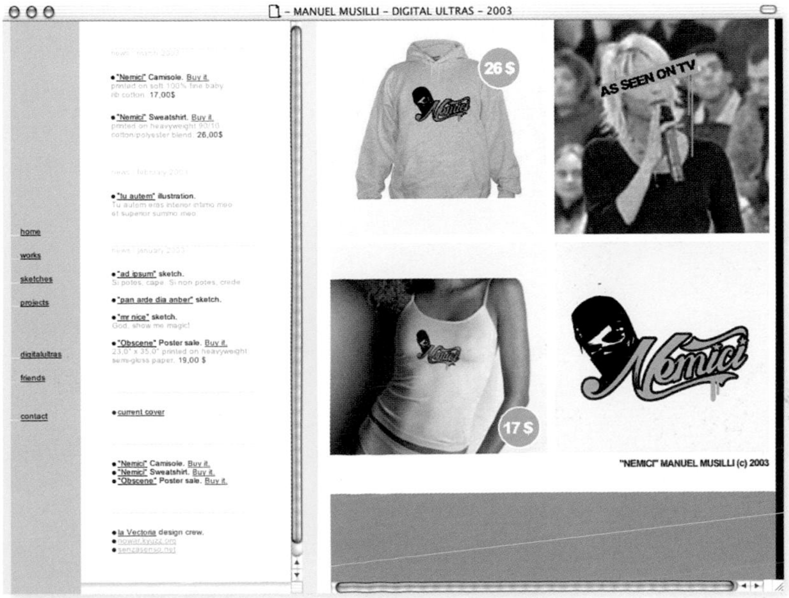

WWW.DIGITALULTRAS.COM
D: MANUEL PERFETTO
A: DIGITALULTRAS, **M:** MANU@MORS.IT

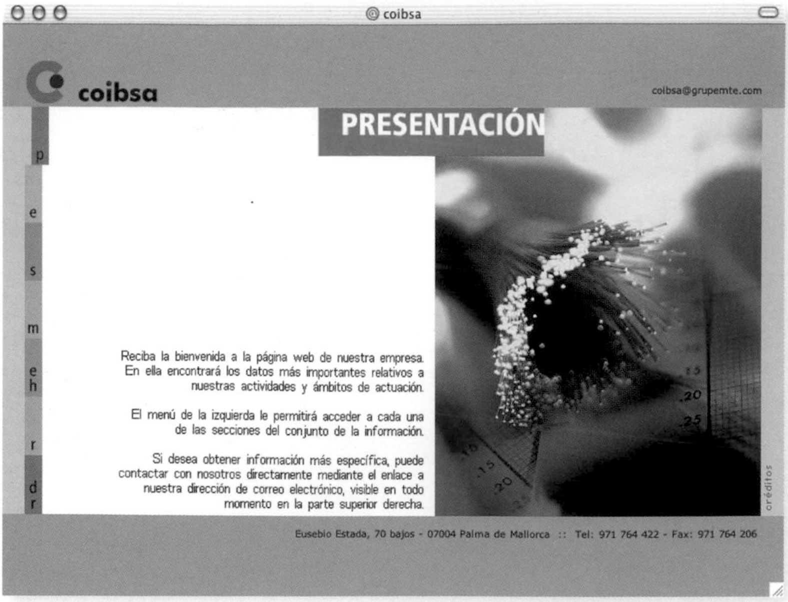

WWW.COIBSA.COM
D: PEDRO VALDEOLMILLOS
A: MELTEMI, **M:** PV@MELTEMI.INFO

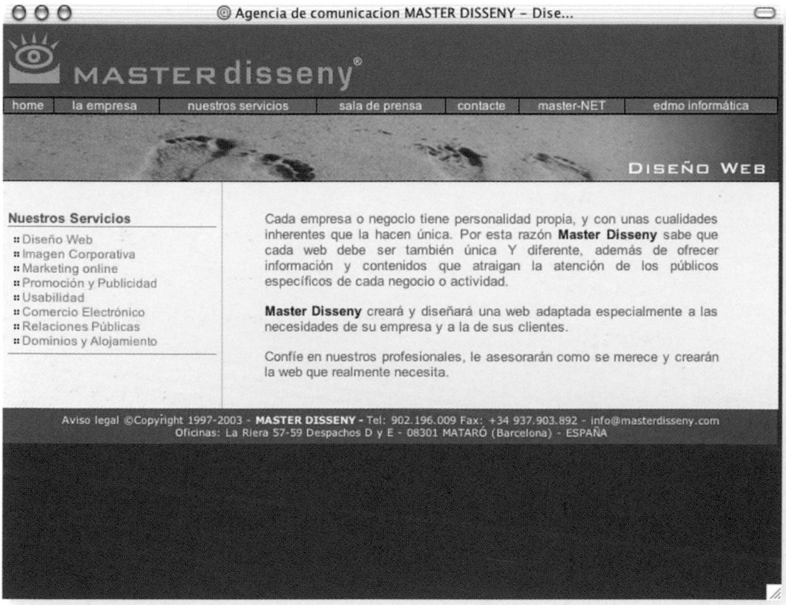

WWW.MASTERDISSENY.COM
D: ABEL CHICA ARDIACA, **C:** JORDI ROCA
A: MASTER DISSENY, **M:** INFO@MASTERDISSENY.COM

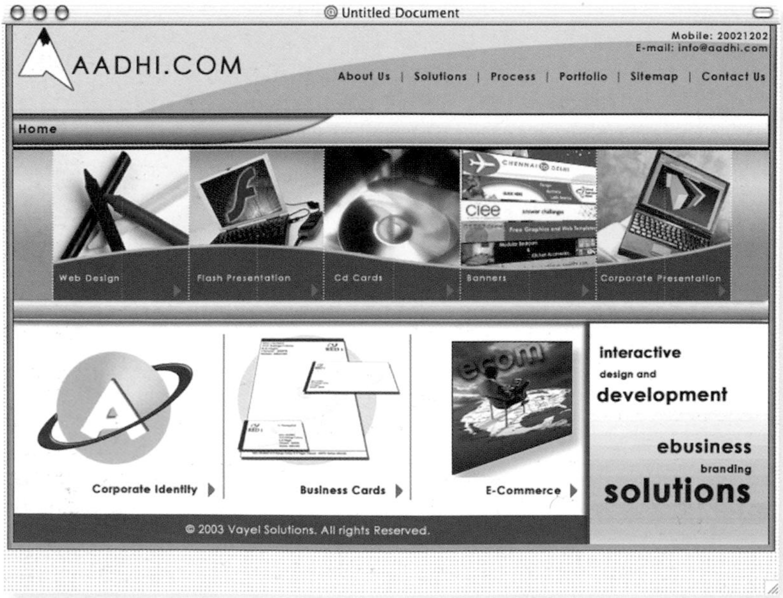

WWW.AADHI.COM
D: G. THANIGAIVEL
A: AADHI, **M:** INFO@AADHI.COM

RECORD2003.BOUN.EDU.TR
D: CAN BURAK BIZER, **C:** BARIS CEKIC
A: 2 FRESH, **M:** CANBURAK@2FRESH.COM

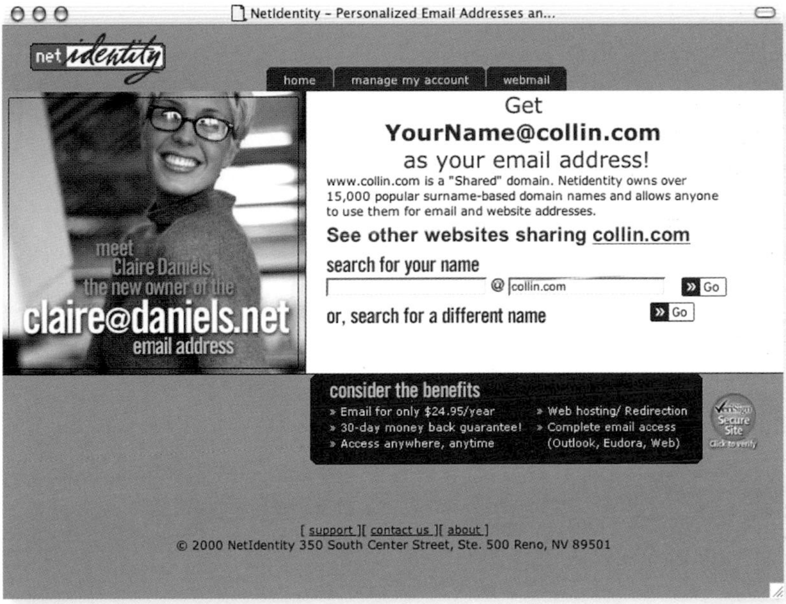

WWW.COLLIN.COM
D: JESSIKA BÄTZ, **C:** JESSIKA BÄTZ, **P:** WEB-ACTS
A: WEB-ACTS, **M:** INFO@WEB-ACTS.DE

WWW.LINKAUTO.IT
D: DANIELE ACCORNERO
M: X19NET@HOTMAIL.COM

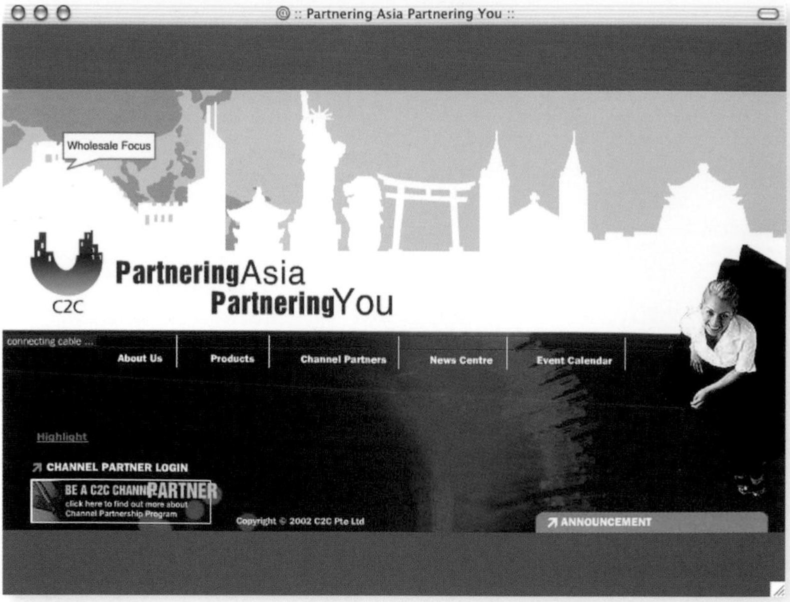

WWW.C2CCN.COM
D: KALINDA LOW, **C:** RAGHU
A: VOXMEDIA PTE LTD, **M:** JOE@VOXMEDIA.COM.SG

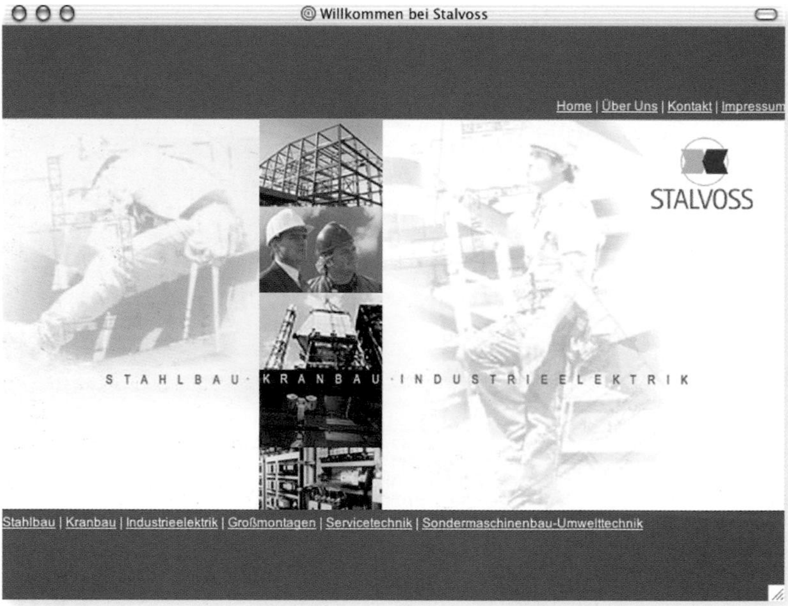

WWW.STALVOSS.DE
D: CHRISTIAN STEIN
A: WERBEAGENTUR HELLMANN, **M:** POST@C74.DE

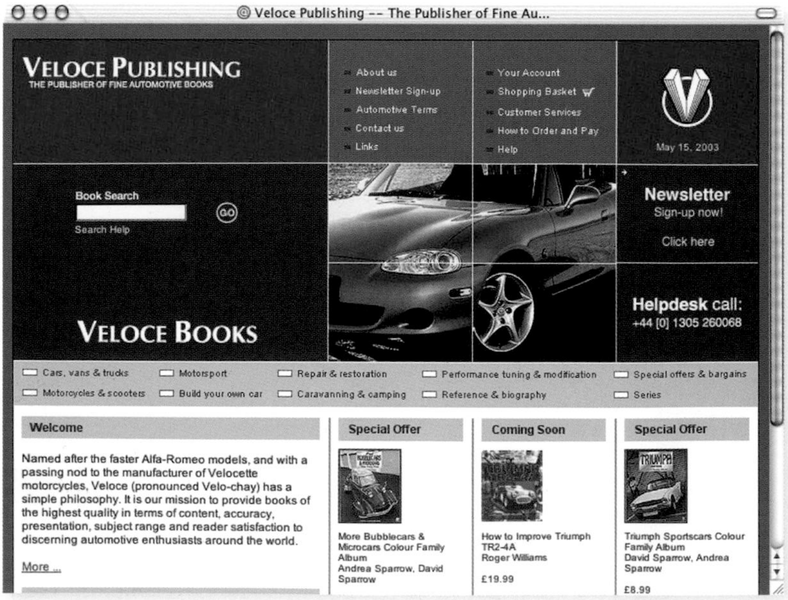

WWW.VELOCE.CO.UK
D: NATHAN KINGSTONE, **C:** DAVID MORLEY, **P:** DAVID MORLEY
A: ASPIN INTERACTIVE LIMITED, **M:** MARCUSP@ASPIN.CO.UK

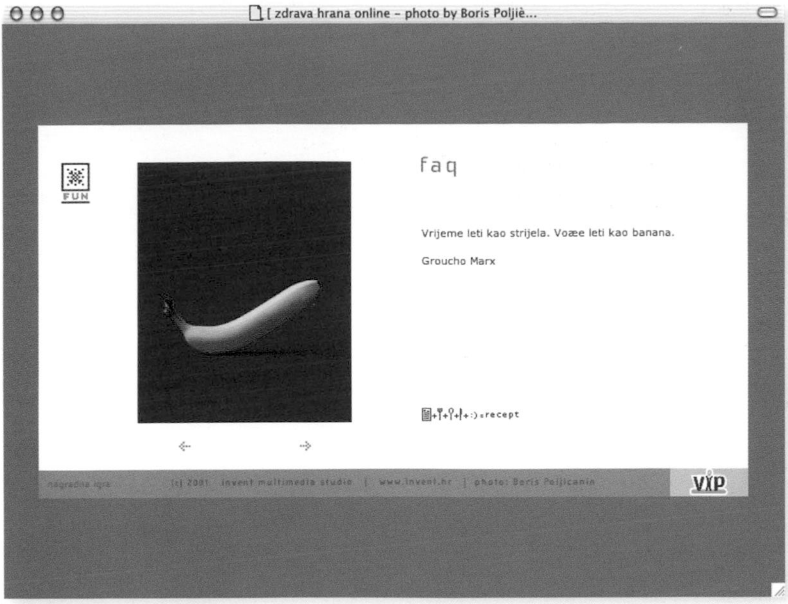

WWW.VEGENOVA.VIP.HR
D: IGOR SKUNCA, **C:** PETRA ZLOVIC
A: INVENT - MULTIMEDIA STUDIO, **M:** IGOR@INVENT.HR

WWW.KEATNG.COM
D: KEAT NG
M: KEATNG@KEATNG.COM

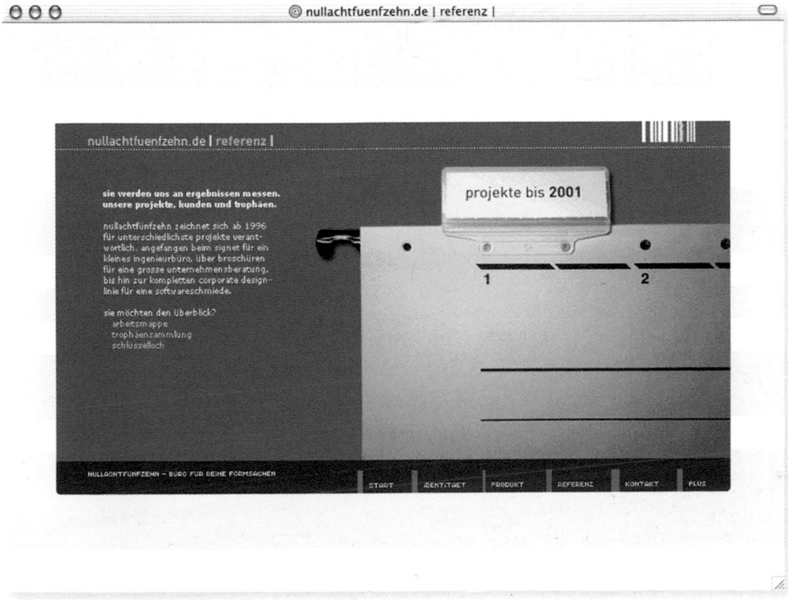

WWW.NULLACHTFUENFZEHN.DE
D: JAN STOLTENHOFF, **C:** ROBERT BÖTTNER, DENIS KAGANE, **P:** JAN STOLTENHOFF
A: NULLACHTFÜNFZEHN, **M:** HALLO@NULLACHTFUENFZEHN.DE

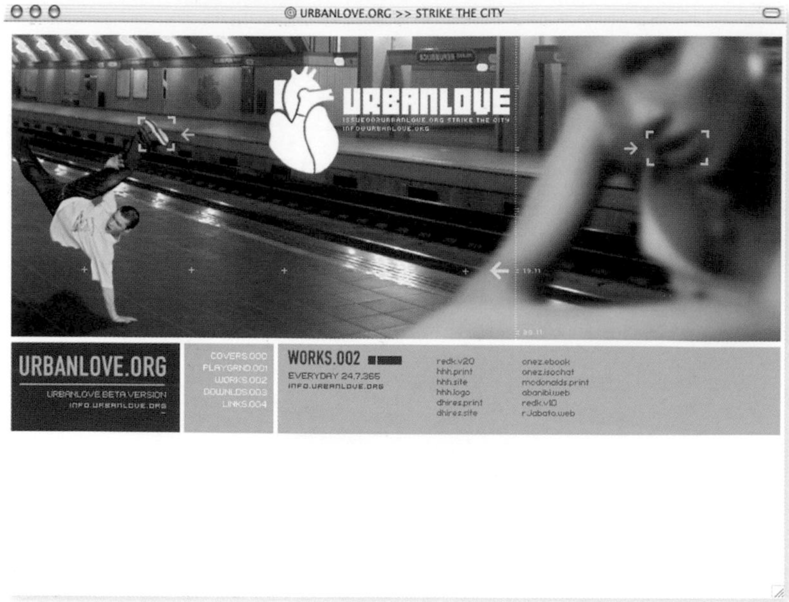

WWW.URBANLOVE.ORG
D: GUSTAVO PONCE RICO
M: TAVO@UR BANLOVE.ORG

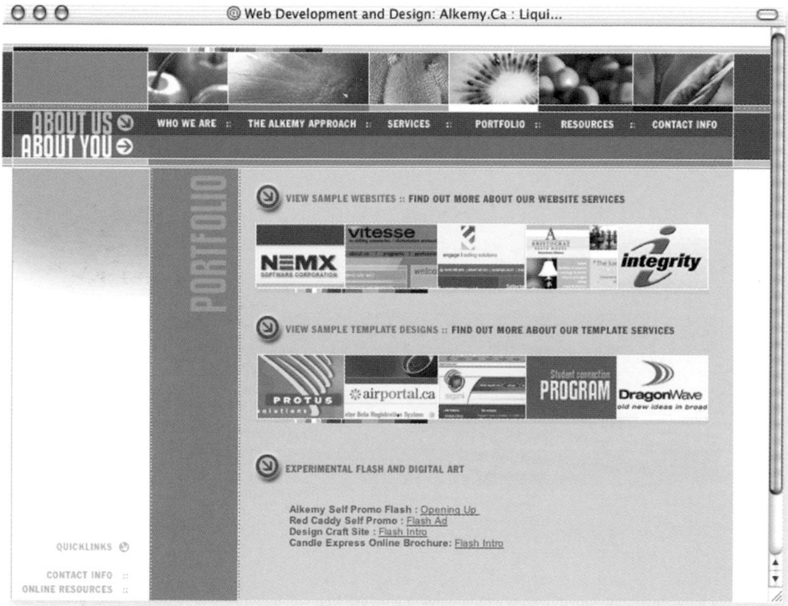

WWW.ALKEMY.CA
D: SARAH BUSSELL
A: ALKEMY, **M:** LUISA.RIOS@ALKEMY.CA

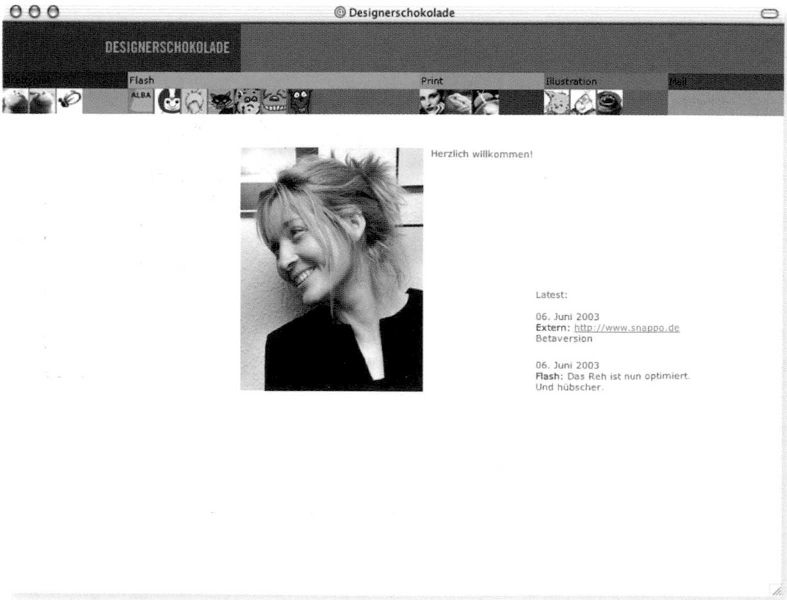

WWW.DESIGNERSCHOKOLA.DE
D: ANGELA PIGL, **C:** ANGELA PIGL/JÜRGEN TEMMING, **P:** ANGELA PIGL
A: DESIGNERSCHOKOLADE, **M:** ANGELA@DESIGNERSCHOKOLA.DE

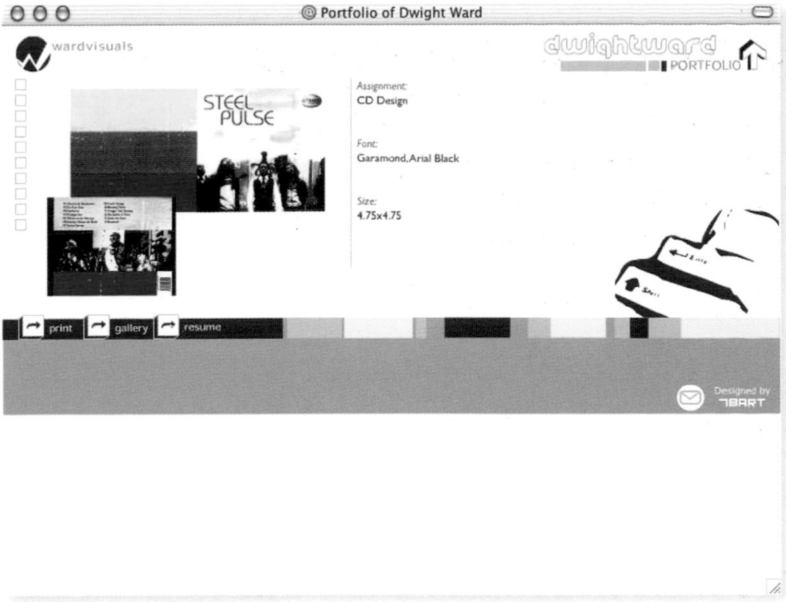

WWW.WARDVISUALS-ARTGALLERY.COM
D: FRANKLIN MORALES
A: BUILDINGBLOCS, **M:** FM78ART@AOL.COM

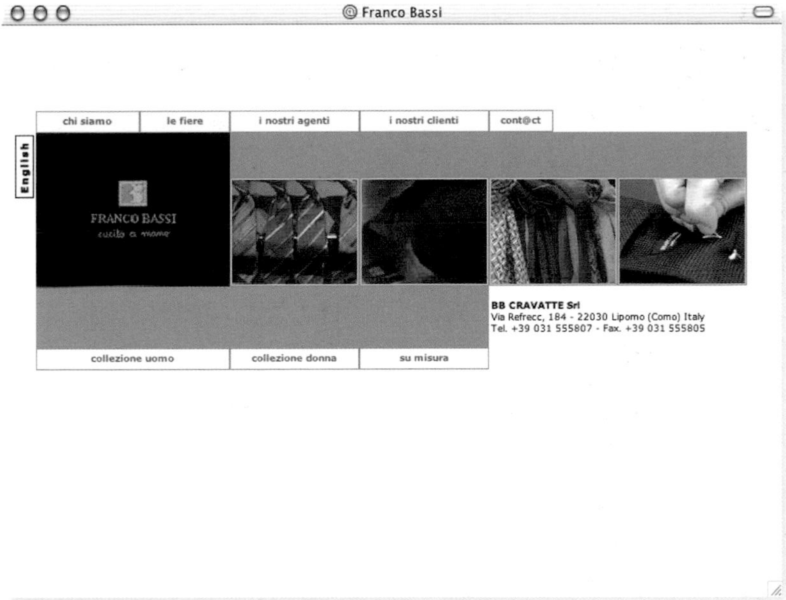

WWW.FRANCOBASSI.COM
D: ORITH KOLODNY
M: OKOLODNY@FASTWEBNET.IT

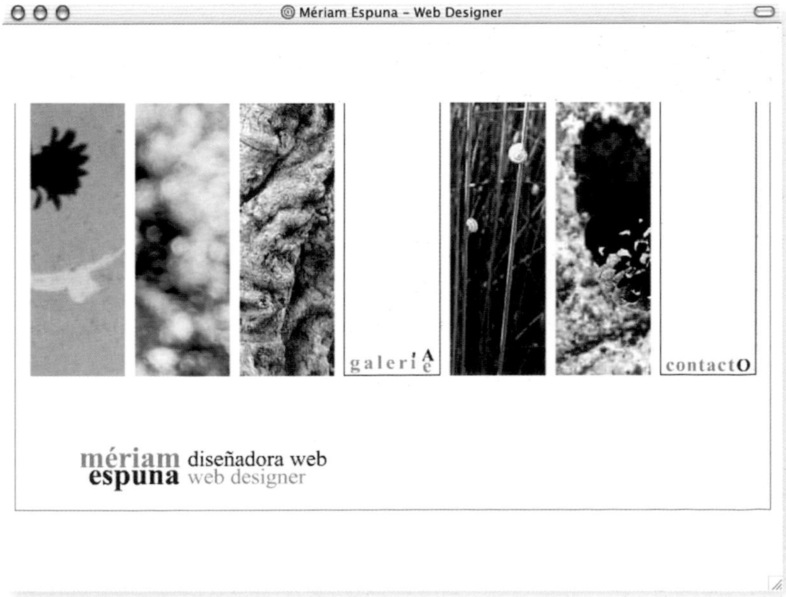

WWW.MERIAM.ESPUNA.ONLINE.FR
D: MÉRIAM ESPUNA
M: MERIAMEG2000@YAHOO.FR

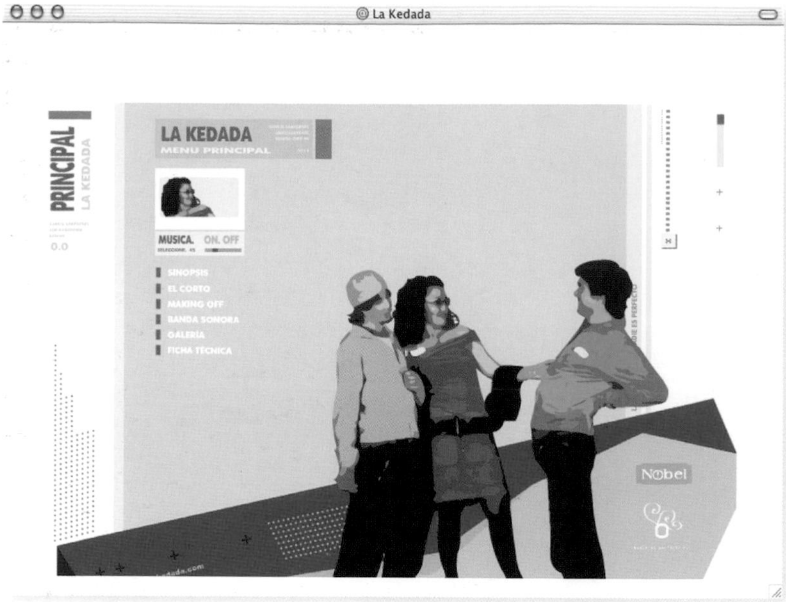

WWW.LAKEDADA.COM
D: JESSICA TRAVIESO SUAREZ, **C:** OSCAR PEREZ PINAZO, **P:** OSCAR PEREZ PINAZO
A: TIERRA VIRTUAL S.L, **M:** INFO@TIERRAVIRTUAL.NET

WWW.MUSA.IT/BRO.HTML
D: FRANCESCO DAL SANTO, **P:** SANDRO MUNZI
A: MUSA S.R.L., **M:** INFO@MUSA.IT

WWW.BITXAS.COM
D: SONIA HERNANDO, **C:** LUIS MARTINEZ, **P:** SONIA HERNANDO
M: SONIA_BITXAS@ARENAGROOVE.ORG

WWW.BUTTERO.IT
D: DANIEL STEFAN
A: COPYPASTE, **M:** DANIEL@COPYPASTE.IT

WWW.JOVOHAZ.HU
D: BENCE CSERNAK
A: BENCIUM, **M:** CSBENCE@BENCIUM.HU

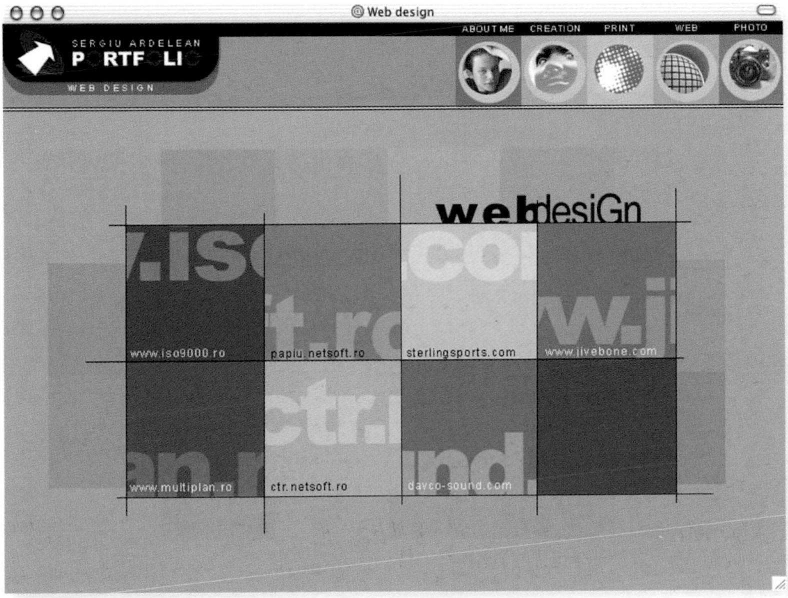

WWW.REEA.NET/SERGIU
D: SERGIU ARDELEAN
M: ASERGIU@FX.RO

WWW.ILCAFFE.CH
D: MICHEL SEELIGER, **C:** MICHEL SEELIGER
A: CHAMELEON GRAPHICS GMBH, **M:** INFO@CHAMELEONGRAPHICS.CH

WWW.LACOMUNACORDOBA.COM
D: DAVID PRIETO
A: DRAMAPLASTIKA, **M:** DAVIDPRIETO@SUPERCABLE.ES

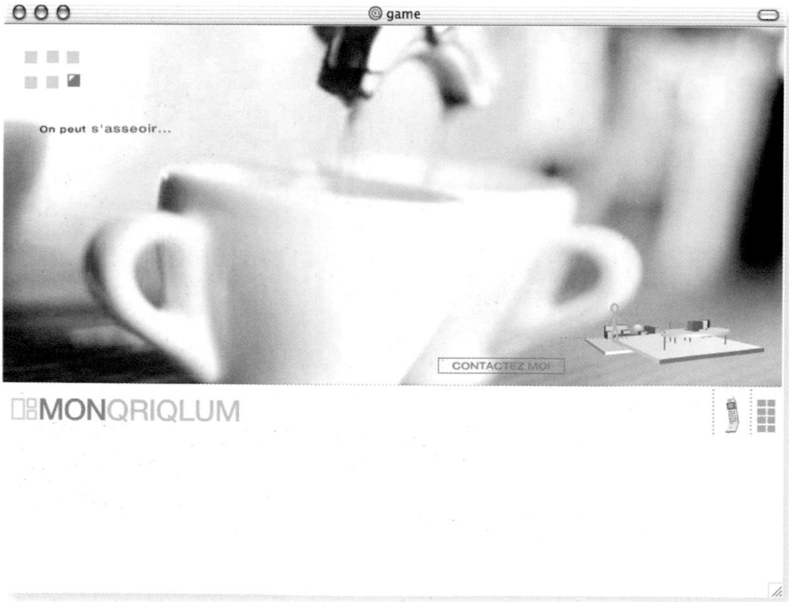

WWW.CHEZ.TISCALI.FR/MONQRIQLUM
D: CHRISTOPHE HUCK
M: CHHUCK@HOTMAIL.COM

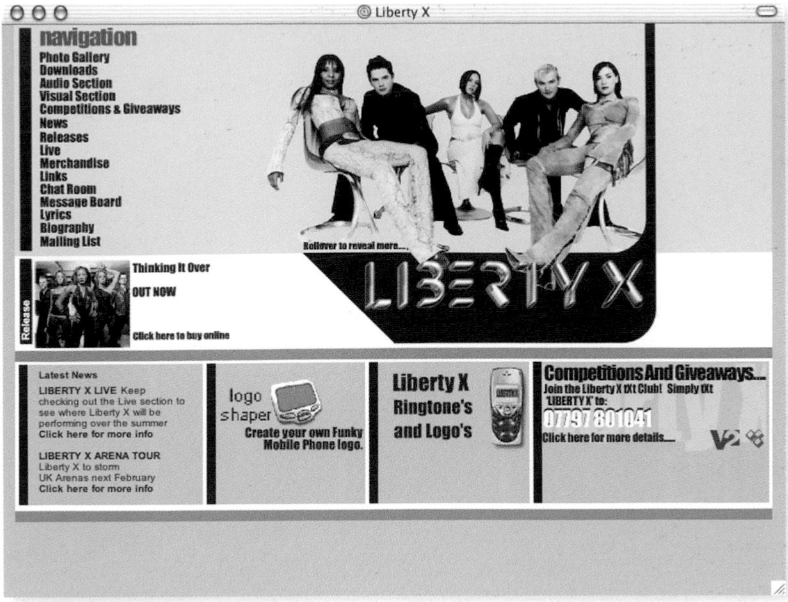

WWW.LIBERTYX.CO.UK
D: STEVEN OAKES
A: DESIGNESTI, **M:** STEVEN@DESIGNESTI.COM

WWW.JACUZZICONVENTION.COM
D: CHRISTIAN KUNZ
M: SCHMIDTLENA@GMX.DE

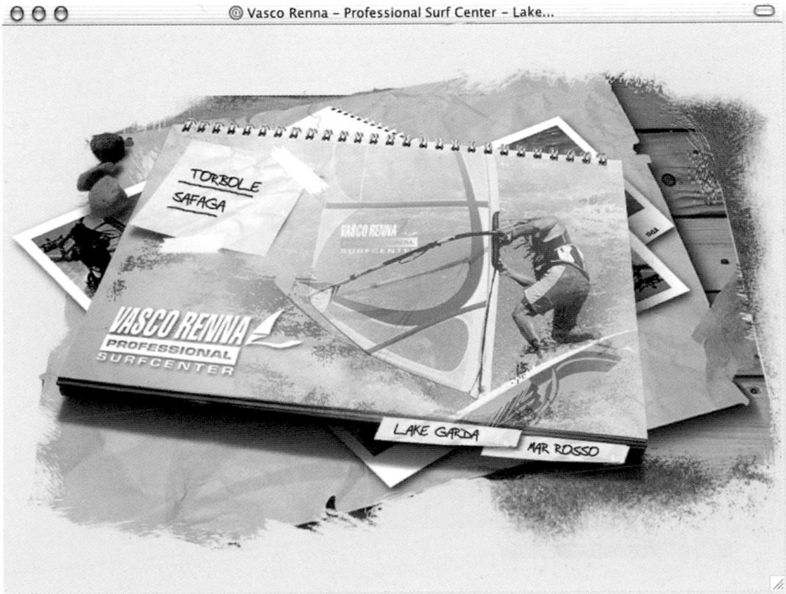

WWW.VASCORENNA.COM
D: LORENZO CATTONI
A: LINEA WEB GRAFFITI2000, **M:** LORENZO.CATTONI@GRAFFITI2000.COM

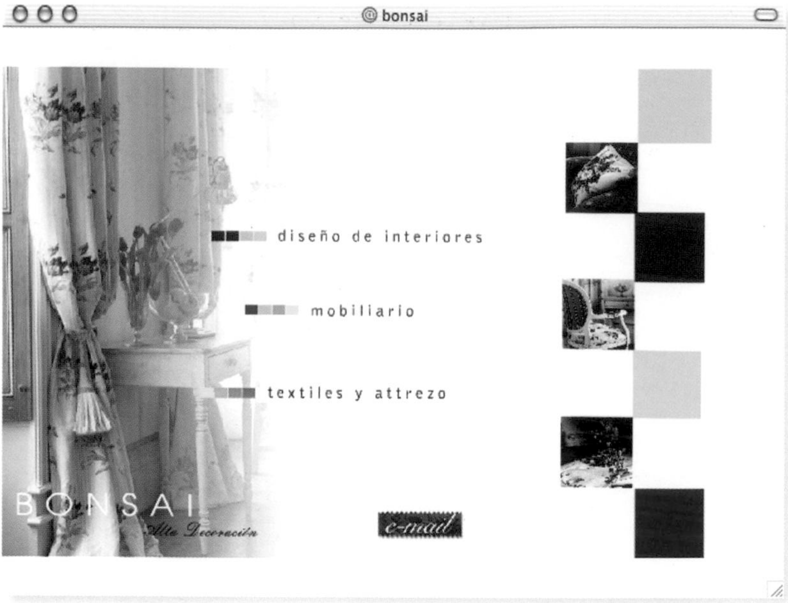

WWW.BONSAIDECORACION.COM
D: CAROLINA GOMEZ, **C:** ROBERTO GONZÁLEZ, **P:** ROBERTO GONZÁLEZ
A: GALERA PUBLICIDAD, **M:** ROBERTOGONZALEZ@GALERAPUBLICIDAD.COM

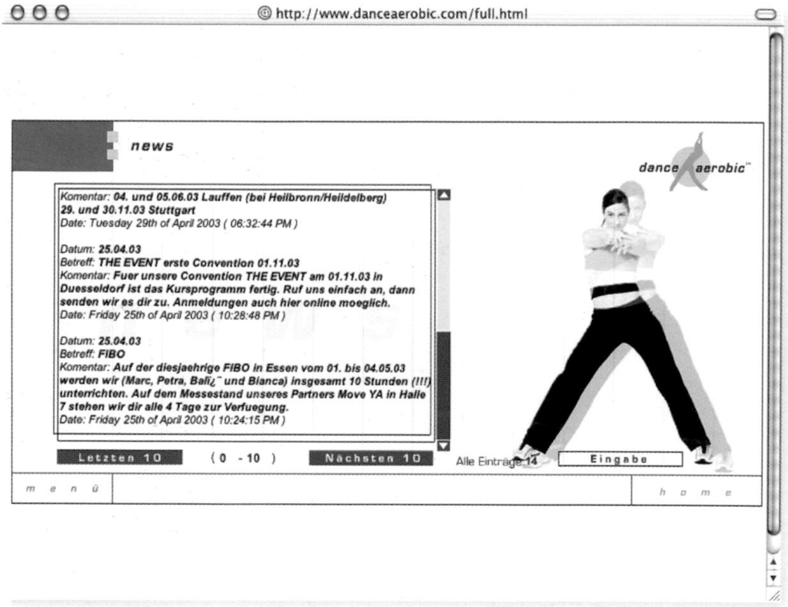

WWW.DANCEAEROBIC.COM
D: GUIDO EICHHOFF
A: ARTBOXX, **M:** GUIDO@ARTBOXX.NET

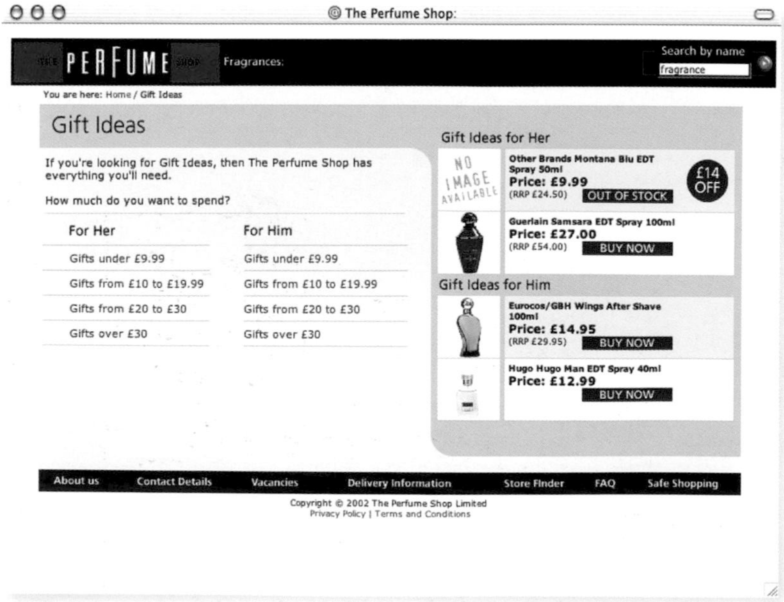

WWW.THEPERFUMESHOP.COM
D: MIKE TAYLOR, **C:** CHRISTIAN WEB
A: AB GRAPHICS, **M:** MIKE@AB-UK.COM

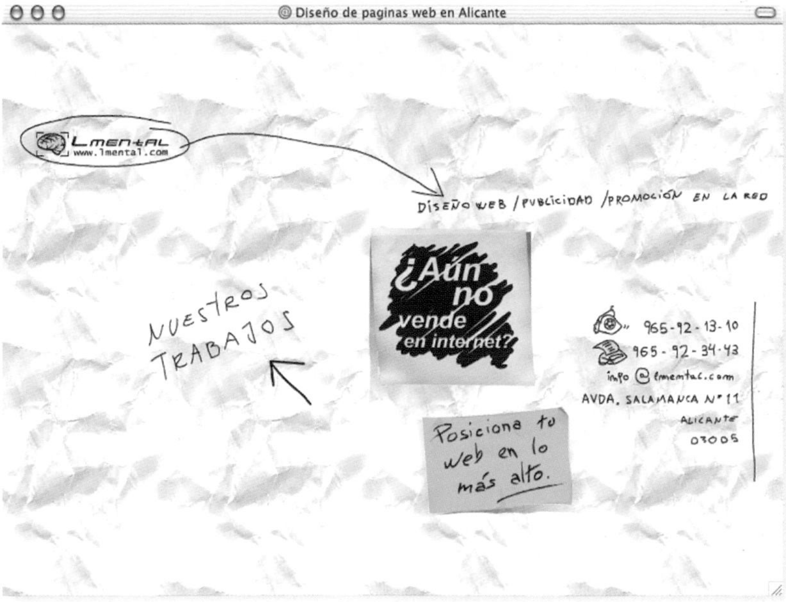

WWW.LMENTAL.COM
D: HÉCTOR GOMIS, **C:** SERGIO FERNANDEZ, **P:** JOSE MANUEL ABELLAN
A: LMENTAL, **M:** INFO@HECTORGOMIS.COM

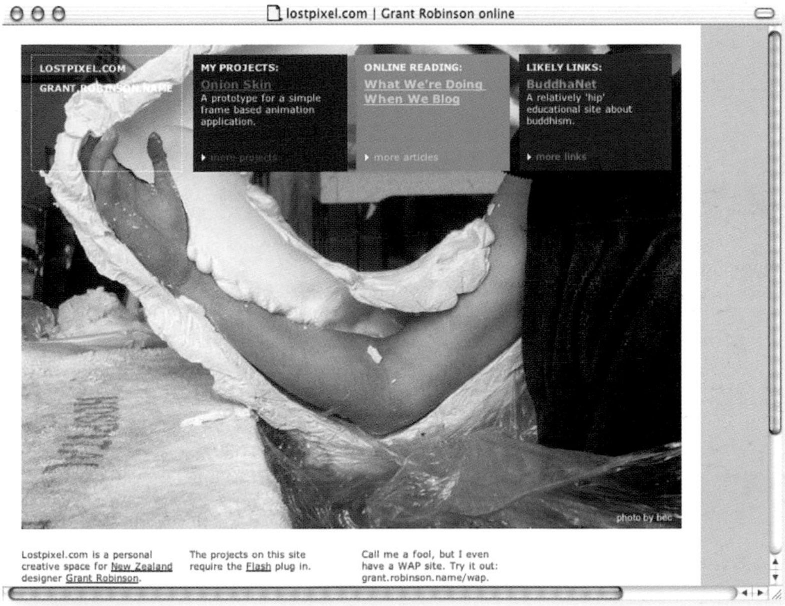

WWW.LOSTPIXEL.COM
D: GRANT ROBINSON
M: GRANT@LOSTPIXEL.COM

WWW.ALTRAVIA.COM
D: SHAUN DE LUCIA, **C:** LUCA SCURIATTI, **P:** ORANGE TREE SRL
A: ORANGE TREE SRL, **M:** S.DELUCIA@ALTRAVIA.COM

WWW.28MM.ORG
D: RACHEL JAMES, **C:** MARCEL KLOMP
M: EDITOR@28MM.ORG

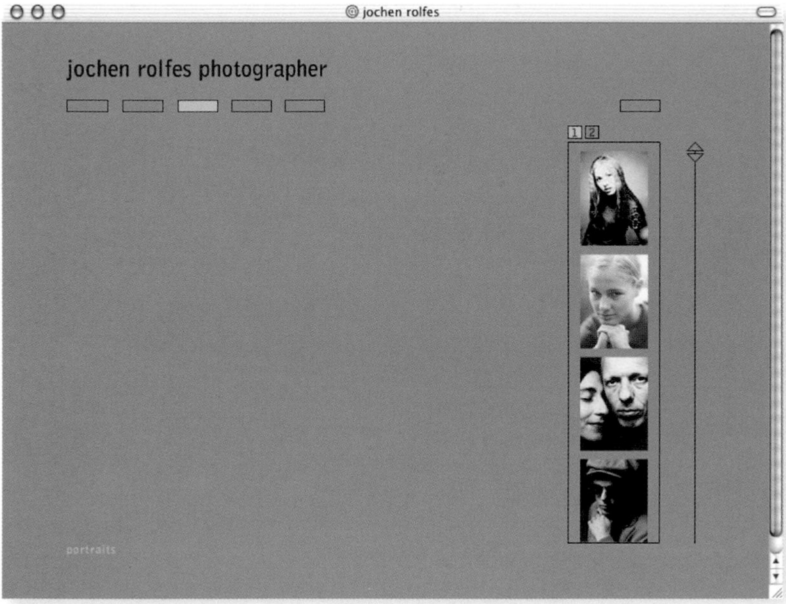

WWW.JOCHENROLFES.DE
D: GUIDO EICHHOFF
A: ARTBOXX, **M:** GUIDO@ARTBOXX.NET

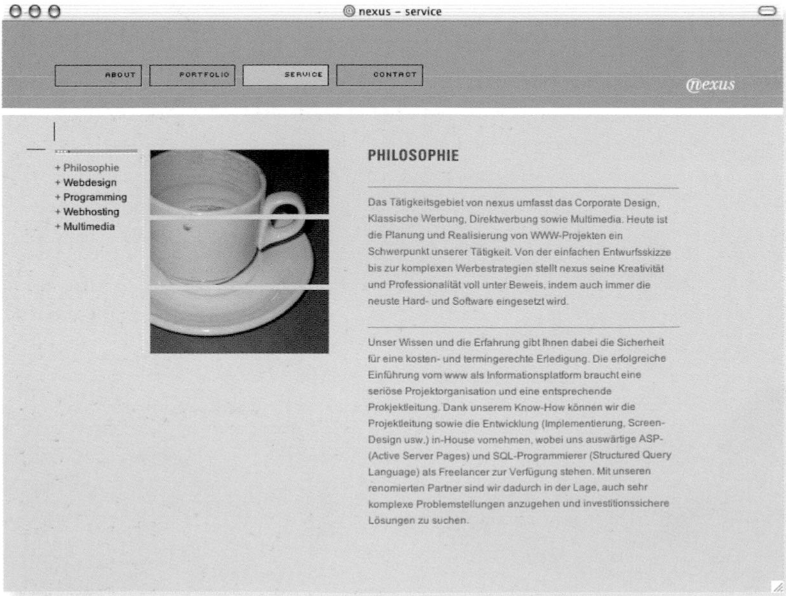

WWW.NCC.CH
D: CORNEL BETSCHART, **C:** CORNEL BETSCHART, **P:** PETER ULRICH
A: NEXUS - CREATIVE COMPANY, **M:** INFO@NCC.CH

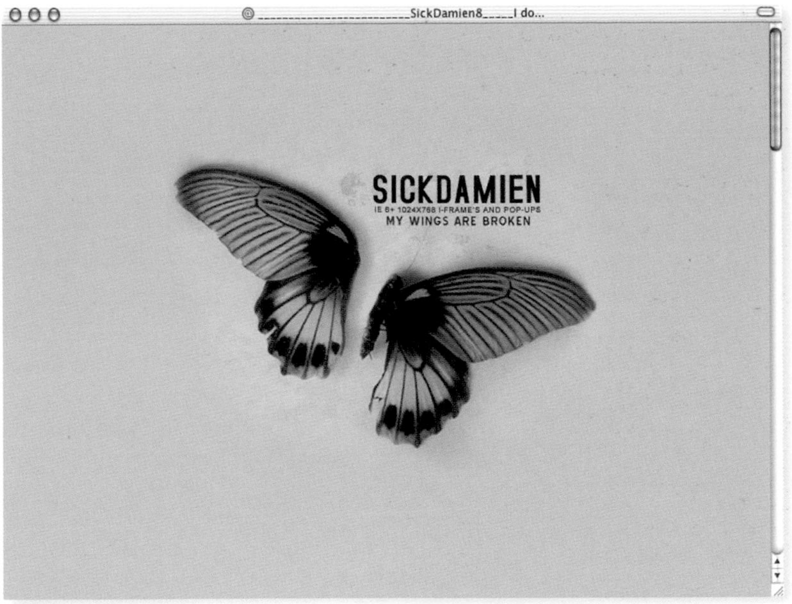

WWW.SICKDAMIEN.NL
D: DAMIEN VAN HOLTEN
M: CONTACT@SICKDAMIEN.NL

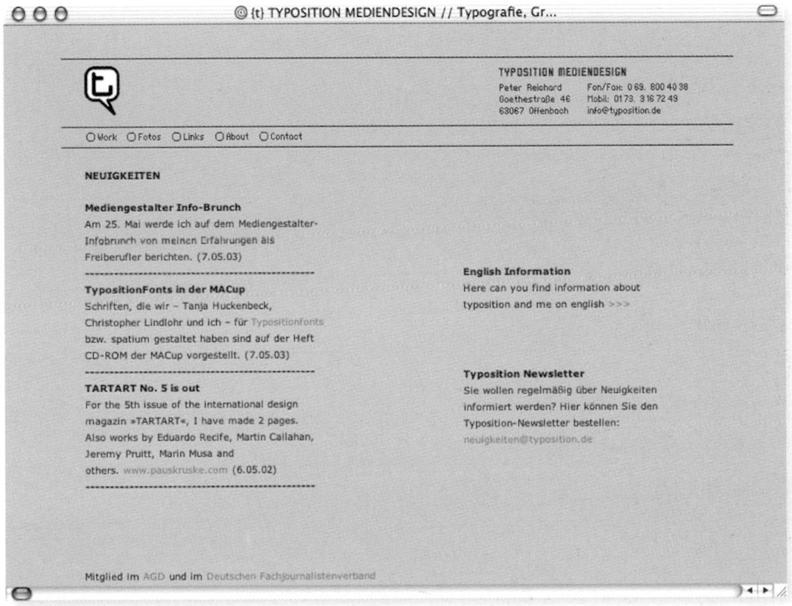

WWW.TYPOSITION.DE
D: PETER REICHARD
A: TYPOSITION MEDIENDESIGN, **M:** INFO@TYPOSITION.DE

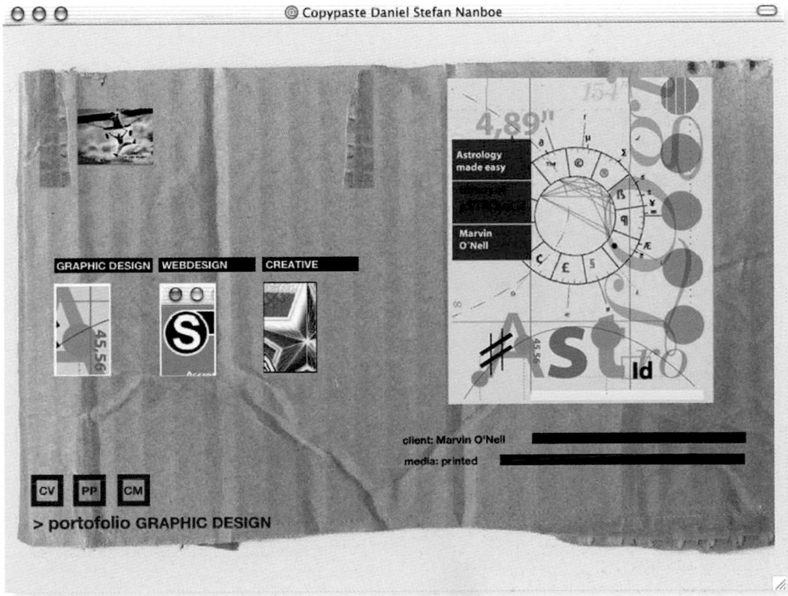

WWW.COPYPASTE.IT
D: DANIEL STEFAN
A: COPYPASTE, **M:** DANIEL@COPYPASTE.IT

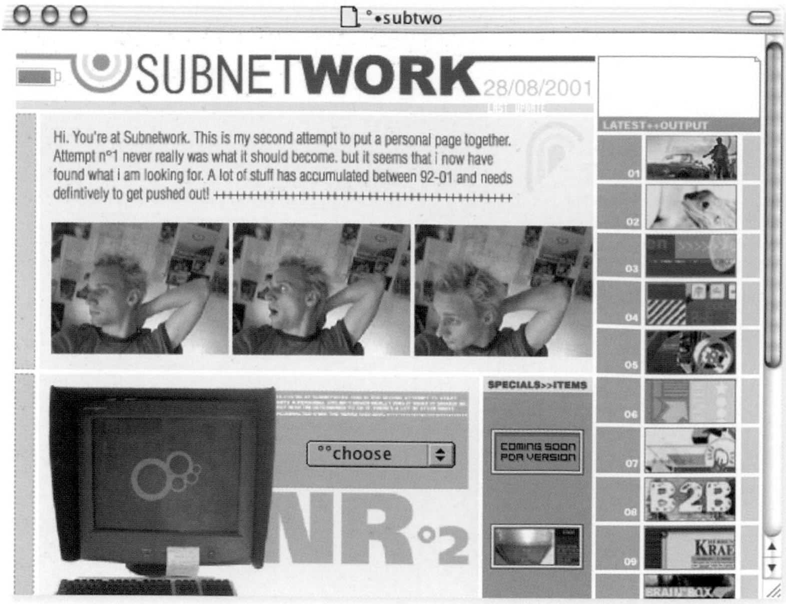

WWW.SUBNETWORK.DE/_IT_COMES
D: PETER BECKER
A: SBNTWRK, **M:** HOISON@GMX.NET

WWW.NULLBOOKING.DE
D: CHRISTIAN BRODACK
A: BRO.DESIGN, **M:** BRO@NULLBOOKING.DE

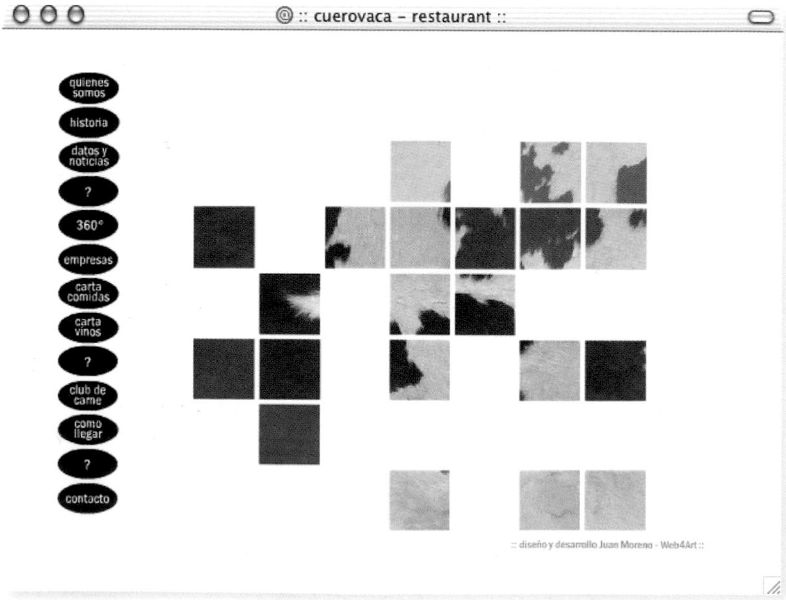

WWW.CUEROVACA.COM
D: JUAN MORENO, **C:** JUAN MORENO, **P:** SABEL GARCÍA
A: WEB4ART, **M:** JUANM@WEB4ART.CL

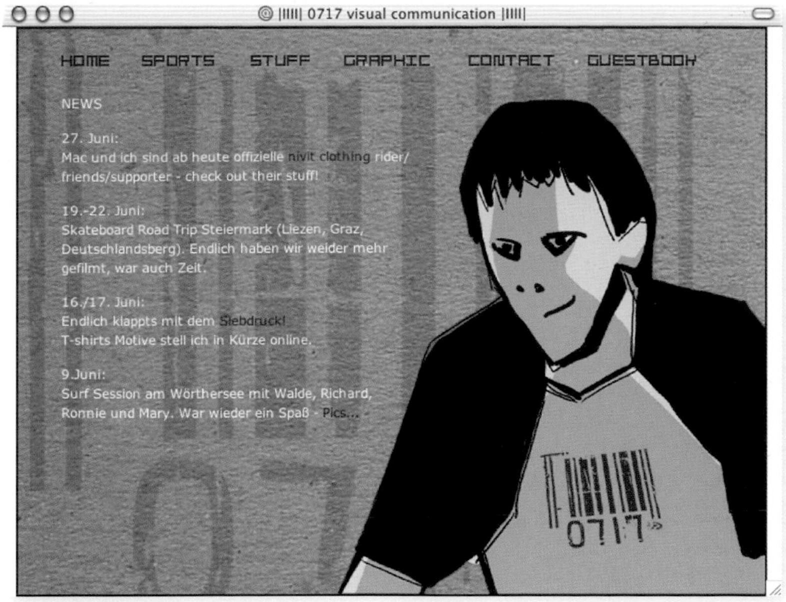

WWW.LILO.KREBERNIK.AT/HTML/HOME.HTML
D: LILO KREBERNIK
A: D:VISION VISUAL COMMUNICATION, **M:** LILO@KREBERNIK.AT

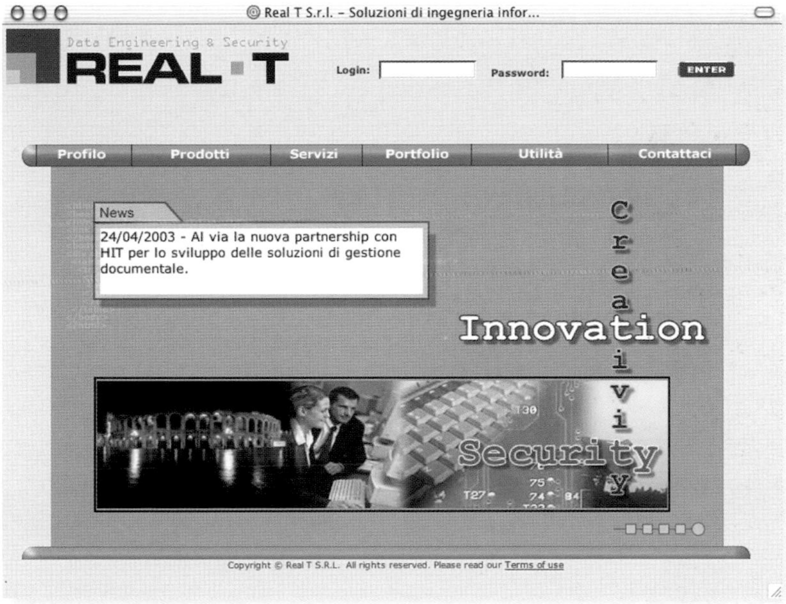

WWW.REALT.IT
D: GIURGEVICH FABRIZIO, **C:** PETRILLI LUIGI, **P:** REAL T
A: REAL T, **M:** PETRILLI.LUIGI@REALT.IT

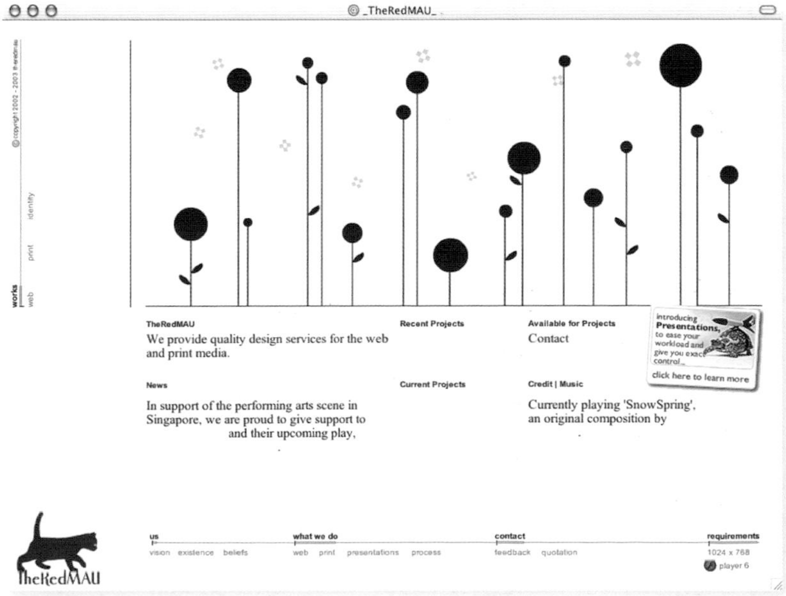

WWW.THEREDMAU.COM
D: JEANNIE TAN
M: JEANNIE@THEREDMAU.COM

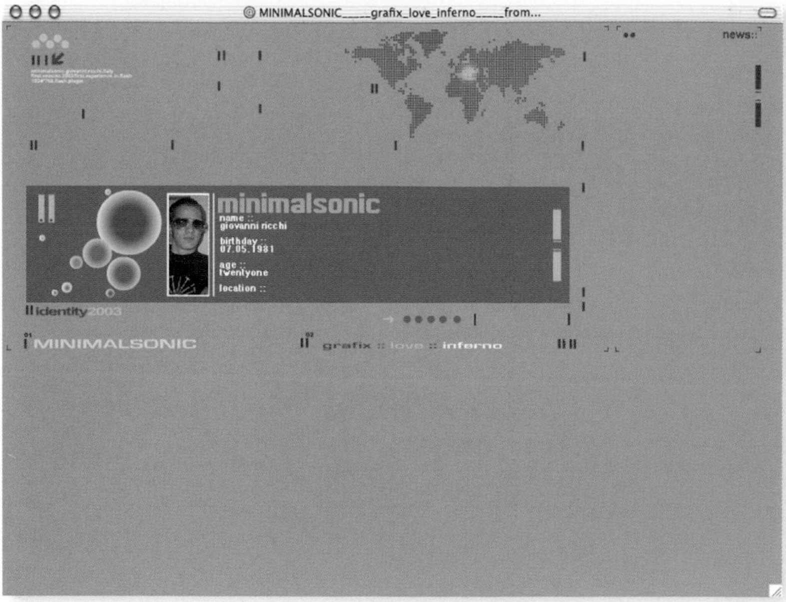

WWW.MINIMALSONIC.NET/VERSION01.HTM
D: GIOVANNI RICCHI
A: MINIMALSONIC, **M:** MINIMALSONIC@HOTMAIL.COM

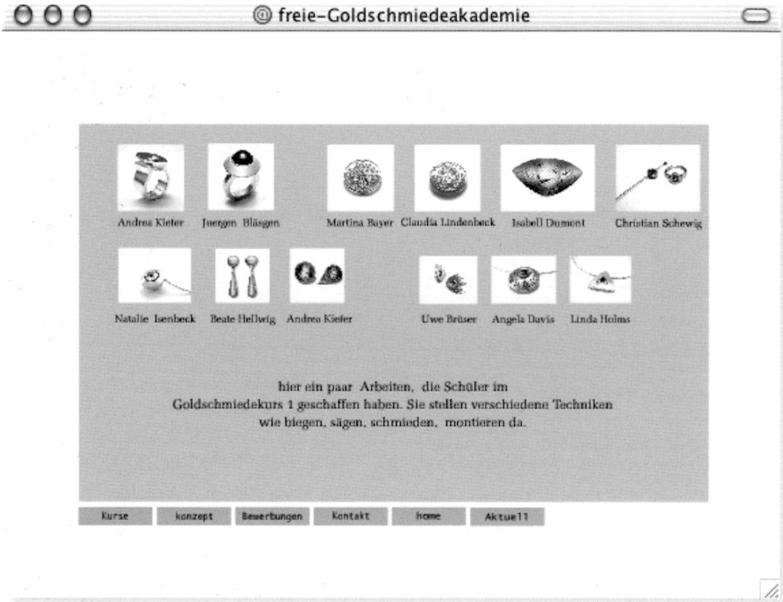

WWW.FREIE-GOLDSCHMIEDEAKADEMIE.COM
D: JOHANNES BRAND
A: BRAND-DESIGN, **M:** JB@BRAND-DESIGN.DE

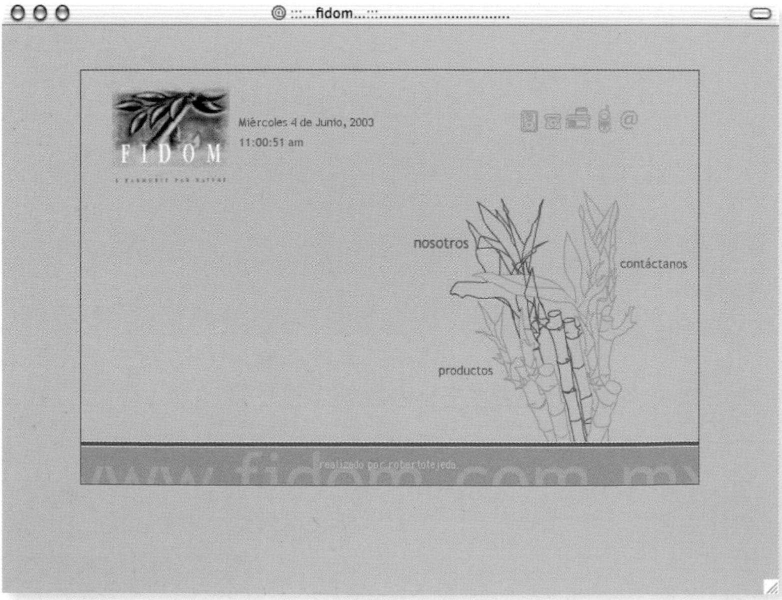

WWW.FIDOM.COM.MX
D: ROBERTO TEJEDA
A: ESFERA, **M:** ROBERTOTEJEDA@ESFERAMULTIMEDIA.COM

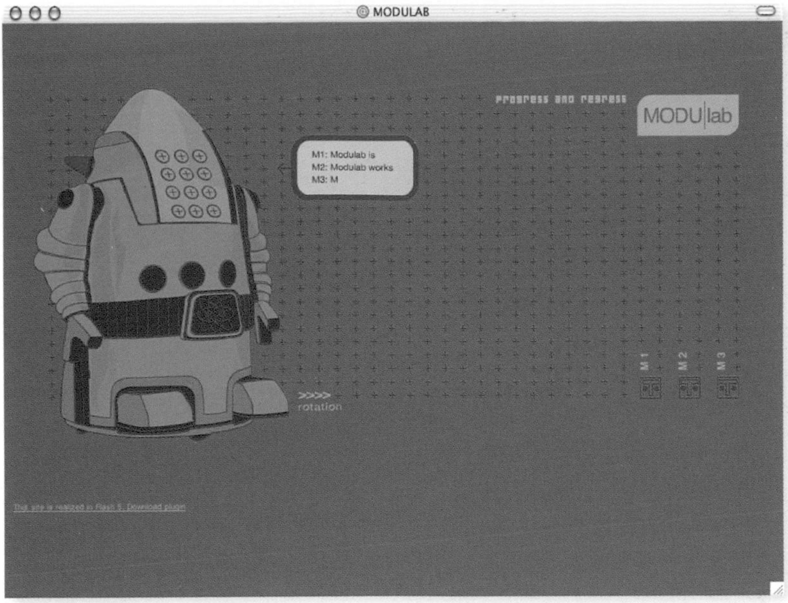

WWW.MODULAB.IT
D: LUCA BIANCONI, **C:** AURELIANO FONTANA, **P:** LUCA BIANCONI
A: MODULAB, **M:** MODULAB@LIBERO.IT

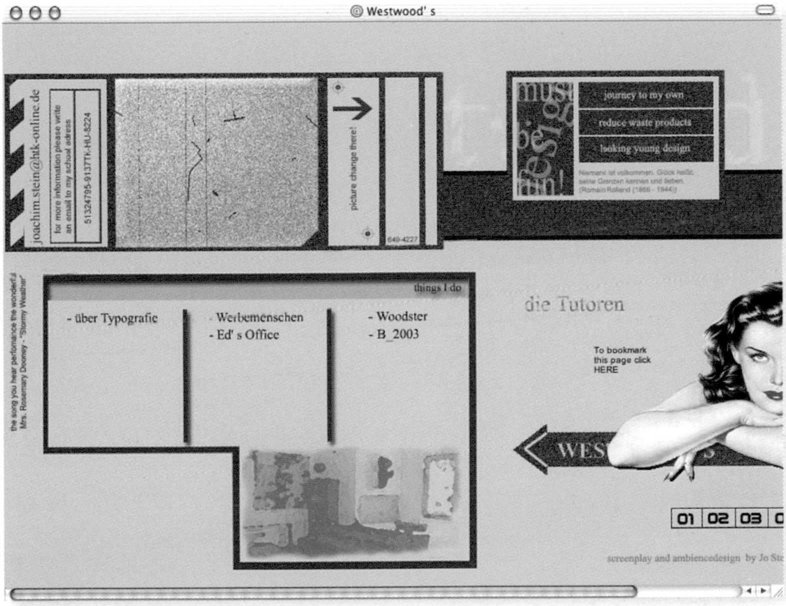

WWW.WESTWOODS.DE
D: JO STEIN, **C:** JO STEIN
M: STEIN-ROEVENICH@T-ONLINE.DE

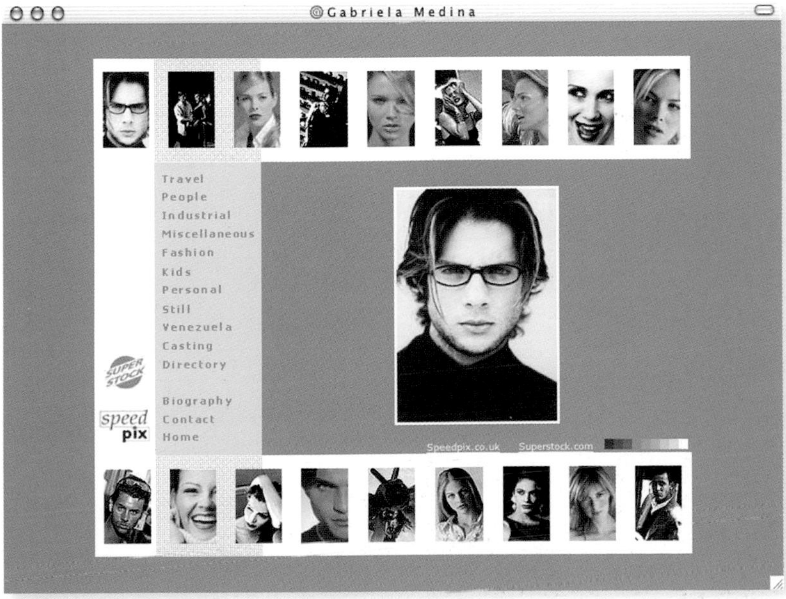

WWW.GABRIELAMEDINA.COM
D: CAROLINA VERA, **C:** CAROLINA VERA, **P:** GABRIELA MEDINA
M: PHOTOGAB@TELCEL.NET.VE

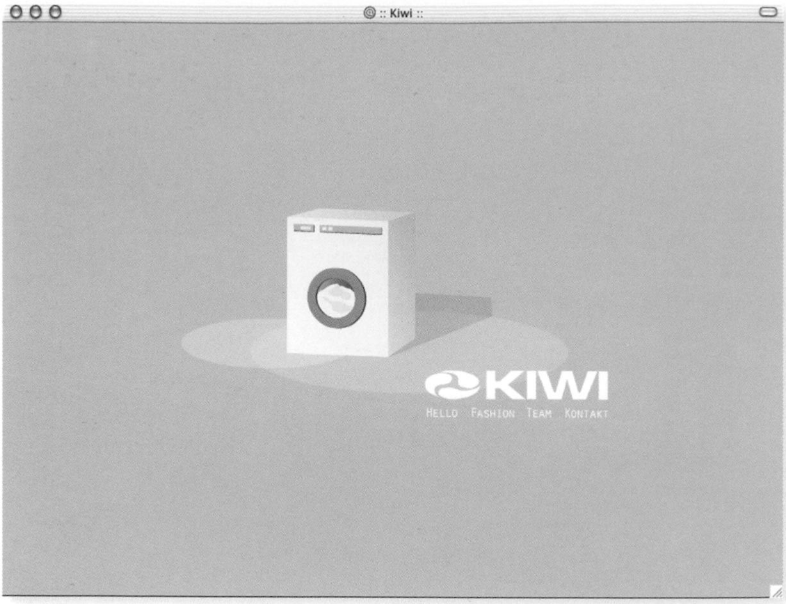

WWW.KIWIS.CH
D: ANITA SCHNEEBERGER, **C:** ANITA SCHNEEBERGER, **P:** MODEAGENTUR WERNER LUTZ
A: OUT MEDIA DESIGN GMBH, **M:** URS@OUT.TO

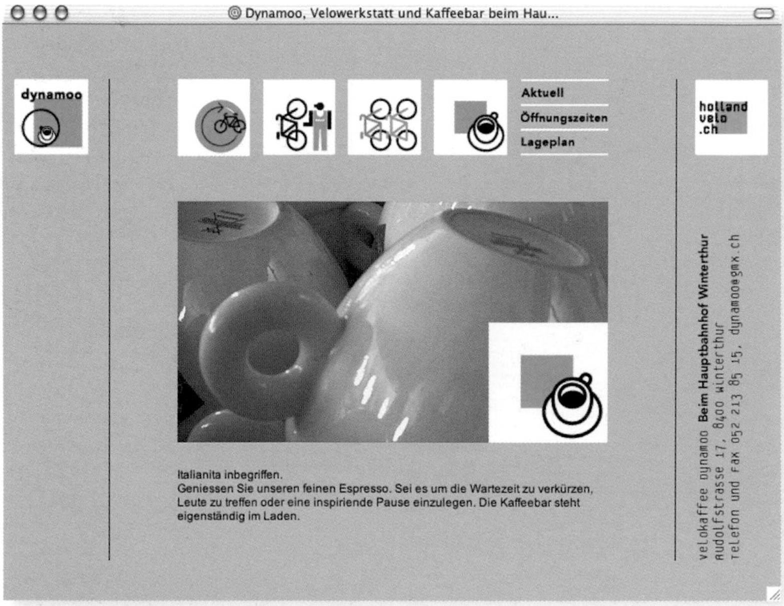

WWW.DYNAMOO.CH/KAFFEEBAR.SHTML
D: THOMAS BRUGGISSER, **C:** SCHMID ROGER, **P:** THOMAS BRUGGISSER / SCHMID ROGER
A: GRAFIKTRAKTOR.CH, **M:** MAILS@ROGER-SCHMID.CH

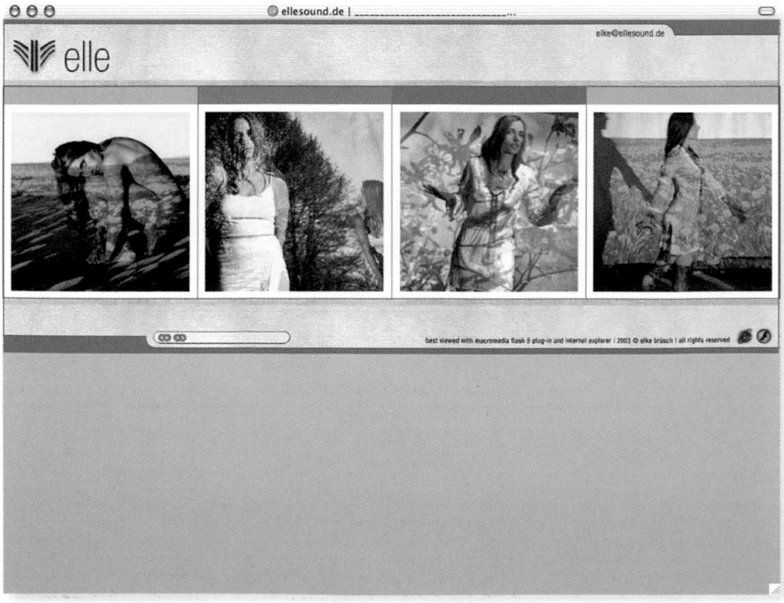

WWW.ELLESOUND.DE
D: SEVERIN BRETTMEISTER
A: FA-RO MARKETING, **M:** SEVERIN@FA-RO.DE

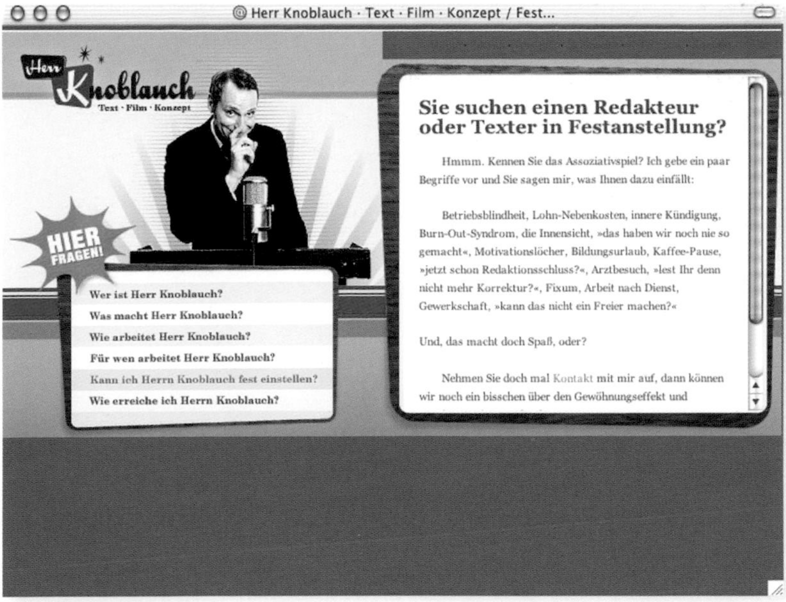

WWW.HERRKNOBLAUCH.DE
D: CHRISTOPH RENNE
A: RPUNKTDESIGN WERBEAGENTUR GMBH, **M:** CHEF@KRYZCOM.DE

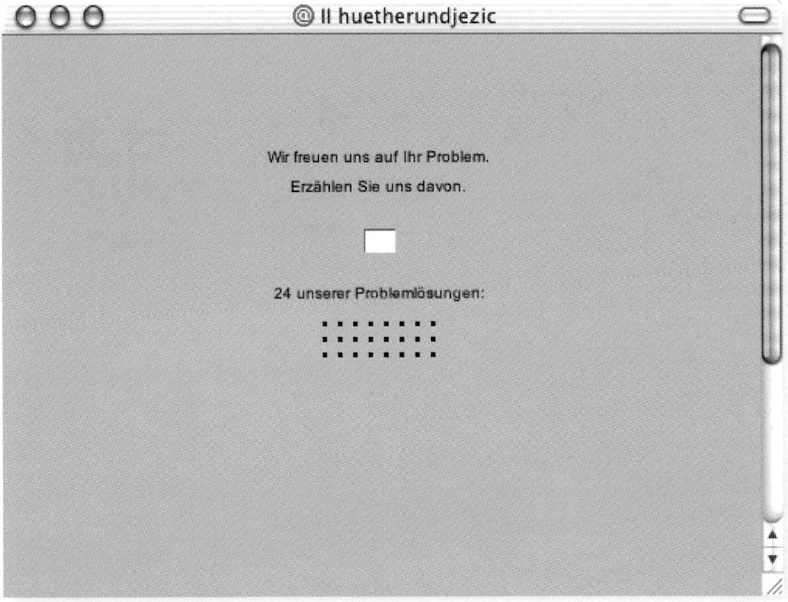

WWW.HUETHERUNDJEZIC.COM
D: BORIS JEZIC, **C:** TIM HUETHER
M: TH@HUETHERUNDJEZIC.COM

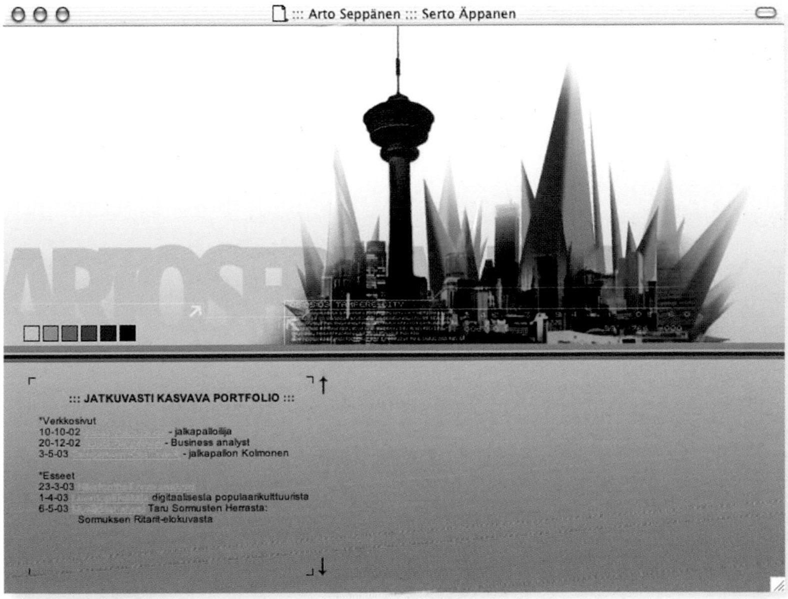

WWW.ARTOSEPPANEN.CJB.NET
D: ARTO SEPPÄNEN
M: ARTO.SEPPANEN@CULT.TPU.FI

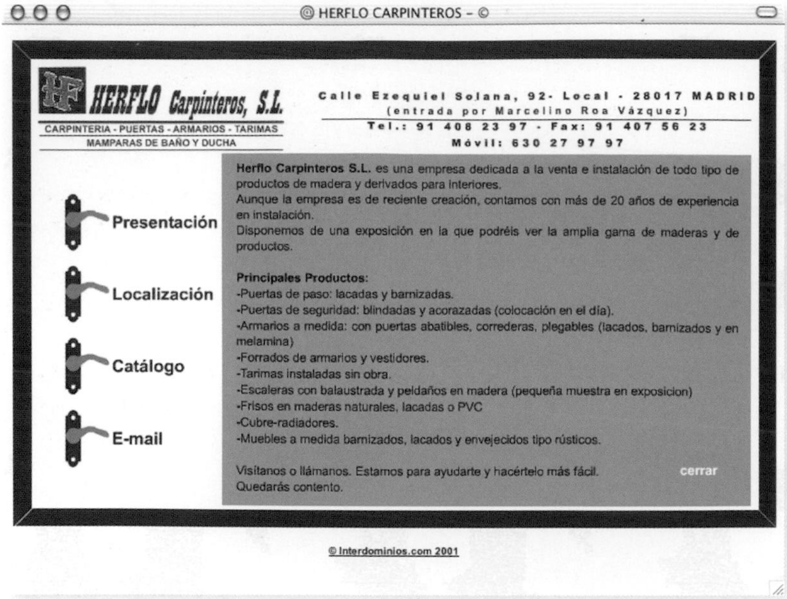

WWW.HERFLO.COM/HERFLO.HTML
D: JOSE MARIA GONZALEZ MOLINETE
M: GRANCHEMA@ARRAKIS.ES

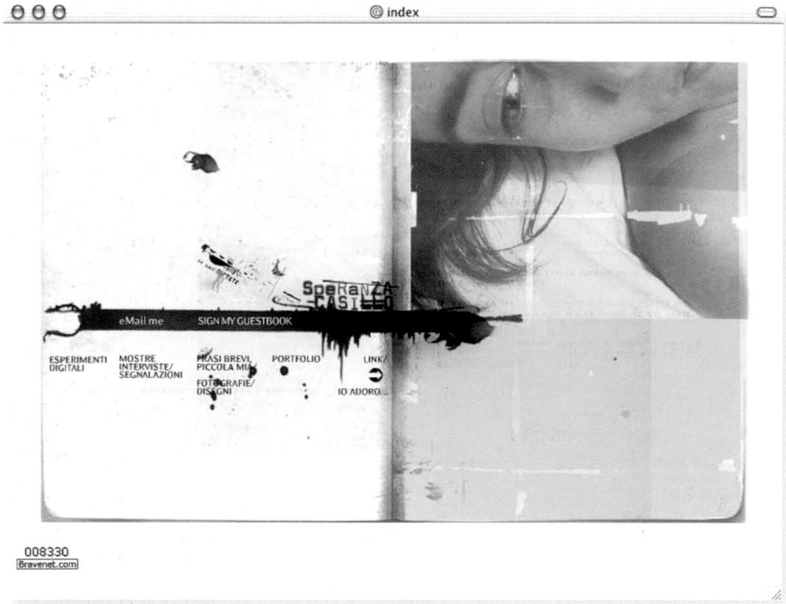

WWW.ARTSERVICE.IT/SPE
D: SPERANZA CASILLO
M: MANDARINA@TISCALINET.IT

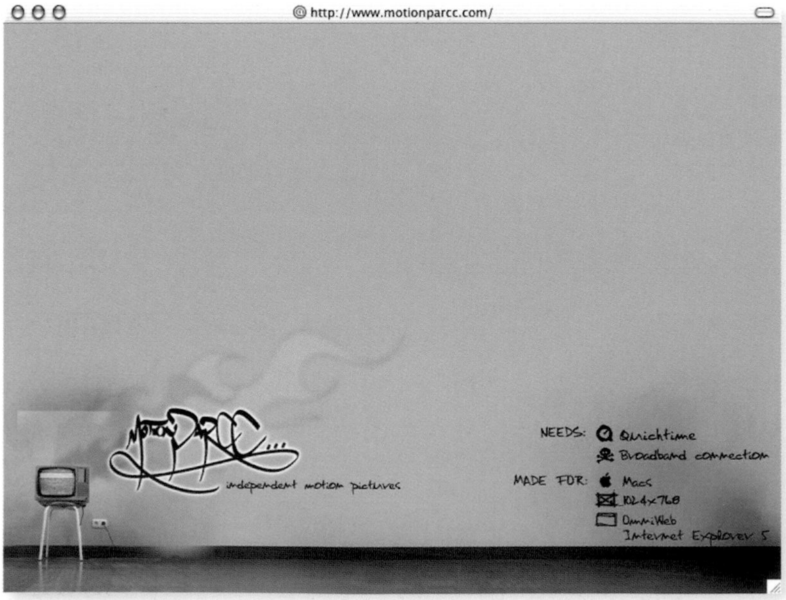

WWW.MOTIONPARCC.COM
D: INDEPENDENTBLUE
A: INDEPENDENTBLUE, **M:** SEBASTIAN@INDEPENDENTBLUE.COM

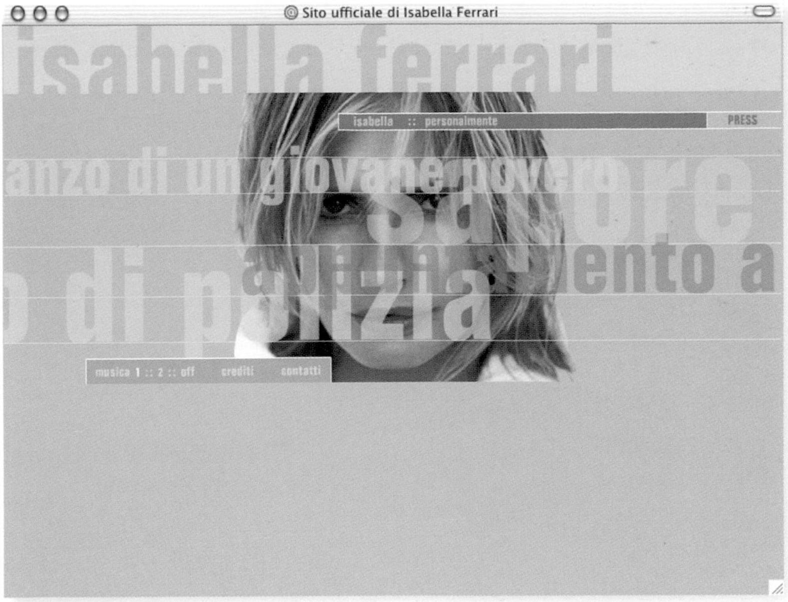

WWW.ISABELLAFERRARI.IT
D: LUCA CORLAITA, **C:** LUCA MARCHETTI, **P:** FEDERICA BEE
A: D-SIGN S.R.L., **M:** LORENZO@D-SIGN.IT

WWW.CUJO.BIZ
D: DIEGO SANZ (KARRAMARRO), **C:** PAULO CARVAJAL, **P:** IÑIGO ROMERA
A: VUDUMEDIA S.L., **M:** KARRAMARRO@VUDUMEDIA.COM

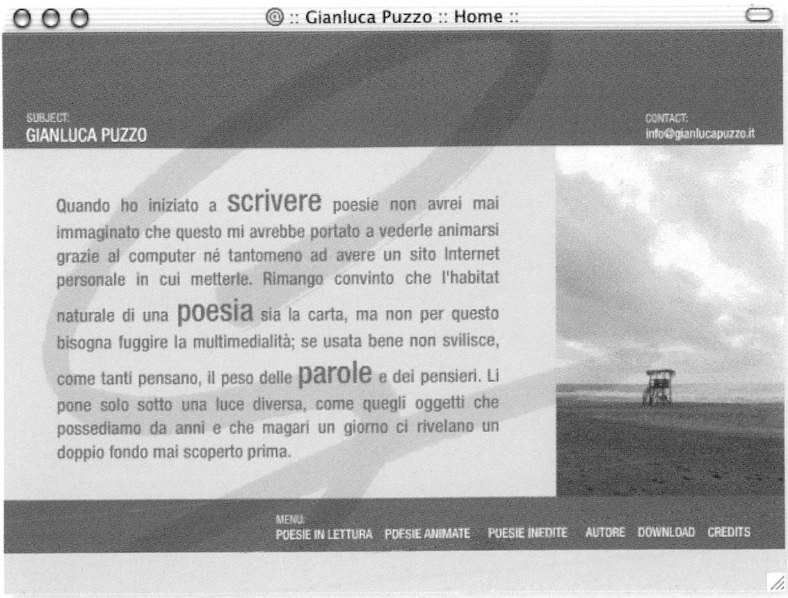

WWW.GIANLUCAPUZZO.IT/HOME.HTM
D: ANDREA CAPERNI
M: INFO@GIANLUCAPUZZO.IT

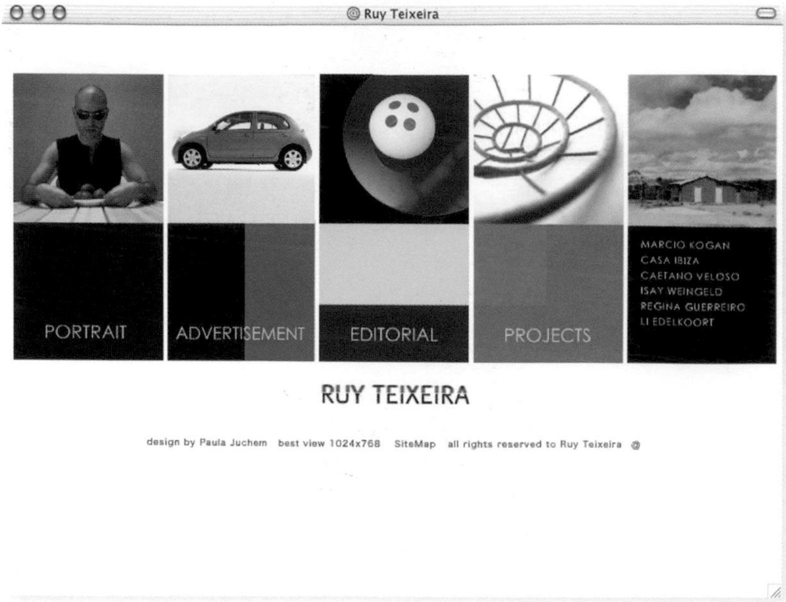
Ruy Teixeira
MARCIO KOGAN
CASA IBIZA
CAETANO VELOSO
ISAY WEINGELD
REGINA GUERREIRO
LI EDELKOORT
PORTRAIT
ADVERTISEMENT
EDITORIAL
PROJECTS
RUY TEIXEIRA
design by Paula Juchem best view 1024x768 SiteMap all rights reserved to Ruy Teixeira

WWW.RUYTEIXEIRA.COM
D: PAULA JUCHEM, **C:** DANIEL CANFIELD, **P:** PAULA JUCHEM
A: STUDIO TEIXEIRA SRL, **M:** DESIGN@PAULAJUCHEM.COM

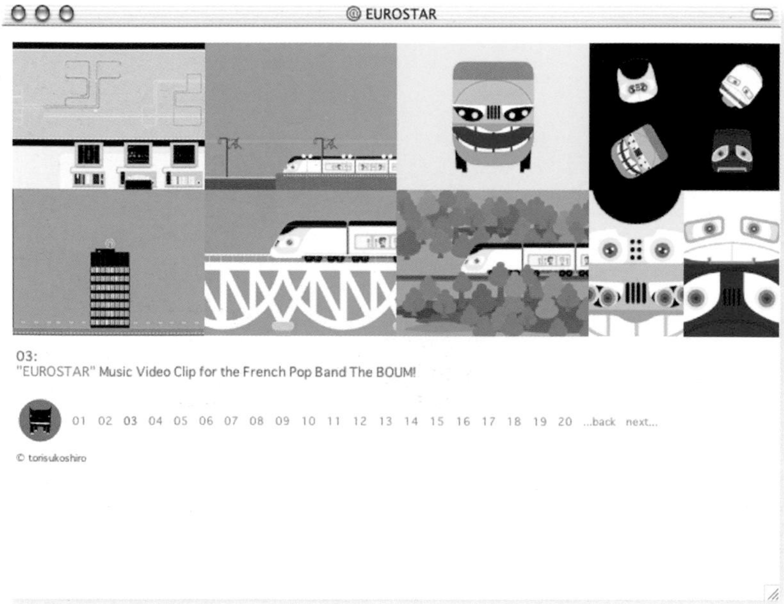
EUROSTAR
03:
"EUROSTAR" Music Video Clip for the French Pop Band The BOUM!
01 02 03 04 05 06 07 08 09 10 11 12 13 14 15 16 17 18 19 20 ...back next...
© torisukoshiro

WWW.TORISUKOSHIRO.COM
D: TORISUKOSHIRO
A: TORISUKOSHIRO, **M:** MISS_PIPI@HELLOKITTY.COM

LARSENPAGE.COM>>Larsen Official Website
© Larsen 2003 > CONTACT > FORUM
www.larsenpage.com

WWW.LARSENPAGE.COM
D: MATTHHEU BREGÈRE
M: MATTLARSEN@LAPOSTE.NET

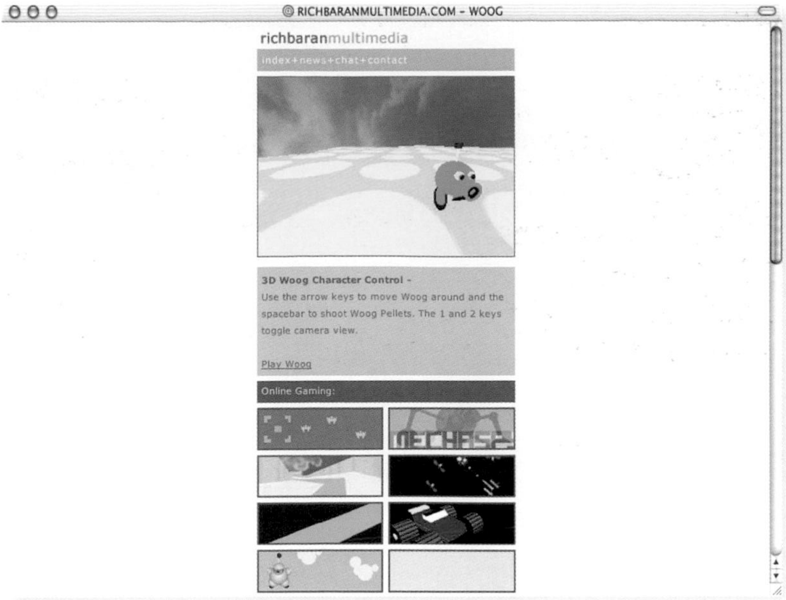

WWW.RICHBARANMULTIMEDIA.COM
D: RICH BARAN
M: RICH@PLASTICALLY.ORG

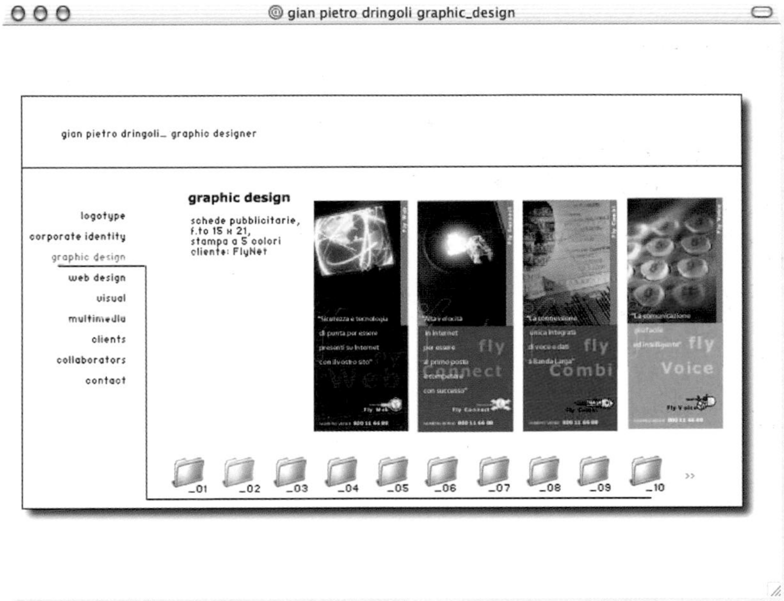

WWW.GIANPIETRODRINGOLI.COM
D: GIAN PIETRO DRINGOLI , **C:** FLYNET
A: GIAN PIETRO DRINGOLI GRAPHIC DESIGN, **M:** INFO@GIANPIETRODRINGOLI.COM

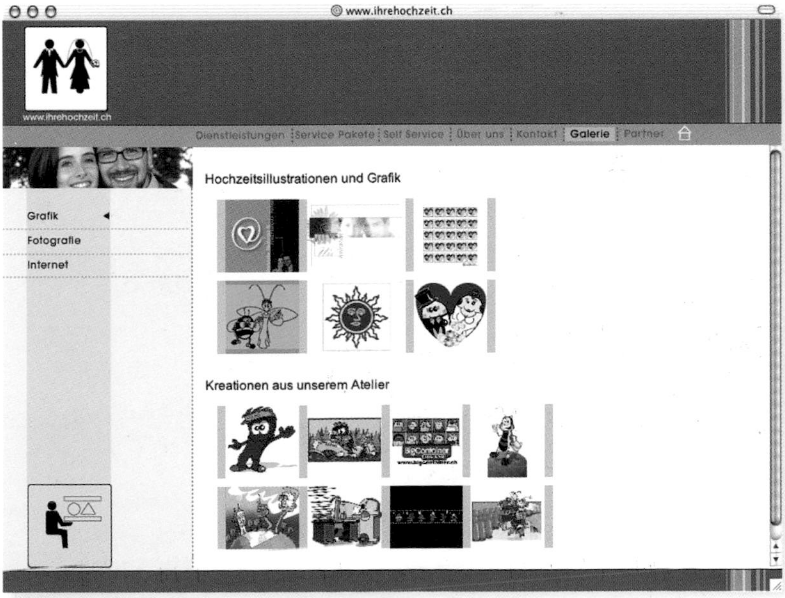

WWW.IHREHOCHZEIT.CH
D: PATRICK SASSINE
A: ACCONCEPT, **M:** P.SASSINE@ACCONCEPT.CH

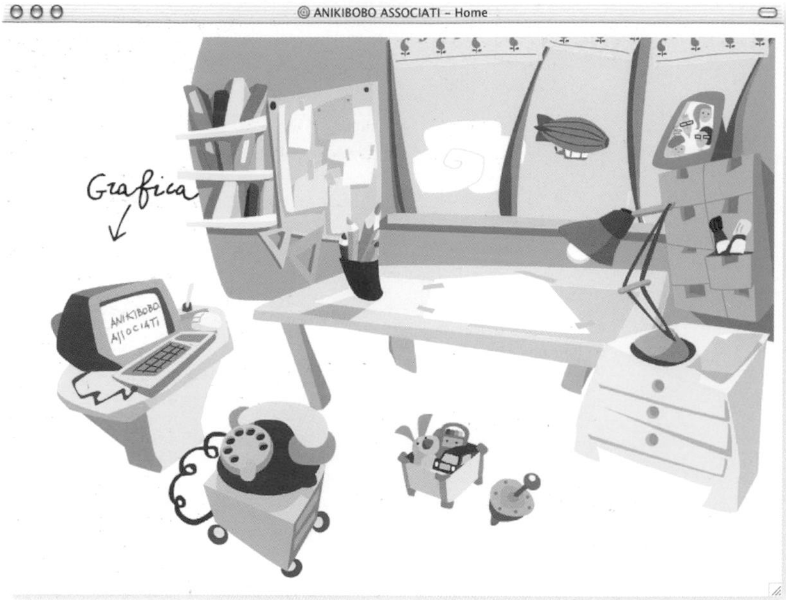

WWW.ANIKIBOBO.IT
D: ANIKIBOBO ASSOCIATI, **C:** PAOLO CAGLIERO
A: ANIKIBOBO ASSOCIATI, **M:** ANIKIBOBO@TISCALI.IT

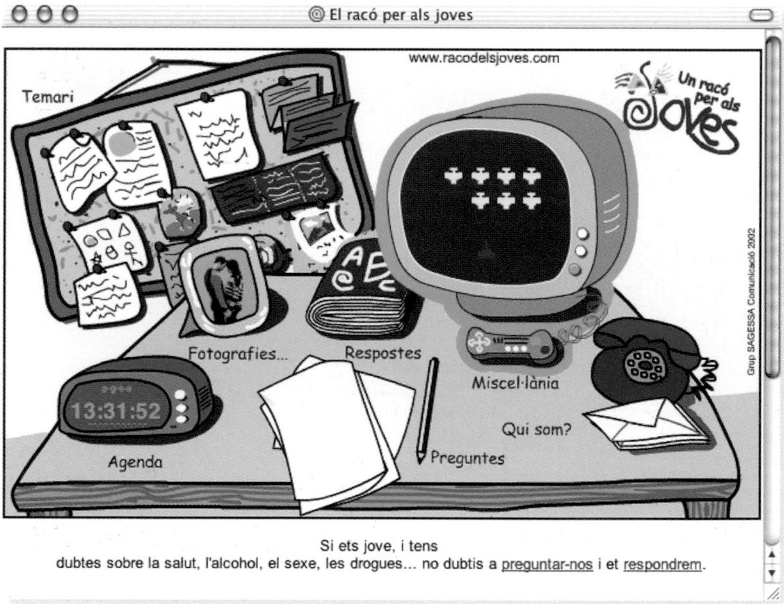

WWW.RACODELSJOVES.COM
D: JOSEP GARCIA CABALLÉ, **C:** JOSEP GARCIA CABALLÉ, **P:** GRUP SAGESSA
A: GRUP SAGESSA, **M:** JGARCIA@GRUPSAGESSA.COM

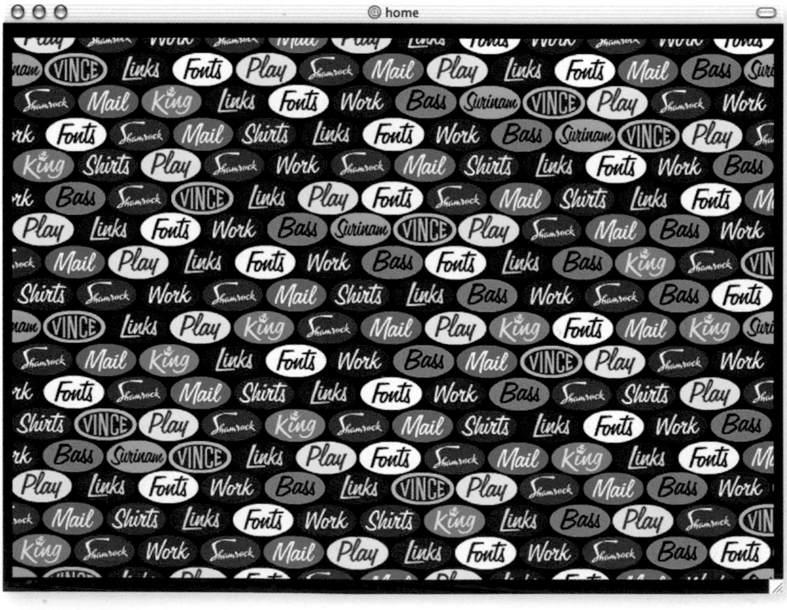

WWW.SHAMROCKING.COM
D: SHAMROCK
A: IMMERZEEL PICTURES, **M:** PASCAL@IMMERZEELPICTURES.COM

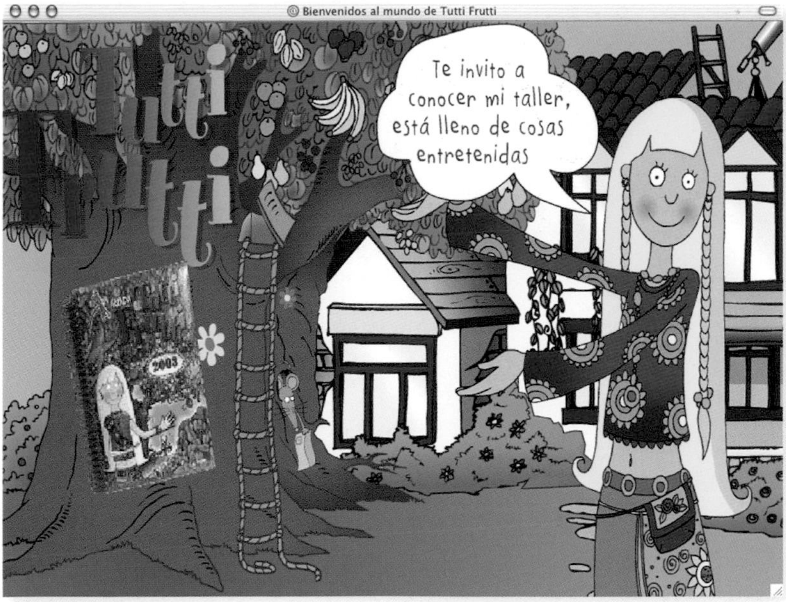

WWW.TUTTIFRUTTI.CL
D: CHRISTIAN CABRERA
A: OVO LTDA., **M:** OVO@OVO.CL

WWW.HOME.KIMO.COM.TW/LUCIUSZIN
D: LUCIUS NICHOLAS WINK
A: IMAGE POWER, **M:** LUCIUS.LUCIUS@MSA.HINET.NET

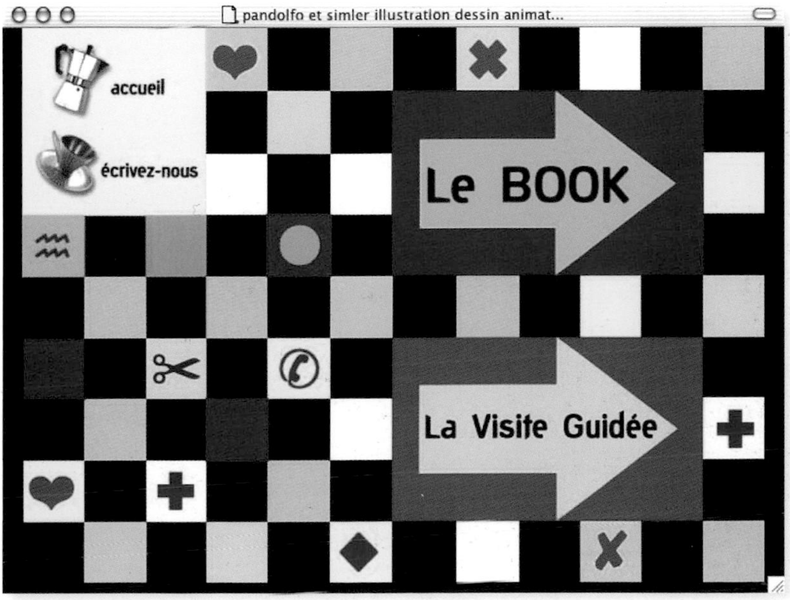

WWW.PANDOLFO-SIMLER.COM
D: PATRICE ELIE ALATIENNE
A: ALATIENNE, **M:** ALATIENNE@WANADOO.FR

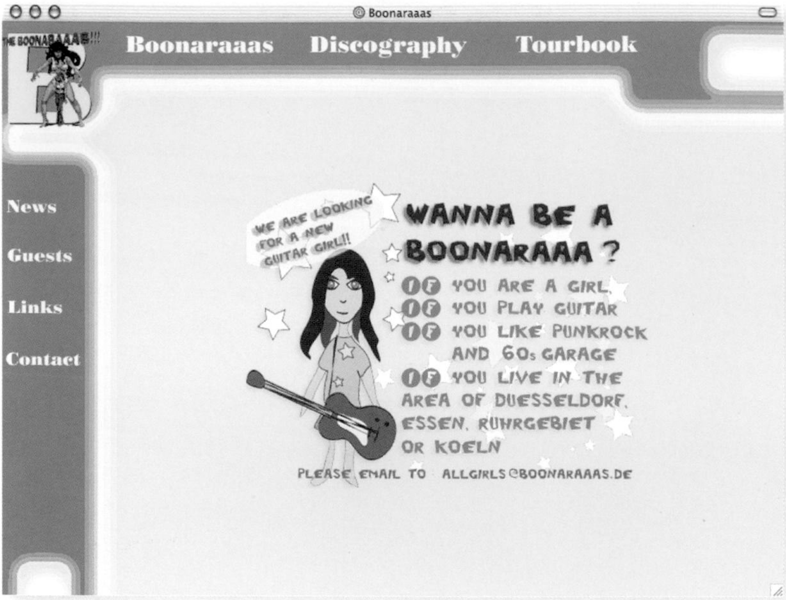

WWW.BOONARAAAS.DE
D: VERONIKA CASPERS
M: LOVERONIKA@HOTMAIL.COM

WWW.LIPTONICETEA.PT/FUSION
D: JOAO FERNANDES, **C:** JOAO FERNANDES, **P:** RUTE FRANÇA
A: VIEW., **M:** JOAO.FERNANDES@VIEW.PT

WWW.VALGANON.COM/SPACEMATH
D: GUSTAVO VALGANON
M: GUSTAVO@VALGANON.COM

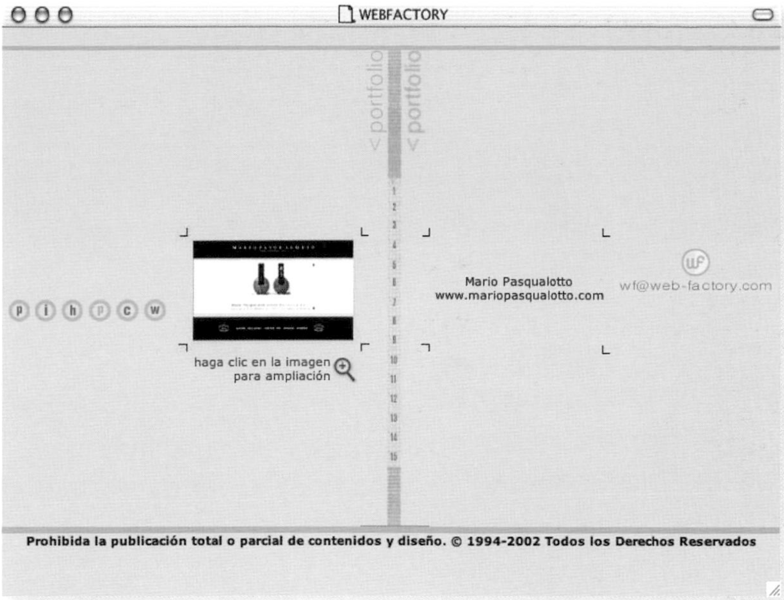

WWW.WEB-FACTORY.COM/WF.HTM.COM
D: WEBFACTORY INTERNET SL
A: WEBFACTORY INTERNET SL, **M:** WF@WEB-FACTORY.COM

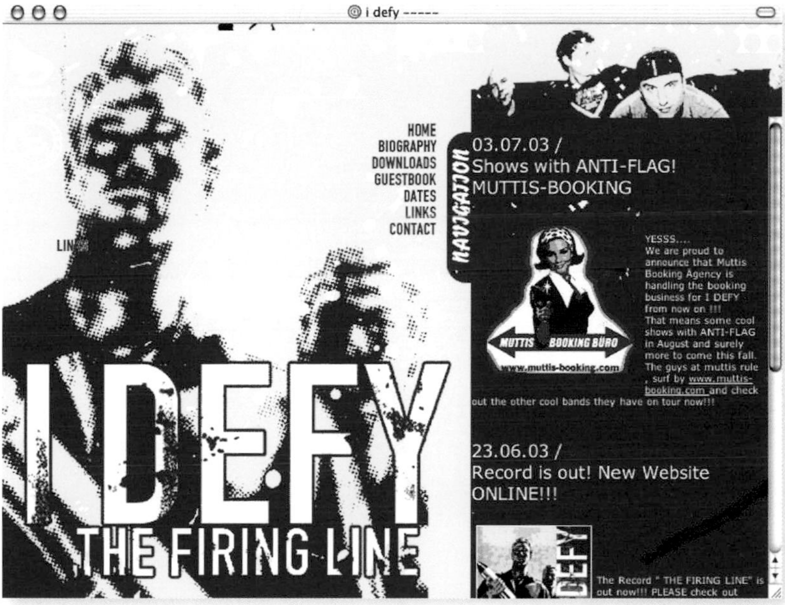

WWW.VEILONLINE.DE/IDEFY/INDEX_MAIN.HTML
D: RAOUL FESTANTE
M: INFO@IDEFY.DE

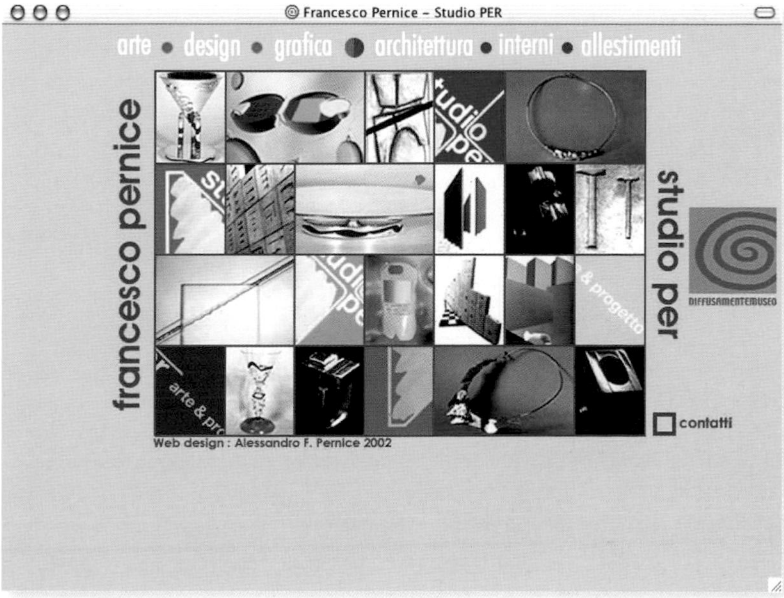

WWW.FRANCESCO-PERNICE.COM
D: ALESSANDRO PERNICE
A: DHARMABUM DESIGN, **M:** AF.PERNICE@TIN.IT

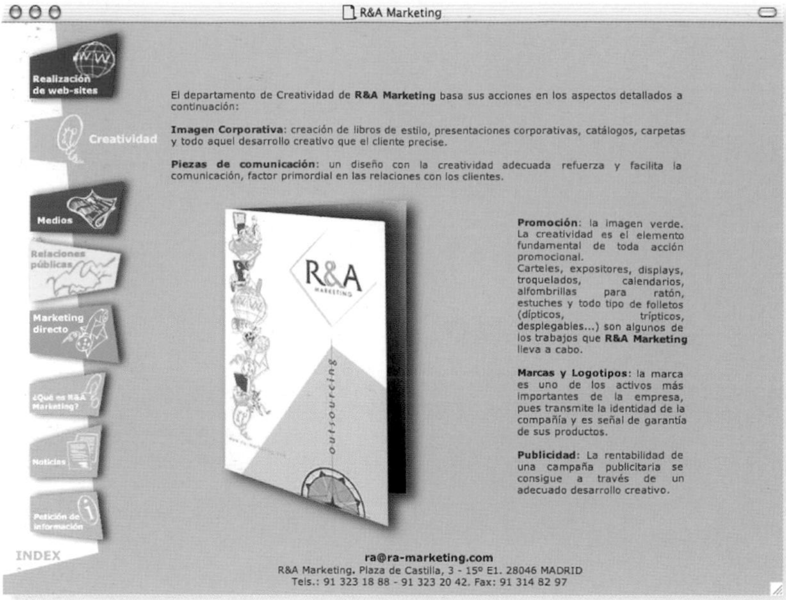

WWW.RA-MARKETING.COM
D: ESTEFANÍA PÉREZ HUERGA
A: R&A MARKETING, **M:** EPH@RA-MARKETING.COM

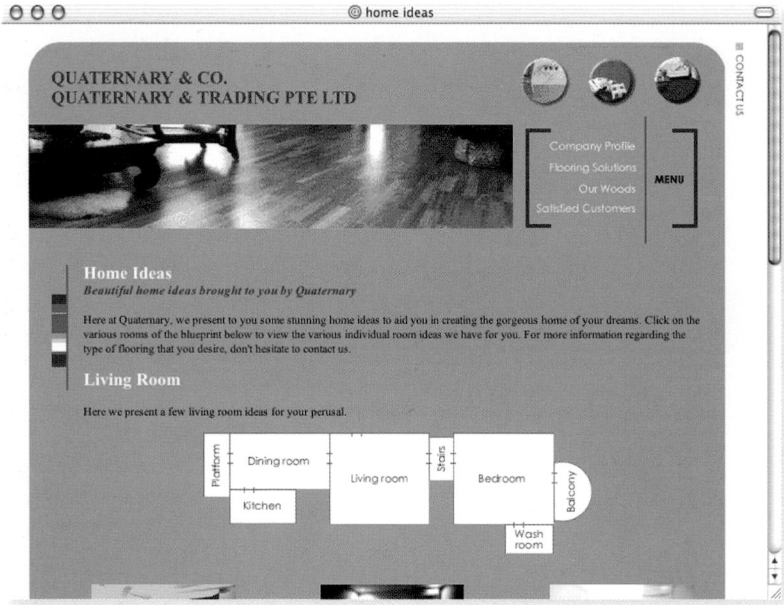

WWW.QUATERNARY-CO.COM
D: JOANNA SUN
A: PUREDIVINITY, **M:** PUREDIVINITY@MAC.COM

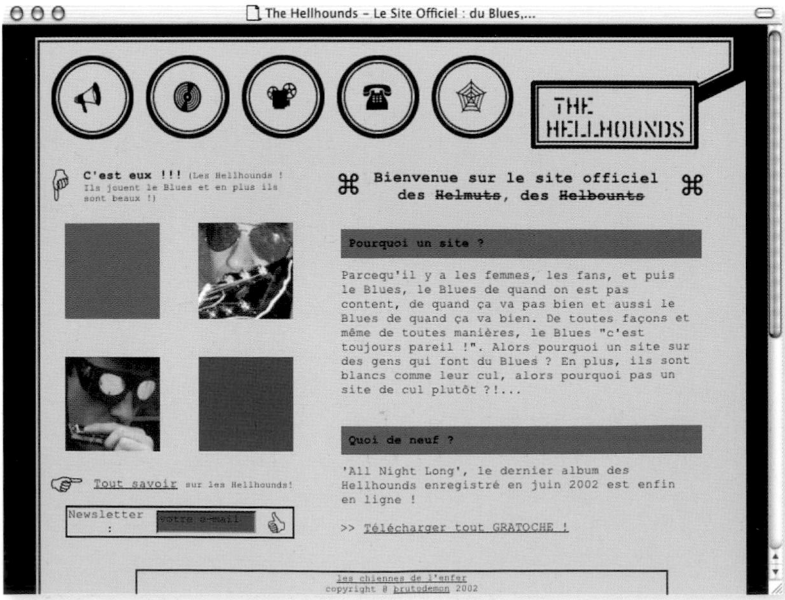

WWW.LESHELLHOUNDS.COM
D: TIMOTHÉE BRUDIEU
A: THE HELLHOUNDS, **M:** BRUTODEMON@LESHELLHOUNDS.COM

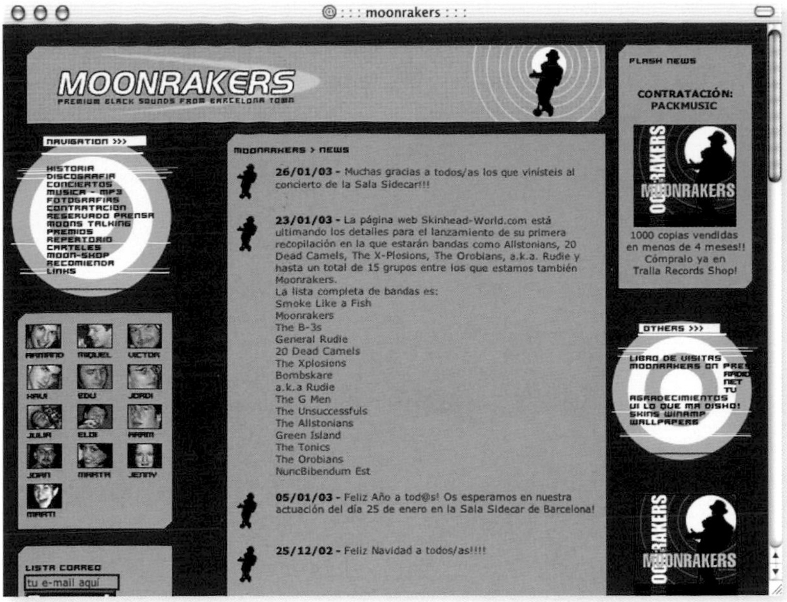

WWW.BOSS-SOUNDS.ORG/MOONRAKERS
D: GIORGIO
M: GIORGIO@BOSS-SOUNDS.ORG

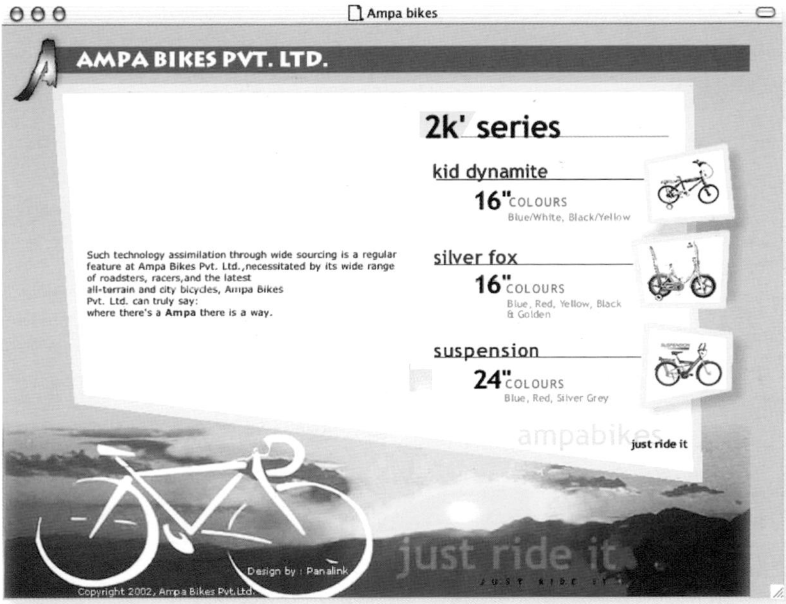

WWW.AMPABIKES.COM
D: AIJAZ HUSAIN, **C:** AKHILESH, **P:** PANALINK
A: PANALINK INFOTECH LTD., **M:** AIJAZ@PANALINKS.COM

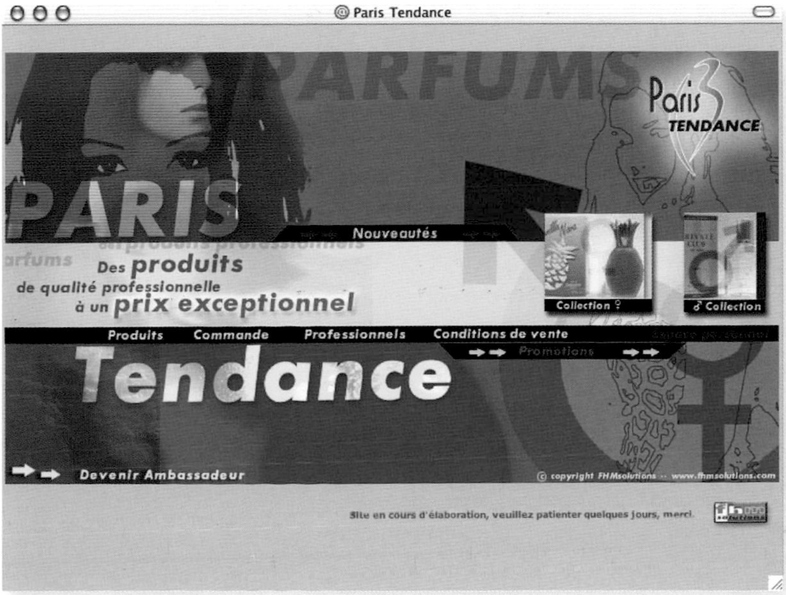

WWW.PARIS-TENDANCE.COM
D: FRANCIS GILLAIN
A: FHMSOLUTIONS, **M:** FGILLAIN@FHMSOLUTIONS.COM

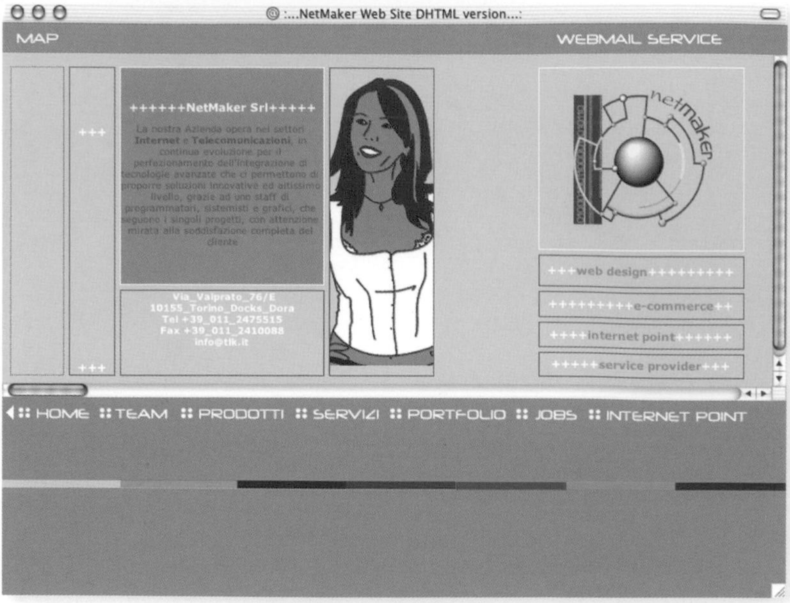

WWW.NETOK.IT
D: PAOLA REVELLO, **C:** CHIARA BUSATTO, **P:** CHIARA BUSATTO
A: NETMAKER SRL, **M:** PAOLA@TLK.IT

WWW.AFTERWEB.COM/JEMA
D: ANDREA FILACCHIONI, **C:** AFTER S.R.L., **P:** ANDREA FILACCHIONI
A: AFTER S.R.L., **M:** ANDREA.FILACCHIONI@AFTER.IT

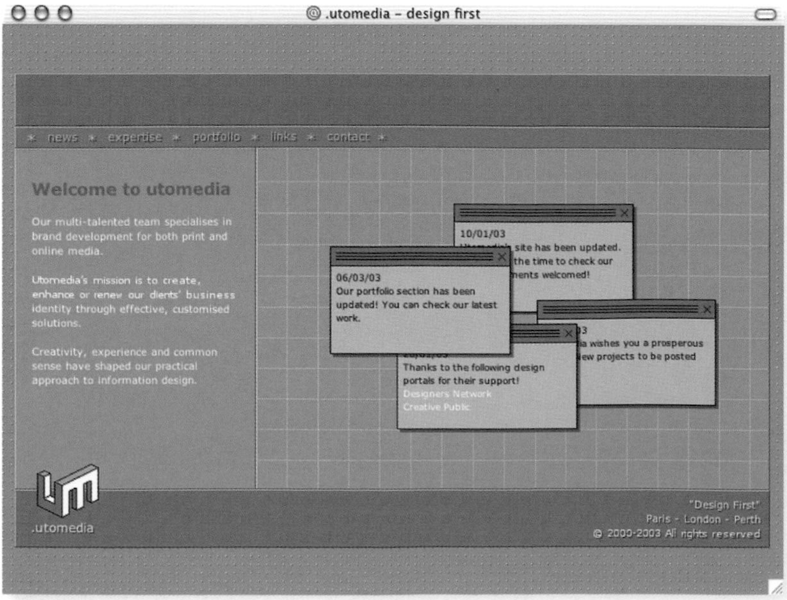

WWW.UTOMEDIA.COM
D: CIRO WILLIAM LULIANO
A: UTOMEDIA, **M:** INFO@UTOMEDIA.COM

WWW.AVONTUUR.COM
D: ROGIER KONING
M: R.KONING75@CHELLO.NL

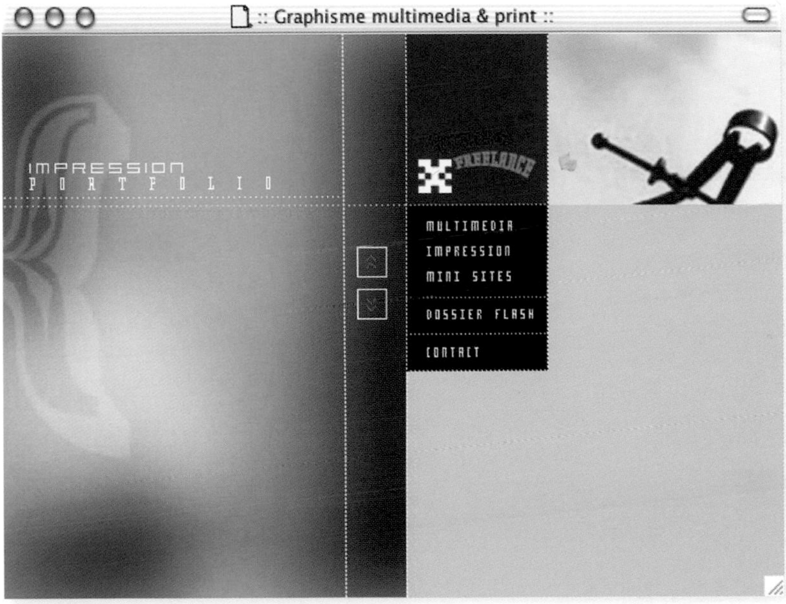

WWW.BRASERO.COM
D: THIERRY SCIARE
A: BRASERO, **M:** SCITY@WANADOO.FR

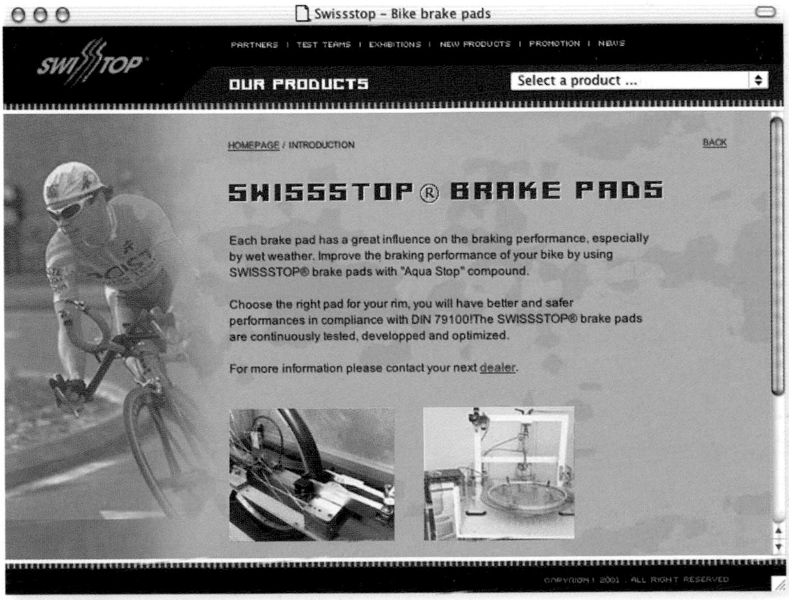

WWW.SWISSSTOP.CH
D: CRISTIANO SIFARI, **C:** CRISTIANO SIFARI, **P:** SERGIO VALOTI
M: CSIFARI@BSVC.NET

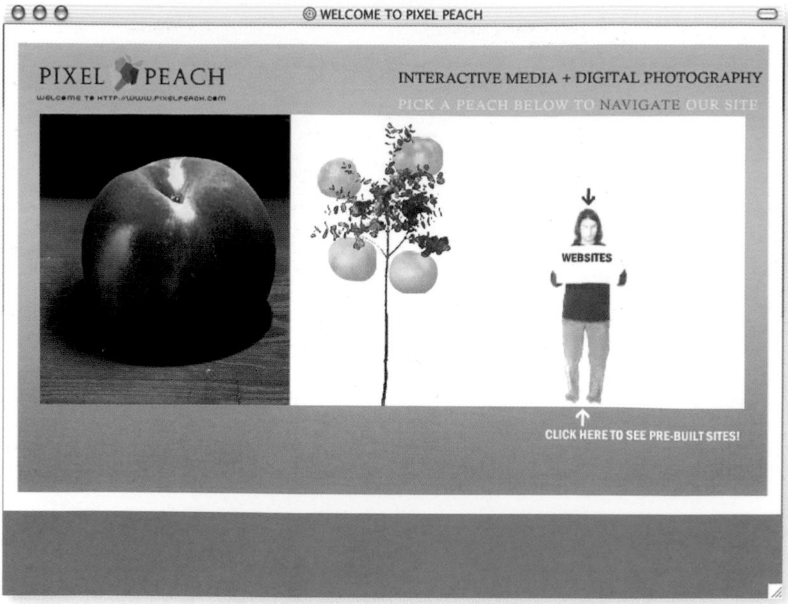

WWW.PIXELPEACH.COM
D: GARY A. DORSEY
A: PIXEL PEACH STUDIO, **M:** GARY@PIXELPEACH.COM

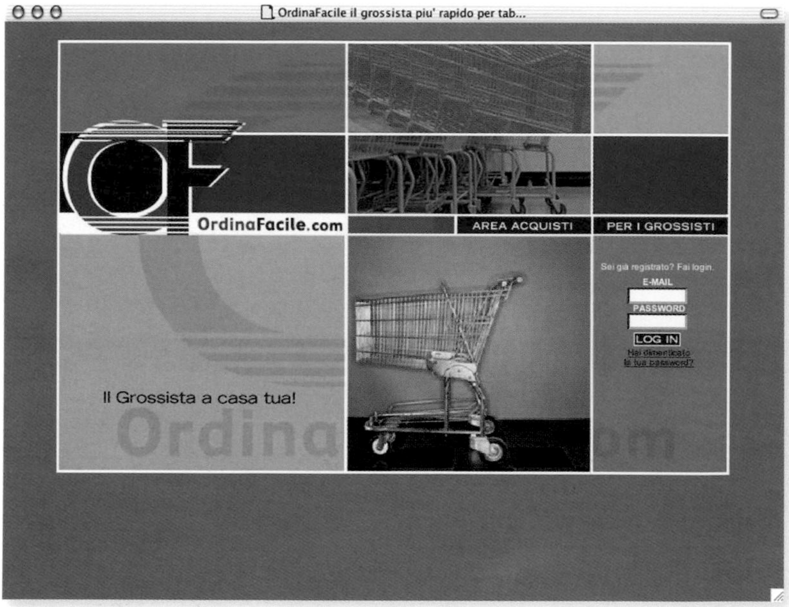

WWW.ORDINAFACILE.IT
D: STEFANO A. SALES, **C:** CHRIS YABU TAKASHI
M: SASALES@BBJ.IT

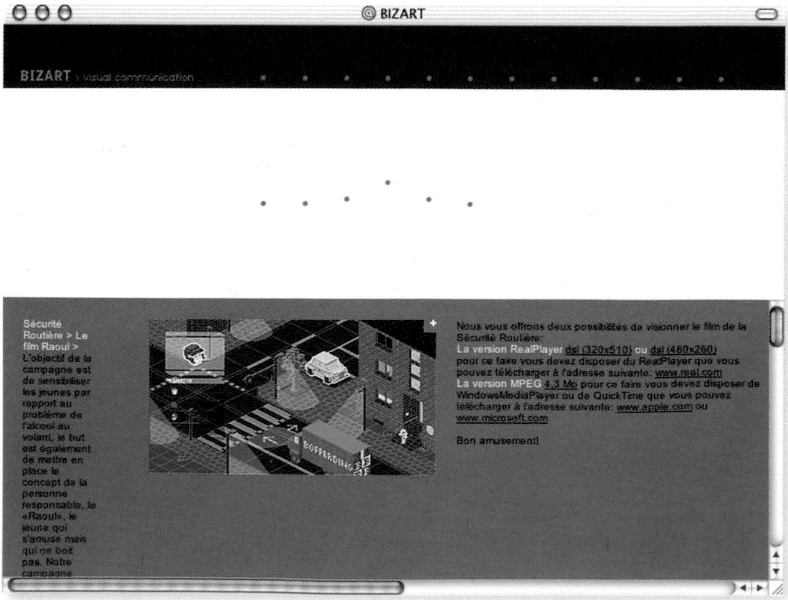

WWW.BIZART.LU
D: LAURENT DAUBACH, **C:** VIKTOR DICK, **P:** ISABELLE CANIVET
A: BIZART, **M:** CONTACT@BIZART.LU

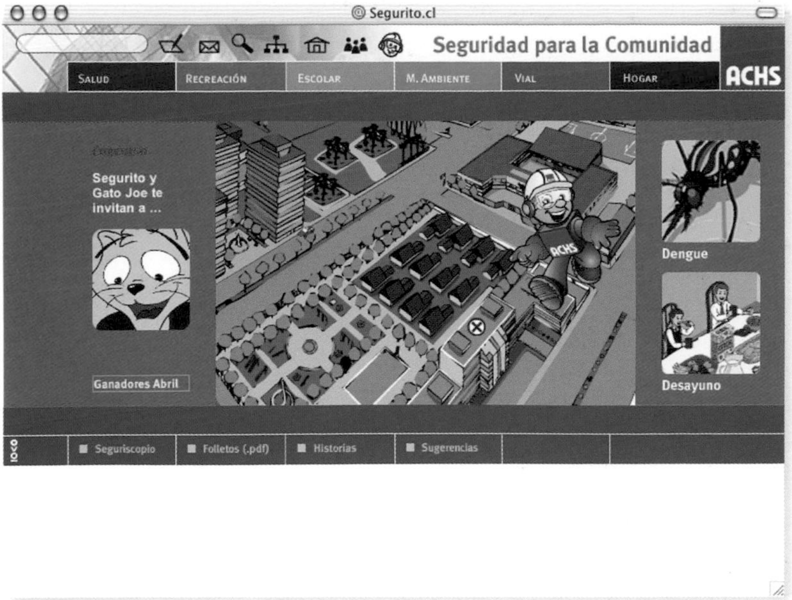

WWW.SEGURITO.CL
D: CHRISTIAN CABRERA, **C:** OVO LTDA., **P:** OVO LTDA.
A: OVO LTDA., **M:** OVO@OVO.CL

WWW.PARASOL-ONLINE.DE
D: KAI GREIM
M: INFO@GRAFIKAI.DE

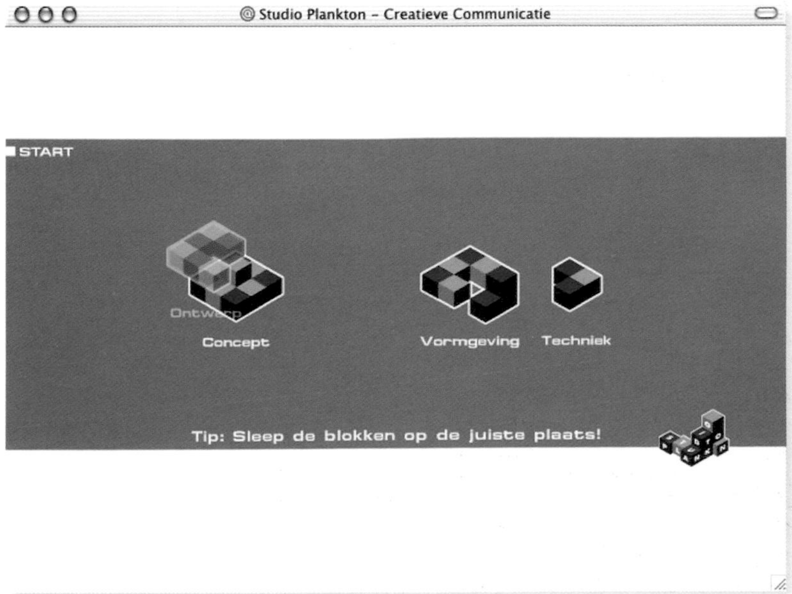

WWW.STUDIOPLANKTON.NL
D: REMCO VAN DER TOORN
A: STUDIO PLANKTON, **M:** REMCO@STUDIOPLANKTON.NL

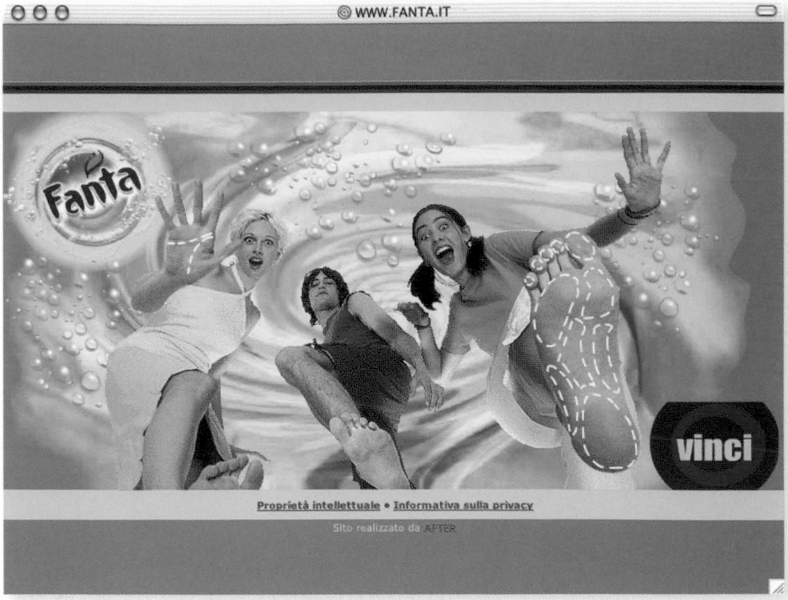

WWW.FANTA.IT
D: SERENELLA DI VITTORIO, **C:** AFTER S.R.L., **P:** ANDREA FILACCHIONI
A: AFTER S.R.L., **M:** ANDREA.FILACCHIONI@AFTER.IT

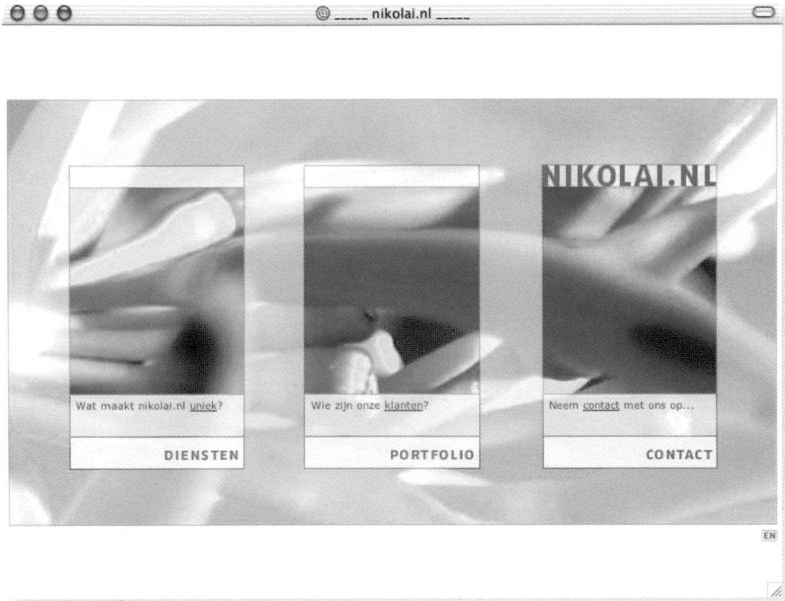

WWW.NIKOLAI.NL
D: NIKOLAI ZAUBER
A: NIKOLAI.NL, **M:** INFO@NIKOLAI.NL

WWW.ALCINOODESIGN.COM
D: NICOLA DESTEFANIS
A: ALCINOODESIGN, **M:** ALCINOO@ALCINOODESIGN.COM

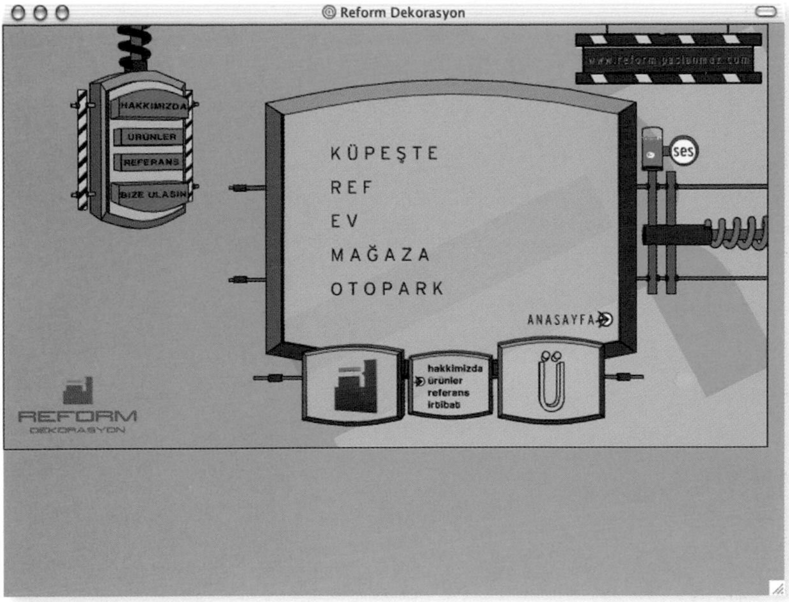

WWW.REFORMPASLANMAZ.COM
D: AROYO METIN
A: 18 DESIGN, **M:** MOSCAR@SUPERONLINE.COM

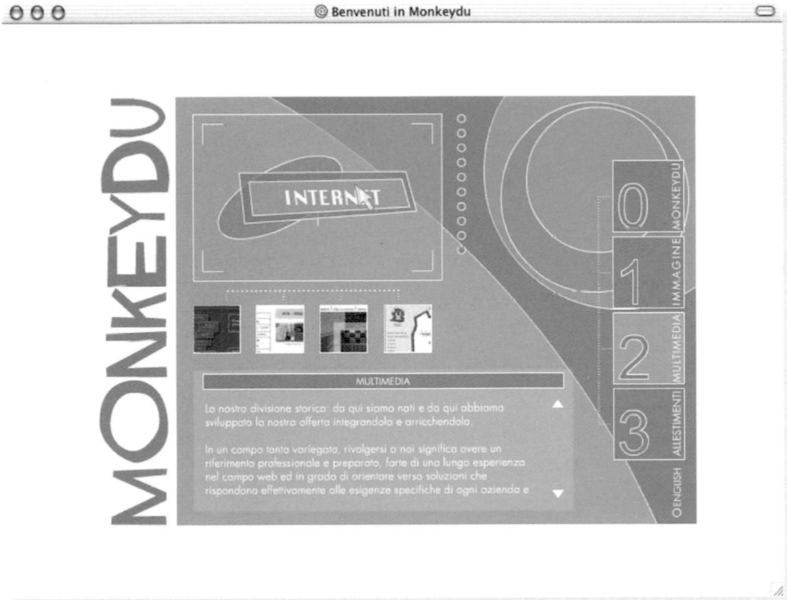

WWW.MONKEYDU.COM
D: MONKEYDU, **C:** CHIARA TORREGGIANI, **P:** MONKEYDU
A: MONKEYDU, **M:** CHIARA@MONKEYDU.COM

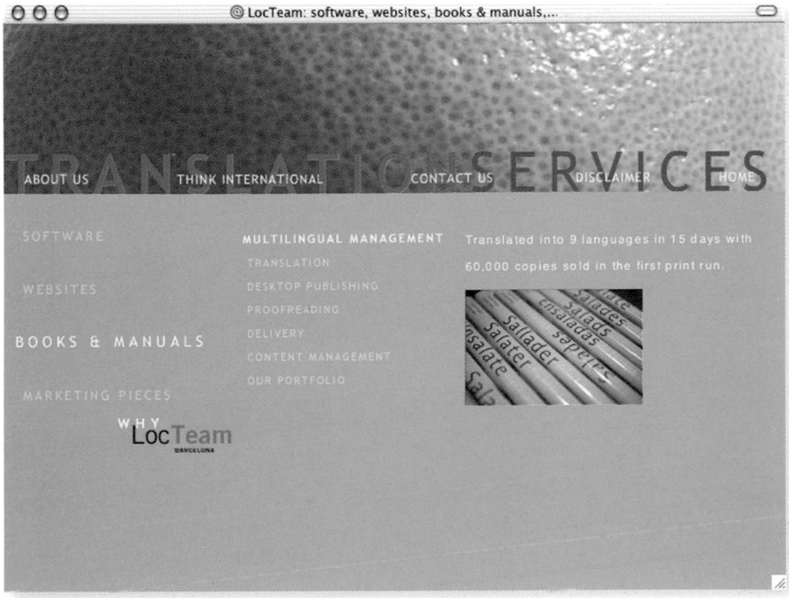

WWW.LOCTEAM.COM
D: ELENA PALLCA, **C:** ALBERT
A: BUENAVISTA STUDIO, **M:** MAIL@BUENAVISTASTUDIO.COM

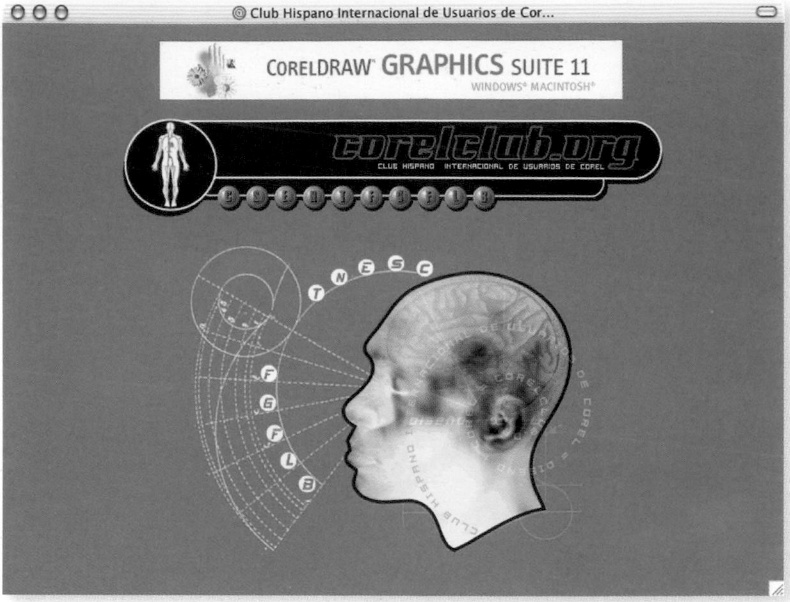

WWW.CORELCLUB.ORG
D: ANNA MARIA LOPEZ LOPEZ
A: ANNA-OM-LINE DISEÑO MULTIMEDIATICO, **M:** ANNA@FASHIONMAS.COM

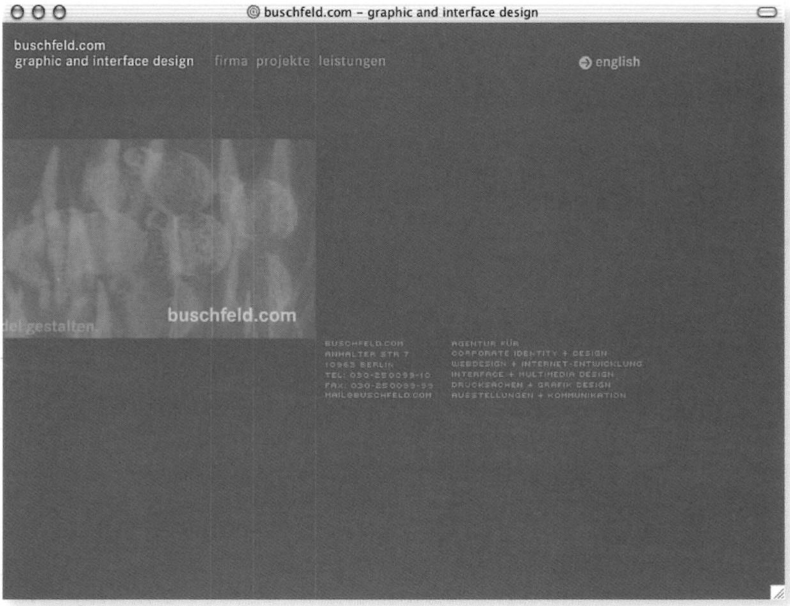

WWW.BUSCHFELD.COM
D: BEN BUSCHFELD
A: BUSCHFELD.COM - GRAPHIC AND INTERFACE DESIGN, **M:** MAIL@BUSCHFELD.COM

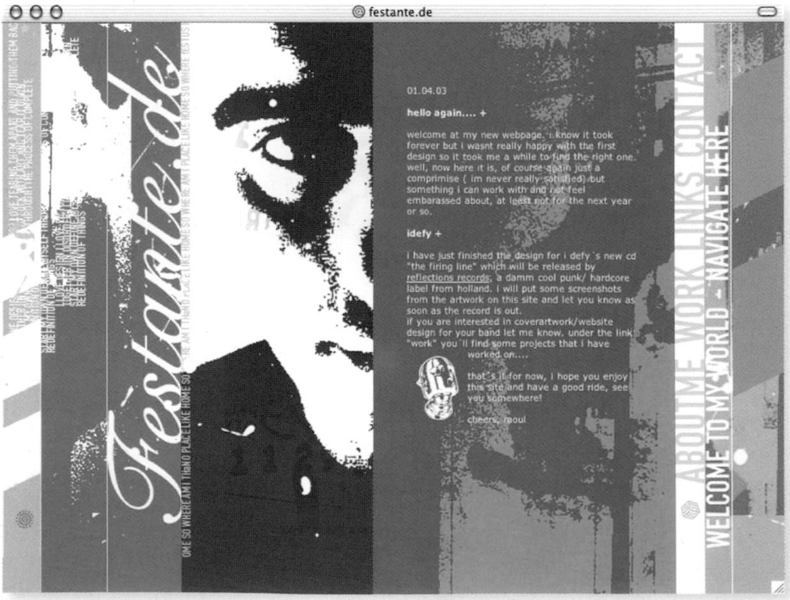

WWW.FESTANTE.DE/INDEX_MAIN.HTM
D: RAOUL FESTANTE
A: FESTANTE, **M:** RAOUL@FESTANTE.DE

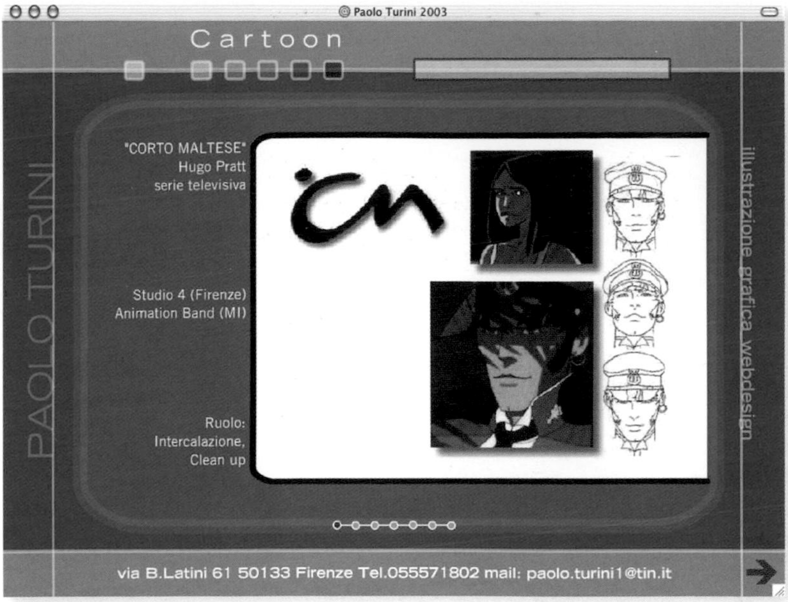

WWW.PAOLOTURINI.COM
D: PAOLO TURINI
A: PAOLO TURINI, **M:** PAOLO.TURINI1@TIN.IT

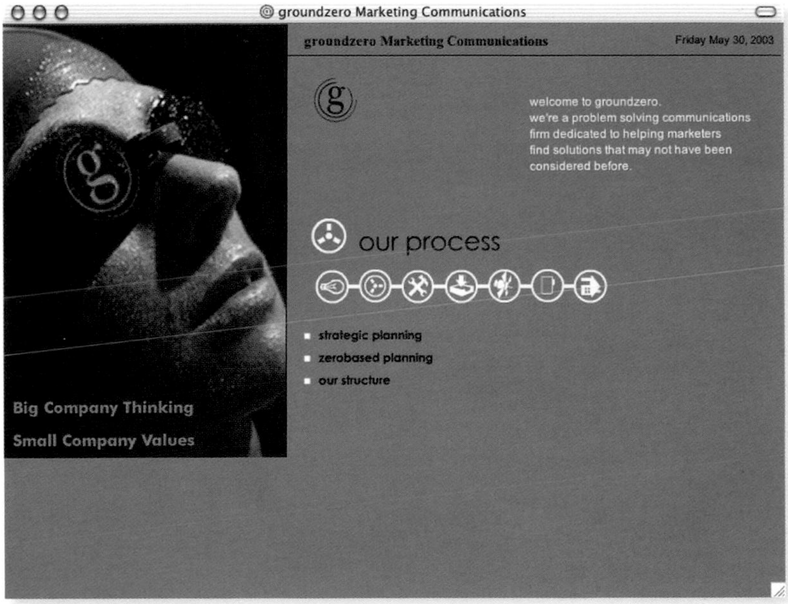

WWW.GROUNDZEROMC.COM
D: DAVE DOBSON
M: DAVEDOBSON@YAHOO.COM

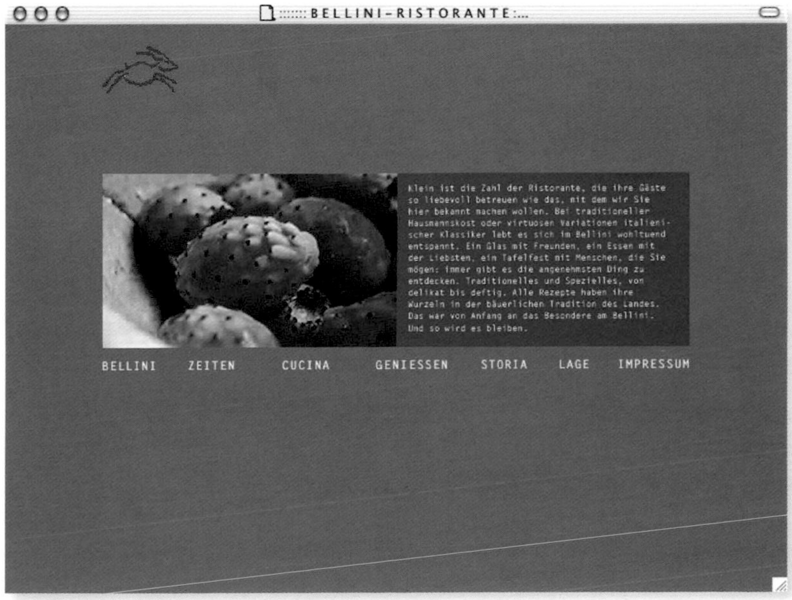

WWW.TOUCHEE.DE/BELLINI
D: WALTER MÖSSLER, **C:** PACO LALUCA, **P:** BAMBOO PRODUCTION
A: TOUCHEE, **M:** INFO@TOUCHEE.DE

WWW.BERNARDI.NET
D: ICCARDO MIGLIAVACCA, **C:** FABIO PIN, **P:** ENRICO DEGRASSI
A: IKON MULTIMEDIA, **M:** RICCARDO@IKON.IT

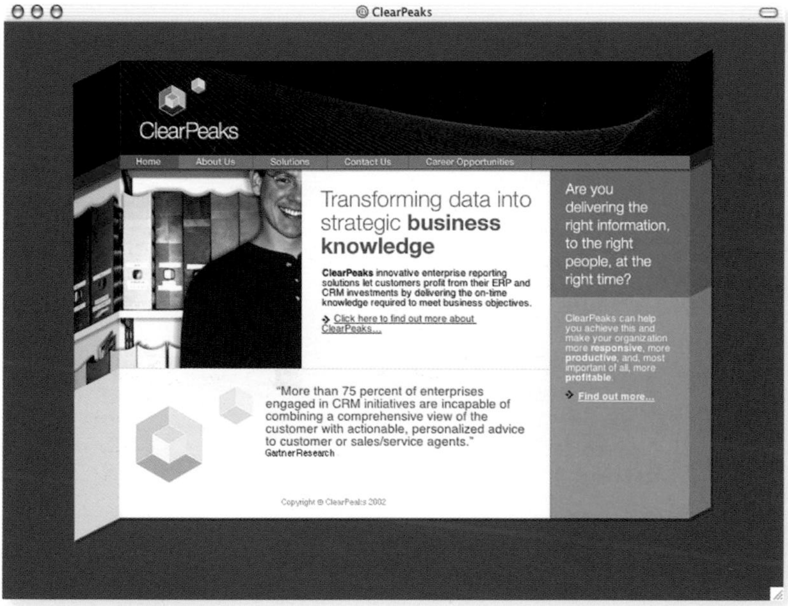

WWW.CLEARPEAKS.COM
D: JUAN CARLOS CAMMAERT
M: JC@CAMMAERT.COM

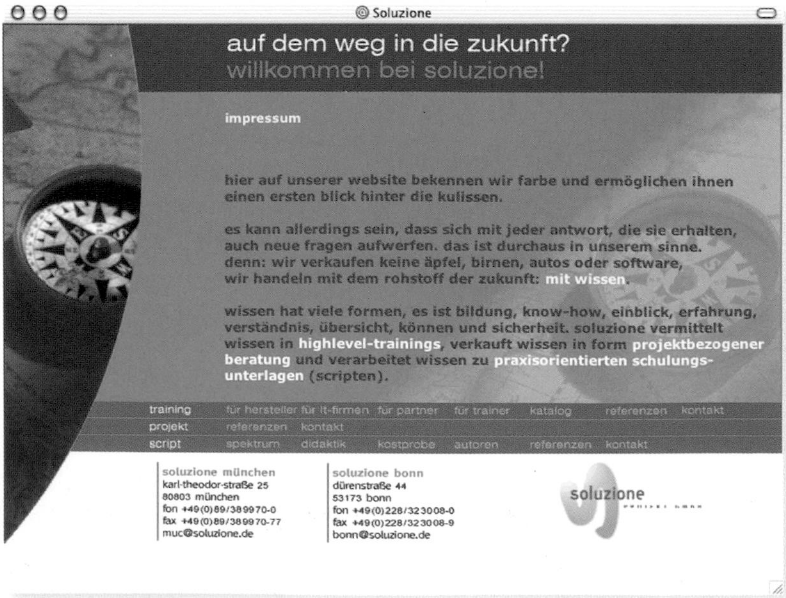

WWW.SOLUZIONE.DE
D: STEFAN BEHRINGER, **C:** JUERGEN WUNDERLE
A: D:\SIGN CREATIVECONCEPTS, **M:** BEHRINGER@DSIGN.DE

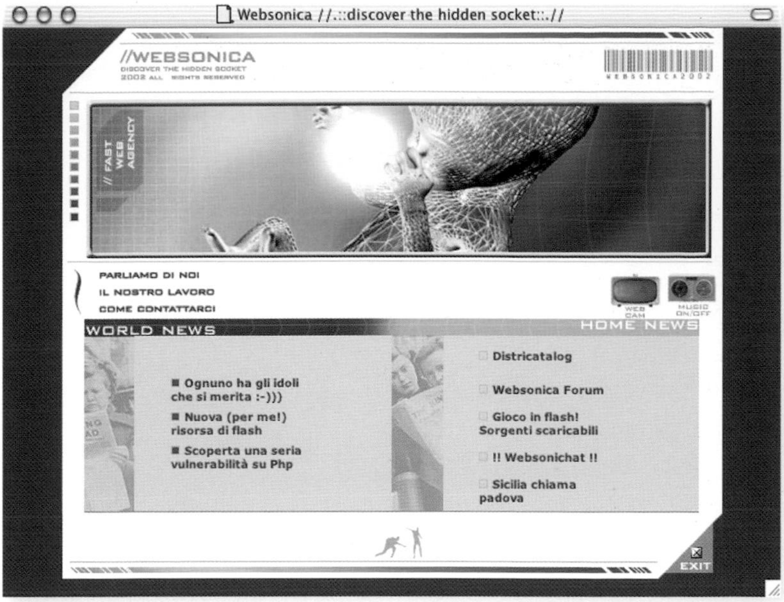

WWW.WEBSONICA.NET/DATA/CHI.PHP
D: GIOVANNI FAGHERAZZI
A: WEBSONICA, **M:** GIO@WEBSONICA.NET

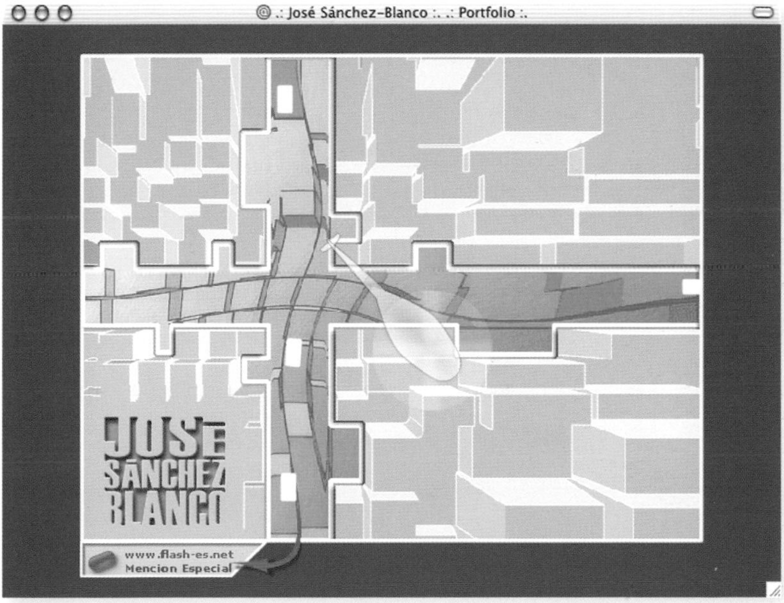

WWW.WEBCINDARIO.COM/JOSETE
D: JOSE SÁNCHEZ-BLANCO
M: JOSETE2002@TELEPOLIS.COM

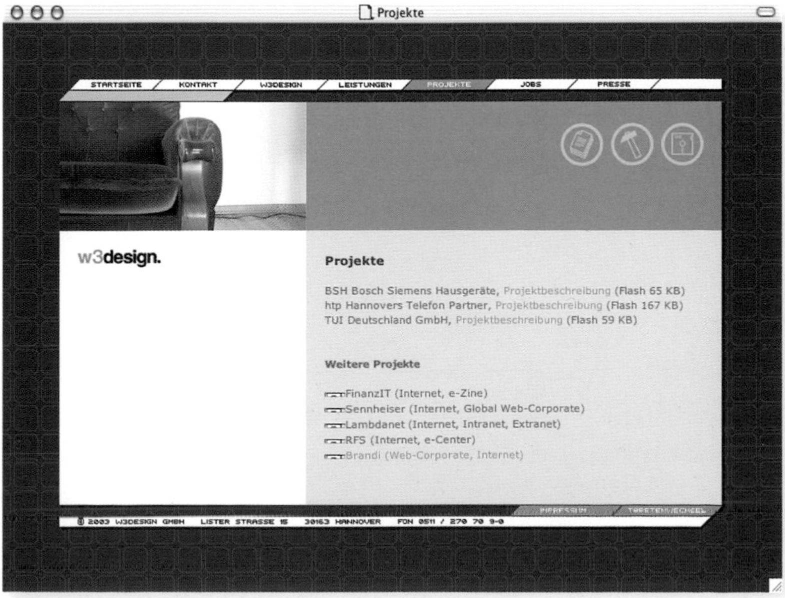

WWW.W3DESIGN.DE
D: BJÖRN PITZSCHKE
A: W3DESIGN GMBH, **M:** BJOERN.PITZSCHKE@W3DESIGN.DE

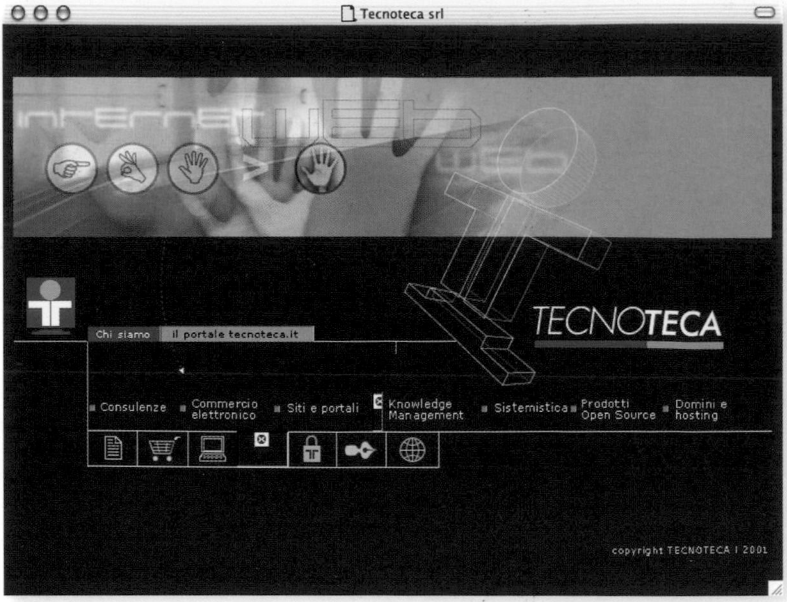

WWW.TECNOTECA.COM
D: DARIA BIASIZZO
A: TECNOTECA SRL, **M:** L.DELLAMARINA@TECNOTECA.IT

WWW.FERRAZ.NET
D: EDUARDO FERRAZ
A: FERRAZ NET PRODUCOES AUDIOVISUAIS, **M:** INFO@FERRAZ.NET

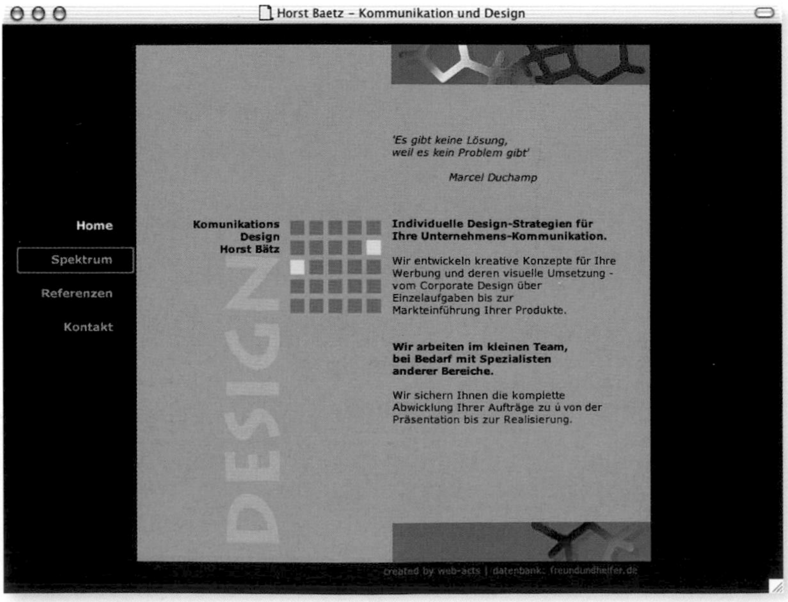

WWW.BAETZDESIGN.DE
D: HORST BÄTZ , JESSIKA BÄTZ, **C:** JESSIKA BÄTZ , TIM SCHOMMER, **P:** WEB-ACTS
A: WEB-ACTS, **M:** INFO@WEB-ACTS.DE

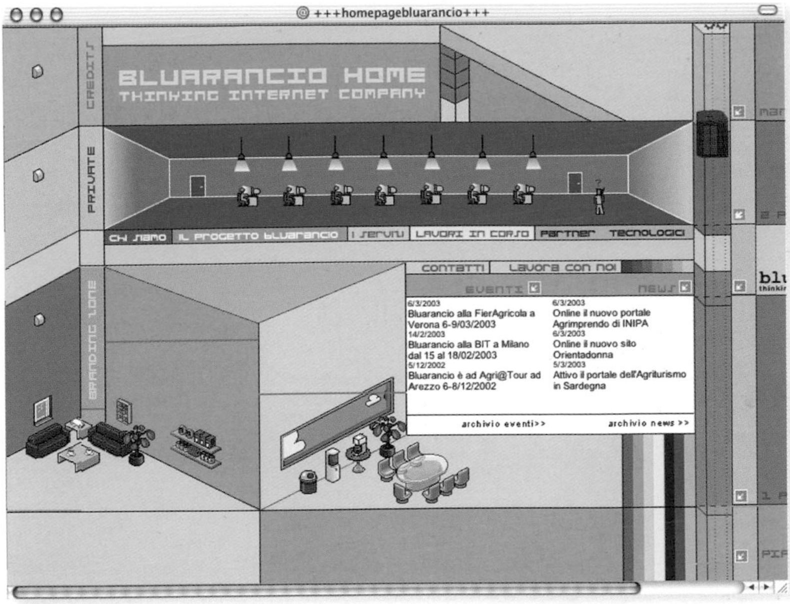

WWW.BLUARANCIO.COM
D: MICHELE CATANI, **C:** LUCA FOSCHI, **P:** MICHELE CATANI
A: BLUARANCIO, **M:** MICHELE.CATANI@BLUARANCIO.COM

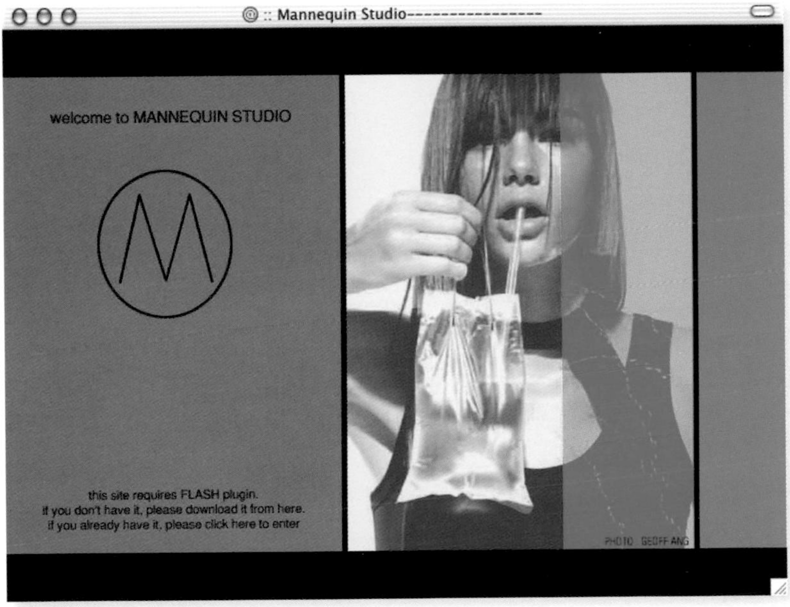

WWW.MANNEQUIN.COM.SG
D: JACK LEE, **C:** JACK LEE, **P:** DAVID BECKER
A: NXSPACE PTE LTD, **M:** TILLMANN@NXSPACE.COM

WWW.CHEB.CO.KR
D: MYUNG-HUN LEE
M: GREGHUNS@LYCOS.CO.KR

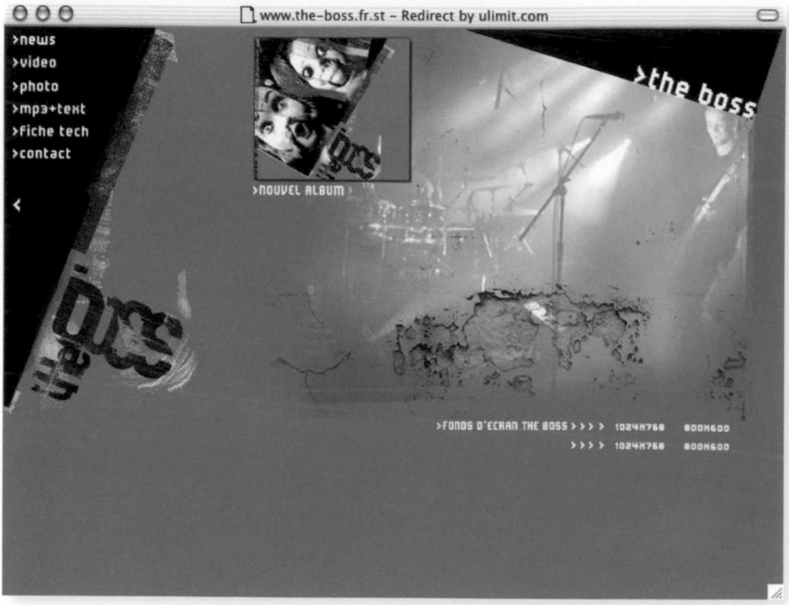

WWW.THE-BOSS.FR.ST
D: SAM HAYLES, **C:** JULIEN MOREL, **P:** JULIEN MOREL
A: DOSE-PRODUCTIONS, **M:** SAM@DOSE-PRODUCTIONS.COM

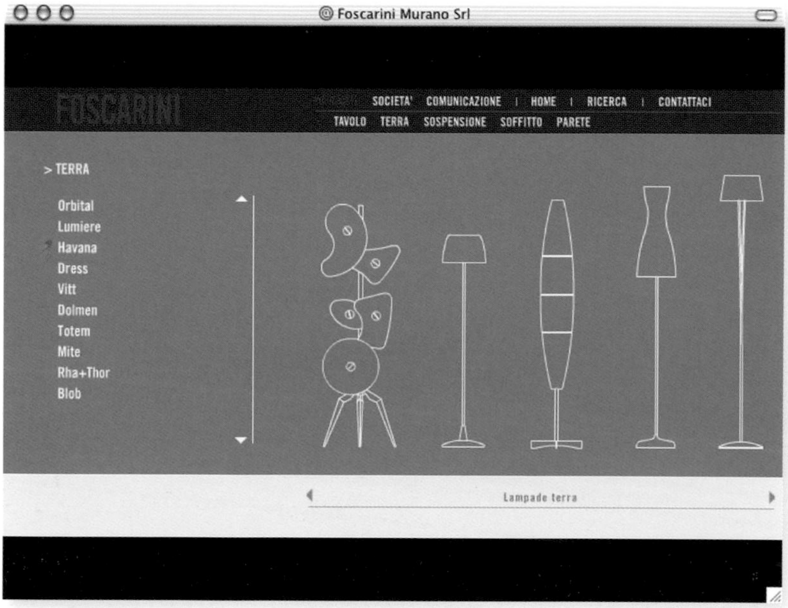

WWW.FOSCARINI.COM
D: MONICA FACCIO, **C:** SEVEN, **P:** FOSCARINI MURANO SRL
A: DESIGNWORK, **M:** MONICA@DESIGNWORK.IT

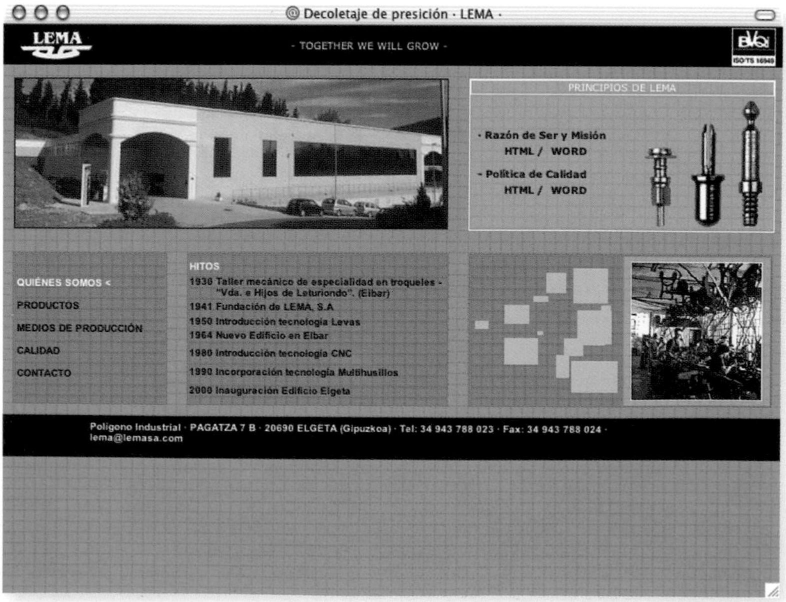

WWW.LEMASA.COM
D: IKER MICHELENA
A: ENTREWEBS, **M:** IMITXELENA@ENTREWEBS.COM

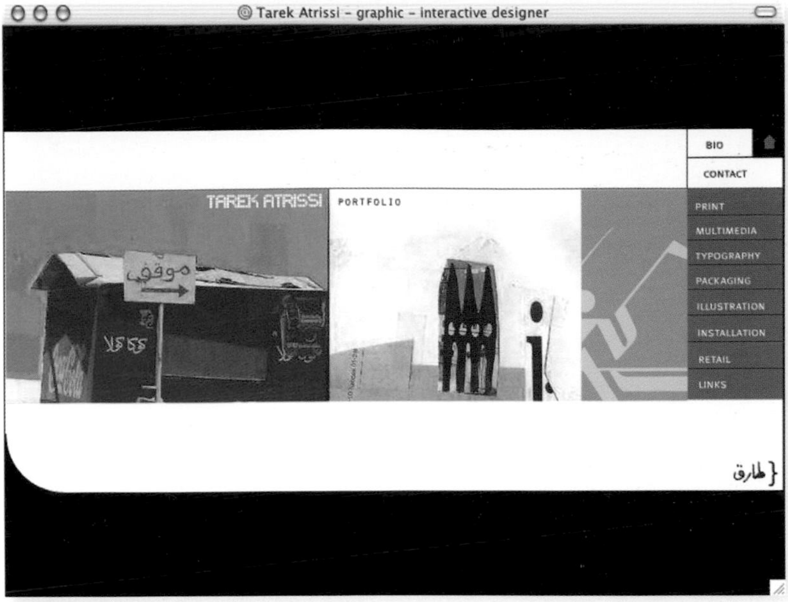

WWW.ATRISSI.COM
D: TAREK ATRISSI
A: TAREK ATRISSI DESIGN, **M:** TAREK@ATRISSI.COM

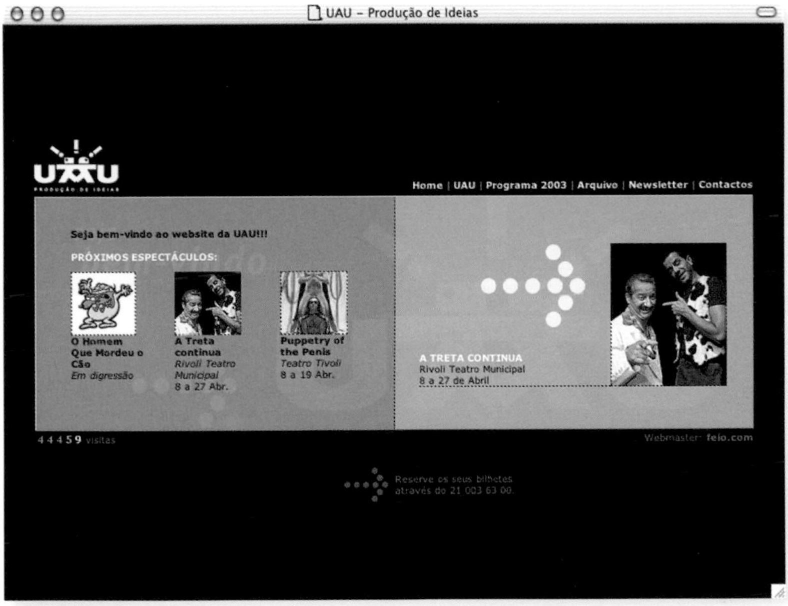

WWW.UAU.PT
D: FILIPE FEIO
A: FILIPE FEIO, **M:** FILIPE@FEIO.COM

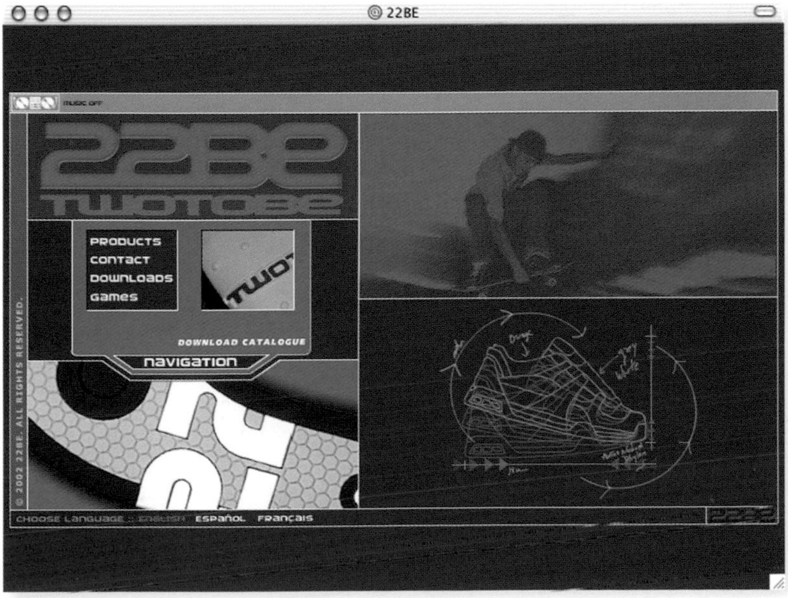

WWW.22BE.COM
D: RICHARD TALUT, **C:** RICHARD TALUT, **P:** RICHARD TALUT & ANA MORENO
A: ESTUDIO ANA MORENO, **M:** RICHARD-STUDIO@MENTA.NET

WWW.SALAMANDRAONLINE.COM
D: LORENTE TÓRTOLA / RODRIGUEZ RIBA, **C:** LORENTE TÓRTOLA, **P:** RODRIGUEZ RIBA
A: EVD, **M:** EVD@SALAMANDRAONLINE.COM

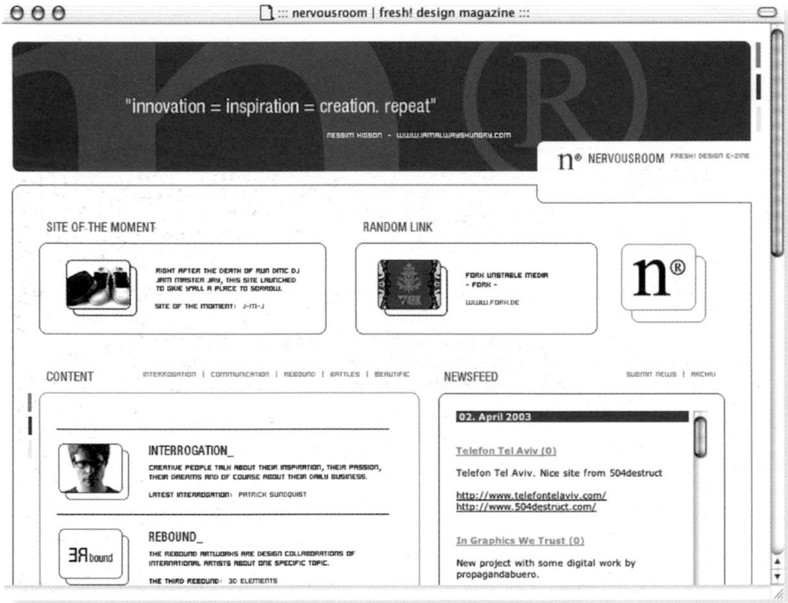

WWW.NERVOUSROOM.COM
D: MATTHIAS GILLE, **C:** DANIEL HARRINGTON
M: MATTHIAS@XTENSIVE.DE

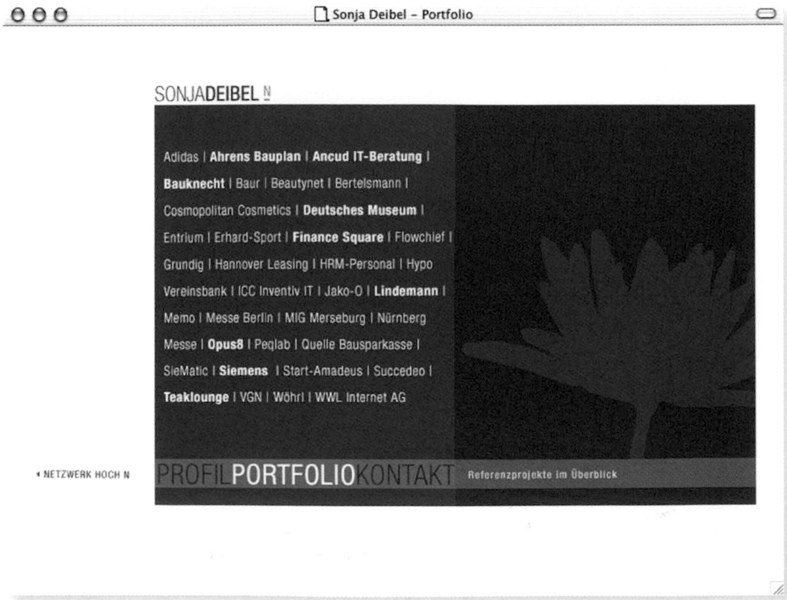

WWW.HOCH-N.DE
D: SONJA DEIBEL, **C:** FABRIZIO GAMBATO, **P:** SONJA DEIBEL - BRIGITTE BEILING
A: NETZWERK HOCH_N, **M:** SD@HOCH-N.DE

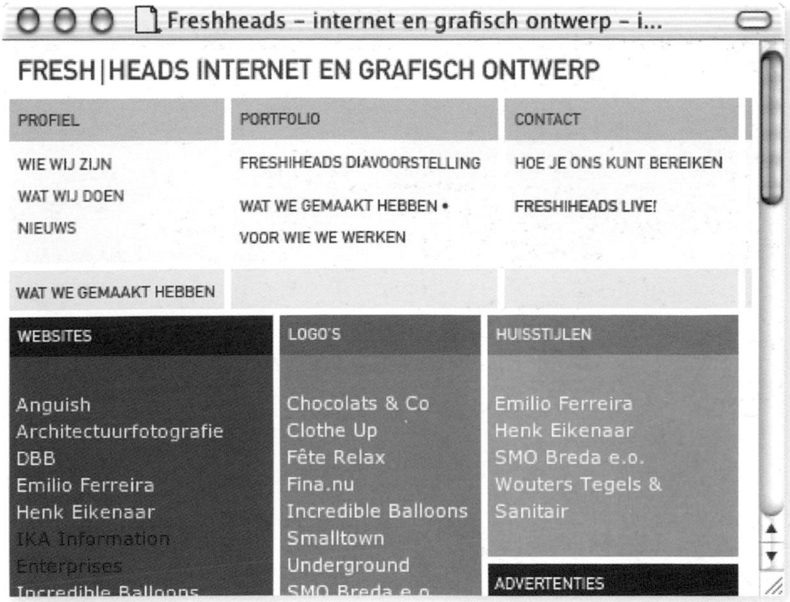

WWW.FRESHHEADS.COM
D: SJOERD EIKENAAR, **C:** JOOST GIELEN
M: JOOST@FRESHHEADS.COM

WWW.THEBEN-TTS.DE
D: BETTINA ROECKLE, **C:** GEORG OEHLER, **P:** GEORG OEHLER
A: RTS RIEGER TEAM, **M:** GEORG.OEHLER@RTS -RIEGERTEAM.DE

WWW.IDEAJUICE.NET
D: MARCO CASSÉ
A: IDEAJUICE, **M:** IDEAJUICE@TIN.IT

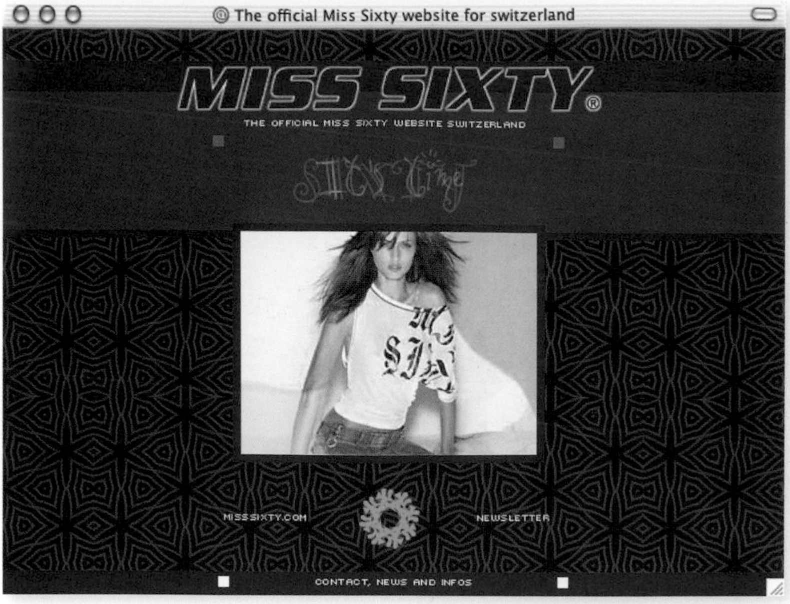

WWW.MISS-SIXTY.CH
D: URS MEYER, **C:** URS MEYER, ANITA SCHNEEBERGER, **P:** MODEAGENTUR WERNER LUTZ
A: OUT MEDIA DESIGN GMBH, **M:** URS@OUT.TO

WWW.FISHANDCHIPS.IT
D: DANIELE PASCERINI
A: FISHANDCHIPS, **M:** DANIELE@FISHANDCHIPS.IT

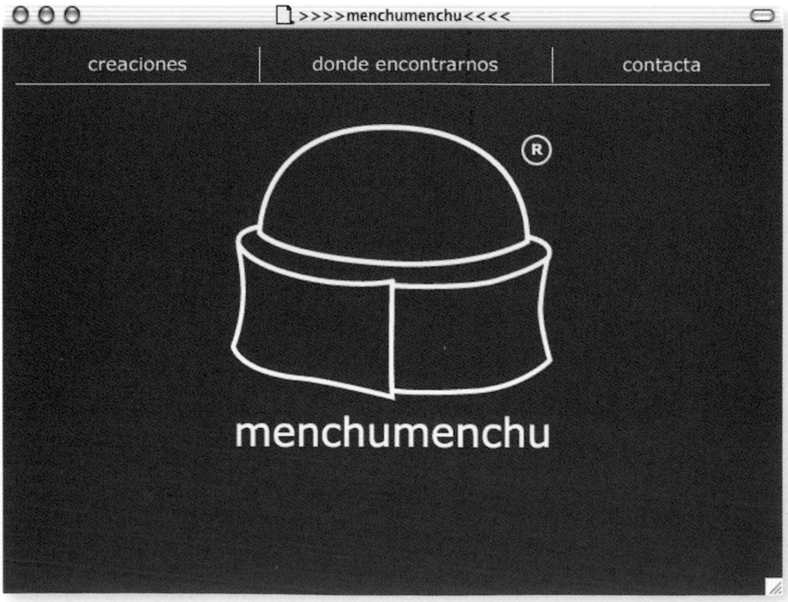

WWW.MENCHUMENCHU.COM
D: CARMEN FERNANDEZ
A: MENCHUMENCHU, **M:** MENCHUMENCHU@MENCHUMENCHU.COM

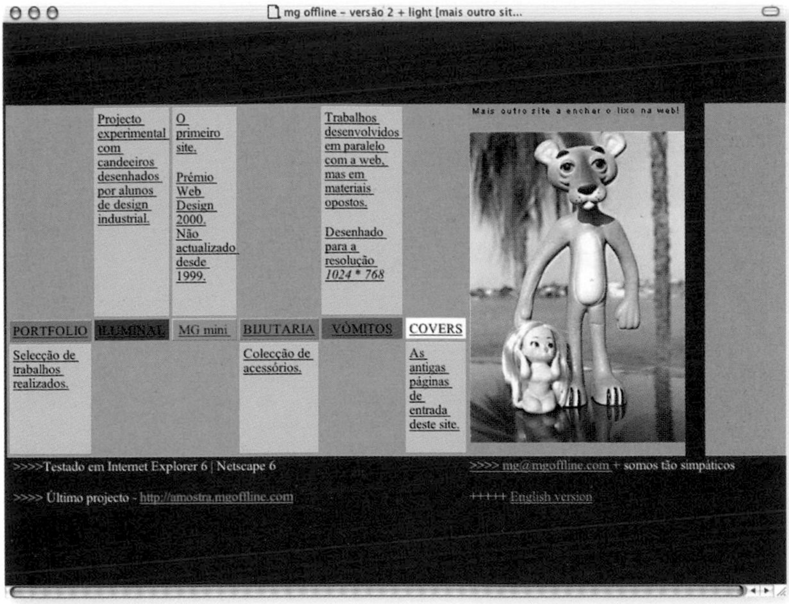

WWW.MGOFFLINE.COM
D: MARGARIDA GIRÃO
M: MARGARIDA@MGOFFLINE.COM

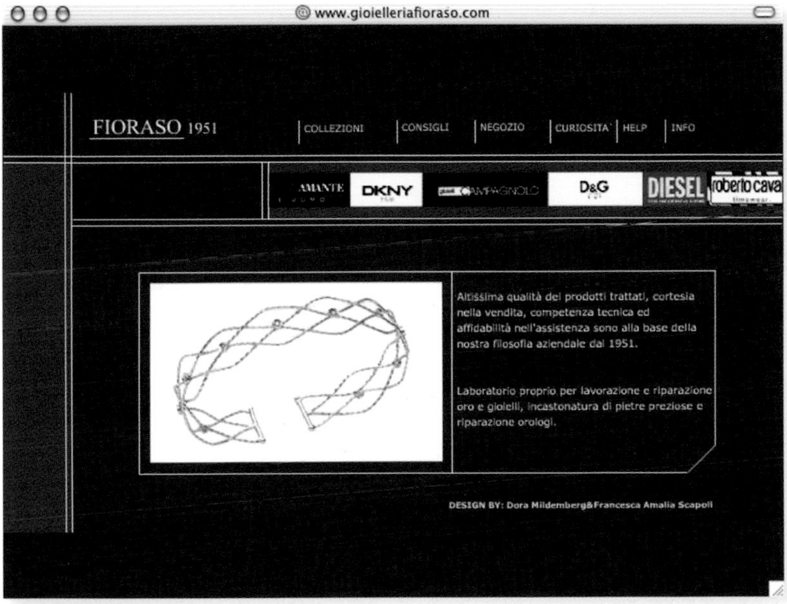

WWW.GIOIELLERIAFIORASO.COM
D: DORA MILDENBERG&FRANCESCA SCAPOLI
M: FRANCESCAMALIA@SUPEREVA.IT

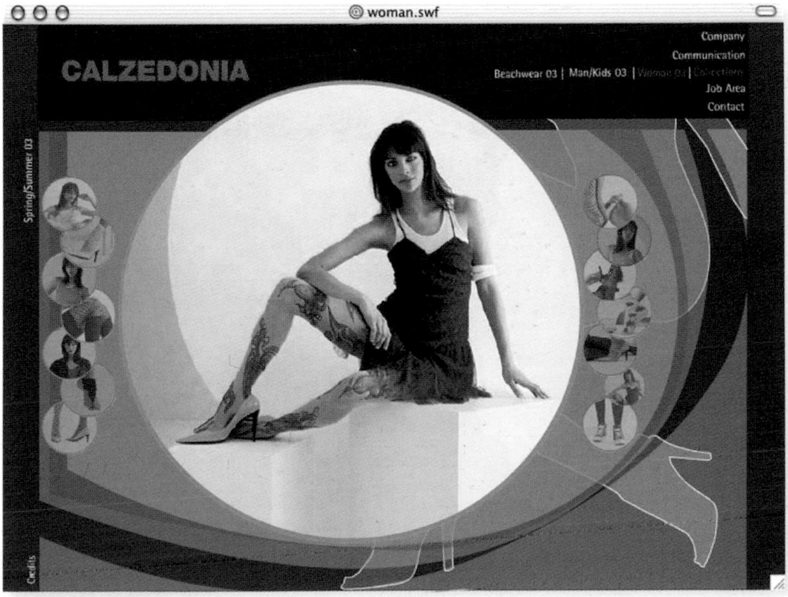

WWW.CALZEDONIA.IT/HOME.SWF
D: WWW.KAST.IT
M: WWW.KAST.IT

WWW.o2DESIGNS.COM
D: IJAN SEMPOI
M: IJANSEMPOI@HOTMAIL.COM

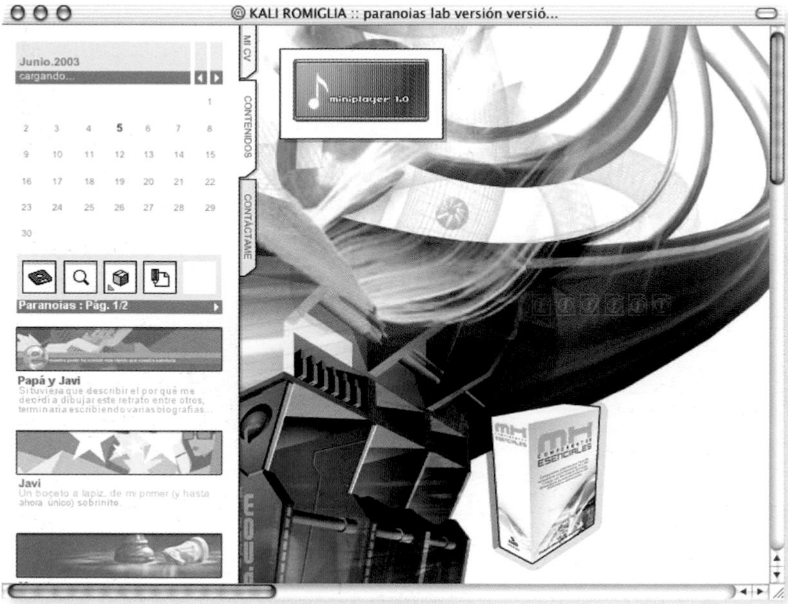

WWW.ROMIGLIA.COM
D: KALI ROMIGLIA
A: ROMIGLIA.COM, **M:** KALI@ROMIGLIA.COM

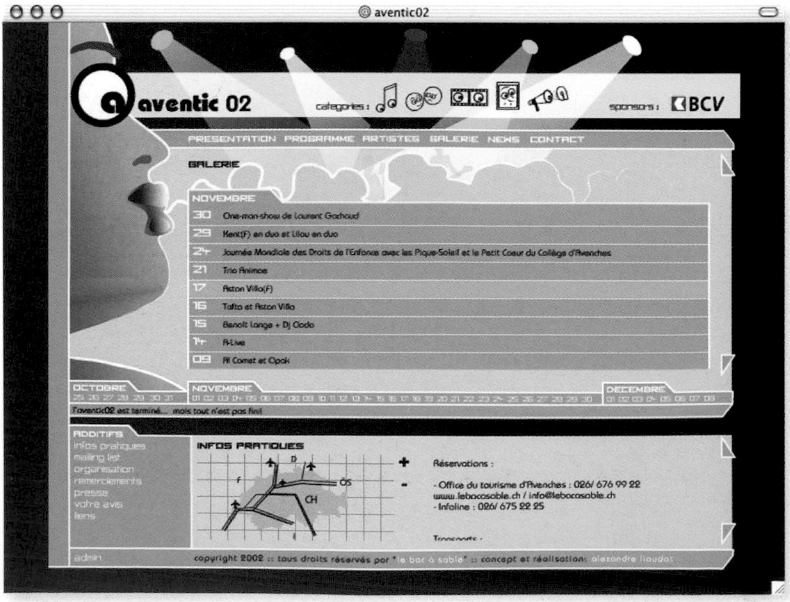

WWW.AVENTICo2.CH/AVENTICo2
D: ALEXANDRE LIAUDAT, **C:** ALEXANDRE LIAUDAT, **P:** AVENTICo2
M: AL.YODA@BLUEWIN.CH

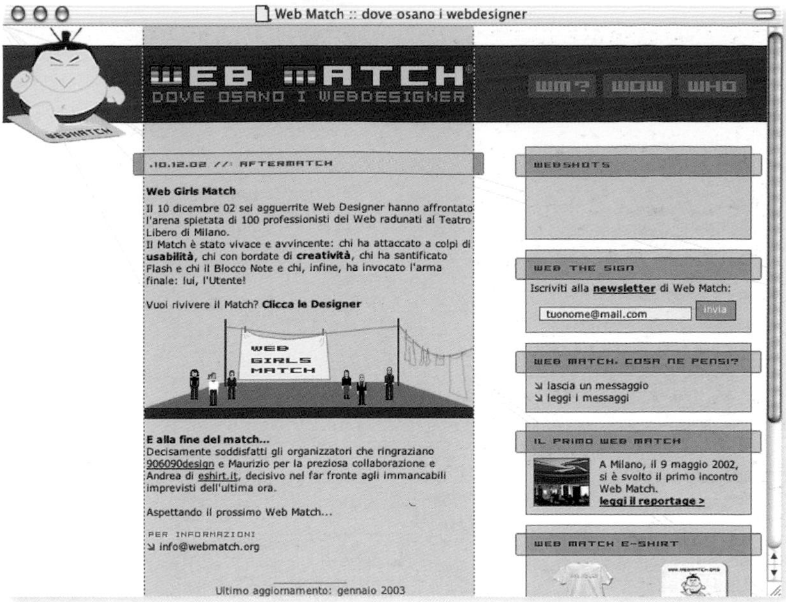

WWW.WEBMATCH.ORG
D: STEFANIA BOJANO
M: STEF@STEFANIABOJANO.NET

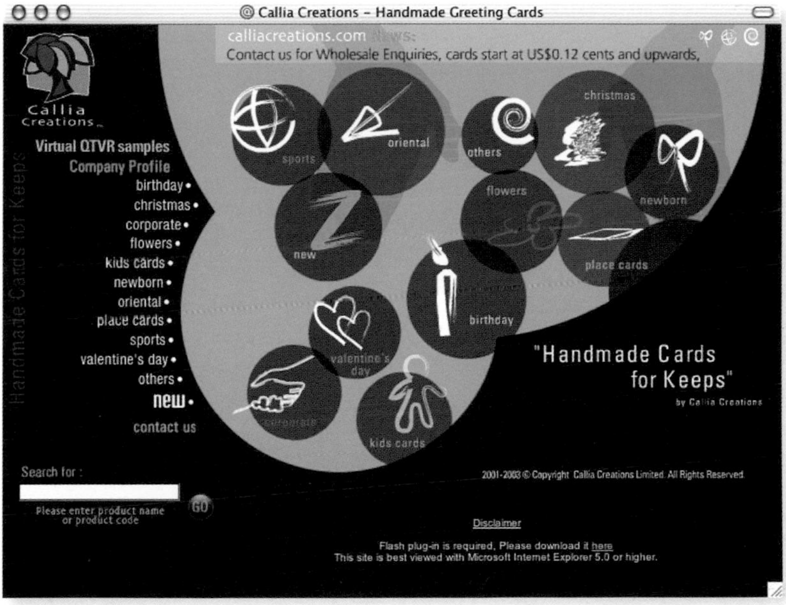

WWW.CALLIACREATIONS.COM
D: SIMONI TAM, **C:** FEDA MAN, **P:** SIMONI TAM
A: HOT DOG TREE LTD., **M:** SIMON@HDTREE.COM.HK

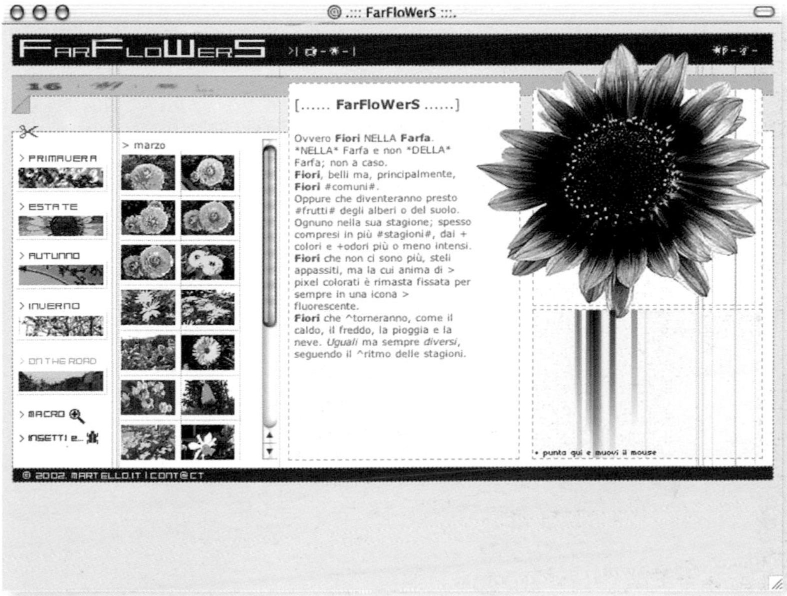

WWW.MARTELLO.IT/FARFLOWERS
D: PASQUALE MARTELLO
A: MARTELLOCARTOON, **M:** P.MARTELLO@RAI.IT

WWW.ARS3.COM
D: FERRAN SENDRA, **C:** MIQUEL ANGLARILL, **P:** ROBERT RAMOS
A: ARS3, M: FERRAN@ARS3.COM

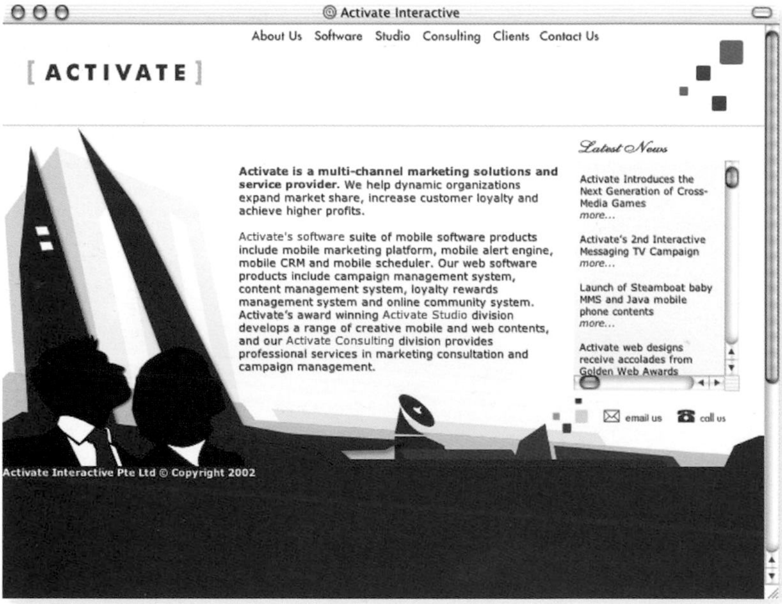

WWW.ACTIVATE.COM.SG
D: ACTIVATE STUDIO TEAM, **C:** ACTIVATE STUDIO TEAM, **P:** JOHN FOO
A: ACTIVATE INTERACTIVE PTE LTD, **M:** STEPHANIE@ACTIVATE.COM.SG

WWW.DOMINO-MNM.DE
D: STEFAN BEHRINGER, **C:** JUERGEN WUNDERLE
A: D:\SIGN CREATIVECONCEPTS, **M:** BEHRINGER@DSIGN.DE

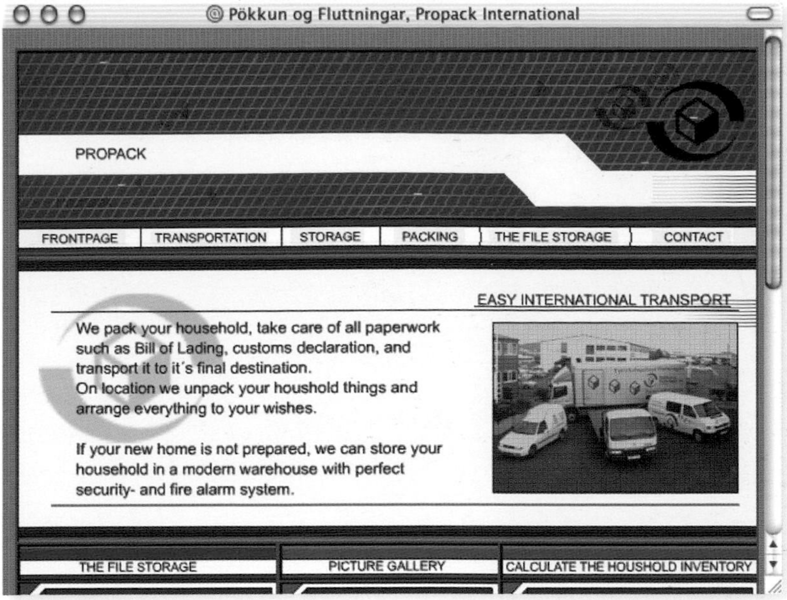

WWW.PROPACK.IS
D: BRYNJAR ELÍ PÁLSSON
A: VIRTUAL DESIGN, **M:** BRYNJAR@VDESIGN.WEB.IS

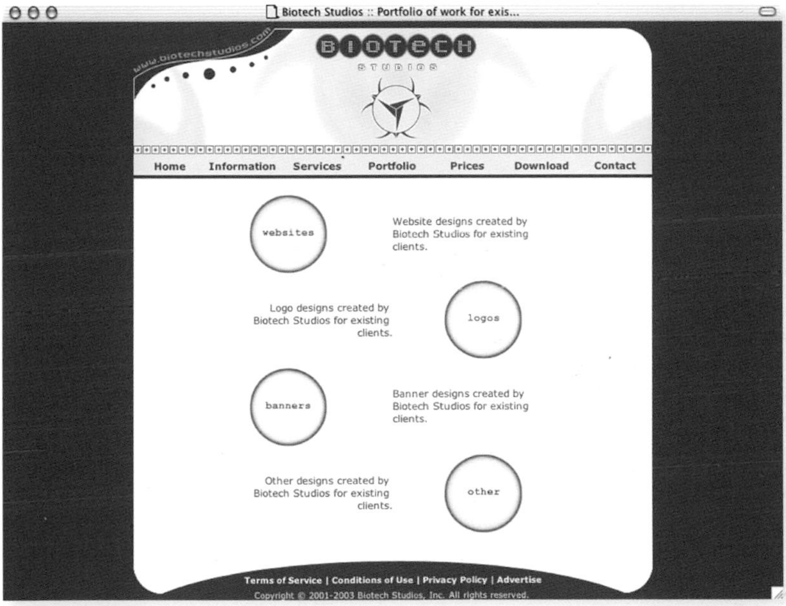

WWW.BIOTECHSTUDIOS.COM
D: DLAIR KADHEM
A: BIOTECHSTUDIOS.COM, **M:** INFO@BIOTECHSTUDIOS.COM

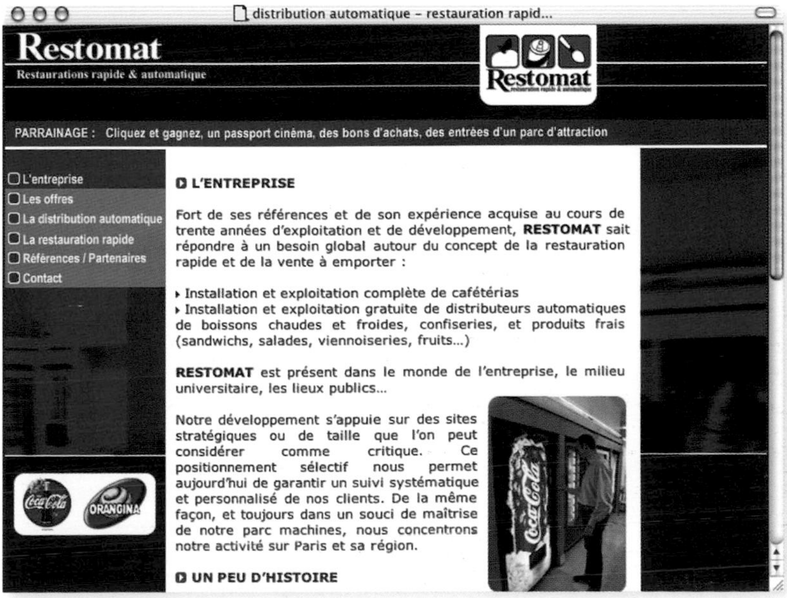

WWW.RESTOMAT.FR
D: JEAN-CHRISTOPHE GILQUIN
A: GOLDENMARKET, **M:** JC@GOLDENMARKET.FR

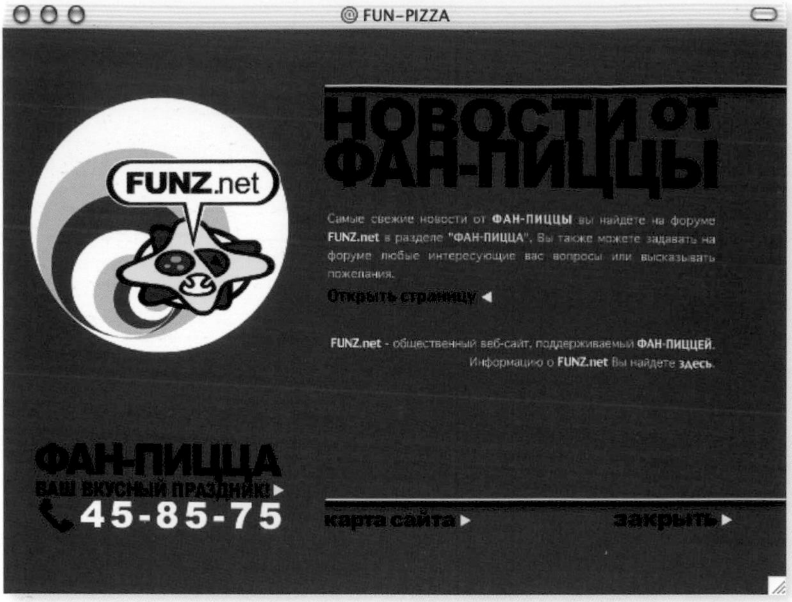

WWW.FUN-PIZZA.RU
D: NACRESTUDIO
A: NACRESTUDIO, **M:** NACRESTUDIO@MAC.COM

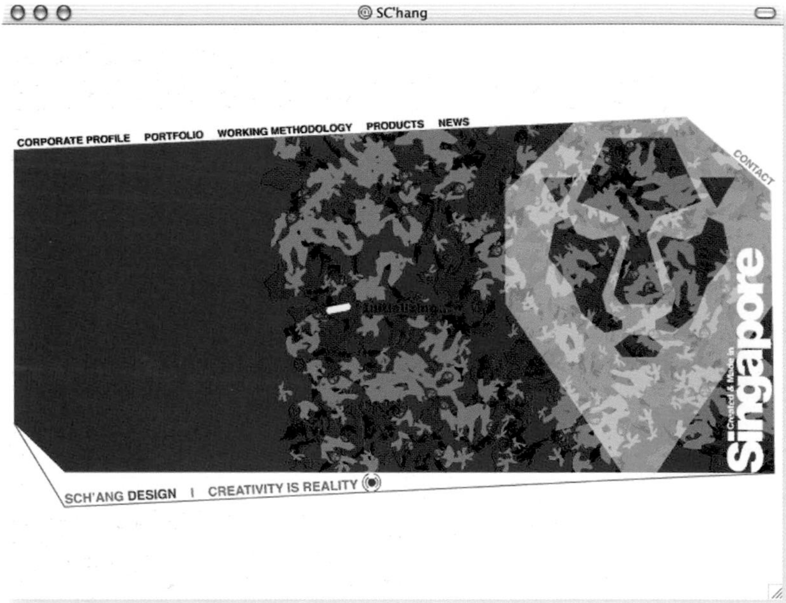

WWW.SCHANG.COM.SG
D: SAMANTHA CHONG, **C:** ALEX CHONG, **P:** JASON LOW
A: SCH'ANG DESIGN, **M:** JASON@SCHANG.COM.SG

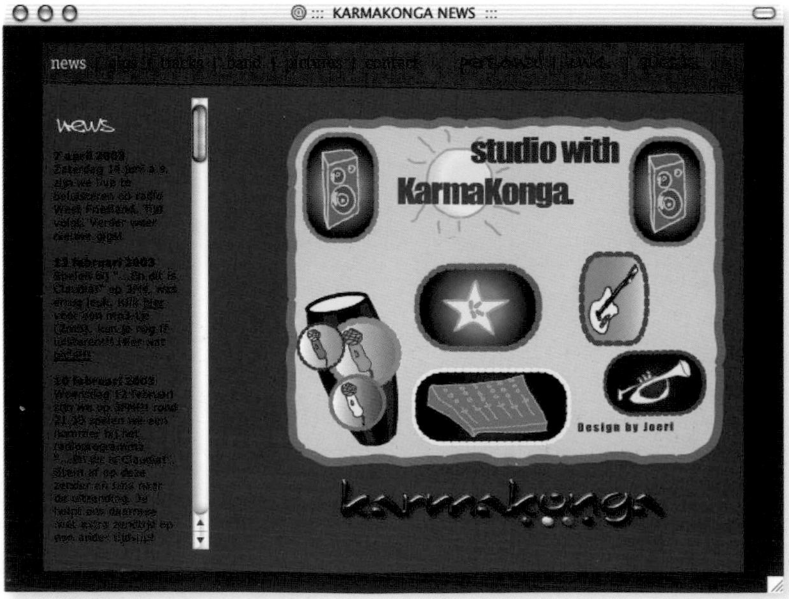

WWW.KARMAKONGA.COM
D: JOERI LANS, **C:** JOERI LANS, **P:** KARMAKONGA
A: THE PARTNERS

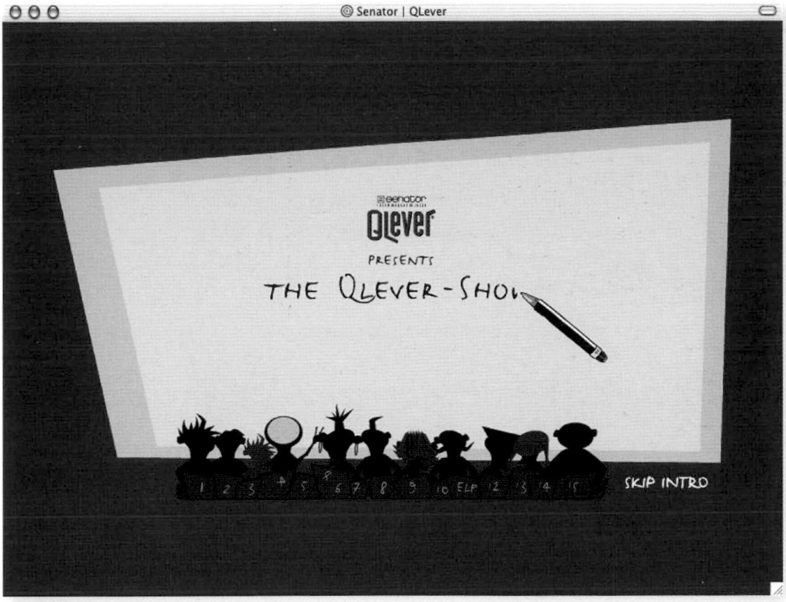

WWW.BE-QLEVER.DE
D: S. MAICHER, **C:** T. JOERRENS, I. SEIDEMANN, P. SCHOLZ, S. NOLTE, **P:** BURG GMBH
A: BURG IT AND MEDIENSERVICES, **M:** STEFAN.MAICHER@BURG-GMBH.DE

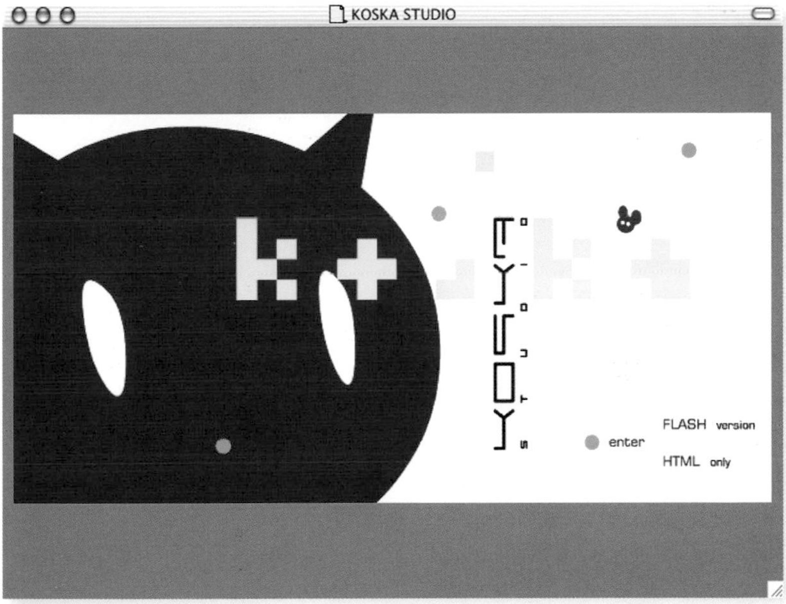

WWW.KOSKASTUDIO.COM
D: AGNES KOSKA
A: KOSKA STUDIO, **M:** MAIL@KOSKASTUDIO.COM

WWW.GAMEC.IT
D: TIZIANO COLOMBI, **C:** MAX INZOLLI, **P:** CONTEMPORANEI
M: TIZIANO.COLOMBI@CONTEMPORANEI.IT

WWW.ACLAIM.COM.SG
D: IVAN MP TAN
A: AC'LAIM!

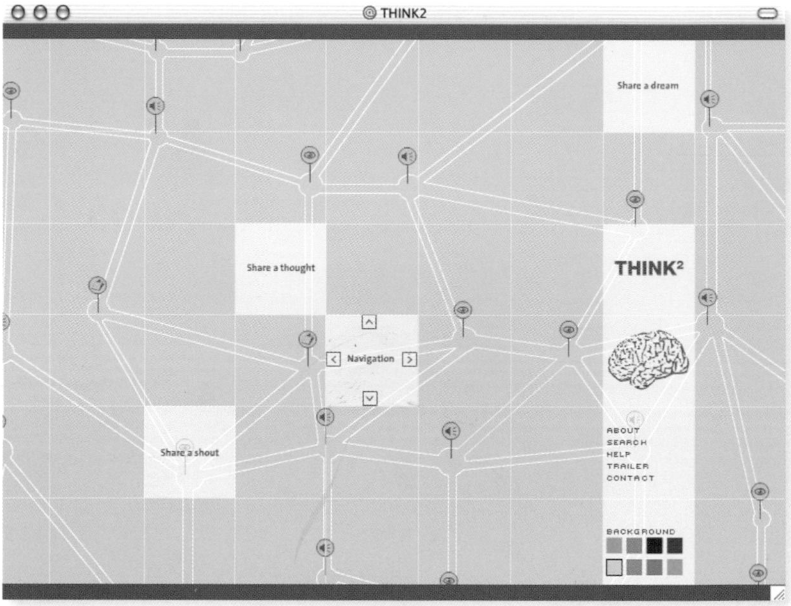

WWW.THINK2.ORG
D: STUDIO ORANGE
A: STUDIO ORANGE, **M:** DIRK@STUDIOORANGE.DE

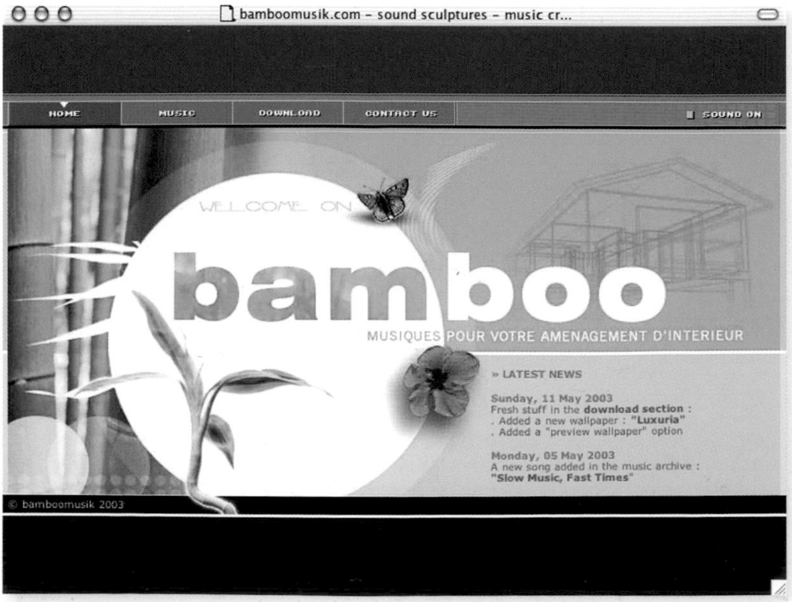

WWW.BAMBOOMUSIK.COM
D: FRÉDÉRIC BERTRAND
M: CONTACT@BAMBOOMUSIK.CJB.NET

WWW.XLTOUCH.COM
D: NICOLAS LAIGNEL, **C:** FRÉDÉRIC LAIGNEL
A: XL TOUCH, **M:** NICOLAS@XLTOUCH.COM

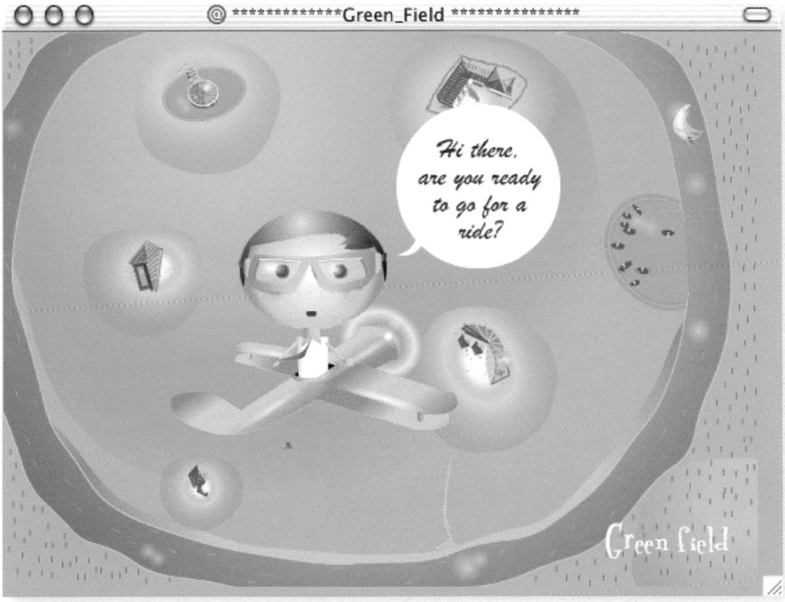

WWW.KS.HE.ST/NEW/MAIN.HTM
D: KIM SENG
A: INTERACTIVE KNOWLEDGE SYSTEMS, **M:** KIMSENG@IKSONLINE.COM

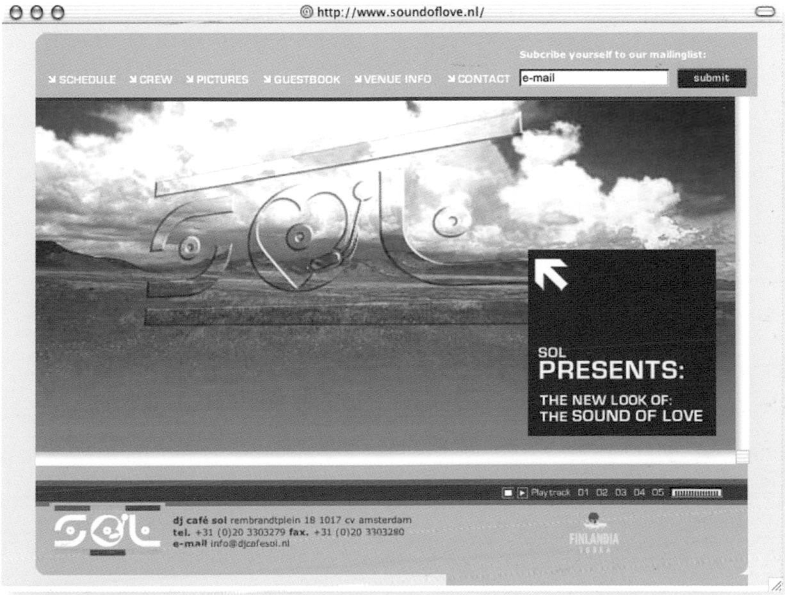

WWW.SOUNDOFLOVE.NL
D: HENK-JAN BERKHOFF
A: A36, M: HENKJAN@A36.NL

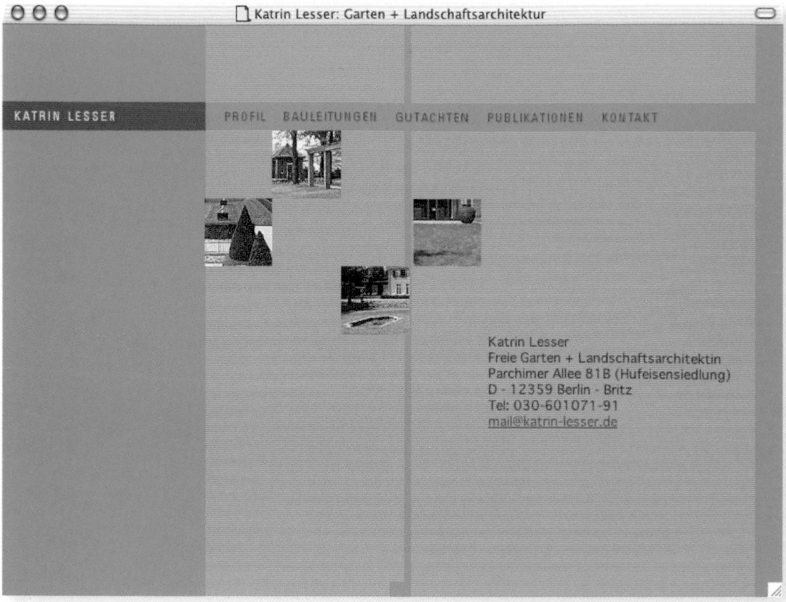

WWW.KATRIN-LESSER.DE
D: BEN BUSCHFELD
A: BUSCHFELD.COM - GRAPHIC AND INTERFACE DESIGN, **M:** MAIL@BUSCHFELD.COM

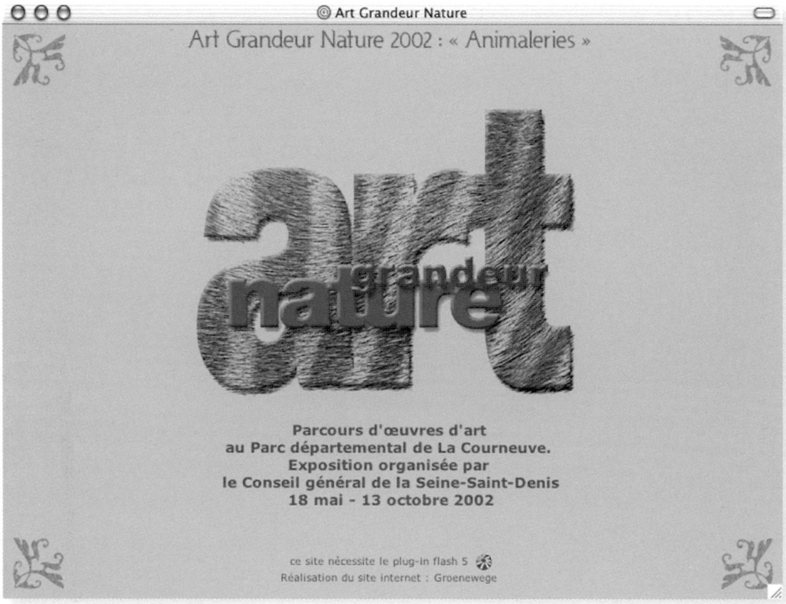

WWW.ART-GRANDEUR-NATURE.COM
D: GUNTHER GROENEWEGE
M: GROENEWEGE@HOTMAIL.COM

WWW.SOLIDTEAM.DE
D: STEFAN FELDHINKEL
A: SOLIDTEAM GMBH, **M:** SFELDHINKEL@SOLIDTEAM.DE

WWW.COLORCARDS.NL
D: REMCO AHNE, **P:** GUUS WOLTERS
A: LOOKAT BV, **M:** INFO@STRAKWERK.NL

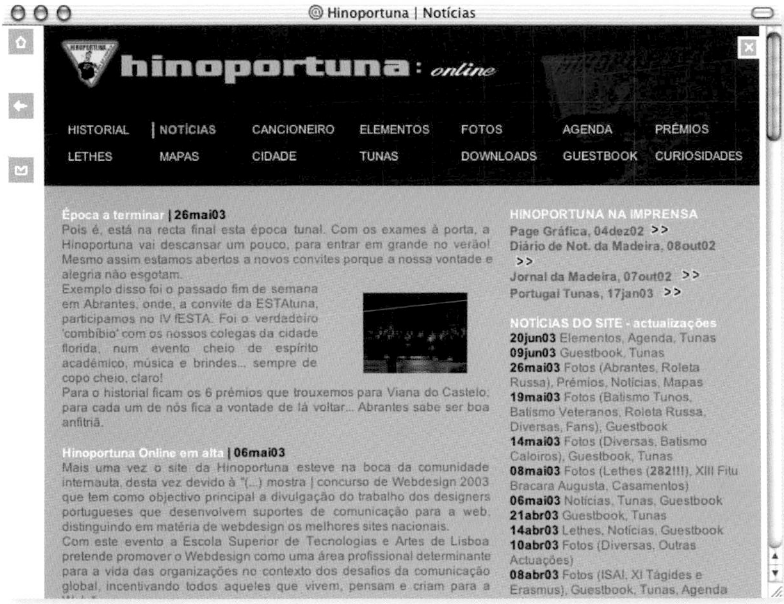

WWW.HINOPORTUNA.COM
D: RICARDO RODRIGUES
M: RICDESIGN@NORTENET.PT

WWW.REDSTR.COM
D: ALEX VALICH
A: REDSTR, **M:** ALEX@REDSTR.COM

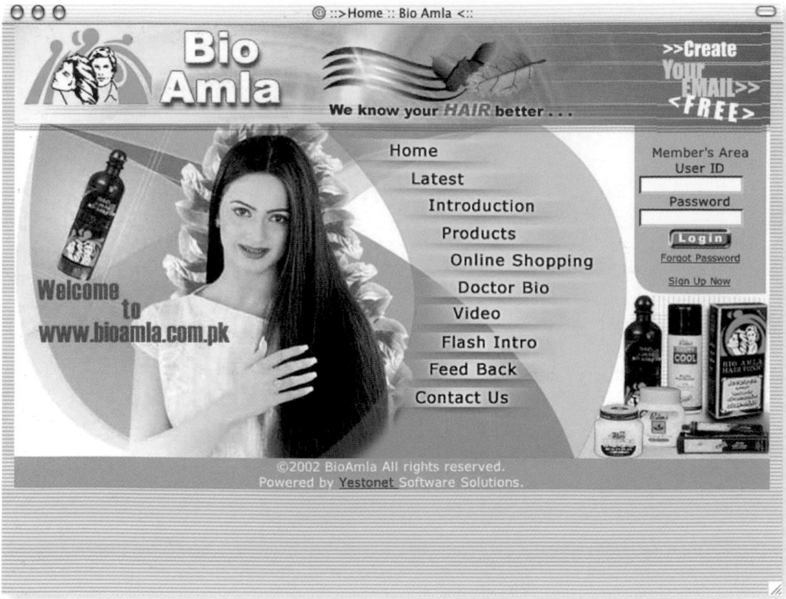

WWW.BIOAMLA.COM.PK
D: IMRAN SUBHANI, **P:** UMBER IBAD
A: YESTONET, **M:** IMRANSUBHANI@HOTMAIL.COM

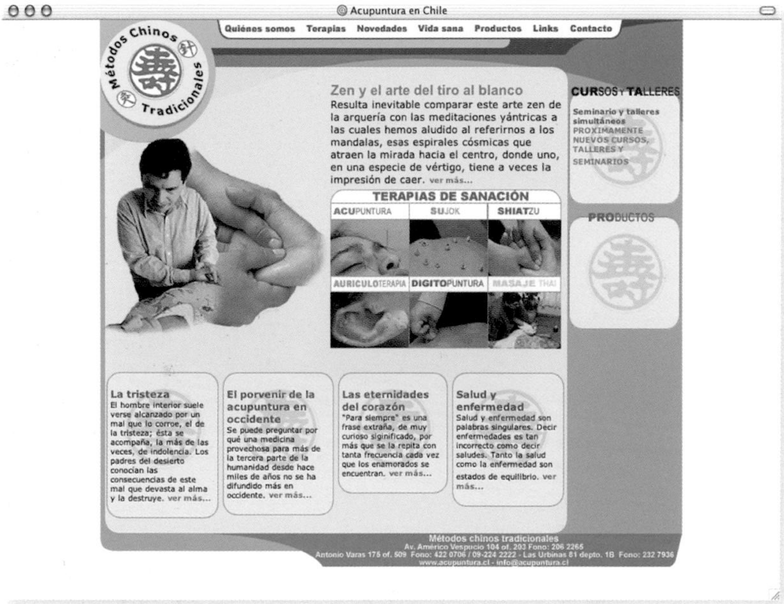

WWW.ACUPUNTURA.CL
D: ALEJANDRO BAEZA LUCO
A: ALEJANDRO BAEZA LUCO, **M:** JANOOPY@PATAGONIACHILE.CL

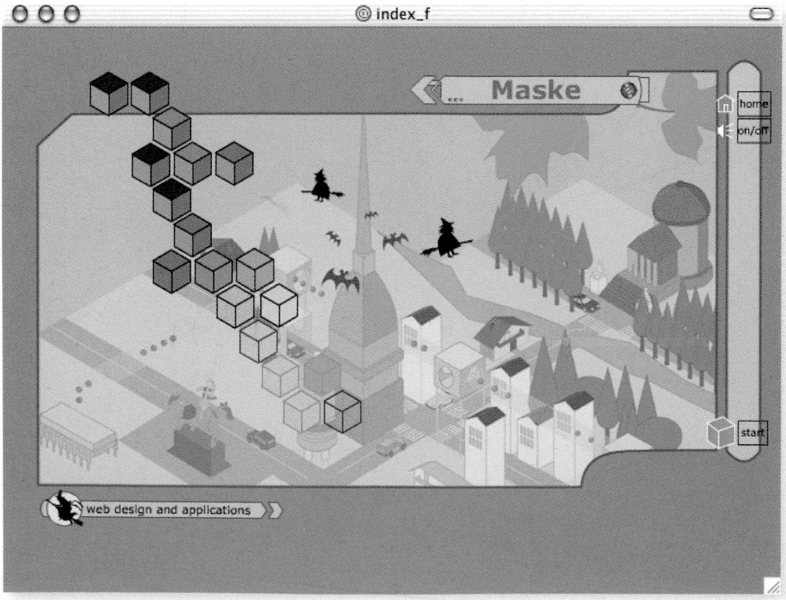

WWW.MASKE.IT/FLASH/INDEX_F.HTML
D: GUIDO TROTTA , SIMONE TROTTA
A: MASKE S.N.C., **M:** INFO@MASKE.IT

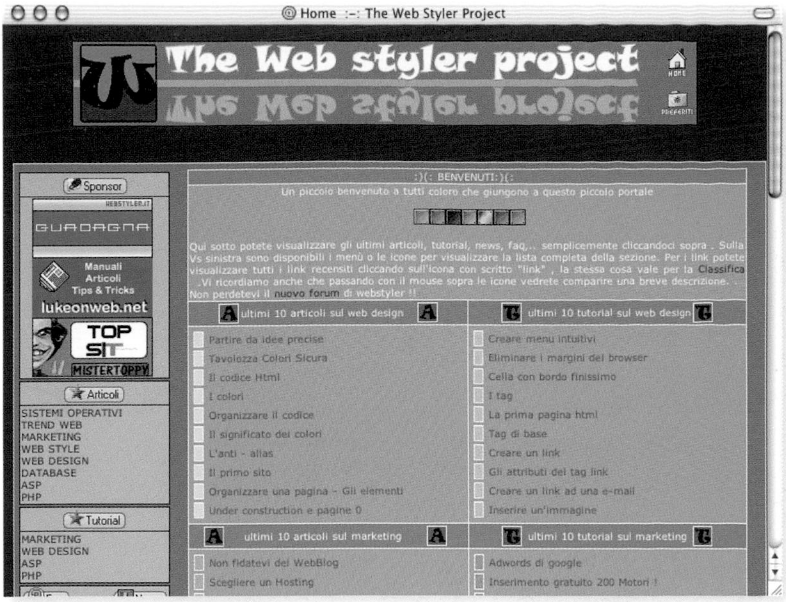

WWW.WEBSTYLER.IT
D: SIMONE CASALIGGI
A: SIMONE CASALIGGI, **M:** SIMONE@CASALIGGI.COM

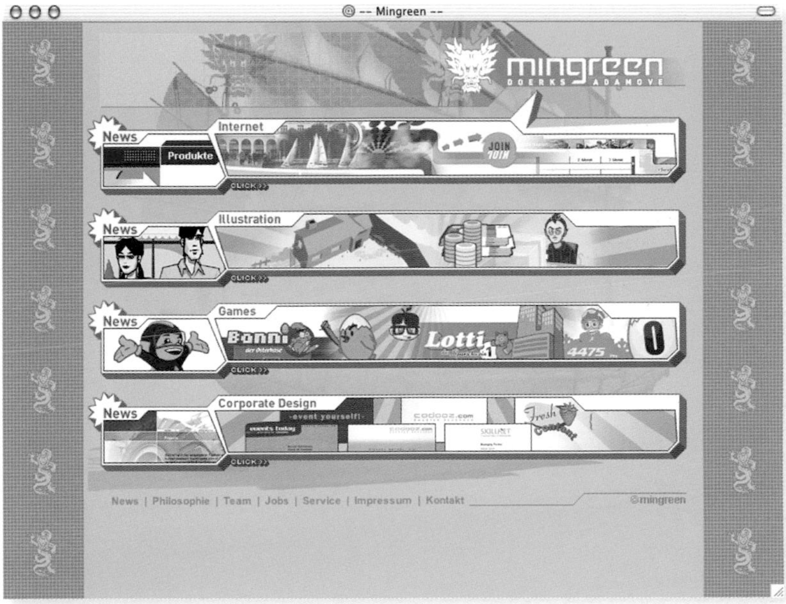

WWW.MINGREEN.COM
D: PATRICK ADAMOVÉ, **C:** STEFAN DOERKS
A: MINGREEN GBR | DOERKS | ADAMOVE, **M:** ADAMOVE@MINGREEN.COM

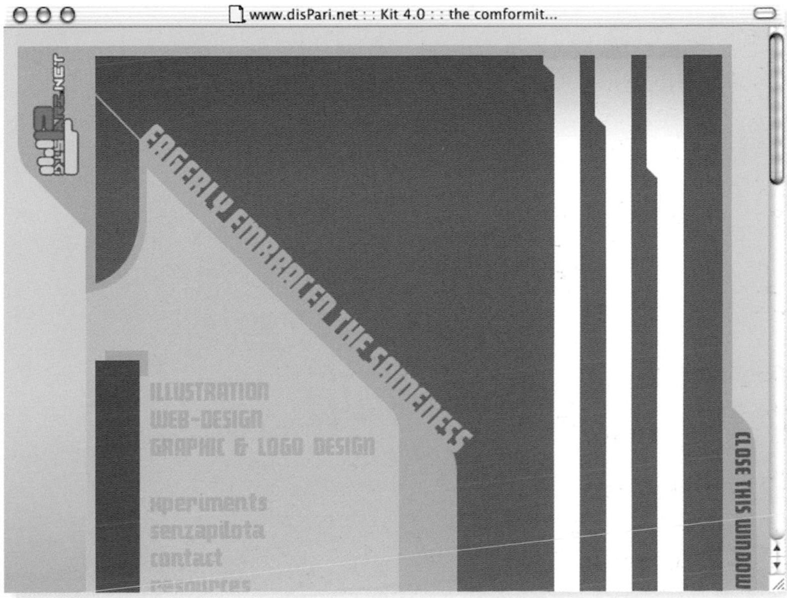

WWW.DISPARI.NET
D: DANILO MORETTI
A: DISPARI.NET, **M:** PARI@DISPARI.NET

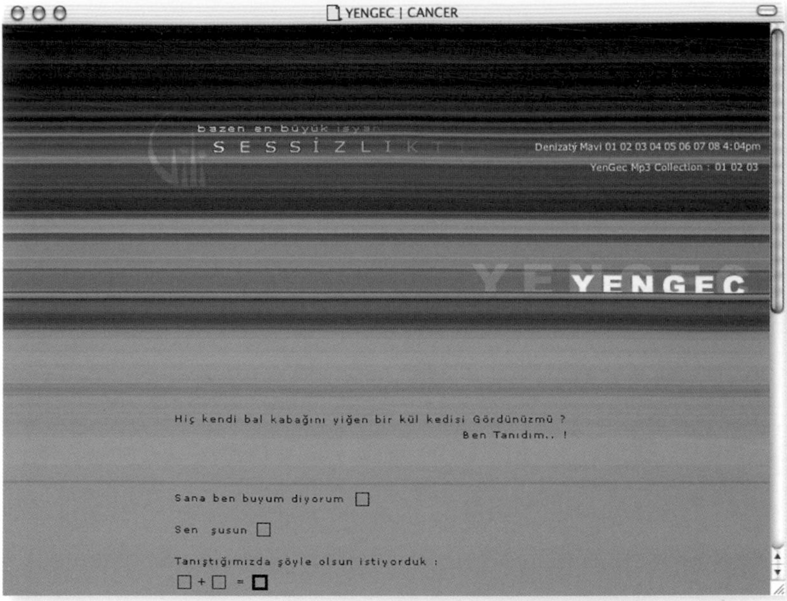

WWW.YENGEC.COM
D: ERHAN POLAT
A: YENGEC NEW GENERATION DESIGN FACTORY, **M:** ERHAN@YENGEC.NET

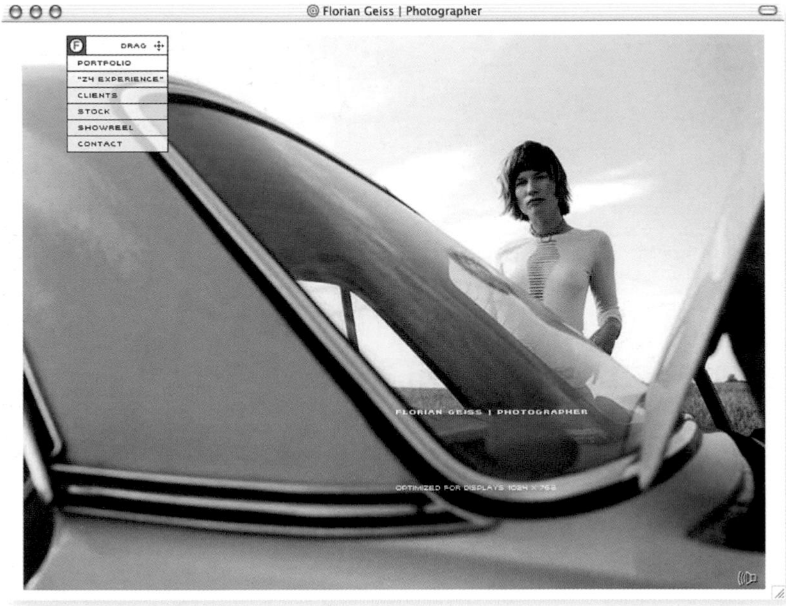

WWW.FLORIANGEISS.COM
D: CHRISTIANE ALT, **C:** ULRICH MÜLLER
M: DESIGN@CHRISALT.COM

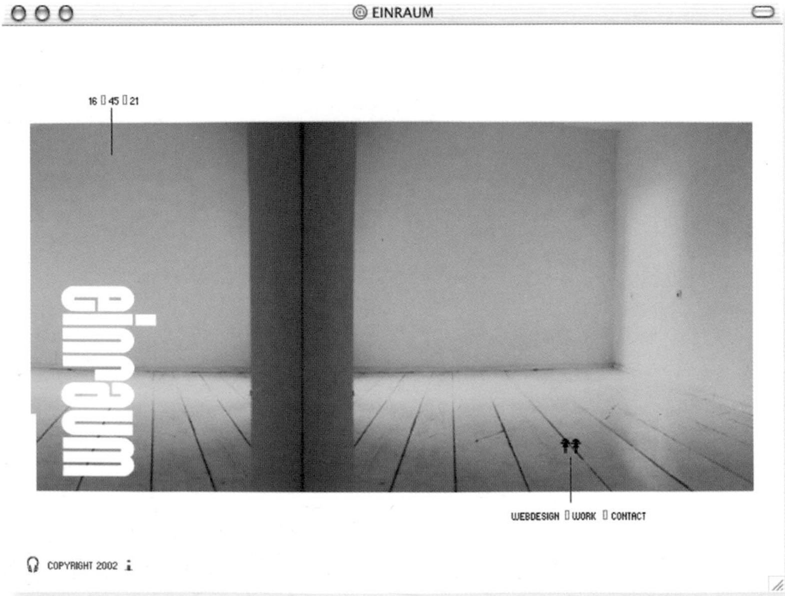

WWW.EINRAUM.DE
D: EINRAUM
A: EINRAUM, **M:** UTEMOLNAR@GMX.NET

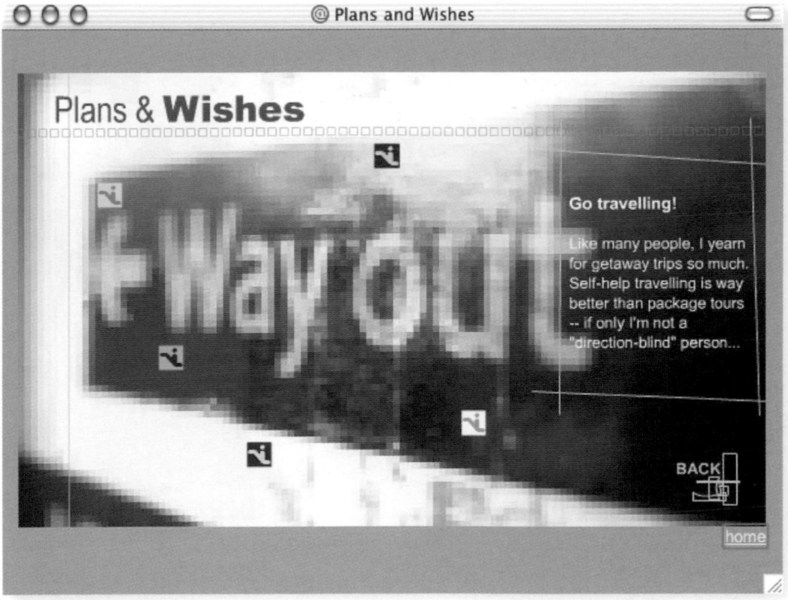

WWW.BIGTHINKHEAD.COM
D: KATHY LO
M: BIGTHINKHEAD@SINATOWN.COM

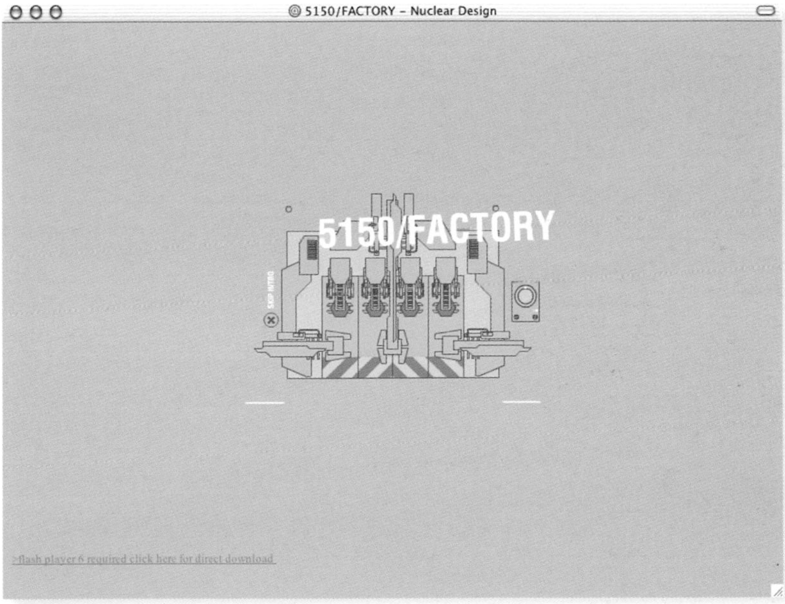

WWW.5150F.COM
D: MATTEO CIVASCHI
A: 5150/FACTORYÔ, **M:** CIVASCHI@5150F.COM

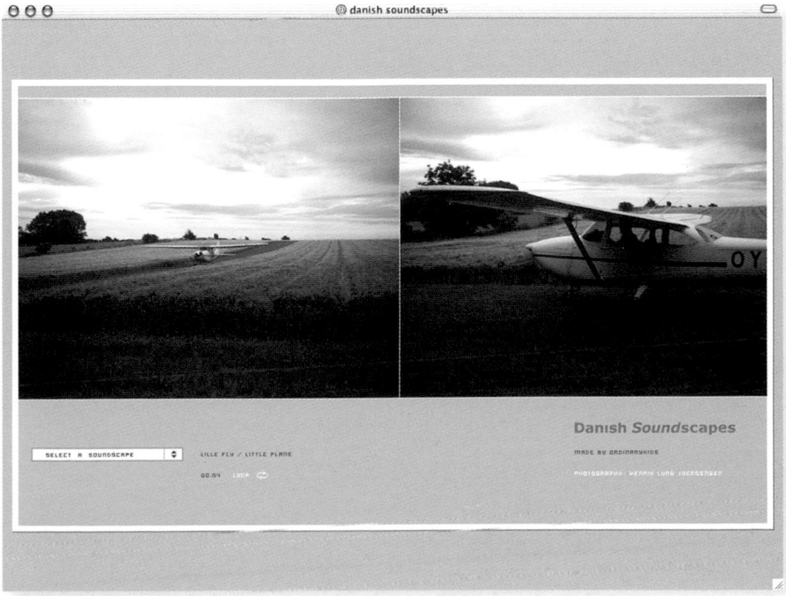

WWW.DANISHSOUNDSCAPES.COM
D: HENRIK LUND JOERGENSEN, C: JASON HERRING, **P:** THORBJOERN KOENIG
A: ORDINARYKIDS, **M:** THORBJOERN@ORDINARYKIDS.COM

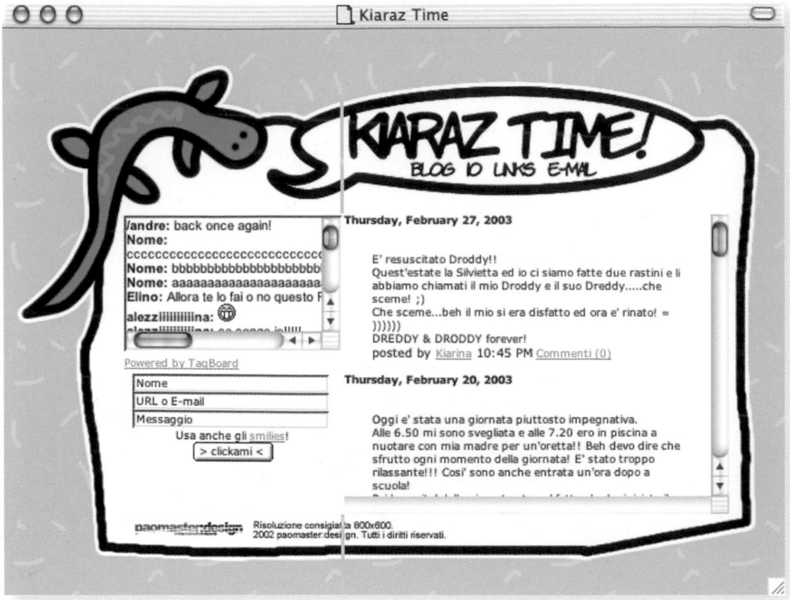

WWW.PAOMASTER.IT/KIARAZTIME
D: ANDREA BAIETTI
A: PAOMASTER:DESIGN, **M:** DESIGN@PAOMASTER.IT

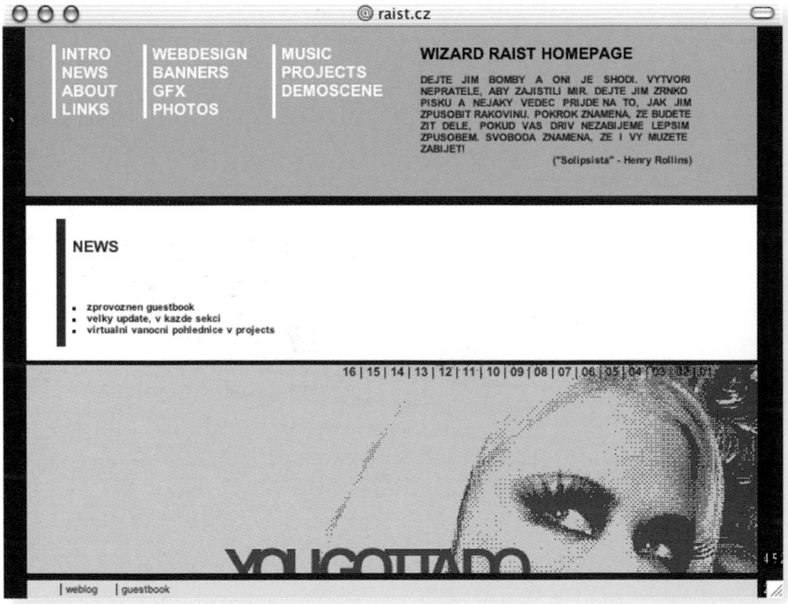

WWW.RAIST.CZ
D: RAIST
M: RAIST@SPOK.CZ

WWW.UNTITLED-DOCUMENT.DE
D: ALEXANDER BAYER
M: ALEXANDERBAYER@WEB.DE

WWW.2DOGDESIGNSTUDIOS.COM
D: SHAWN BENDINELLI
A: 2DOG DESIGN STUDIOS, **M:** SHAWN@2DOGDESIGNSTUDIOS.COM

WWW.FOCANTI.COM/LOS-ROQUES/INDEX.HTM
D: FRANCESCO GUIDI / SILVIA BENDINELLI, **P:** POSADA LA LAGUNA

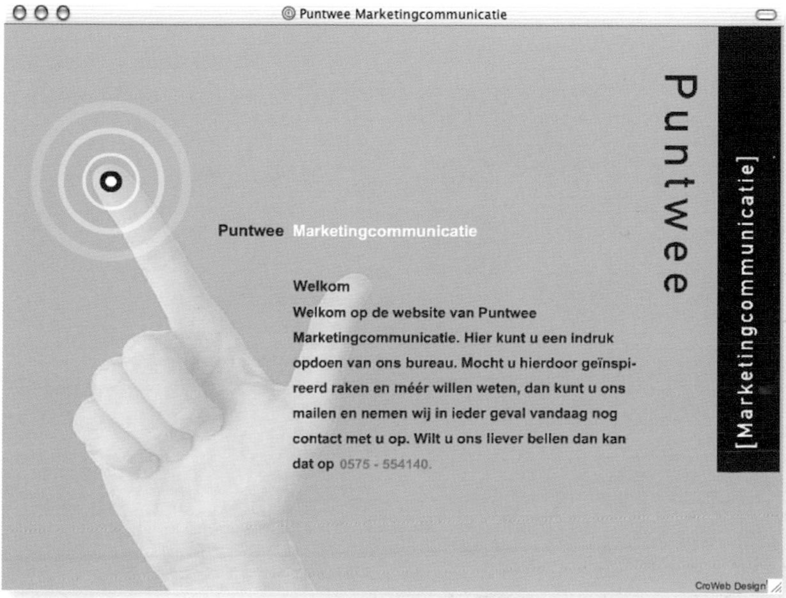

WWW.PUNTWEE.NL
D: CAROLINE VAN DEN BERG
A: CROWEB DESIGN, **M:** INFO@CROWEB.NL

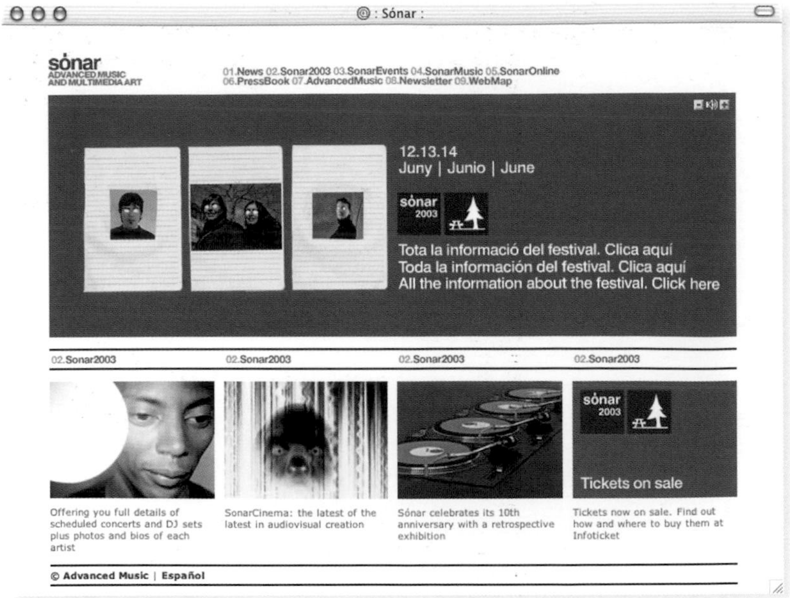

WWW.ANNUO.ORG
D: DANIEL COSTAS, **C:** RAMÓN ORDAX
A: ANNUO, **M:** ANNUO@ALEN-SL.ES

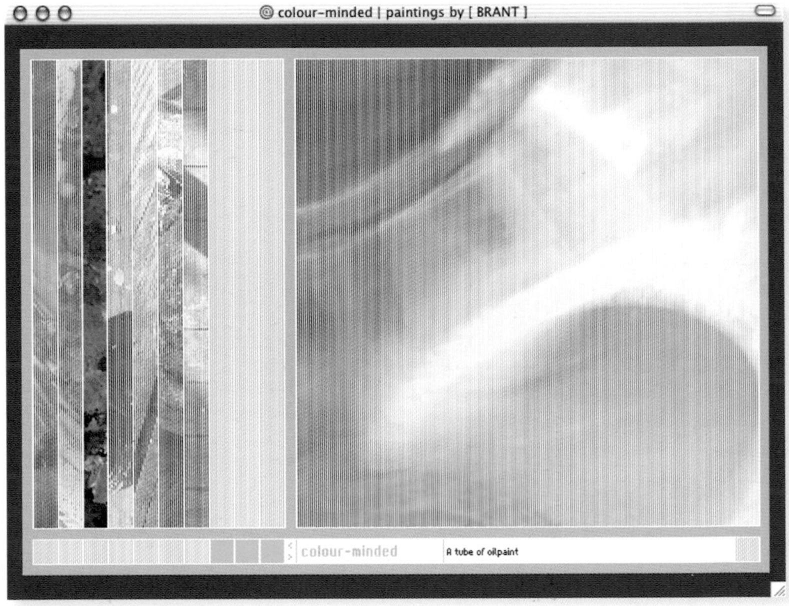

WWW.COLOUR-MINDED.COM
D: HIPATRIP
M: BRANT@COLOUR-MINDED.COM

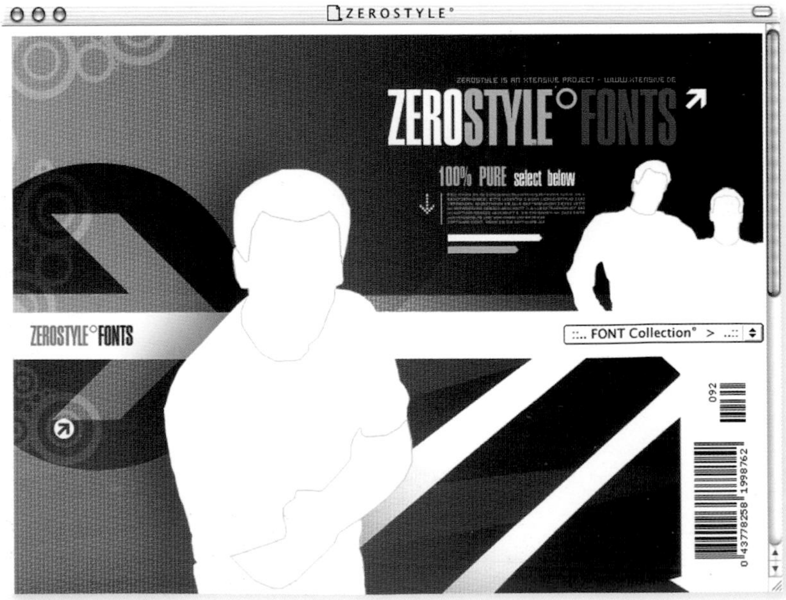

WWW.ZEROSTYLE.DE
D: MATTHIAS GILLE
M: MATTHIAS@XTENSIVE.DE

WWW.BRAINTWISTING.COM
D: DANIELE CASCONE
M: KASKO@CIAOWEB.IT

WWW.ZALEAEQUITACION.COM
D: BERNARDO BARAGAÑO MOSLARES
A: START UP S.L., **M:** FONDAQUE@YAHOO.ES)

WWW.SIMONAM.COM
D: ANTONELLO COGHE
A: RADIO TIME SRL, **M:** ANTONELLO@FASHIONFM.IT

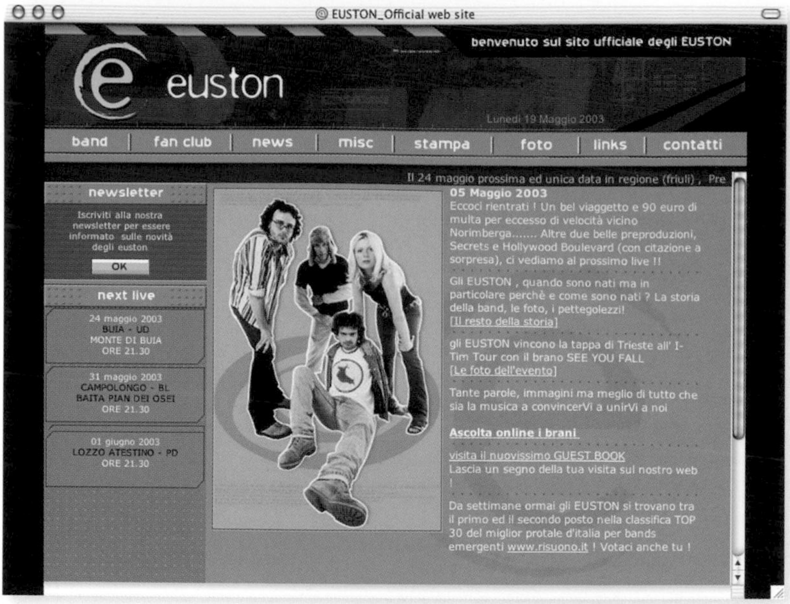

WWW.EUSTON.IT
D: ENRICO CAMPANER, **C:** SIMONE PITTIS , **P:** GIORGIO RANCIARO
A: ENRICO CAMPANER, **M:** ECAMPANER@HOTMAIL.COM

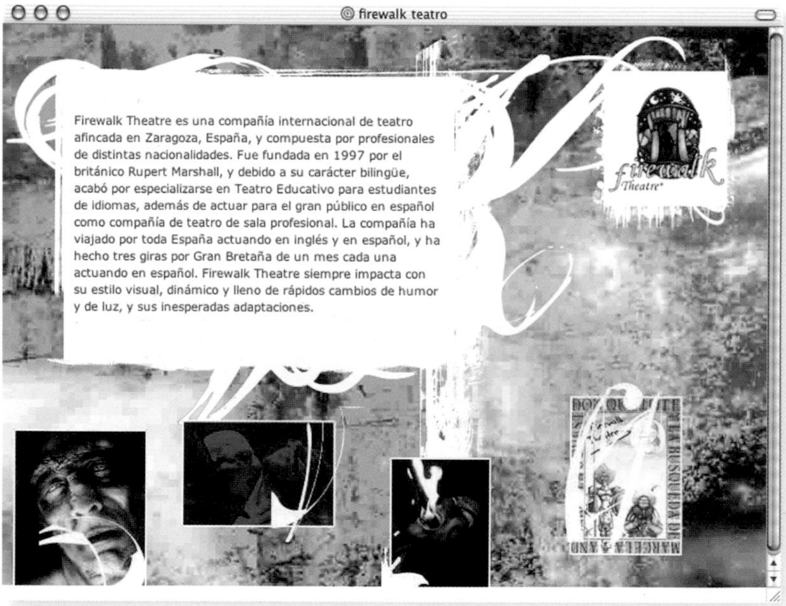

WWW.ACTIVSTUDIO.COM/CLIENTES
D: PARDO RUBIO, **C:** IVAN RUBIO, **P:** IVAN RUBIO
A: ACTIVSTUDIO, **M:** IVANRUBIO@ACTIVSTUDIO.COM

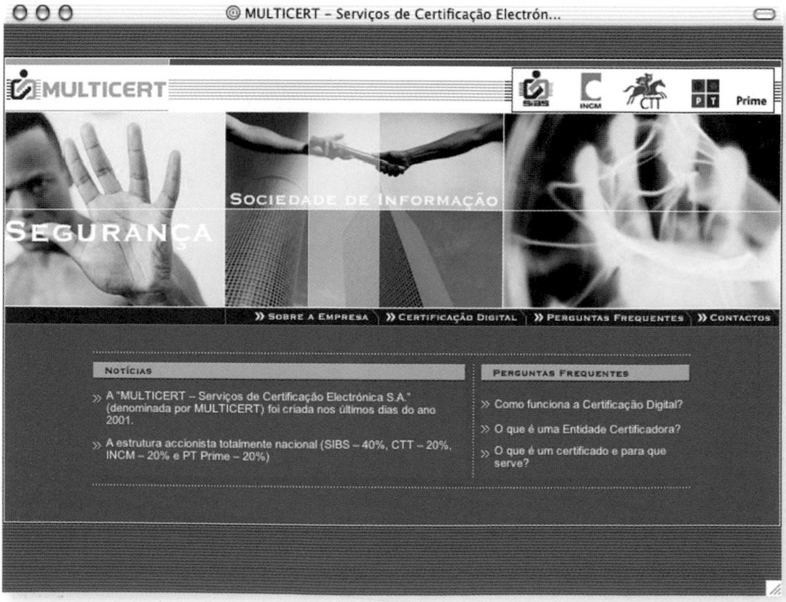

WWW.MULTICERT.COM
D: ALEXANDRA ROCHA, **C:** JOÃO FERNANDEZ, **P:** VÍTOR MAGALHÃES
A: MULTICERT, **M:** ALEXANDRA.ROCHA@INFOPULSE.PT

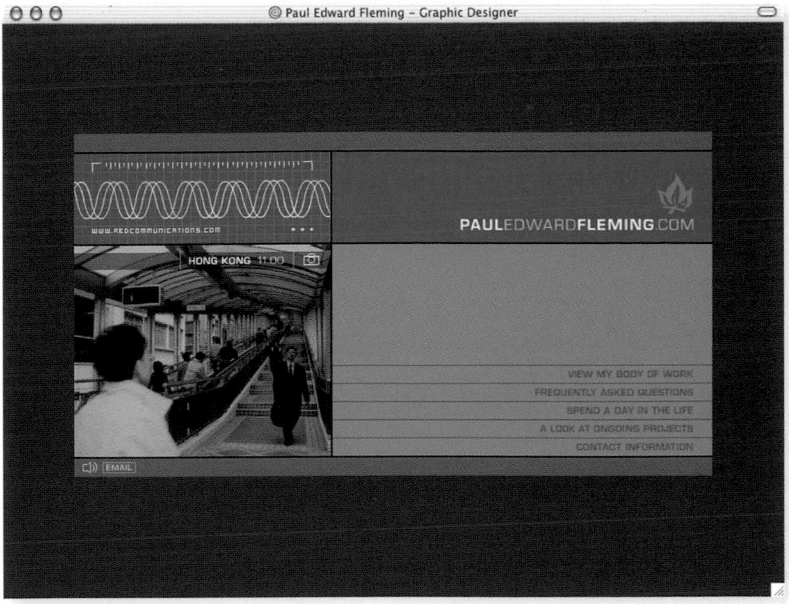

WWW.PAULEDWARDFLEMING.COM
D: PAUL EDWARD FLEMING
A: PAUL EDWARD FLEMING, **M:** PAUL@PAULEDWARDFLEMING.COM

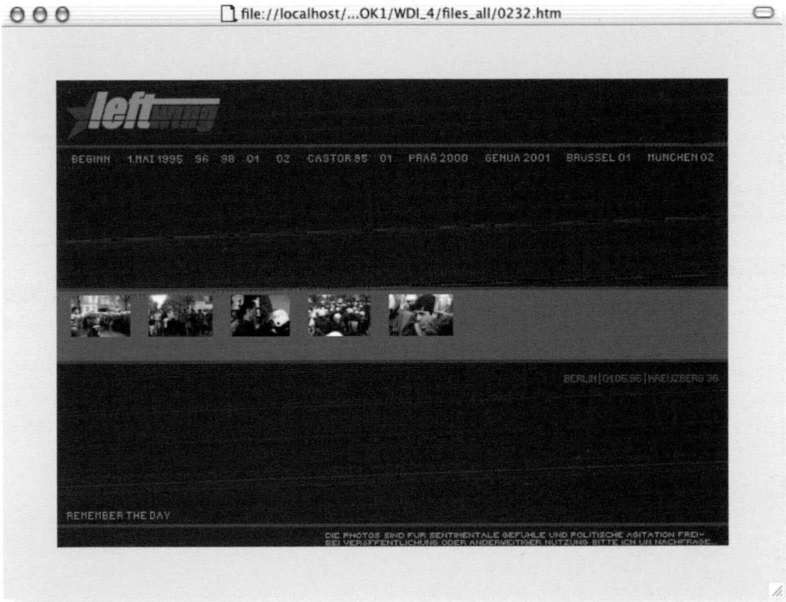

WWW.LEFTWING.DE
D: TOBIAS PFORTE, **C:** TOBIAS PFORTE

WWW.ANDRESGIMENOHCS.COM/INDEX2_EN.HTML
D: NATHALIE GARCIA
M: NATHALIE@ZINK.ES

WWW.E-LLUMINATION.NET
D: ERIC STEUTEN
A: ELLUMINATION, **M:** ERIC@E-LLUMINATION.NET

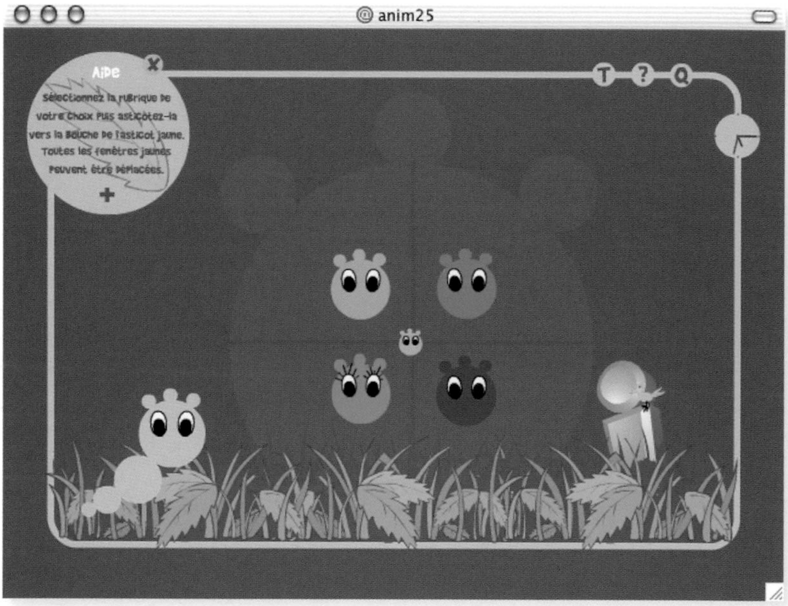

WWW.ASTICONET.COM
D: FRÉDÉRIC EMAILLE
A: ASTICONET.COM, **M:** CONTACT@ASTICONET.COM

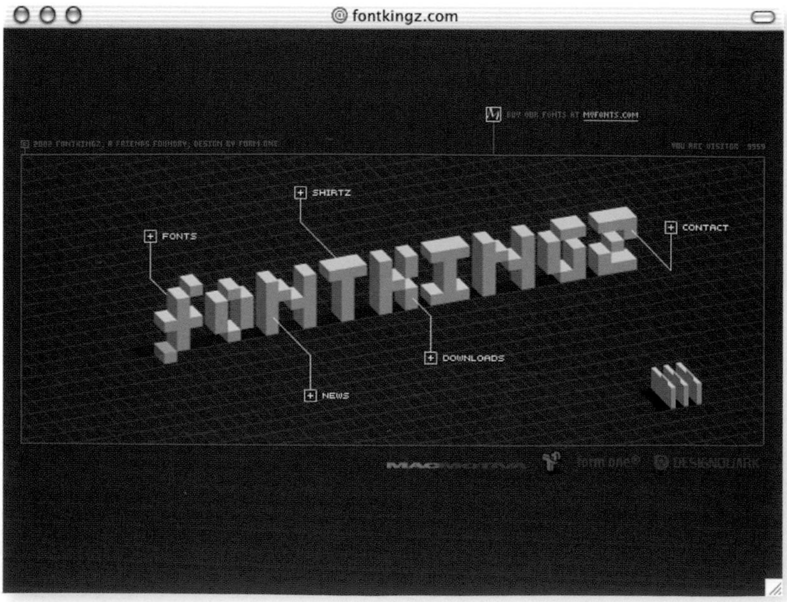

WWW.FONTKINGZ.COM
D: CARLO KRÜGER
A: FORM ONE, **M:** KRUEGER@FORM-ONE.DE

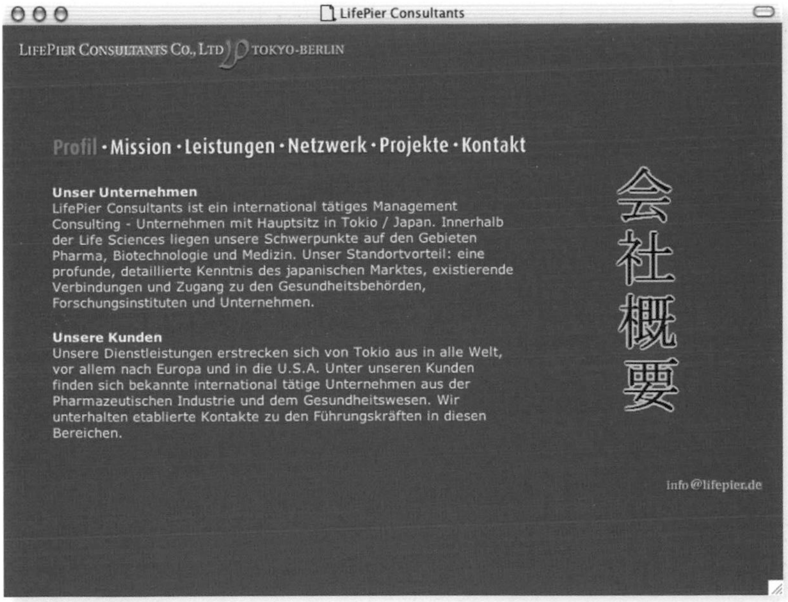

WWW.LIFEPIER.DE
D: BEN BUSCHFELD
A: BUSCHFELD.COM - GRAPHIC AND INTERFACE DESIGN, **M:** INFO@LIFEPIER.DE

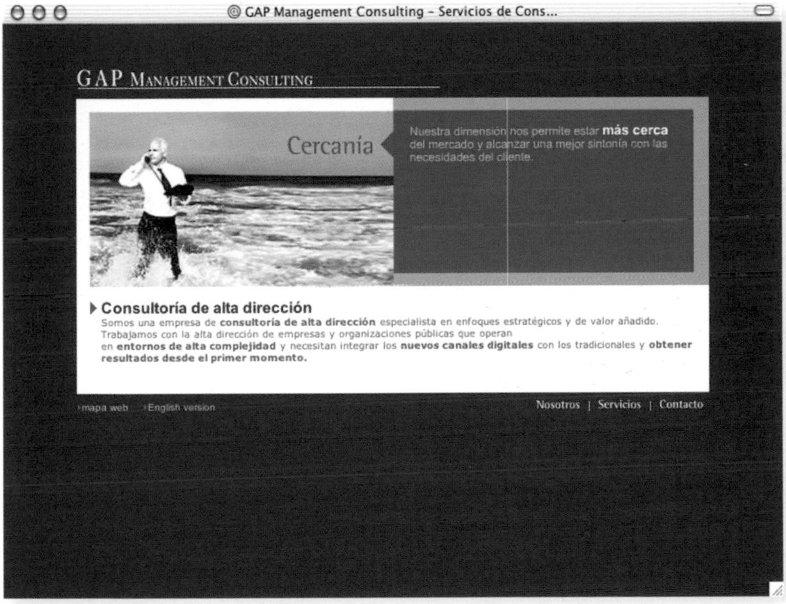

WWW.GAPMC.COM
D: DANIEL MARTIN
A: FUTURESPACE

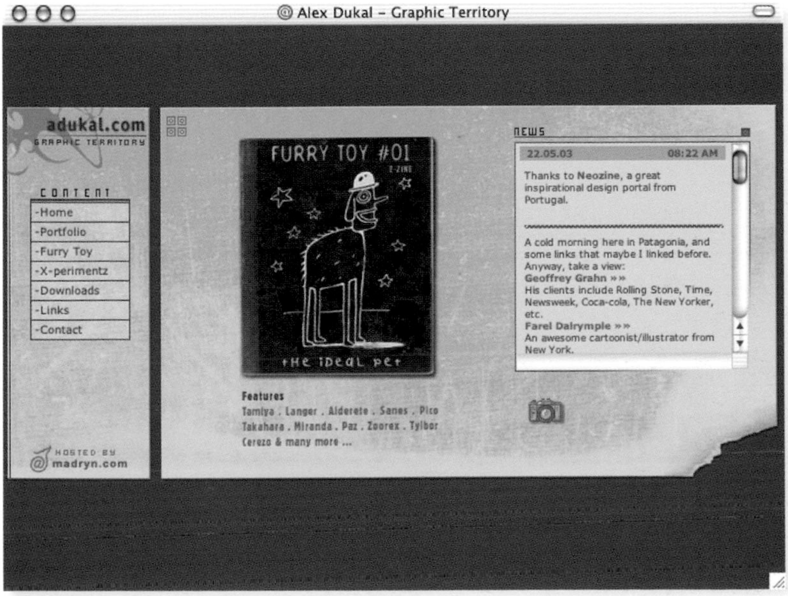

WWW.ADUKAL.COM
D: ALEX DUKAL
M: ADUKAL@ADUKAL.COM

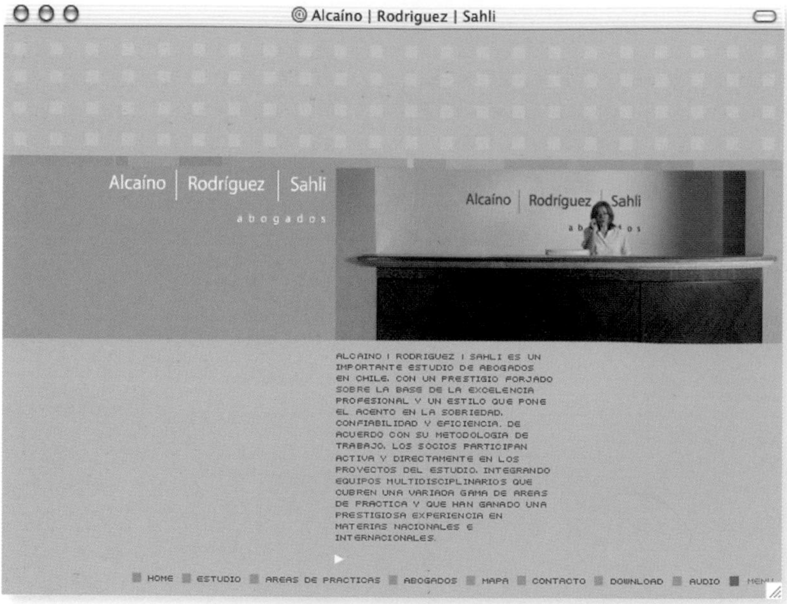

WWW.ARYS.CL
D: CHRISTIAN SOTO INOSTROZA, **C:** CHRISTIAN SOTO INOSTROZA, **P:** IVAN VILLALOBOS
A: COMANDO ZETA , **M:** ZETASOTO@VTR.NET

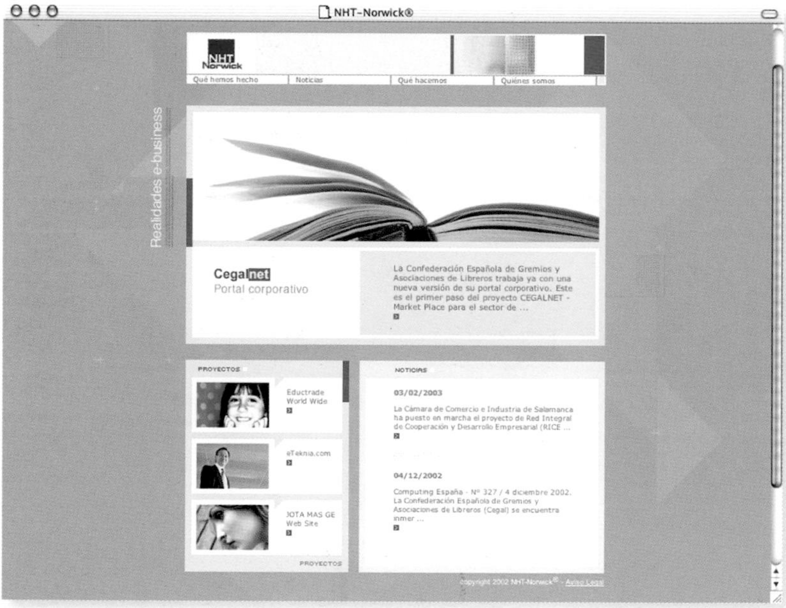

WWW.NHT-NORWICK.COM
D: ANTONIO BALLESTEROS, **C:** MARIA DIAZ, **P:** NHT-NORWICK
A: NHT-NORWICK, **M:** ABALLESTEROS@NHT-NORWICK.NET

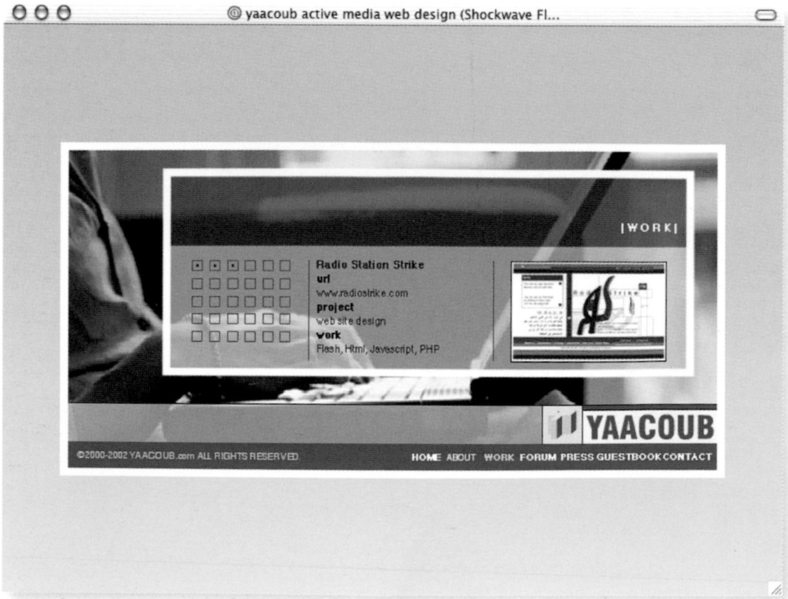

WWW.YAACOUB.COM
D: PIERRE YAACOUB, **C:** BAXTER YAZBEK, **P:** NISSRIN HASSANIYEH
A: YAACOUB.COM, **M:** PIERRE@YAACOUB.COM

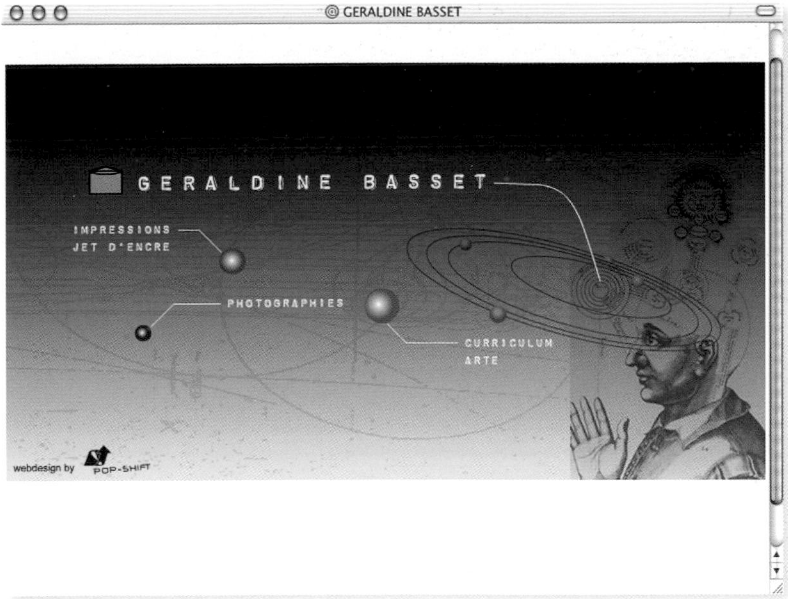

WWW.GERALDINEBASSET.COM
D: JEAN-CHRISTOPHE LANTIER, **C:** NICOLAS BRIGNOL
A: POP-SHIFT

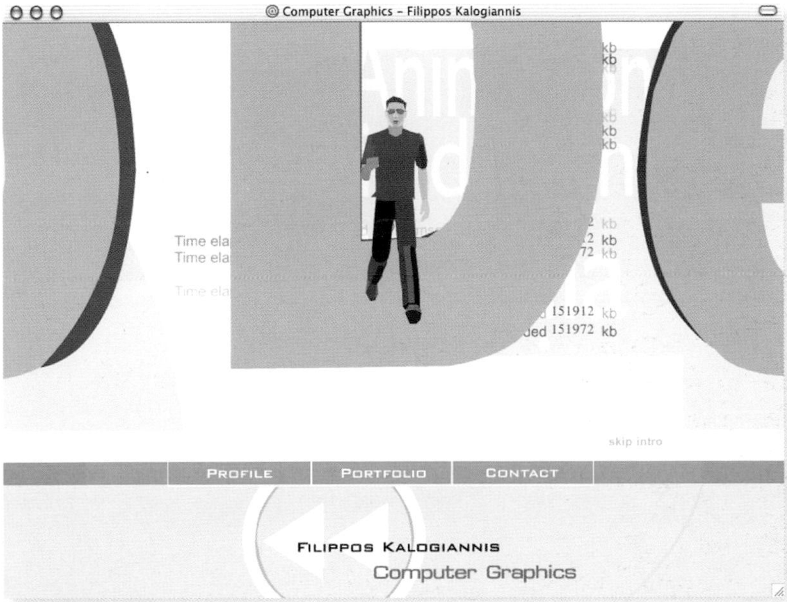

WWW.FILIPPOSART.GR
D: FILIPPOS KALOGIANNIS
A: FILIPPOS ART, **M:** INFO@FILIPPOSART.GR

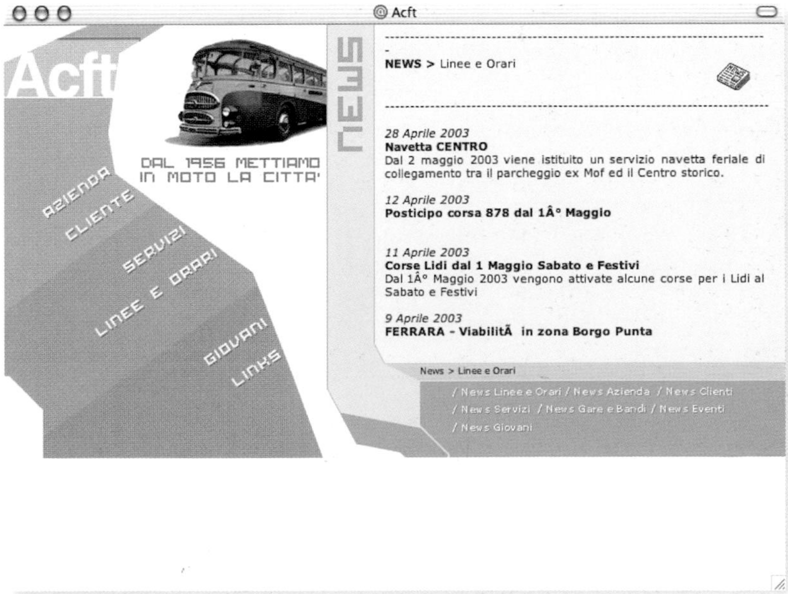

WWW.ACFT.IT/HOME.ASP
D: PACO ZANE, **C:** ANDREA GRECO, **P:** SANDRO LOVADINA
A: VENICECOM, **M:** PZANE@VENICECOM.IT

WWW.RAFFAELERUSSO.COM
D: RAFFAELE RUSSO
A: DEFSIGN, **M:** INFO@RAFFAELERUSSO.COM

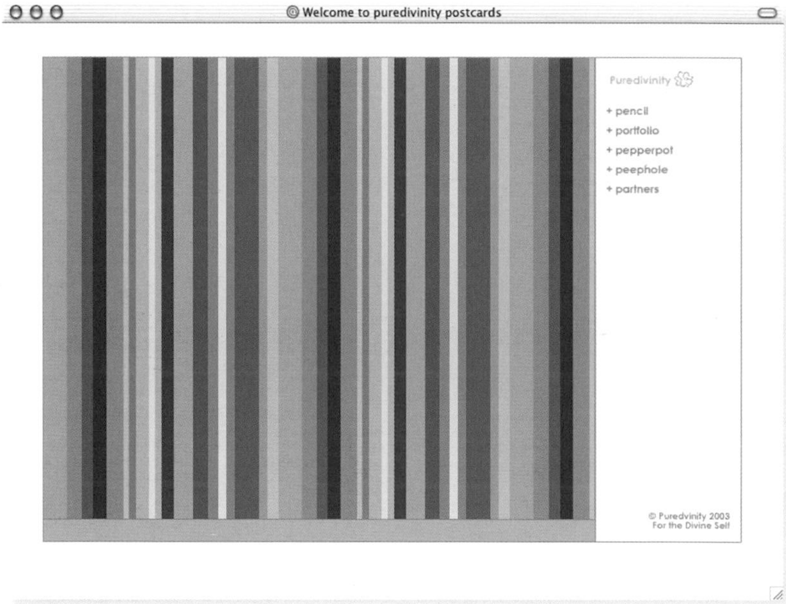

WWW.PUREDIVINITY.CJB.NET
D: JOANNA SUN
A: PUREDIVINITY, **M:** PUREDIVINITY@MAC.COM

WWW.SCHUDELDRUCK.CH
D: MICHEL SEELIGER & SABINA MALER, **C:** MICHEL SEELIGER
A: CHAMELEON GRAPHICS GMBH, **M:** INFO@CHAMELEONGRAPHICS.CH

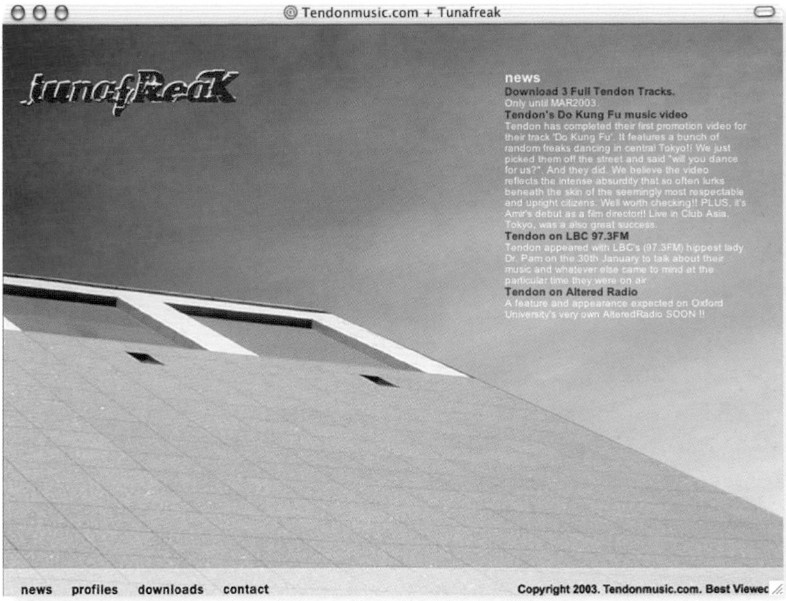

WWW.TENDONMUSIC.COM
D: EUGENE LOW
A: INKBOMB, **M:** THEZEROHOUR@HOTMAIL.COM

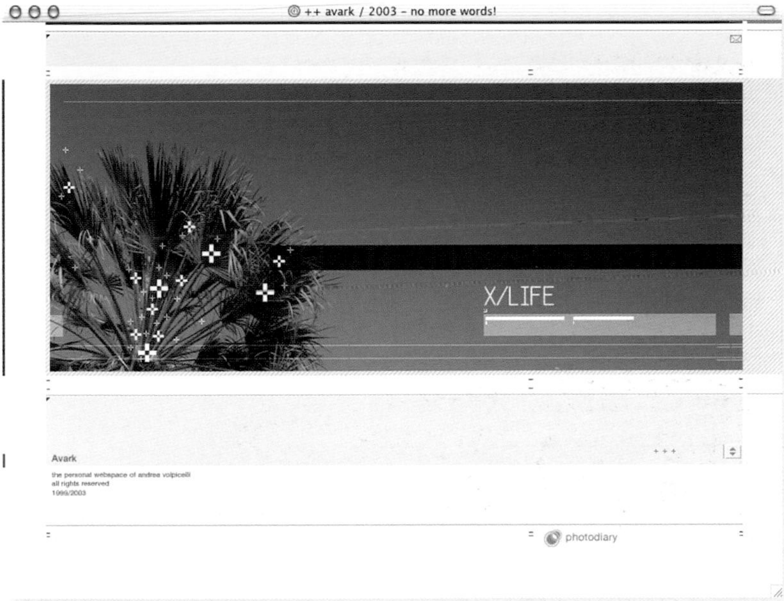

WWW.ARKIMEDIA.NET/AVARK/AVARK.ASP
D: ANDREA VOLPICELLI
M: ANDREA.VOLPICELLI@TIN.IT

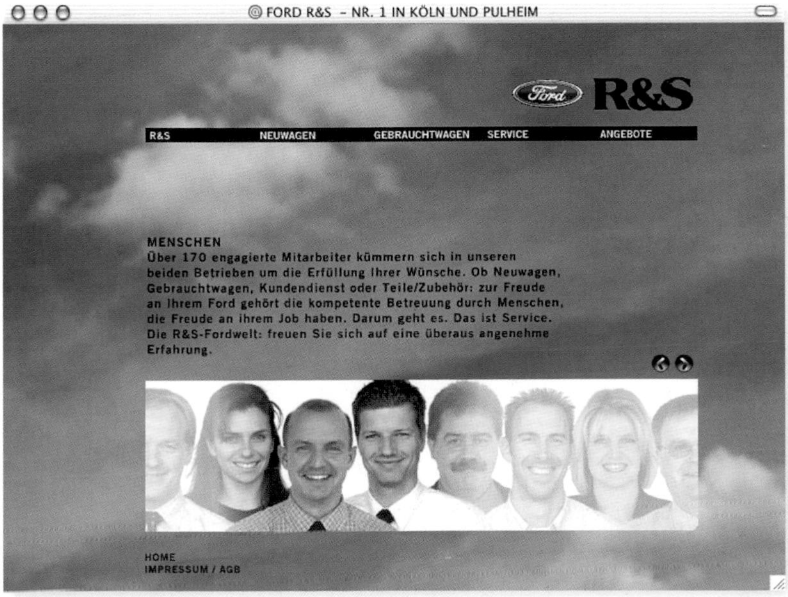

WWW.RSMOBILE.DE/MAIN.HTML
D: WALTER MÖSSLER, **C:** PACO LALUCA, **P:** PACO LALUCA
A: TOUCHEE, **M:** INFO@TOUCHEE.DE

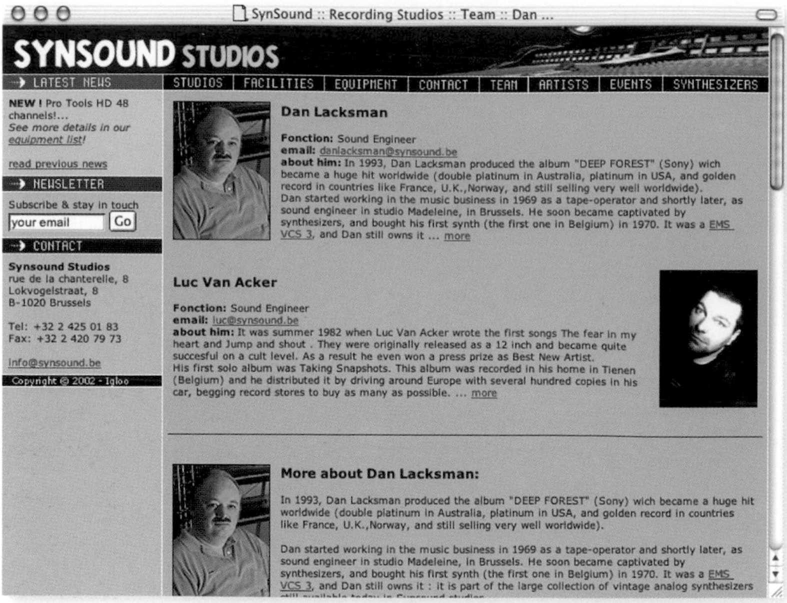

WWW.SYNSOUND.BE
D: ANTOINE GATTOLLIAT
A: IGLOO, **M:** ANTOINE@IGLOO.BE

WWW.PRODIGOWEB.NET
D: FRANCISCO GÓMEZ
A: PRODIGO-MULTIMEDIA, **M:** PRODIGO@PRODIGOWEB.NET

WWW.KONTRASTMITTEL.DE
D: DIRK HEINEMANN, **C:** HENNING LEFELDT
A: IMP, **M:** WWW.IMPARTNER.DE

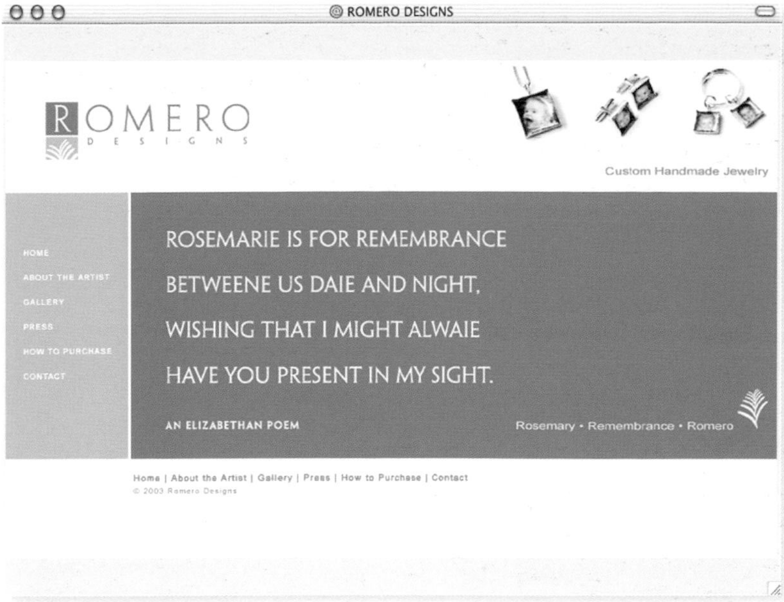

WWW.ROMERODESIGNS.COM
D: RHONDA KIM, **P:** MICK WALSH
A: WALSH PRODUCTIONS INC., **M:** INFO@WPINYC.COM

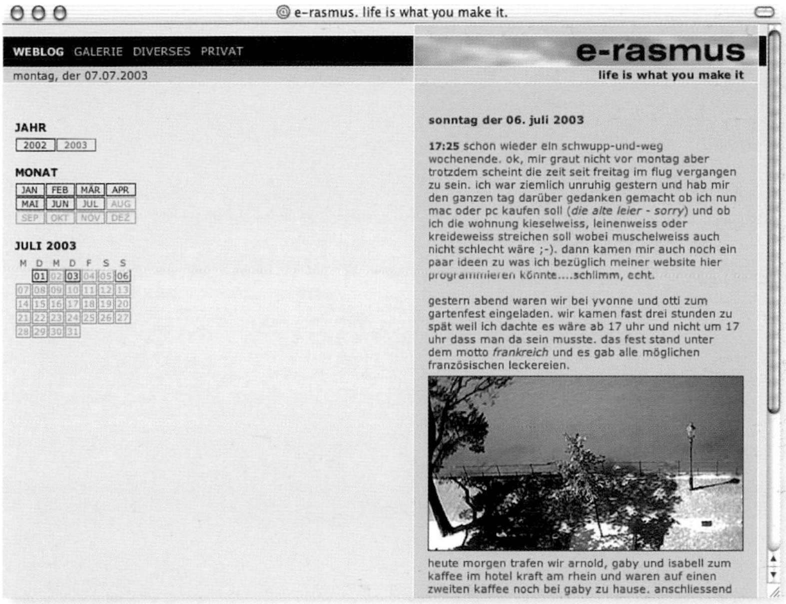

WWW.E-RASMUS.DE
D: MATTHIAS MAIER
M: MATTE@E-RASMUS.DE

WWW.MAGNETICA.IT
D: MAGNETICA DEVELOPMENT, **C:** EMILIANO GUSMINI, **P:** MAGNETICA DEVELOPMENT
A: MAGNETICA DEVELOPMENT, **M:** INFO@MAGNETICA.IT

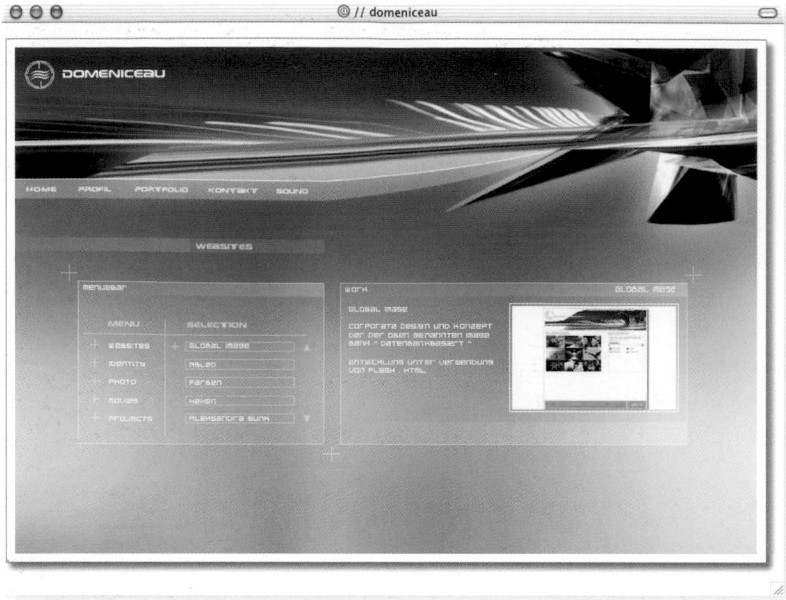

WWW.DOMENICEAU.DE
D: DOMINIK WELTERS
M: DOMINIK@DOMENICEAU.DE

WWW.TRIPOLY.COM
D: ISAAC DE LA POMPA, **C:** RUBÉN VILLORIA, **P:** TRIPOLY
A: TRIPOLY, **M:** ISAAC@TRIPOLY.COM

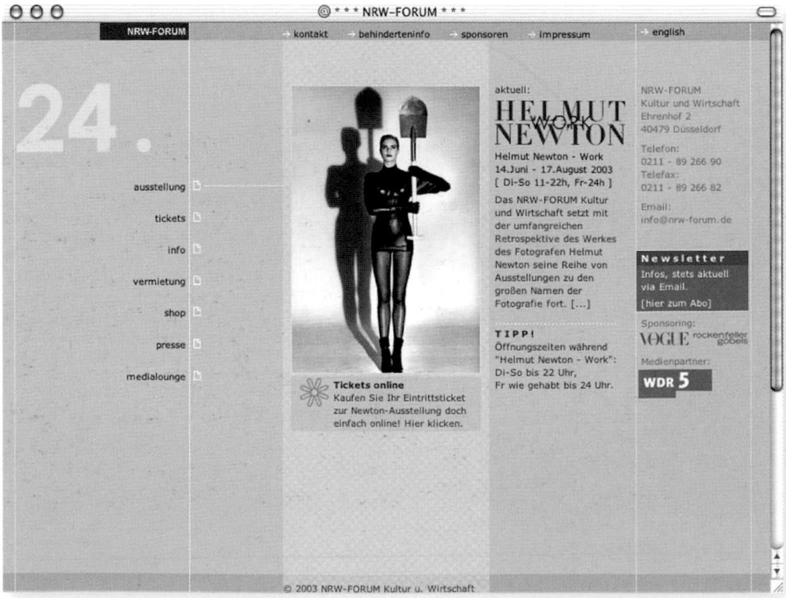

WWW.NRW-FORUM.DE
D: CHRIS & KATRIN BRACKMANN, **C:** KATRIN BRACKMANN
A: OZ DESIGN, **M:** KA@OZ-ZONE.DE

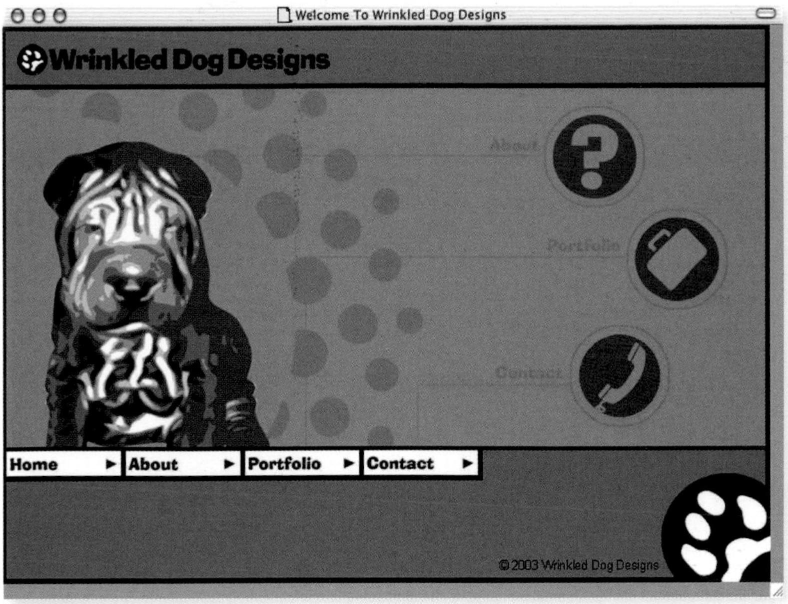

WWW.WRINKLEDDOGDESIGNS.COM
D: CHAS MINNICH
A: WRINKLED DOG DESIGNS, **M:** CHAS@WRINKLEDDOGDESIGNS.COM

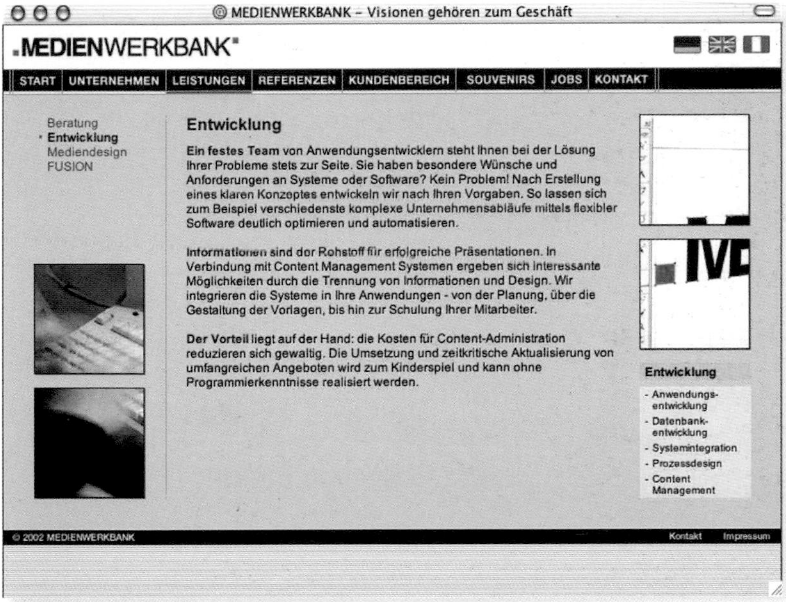

WWW.MEDIENWERKBANK.DE
D: PATRICK JÖST, ENRICO THIES, SIRKO STENZ, **C:** ALLAN GRUNERT, **P:** PATRICK JÖST
A: MEDIENWERKBANK, **M:** PJ@MEDIENWERKBANK.DE

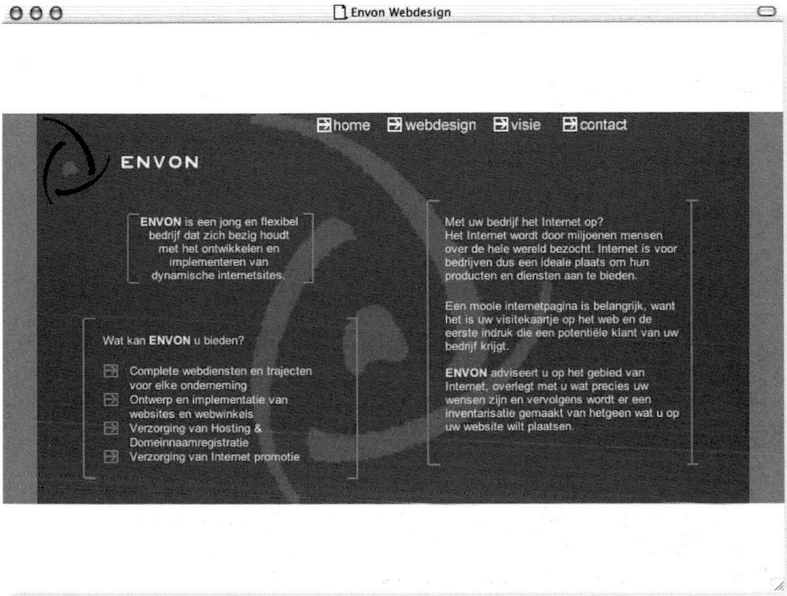

WWW.ENVON.NL
D: ERWIN VELTHOEN
A: ENVON, **M:** ERWIN@ENVON.NL

WWW.VILLAGE.IT
D: ILARIA BOZ, **C:** SERGIO FAZIO, **P:** SERGIO FAZIO
A: VILLAGE, **M:** ASSUE@VILLAGE.IT

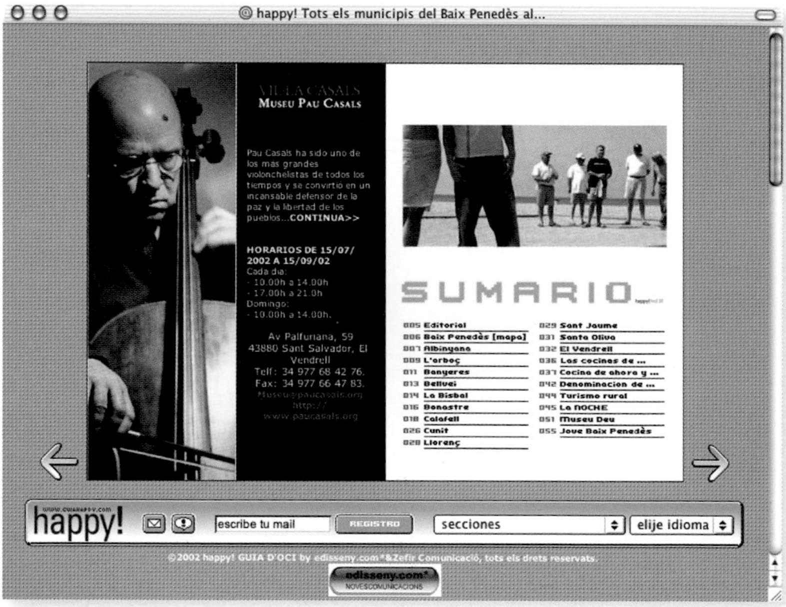

WWW.GUIAHAPPY.COM
D: EMILIO GARCIA VAZ
A: EDISSENY.COM*, **M:** INFO@EDISSENY.COM

WWW.EWA-PRODUCTIONS.DE
D: HENRIK NIBBE, **C:** SVEN GROẞJOHANN, **P:** EWA-PRODUCTIONS GMBH
A: EWA-PRODUCTIONS GMBH, **M:** HN@EWA-PRODUCTIONS.DE

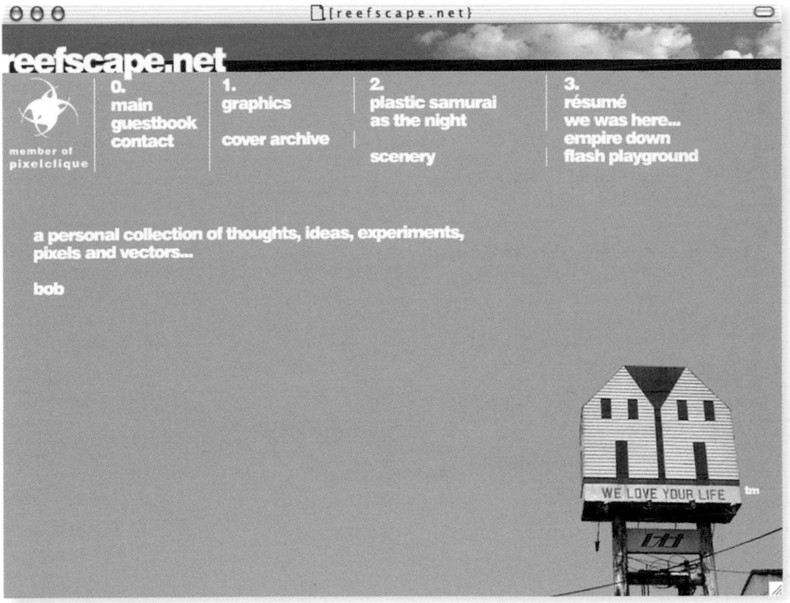

WWW.REEFSCAPE.NET
D: BOB CORPORAAL
M: ITS_THE_WEBDESIGN_INDEX@REEFSCAPE.NET

WWW.UNTITLED-DOC.DE
D: BURAK YILDIRIM
A: BRAINTRANSFER, **M:** BURAK.YILDIRIM@BRAINTRANSFER.DE

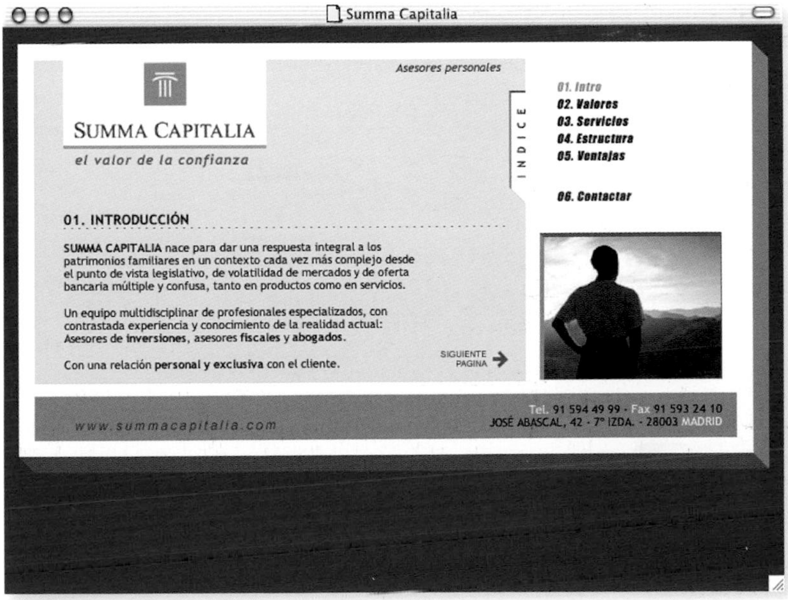

WWW.SUMMACAPITALIA.COM
D: JUANJO PALACIOS
A: IFI, **M:** JUANJO_P@YAHOO.COM

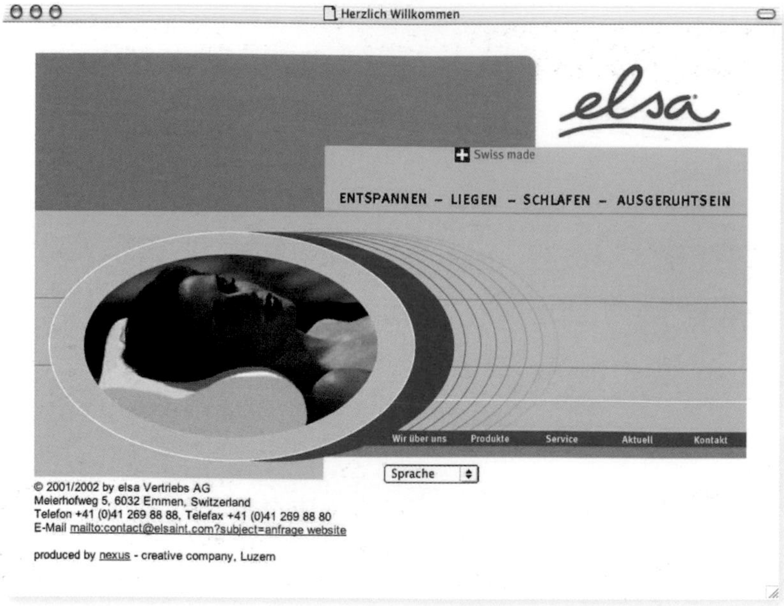

WWW.ELSAINT.COM
D: CORNEL BETSCHART, **C:** PETER ULRICH, **P:** CORNEL BETSCHART
A: NEXUS - CREATIVE COMPANY, **M:** INFO@NCC.CH

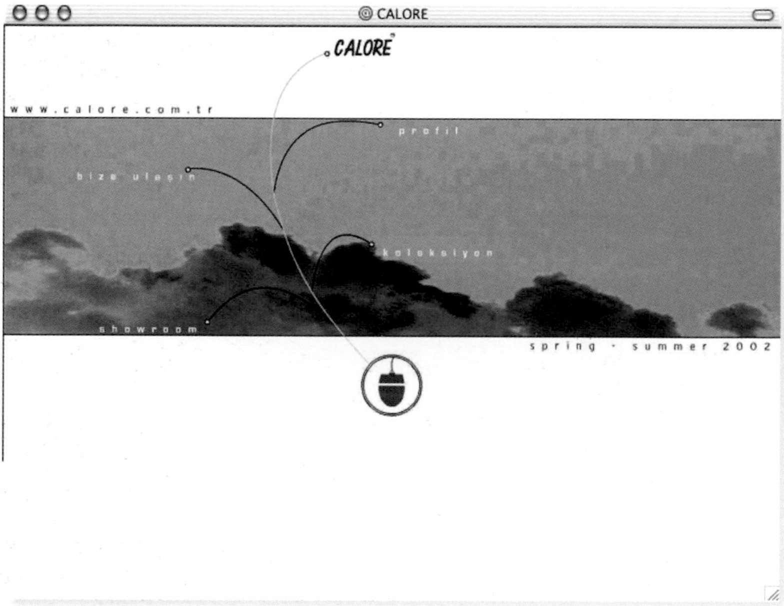

WWW.CALORE.COM.TR
D: AROYO METIN
A: 18 DESIGN, **M:** MOSCAR@SUPERONLINE.COM

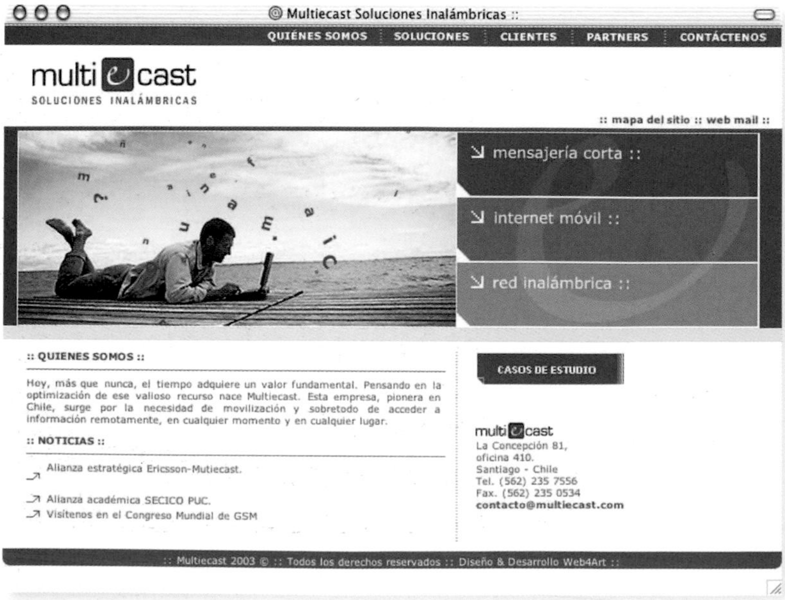

WWW.MULTIECAST.COM
D: JUAN MORENO, **C:** JUAN MORENO, **P:** LUPE SANTOS
A: WEB4ART, **M:** JUANM@WEB4ART.CL

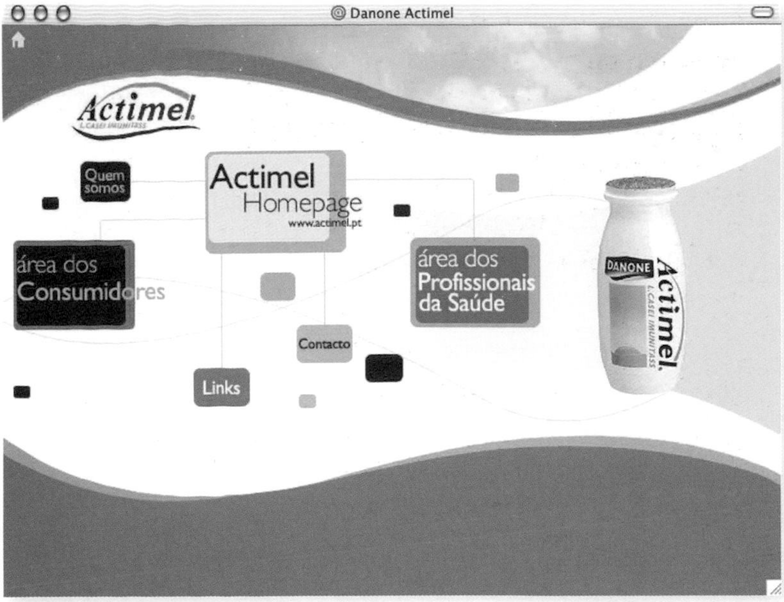

WWW.ACTIMEL.PT
D: JOAO FERNANDES, **C:** JOAO FERNANDES, **P:** JEAN SANTOS
A: VIEW., **M:** JOAO.FERNANDES@VIEW.PT

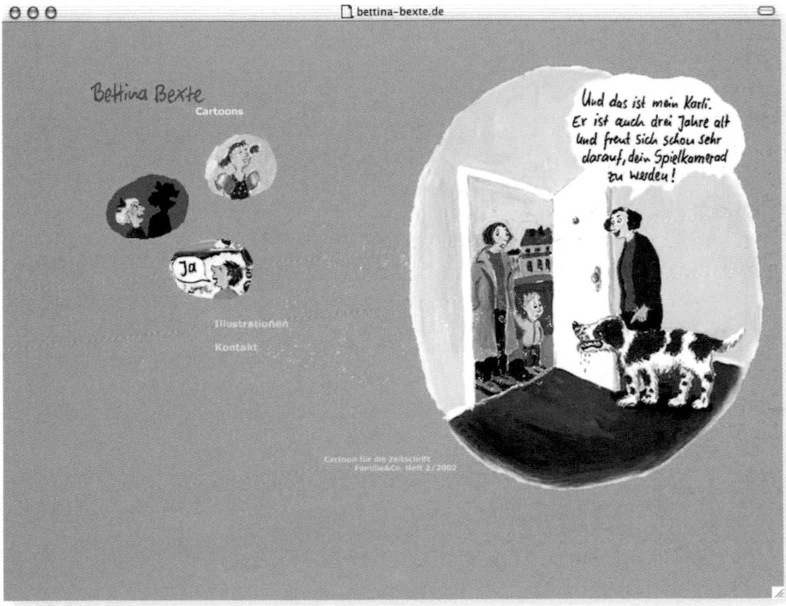

WWW.BETTINA-BEXTE.DE
D: BETTINA BEXTE, **C:** MICHAEL RIPPL, **P:** BETTINA BEXTE
A: POOL-WEBDESIGN, **M:** BETTINA.BEXTE@T-ONLINE.DE

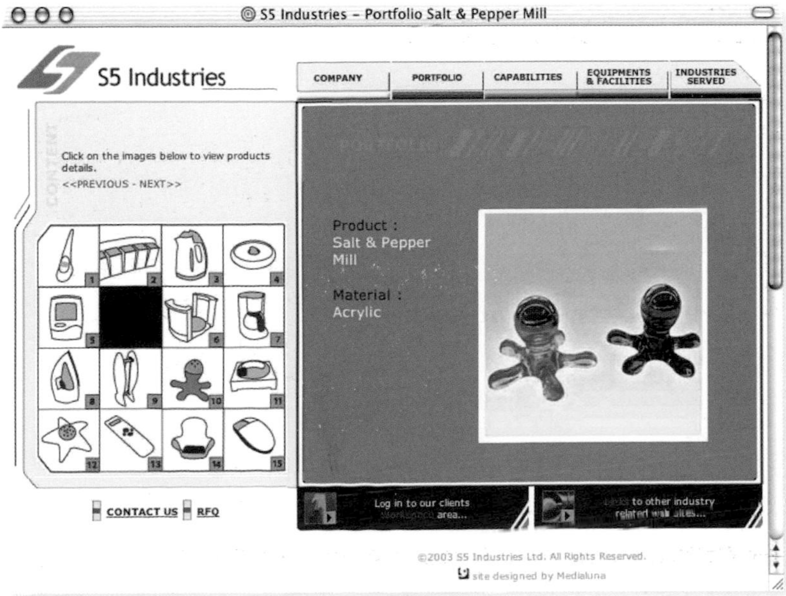

WWW.S5INDUSTRIES.COM
D: ALESSANDRA PORTA
A: MEDIALUNA, **M:** APORTA@LOMBARDIACOM.IT

WWW.NOW8.DE
D: MICHAEL GALLER
A: NOW8, **M:** MG@NOW8.DE

WWW.HOLLANDVELO.CH/DEUTSCH/HOME.SHTML
D: THOMAS BRUGGISSER, **C:** SCHMID ROGER, **P:** THOMAS BRUGGISSER / SCHMID ROGER
A: GRAFIKTRAKTOR.CH, **M:** MAILS@ROGER-SCHMID.CH

WWW.ALTRETTANTO.CH
D: MICHEL FRIES, **P:** MICHEL FRIES / SCHMID ROGER
A: MICHEL FRIES, **M:** MAILS@ROGER-SCHMID.CH

WWW.SHARKYDESIGN.NET
D: SHARKY, **C:** FRANÇOIS RENÉ
A: SHARKY DESIGN, **M:** SHARKYDESIGN@HOTMAIL.COM

WWW.ESTASLOCO.COM
D: JAVIER GRIÑÁN LACACI, **C:** FERNANDO BONILLA, **P:** JOAQUÍN PAREJO
A: ESTASLOCO.COM, **M:** JGLACACI@ESTASLOCO.COM

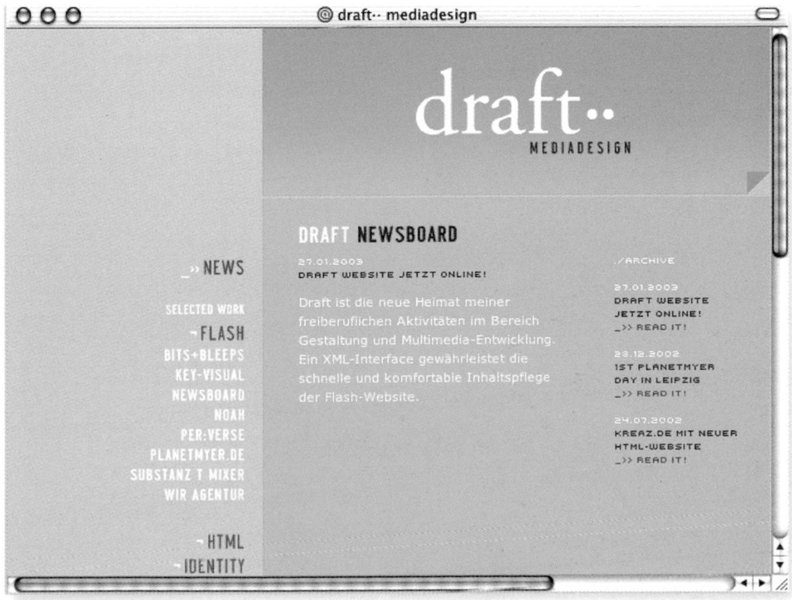

WWW.DRAFT.DEV-LAB.NET
D: KLAUS GROTZ
A: DRAFT MEDIADESIGN, **M:** KG@DEV-LAB.NET

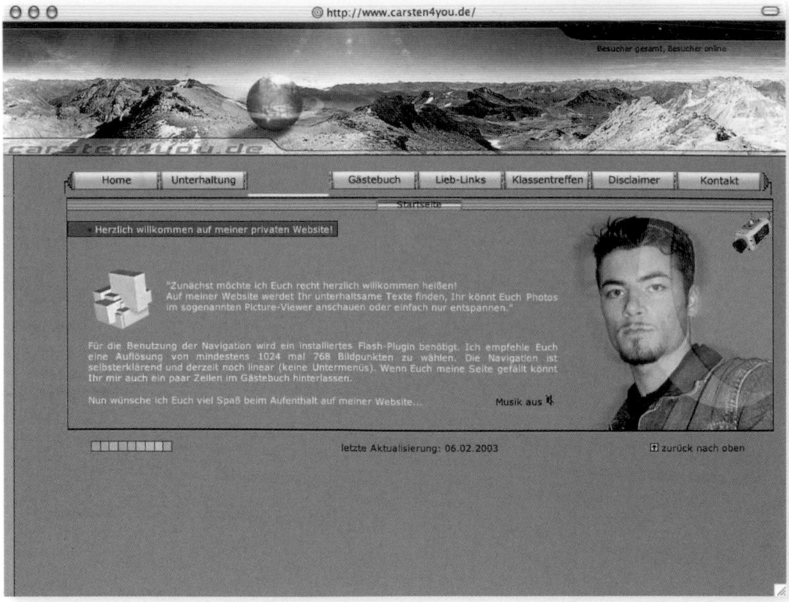

WWW.CARSTEN4YOU.DE
D: DOMINIC BEINENZ, **C:** CARSTEN LINDSTEDT
A: NEXORM, **M:** CU2NITE@YOURWAP.COM

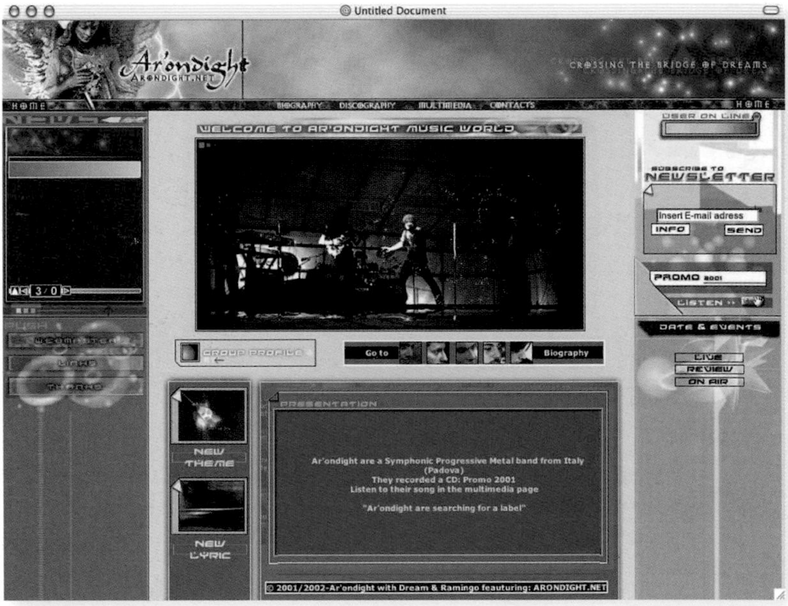

WWW.ARONDIGHT.NET
D: RAMINGO, **C:** DREAM
M: RAMINGOS@EMAIL.IT

WWW.JACKIECHANZONE.VIRTUALAVE.NET
D: GARY CHEAH
A: GARY CHEAHV, **M:** GARY_CHEAH@YAHOO.COM

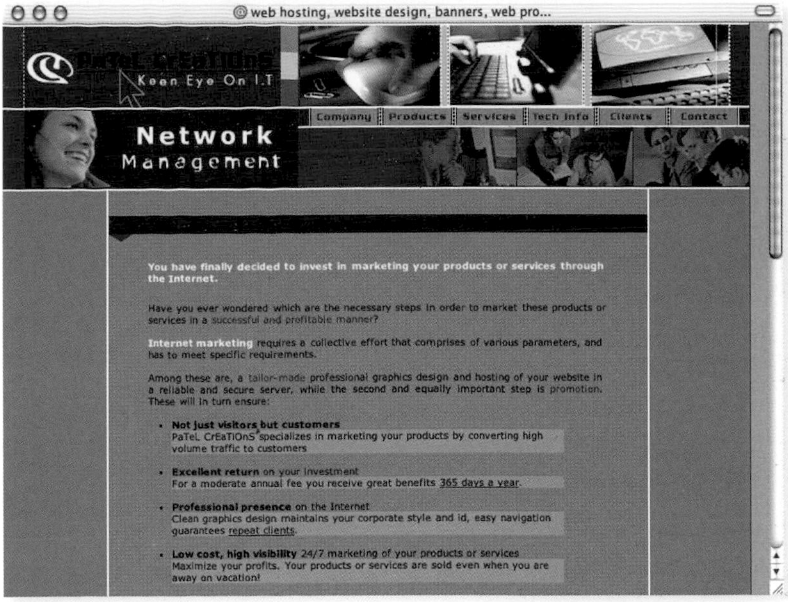

WWW.PATELCREATIONS.NET
D: YOUSUF PATEL, IMRAN SIDDIQUI, **C:** YOUSUF PATEL, IMRAN SIDDIQUI, **P:** BRAHIM
A: PATEL CREATIONS, **M:** INFO@PATELCREATIONS.NET

WWW.BSSG.CH
D: ANDREAS ALTENBURGER
A: NETZ.WERK, INTERNETAGENTUR ST.GALLEN, **M:** OFFICE@NETZ.WERK.CH

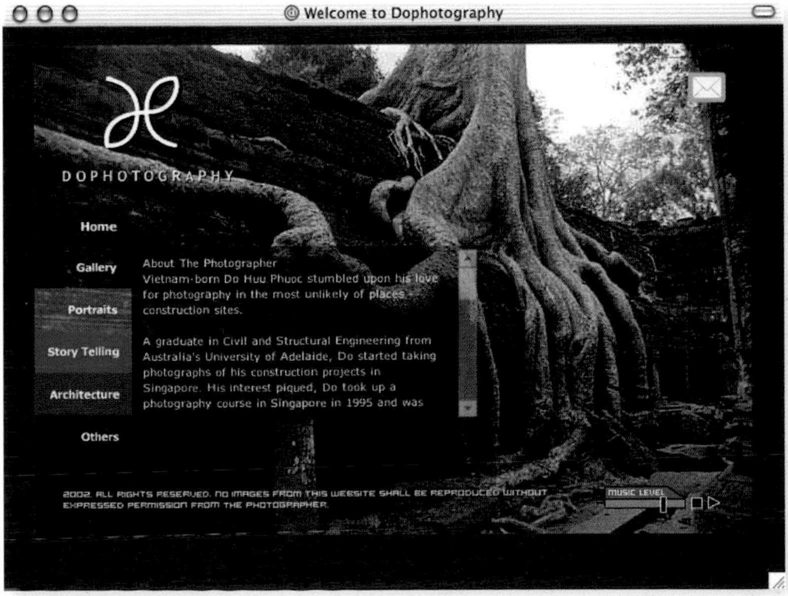

WWW.DOPHOTOGRAPHY.COM
D: TAN BRYAN
A: TOUCHMOTION PTE LTD, **M:** BRYAN@TOUCHMOTION.COM

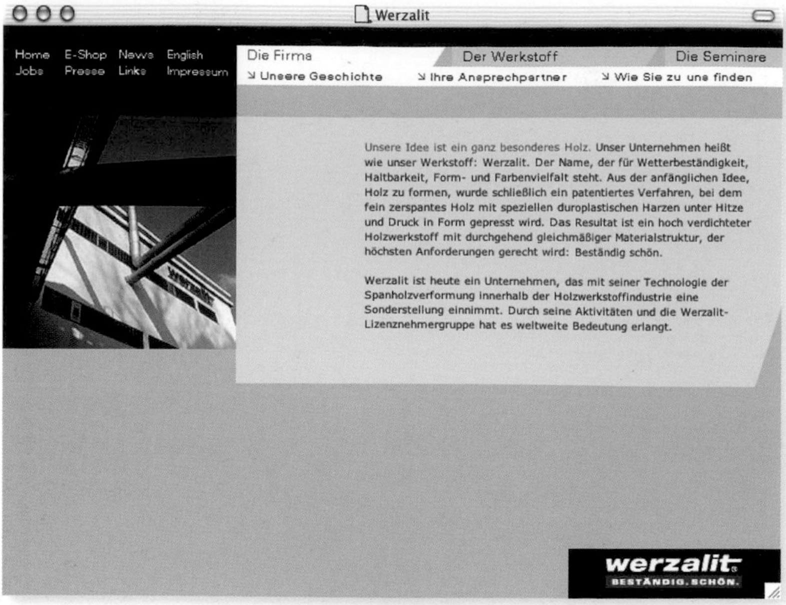

WWW.WERZALIT.COM
D: CLAUDIA GLOECKLER, **C:** NICO WECKERLE, **P:** NICO WECKERLE
A: RTS RIEGER TEAM, **M:** GEORG.OEHLER@RTS-RIEGERTEAM.DE

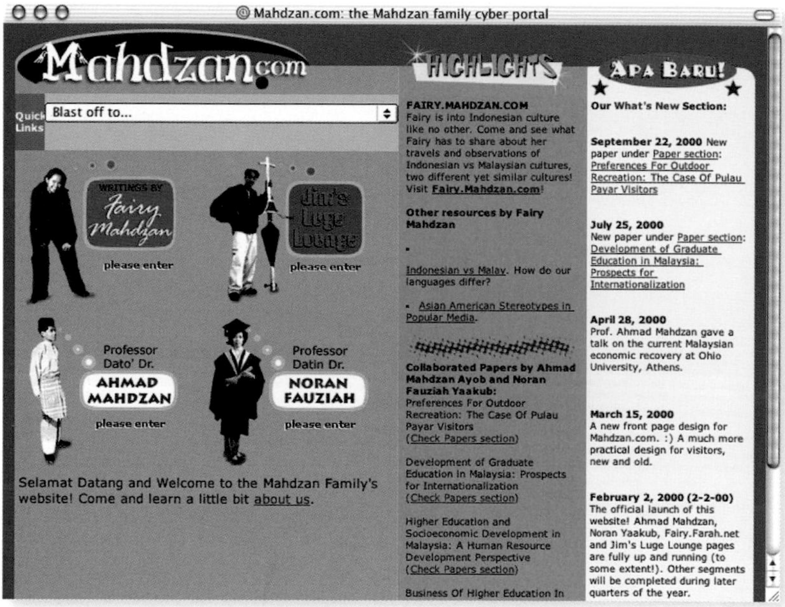

WWW.MAHDZAN.COM
D: FARAH 'FAIRY' MAHDZAN
A: MAHDZAN.COM, **M:** FAIRY@MAHDZAN.COM

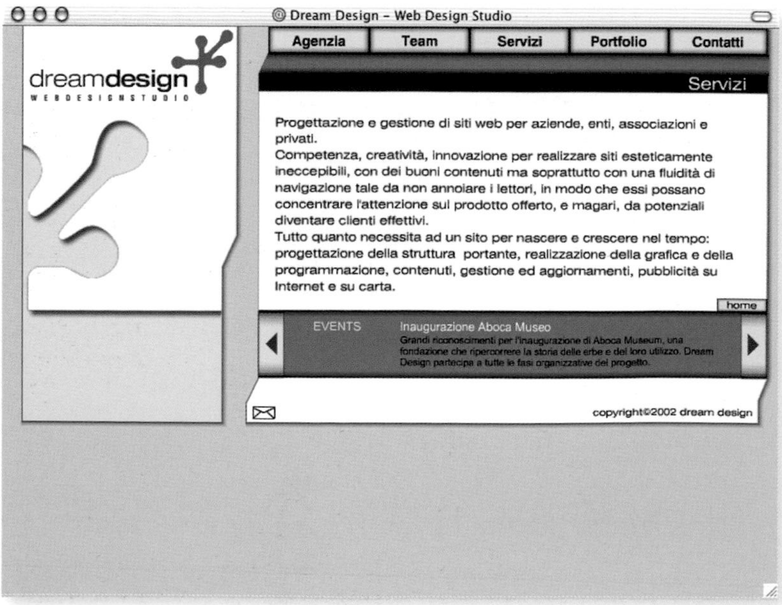

WWW.DREAMDESIGN.IT
D: LORENZO MERCATI, **C:** LORENZO MERCATI, **P:** DREAMDESIGN
A: DREAMDESIGN, **M:** INFO@DREAMDESIGN.IT

WWW.CCC-ACAM.IT/AZIENDA/AZIENDA.PHP
D: ELISABETTA MORO, **C:** GIOVANNI GANASSIN, **P:** SANDRO LOVADINA
A: VENICECOM, **M:** EMORO@VENICECOM.IT

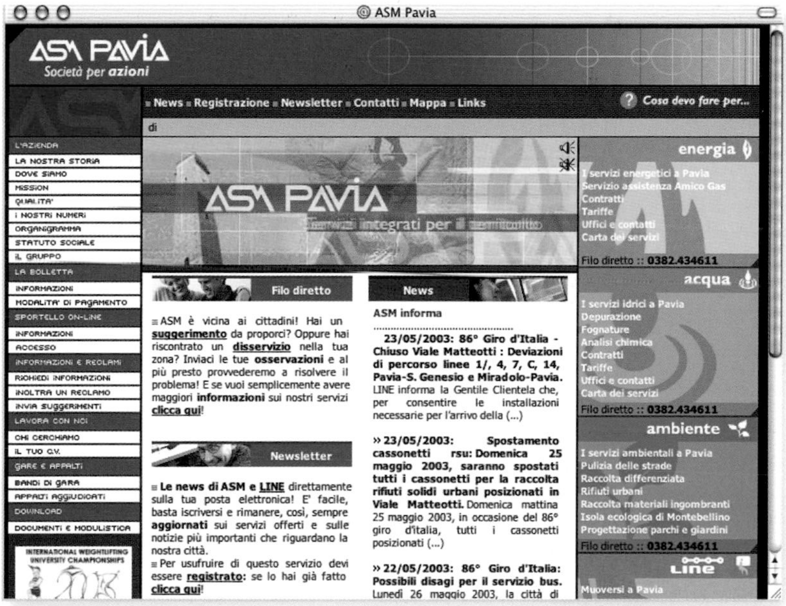

WWW.ASM.PV.IT
D: DANIELE FERRETTI, WALTER RITRIVI, **C:** LUCA STACCHIO
A: NETA, **M:** INFO@NETANET.IT

WWW.STORIEDIWEB.IT
D: FRANCESCA MORBIDELLI
A: FRANCESCA MORBIDELLI, **M:** FRANCESCA.MOR@TIN.IT

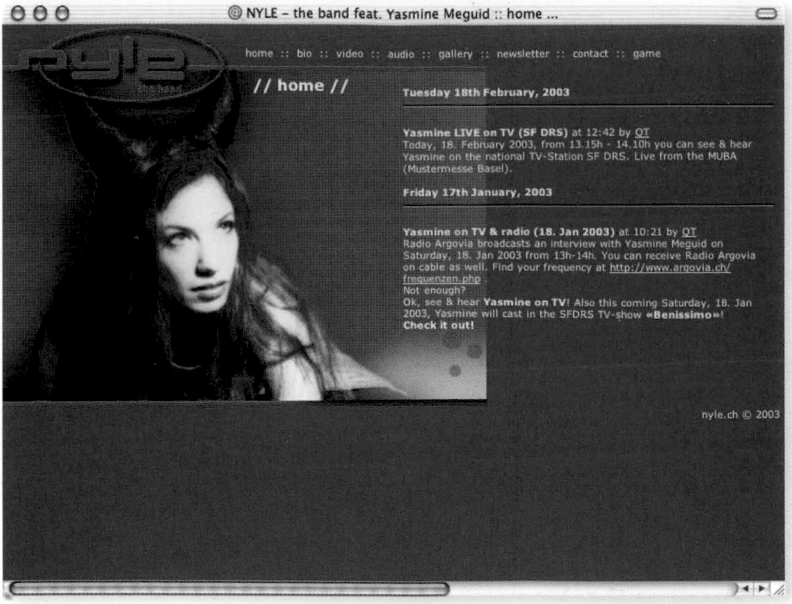

WWW.NYLE.CH
D: MARTIN KUTTER
A: WEBSOLUTIONS MARTIN KUTTER [WMK], **M:** INFO@WMK.CH

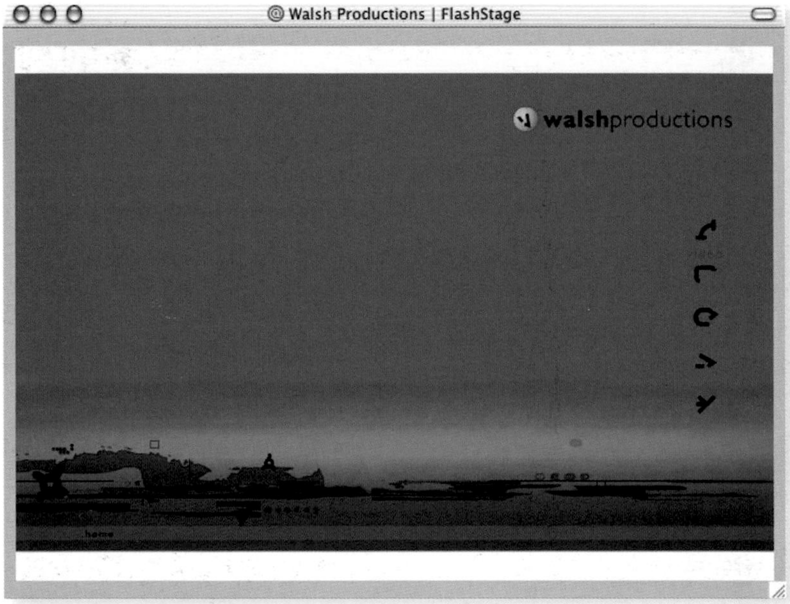

WWW.WPINYC.COM/FLASHSTAGE.HTML
D: MICK WALSH
A: WALSH PRODUCTIONS, INC., **M:** INFO@WPINYC.COM

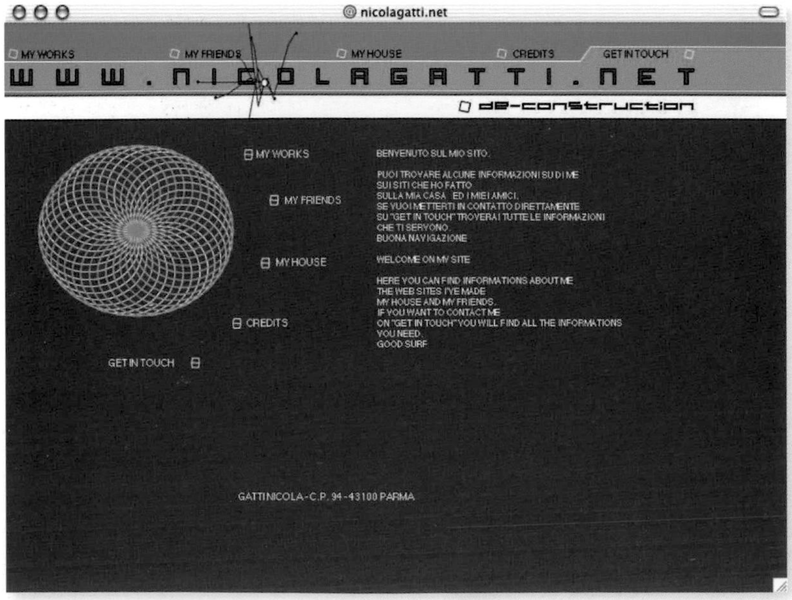

WWW.NICOLAGATTI.NET
D: NICOLA GATTI
A: NICOLAGATTI.NET, **M:** INFO@NICOLAGATTI.NET

WWW.INTERNETIXOY.FI
D: ROBERT BLOMERUS, **C:** JARI LANKINEN, **P:** NITERNETIX OY
A: INTERNETIX OY, **M:** ROBERT.BLOMERUS@INTERNETIXOY.FI

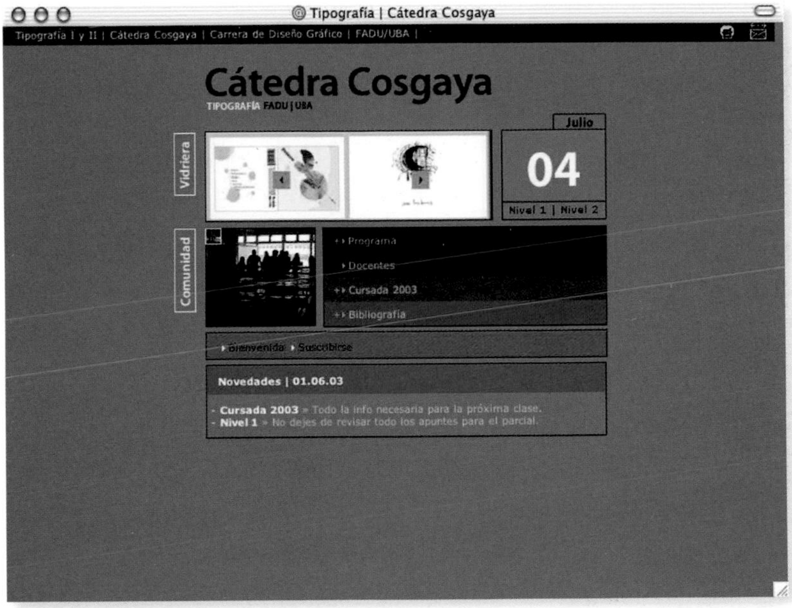

WWW.CATEDRACOSGAYA.COM.AR
D: LEONARDO SPINETTO, **C:** LEONARDO SPINETTO, **P:** CÁTEDRA COSGAYA
A: CÁTEDRA COSGAYA, **M:** WEBMASTER@CATEDRACOSGAYA.COM.AR

WWW.XTEAM.CL
D: LUIS BARRERA, **C:** PATRICIO MILAN, **P:** LUIS BARRERA
A: ANATOMICO, **M:** ANATOMICO@ANATOMICO.CL

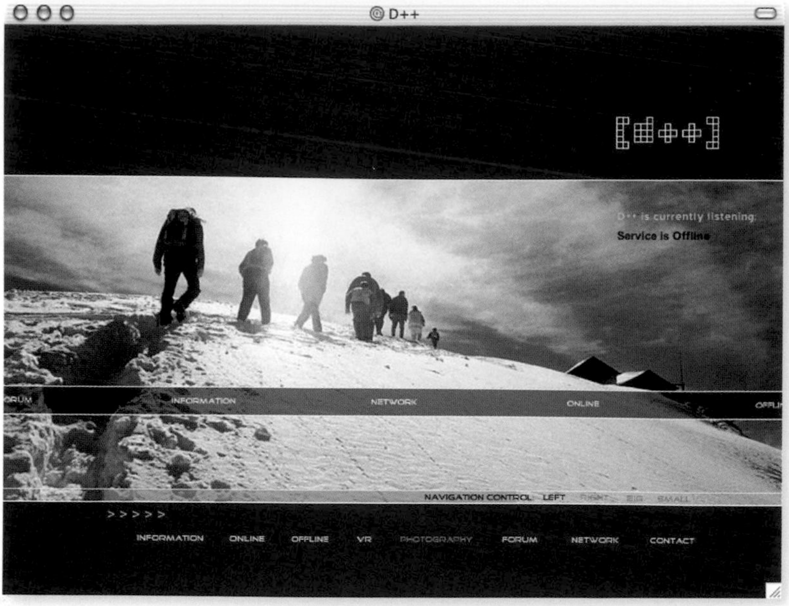

WWW.DPLUSPLUS.DE
D: DAVID WEBER, **C:** DAVID WEBER, **P:** D++
A: D++, **M:** INFO@DPLUSPLUS.DE

WWW.BRANDEVOORT.COM
D: PP CORNELISSEN
A: TRIMEDIA INTERACTIVE PROJECTS, **M:** PP.CORNELISSEN@TRIMEDIA.NL

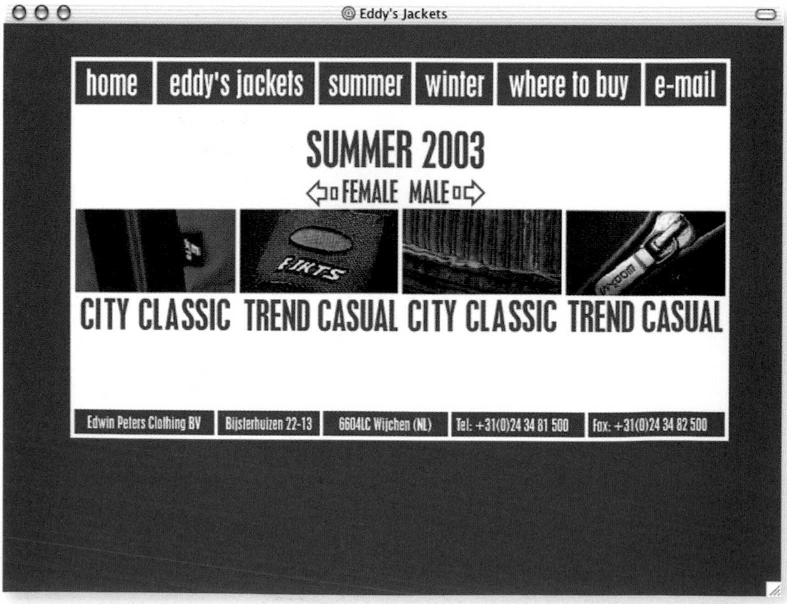

WWW.EDDYSJACKETS.COM
D: LEO HAMERS
A: YAIKZ!, **M:** INFO@YAIKZ.NL

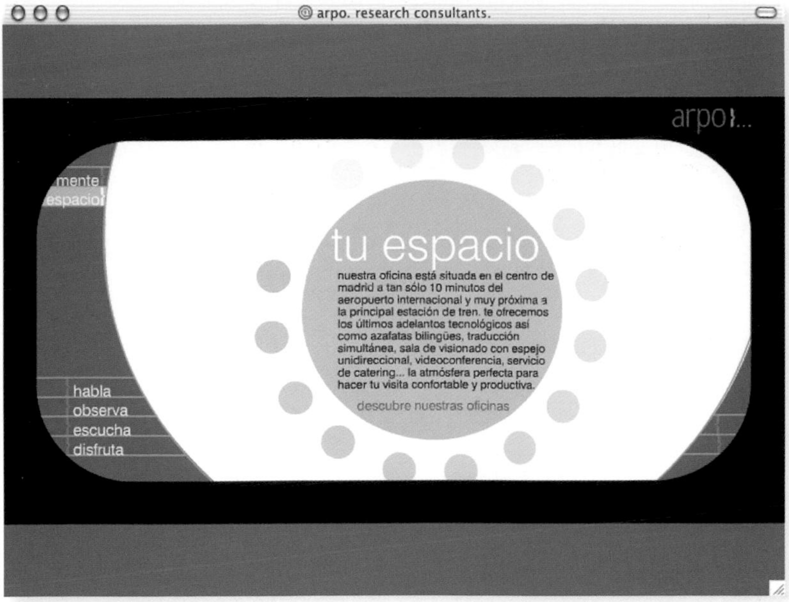

WWW.ARPO.ES
D: BETTINA IHLE, **C:** JAVIER QUER
M: JAVIERQUER@TELEFONICA.NET

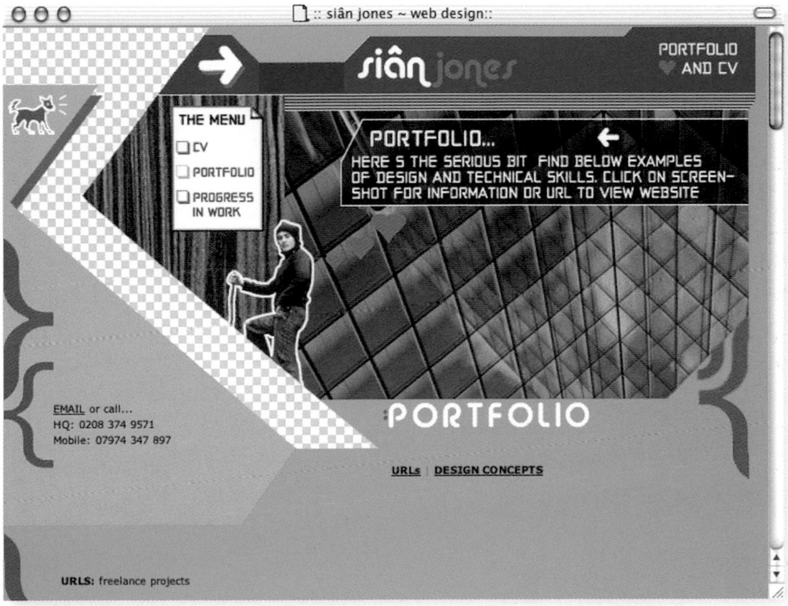

WWW.SIANJONES.NET
D: SIAN JONES
A: SIAN JONES, **M:** SIAN@SIANJONES.NET

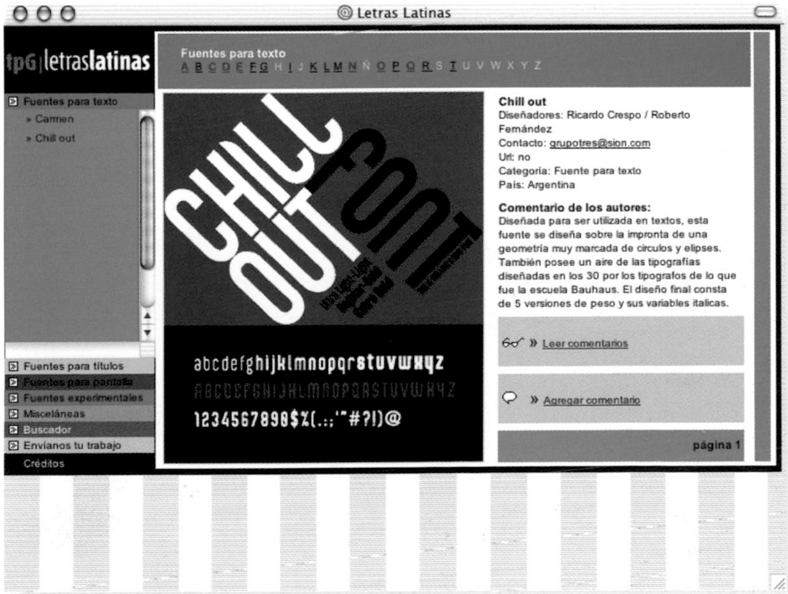

WWW.LETRASLATINAS.COM
D: LEONARDO SPINETTO, MARÍA LAURA CHIESA, NATALIA FERNANDEZ
A: LETRASLATINAS, **M:** LS@LETRASLATINAS

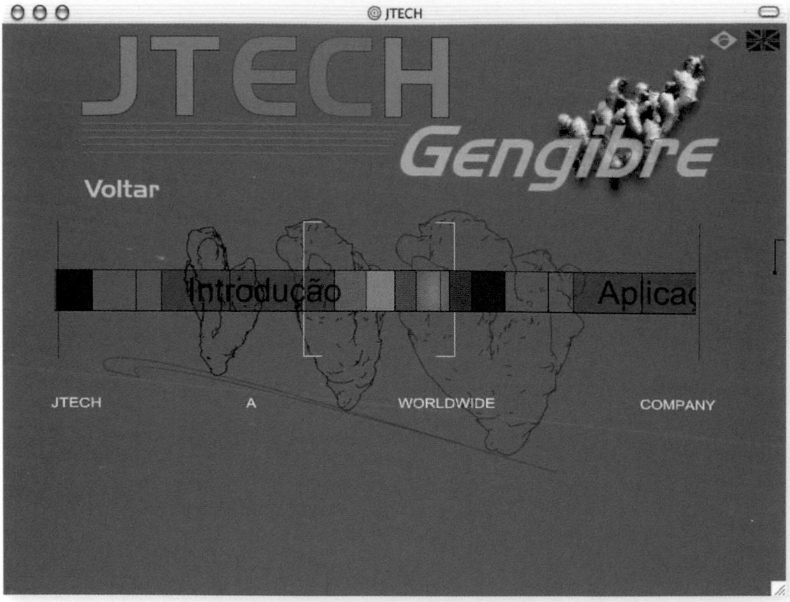

WWW.JTECH.COM.BR
D: PEDRO JAFET, **C:** PEDRO JAFET, **P:** JTECH
A: PEDRO JAFET, **M:** JAFET@UOL.COM.BR

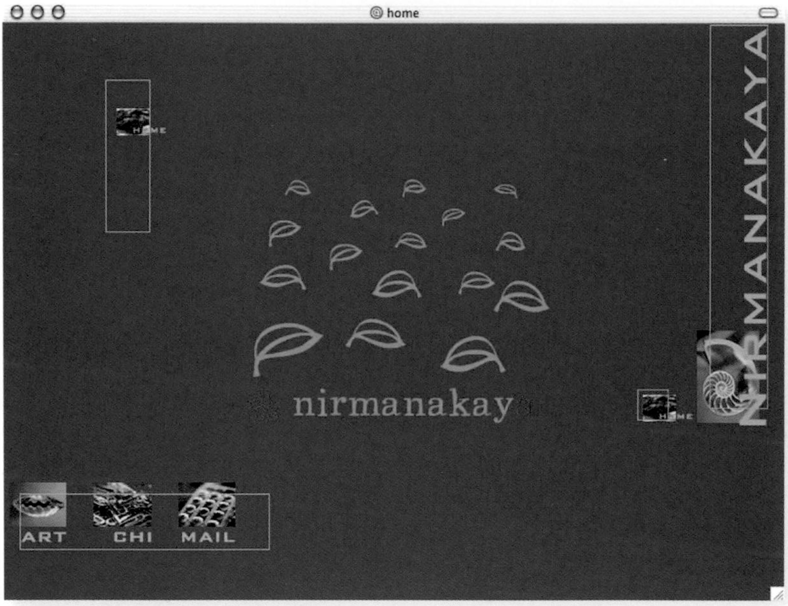

WWW.NIRMANAKAYA.NET
D: OLIVIA DEL BUFALO, **C:** NIRMANAKAYA, **P:** NIRMANAKAYA
A: NIRMANAKAYA, **M:** NIRMANAKAYA@TISCALINET.IT

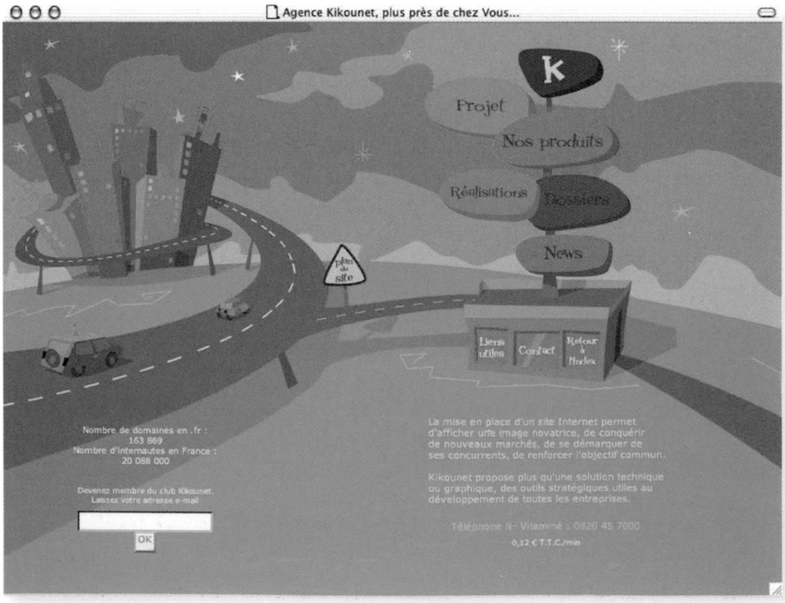

WWW.KIKOUNET.COM
D: KIKOUNET
A: KIKOUNET SARL, **M:** CONTACT@KIKOUNET.COM

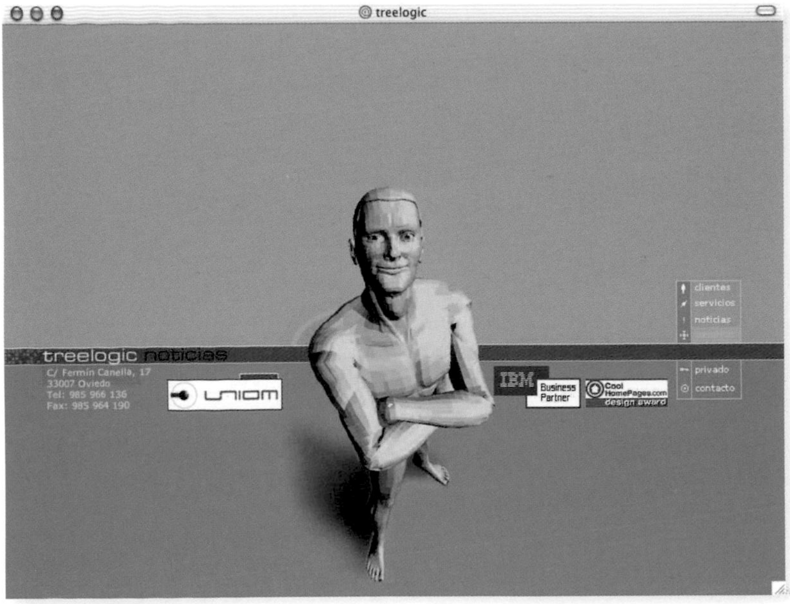

WWW.TREELOGIC.COM
D: RODOLFO GARCIA
A: TREELOGIC, **M:** RODOLFO@TREELOGIC.COM

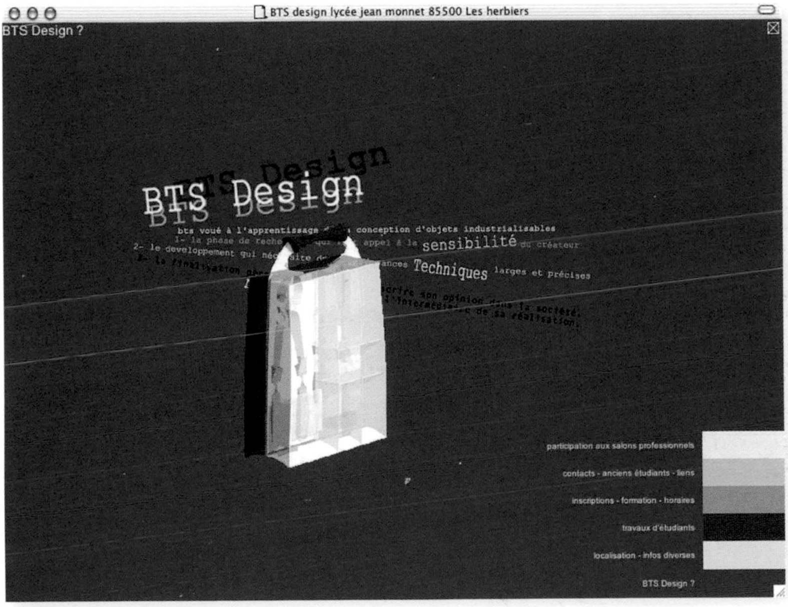

WWW.BTSDESIGN.COM
D: GAILLE MANU
M: EGAILLE@EXCITE.COM

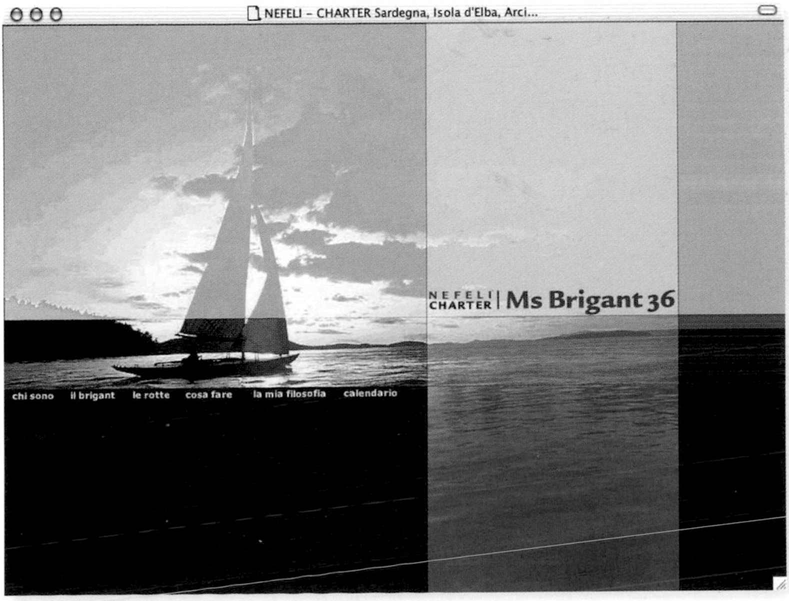

WWW.NEFELI-CHARTER.IT
D: GABRIELE STAMPA
A: OFFICINEGENERALI.IT, **M:** INFO@NEFELI-CHARTER.IT

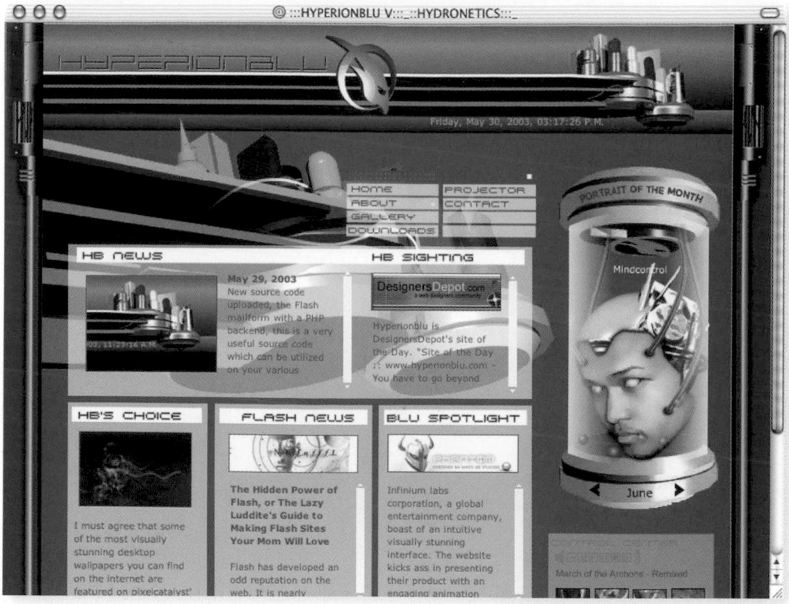

WWW.HYPERIONBLU.COM
D: STANLEY COLOMA
A: CREATIVE SYNERGY INC., **M:** SCOLOMA@CREATIVE-SYNERGY.COM

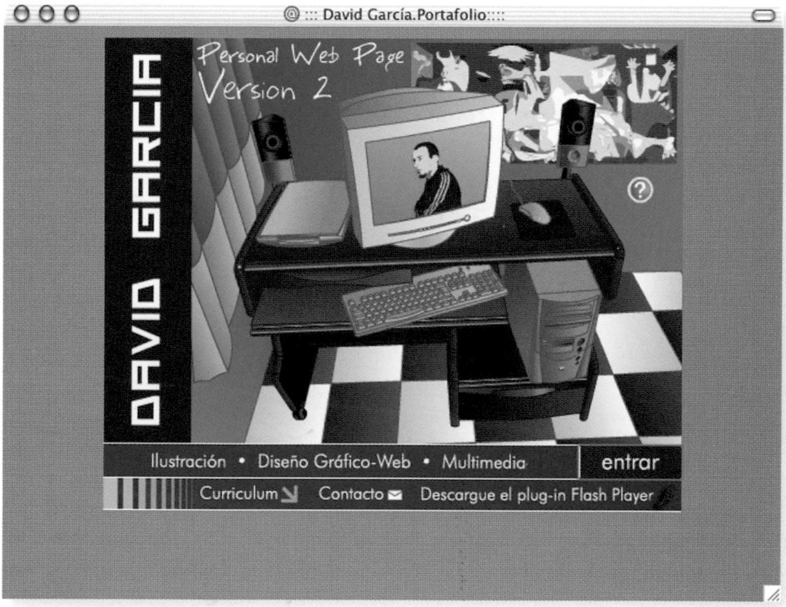

WWW.DGARCIA.YUBARTA.COM
D: CEREZO GARCÍA
A: YUBARTA TECHNOLOGIES, **M:** INFO@YUBARTA.COM

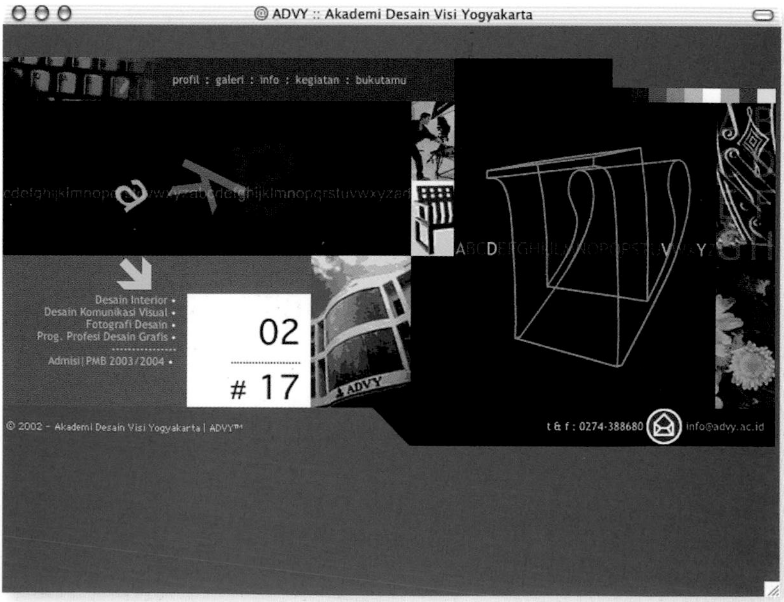

WWW.ADVY.AC.ID
D: DIEN SYAIFUDIEN, **P:** TEAM ADVY
A: JAGONYA WEB INDONESIA, **M:** DIEN@JAGONYA.WEB.ID

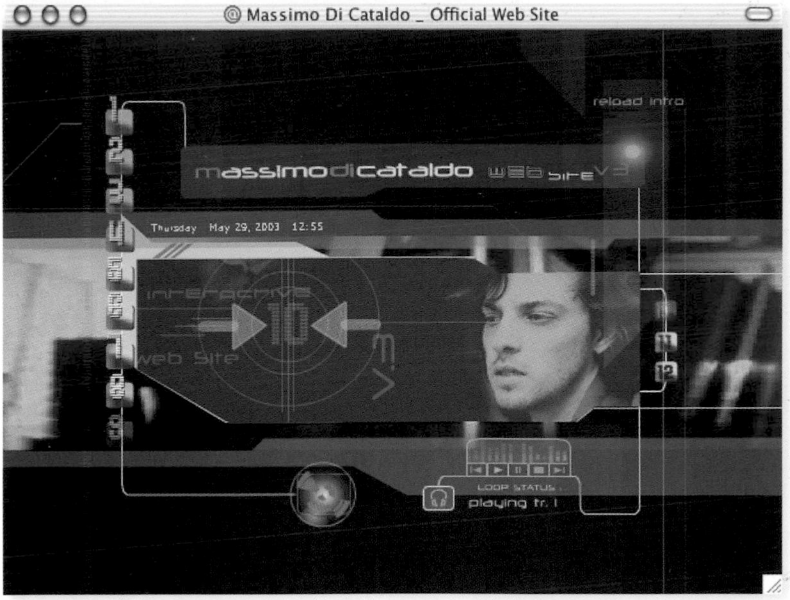

WWW.MASSIMODICATALDO.IT
D: ANNA LAURA MILLACCI
A: ALAMI MULTIMEDIA DI ANNA LAURA MILLACCI, **M:** INFO@ALAMIMULTIMEDIA.COM

WWW.TRUETECH.COM.BR
D: PEDRO JAFET / DENIS SANTOS, **C:** PEDRO JAFET, **P:** TRUETECH
A: TRUETECH, **M:** JAFET@TRUETECH.COM.BR

WWW.ASTRO.COM.MY
D: KAKIT TAN, **C:** FAIRY, **P:** KAKIT TAN
A: AMP SDN BHD, **M:** KAH-KIT_TAN@ASTRO.COM.MY

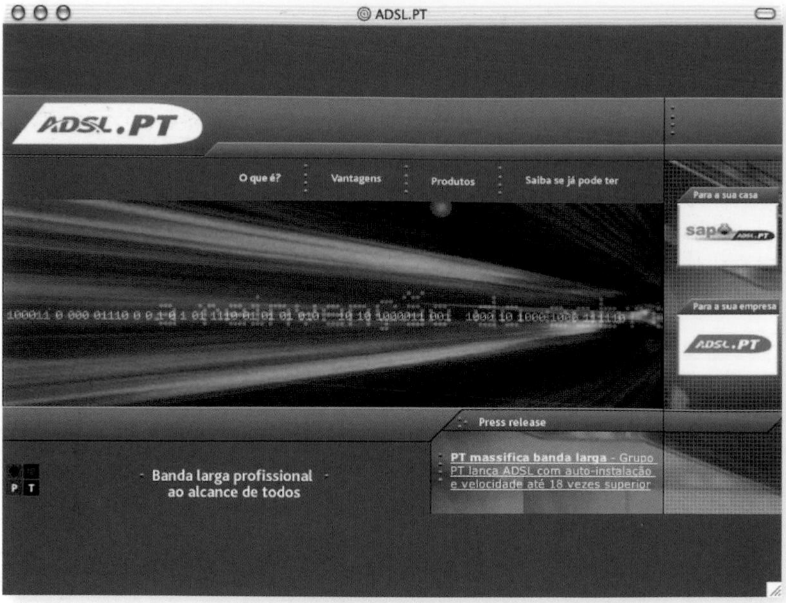

WWW.ADSL.PT
D: ALEXANDRA ROCHA, **C:** JOÃO FERNANDEZ, **P:** VÍTOR MAGALHÃES
A: INFOPULSE PORTUGAL, **M:** ALEXANDRA.ROCHA@INFOPULSE.PT

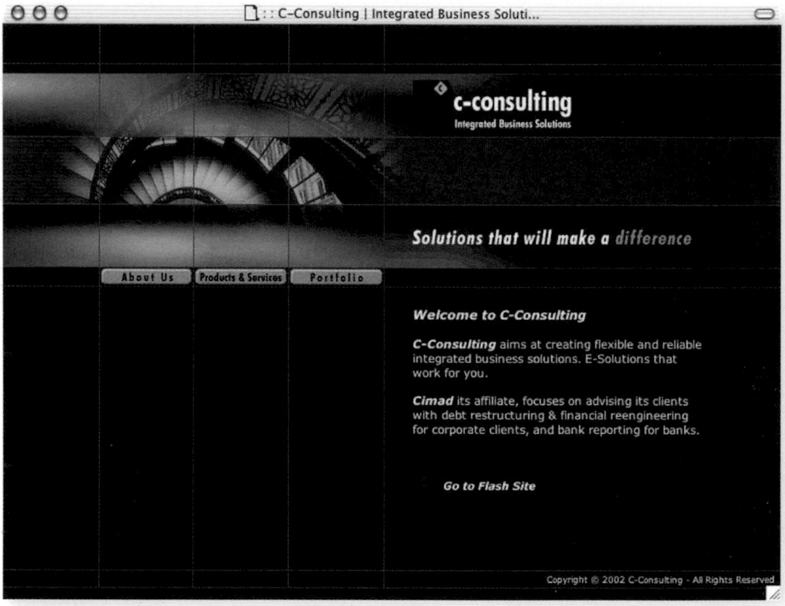

WWW.C-CONSULTING.CO.ID
D: MUSWARDI, **C:** KUSWALUYARDI, **P:** PETER VERHEZEN
A: C-CONSULTING, **M:** MUSWARDI@C-CONSULTING.CO.ID

WWW.OMNIWEAR.COM
D: RICARDO FERREIRA, **C:** RICARDO FERREIRA, **P:** EDUARDO FREITAS
M: FERREIRANET@MSN.COM

WWW.MINIATURE-EARTH.COM
D: ALLYSSON ORESTES LUCCA
A: LUCCAICO., **M:** LUCCA@LUCCACO.COM

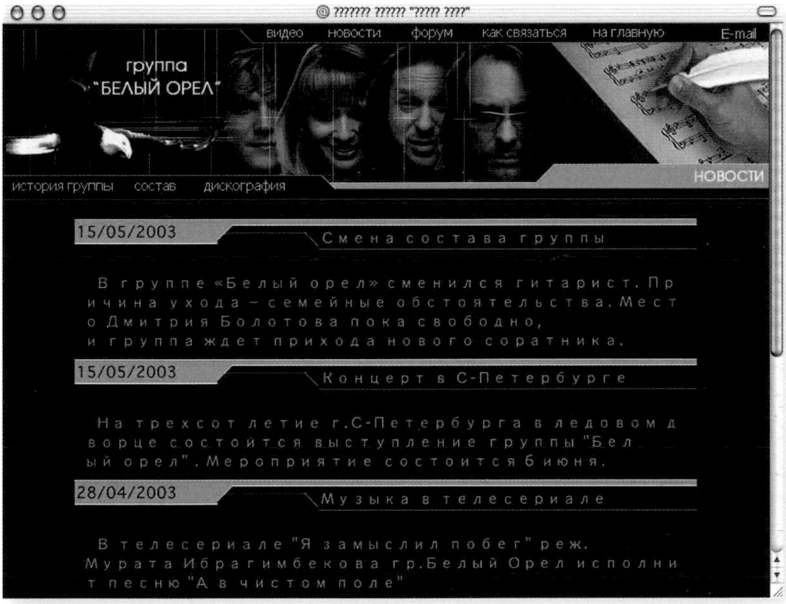

WWW.W-EAGLE.RU
D: ZHUKOV ALEXANDER, **C:** GREBENNIKOV ALEXANDER, **P:** SHUCHOV ALEXANDER
M: ALEX_ZHUKOV@INBOX.RU

WWW.VILLASPUNTAIXTAPA.COM.MX
C: RICARDO PACHECO / HECTOR VILLASEÑOR
A: WAREBOX, **M:** LREYES@WAREBOX.COM

WWW.TURISMOGROVE.COM
D: JOSÉ MANUEL GONZÁLEZ
A: IMAXINA, **M:** GLEZX2@HOTMAIL.COM

WWW.MAGICGEOX.COM
D: NETHOUSE
A: NETHOUSE, **M:** RELAZIONI.ESTERNE@NETHOUSE.IT

WWW.GRAPEFRUITMOON.CZ
D: LACMO
M: LACMO@EMAIL.CZ

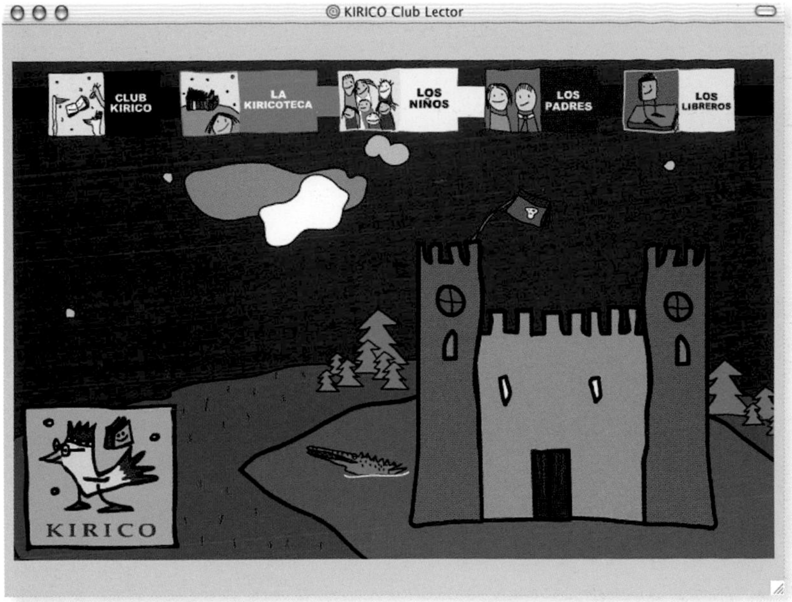

WWW.CLUBKIRICO.COM
D: ANTONIO BALLESTEROS KEREJETA, **C:** ANAROSA MIGUEL, **P:** CLUB KIRICO
A: NHT-NORWICK, **M:** ABALLESTEROS@NHT-NORWICK.NET

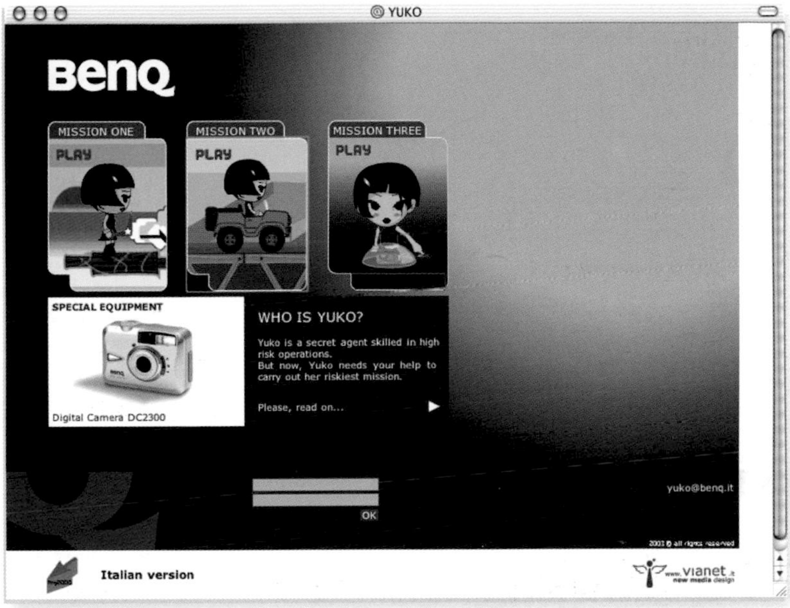

WWW.YUKO-BENQ.COM
D: SIMONE LEGNO, **C:** EMANUELE PETRUNGARO, FABIO GALLO, **P:** LUCA SIMEONE
A: VIANET, **M:** LUCA@VIANET.IT

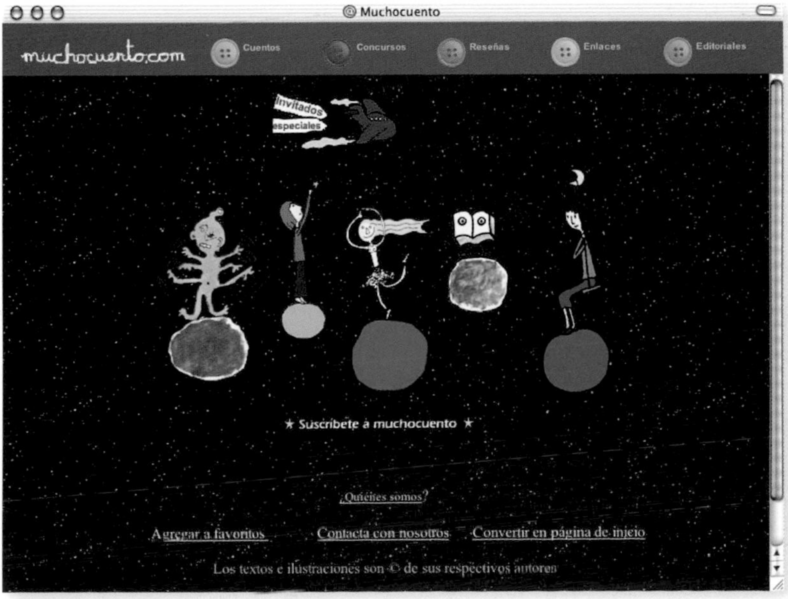

WWW.MUCHOCUENTO.COM
D: OLGA ÁLVAREZ
A: MUCHOCUENTO, **M:** LJMENENDEZ@MUCHOCUENTO.COM

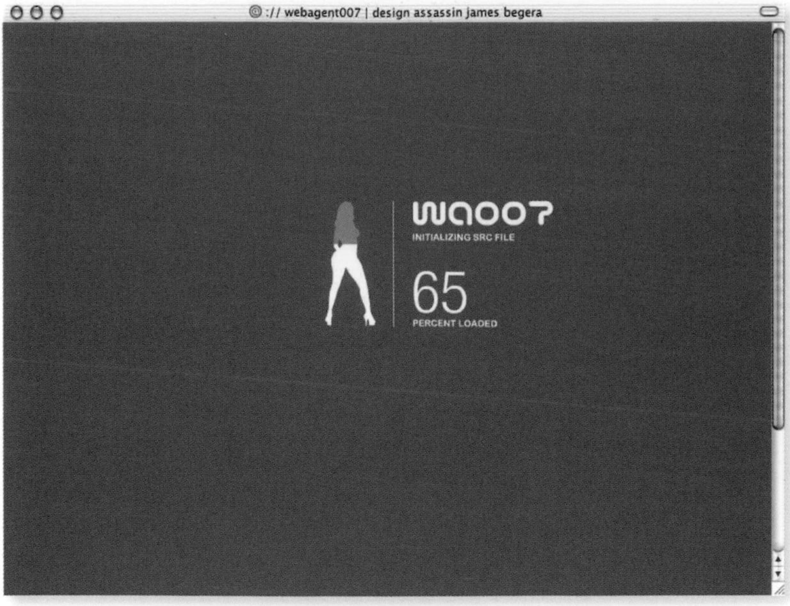

WWW.WEBAGENT007.COM
D: JAMES BEGERA
M: MAURICIO160@HOTMAIL.COM

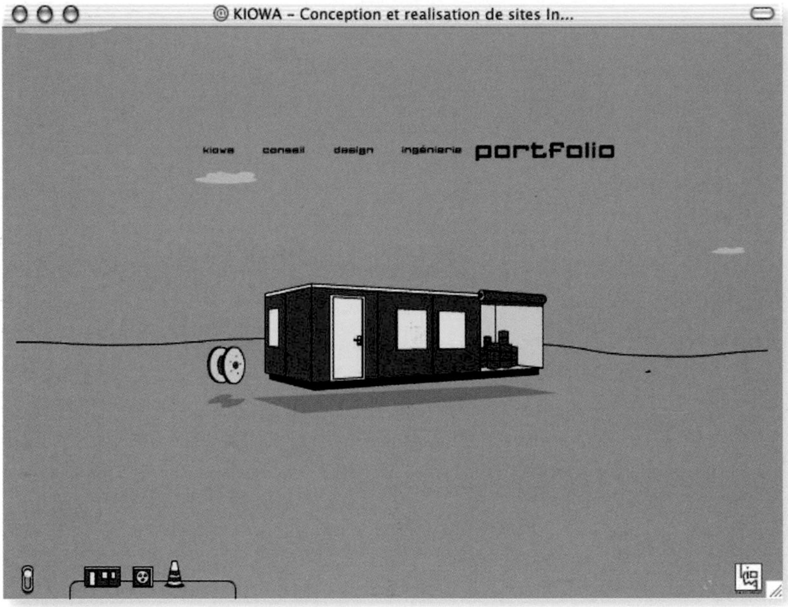

WWW.KIOWA.FR
D: LAURENCE BARREY, **C:** CHRISTOPHE PERRIN
A: KIOWA, **M:** ANNE@KIOWA.FR

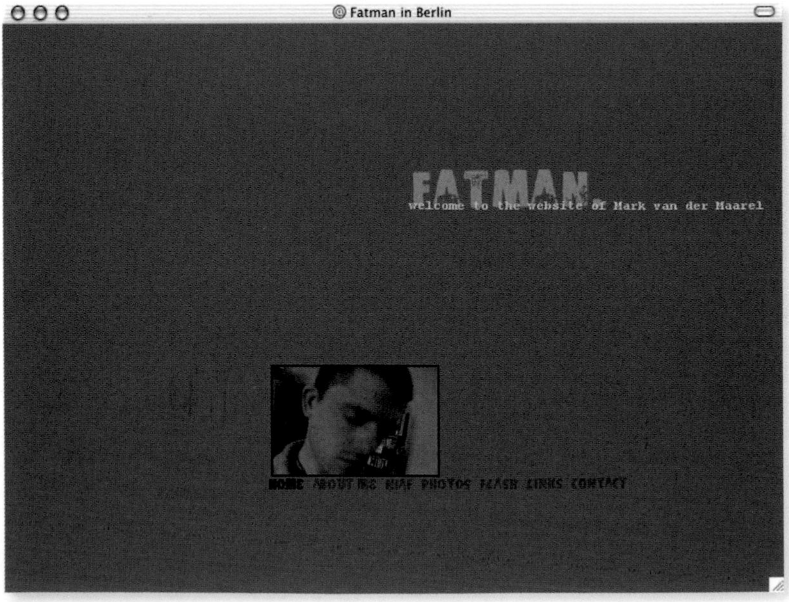

WWW.FATMANINBERLIN.DE
D: MARK VAN DER MAAREL
M: M_V_D_M@YAHOO.COM

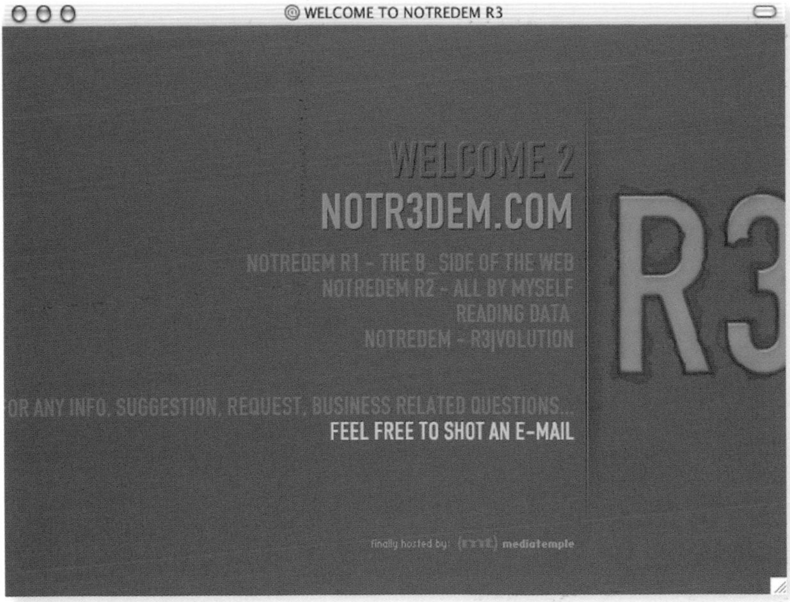
WELCOME TO NOTREDEM R3
WELCOME 2
NOTR3DEM.COM
NOTREDEM R1 - THE B_SIDE OF THE WEB
NOTREDEM R2 - ALL BY MYSELF
READING DATA
NOTREDEM - R3|VOLUTION
R3
OR ANY INFO, SUGGESTION, REQUEST, BUSINESS RELATED QUESTIONS...
FEEL FREE TO SHOT AN E-MAIL
finally hosted by: mediatemple

WWW.NOTREDEM.COM
D: DEMZ
A: NOTREDEM, **M:** DEM@NOTREDEM.COM

OSK DISSENY GRAFIC
OSK
dissenygràfic
© Óscar Latre i Andreu | 680 34 46 91 | olatre@menta.net

WWW.TELEFONICA.NET/WEB/OSK
D: OSCAR LATRE ANDREU
M: OLATRE@MENTA.NET

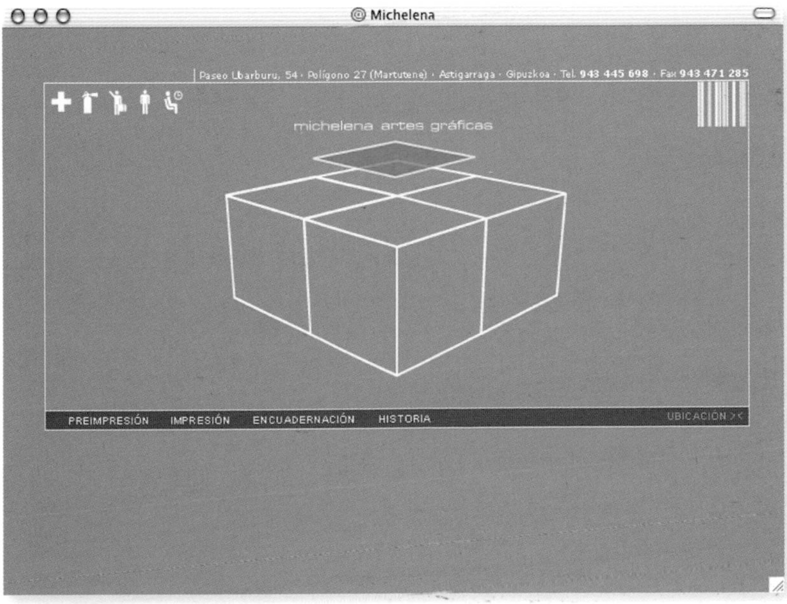
Michelena
Paseo Ubarburu, 54 · Polígono 27 (Martutene) · Astigarraga · Gipuzkoa · Tel. 943 445 698 · Fax 943 471 285
michelena artes gráficas
PREIMPRESIÓN
IMPRESIÓN
ENCUADERNACIÓN
HISTORIA
UBICACIÓN

WWW.MICHAG.ES
D: IKER MICHELENA BARRIO
A: ENTREWEBS, **M:** IMITXELENA@ENTREWEBS.COM

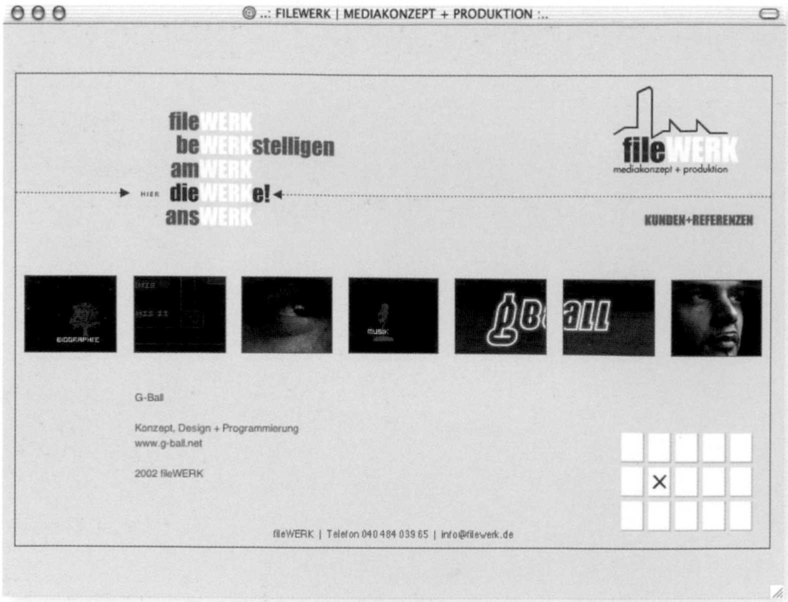

WWW.FILEWERK.DE
D: KAI WEISSER
A: FILEWERK, **M:** KAI.WEISSER@FILEWERK.DE

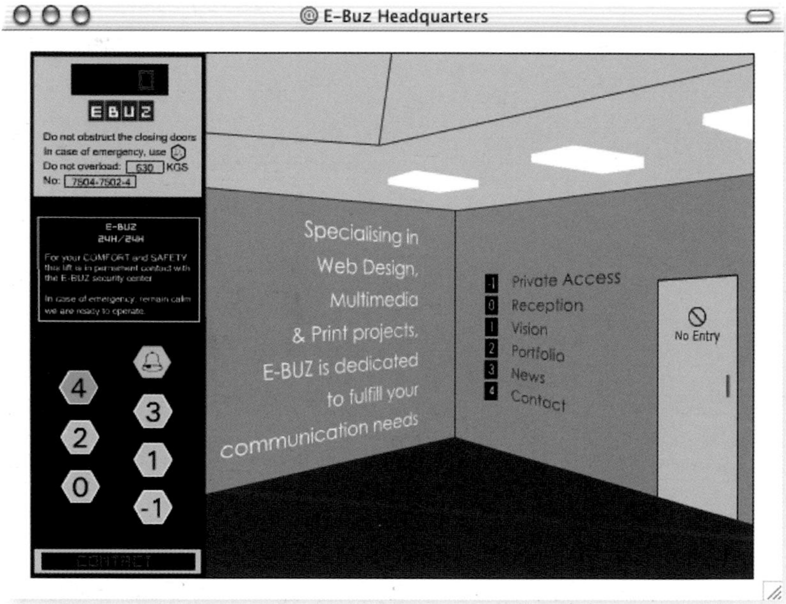

WWW.E-BUZ.COM
D: MICHAEL MONTMORIL
M: MICHAEL@E-BUZ.COM

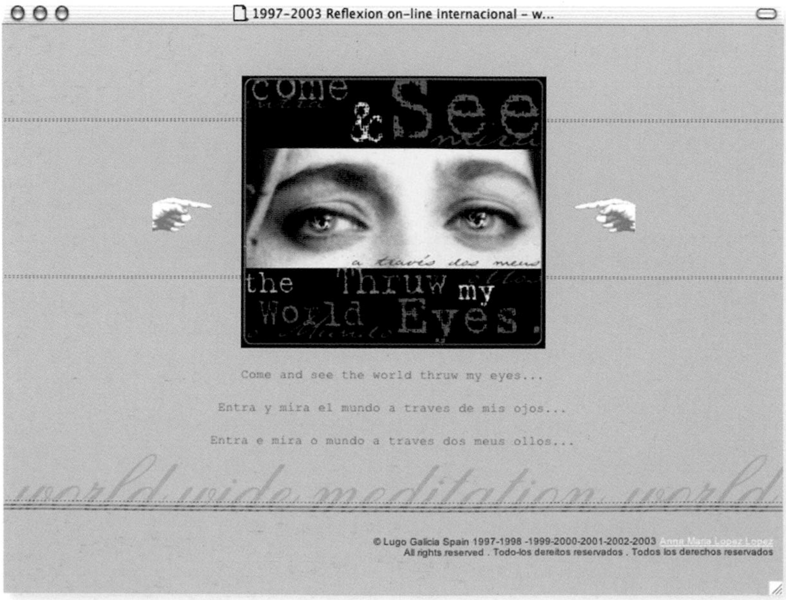

WWW.REFLEXION.ORG
D: ANNA MARIA LOPEZ LOPEZ
A: ANNA-OM-LINE DISEÑO MULTIMEDIATICO, **M:** ANNA@FASHIONMAS.COM

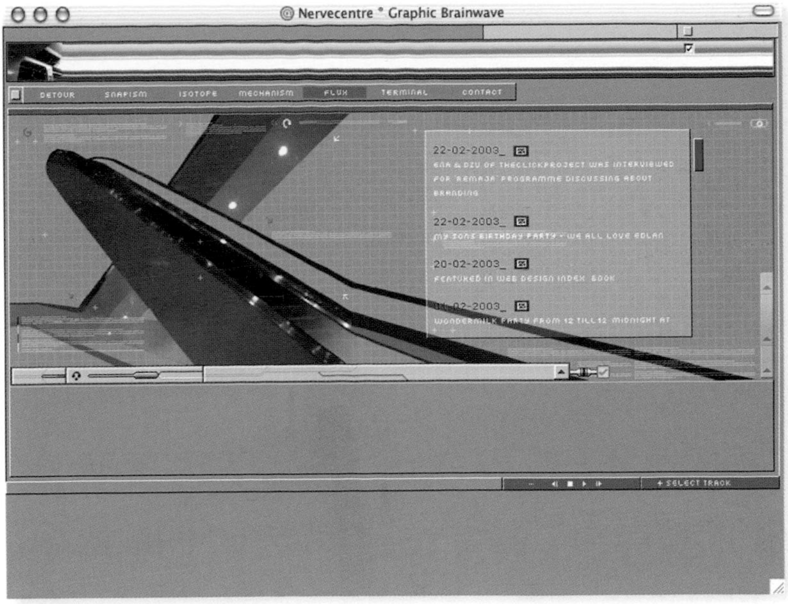

WWW.SYAM.LY
D: RUSHDI AHMAD SYAMLY
A: NERVECENTRE GRAPHIC BRAINWAVE, **M:** SYAMLY@SYAM.LY

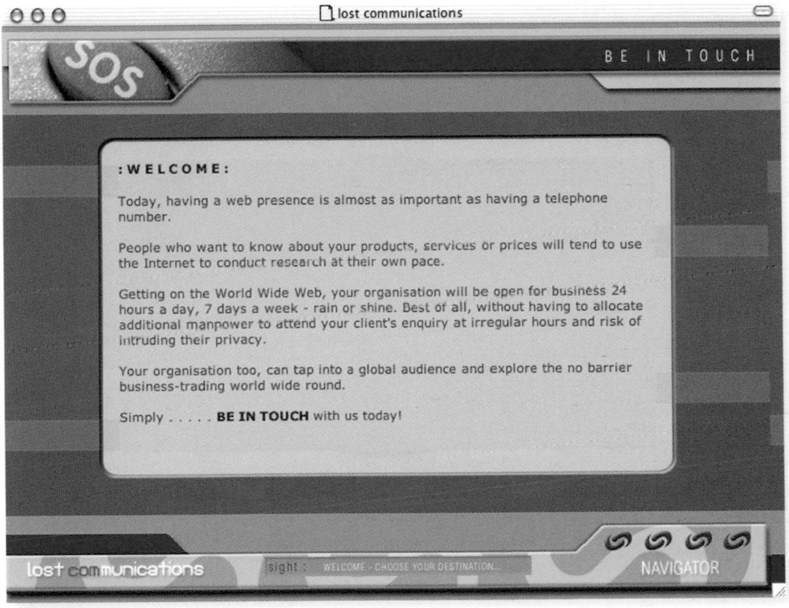

WWW.LOST-COM.COM
D: ORBITANT

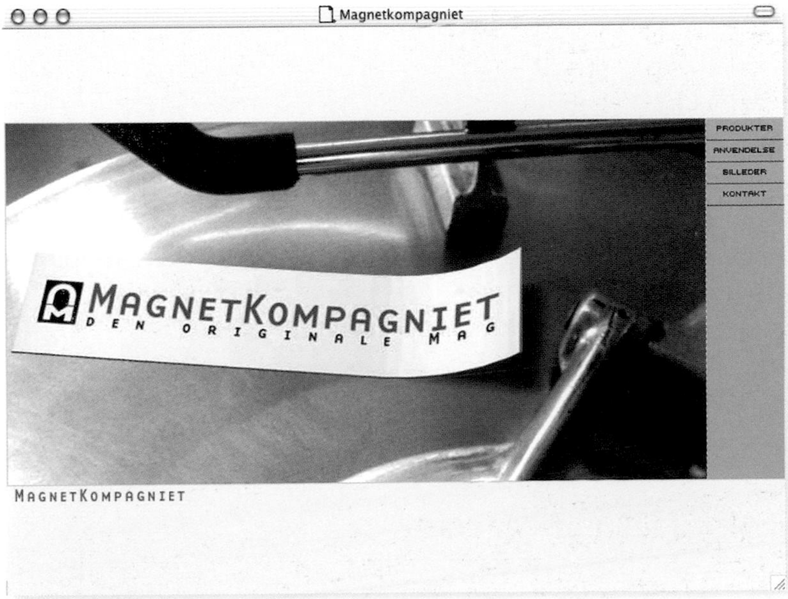

WWW.MAGNETKOMPAGNIET.DK
D: ANDERS OJGAARD
A: ANDERS OJGAARD KOMMUNIKATION, **M:** ANDERS@OJGAARD.DK

WWW.ANDRE-SOBOTT.DE
D: ANDRÉ SOBOTT
M: MAIL@ANDRE-SOBOTT.DE

WWW.MATTIA77.COM/MATV3.HTM
D: MATTIA DELL'ERA
A: MATTIA DELL'ERA, **M:** MATTIA8@EMAIL.IT

WWW.SURF108.COM
D: ENZO DE ROSA, **C:** CHRIS, **P:** ENZO & CHRIS
A: SURF, **M:** INFO@SURFTHENET.IT

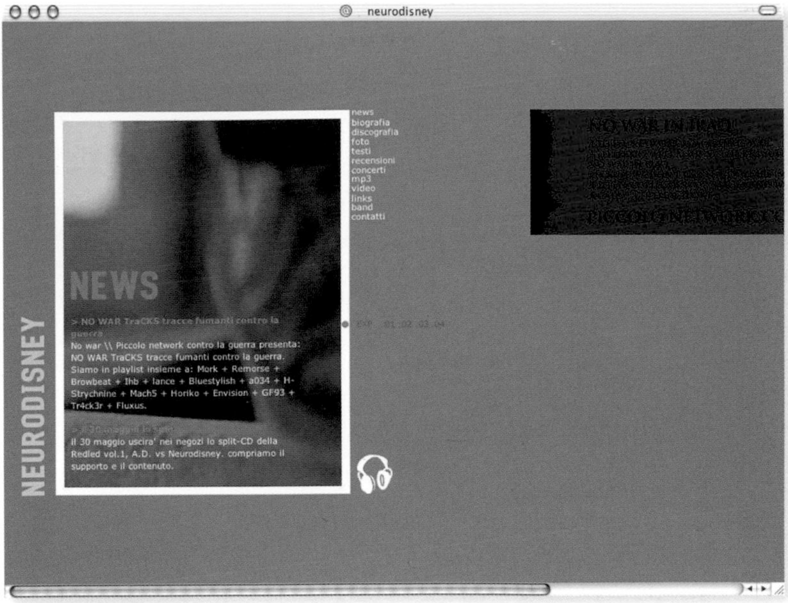

WWW.NEURODISNEY.COM
D: FRANCESCO DI GRAVINA
M: FRANCESCO.DIGRAVINA@LEFTLOFT.COM

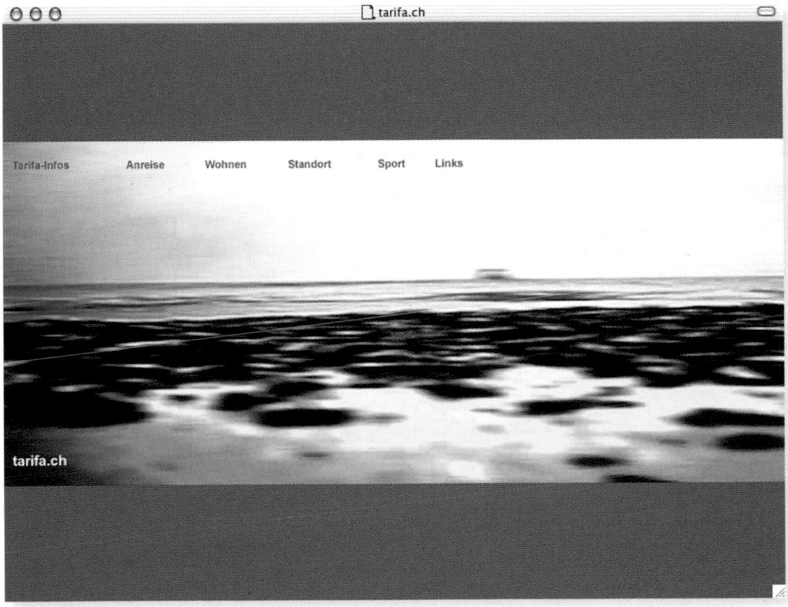

WWW.TARIFA.CH
D: DAVID TRMAL
A: STRANDGUT.CH, **M:** INFO@STRANDGUT.CH

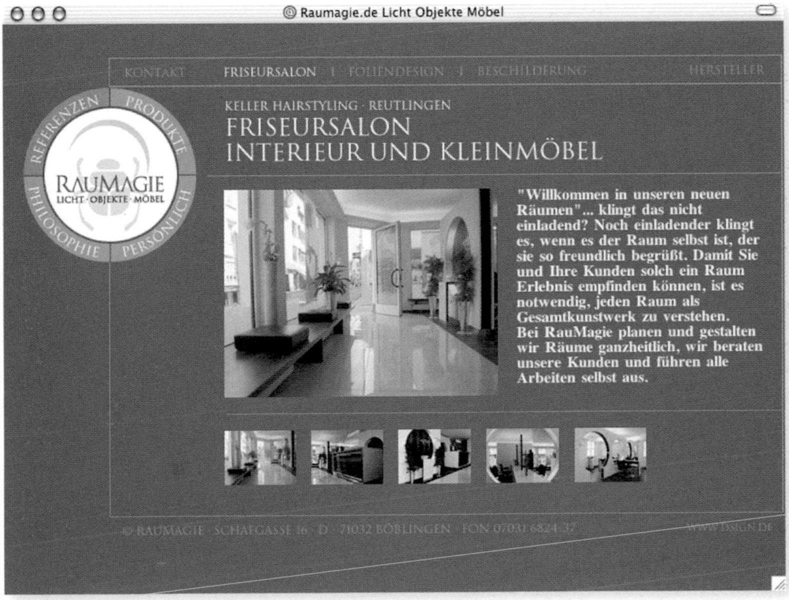

WWW.RAUMAGIE.DE
D: STEFAN BEHRINGER, **C:** JUERGEN WUNDERLE
A: D:\SIGN CREATIVECONCEPTS, **M:** BEHRINGER@DSIGN.DE

WWW.SILICIUM.NL
D: NIELS POLAK
A: SILICIUM INTERACTIEF, **M:** NIELS@SILICIUM.NL

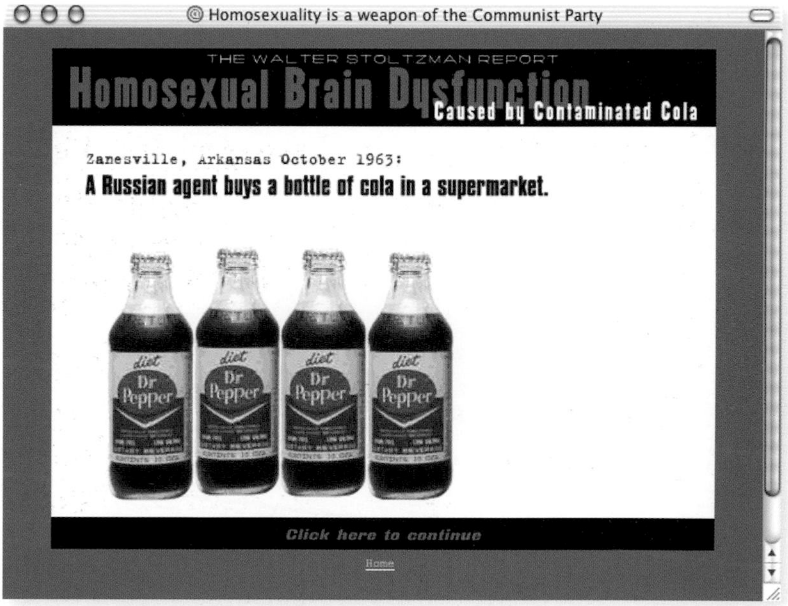

WWW.GEOCITIES.COM/UFOCONSPIRACYWATCH/NEWFILES/INDEX2.HTML
D: CHRISTIAN LEMBOURN
A: CHRISTIAN LEMBOURN, **M:** CHRISTIAN@LEMBOURN.DK

WWW.CDWART.COM
D: CHRISTIAN CALDWELL
A: CDW/ART>PUBLICENTRO, **M:** INFO@CDWART.COM

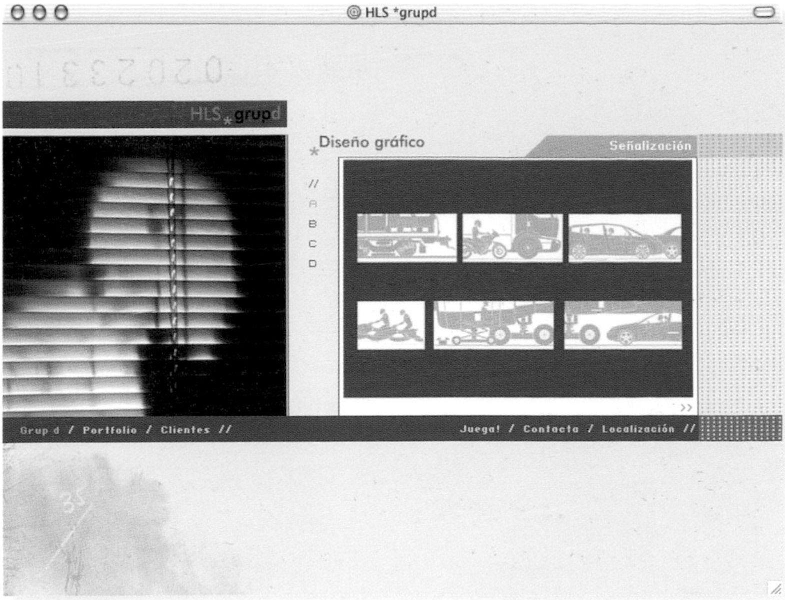

WWW.GRUPD.COM
D: ROGER CORTÈS RIERA
A: GRUPD, **M:** RCORTES@GRUPD.COM

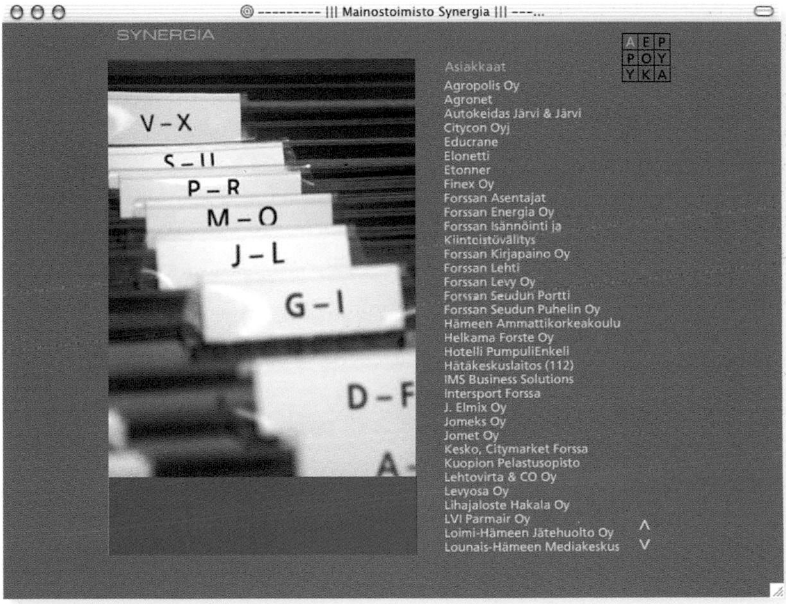

WWW.MAINOSSYNERGIA.COM/MAIN.HTML
D: SUSANNA KAHARINEN, **C:** SATU KIVIOJA, **P:** RAMI TIIHONEN
A: MAINOSTOIMISTO SYNERGIA, **M:** SATU.KIVIOJA@MAINOSSYNERGIA.COM

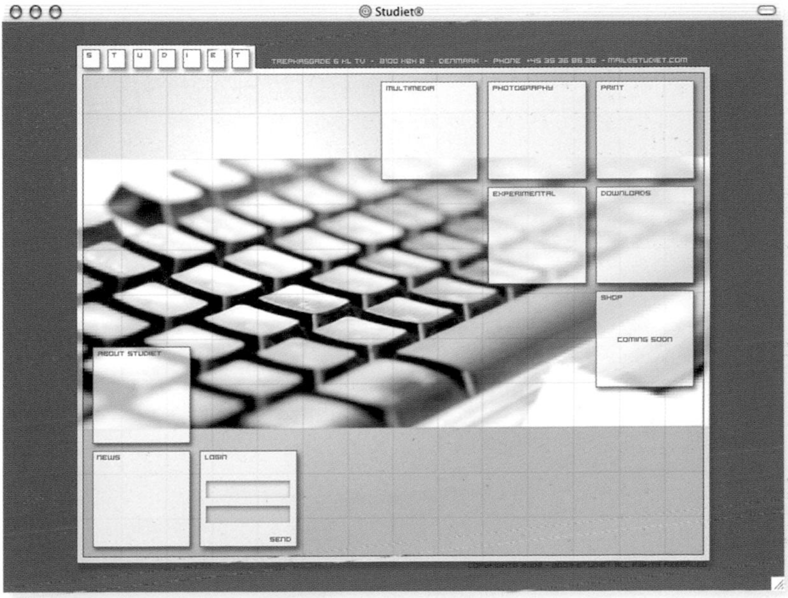

WWW.STUDIET.COM
D: STEVIE LAUX
A: STUDIET, **M:** STEVIE@STUDIET.COM

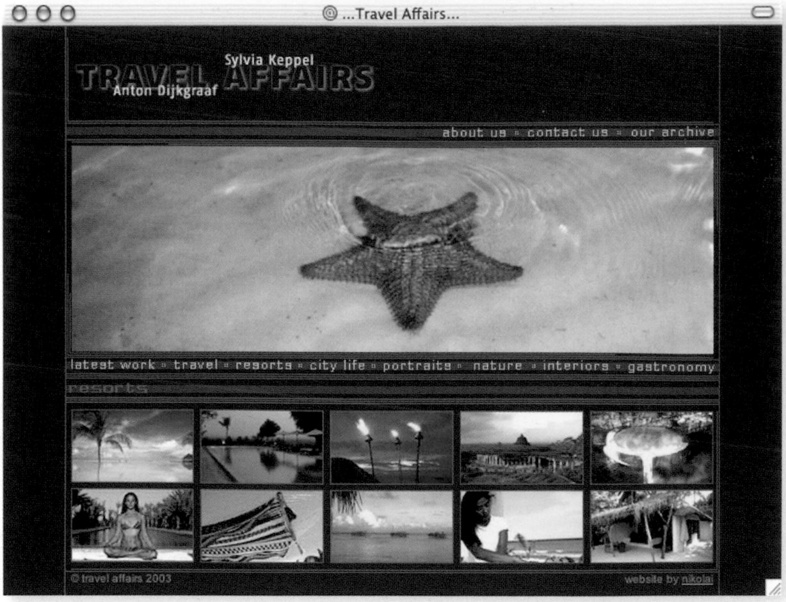

WWW.TRAVELAFFAIRS.NL
D: NIKOLAI ZAUBER
A: CYBERWORKS, **M:** NZAUBER@HOTMAIL.COM

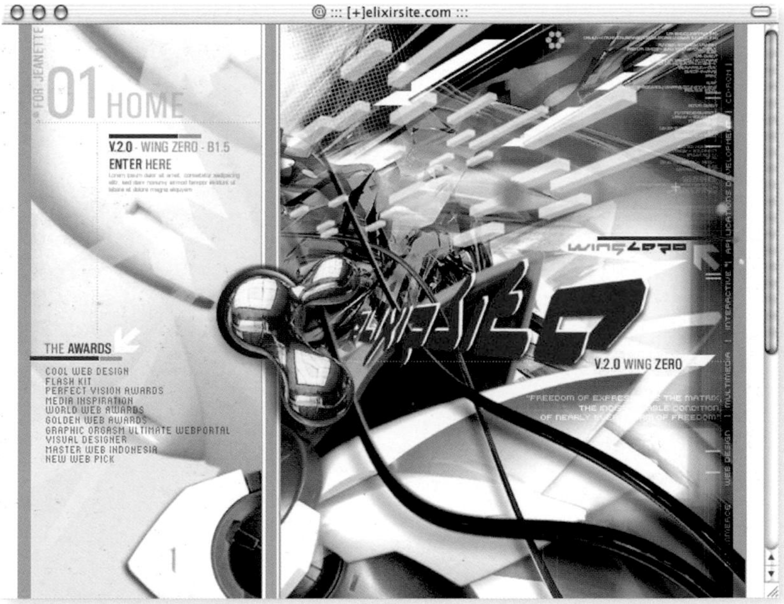

WWW.ELIXIRSITE.COM
D: CALVIN CUN-CUN KIZANA
A: ELIXIRSITE, **M:** CALVIN@ELIXIRSITE.COM

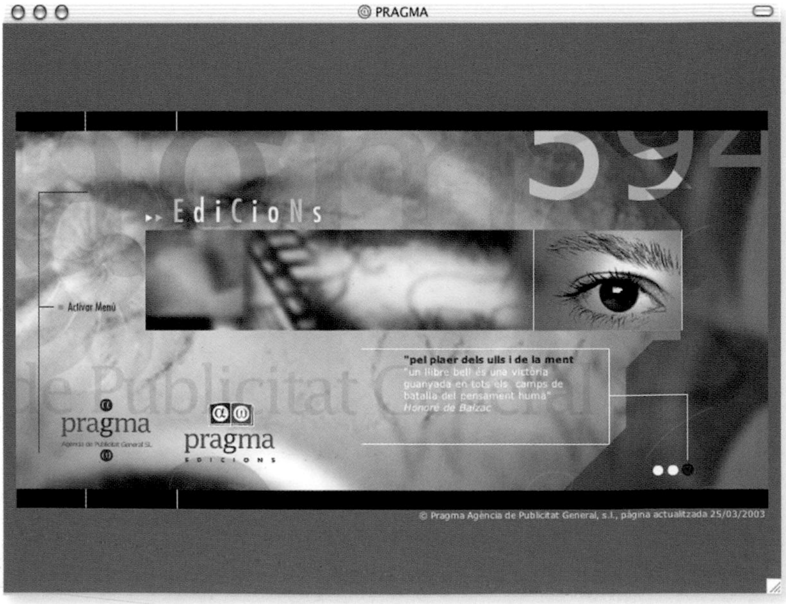

WWW.PRAGMAPUBLICITAT.COM
D: IVAN, SALVA, ASIER, **C:** IVAN, SALVA, ASIER, **P:** SALVA
A: PRAGMA AGENCIA DE PUBLICITAT GENERAL, **M:** PRAGMA@PRAGMAPUBLICITAT.COM

WWW.EYE.SOOLID.IT
D: ALBERTI ALBERTO, **C:** COTTAFAVI PIETRO, **P:** SOOLID DESIGN
A: SOOLID DESIGN, **M:** INFO@SOOLID.IT

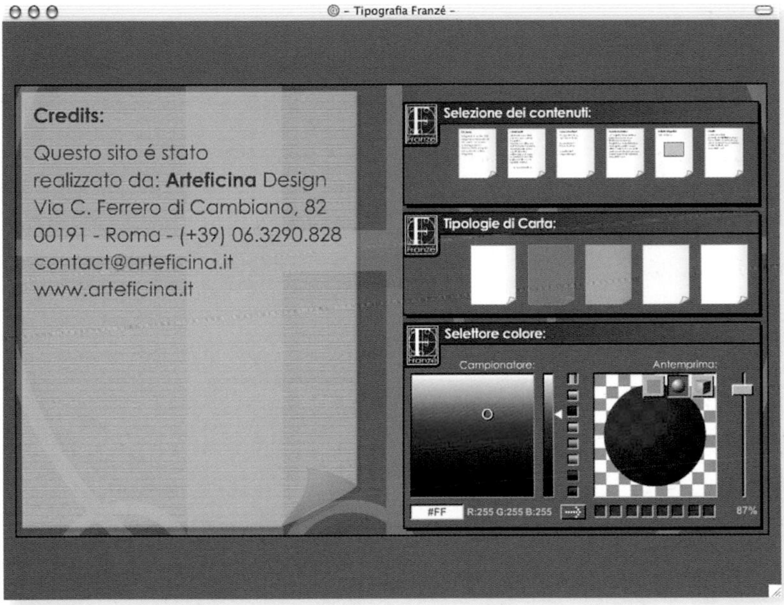

WWW.FRANZE.IT
D: JACOPO PIETRINFERNI
A: ARTEFICINA DESIGN, **M:** CONTACT@ARTEFICINA.IT

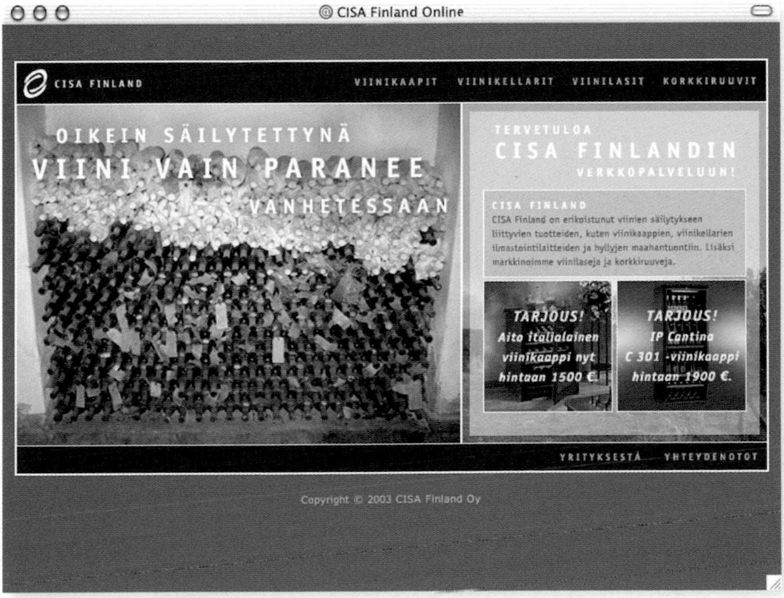

WWW.CISA.FI
D: GUSTAF FROM
M: GUSTAF.FROM@KOLUMBUS.FI

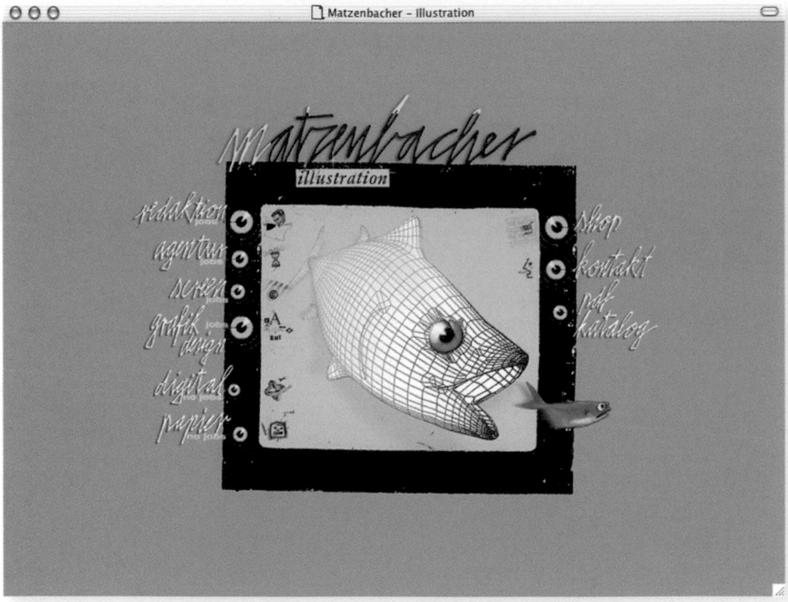

WWW.MATZENBACHER.DE
D: DANIEL MATZENBACHER, **C:** STEFFEN BARANIAK
A: MATZENBACHER ILLUSTRATION, **M:** CUT@MATZENBACHER.COM

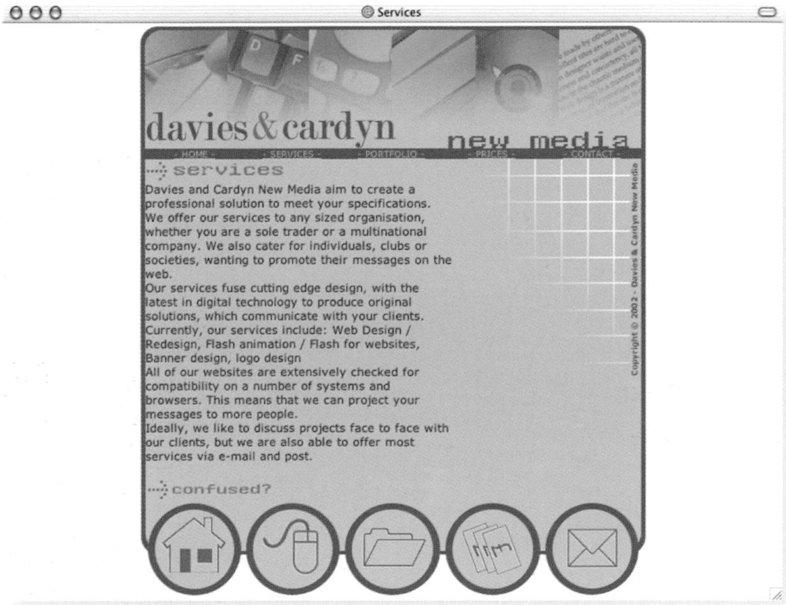

WWW.DAVIESANDCARDYN.COM/INDEX2.HTM
D: JOHN DAVIES / NICK CARDYN
A: DAVIES AND CARDYN NEW MEDIA, **M:** JOHN@DAVIESANDCARDYN.COM

WWW.MOEBEL.BUECOM.DE
D: ANDREAS KYRLOGLOU, **P:** IDEA TERRA
A: IDEA TERRA, **M:** ANDI@IDEA-TERRA.COM

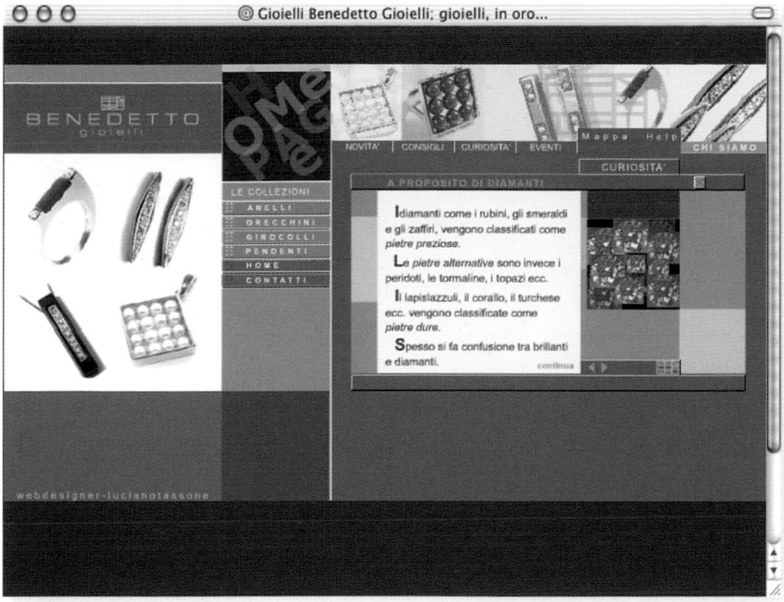

WWW.BENEDETTOGIOIELLI.IT
D: LUCIANO TASSONE
M: TAXON@KATAMAIL.COM

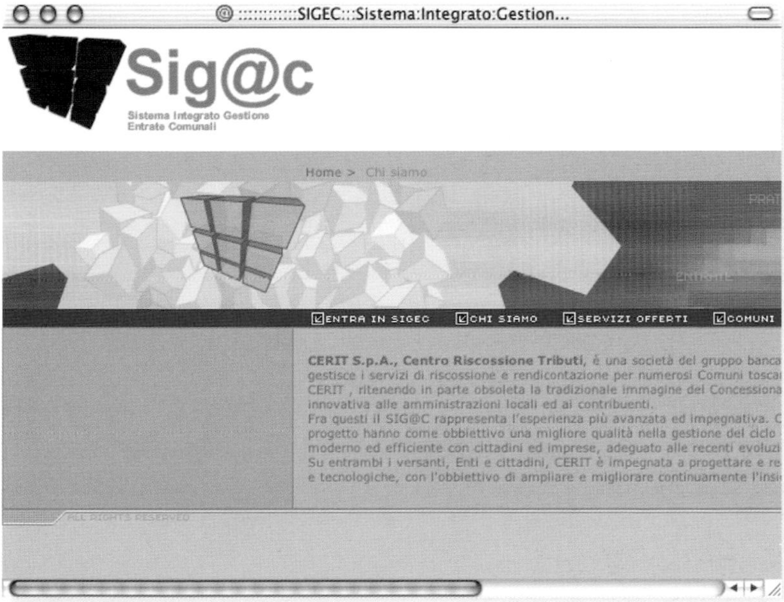

WWW.CERITRIB.IT/SIGEC/INDEX.HTML
D: LUCIANO LIMOLI
A: ANDERSEN, **M:** LULIMOLI@BRAXTON.COM

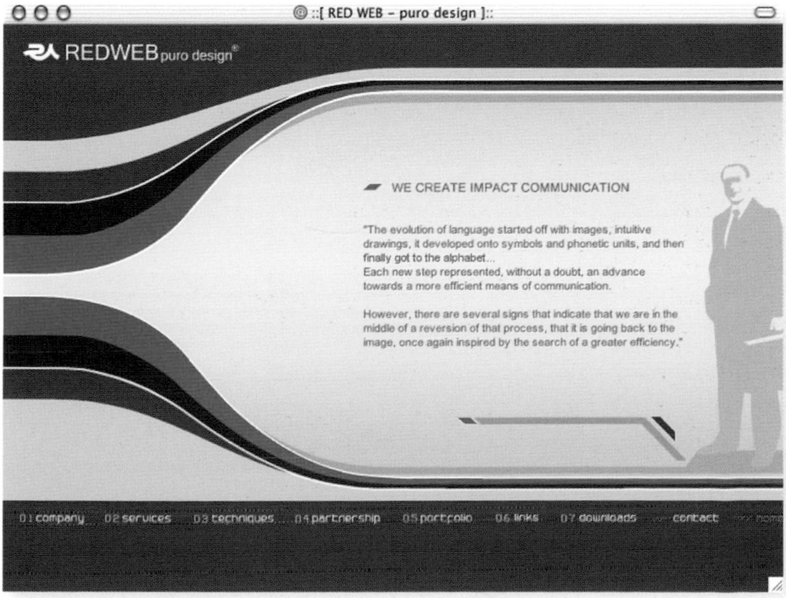

WWW.REDWEB.PT
D: LEONARDO GUICHON, PEDRO NUNES, **C:** DINIS QUELHAS
A: REDWEB, **M:** DINIS.QUELHAS@REDWEB.PT

WWW.Q-BOARDING.DE.VU
D: STEFAN STOLTMANN, SEBASTIAN BECKER, **C:** STOLTMANN, BECKER, **P:** BECKER
A: TST - STUDIOS, **M:** BECKERSEBASTIAN@WEB.DE

WWW.NODOMODA.ES
D: BORILLO & CÉSPEDES, **C:** SALVADOR K.TA, **P:** FASHCAT S.L
A: FASHCAT S.L, **M:** MARTIN@FASHCAT.COM

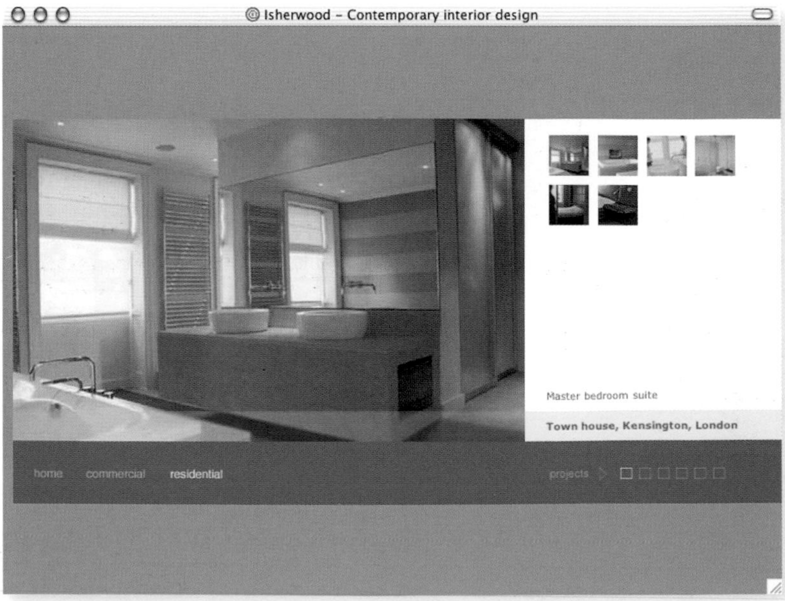

WWW.ISHERWOODINTERIORDESIGN.COM
D: SCOTT GRAHAM, **C:** NATALIE O'DONOVAN, **P:** SCOTT GRAHAM
A: CYAN CREATIVE, **M:** EMAIL@CYANCREATIVE.COM

WWW.ORSINOMOTORS.IT
D: LOGICAL NET
A: LOGICAL NET, **M:** INFO@LOGICAL.IT

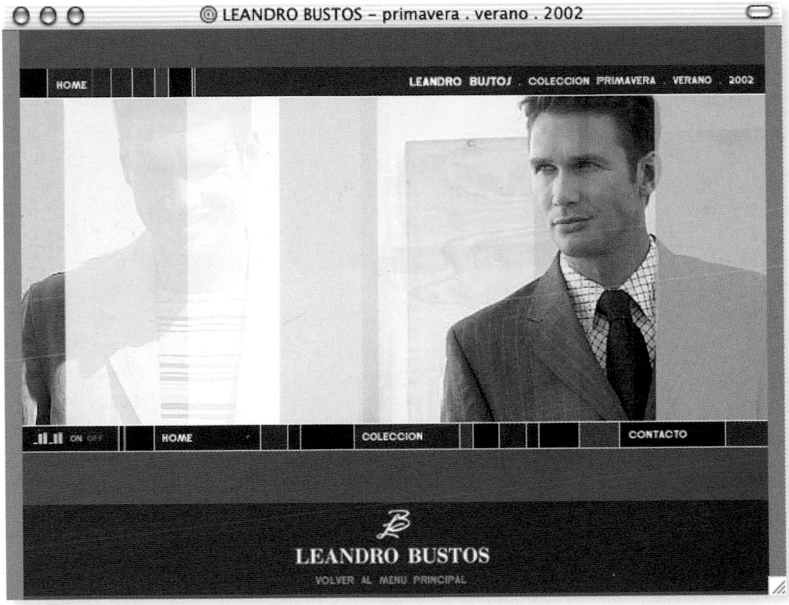

WWW.LEANDROBUSTOS.COM
D: BORILLO & CÉSPEDES, **C:** SALVADOR K.TA, **P:** FASHCAT S.L
A: FASHCAT S.L, **M:** MARTIN@FASHCAT.COM

WWW.PLAYCREATIVIDAD.COM
D: DAVID GARCIA, **C:** IVAN CAÑO, TOMÁS GARCIA, **P:** EFRÉN GARCÍA
A: PLAY CREATIVIDAD, **M:** DAVID@PLAYCREATIVIDAD.COM

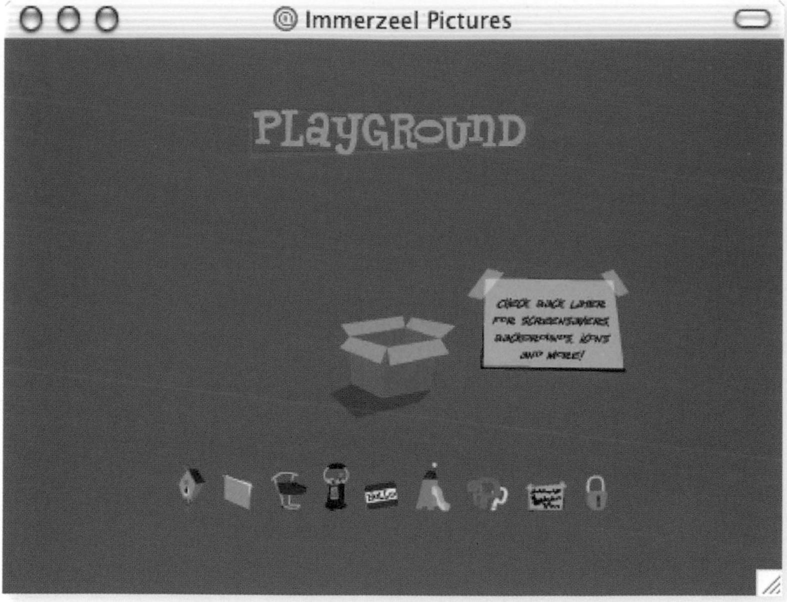

WWW.IMMERZEELPICTURES.COM
D: PASCAL IMMERZEEL
A: IMMERZEEL PICTURES, **M:** PASCAL@IMMERZEELPICTURES.COM

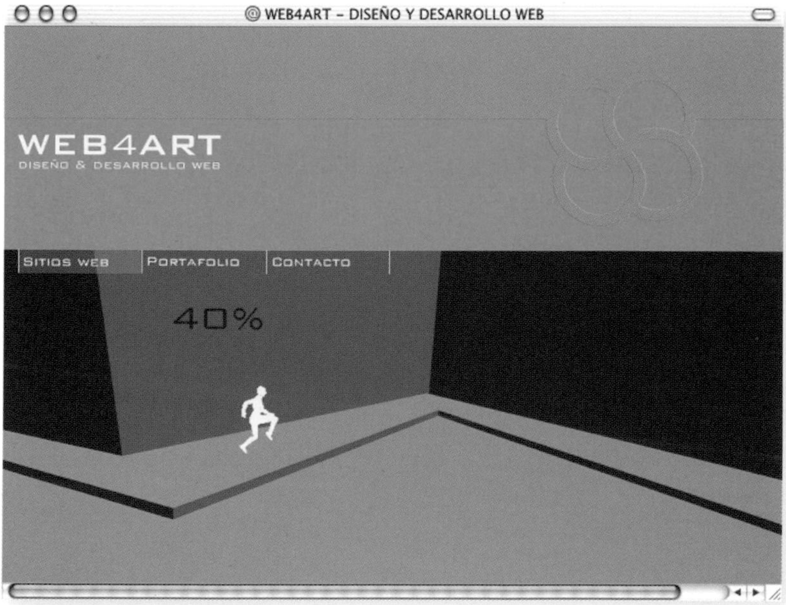

WWW.WEB4ART.CL
D: JUAN MORENO, **C:** JUAN MORENO, **P:** ISABEL GARCÍA
A: WEB4ART, **M:** JUANM@WEB4ART.CL

WWW.CEDARSEED.COM
D: JOUMANA MEDLEJ
M: MANA@CEDARSEED.COM

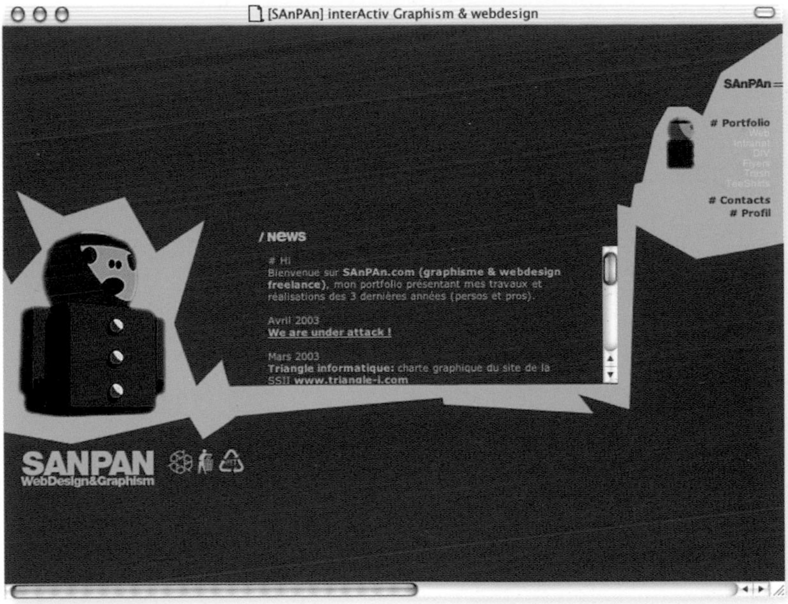

WWW.SANPAN.COM
D: SANPAN
A: SANPAN WDA, **M:** SANPAN@FREE.FR

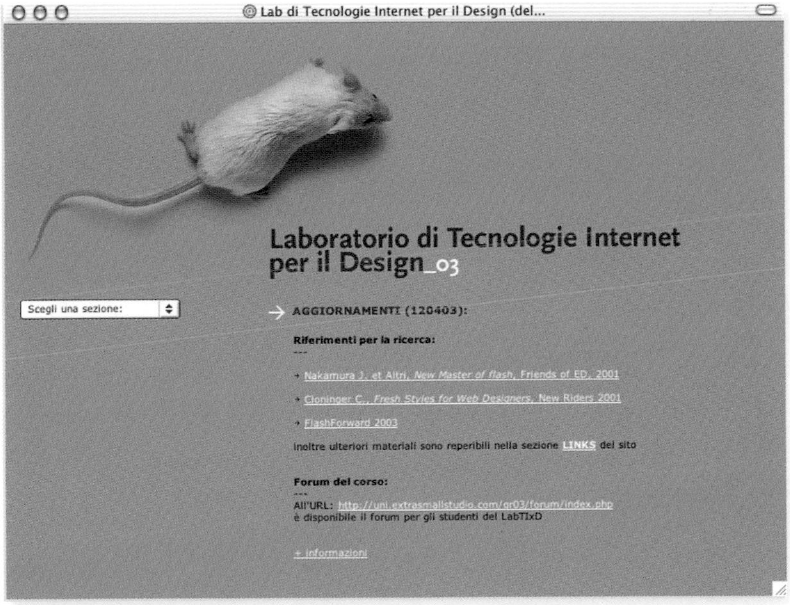

WWW.CS.UNIBO.IT/~BOLLINI/LABTIXD03/
D: LETIZIA BOLLINI
A: EXTRASMALL STUDIO, **M:** BOLLINI@EXTRASMALL.NET

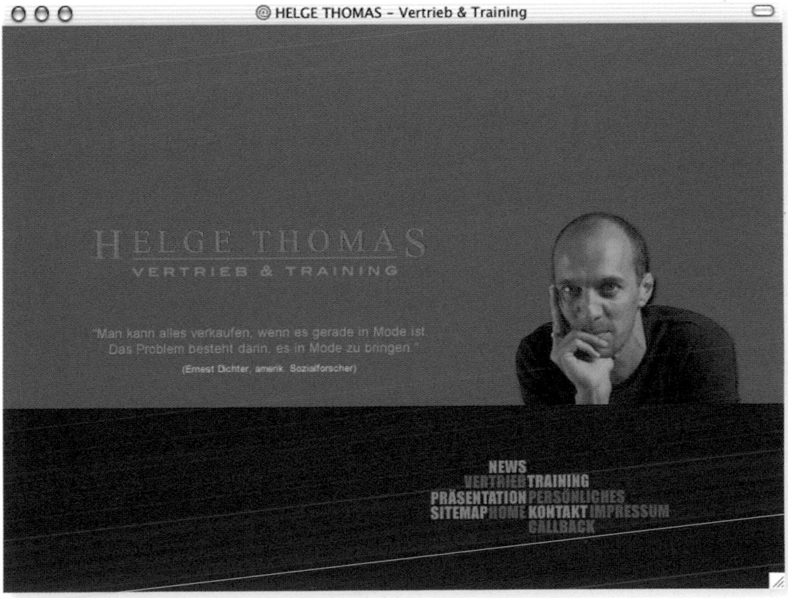

WWW.HELGE-THOMAS.DE
D: THOMAS HAAF
A: SMART-SIGN.COM, **M:** INFO@SMART-SIGN.COM

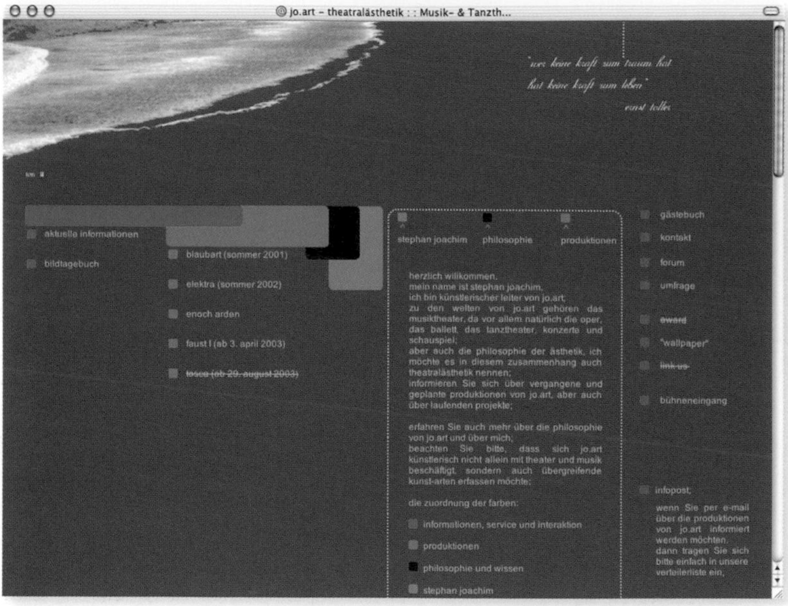

WWW.JO-ART.DE
D: STEPHAN JOACHIM
M: STEPHAN-JOACHIM@JO-ART.DE

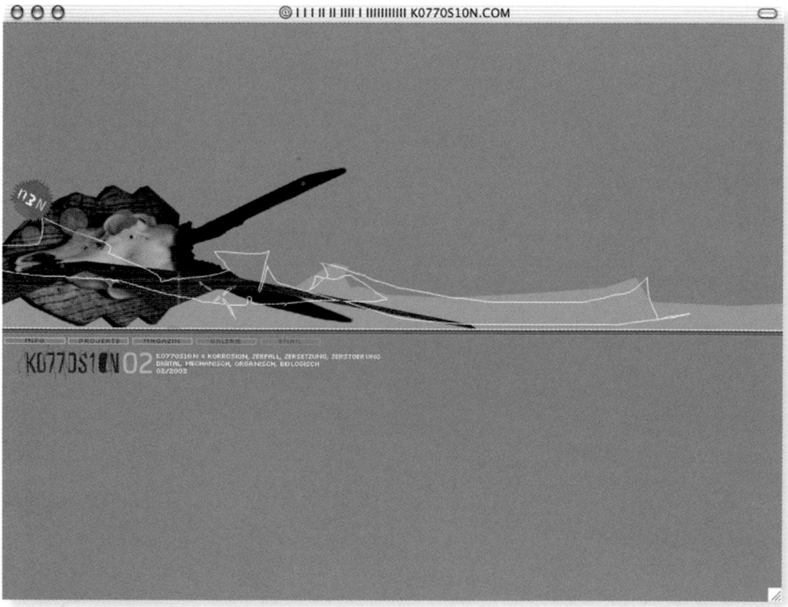

WWW.K0770S10N.COM
D: ALEXANDER BRAUN
M: INFO@ALEXBRAUN.DE

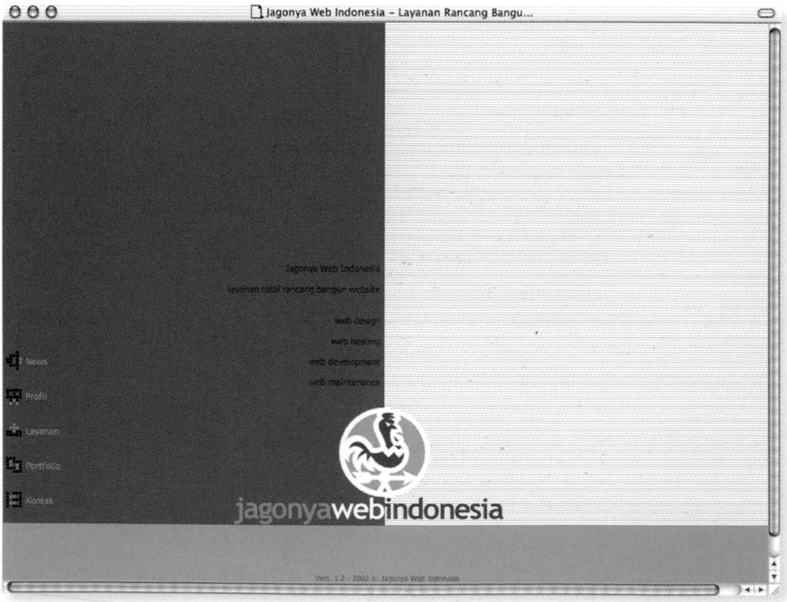

WWW.JAGONYA.WEB.ID
D: DIEN SYAIFUDIEN
A: JAGONYA WEB INDONESIA, **M:** DIEN@JAGONYA.WEB.ID

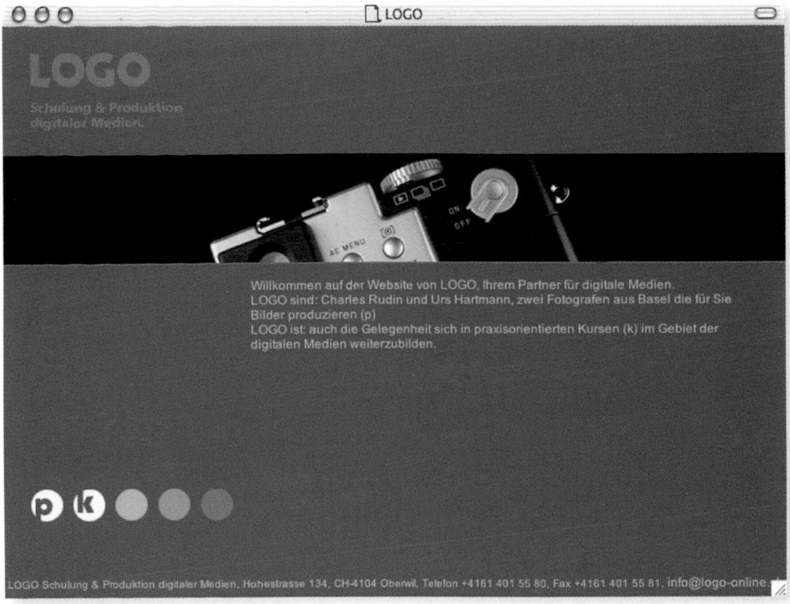

WWW.LOGO-ONLINE.CH
D: MICHEL SEELIGER
A: CHAMELEON GRAPHICS GMBH, **M:** INFO@CHAMELEONGRAPHICS.CH

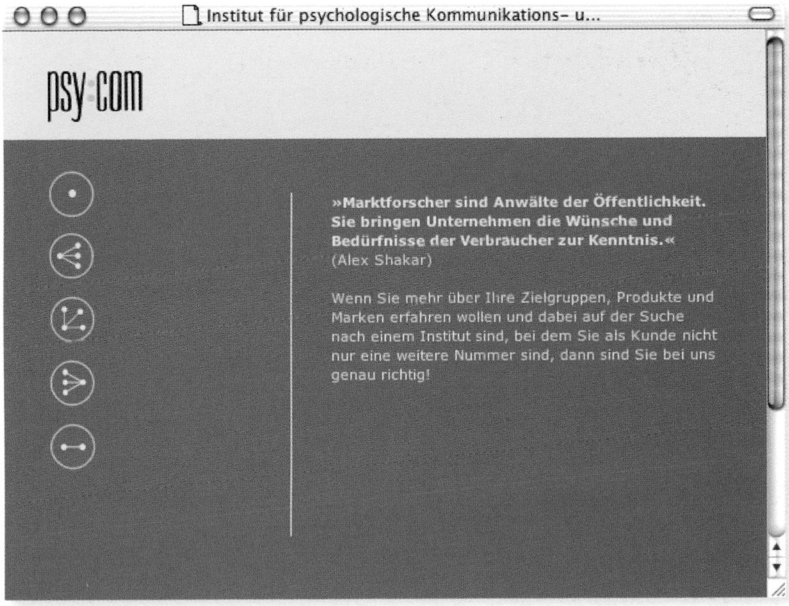

WWW.PSYCOM-ONLINE.DE
D: PETER REICHARD
A: TYPOSITION MEDIENDESIGN, **M:** INFO@TYPOSITIONFONTS.DE

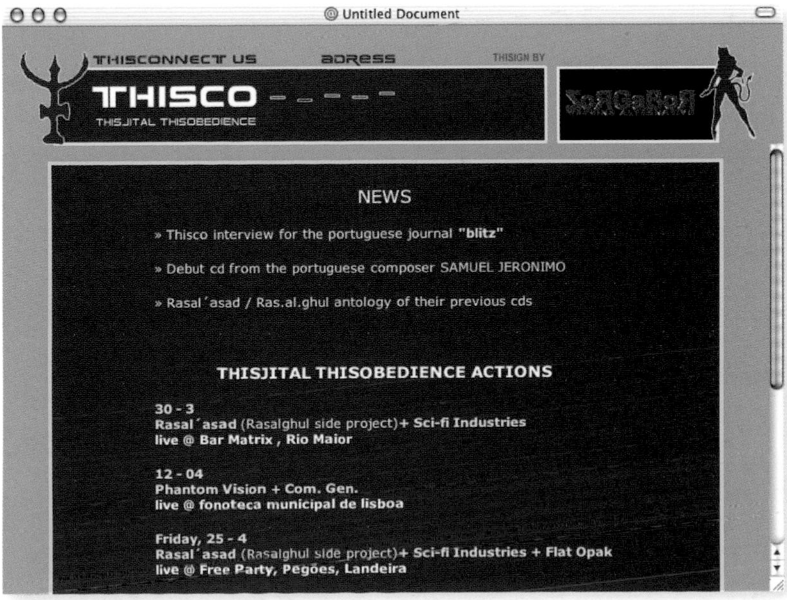

WWW.THISCO.NET
D: CARLOS PROENCA
M: CARLOSPROENCA@THISCO.NET

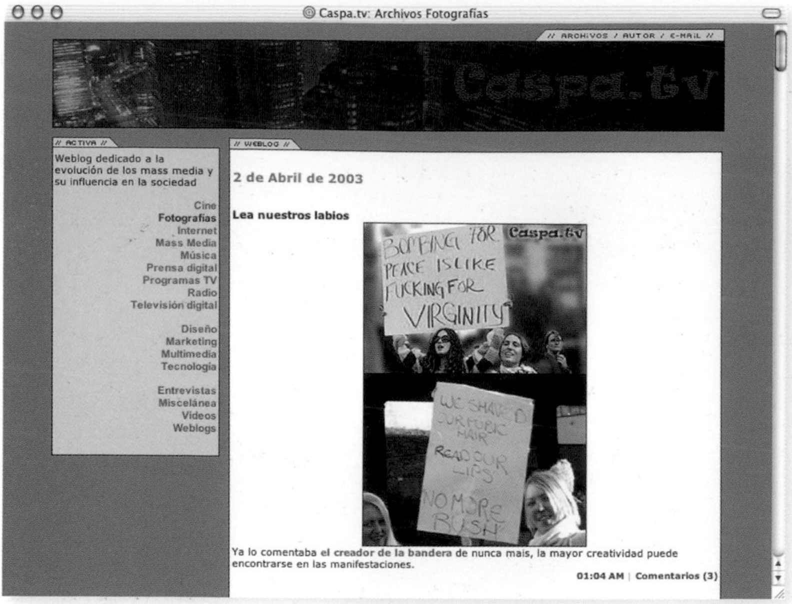

WWW.CASPA.TV
D: ANTONIO DELGADO BARRERA
M: DELETE@CASPA.TV

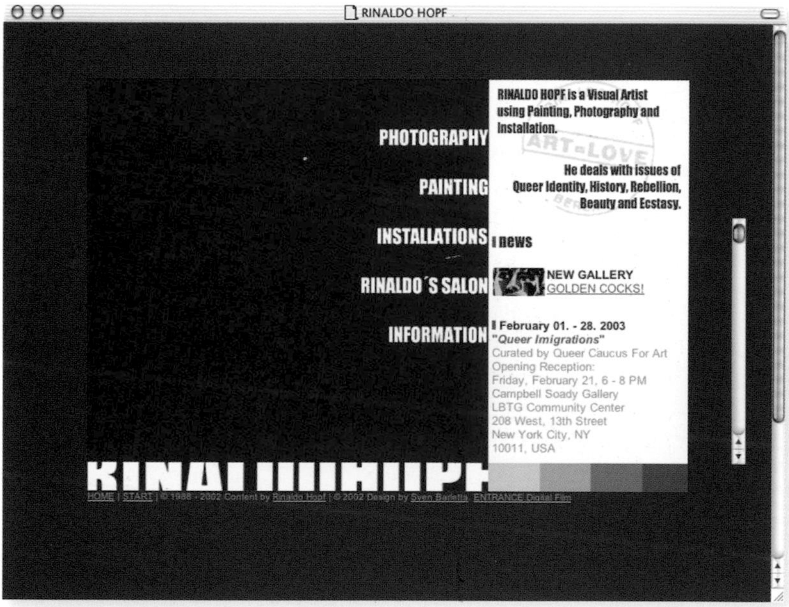

WWW.RINALDOHOPF.COM
D: SVEN BARLETTA
A: ENTRANCE DIGITAL FILM, **M:** BARLETTA@ENTRANCEDIGITALFILM.COM

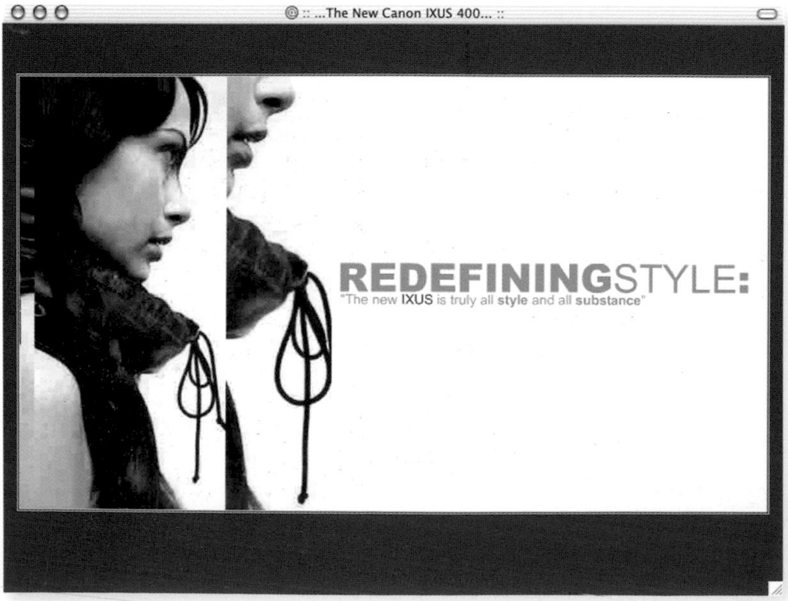

WWW.MYDIGITALCAM.COM
D: IVAN MP TAN, SARAH HO, **C:** KONG SUGIN
A: KONG SUGIN, **M:** IVAN@ACLAIM.COM.SG

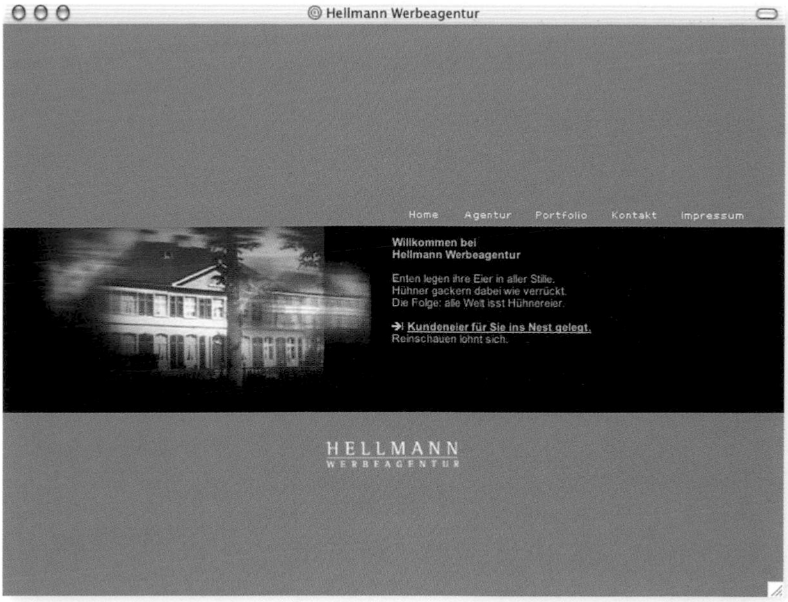

WWW.HELLMANN-GMBH.DE
D: CHRISTIAN STEIN
A: HELLMANN GMBH, **M:** C.STEIN@HELLMANN-GMBH.DE

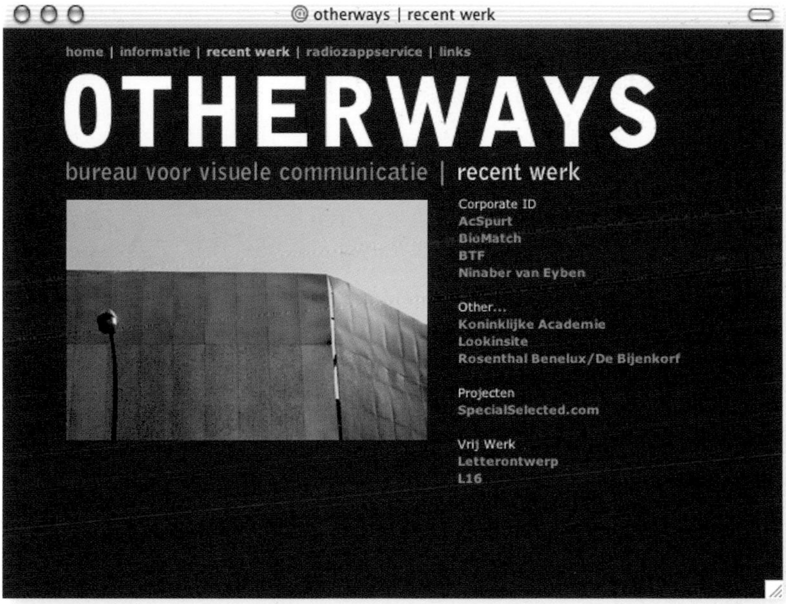

WWW.OTHERWAYS.NL
D: DONALD ROOS
A: OTHERWAYS, **M:** DONALD.ROOS@OTHERWAYS.NL

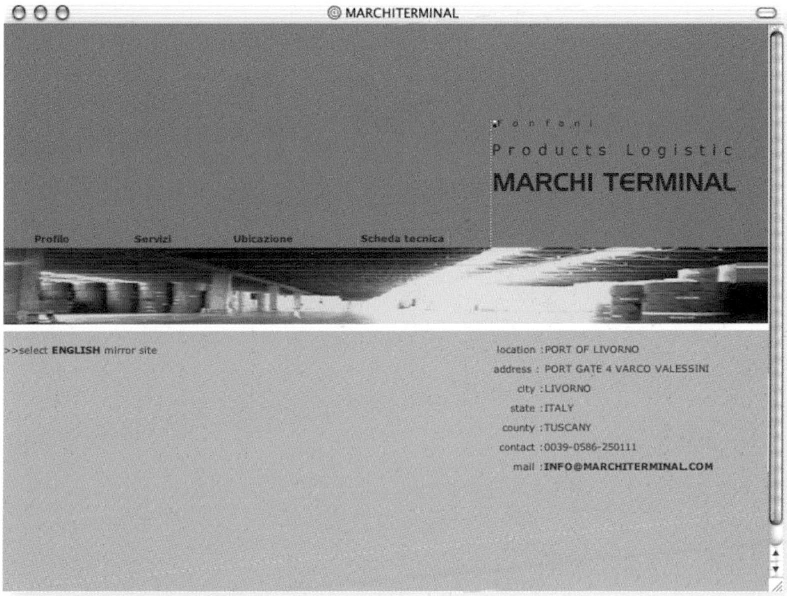

WWW.MARCHITERMINAL.COM
D: GABRIELE STAMPA
M: INFO@OFFICINEGENERALI.IT

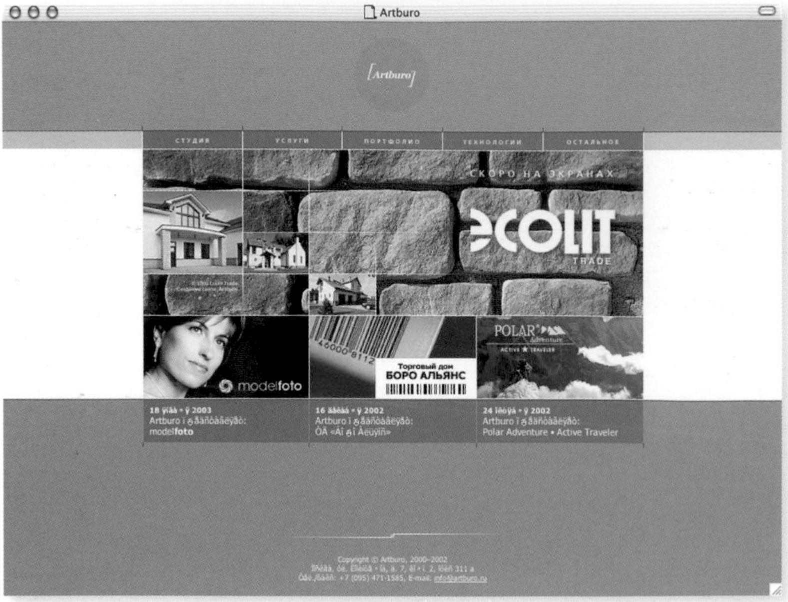

WWW.ARTBURO.RU
D: ALEXANDER METEL'KOV, **C:** IGOR VLASOV, **P:** MAXIM NAUMKIN
A: ARTBURO, **M:** INFO@ARTBURO.RU

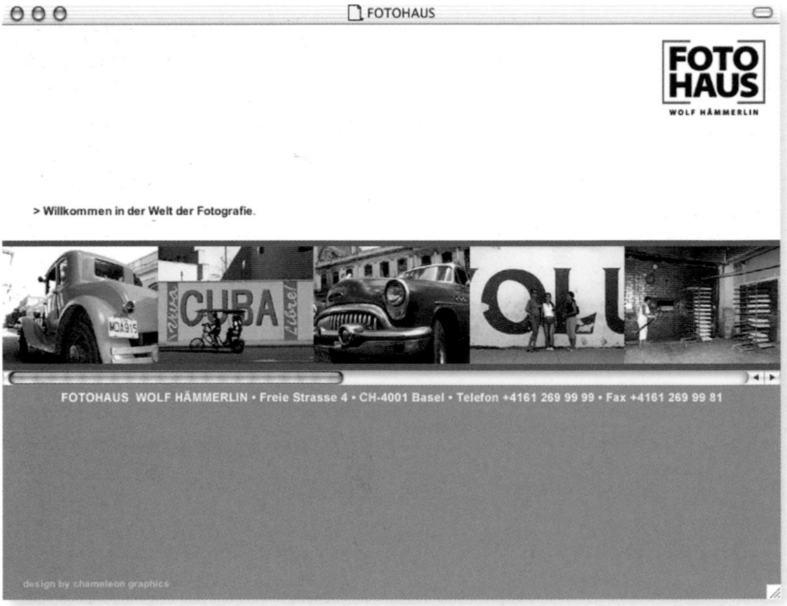

WWW.FOTOHAUS.CH
D: MICHEL SEELIGER
A: CHAMELEON GRAPHICS GMBH, **M:** INFO@CHAMELEONGRAPHICS.CH

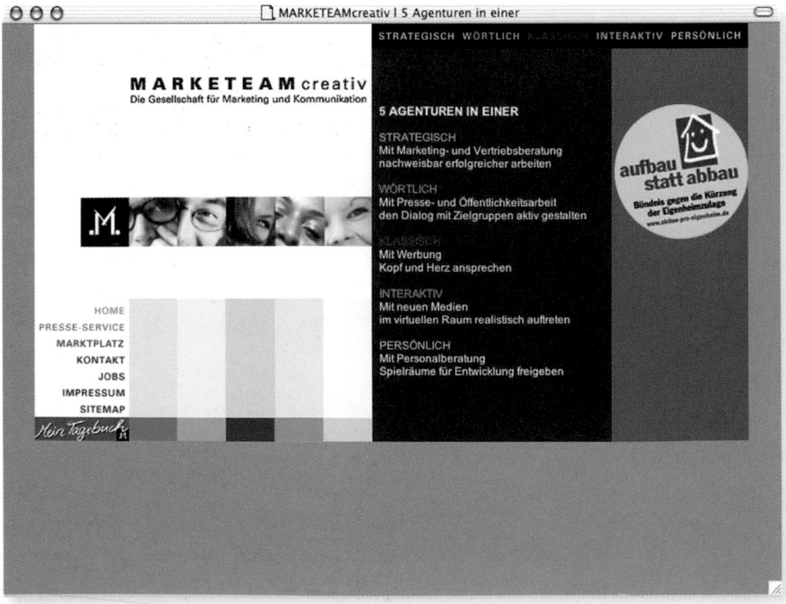

WWW.MARKETEAMCREATIV.DE
D: PETRA SCHNEIDER, **C:** PETRA SCHNEIDER, **P:** MARKETEAMCREATIV
A: MARKETEAMCREATIV, **M:** P-SCHNEIDER@MARKETEAMCREATIV.DE

WWW.NONEOFTHEM.IT
D: FRANCESCO DAL SANTO
A: SANTEX MEDIA, **M:** CESCO@NONEOFTHEM.IT

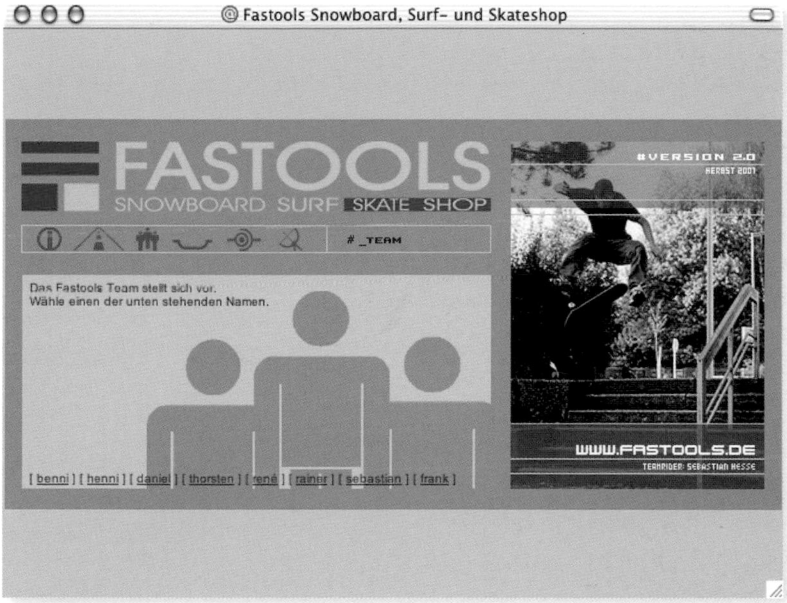

WWW.FASTOOLS.DE
D: CHRISTIAN STEIN
M: POST@C74.DE

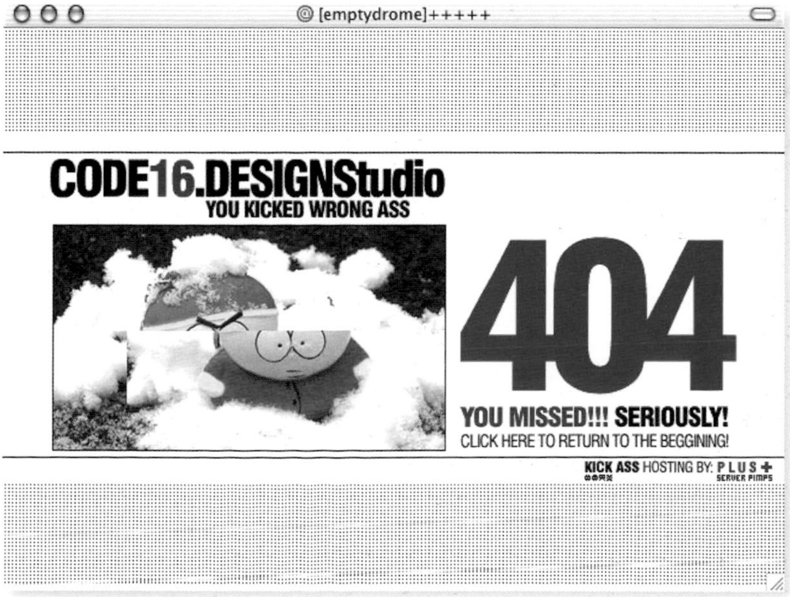

WWW.EMPTYDROME.COM
D: J.POU
A: EMPTYDROME, **M:** J.POU@EMPTYDROME.COM

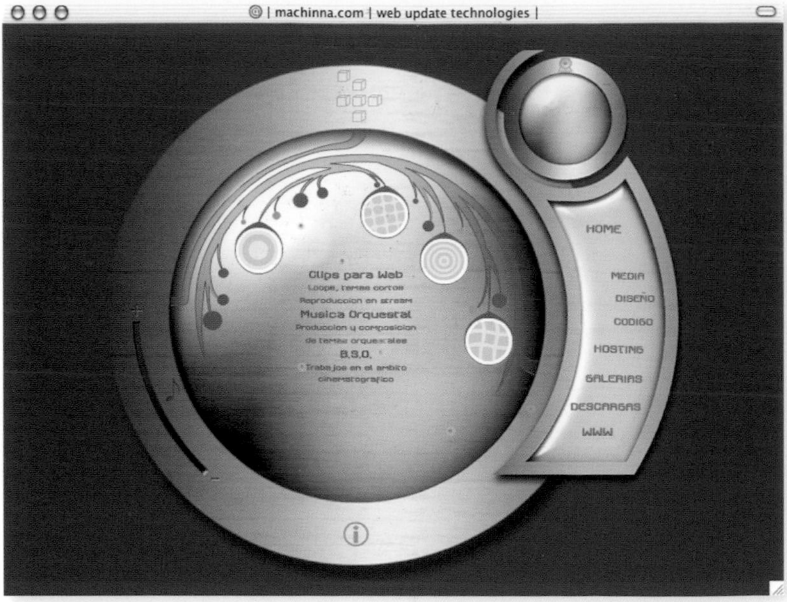

WWW.MACHINNA.COM
D: INGRID SUMSI MOLINA, **C:** LUCAS VAN DER KROON, **P:** DAVID MENDOZA
A: MACHINNA.COM, **M:** DESIGN@MACHINNA.COM

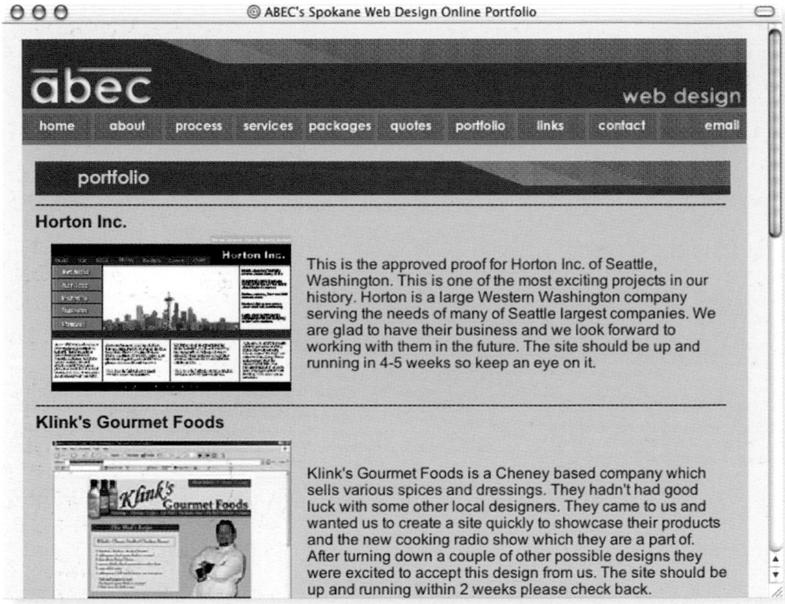

WWW.ABECTECH.COM
D: RYAN STEMKOSKI
A: ABEC WEB DESIGN GROUP, **M:** RYAN@ABECTECH.COM

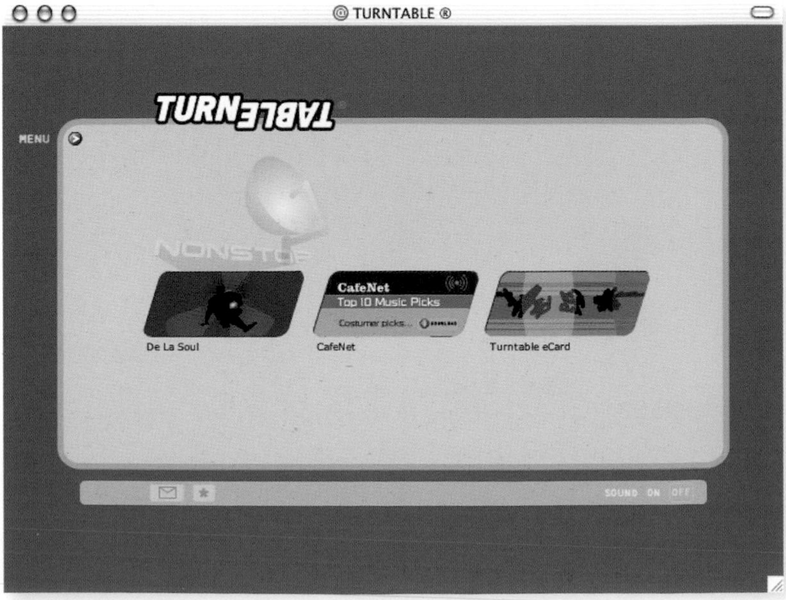

WWW.TURNTABLE.COM
D: PHILIP FIERLINGER
A: TURNTABLE, **M:** PHILIP@TURNTABLE.COM

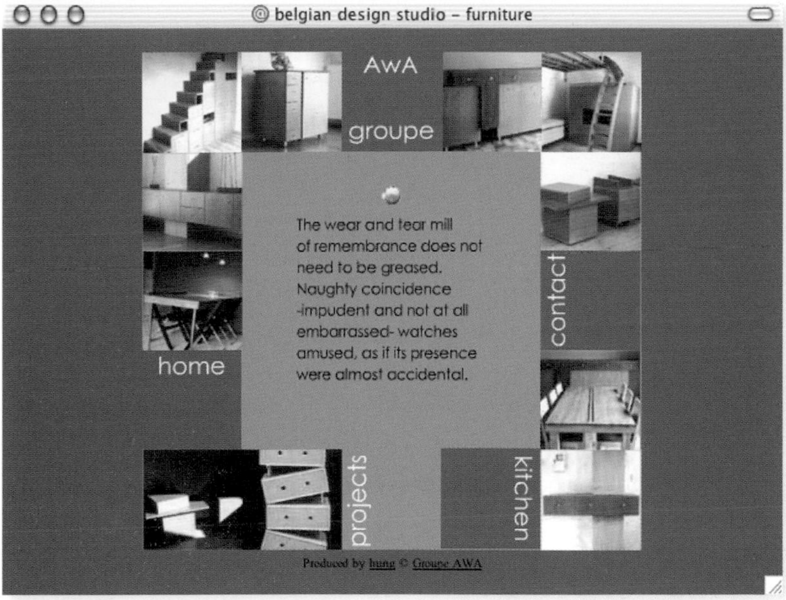

WWW.AWA.BE
D: HUNG TRAN VAN
A: HUNG, **M:** HUNG@HUNG.BE

WWW.EXTRASMALL.NET
D: LETIZIA BOLLINI
A: EXTRASMALL STUDIO, **M:** BOLLINI@EXTRASMALL.NET

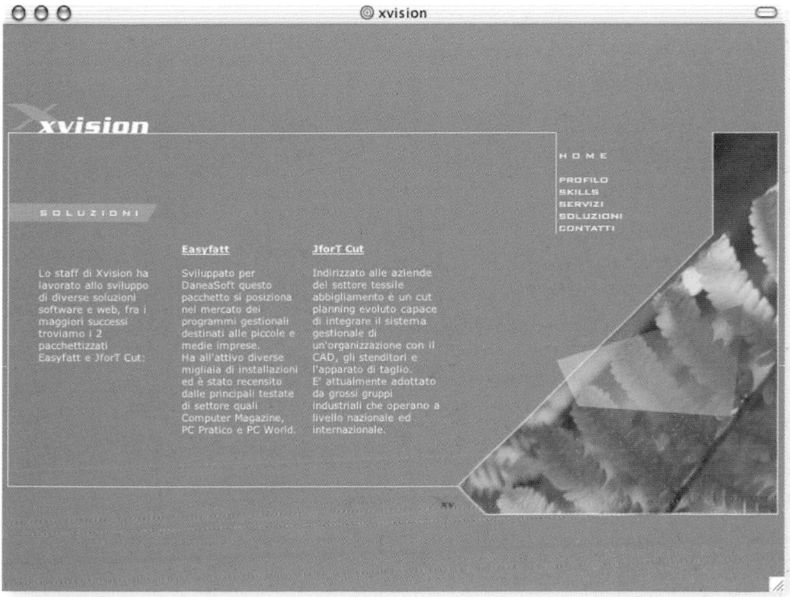

WWW.XVISION.IT
D: LAMBERTO SALVAN
M: INFO@XVISION.IT

WWW.NXSPACE.COM
D: JACK LEE, C: JACK LEE, **P:** DAVID BECKER
A: NXSPACE PTE LTD, **M:** TILLMANN@NXSPACE.COM

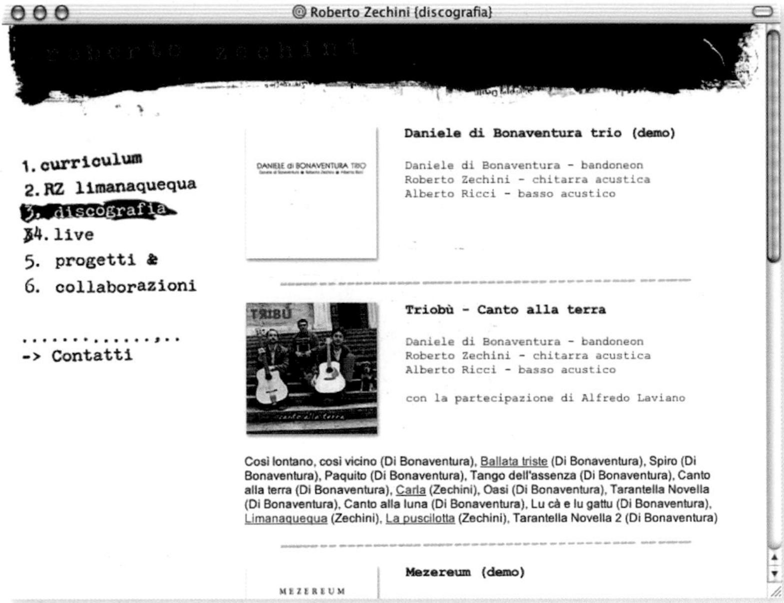

WWW.ROBERTOZECHINI.IT
D: DEMETRIO MANCINI
M: DEMETRIOMANCINI@LIBERO.IT

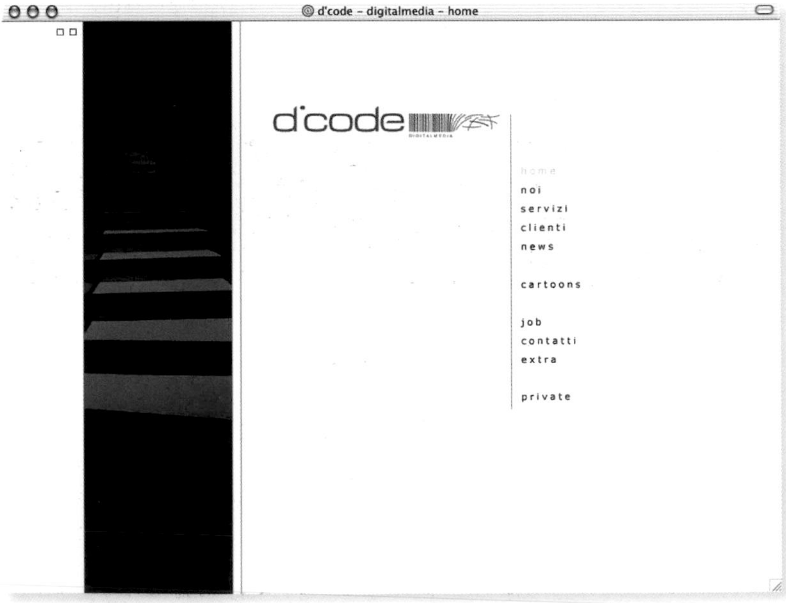

WWW.D-CODE.IT
D: CYRUS KHANIDE
A: D'CODE - DIGITALMEDIA, **M:** CYRUS.KHANIDE@D-CODE.IT

WWW.CODINGO.DE
D: JÜRGEN TEMMING
A: CODINGO, **M:** TEMMING@CODINGO.DE

WWW.METTLERBAU.CH
D: ERIK SÜSSKIND
A: SÜSSKIND SGD, **M:** SGD@SUESSKIND.CH

WWW.EROTICPEOPLE.CH/INDEX33.HTML
D: MEYER LIECHTI UND PARTNER, **C:** MARTIN MEYER, **P:** EROTICPEOPLE-TEAM
A: MEYER LIECHTI UND PARTNER, **M:** INFO@MEYER-LIECHTI.CH

WWW.RODAM.DE
D: THOMAS RICKER, **C:** JÜRGEN EBBING
A: ROSALES GMBH, **M:** J.EBBING@MEDIAHAUS.DE

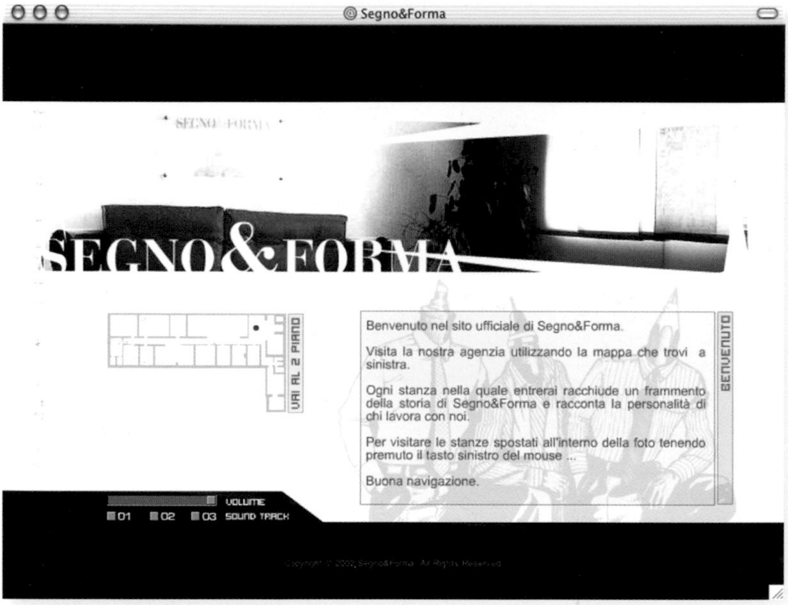

WWW.SEGNOEFORMA.IT
D: DANIELE LODI RIZZINI, **C:** DANIELE GIUSTI, **P:** DANIELE LODI RIZZINI
A: SEGNO&FORMA, **M:** DANIELE@SEGNOEFORMA.IT

WWW.QUARTETTOEUPHORIA.IT/INDEX2.HTML
D: GIAN PIETRO DRINGOLI, **C:** TAVANTI, **P:** QUARTETTO EUPHORIA
A: GRAPHIC DESIGN - GIAN PIETRO DRINGOLI, **M:** INFO@GIANPIETRODRINGOLI.COM

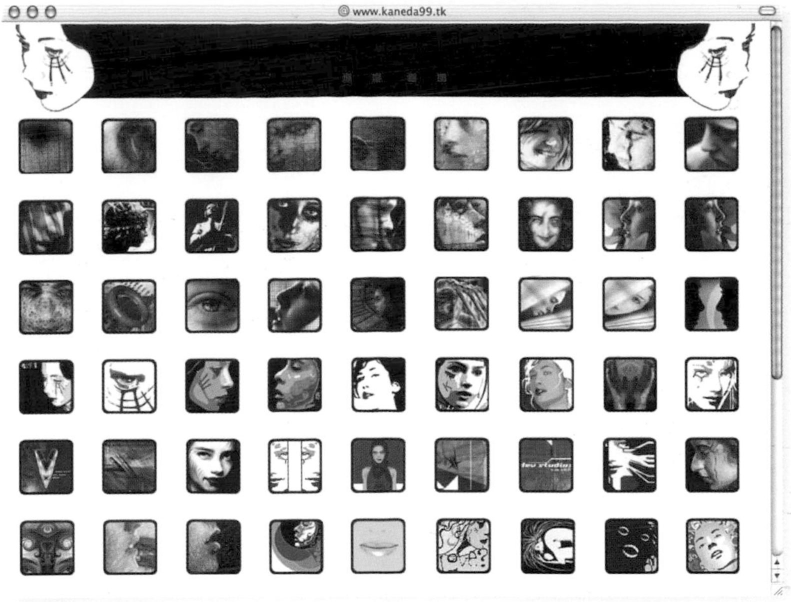

WWW.KANEDA99.TK
D: ALESSANDRO KANEDA99
A: COM & C, **M:** KANEDA99@INWIND.IT

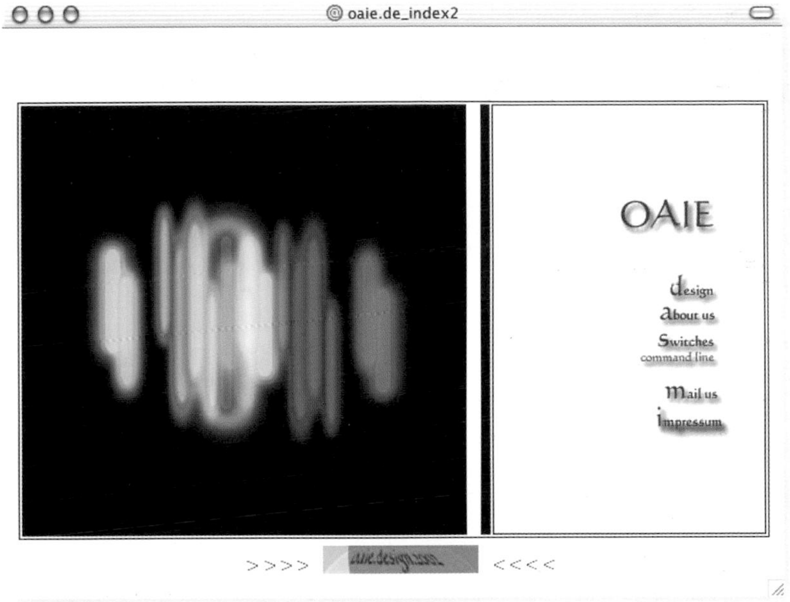

WWW.OAIE.DE
D: ION OAIE
M: ION@OAIE.DE

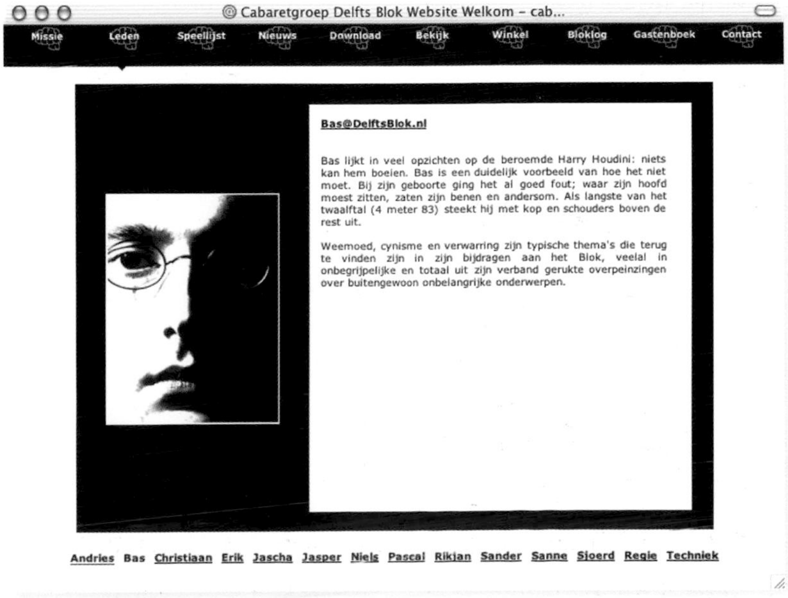

WWW.DELFTSBLOK.NL
D: ERIK THOMASSEN
A: DELFTS BLOK, **M:** ERIK@DELFTSBLOK.NL

WWW.SITANDDIE.COM
D: PEDRO J. SAAVEDRA MACÍAS, **C:** PEDRO J. SAAVEDRA MACÍAS, **P:** SIT AND DIE
A: SIT AND DIE, **M:** SITANDDIE@SITANDDIE.COM

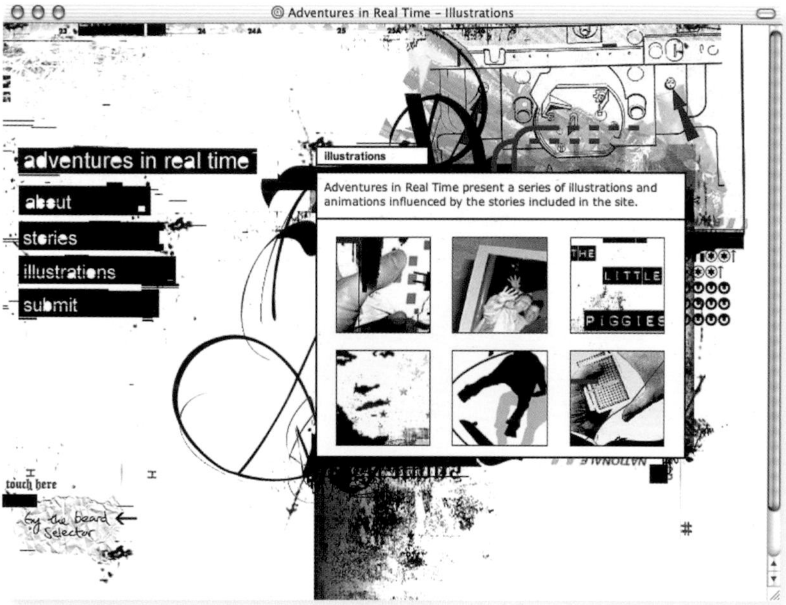

WWW.ADVENTURESINREALTIME.CO.UK
D: RICHARD HALL
A: CANNIBAL, **M:** RICHCANNIBAL@HOTMAIL.COM

WWW.SAFILO.COM
D: CLAUDIO CUGIA
M: CUGIAC@SAFILO.COM

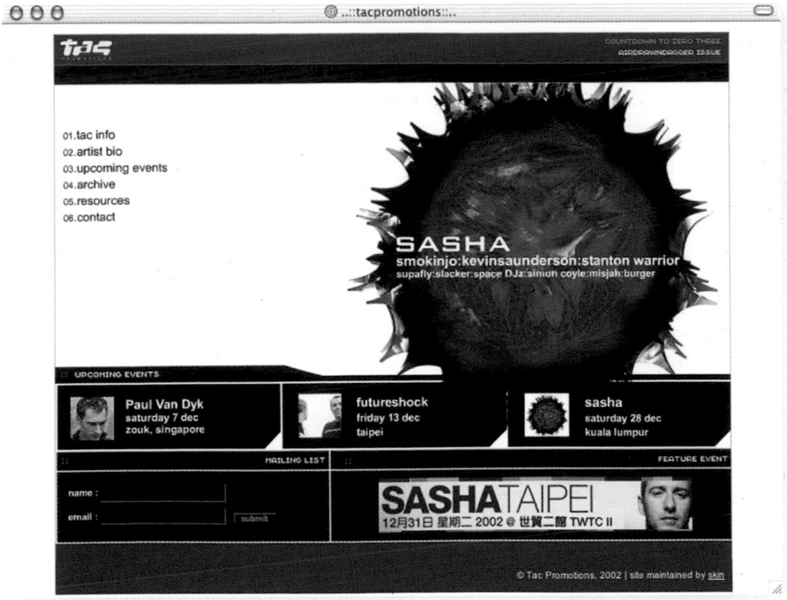

WWW.TACPROMOTIONS.COM
D: KEN CHAN
A: MEEK, **M:** AFRO@IAMMEEK.COM

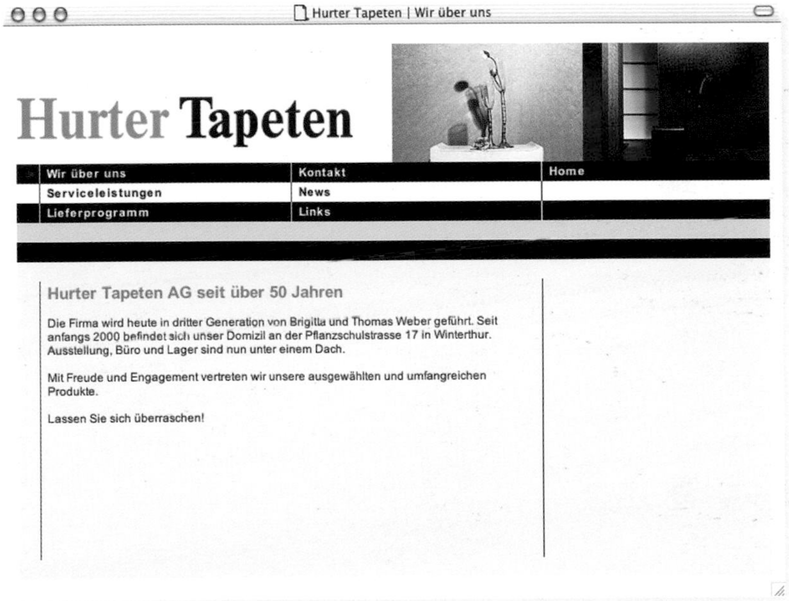

WWW.HURTERTAPETEN.CH
D: ROGER SCHMID
A: WWW.ROGER-SCHMID.CH, **M:** MAILS@ROGER-SCHMID.CH

WWW.SONORAMA-ARANDA.COM
D: JOSÉ LUIS DOMINGUEZ MONGE, **C:** FELIPE GAYUBO, **P:** RAFAEL GONZÁLEZ
M: JLDOMINGUEZ@MASMADERA.NET

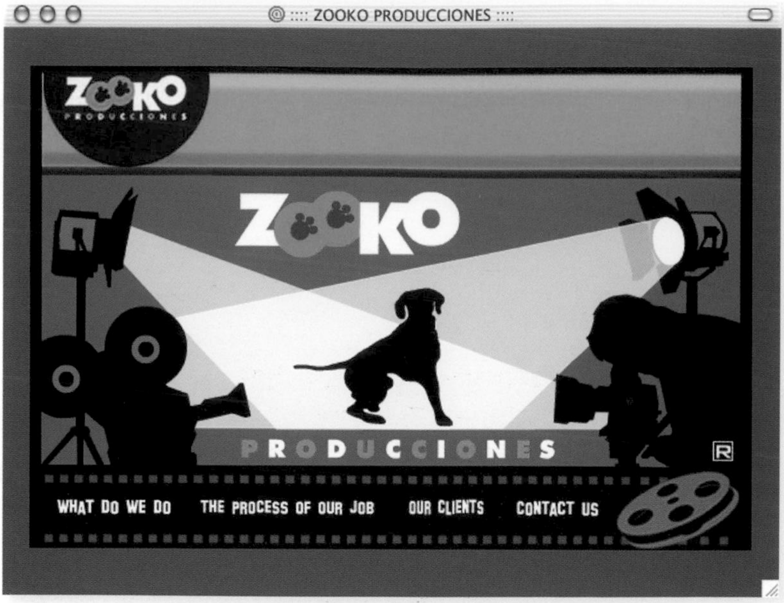

WWW.ZOOKOPRODUCCIONES.COM
D: DANIEL MARTINEZ
M: GROTESCO@WANADOO.ES

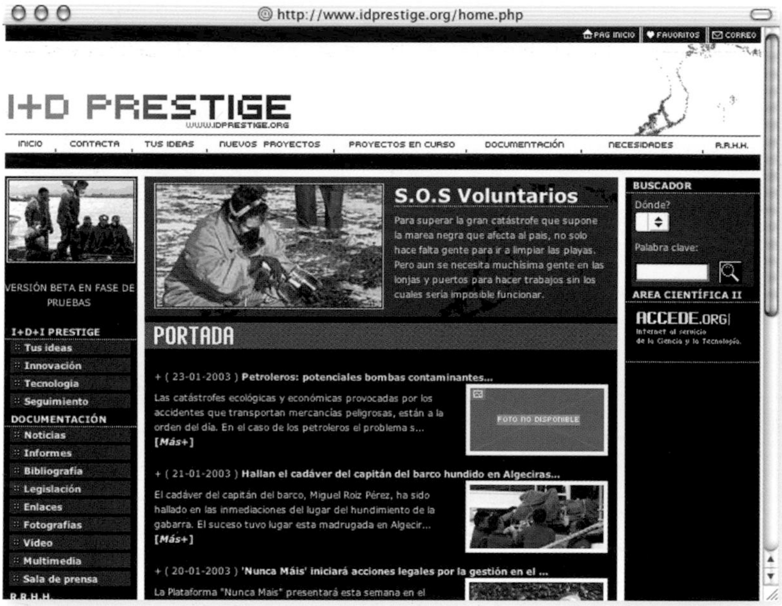

WWW.IDPRESTIGE.ORG
D: EMILIO GARCIA VAZ
A: EDISSENY.COM*, **M:** INFO@EDISSENY.COM

WWW.CUBODUPLA.COM
D: CUBODUPLA
A: CUBODUPLA, **M:** INFO@CUBODUPLA.COM

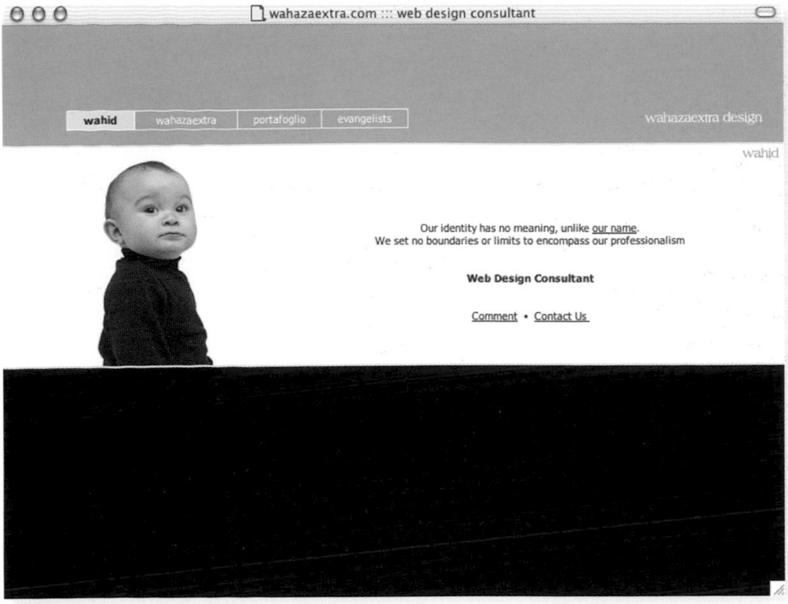

WWW.WAHAZAEXTRA.COM
D: MOHD HISHAM SALEH
A: WAHAZA EXTRA DESIGN STUDIO, **M:** DESIGNCONSULTANT@WAHAZAEXTRA.COM

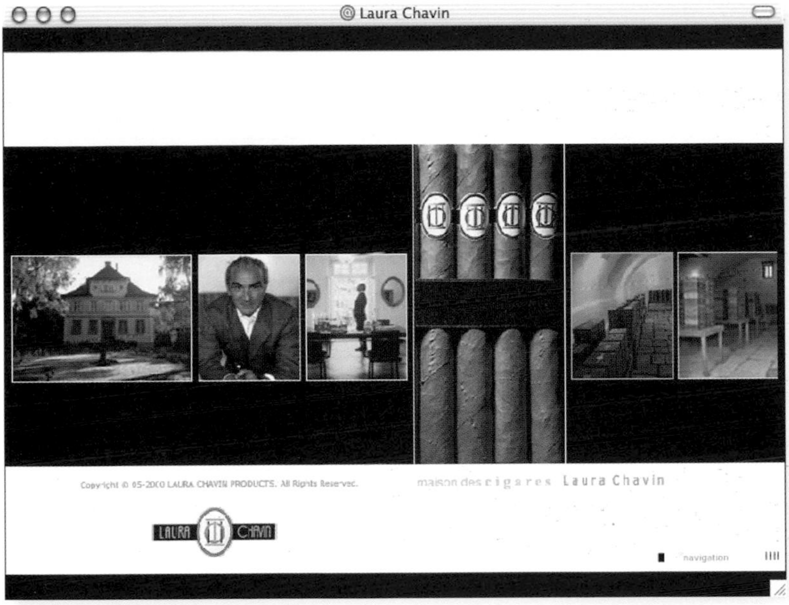

WWW.LAURA-CHAVIN.COM/FLASH_D
D: HERWART KONNERTH
A: ITV2, M: MAIL@ITV2.DE

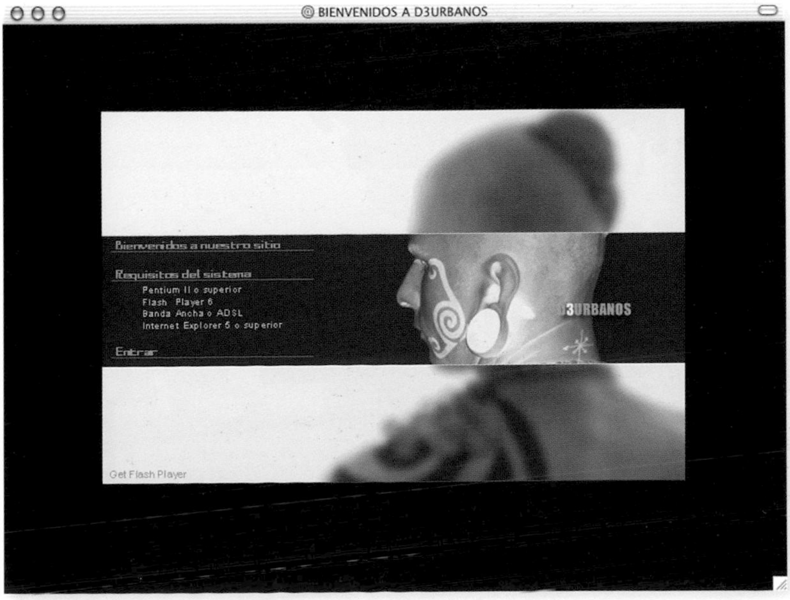

WWW.D3U.CL
D: ALVARO CALDERA, **C:** MARCO MARTINEZ, **P:** JOSE LUIS RAMOS
A: D3URBANOS, **M:** ACALDERA@D3U.CL

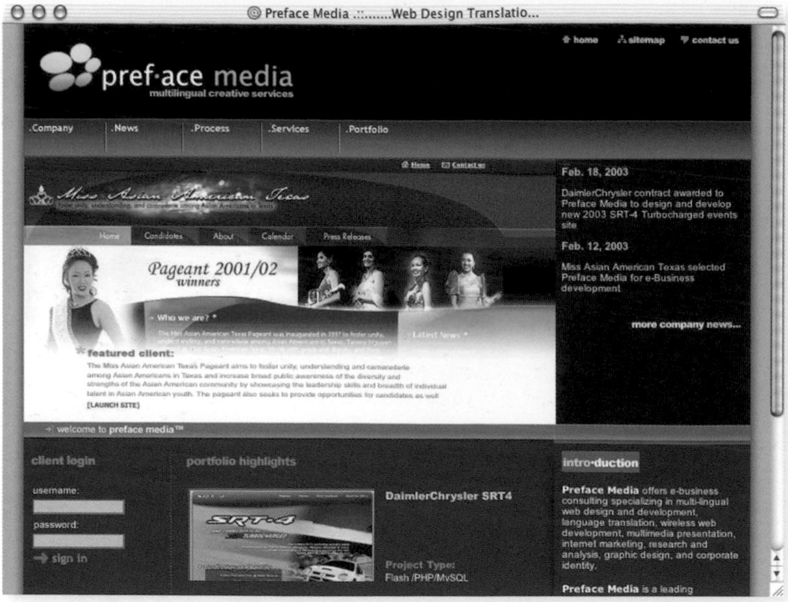

WWW.PREFACEMEDIA.COM
D: KEVIN YAO
A: PREFACE MEDIA, INC., **M:** KY@PREFACEMEDIA.COM

WWW.AUGENBLUTEN.COM
D: INTERFACES - SYMPOSIUM UEBER SCHRIFT UND SPRACHE
A: INTERFACES - SYMPOSIUM UEBER SCHRIFT UND SPRACHE, **M:** AXEL@AUGENBLUTEN.COM

WWW.PCSIWA12.RETT.POLIMI.IT/~PHDDI/
D: LETIZIA BOLLINI
M: INFO@EXTRASMALL.NET

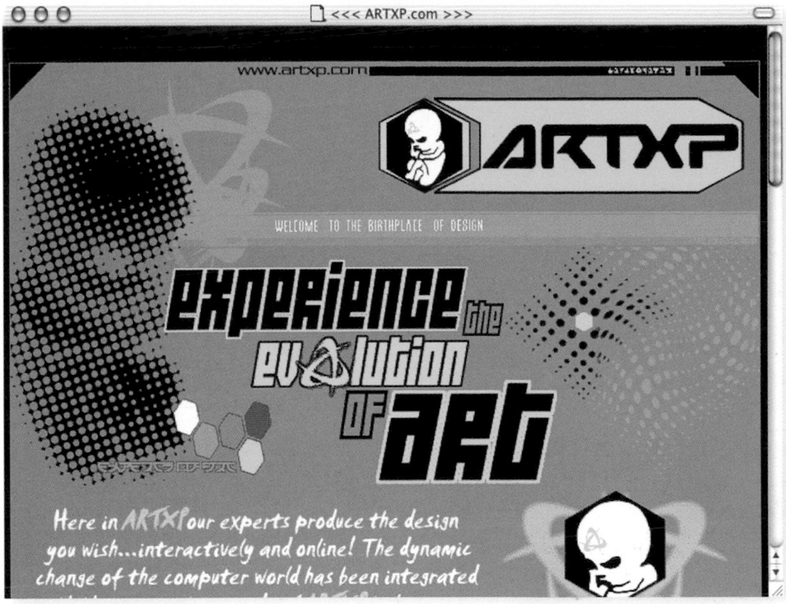

WWW.ARTXP.COM
D: ILKER YOLDAS
A: ARTXP.COM, **M:** ILKER@ARTXP.COM

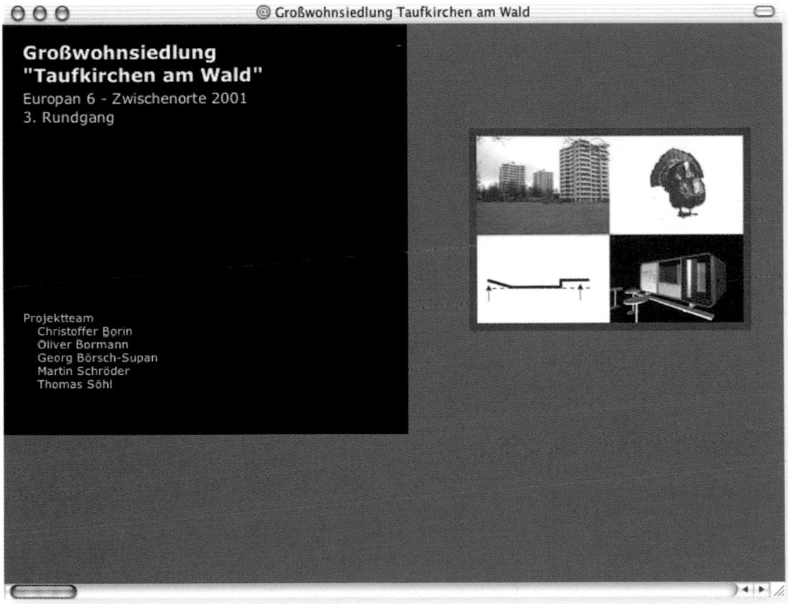

WWW.PROCESSYELLOW.DE
D: CHRISTOPH PACKHIESER
A: KALT8 KONZEPT, **M:** WIR@KALT8.DE

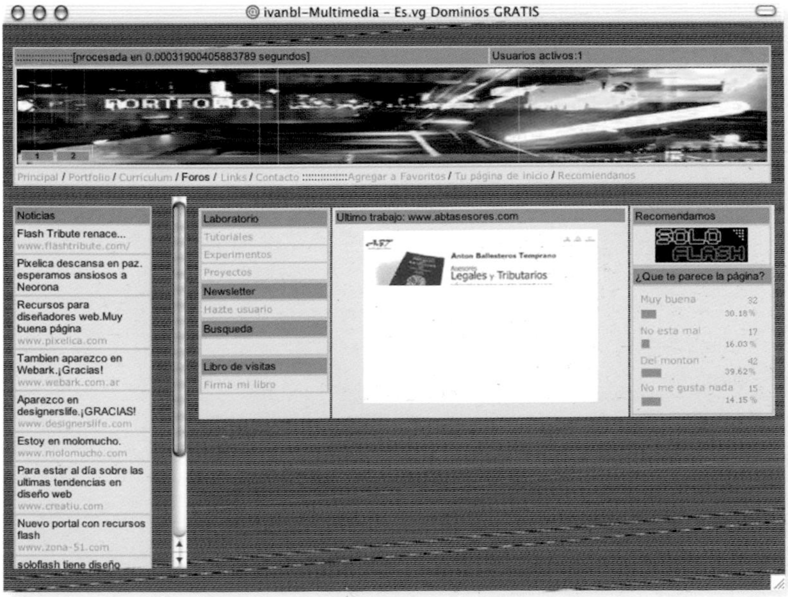

WWW.IVANBL.ES.VG
D: IVAN BLANCO
A: IVANBL

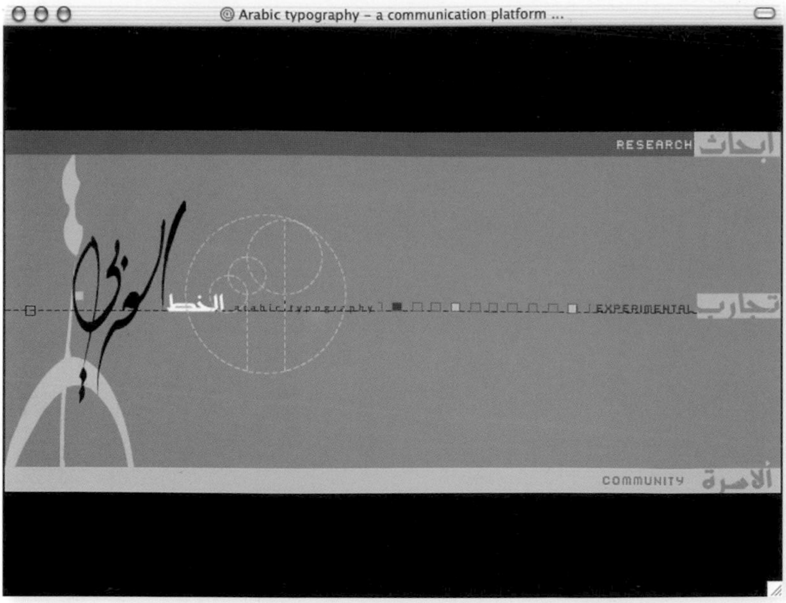

WWW.ARABICTYPOGRAPHY.COM
D: TAREK ATRISSI, **C:** TAREK ATRISSI & PAUL KLOK, **P:** TAREK ATRISSI
A: TAREK ATRISSI DESIGN, **M:** TAREK@ATRISSI.COM

WWW.ZORGPROFESSIONALS.NL
D: FLORIEN WILDEMAN, **C:** FLORIEN WILDEMAN, **P:** FUNKTIEMEDIAIR
A: FLO PRODUCTIONS, **M:** FLORIEN@FLO-PRODUCTIONS.NL

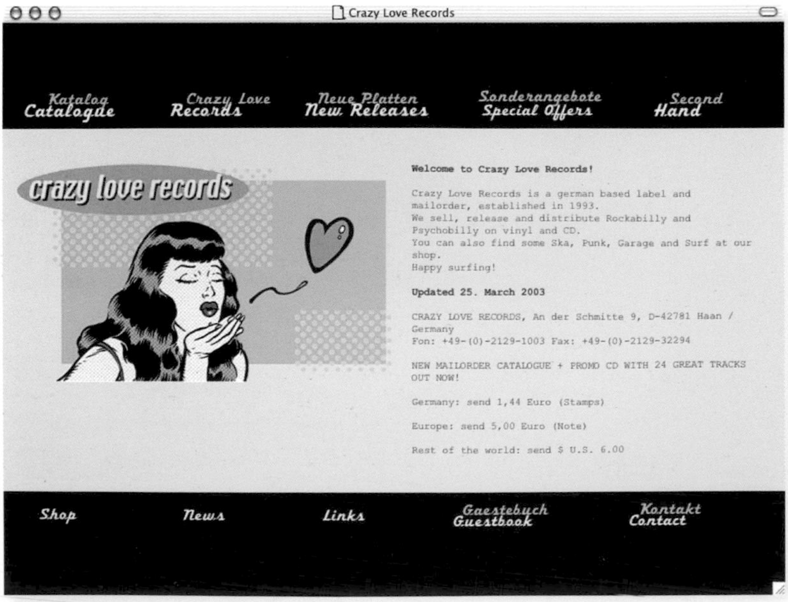

WWW.CRAZYLOVERECORDS.DE
D: VERONIKA CASPERS
M: LOVERONIKA@HOTMAIL.COM

WWW.KAMMERSOLISTEN.CH
D: PIT MÜLLER
A: PIT DESIGN, **M:** PETER.MUELLER@DATAZUG.CH

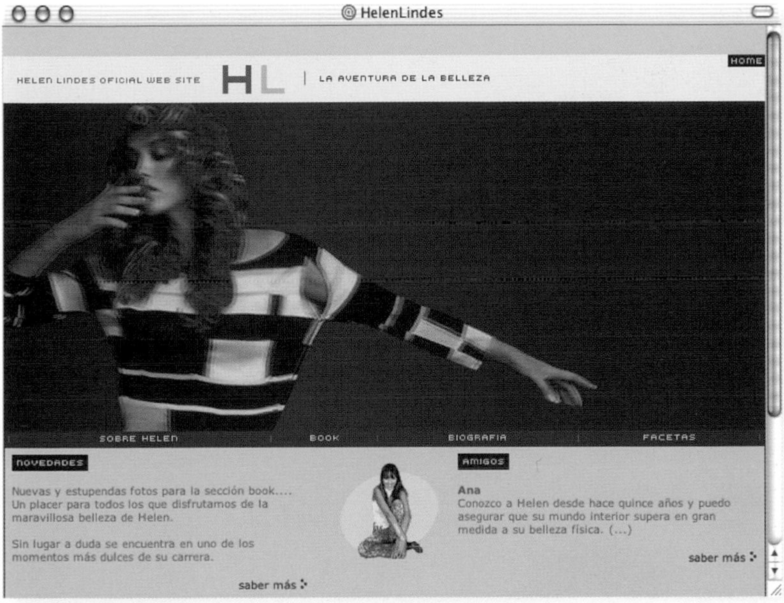

WWW.HELENLINDES.COM
D: MANUEL OTERO
A: MUTADOR, **M:** INFO@MUTADOR.COM

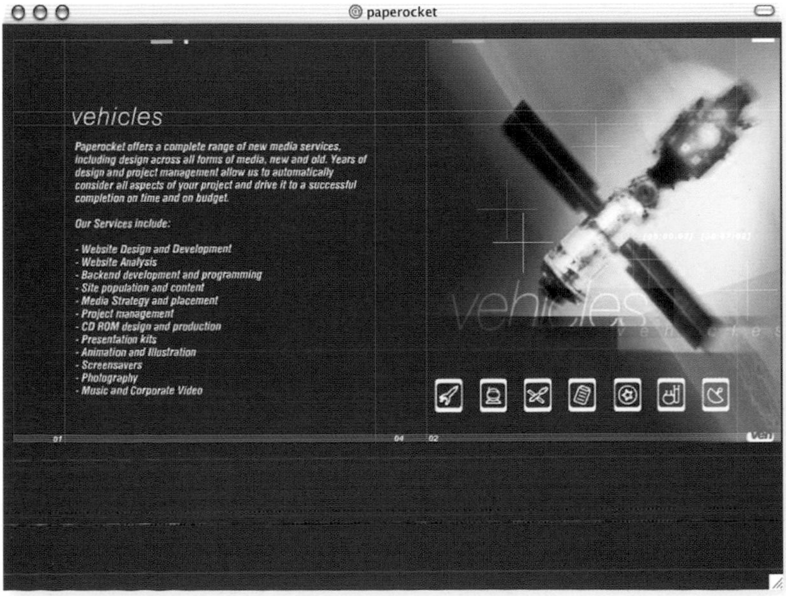

WWW.PAPEROCKET.COM
D: PAUL JASON, **C:** RIK PETERS & PAUL JASON, **P:** RIK PETERS
A: PAPEROCKET, **M:** PAUL@PAPEROCKET.COM

WWW.SONY-ASIA.COM/WEGADRSERIES/WEGA.HTML
D: IVAN MP TAN, CHARLENE LEUNG, **C:** LYNDONN OH, **P:** PAUL KAN
A: AC'LAIM, **M:** IVAN@ACLAIM.COM.SG

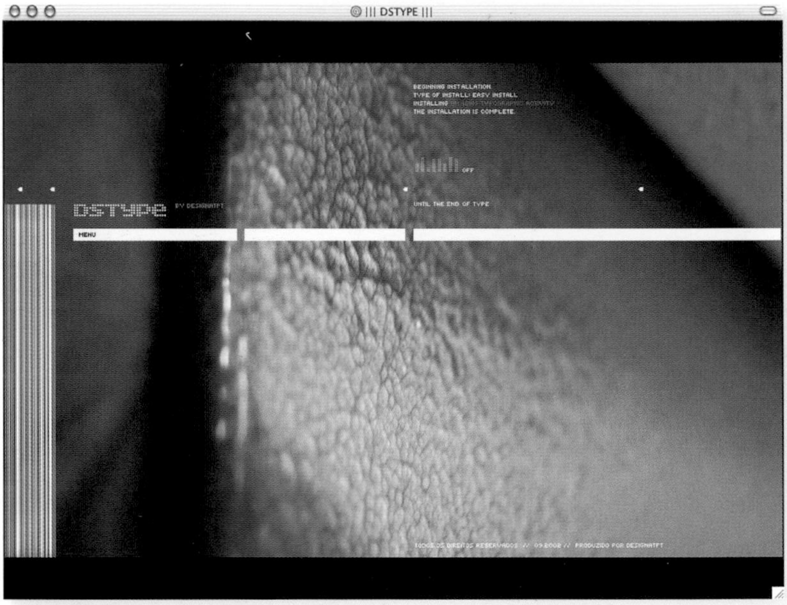

WWW.DSTYPE.COM
D: DESIGN ATPT
A: DESIGN ATPT, **M:** INFO@DESIGNATPT.PT

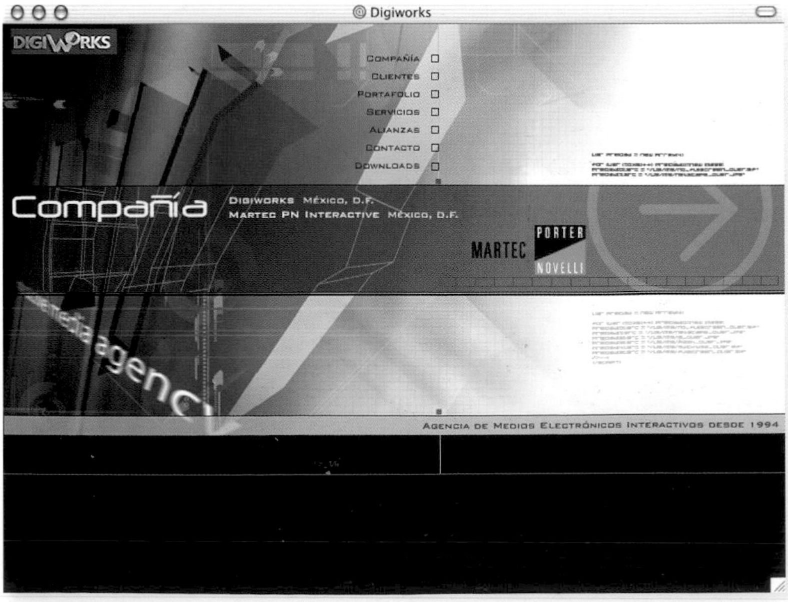

WWW.DIGIWORKS.COM.MX
D: ABRAHAM GONZALEZ, **C:** RICHARD BEHAR
A: DIGIWORKS, **M:** GRIDEX@SOFTHOME.NET

WWW.NETICA.FR
D: PIERRE-HENRI PHAM
A: NETICA.FR, **M:** PH@NETICA.FR

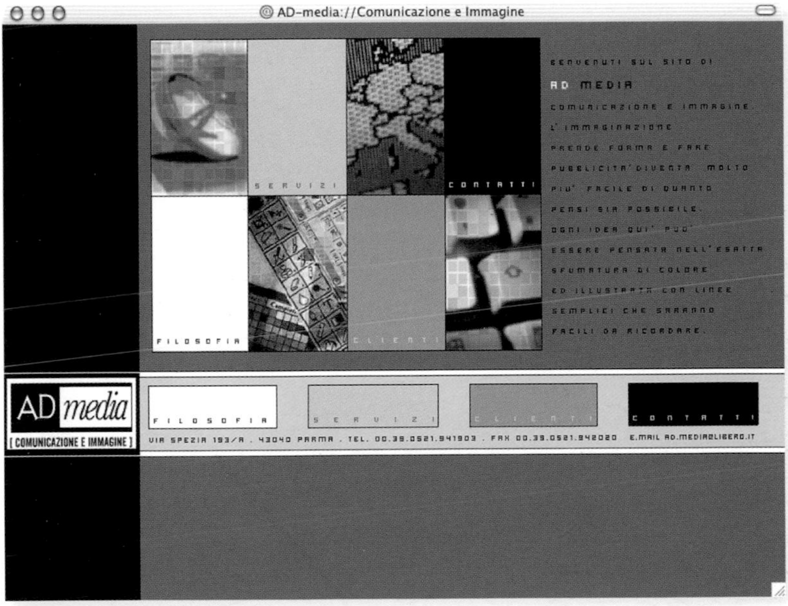

WWW.ADMEDIAONLINE.IT
D: NICOLA GATTI, **C:** NICOLA GATTI, **P:** SPAGGIARI MARIA GRAZIA
A: ADMEDIA, **M:** NICOLA@ADMEDIAONLINE.IT

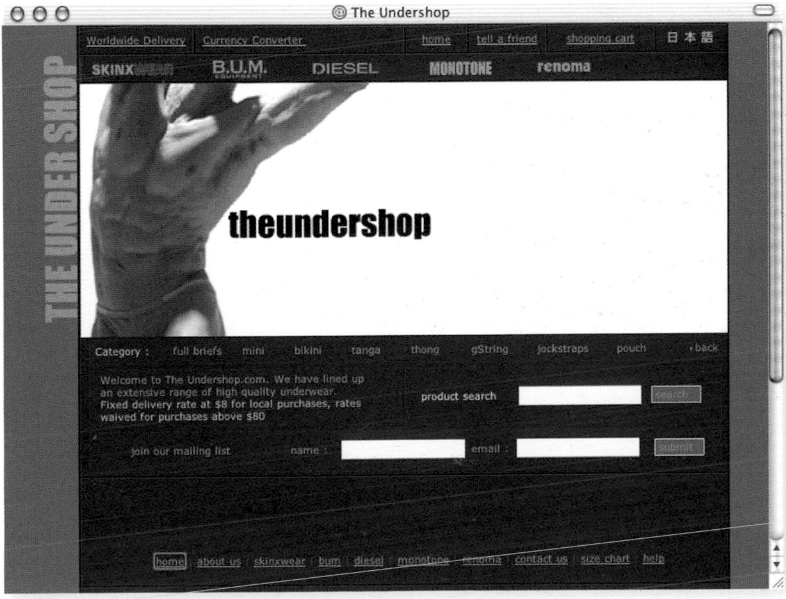

WWW.THEUNDERSHOP.COM
D: KEN CHAN, **C:** RAYMOND LIAN, **P:** ALDRICH KOH
A: MEEK, **M:** SKIN@PACIFIC.NET.SG

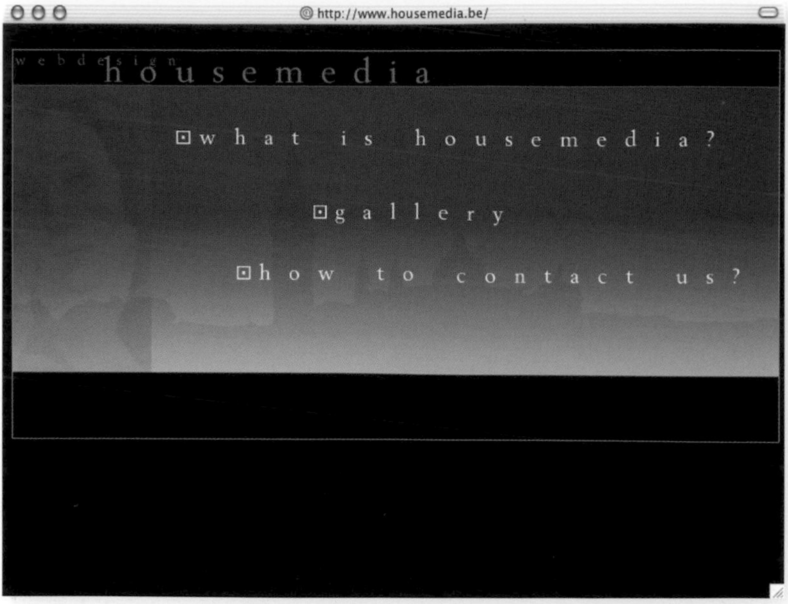

WWW.HOUSEMEDIA.BE
D: TIMOTHY DE PAEPE
A: HOUSEMEDIA, **M:** TIMDEPAEPE@SKYNET.BE

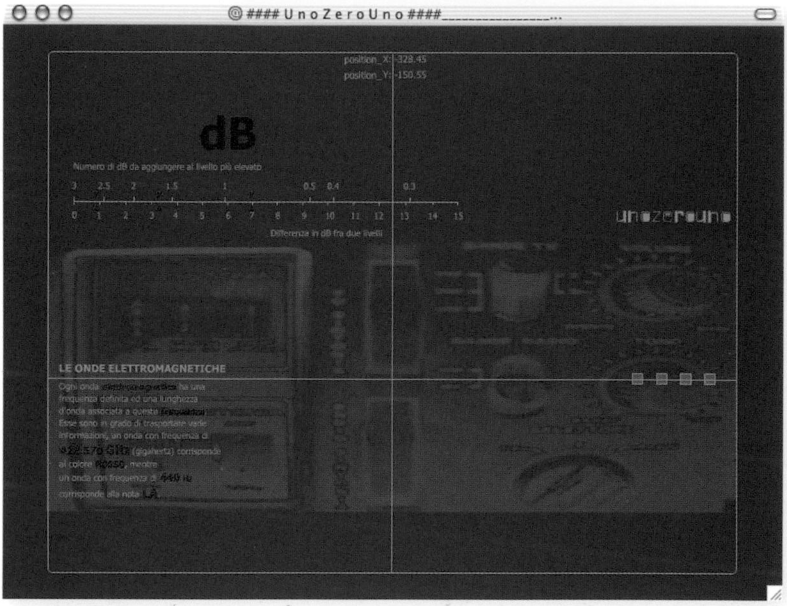

WWW.DIGILANDER.LIBERO.IT/UNOZEROUNO/SITO2002/1024X768.HTML
D: ROSARIO GRIECO
M: SNOUT@LIBERO.IT

WWW.URSOPUBBLICITA.IT
D: MONTSERRAT COLL VILLAR
A: URSO PUBBLICITÀ, **M:** MONTSE@URSOPUBBLICITA.IT

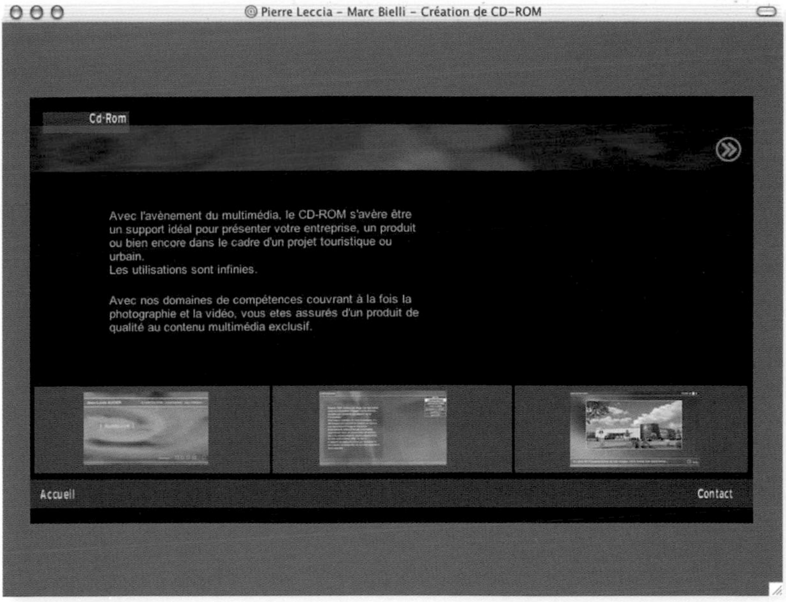

WWW.PIERRE-LECCIA.NET
D: PIERRE LECCIA
M: LECCIA.P@LAPOSTE.NET

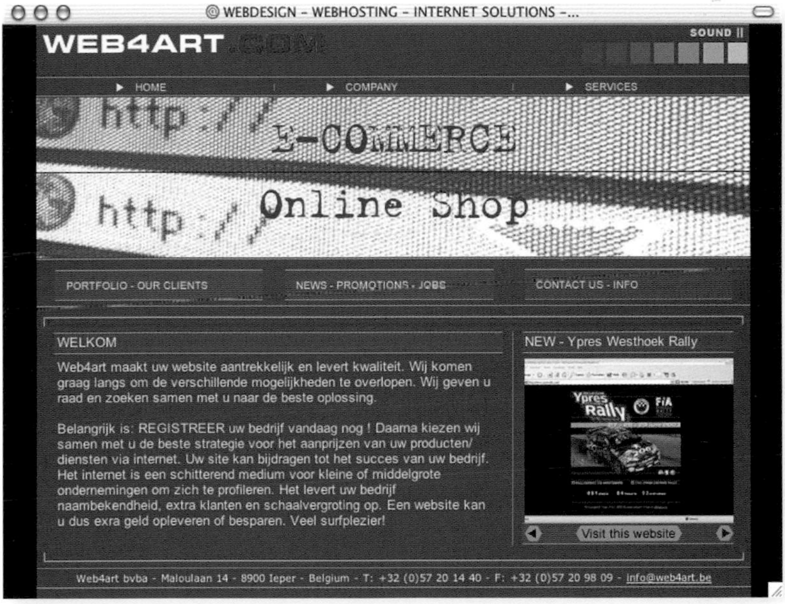

WWW.WEB4ART.BE
D: STEVE SNICK
A: WEB4ART BVBA, **M:** INFO@WEB4ART.BE

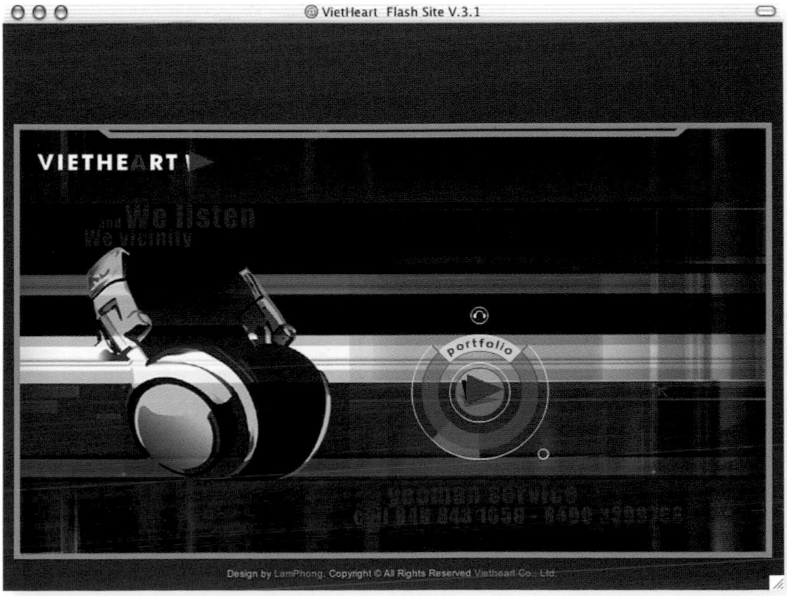

WWW.VIETHEARTTEAM.COM
D: FUNGLIN
A: VIETHEART CO., LTD, **M:** SALES@VIETHEARTTEAM.COM

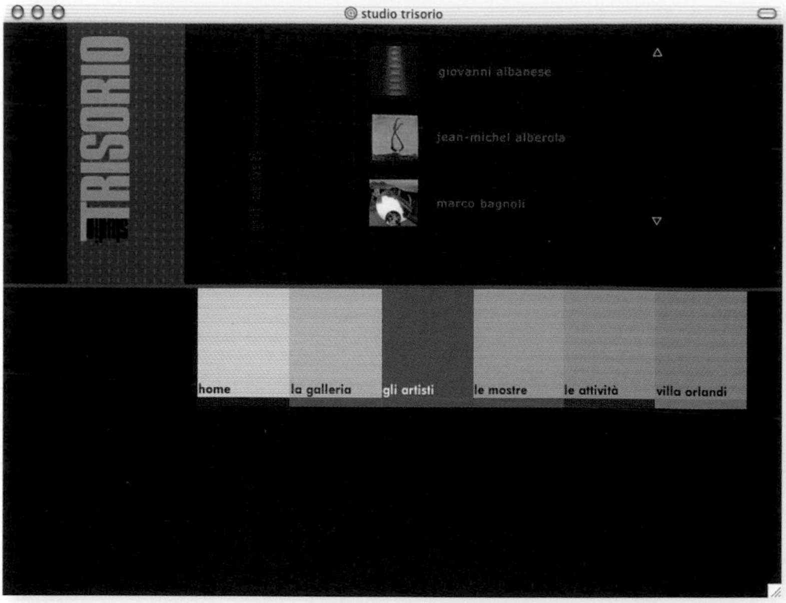

WWW.STUDIOTRISORIO.COM
D: CHIARA BOSCOTRECASE
A: JIOLAHY, **M:** INFO@JIOLAHY.IT

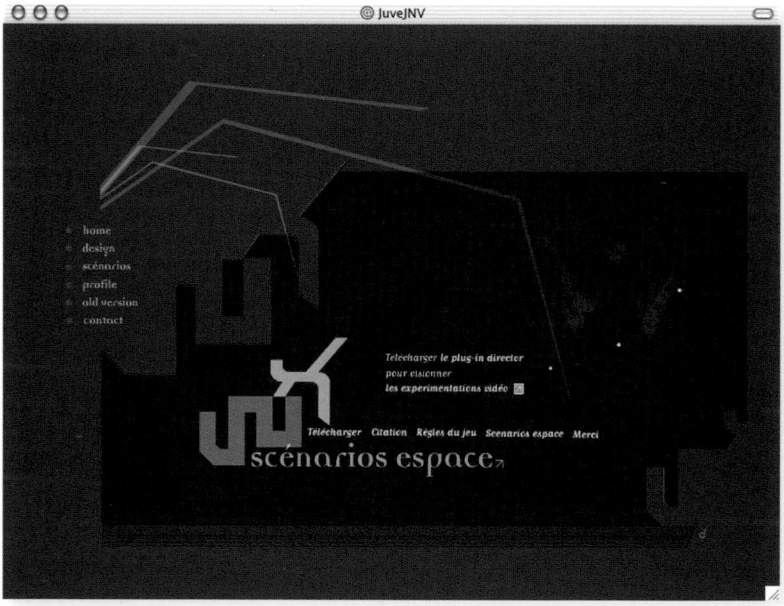

WWW.JUVEJNV.FREE.FR
D: JULIETTE NICOLAS-VULLIERME
M: JUVEJNV@FREE.FR

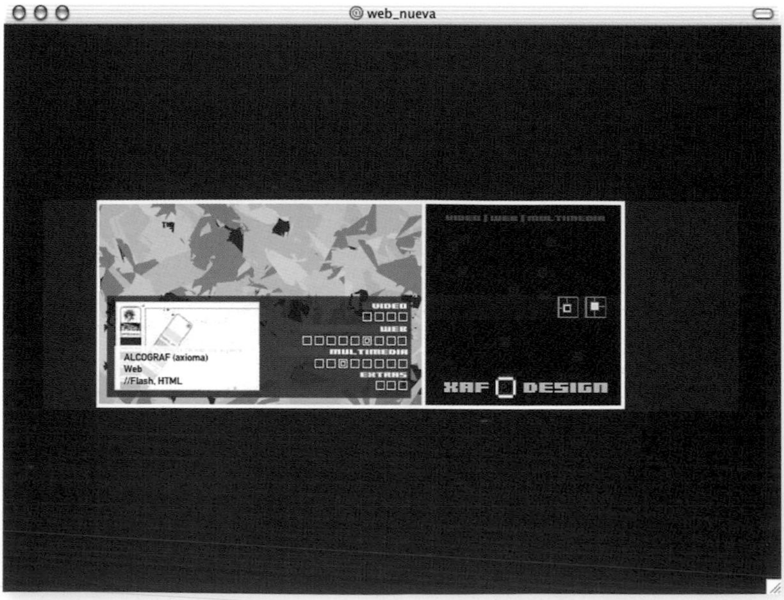

WWW.XAFDESIGN.COM
D: XAVI ROYO
A: XAFDESIGN, **M:** XAVI@XAFDESIGN.COM

WWW.DESIGNSTUDIO360.DE
D: RICHARD SUMMERS
A: DESIGNSTUDIO 360, **M:** WEBMASTER@DESIGNSTUDIO360.DE

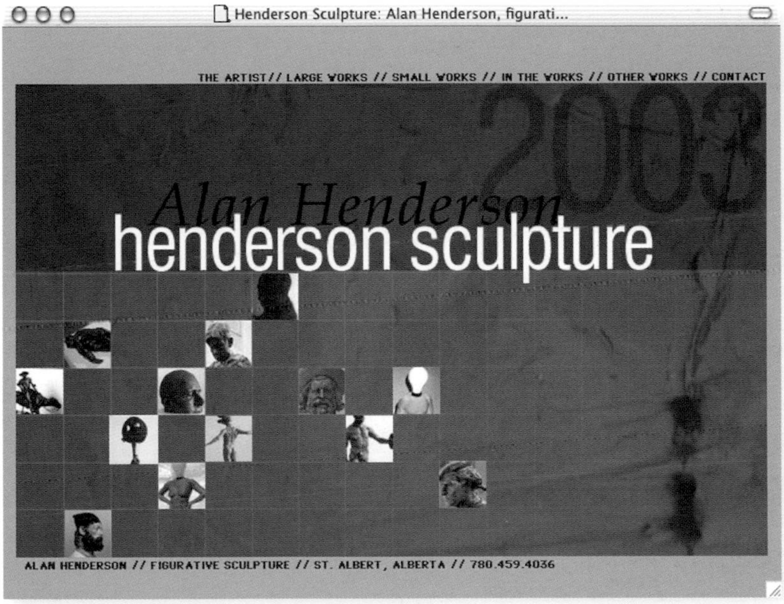

WWW.HENDERSONSCULPTURE.COM
D: DAWN CAMPBELL
A: ACCORD SYSTEMS GROUP LTD., **M:** DAWN@ACCORDSYSTEMS.COM

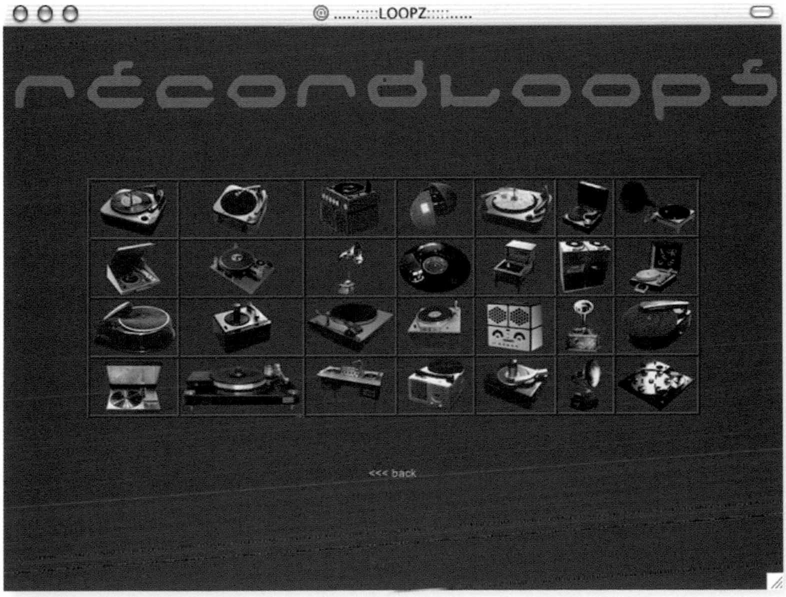

WWW.RECORDLOOPS.COM
D: BATCHAS
A: SP-MULTIMEDIA, **M:** INFO@RECORDLOOPS.COM

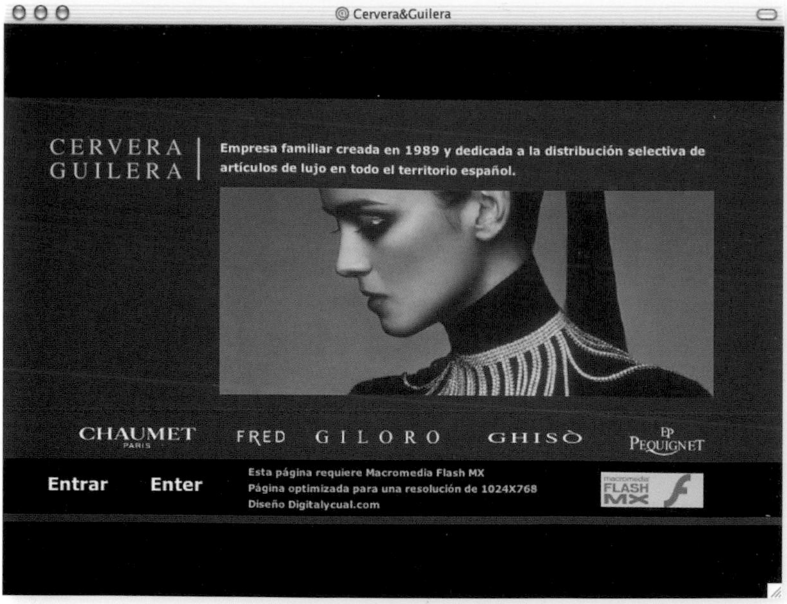

WWW.CERVERAGUILERA.COM
D: JUAN LINARES, **C:** JOAN SALMERON, **P:** VICKY PRENAFETA
A: DIGITALYCUAL, **M:** INFO@DIGITALYCIAL.COM

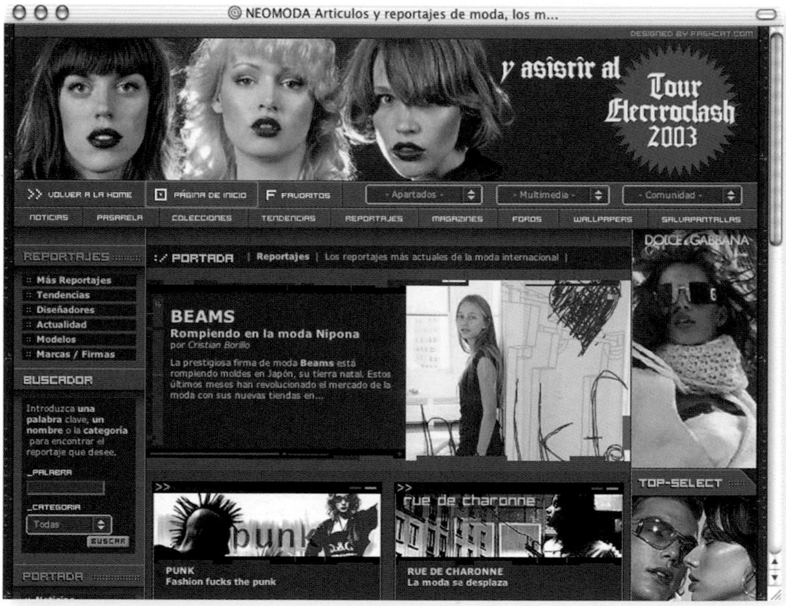

WWW.NEOMODA.COM
D: BORILLO & CÉSPEDES, **C:** SALVADOR K.TA, **P:** FASHCAT S.L
A: FASHCAT S.L, **M:** MARTIN@FASHCAT.COM

WWW.KUZU.COM.TR
D: KEREM AKBARCI
A: 18 DESIGN, **M:** MOSCAR@SUPERONLINE.COM

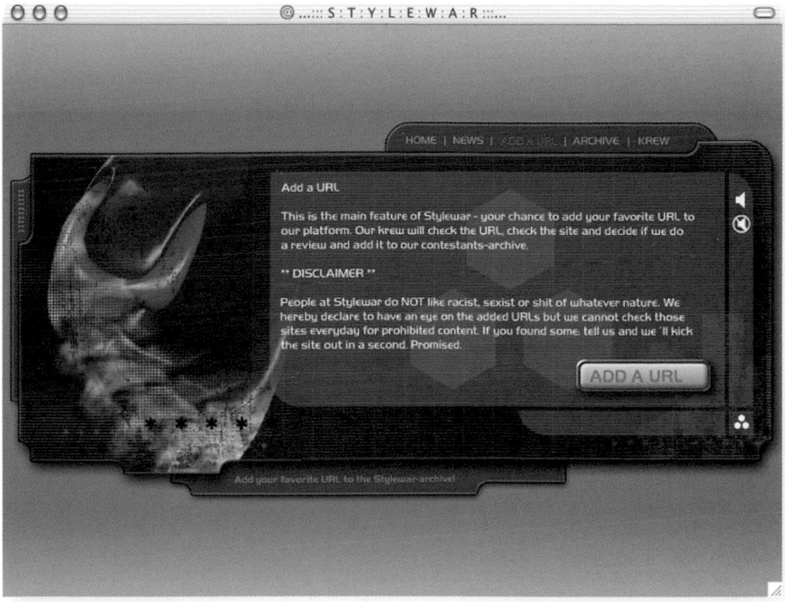

WWW.STYLEWAR.DE
D: CHRISTOPH RENNE
A: KRYZCOM INC., **M:** CHEF@KRYZCOM.DE

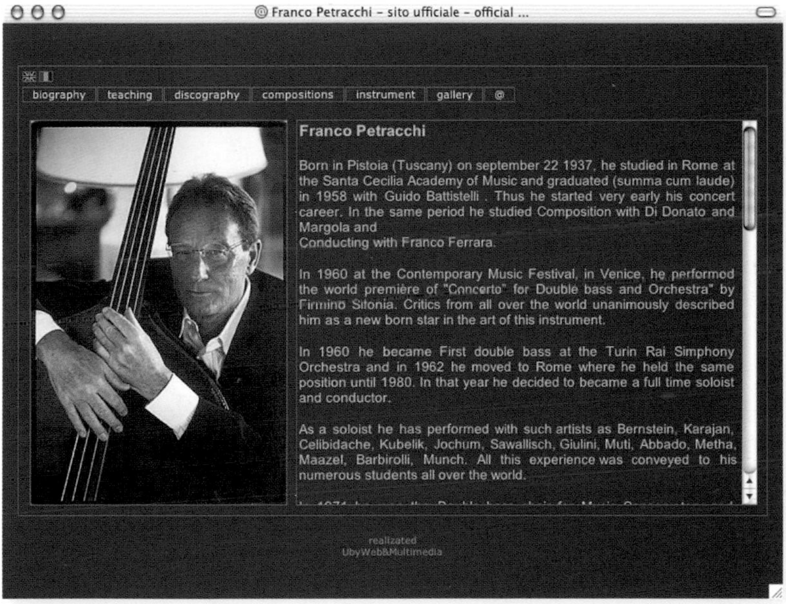

WWW.FRANCOPETRACCHI.COM
D: PONZIO UBALDO
A: UBYWEB&MULTIMEDIA, **M:** UBALDO@PONZIO.IT

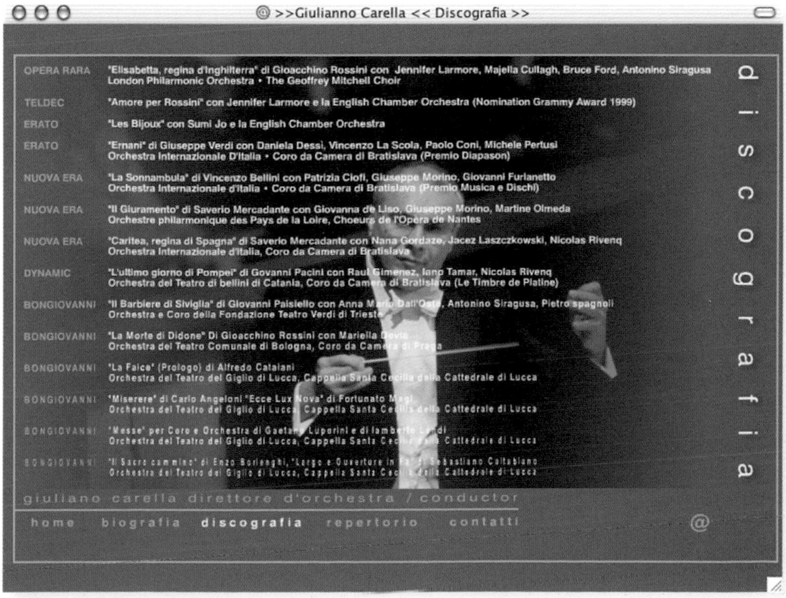

WWW.GIULIANOCARELLA.IT
D: FRANCESCO GUIDI, **P:** GIULIANO CARELLA
A: ELGON GRAFICA, **M:** INFO@ELGON.IT

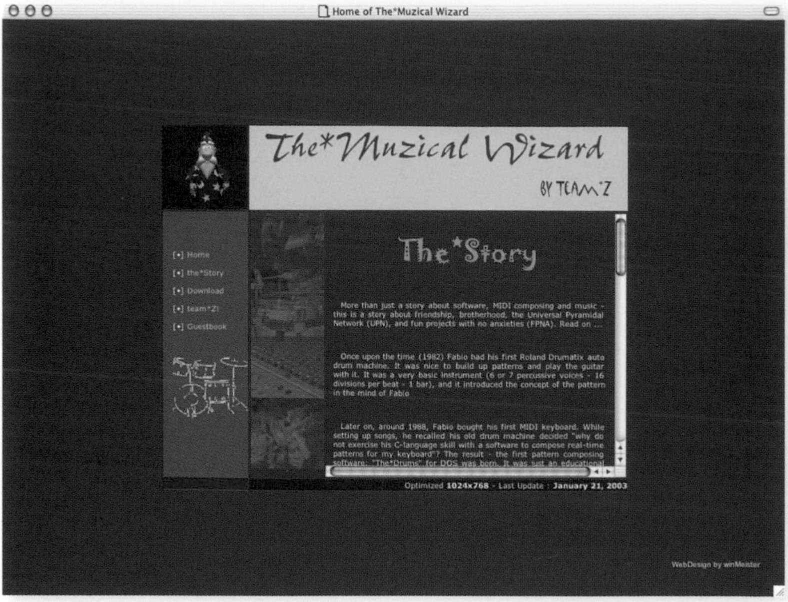

WWW.MCLINK.IT/PERSONAL/MC3796
D: FABIO MARZOCCA
M: MARZOCCA@MCLINK.IT

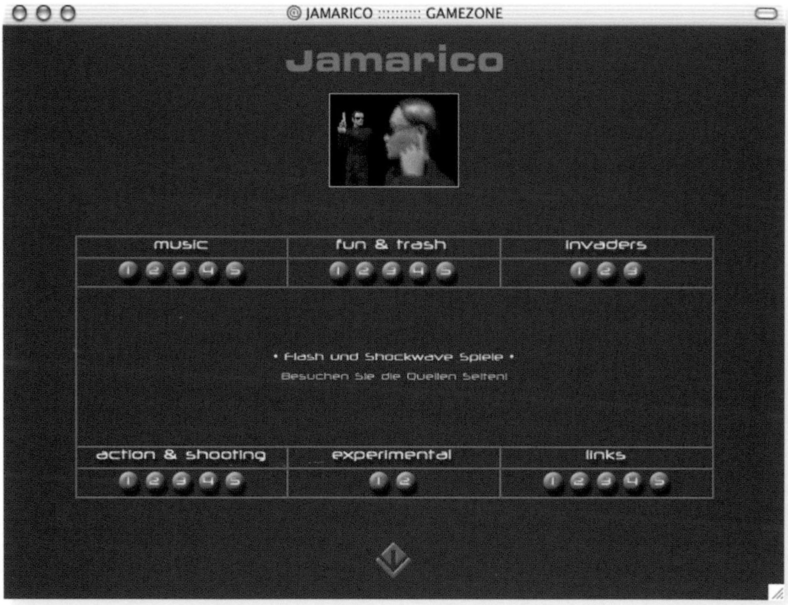

WWW.JAMARICO.CH
D: BATCHAS
A: SP-MULTIMEDIA, **M:** INFO@SP-MULTIMEDIA.COM

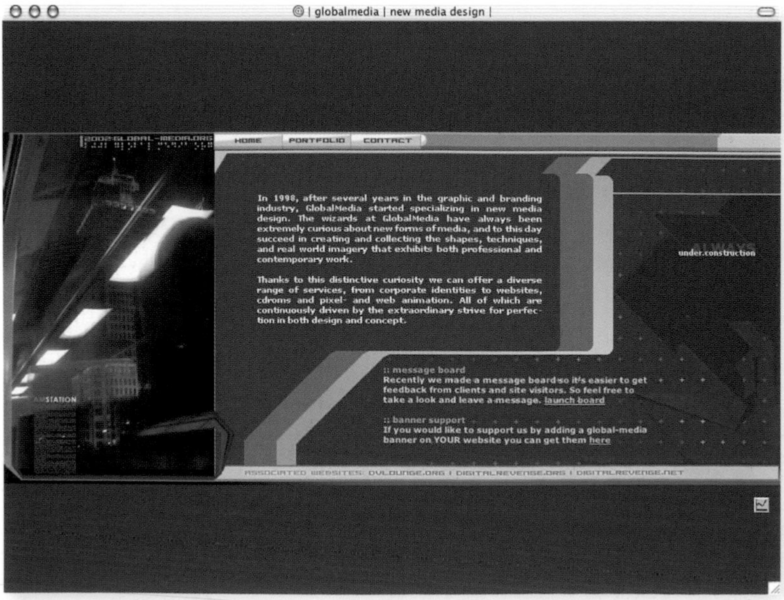

WWW.GLOBAL-MEDIA.ORG
D: D.J. VAN BALLEGOOIJEN
A: GLOBALMEDIA, **M:** DADJ@DIGITALREVENGE.ORG

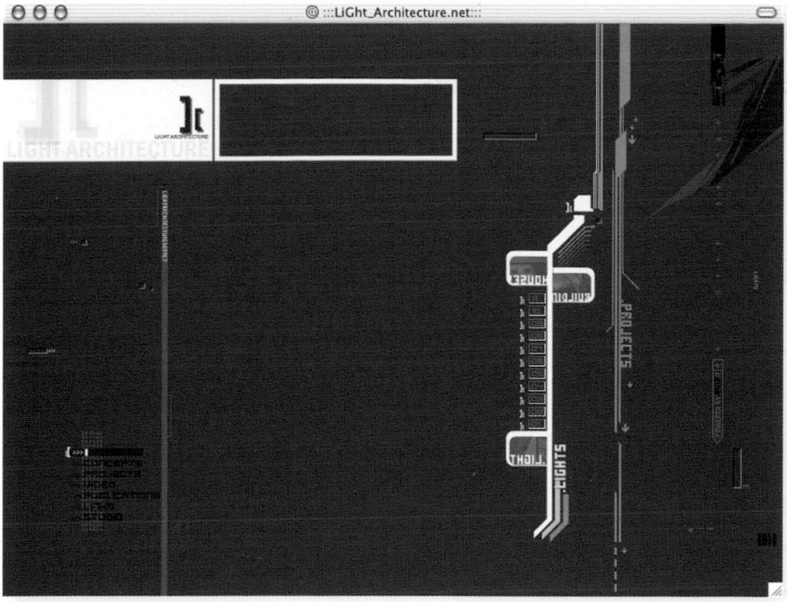

WWW.LIGHTARCHITECTURE.NET
D: STEFANO PEDRETTI
A: PULPIT, **M:** PEDRO@PULPIT.IT

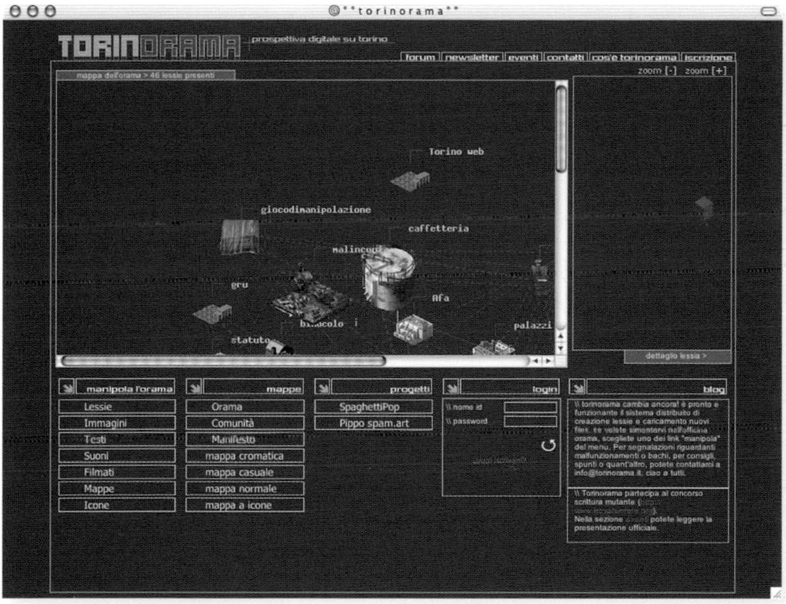

WWW.TORINORAMA.IT
D: DAVID BOARDMAN
M: INFO@TORINORAMA.ITA

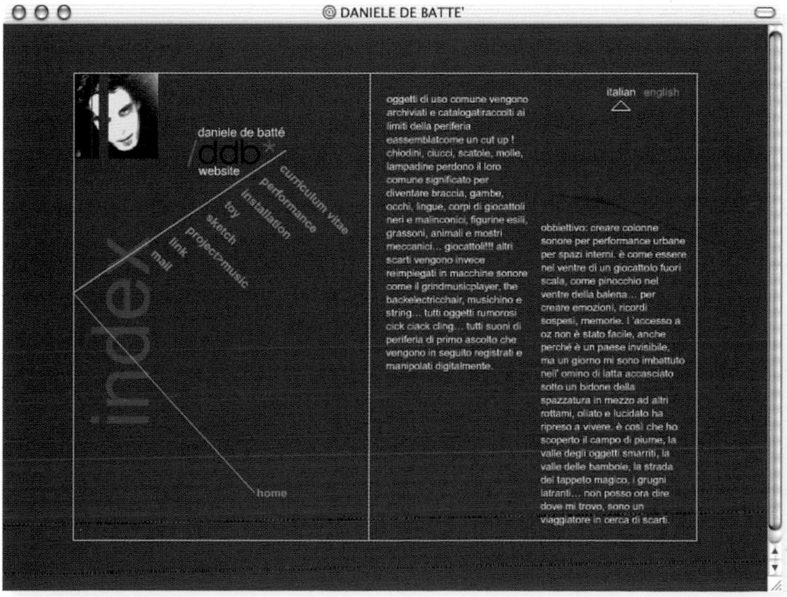

WWW.WALK.TO/DANY
D: DANIELE DE BATTÉ
M: DANIELEDEBATTE@LIBERO.IT

WWW.HOTKNIVES.NET
D: RALF KOPPELKAMP
A: SCORCHA MEDIASERVICE, **M:** RK@SCORCHA.DE

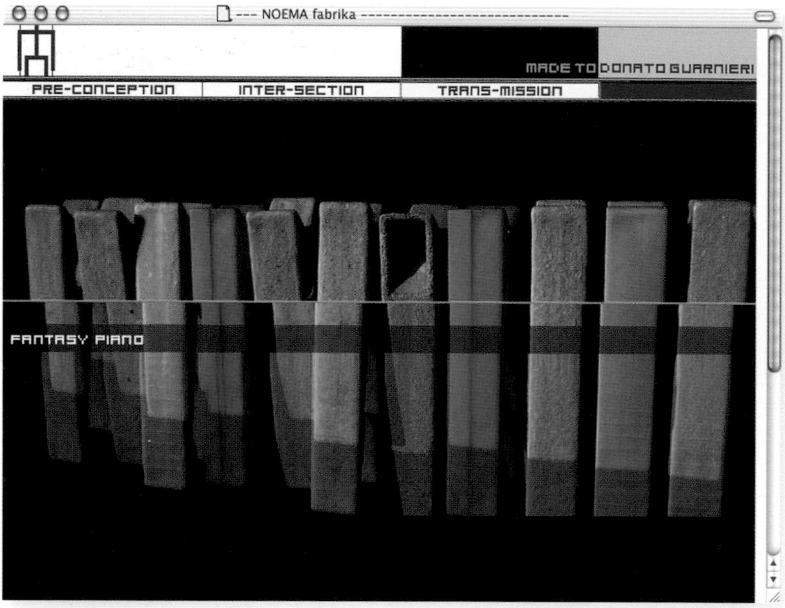

WWW.NOEMAGENCY.COM/FABRIKA/PIANO.HTM
D: GUARNIERI DONATO
M: FREMDA@ONEONLINE.IT

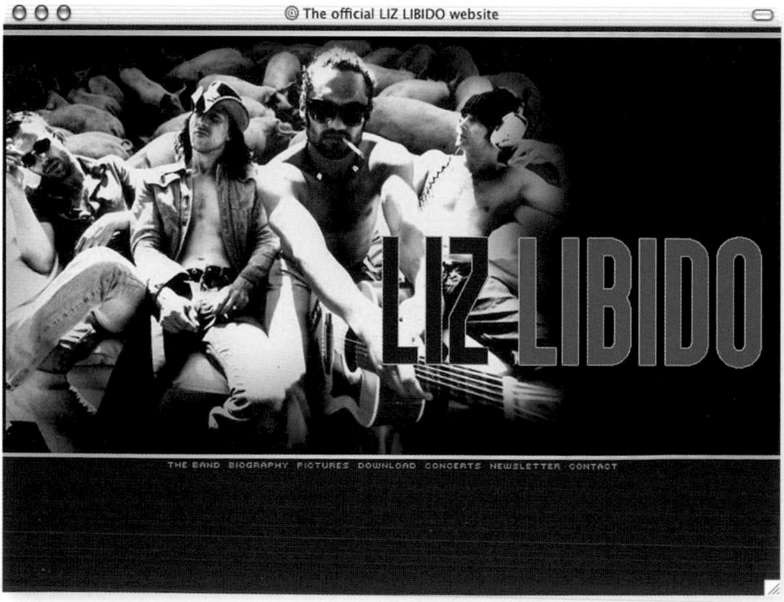

WWW.LIZLIBIDO.COM
D: URS MEYER, **C:** OLIVER ZAHORKA, **P:** LIZ LIBIDO
A: OUT MEDIA DESIGN GMBH, **M:** URS@OUT.TO

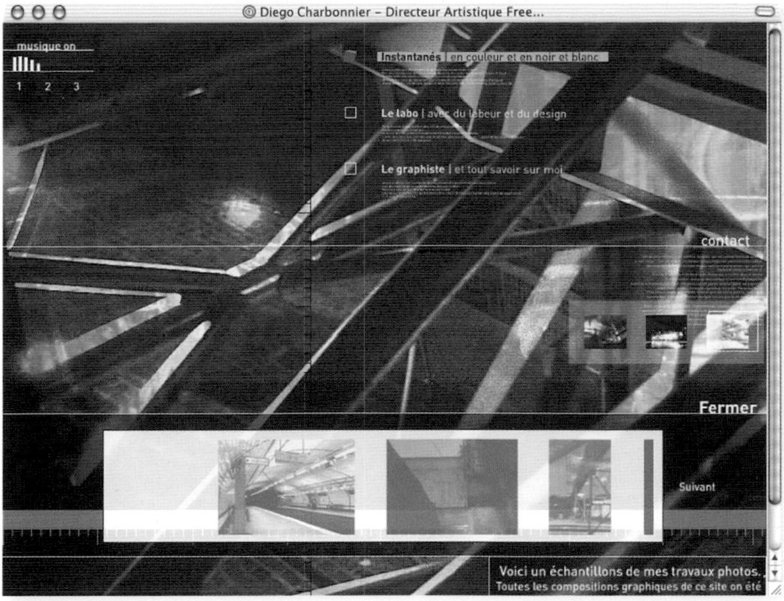

WWW.DIEGOC.NET
D: DIEGO CHARBONNIER
A: DIEGOC.NET, **M:** DIEGO@DIEGOC.NET

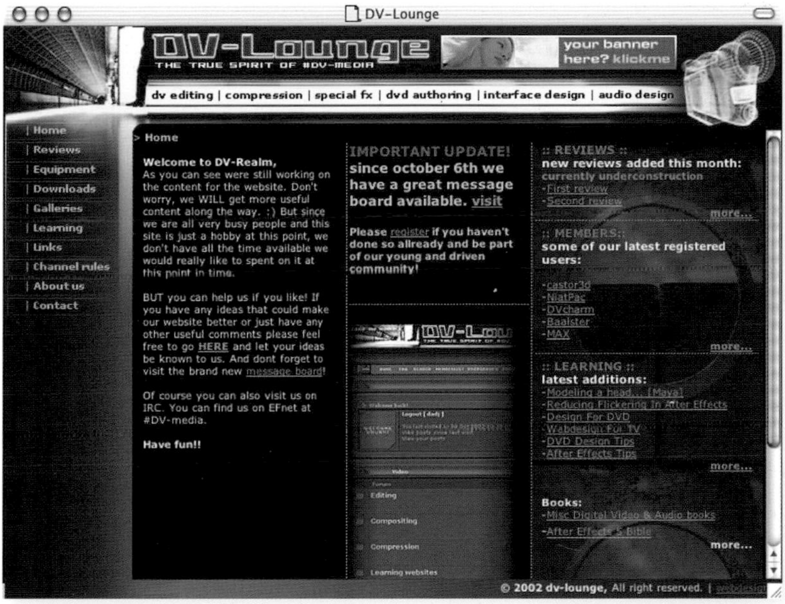

WWW.DVLOUNGE.NET
D: DAVID VAN BALLEGOOIJEN
A: GLOBALMEDIA, **M:** DJ@DRWILCO.NET

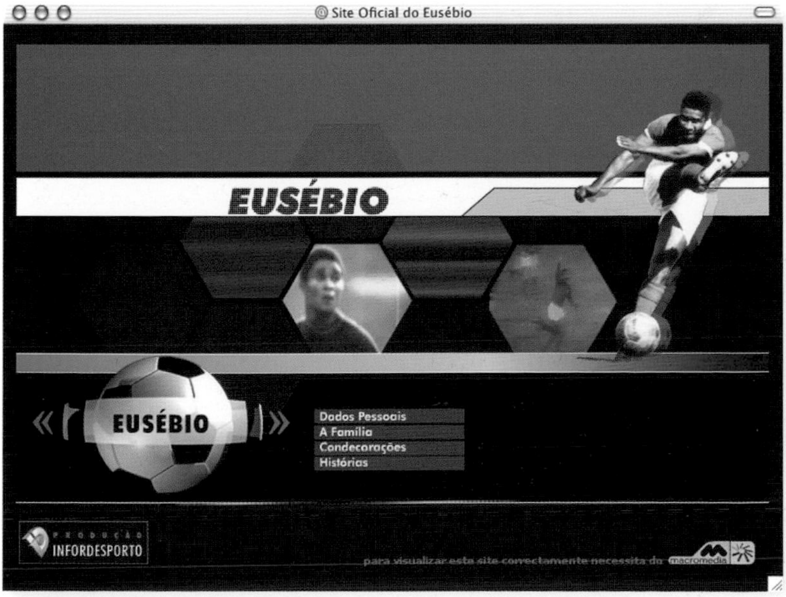

WWW.INFORDESPORTO.SAPO.PT/EUSEBIO/
D: ANA CARVALHO, **C:** HUGO RIBEIRO
A: IANA34, **M:** IANA34@NETCABO.PT

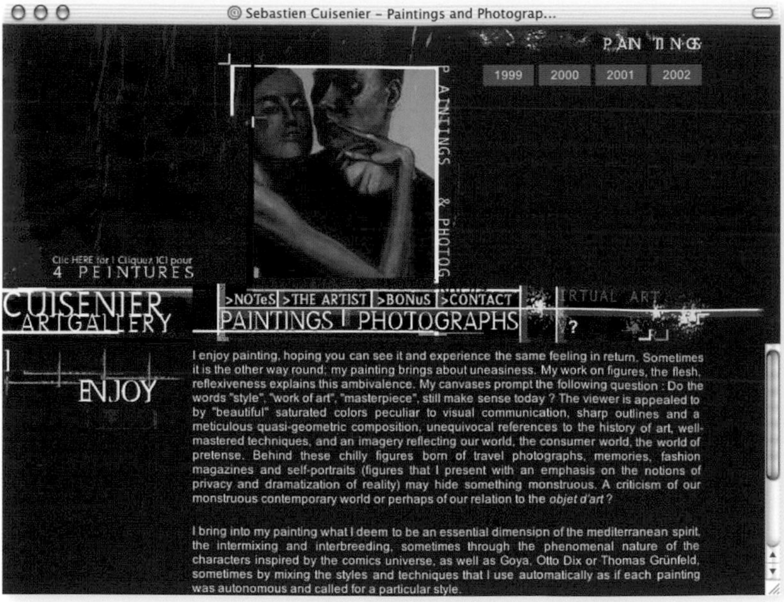

WWW.CUISENIER-ARTGALLERY.COM
D: SAM HAYLES, **C:** JULIEN MOREL, **P:** SEBASTIEN CUISENIER
A: DOSE-PRODUCTIONS, **M:** SAM@DOSE-PRODUCTIONS.COM

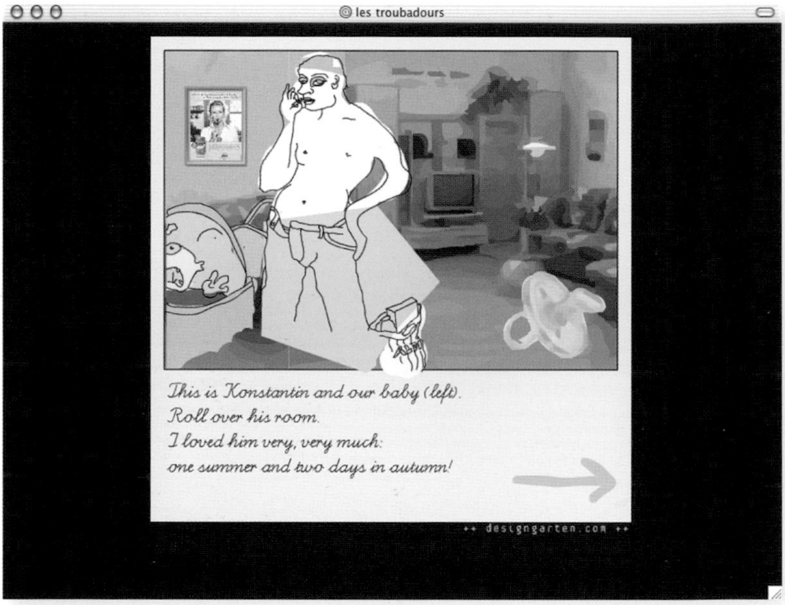

WWW.DESIGNGARTEN.DE
D: CONSTANZE VON GERSDORFF

WWW.BIZARREPUBLIC.COM
D: WILMA WOO WEISSMANN, **C:** RASTO JANKO, **P:** MAROS HECKO
A: EVOLUTION FATAL DIVISION

WWW.SASSINE.CH/HOCHZEIT
D: PATRICK SASSINE
A: ACCONCEPT, **M:** P.SASSINE@ACCONCEPT.CH

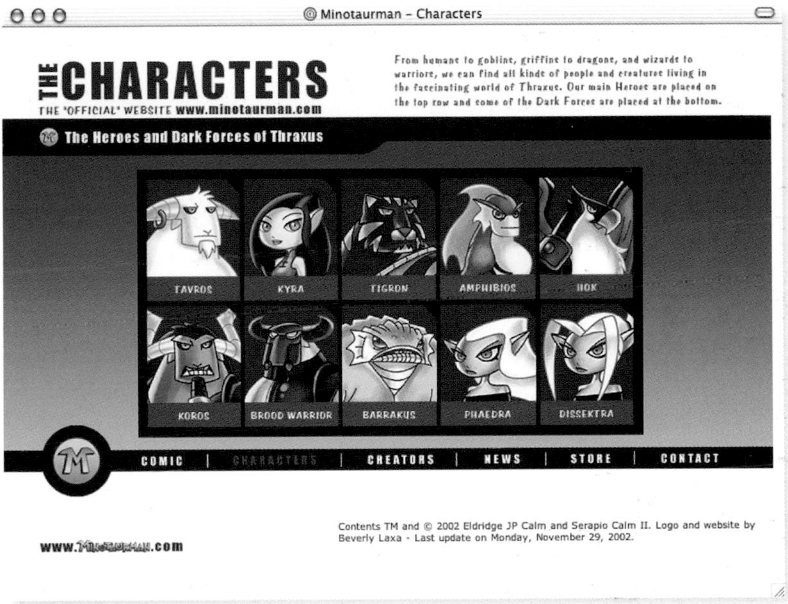

WWW.MINOTAURMAN.COM
D: BEVERLY LAXA
A: BEV-L DESIGN, **M:** BEVERLYLAXA@HOTMAIL.COM

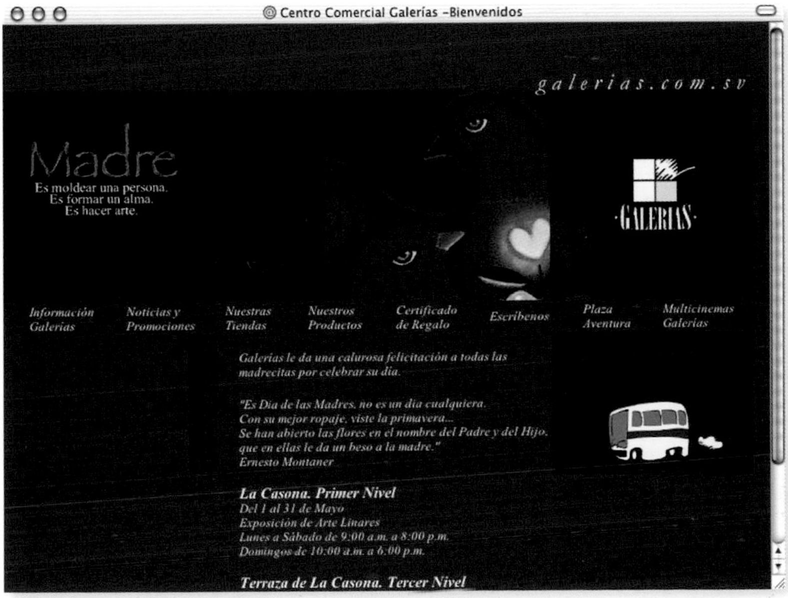

WWW.GALERIAS.COM.SV
D: ADRIAN HERNANDEZ, **C:** ADOLFO MATUS, **P:** GERARDO MEJIA
A: WEB INFORMATICA, **M:** RPALOMO@WEB-INFORMATICA.COM

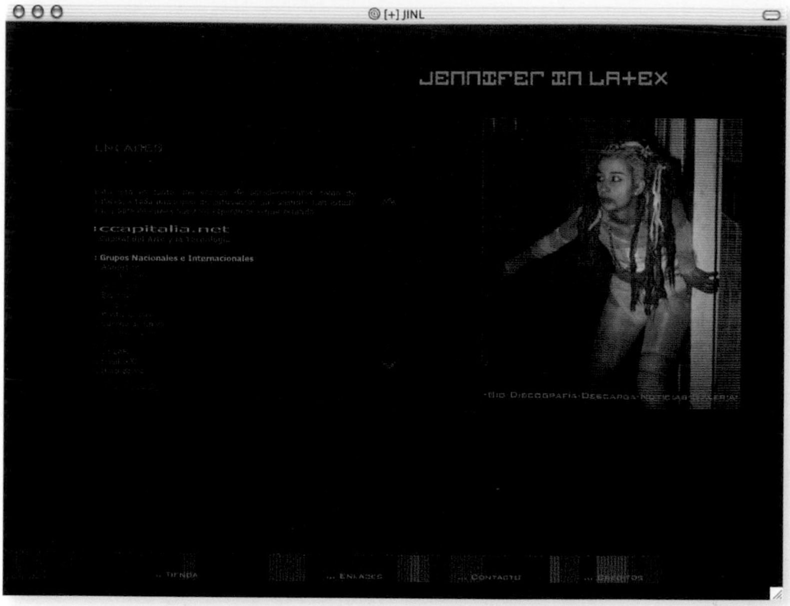

WWW.JENNIFERINLATEX.COM
D: CAROLINA ALCALÁ, **C:** ADOLFO GARCÍA
A: 2INWEB, **M:** CAROLINA@2INWEB.COM

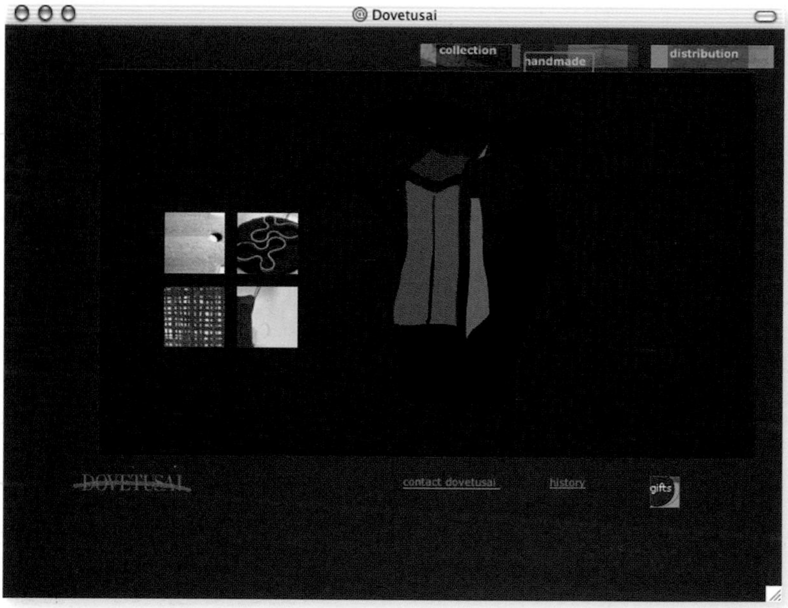

WWW.DOVETUSAI.IT
D: PAULA JUCHEM, **C:** DANIEL CANFIELD, **P:** PAULA JUCHEM
A: STUDIO TEIXEIRA SRL, **M:** DESIGN@PAULAJUCHEM.COM

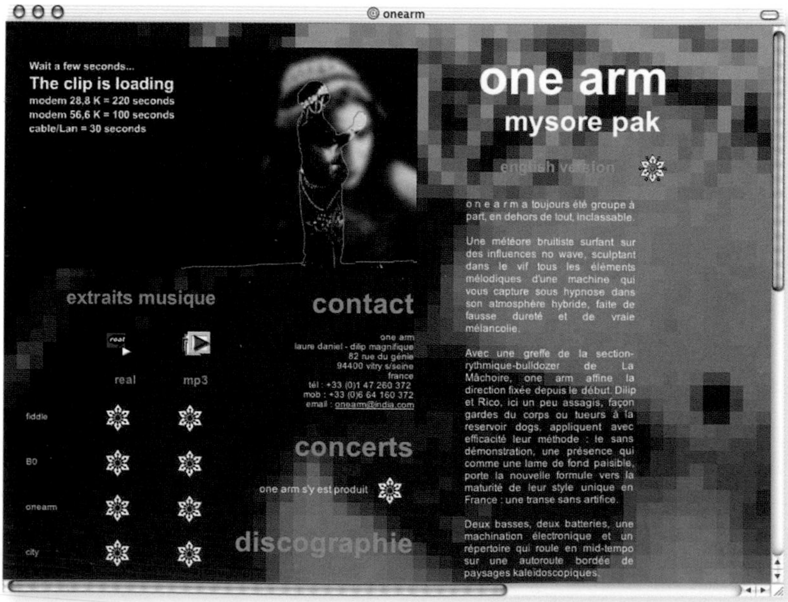

WWW.ONEARM.NET
D: OLIVIER VALLA
A: O-V-O

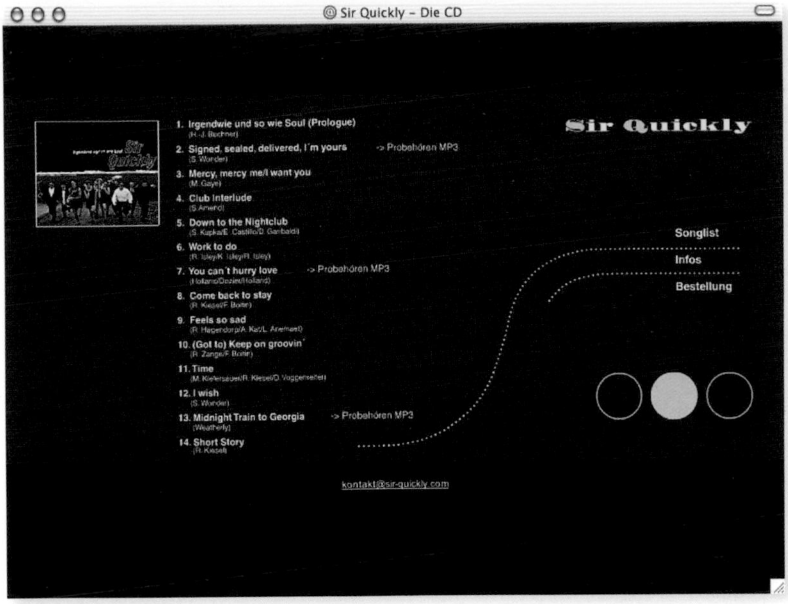

WWW.SIR-QUICKLY.COM
D: SEVERIN BRETTMEISTER
A: FA-RO MARKETING, **M:** SEVERIN@FA-RO.DE

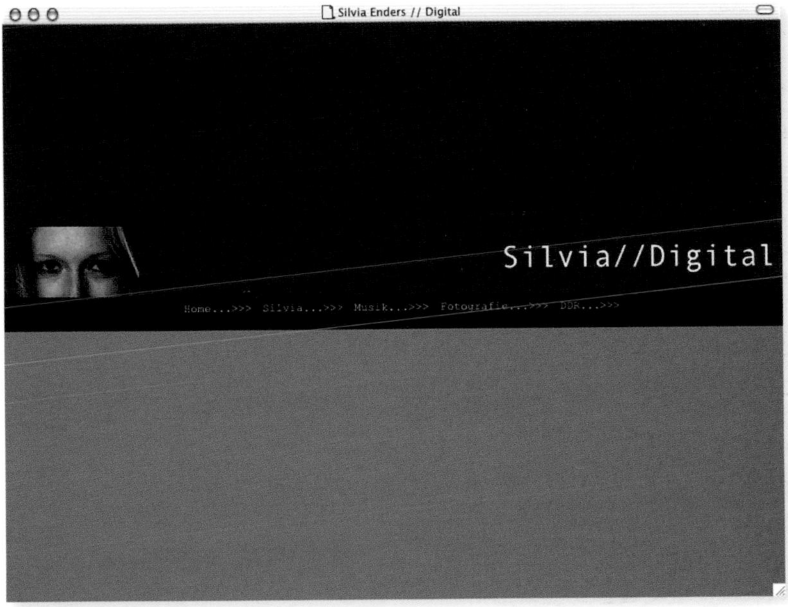

WWW.SILVIA-DIGITAL.DE
D: CLAUDIUS KONRAD
M: CK@CKONRAD.DE

WWW.MEMBERS.JCOM.HOME.NE.JP/NARAJIN/JAINA/ARTS.HTML
D: JIN NARA
M: NARAJIN@JCOM.HOME.NE.JP

WWW.DESIGNGARTEN.COM
D: CONSTANZE V. GERSDORFF
M: ROSINEN@WEB.DE

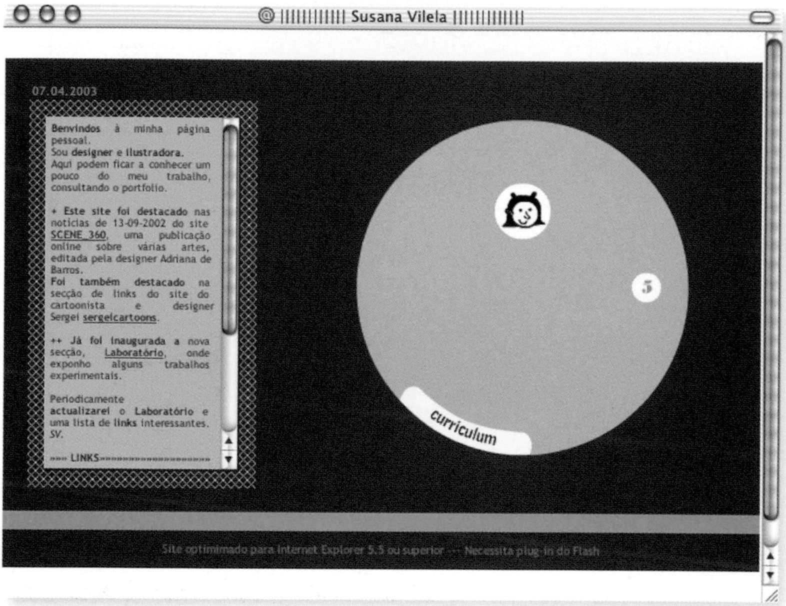

WWW.SUSANAVILELA.PLANETACLIX.PT
D: SUSANA VILELA
M: SUSANAVILELA@CLIX.PT

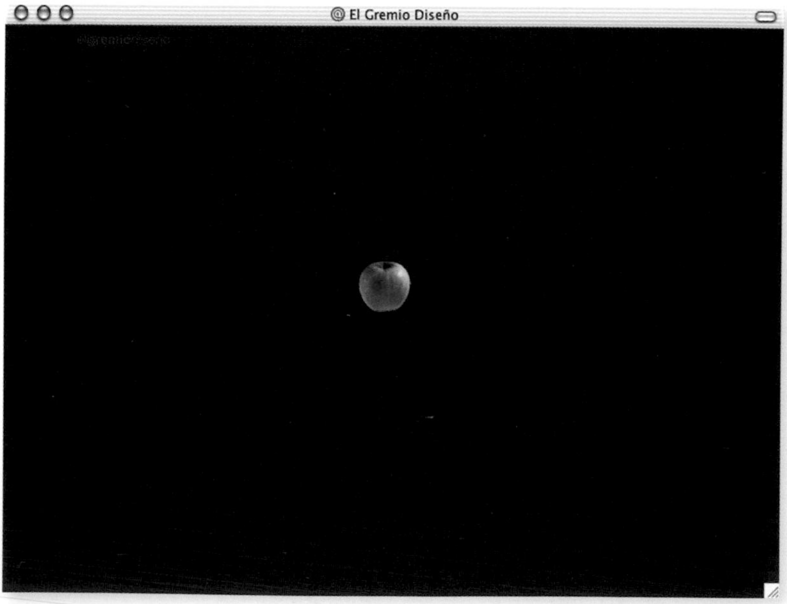

WWW.ELGREMIO.ORG
D: JUAN IGNACIO FLORES TARANCÓN, **C:** SILVIA DE NOVA, **P:** EL GREMIO DISEÑO
A: EL GREMIO DISEÑO, **M:** JUANFLORES@ELGREMIO.ORG

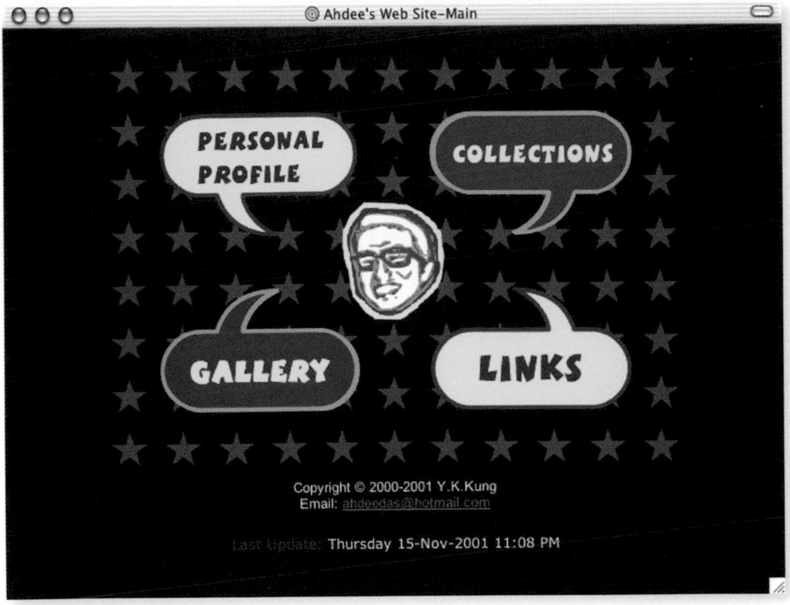

WWW.SABAH.NET.MY/AHDEEDAS
D: YK KUNG
M: AHDEEDAS@TM.NET.MY

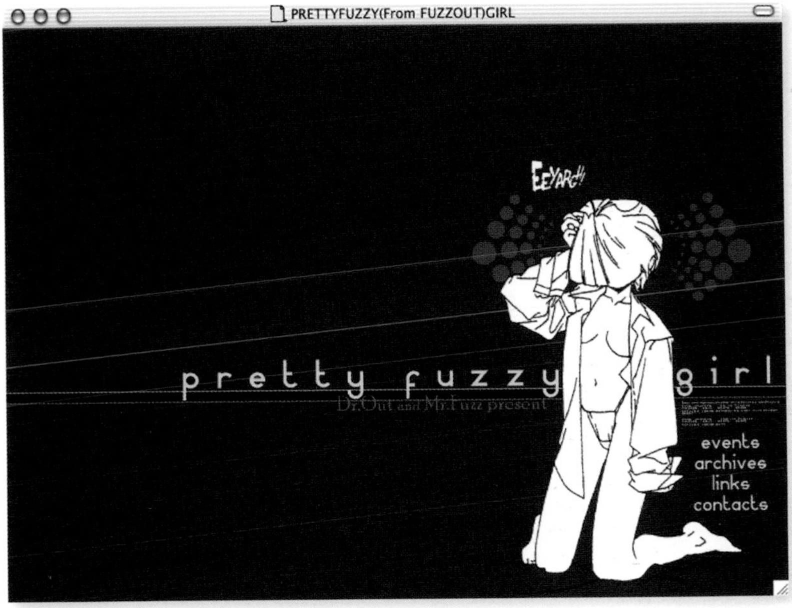

WWW.FUZZOUT.COM/2002/09_NOVEMBRE2002/_MAIN/INDEX.HTML
D: EMMANUEL BLONDEAU
M: MR.FUZZ@FUZZOUT.COM

WWW.YAMSPLAYGROUND.COM
D: JENS LOFBERG
M: JENSLOFBERG@WANADOO.FR

WWW.CMKARTING.COM
D: MAITE CAMACHO PÉREZ
A: ESTUDIO MAMÁS, **M:** MARIO@ESTUDIOMAMAS.COM

WWW.YAIKZ.NL
D: LEO HAMERS
A: YAIKZ!, **M:** INFO@YAIKZ.NL

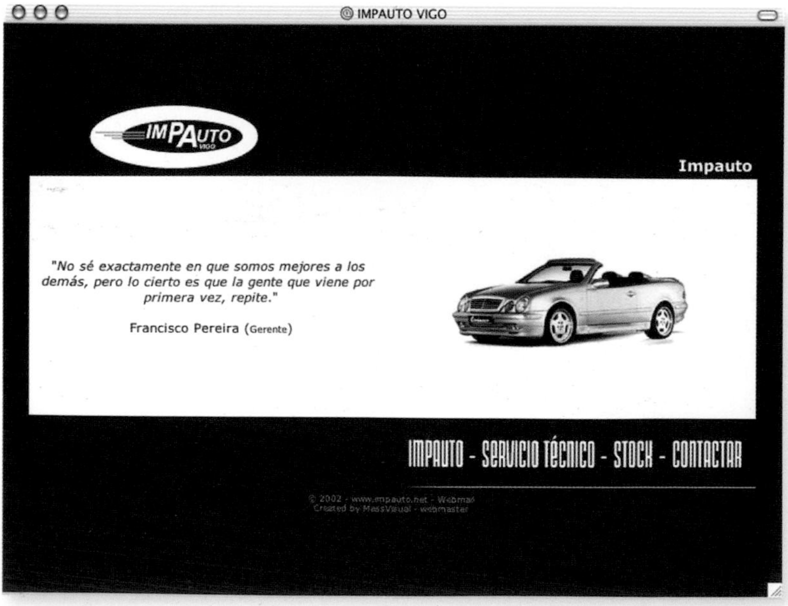

WWW.IMPAUTO.NET
D: TOTI MAGDALENA, **P:** ISAAC GONZÁLEZ
A: MASSVISUAL, **M:** GERENTE@MASSVISUAL.COM

WWW.TREKKING.DOLO-ALP.COM
D: SARA PÖRNBACHER
M: SARILE@GMX.NET

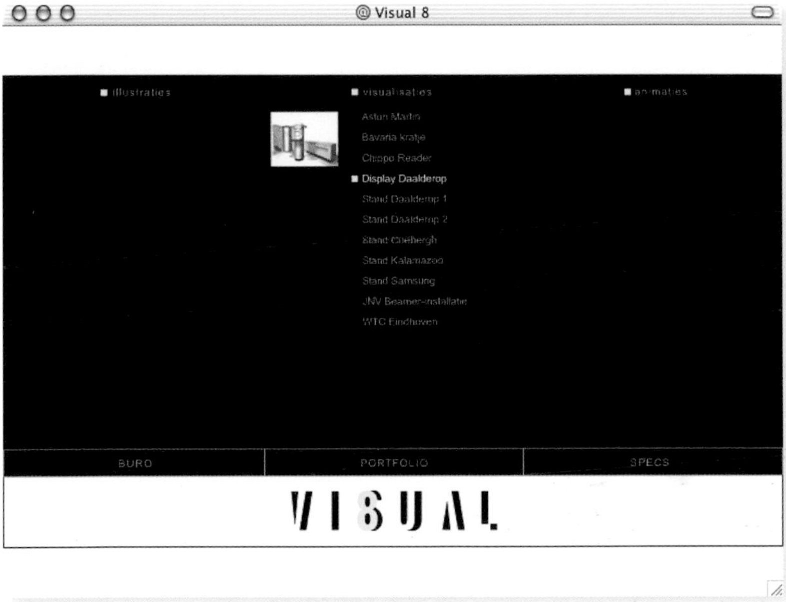

WWW.VISUAL8.NL
D: LEO HAMERS
A: YAIKZ!, **M:** INFO@YAIKZ.NL

WWW.PERTEMAD.COM
D: VANESA RUBIO, **C:** ALBERTO VICENTE, **P:** JESÚS VICENTE JORDANA
A: IDENET INTERNET & MULTIMEDIA CONSULTING S.L., **M:** JVICENTE@IDENET.NET

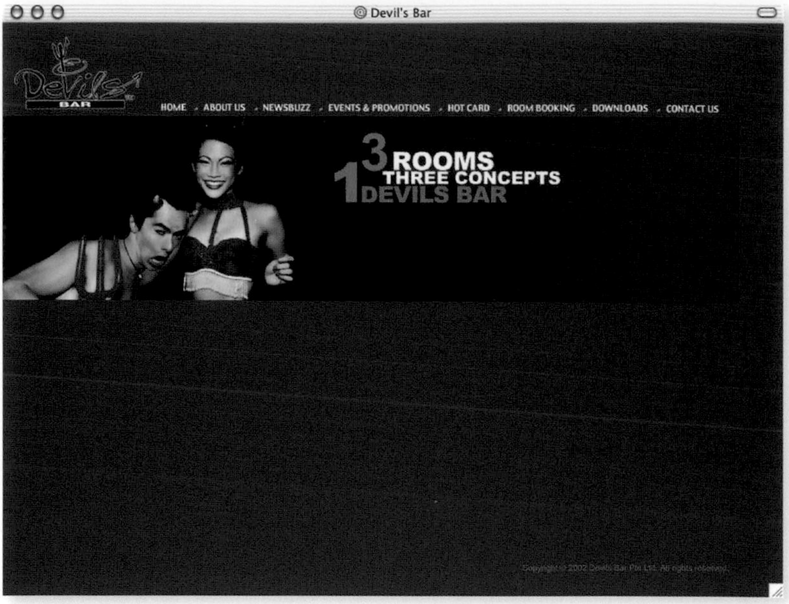

WWW.DEVILSBAR.COM.SG
D: PRESTON TAN, **C:** JESRINE LEE, **P:** PRESTON TAN
M: ESKIMOS@MAC.COM

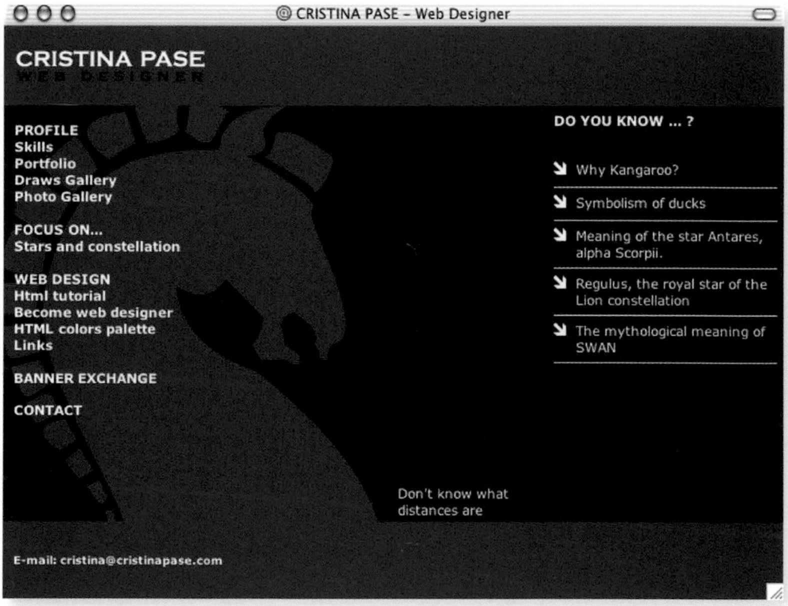

WWW.CRISTINAPASE.COM
D: CRISTINA PASE
M: CRISTINA@CRISTINAPASE.COM

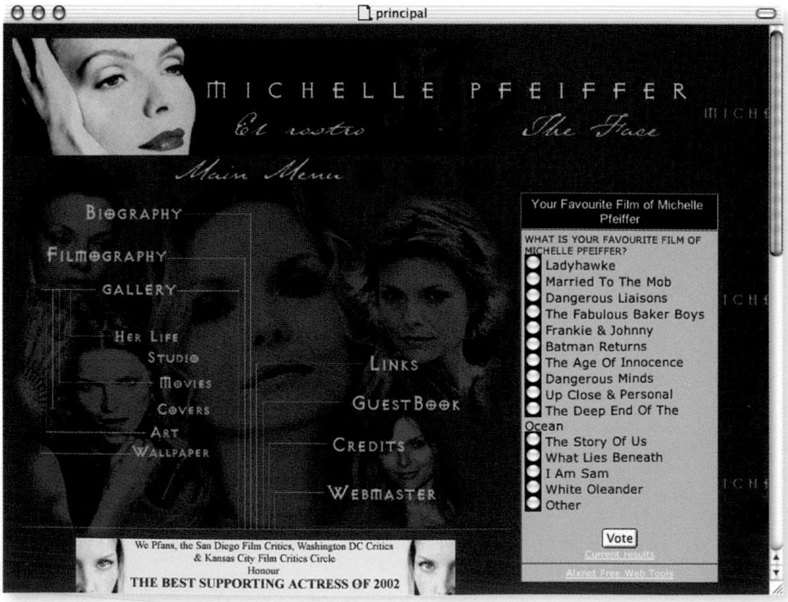

WWW.IESPANA.ES/PFEIFFER-THEFACE
D: FRANCISCO GONZALEZ SANCHEZ
M: DANGERART25@HOTMAIL.COM

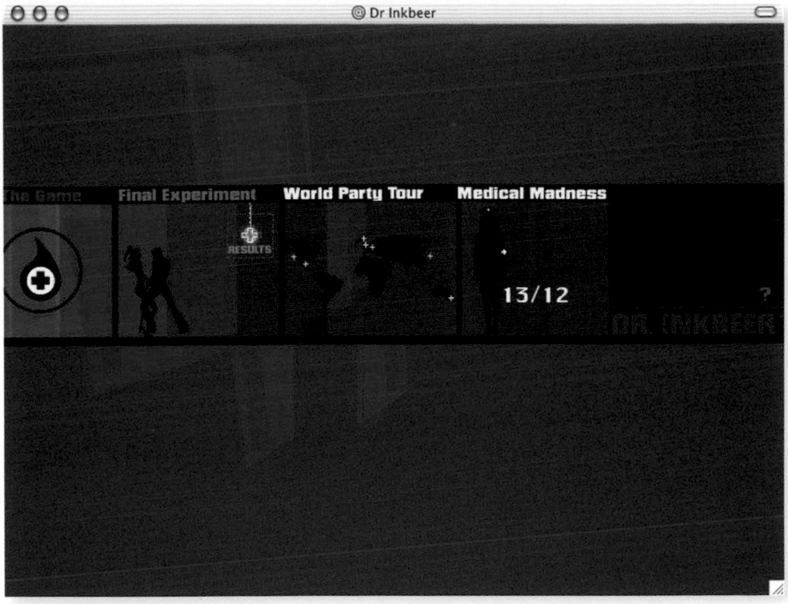

WWW.DR-INKBEER.COM
D: JEN BOXER, WINNE LOH, **C:** ANDY NAYLOR
A: EURORSCG, **M:** JEN@BOXERCOX.COM

WWW.CREATYPE.NL
D: LEENHEER, **C:** NIELS
A: CREATYPE, **M:** STUDIO@CREATYPE.NL

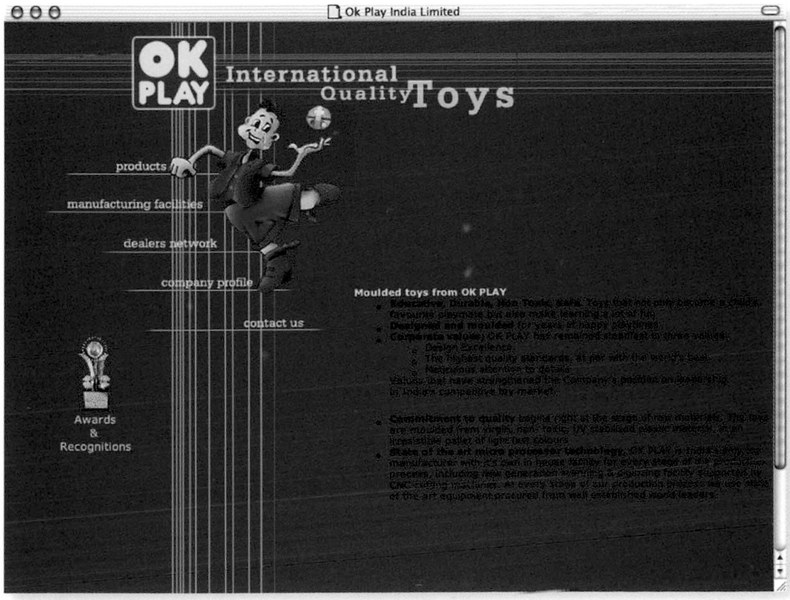

WWW.OKPLAYINDIA.COM
D: MANOJ MAURYA, **C:** MANOJ MAURYA, **P:** OK PLAY INDIA PVT. LTD.
A: PIXEL2PIXEL, **M:** PIXEL2PIXEL@REDIFFMAIL.COM

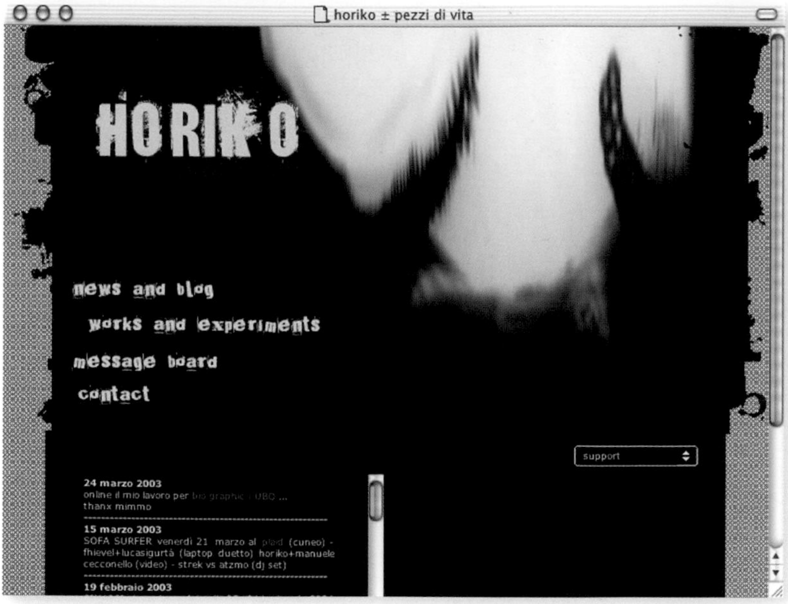

WWW.HORIKO.ORG/LAYOUT.HTM
D: DAVIDE BERNARDI
M: INFO@HORIKO.ORG

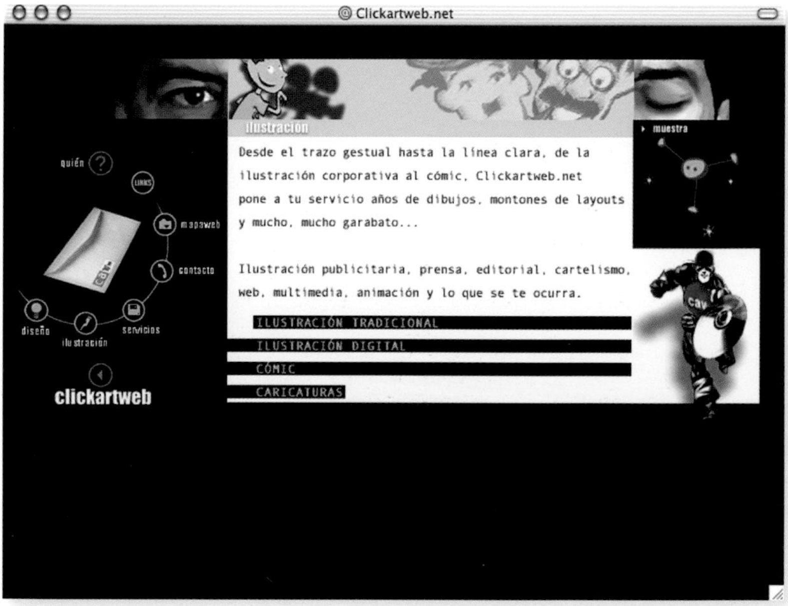

WWW.CLICKARTWEB.NET
D: CARLOS PARAMOS
A: CLICKARTWEB, **M:** CARLOS@CLICKARTWEB.NET

WWW.SPAZIOINWIND.LIBERO.IT/KIXARTS
D: LUIGI PANTUSA
A: KIXART'S, **M:** LUIGIPANTUSA@INWIND.IT

WWW.LEPIANISTE-LEFILM.COM
D: NICOLAS DELAPLACE
A: MATYS, **M:** WWW.LEPIANISTE-LEFILM.COM

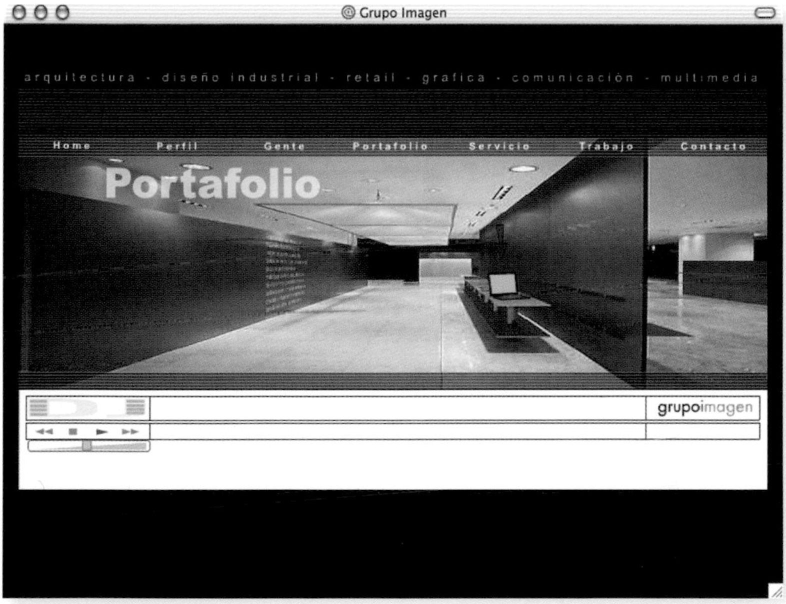

WWW.GRUPOIMAGEN.CL
D: ALVARO CALDERA, **C:** JORDI NIETO, **P:** ALVARO CALDERA
A: GRUPOIMAGEN, **M:** ACALDERA@GRUPOIMAGEN.CL

WWW.HOMODIGITALIS.COM
D: BERNARDO RIVAVELARDE, **C:** LUIS HERRERO & BELÉN GARCÍA, **P:** LUIS HERRERO
A: CON MEDIA LAB, **M:** LUISO2K@HOTMAIL.COM

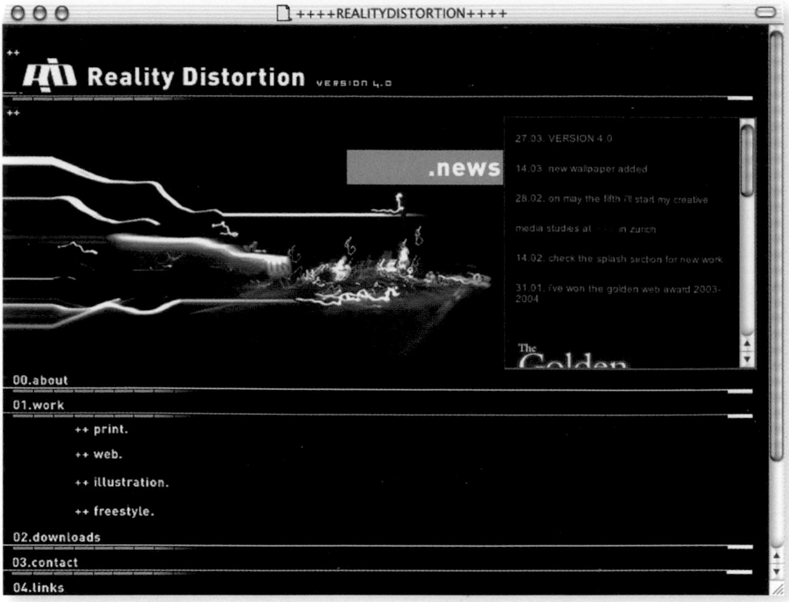

WWW.REALITYDISTORTION.CH
D: ALESSANDRO MATTARELLI
M: MATTARELLI@REALITYDISTORTION.CH

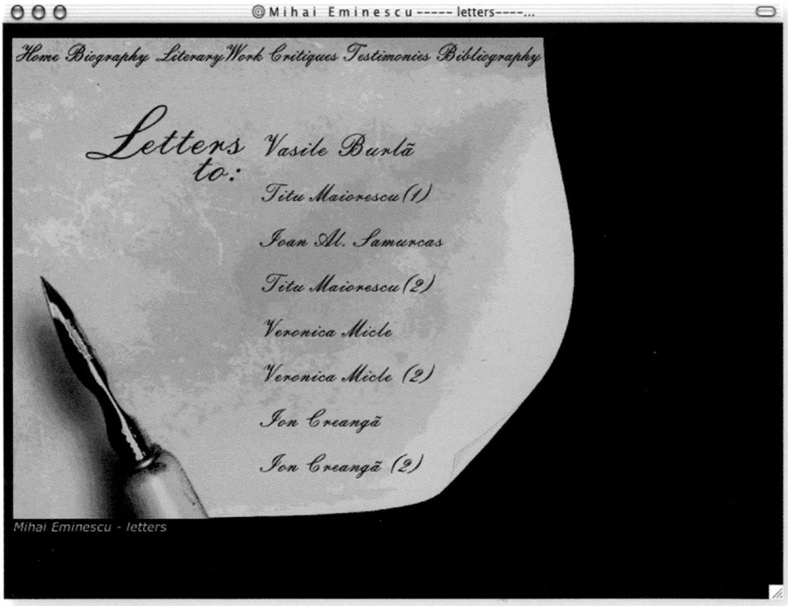

WWW.MIHAIEMINESCU.RO
D: CATALIN ILINCA, **C:** ITC ROMANIA, **P:** LIBRA CULTURAL FOUNDATION
A: MEDIA9, **M:** OFFICE@MEDIA9.RO

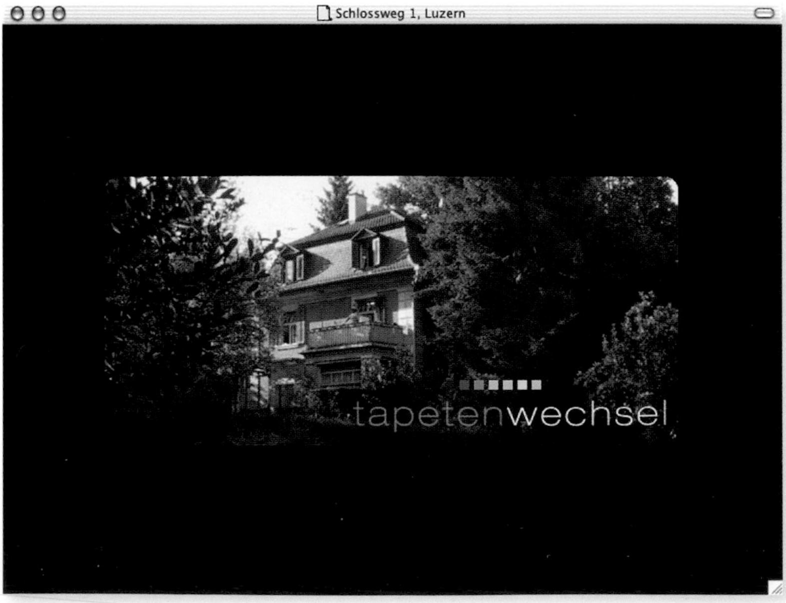

WWW.SCHLOSSWEG.COM
D: PETER ULRICH
A: NEXUS - CREATIVE COMPANY, **M:** INFO@NCC.CH

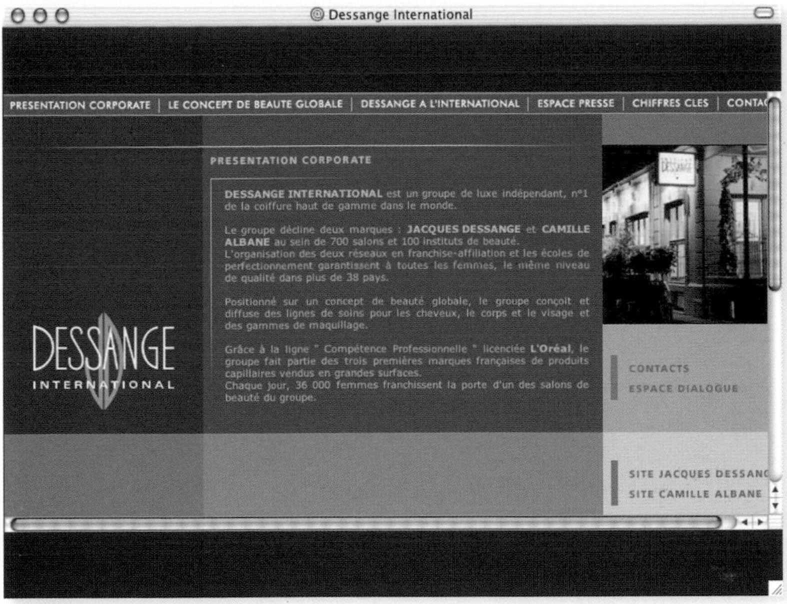

WWW.DESSANGE-INTERNATIONAL.COM
D: COSTARD HUGO
A: IDEA COMMUNICATION, **M:** REF@IDEA-COMMUNICATION.COM

WWW.AFAR4.COM
D: JUAN ALBERTO GARCÍA DE CUBAS, CARLOS NAVALÓN CASADO **C:** D. SÁNCHEZ CASADO
M: DSANCHEZ@AFI.ES

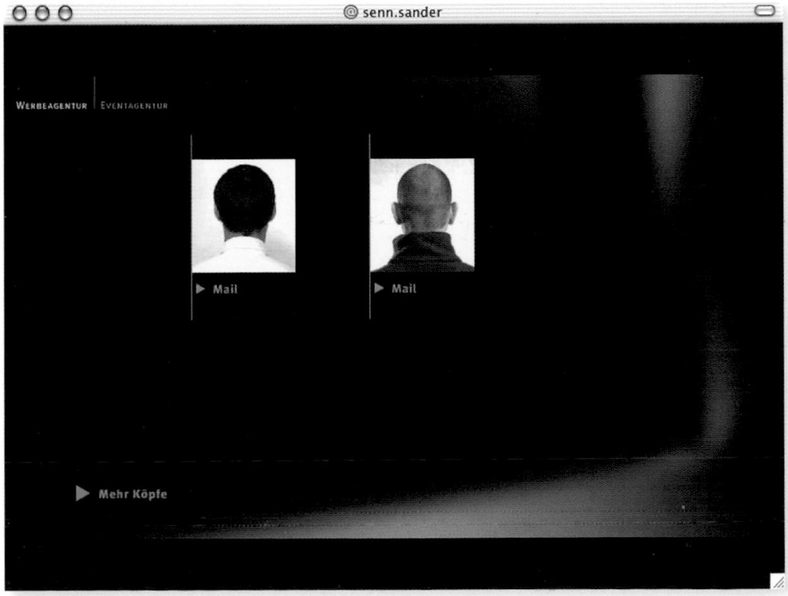

WWW.SENNSANDER.DE
D: ULRIKE BUNK, **P:** ELECTRIC UMBRELLA
A: SENN.SANDER WERBEAGENTUR, **M:** BUNK@SENNSANDER.DE

WWW.CONTDIV.COM
D: MIKE HEADLEY
M: MIKE@CONTDIV.COM

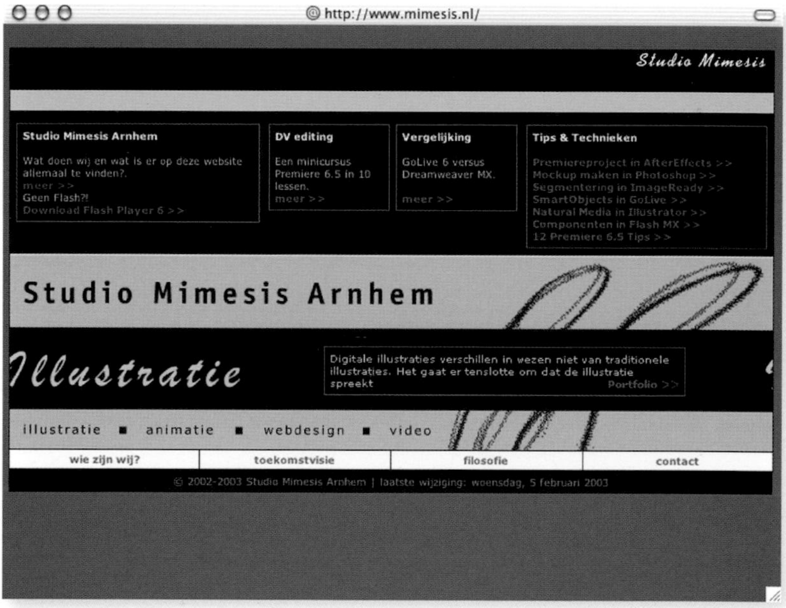

WWW.MIMESIS.NL
D: HENK VAN DEN HEUVEL
M: MIMESIS@CHELLO.NL

WWW.SIMBOLOSDELPODER.CENTROAFFARIAREZZO.IT/INDEX2.HTML
D: GIAN PIETRO DRINGOLI, **C:** TAVANTI, **P:** CENTRO AFFARI AREZZO
A: GRAPHIC DESIGN - DRINGOLI, **M:** INFO@GIANPIETRODRINGOLI.COM

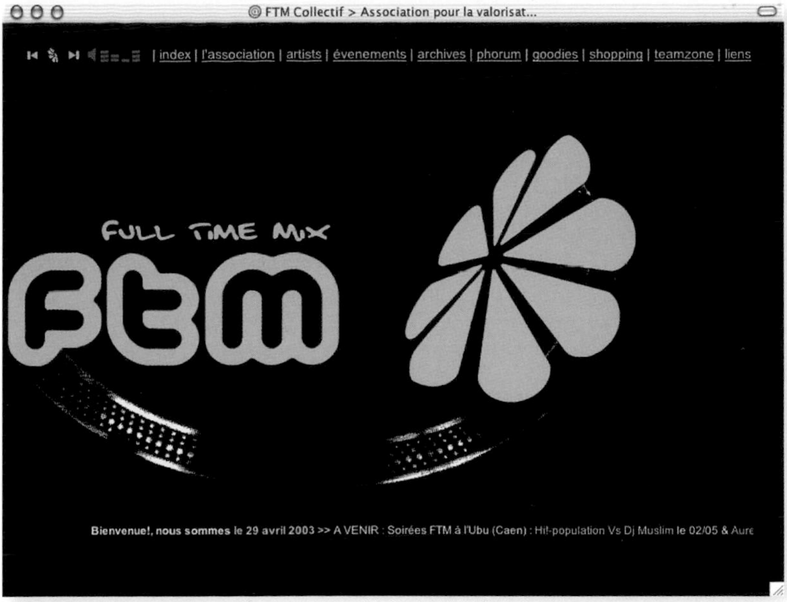

WWW.FTMCOLLECTIF.ORG
D: UGO QUAISSE
M: UGO.QUAISSE@LAPOSTE.NET

WWW.MODERNE-REKLAME.DE
D: GABI MUELLER, KARL MUELLER
A: MODERNE REKLAME, **M:** INFO@MODERNE-REKLAME.DE

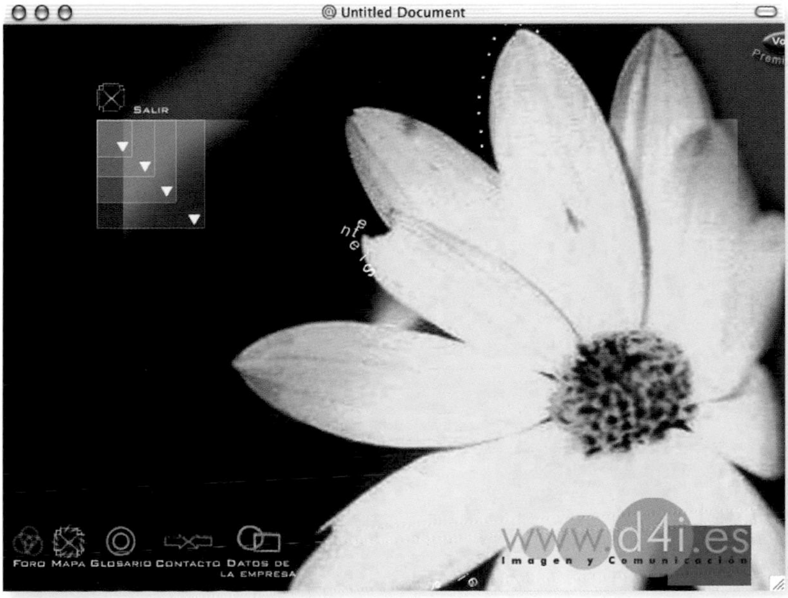

WWW.D4I.ES
D: ARANTZAZU BAYON, **C:** ANTONIO MUÑOZ, **P:** ESTIBALITZ BAYON
A: D4 IMAGEN Y COMUNICACIÓN, **M:** A_BAYON@D4I.ES

WWW.EALMINAR.COM
D: CARLOS ZARAGOZA KOBLISCHEK
A: PLENUMWEB, **M:** INFO@PLENUMWEB.COM

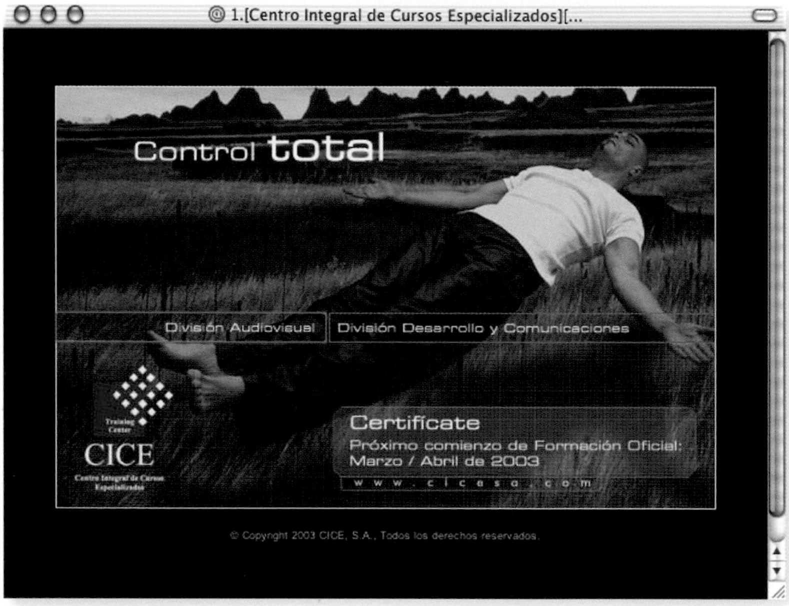

WWW.CICESA.COM
D: JORGE ARBOLEYA Y NANCY PORZIO, **C:** JORGE ARBOLEYA, **P:** MARCO A. FERNÁNDEZ
M: J.ARBOLEYA@ARTERALIA.COM

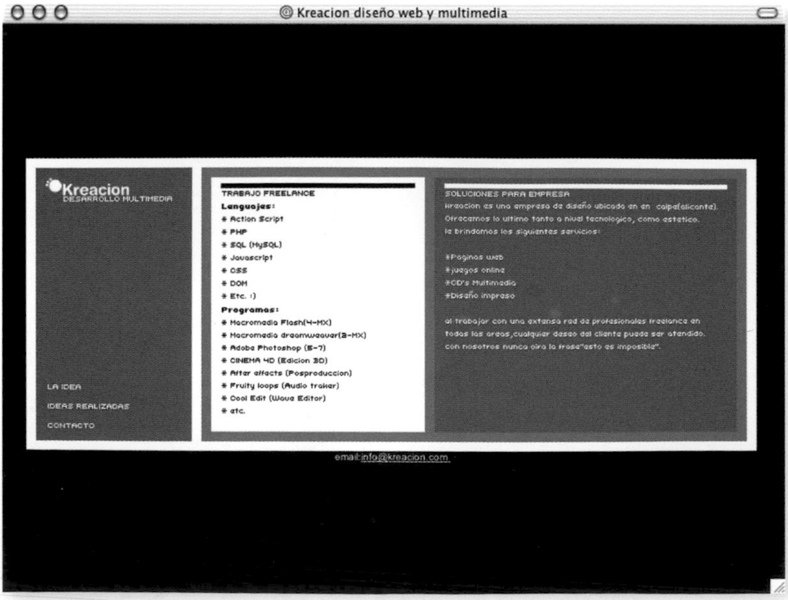

WWW.KREACION.COM
D: MIGUEL HAHN
A: KREACION, **M:** INFO@KREACION.COM

WWW.COCA-COLA.NL/DANCE
D: JURRIAAN VAN BOKHOVEN / ROEL TER VOORT, **C:** NEIL YOUNG, **P:** BREGO KELLER
A: CLOCKWORK, **M:** JURRIAAN@CLOCKWORK.NL

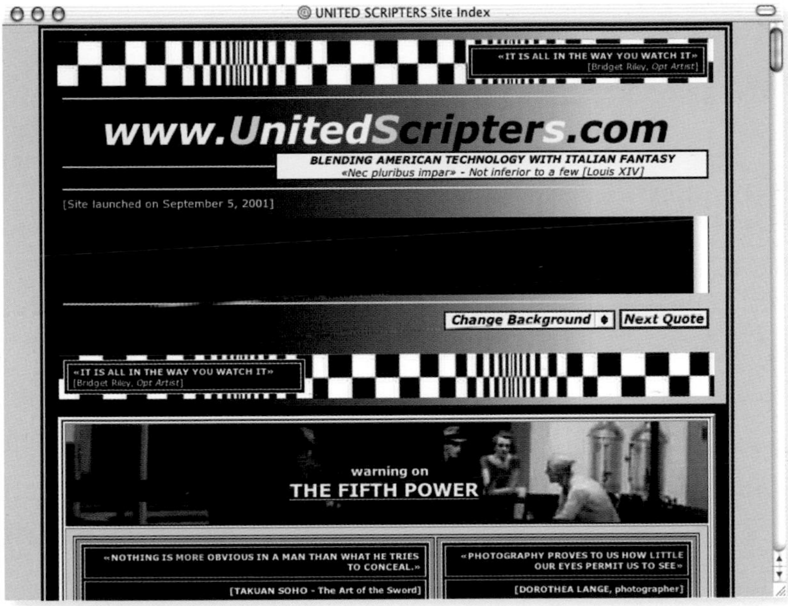

WWW.UNITEDSCRIPTERS.COM/LIST.HTML
D: ALBERTO VALLINI
A: UNITEDSCRIPTERS, **M:** WEBMASTER@UNITEDSCRIPTERS.COM

WWW.LUCACASADEI.IT
D: DANIELE PASCERINI, **P:** ENDURANCE S.R.L.
A: FISHANDCHIPS, **M:** DANIELE@FISHANDCHIPS.IT

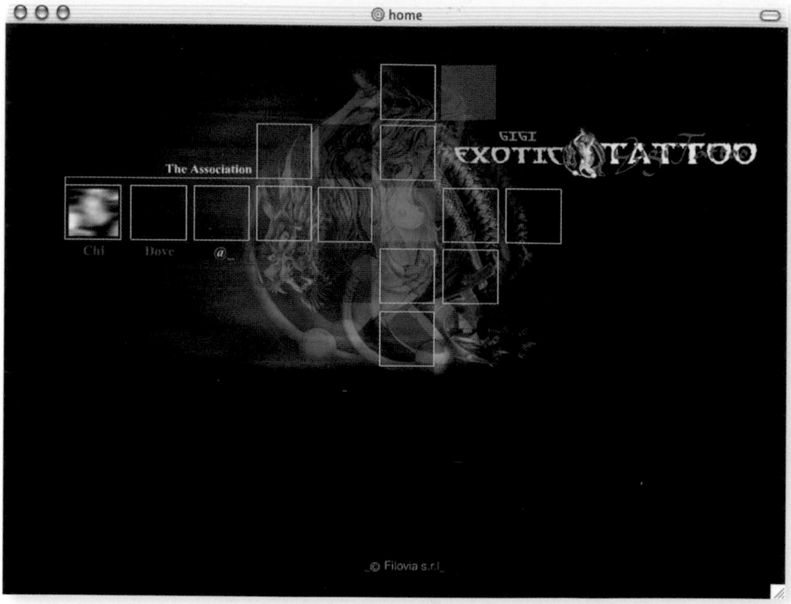

WWW.GIGITATTOO.IT
D: ALESSANDRO CIRILLO
A: AGENZIA PUBBL. FILOVIAS.R.L., **M:** ALESFLY@TISCALINET.IT

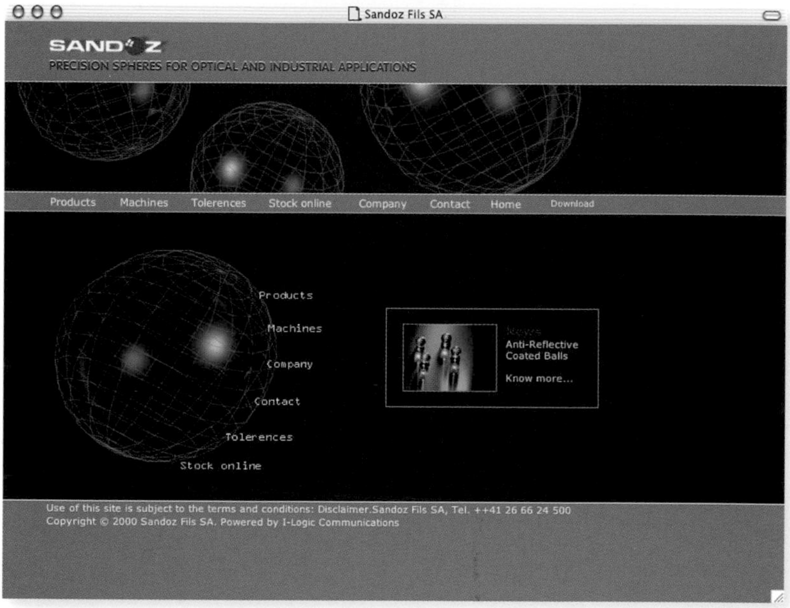

WWW.SANDOZ.CH
D: J.FREIBURGHAUS
A: I-LOGIC COMMUNICATONS, **M:** JF@I-LOGIC.CH

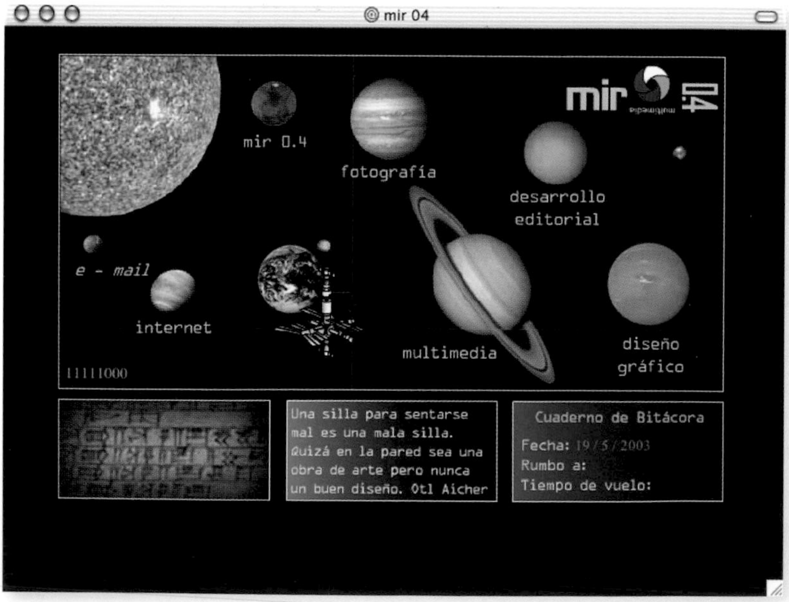

WWW.MIR04.COM
D: MÉNDEZ MARCOS
A: MIR04 MULTIMEDIA, **M:** MIR04@MIR04.COM

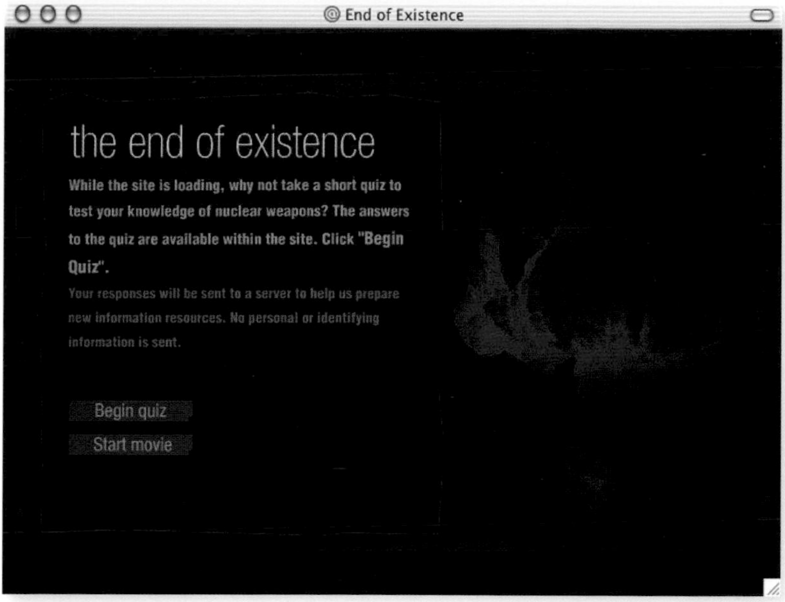

WWW.ENDOFEXISTENCE.ORG
D: TONY KE
M: KEONE@KEICON.COM

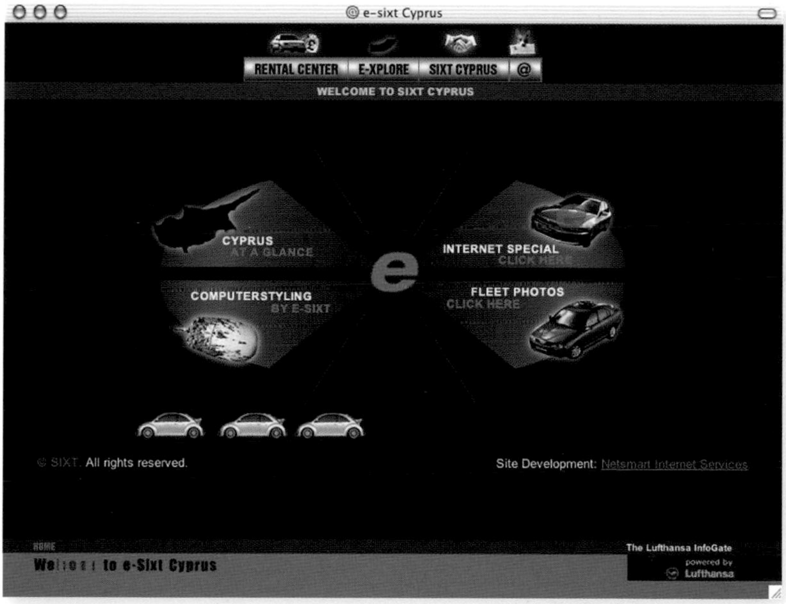

WWW.SIXT.COM.CY
D: RICHARD LIAN
A: NETSMART, **M:** INFO@LIAN.BIZ

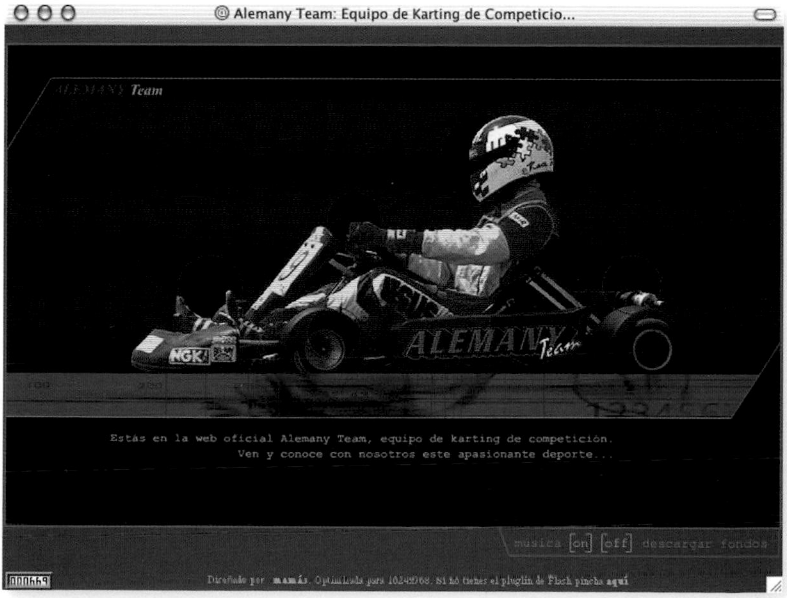

WWW.ALEMANYTEAM.COM
D: MAITE CAMACHO PÉREZ, **C:** MARIO GUTIÉRREZ
A: ESTUDIO MAMÁS, **M:** MAITE@ESTUDIOMAMAS.COM

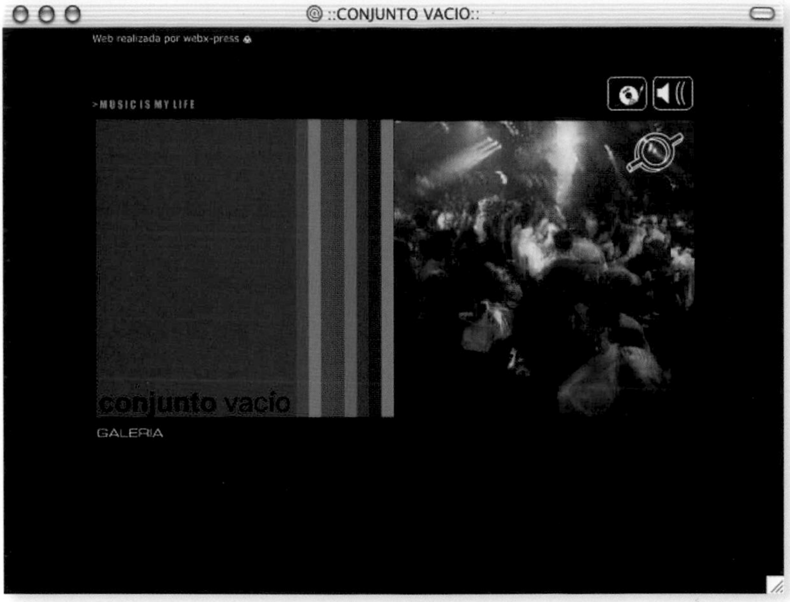

WWW.CONJUNTOVACIO.NET
D: GONZALO ESTEBAN
A: WEBX-PRESS, **M:** WEBX-PRESS@WANADOO.ES

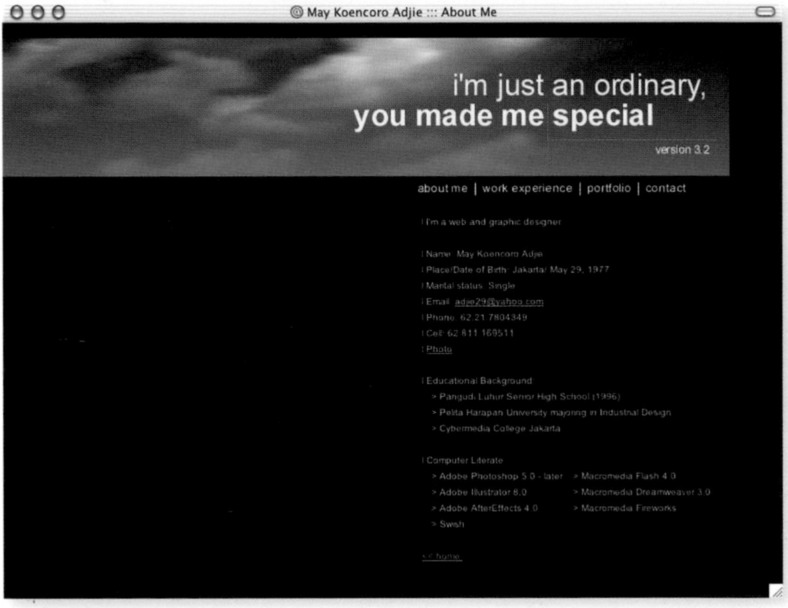

WWW.GEOCITIES.COM/ADJIE29
D: MAY KOENCORO ADJIE
A: ADJIEWEBFOLIO, **M:** ADJIEWEBFOLIO@HOTMAIL.COM

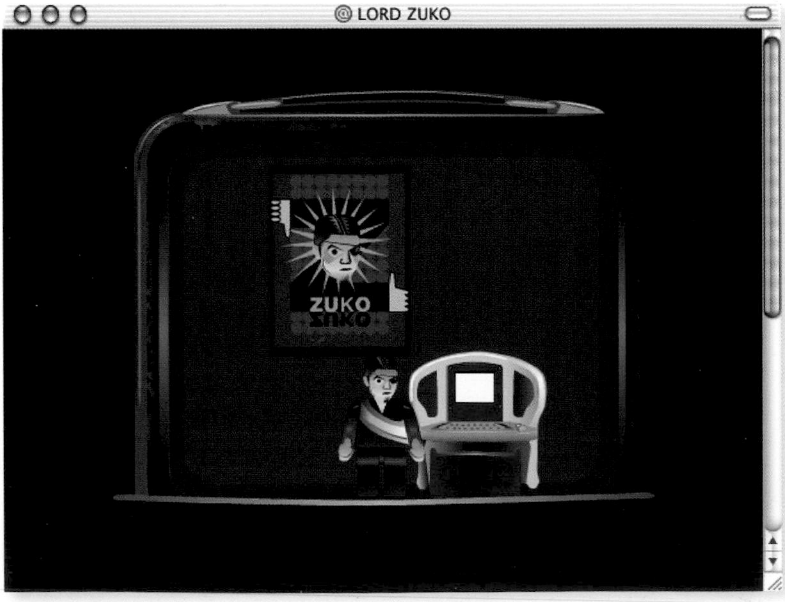

WWW.LORDZUKO.COM.AR
D: LUCIO PALETTA, **P:** GABRIEL LICHTMANN - ALEJANDRO ZUCCO
M: CANDIDATO@LORDZUKO.COM.AR

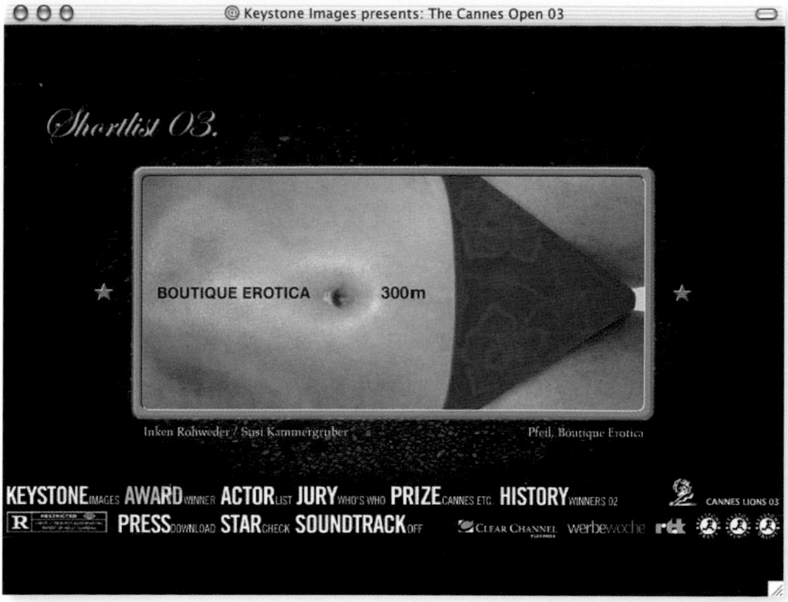

WWW.CANNES-OPEN.CH
D: MARC RINDERKNECHT
A: JUNG VON MATT/LIMMAT AG, **M:** MARC.RINDERKNECHT@JVM.CH

WWW.HOTELARCOVEGGIO.IT
D: ANTONELLO COGHE
A: RADIO TIME SRL, **M:** ANTONELLO@FASHIONFM.IT

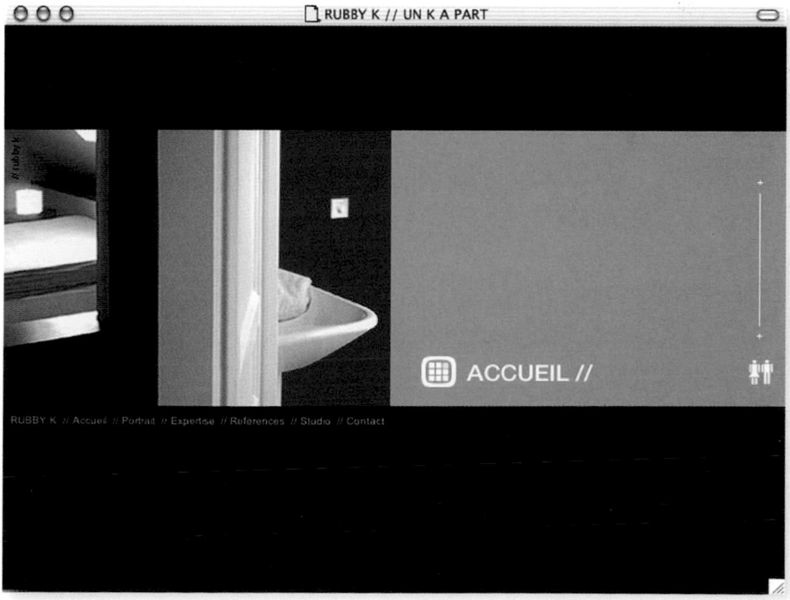

WWW.RUBBYK.COM
D: MICKEAL JAMET, **C:** NICOLAS LAIGNEL
A: RUBBY K, **M:** NICOLAS@XLTOUCH.COM

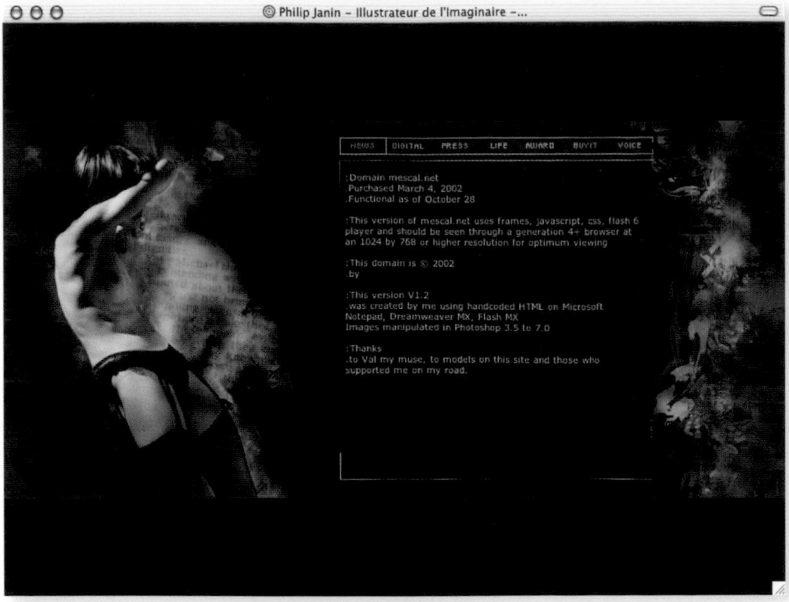

WWW.MESCAL.NET/MAIN/INDEXFRAME.HTML
D: PHILIP JANIN
A: MESCAL Y TEQUILA, **M:** PHILIP@GRAPHIKILLERS.COM

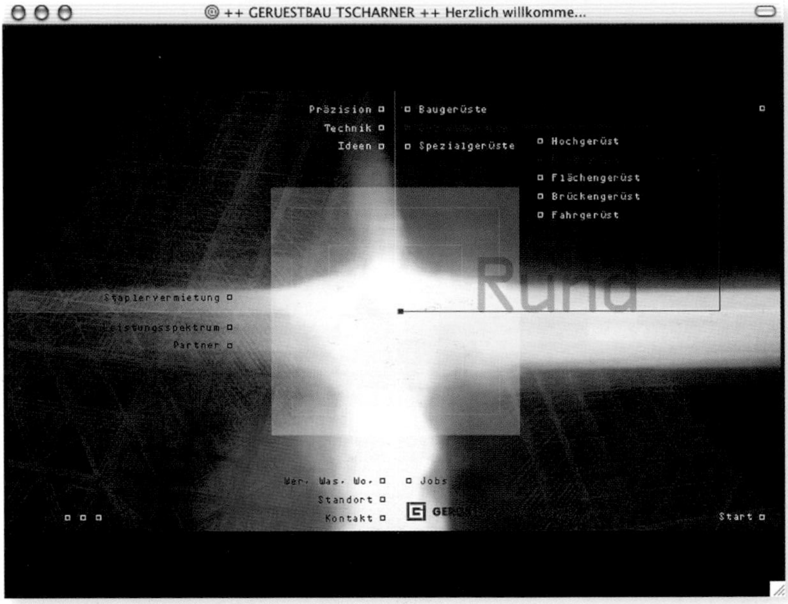

WWW.GERUESTBAU-TSCHARNER.CH
D: ERIK SÜSSKIND, **C:** MARTIN FRICK, **P:** SÜSSKIND SGD CHUR
A: SÜSSKIND SGD CHUR, **M:** SGD@SUESSKIND.CH

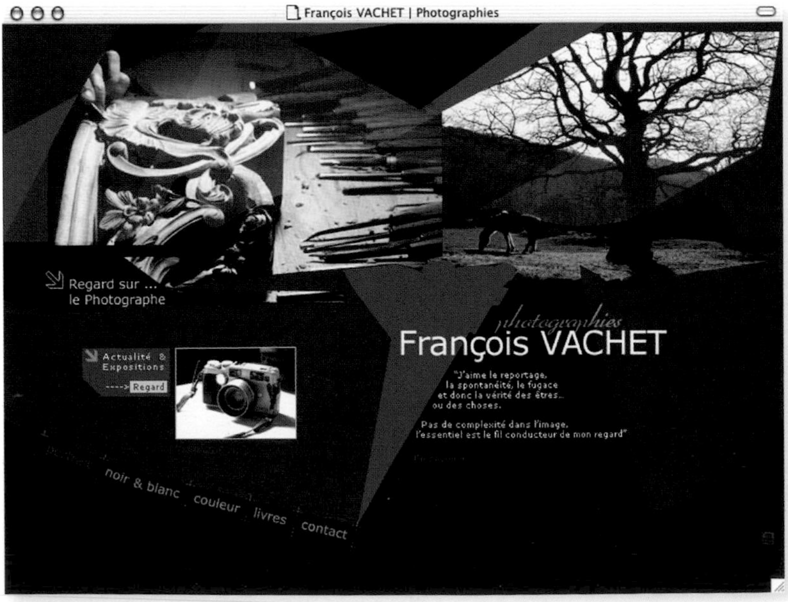

WWW.REGARD-PHOTO.COM
D: STEPHANE SEGURA
A: ACTIVELAB, **M:** CONTACT@ACTIVELAB.NET

WWW.MIRNET.COM.MY
D: EUGENE FOO
A: MIRNET, **M:** FOOJINYEN@MIRNET.COM.MY

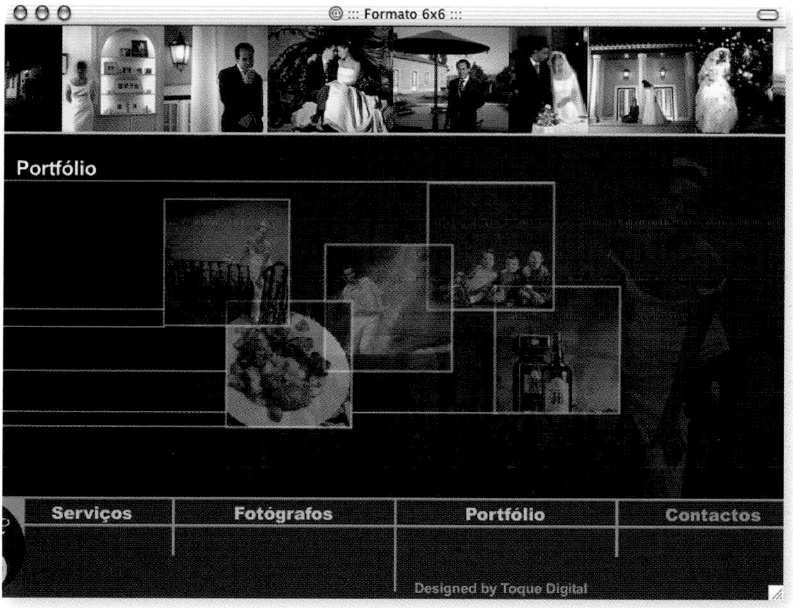

WWW.FORMATO6X6.COM
D: FLAVIO SERRA GRANJA
A: TOQUE DIGITAL, **M:** TOQUE@TOQUEDIGITAL.COM

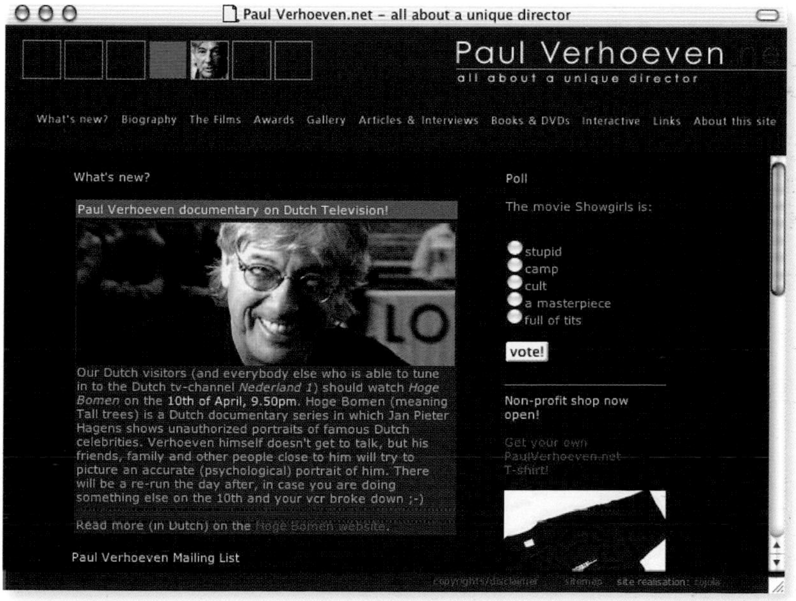

WWW.PAULVERHOEVEN.NET
D: ROBIN AKA ROJOLA
A: ROJOLA DESIGN, **M:** ROJOLA@PAULVERHOEVEN.NET

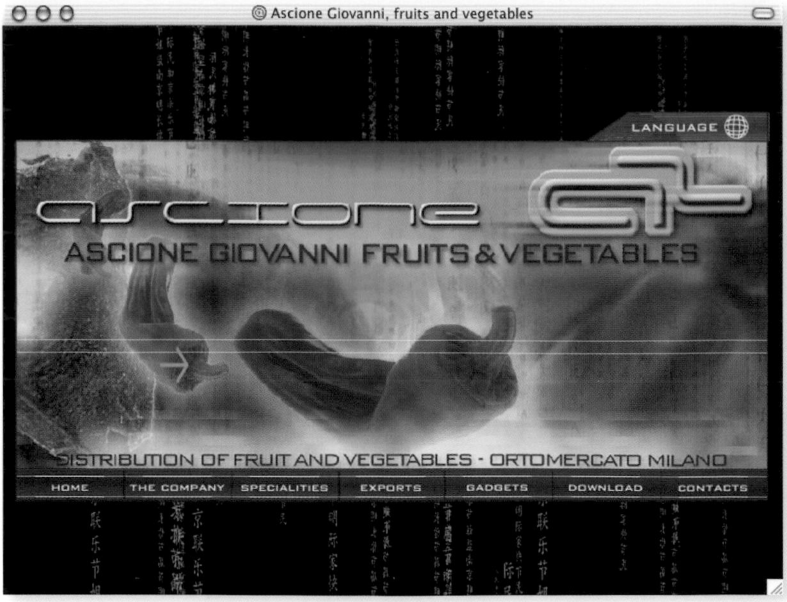

WWW.ASCIONE.BIZ/INGLESE/HOME.HTML
D: MARIO DONADONI, **C:** MASSIMILIANO LO PORCHIO, **P:** GIOVANNI ASCIONE
A: NITENS, **M:** INFO@NITENS.COM

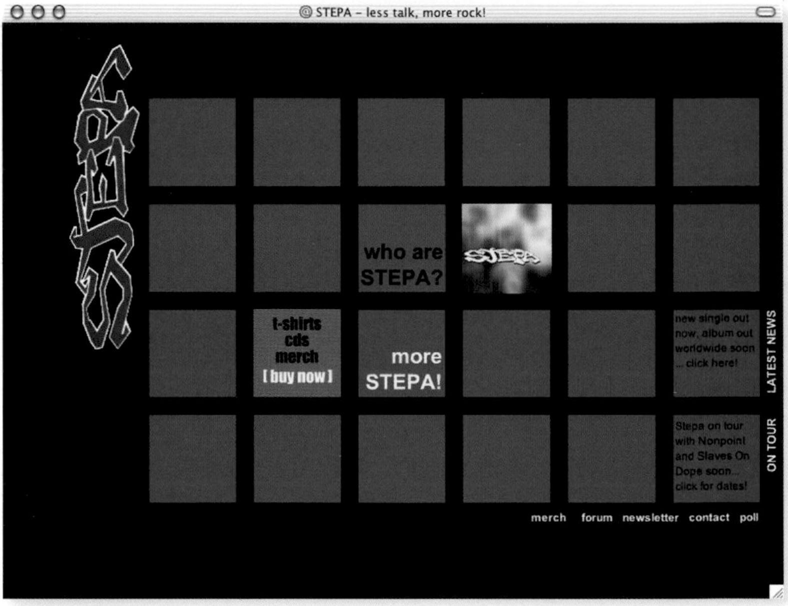

WWW.STEPAMUSIC.COM
D: ERIK DANIELS
M: SALTYSHIT@STEPA2.COM

WWW.CRISTAL.CL
D: FLAVIO PARRA, **C:** GUILLERMO PEREZ, **P:** JUAN SALDIVAR
A: PROMOPLAN S.A, **M:** FPARRA@PROMOPLAN.CL

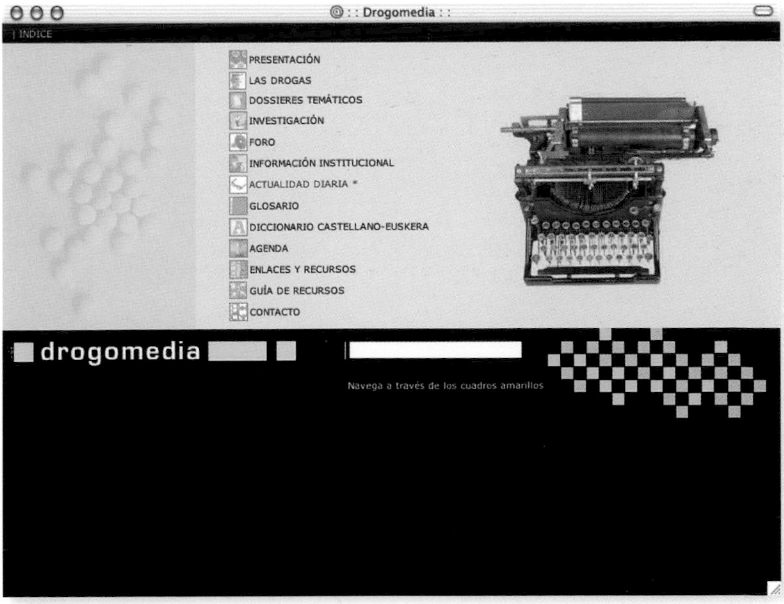

WWW.DROGOMEDIA.COM
D: IKER MICHELENA BARRIO
A: ENTREWEBS, **M:** IMITXELENA@ENTREWEBS.COM

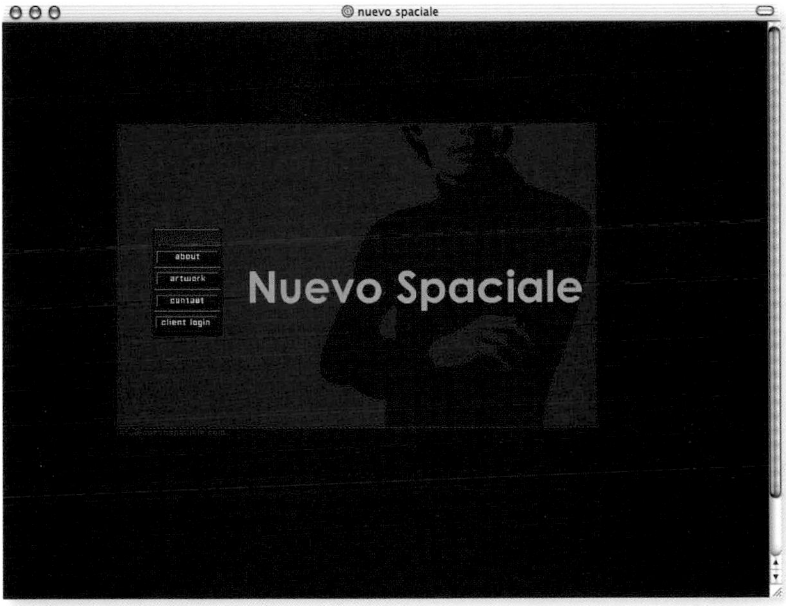

WWW.NUEVOSPACIALE.COM
D: DERK VAN REES, **C:** DERK VAN REES, **P:** ELSBETH LEUPEN
A: NUEVO SPACIALE, **M:** SPACIALE@XS4ALL.NL

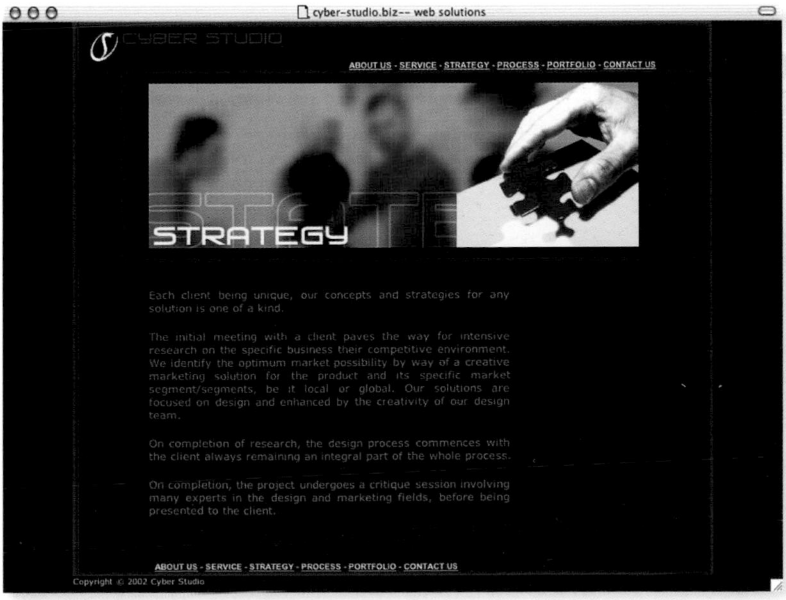

WWW.CYBER-STUDIO.BIZ
D: CYBERSTUDIO TEAM
A: CYBERSTUDIO TEAM, **M:** SADNESSAJ@YAHOO.COM

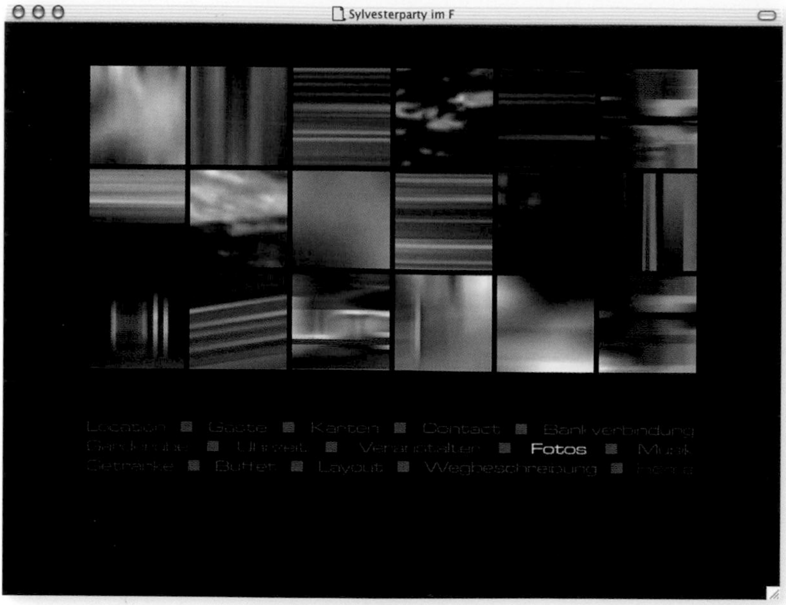

WWW.FUERSTENSAAL.DE
D: THOMAS HONKOMP
M: HONKOMP@WEB.DE

WWW.STUDIOMAGIKO.COM
D: ALESSANDRO CIRILLO
M: ALESFLY@TISCALINET.IT

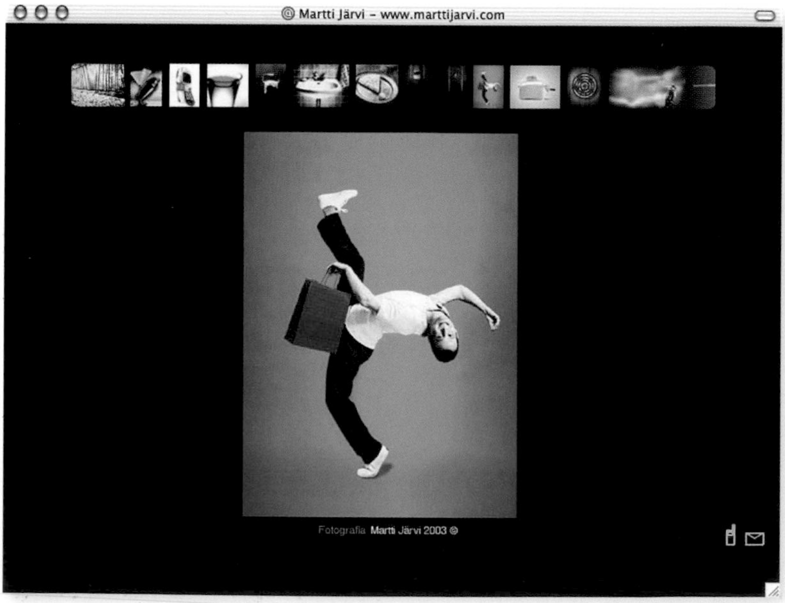

WWW.MARTTIJARVI.COM
D: CHRISTIAN CHAMPAGNE
M: CHAMPAGNE@MIDNIGHTSUNRECORDINGS.COM

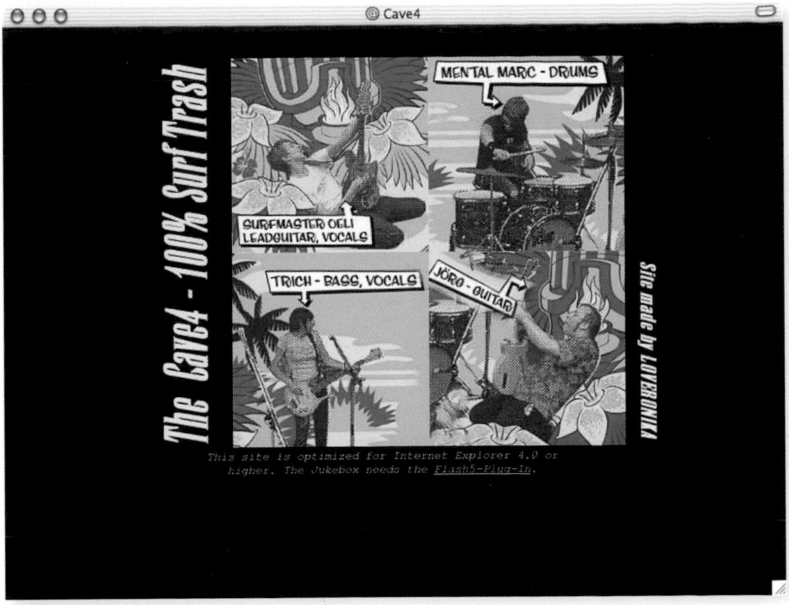

WWW.CAVE4.DE
D: VERONIKA CASPERS
M: LOVERONIKA@HOTMAIL.COM

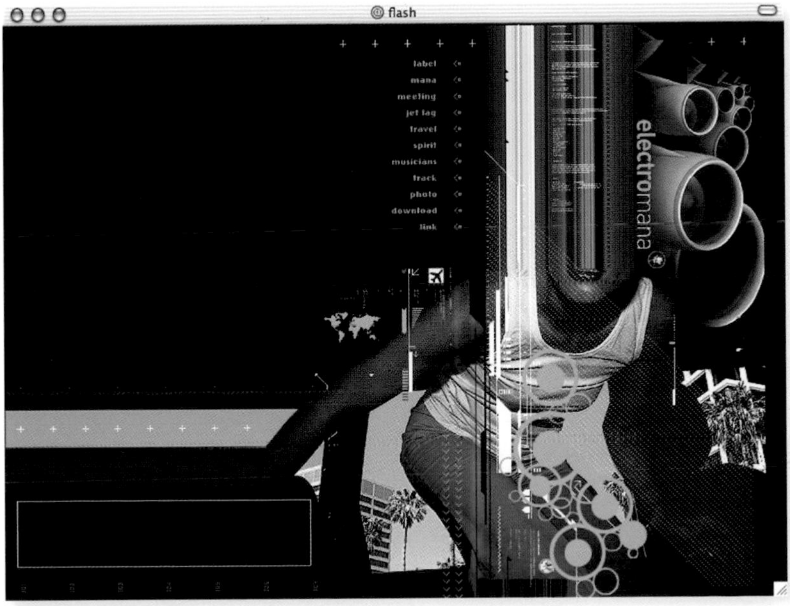

WWW.ELECTROMANA.COM
D: SHARKY, **C:** TOM BOUILLUT, **P:** GEORGE V RECORDS
A: SHARKY DESIGN, **M:** SHARKYDESIGN@HOTMAIL.COM

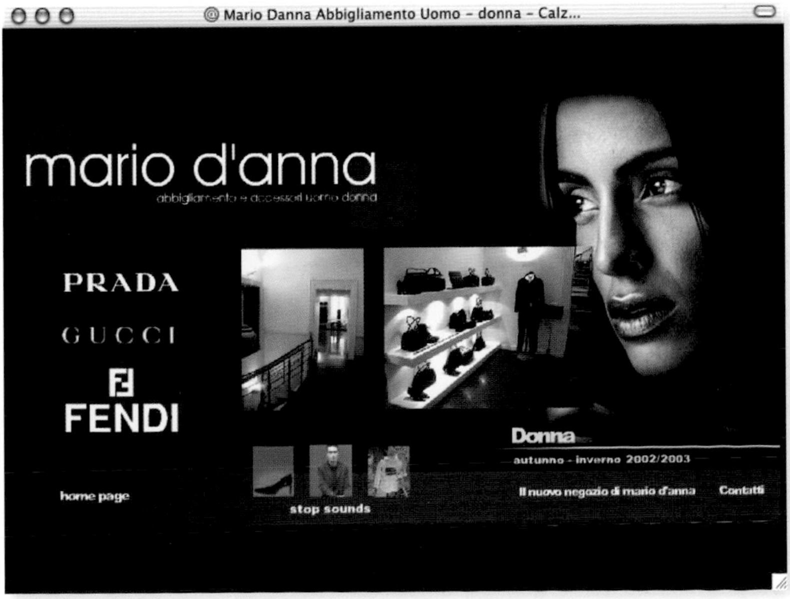

WWW.MARIODANNA.IT
D: VINCENZO MORIELLO, **C:** RAFFAELE PAPIRO, **P:** WORK IN PROGRESS
A: WORK IN PROGRESS, **M:** INFO@WKPROGRESS.COM

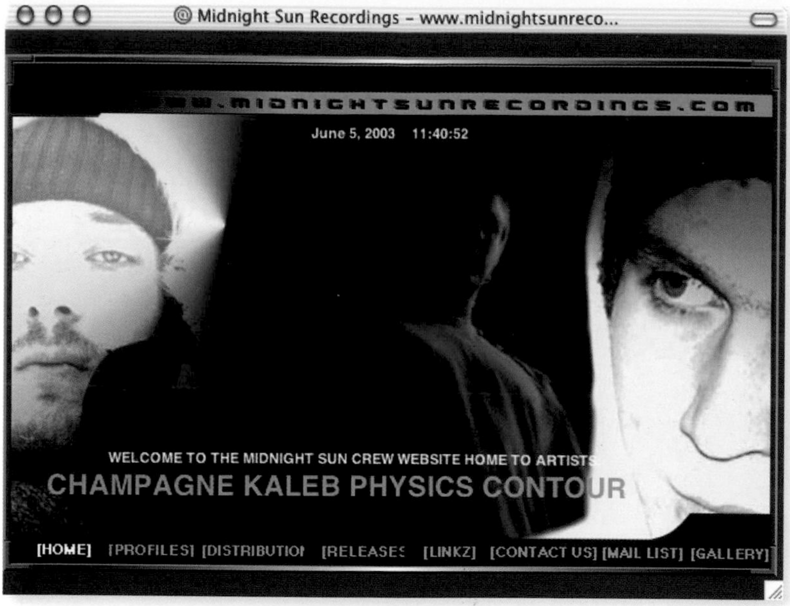

WWW.MIDNIGHTSUNRECORDINGS.COM
D: CHRISTIAN CHAMPAGNE
A: MIDNIGHT SUN RECORDINGS, **M:** CHAMPAGNE@MIDNIGHTSUNRECORDINGS.COM

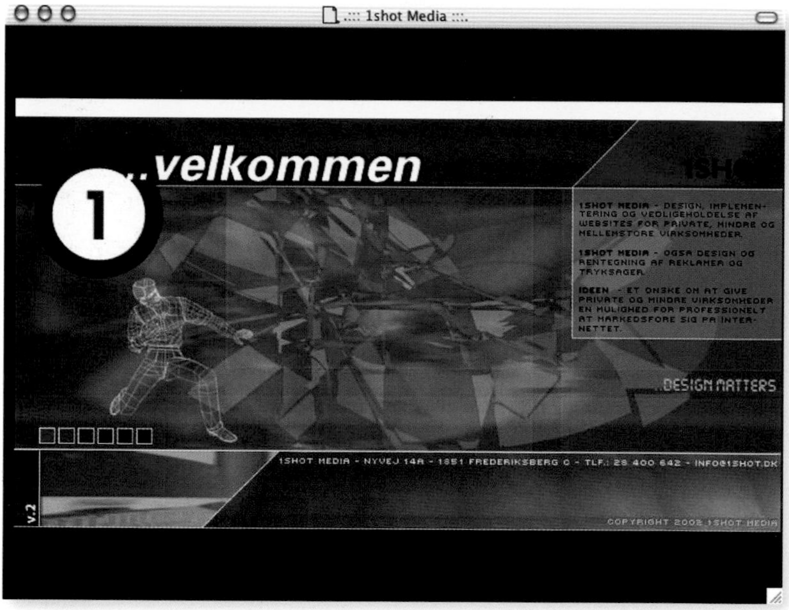

WWW.1SHOT.DK
D: MARCELO ZAGAL
A: 1SHOT MEDIA, **M:** MZH@1SHOT.DK

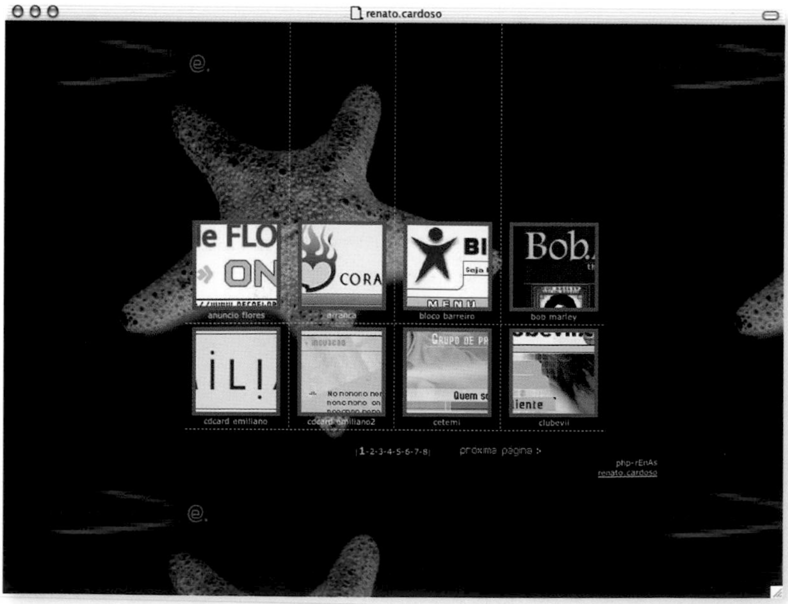

WWW.RENATOCARDOSO.COM
D: RENATO CARDOSO, **C:** RENATO CAVALLARI
M: RENATO@RENATOCARDOSO.COM

WWW.DRUMECSTASY.COM
D: PHIL, **C:** MIKHAIL, **P:** PHIL
A: DATA, **M:** MIKHAIL@DATA.MINSK.BY

WWW.COM-OCEAN.COM
D: SAM HAYLES, **C:** SAM HAYLES, **P:** HERVÉ SEURIN
A: COM-OCEAN, **M:** SAM@COM-OCEAN.COM

WWW.ANGELMAI.COM
D: ANGELMAI, **C:** TONY WHA, **P:** ANGELMAI
A: TEGA, **M:** OEDYWHA@SO-NET.NET.TW

WWW.NOW-I-DECIDED-TO-SPEAK-WITH-THE-SILENCE.COM
D: ANDREA TONIOLO, **C:** GIANPAOLO D'AMICO, **P:** ANDREA TONIOLO
M: ANDREA.TONIOLO@EIENFILMS.COM

WWW.CATERINALUCCHI.IT
D: MATTIA LUMINI, **P:** YYKK SNC
A: YYKK SNC, **M:** INFO@YYKK.COM

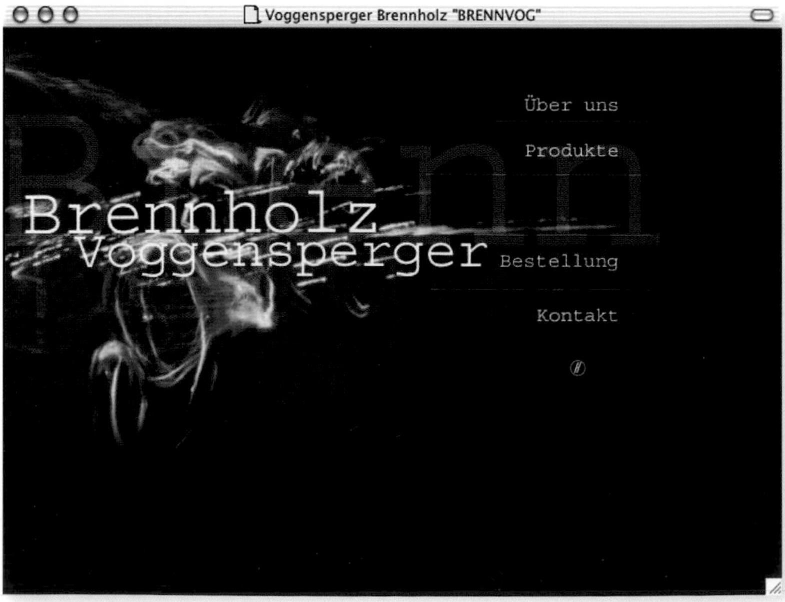

WWW.BRENNVOG.CH
D: THOMAS HAFNER
A: GRAPHICHOUSE, **M:** INFO@GRAPHICHOUSE.CH

WWW.PITCHSHIFTER.COM
D: SAM HAYLES, **C:** JULIEN MOREL, **P:** JS CLAYDEN
A: DOSE-PRODUCTIONS.COM, **M:** SAM@DOSE-PRODUCTIONS.COM

WWW.IN-DESIGN.RU/IN_ENGL.HTM
D: ARKADY OPOCHANSKY, **C:** ARKADY OPOCHANSKY, **P:** IN-DESIGN
A: IN-DESIGN, **M:** INFO@IN-DESIGN.RU

WWW.MARCATLAN.COM
D: MARC ATLAN
A: MARC ATLAN DESIGN, INC., **M:** MARC@MARCATLAN.COM

WWW.VIETUAL.ORG
D: MINH-THAI, **C:** NGÔ HÔNG-QUYÊN, **P:** PTERODACTYLE.COM
A: VIETUAL STUDIO, **M:** THAI@VIETUAL.ORG

WWW.DSM.COM.TR
D: HAKAN KIZILDAG
A: CARSOWEBDESIGN, **M:** HAKAN@HAKANKIZILDAG.COM

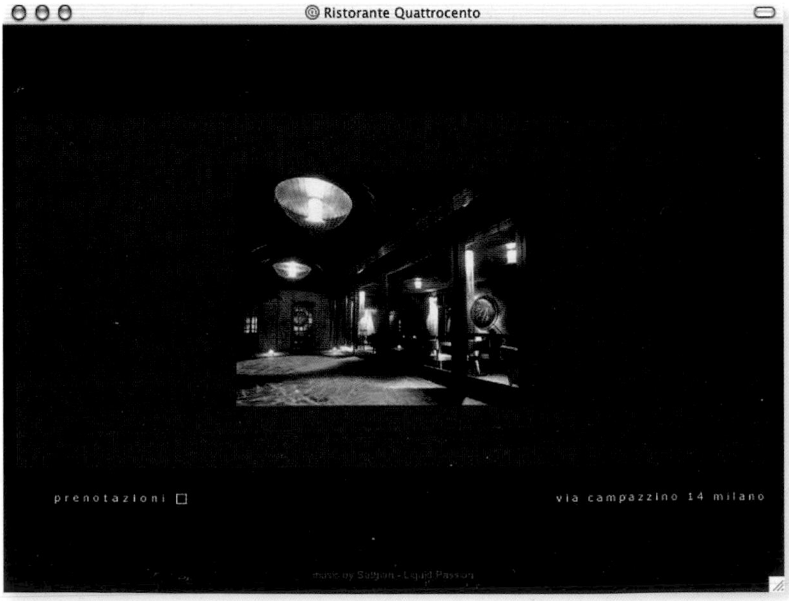

WWW.4CENTO.COM
D: PAULA JUCHEM, **C:** ANDRE LOHMANN, **P:** PAULA JUCHEM
A: STUDIO TEIXEIRA SRL, **M:** DESIGN@PAULAJUCHEM.COM

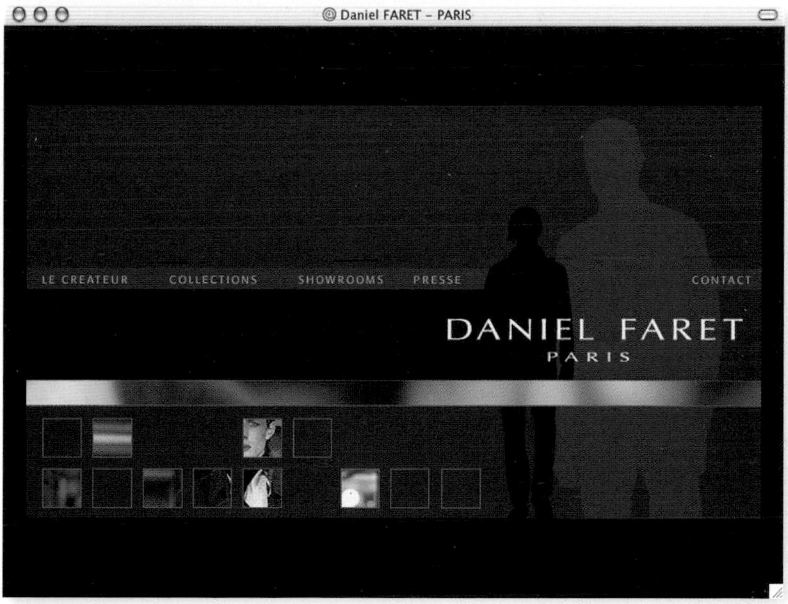

WWW.DANIELFARET.COM
D: FRANCIS GILLAIN
A: FHMSOLUTIONS, **M:** FGILLAIN@FHMSOLUTIONS.COM

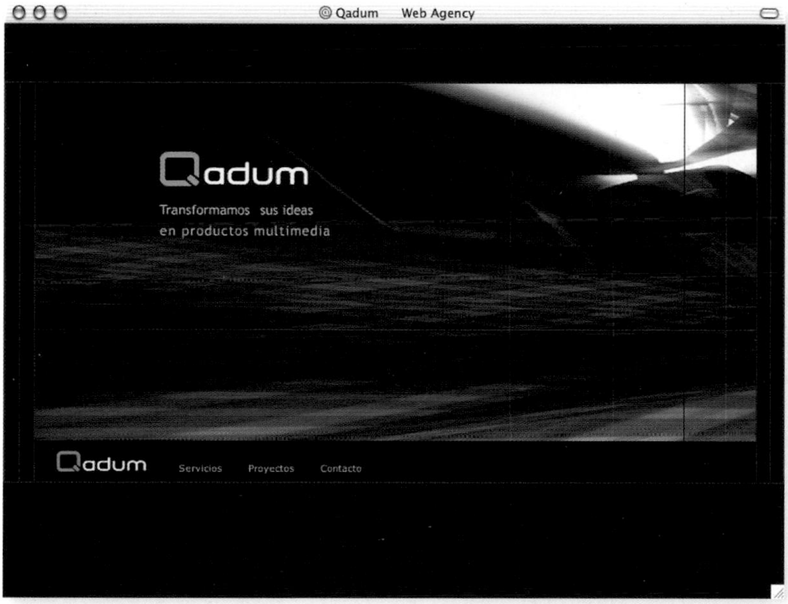

WWW.QADUM.COM
D: MERCÈ CARRASCOSA, **C:** EDUARD GRAU, **P:** QADUM
A: QADUM, **M:** INFO@QADUM.COM

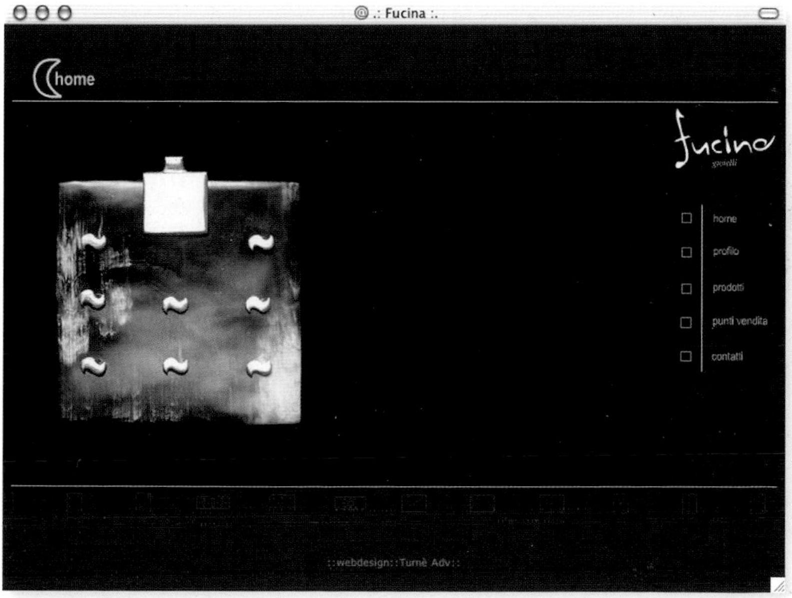

WWW.E-FUCINA.IT
D: MARCO TRAMONTANO, **C:** MARCO TRAMONTANO, **P:** TURNE
A: MARCOTRAMONTANO.COM, **M:** CONTATTI@MARCOTRAMONTANO.COM

WWW.GRAFFITI.FR
D: GRAFFITI, **C:** I'MEDIA, **P:** PATRICK LEBRUN
A: GRAFFITI, **M:** CREA@GRAFFITI.FR

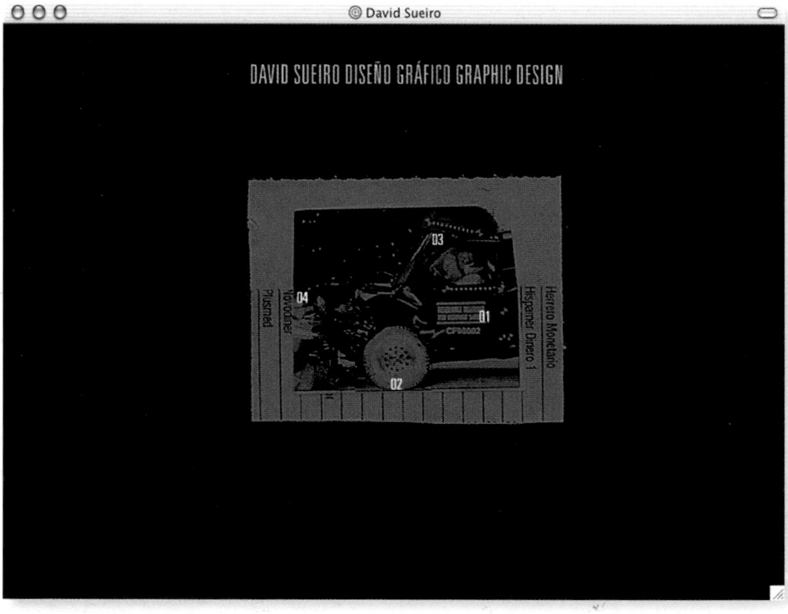

WWW.DAVID.SUEIRO.COM
D: DAVID SUEIRO
A: DSDG, **M:** DAVID@SUEIRO.COM

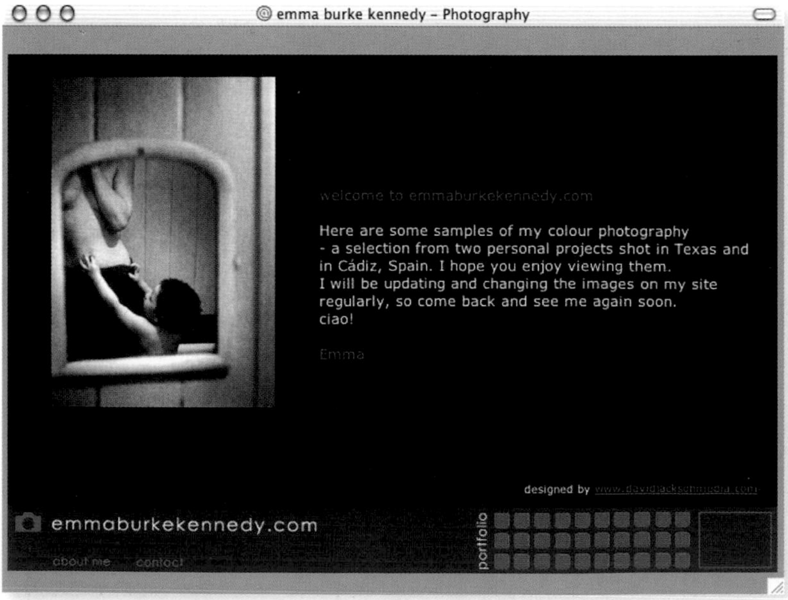

WWW.EMMABURKEKENNEDY.COM
D: DAVID JACKSON
M: DAVE@DAVIDJACKSONMEDIA.COM

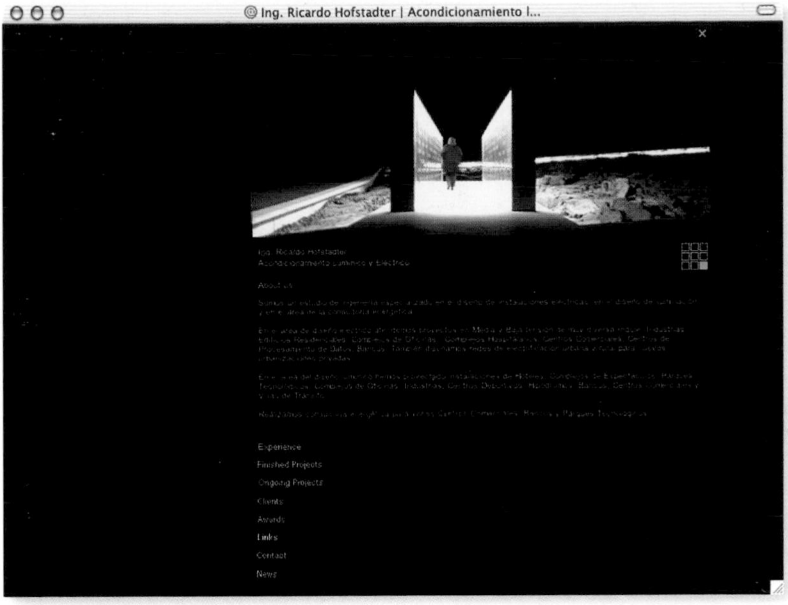

WWW.SPAZIOINWIND.LIBERO.IT/G_CAMARDA/
D: GIULIANO CAMARDA
M: GCAMARDA@INWIND.IT

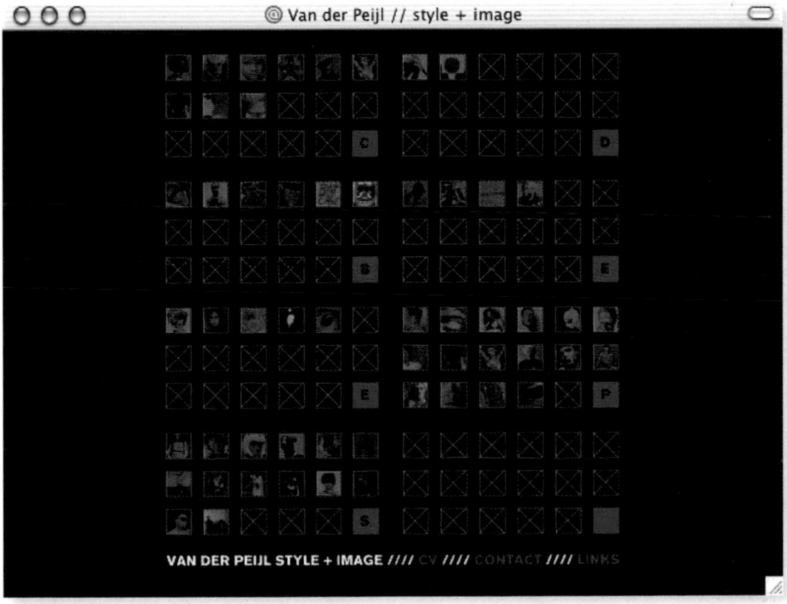

WWW.VANDERPEIJL.COM
D: YACCO VIJN, **C:** YACCO VIJN, **P:** HANS VAN DIJK
A: SKIPINTRO, **M:** YACCO@SKIPINTRO.NL

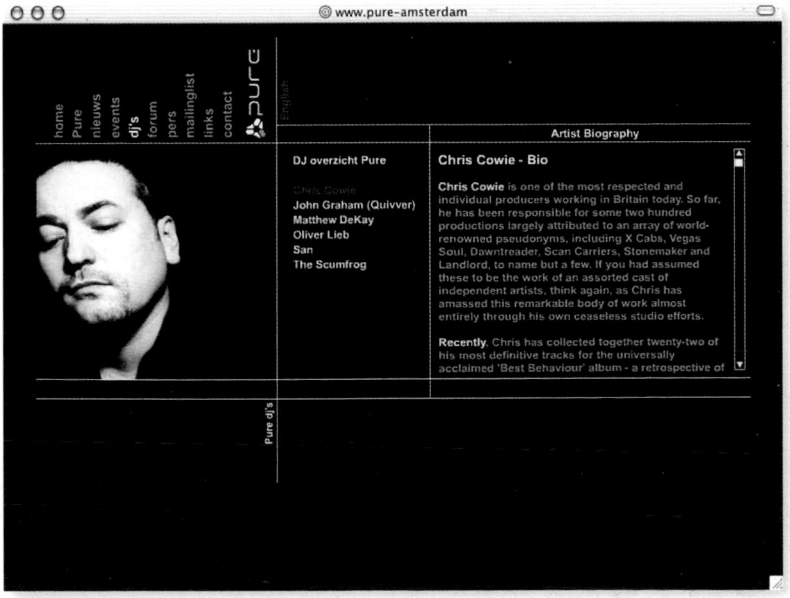

WWW.PURE-ANTWERP.COM
D: MIKE MOORMAN, **C:** MIKE MOORMAN, **P:** NAVESTUDIO
A: NAVELSTUDIO, **M:** ERIK@NAVELSTUDIO.NL

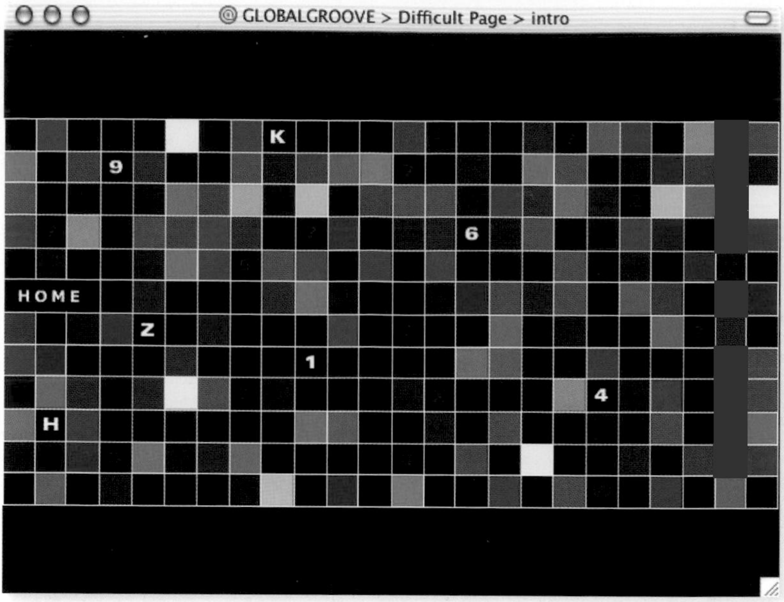

WWW.GLOBALGROOVE.IT
D: GLOBALGROOVE
A: GLOBALGROOVE, **M:** INFO@GLOBALGROOVE.IT

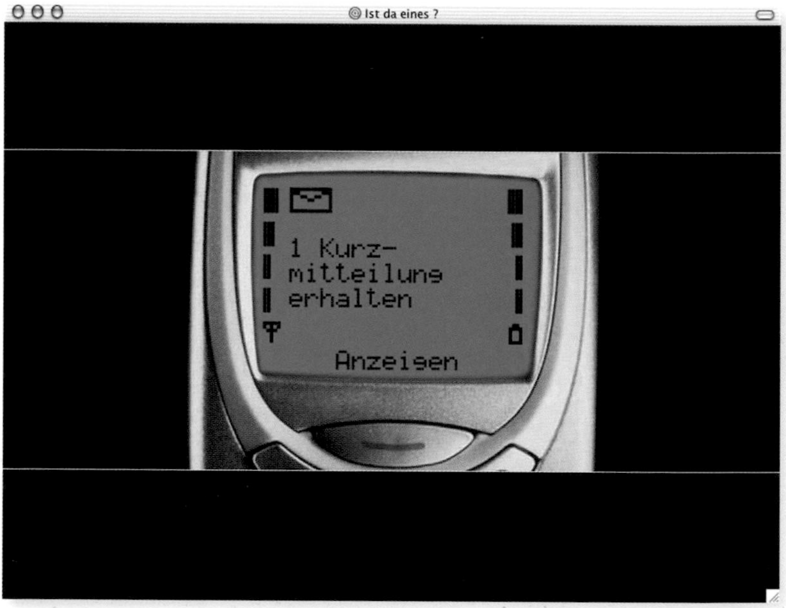

WWW.ISTDAEINES.AT
D: JÖRG WUKONIG
A: WUKONIG.COM, **M:** JOERG@WUKONIG.COM

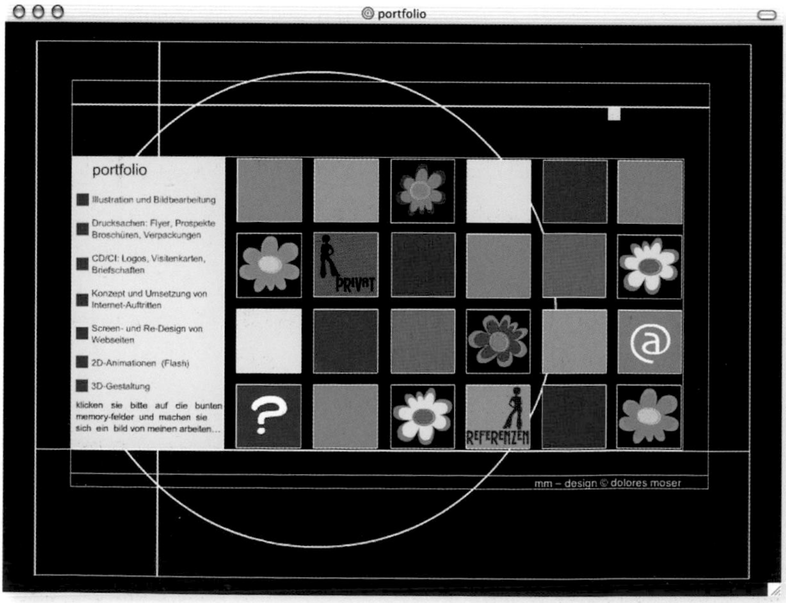

WWW.MMD-MULTIMEDIA.CH
D: DOLORES MOSER
A: MM-DESIGN, **M:** MOSER@MMD-MULTIMEDIA.CH

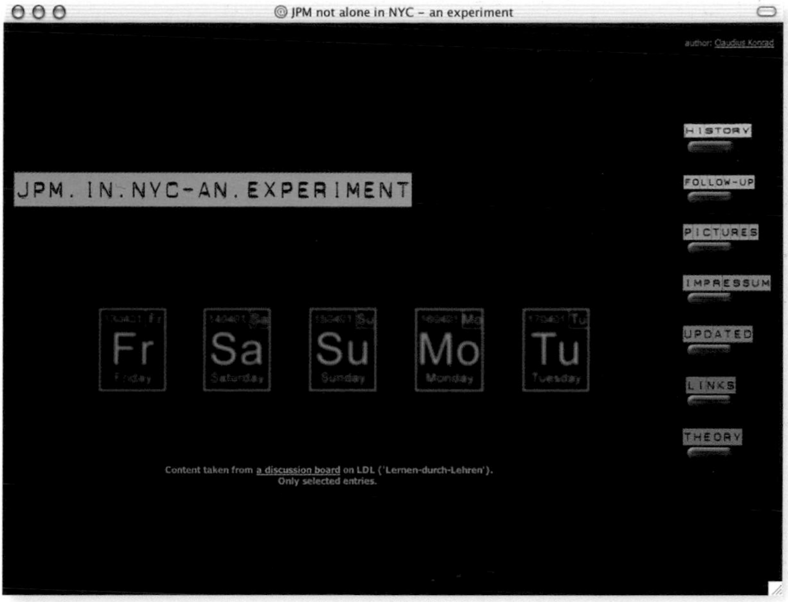

WWW.CKONRAD.DE/JPM.HTML
D: CLAUDIUS KONRAD
M: CK@CKONRAD.DE

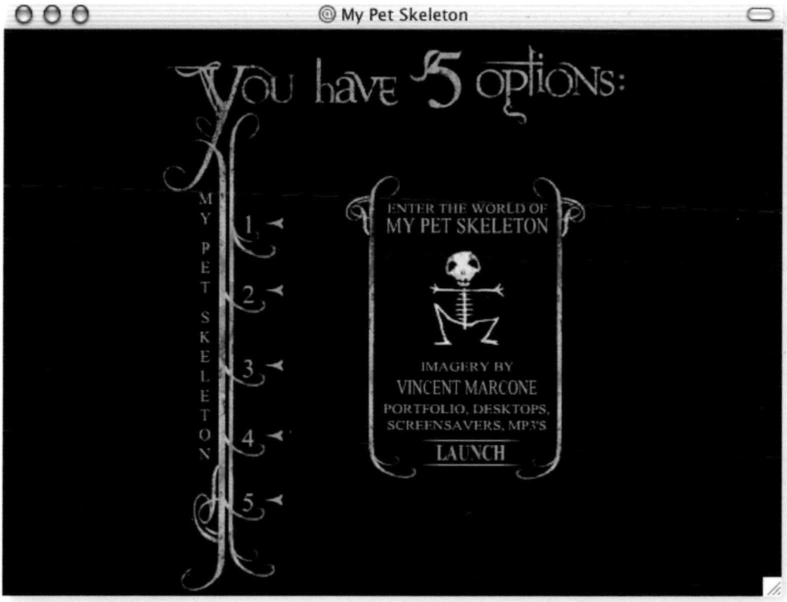

WWW.MYPETSKELETON.COM
D: VINCENT MARCONE

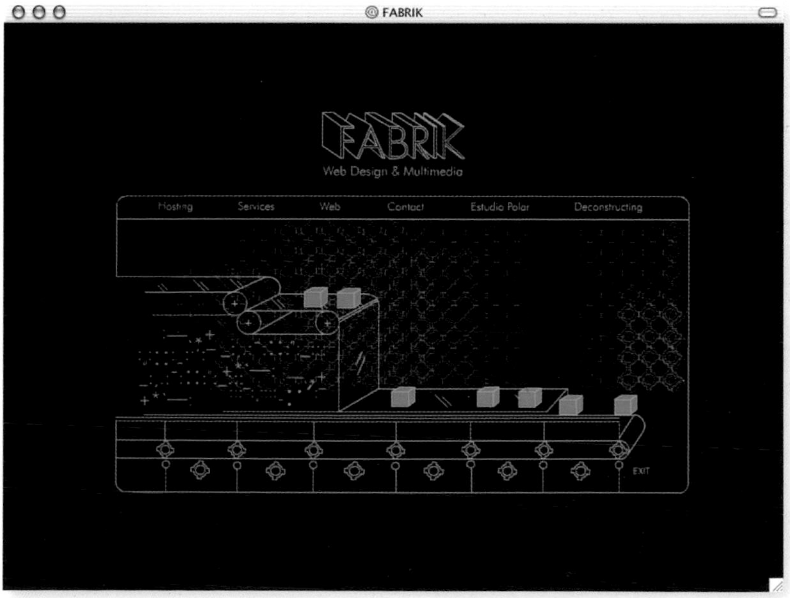

WWW.FABRIK.COM.AR
D: VANESA LEVACOV / LEANDRO SALVATI, **C:** VANESA LEVACOV, **P:** VANESA LEVACOV
A: FABRIK WEB DESIGN, **M:** INFO@FABRIK.COM.AR

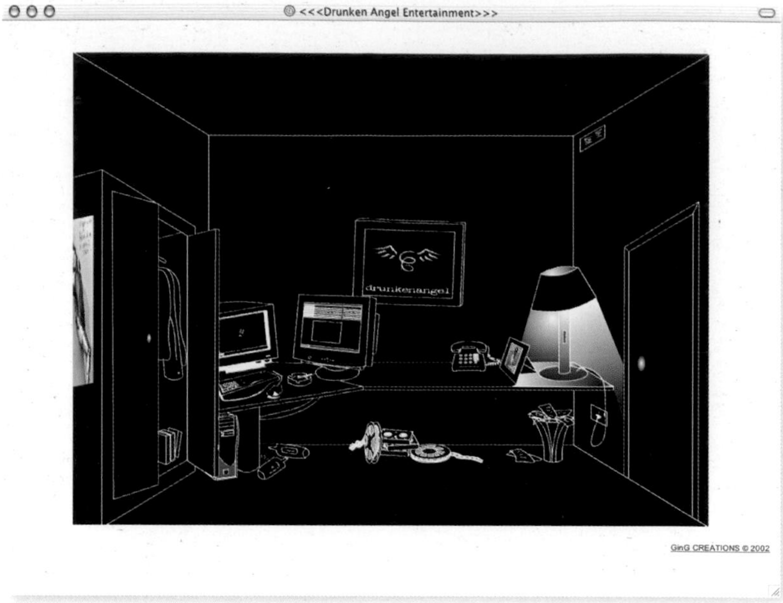

WWW.DRUNKENANGEL.NET
D: FRANCO VELLA
A: GING CREATIONS, **M:** JP@DRUNKENANGEL.NET

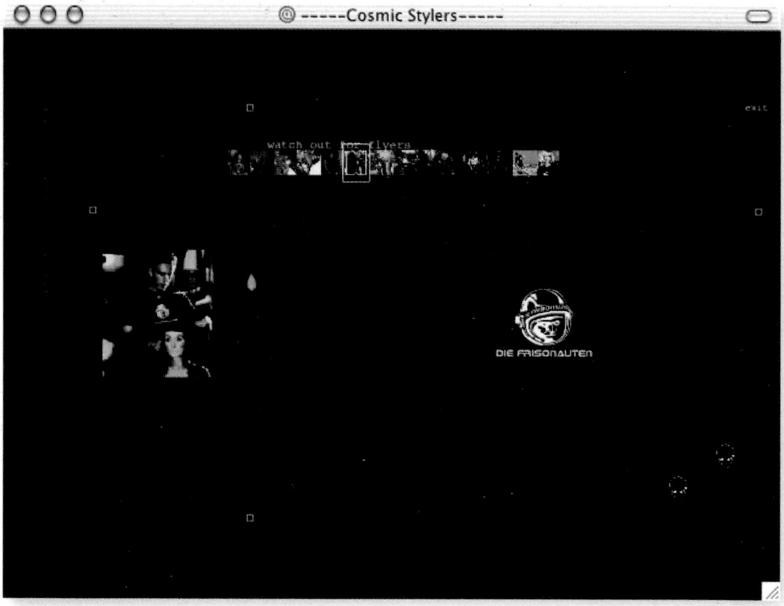

WWW.COSMIC-STYLERS.DE
D: QULIXX & ENOISE
A: QULIXX & ENOISE, **M:** SVEN@QULIXX.DE

WWW.INTERLEUCINA.ORG
D: ROS RODRIGO
M: ROS@INTERLEUCINA.ORG

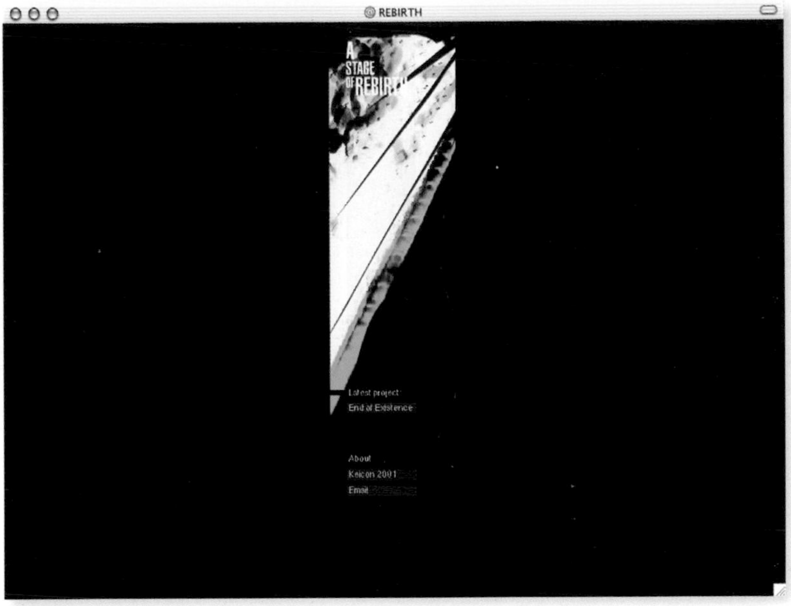

WWW.KEICON.COM
D: TONY KE
M: KEONE@KEICON.COM

WWW.IESPANA.ES/DOBERMAN
D: DoBERMAN, **C:** JAIRO, **P:** JAIRO
M: DoBERMAN@LYCOS.ES

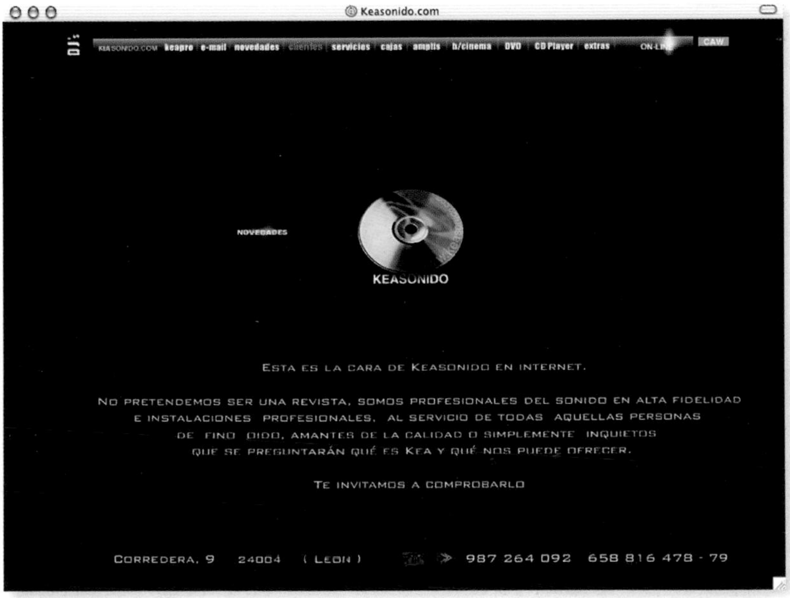

WWW.KEASONIDO.COM
D: CARLOS PARAMOS
A: CLICKARTWEB, **M:** CARLOS@CLICKARTWEB.NET

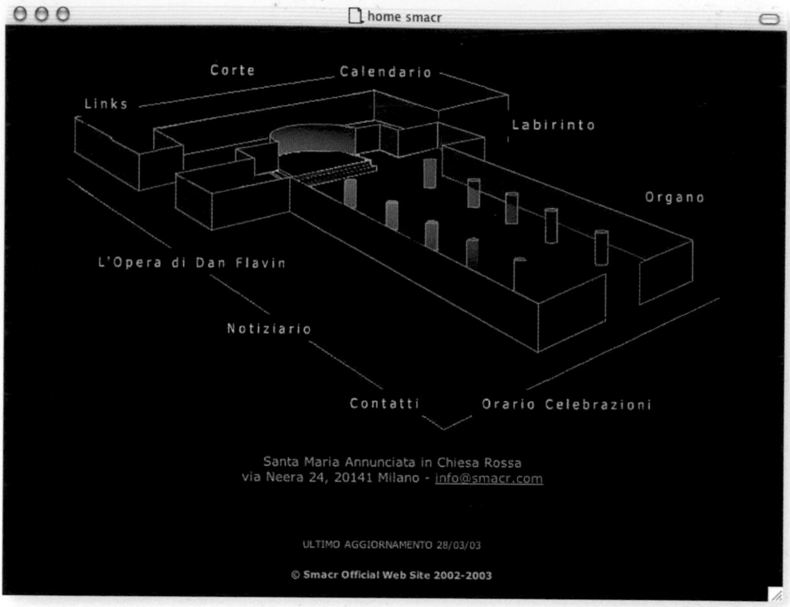

WWW.SMACR.COM
D: GIACOMO ROSSI
M: GIACOMO.ROSSI@LIBERO.IT

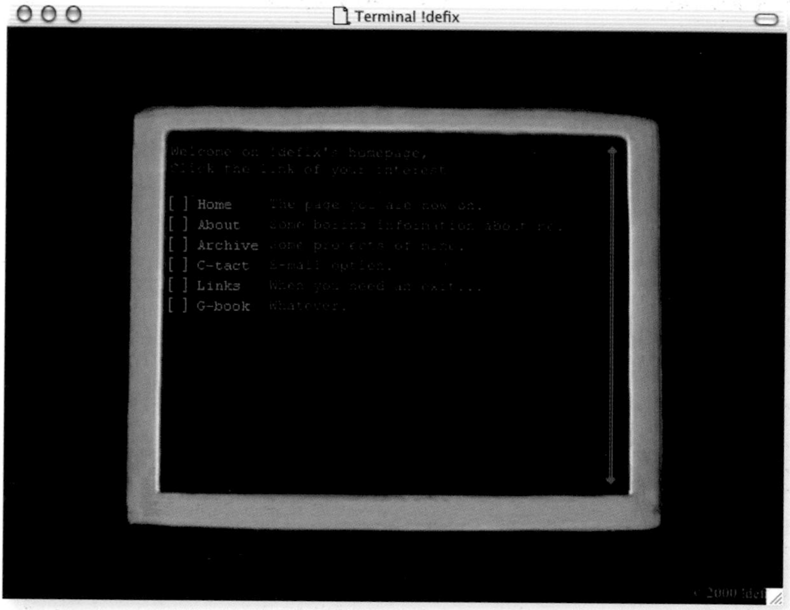

WWW.SARIN.NET/~IDEFIX
D: JACCO VINKE
M: IDEFIX@DWAAL.NET

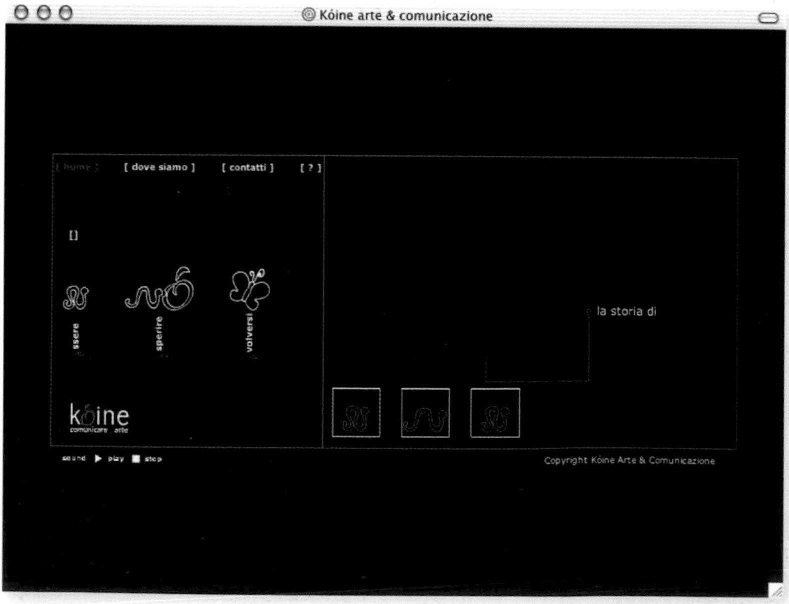

WWW.STUDIOKOINE.IT
D: DARIO GIGLIUCCI, **C:** MARCO POLLICE - ALFREDO ESPOSITO, **P:** CIRO VECCHIARINI
A: KOINE ARTE & COMUNICAZIONE, **M:** INFO@STUDIOKOINE.IT

INDEX

GERMANY

GREAT BRITAIN

GREECE

HONG KONG

HUNGARY

ICELAND

INDIA

INDONESIA

IRAN

IRELAND

ITALY

NEW ZEALAND

PAKISTAN

PHILLIPINES

PORTUGAL

ROMANIA

RUSSIA

SINGAPORE

SLOVAKIA

SOUTH KOREA

SPAIN

VENEZUELA

VIETNAM